Clashing Views on Controversial

Issues in
Social Psychology

TAKING SIDES

Clashing Views on Controversial

Issues in
Social Psychology

Selected, Edited, and with Introductions by

Jason A. Nier
Connecticut College

McGraw-Hill/Dushkin
A Division of The McGraw-Hill Companies

To my parents

Photo Acknowledgment
Cover image: photos.com

Cover Art Acknowledgment
Charles Vitelli

Library of Congress Cataloging-in-Publication Data
Main entry under title:
Taking sides: clashing views on controversial social psychological issues/selected, edited, and with introductions by Jason A. Nier.—1st ed.
Includes bibliographical references and index.
1. Social Psychology-United States. I. Nier, Jason A., *comp.*
370.973
0-07-297879-1
ISSN: 1550-6169

Printed on Recycled Paper

Preface

Human beings are inherently social creatures, and this book examines many important questions about the social nature of our existence from the unique perspective of social psychology. This book includes both classic readings that have been influential in the development of the field, such as Leon Festinger's seminal study examining cognitive dissonance, as well as more contemporary selections that tackle topical issues, such as Brad Bushman and Craig Anderson's research examining the impact of the mass media on aggression.

Like all books in the Taking Sides series, all of the readings are organized around controversial questions with each reading presenting one side of the argument. In the realm of social psychology, debate has swirled around questions such as "Does true altruism exist?" and "Does cognitive dissonance explain why behavior can change attitudes?" Both of these issues, along with many others, have been included in this book. Another distinctive feature of the book is the inclusion of several *applied* questions, which are titled "Applying Social Psychology." You may find these selections particularly engaging since they demonstrate the relevance of social psychological research to the "real world."

Also, in many cases the selections that you read are the original reports of research. While some of these selections have been edited due to space constraints, you should nonetheless benefit from reading the first-hand description of research rather than a second-hand interpretation of it. Reading the original research should allow you to understand the strengths and weaknesses of the studies that are described and ultimately allow you to decide for yourself about the validity of each perspective.

Plan of the book   The book is comprised of 18 different controversial issues in the field of social psychology. Each issue begins with an *issue introduction* that will provide you with the background necessary to understand the context of the debate and its importance to social psychology. In addition to the two readings that address each perspective on the debate, *challenge questions* are also included for each issue, which are designed to stimulate critical thinking and spark thought-provoking discussions. If you are interested in learning more about a particular issue, you can refer to a set of Web sites that contain additional resources and information.

The 18 issues are organized into four different sections. The first section of the book deals with ethical issues in social psychology. Each of the next three sections reflects one of the major subfields within social psychology. One section examines some of the debates surrounding research in *social cognition*, another section address contentious issues in *social influence* research, and the final portion of the book investigates the controversies in *social relations*.

A word to the instructor   An Instructor's *Manual with Test Questions* (multiple choice and essay) is available through the publishers for the instructor using Taking Sides in the classroom. A general guidebook, *Using Taking Sides in the Classroom*, which discusses methods and techniques for integrating the pro-con approach into any classroom setting, is also available. An online version of *Using Taking Sides in the Classroom* and a correspondence service for Taking Sides adopters can be found at http://www.dushkin.com/usingts/.

Taking Sides: Clashing Views on Controversial Issues in Social Psychology is only one title in the Taking Sides series. If you are interested in seeing the table of contents for any of these other titles, please visit the Taking Sides Web site at http://www/dushkin.com/takingsides/.

Acknowledgements   I would like to thank Tabitha and my parents for their moral and emotional support throughout this project. I would also like to thank Joan Chrisler, Donelson Forsyth, Samuel Gaertner, and Jefferson Singer for their helpful comments on the earlier versions of the materials for this book. I would like to thank Theodore Knight, Larry Loeppke, and Jill Peter at McGraw Hill/Dushkin for their advice and encouragement.

Jason A. Nier
Connecticut College

Contents In Brief

Contents

Journalist James Geary discusses research that has examined the effectiveness of various lie detection schemes. Although the average person is not very adept at detecting lies, according to the research of psychologist Paul Ekman, people can be trained to detect the cues to deceit and become quite good at detecting lies. Social psychologist Bella M. DePaulo agrees that the average person is not a very reliable lie detector. However, DePaulo believes that improving people's lie detection skills is not as straightforward as it may seem.

Psychiatrist Richard Kluft believes that repressed and recovered memories are real, and often reflect real instances of trauma and abuse. Cognitive psychologist Elizabeth Loftus argues that false memories can be created with surprising ease. As a result many repressed and recovered memories many not reflect real traumatic or abusive events.

PART 3   SOCIAL INFLUENCE   177

Social psychologists Alice Eagly and Wendy Wood argue that gender differences can be explained by the different social roles that women and men occupy in society. Evolutionary psychologist David Buss believes that gender differences reflect the different adaptive challenges women and men have faced in human evolutionary history.

Social psychologists John P. Sabini and Maury Silver believe that the Obedience Experiments captured the most important psychological aspects of the Holocaust, by demonstrating that normal people can be made to harm others with alarming ease. Psychotherapist Florence R. Miale and political scientist Michael Selzer believe that Milgram's results are not as convincing as is often believed. They contend that the findings of these controversial experiments can be explained by individual differences in participants' willingness to inflict pain on others.

Social psychologists Craig Haney and Philip Zimbardo, believe that the results of the Stanford Prison Experiment should inform U.S. prison policy. Behavioral geneticist David T. Lykken argues that the experiment was not realistic enough to say anything meaningful about real prison life and that personality factors are more important in determining the behavior of prisoners.

Social psychologist Anthony Pratkanis argues that research claiming to demonstrate the efficacy of subliminal persuasion is either fraudulent or flawed. Carefully controlled experiments do not demonstrate that subliminal persuasion can have any effect on behavior. Nicholas Epley, Kenneth Savitsky, and Robert Kachelski agree that much of the research examining subliminal persuasion is flawed. However, more recent research using better methodologies has demonstrated that subliminal stimuli can influence behavior.

Psychologist Trudy Solomon argues that well-known social psychological principles may explain the process by which brainwashing can occur. Also Solomon argues that some religious movements, generally referred to as cults, use these principles to recruit new members. Sociologist James T. Richardson believes that social psychological principles do not necessarily suggest that brainwashing is commonly used in new religious movements. Instead he believes that these organizations use the same the recruitment tactics used by many organizations and therefore cannot be considered "brainwashing."

PART 4   SOCIAL RELATIONS   291

Social psychologist Patricia G. Devine argues that some forms of stereotyping may be automatic and therefore inevitable. In order to prevent these automatic stereotypes from being biased, whites must make a conscious effort to avoid responding in a prejudicial manner. Social psychologists Lorella Lepore and Rupert Brown believe that automatic stereotyping may not be so universal and automatic as Patricia Devine believes. Some whites may be more likely to engage in automatic stereotyping than others, and as a result stereotyping is not necessarily inevitable among all whites.

Lee Jussim, Clark McCauley, and Yueh-Ting Lee believe that stereotypes have been stereotyped. Stereotypes are not always inaccurate and do not invariably lead to biased judgments of others, as most social psychologists seem to believe. Charles Stangor draws a distinction between the *content* accuracy and *application* accuracy in the use of stereotypes. According to Stangor, even if the content of a stereotype is accurate, using the stereotype to judge others will still likely yield inaccurate perceptions.

Social psychologist C. Daniel Batson and his colleagues believe that people sometimes help for purely altruistic reasons. He proposes that empathy is the key factor responsible for altruism and describes the results of an experiment that supports his position. Social psychologist Robert Cialdini and his colleagues are not convinced that empathy alone can motivate helping. He proposes an alternative explanation, called the Negative State Relief Model, which proposes that people help others in order to make themselves feel better.

Brad Bushman and Craig Anderson contend that an overwhelming amount of research indicates that media violence is a significant cause of violent and aggressive behavior. Despite this overwhelming evidence, media corporations irresponsibly downplay the impact that media violence may have. Jonathon Freedman argues that the evidence linking aggression to media violence is not as strong as is it believed to be. Psychologists who contend that such a link has been proven are misunderstanding or misrepresenting what the data actually indicates.

According to David Buss and his colleagues, men and women have evolved different emotional reactions to the infidelity of their partners in response to different reproductive challenges. Men are likely to be particularly bothered by their partner's sexual infidelity while women are likely to be particularly bothered by emotional infidelity. Christine Harris and Nicholas Christenfeld argue that there is a serious methodological problem in the study described by David Buss and his colleagues. They are skeptic of the evolutionary interpretation.

Introduction

Jason A. Nier

Social psychology is an ambitious discipline. From the birth of the field over a 100 years ago, social psychologists have not shied away from the fundamental questions about human nature. In fact the first social psychological experiment, conducted by Max Ringleman in the 1880s (Kravitz & Martin, 1986), was designed to determine whether people are more productive when working together as a group—an ambitious and important question and one that would foretell the ambition of social psychologists 100 years later.

Unresolved Issues

But despite this vigorous commitment to addressing big questions about human nature, many important questions about social thought and behavior remain unanswered by social psychologists. This book and the selections that you will read are designed to stimulate critical thinking by encouraging you to carefully examine each debate from different perspectives. Sometimes you may conclude that one perspective is right and another is wrong. At other times, you may feel that there is an element of truth to both viewpoints after reading the selections. Regardless of your feelings about the validity of each position, the process of examining both sides of the debate will leave you with a more critical understanding of each issue. After having read both sides of each argument, you can weigh the merits of each position and make a decision for yourself as to which argument is more convincing.

But how do social psychologists attempt to answer these unresolved questions? At first glance it may seem as if we can rely on common sense and intuition to settle social psychological questions. After all, we are all social beings, and we have our own beliefs about the world, that we have formed on the basis of own personal experiences. Perhaps these commonsense beliefs are sufficient to understand our social environment. While intuition and commonsense are valuable for understanding our social world, they may sometimes be mistaken, as you will read in Issue 4. In fact there is a great deal of social psychological research that documents the reasons why our beliefs and intuitions are imperfect. As a result, social psychologists use data from carefully controlled studies, rather than intuition or commonsense, to answer enduring questions about human nature.

A Focus on Experimentation

What kind of data do social psychologists examine? Perhaps the single most distinctive aspect of social psychology, which separates it from many other social sciences, is the focus on experimentation. Experiments are still the most preferred method among social psychologists. As you have probably already learned in your other psychology classes, in a true experiment participants are randomly assigned to different experimental conditions. In each condition, participants are exposed to slightly different circumstances. For example, if you were interested in the effect of heat on aggressive behavior, then you might randomly assign some participants to a hot room and others to a cool room and then measure the level of aggression among participants in each condition. If you observed that participants who were randomly assigned to the hot room were more aggressive than participants in the cool room, then you could infer the higher room temperature causes aggressive behavior. Only in an experiment such as this, where participants are randomly assigned to different conditions, can you conclude that one variable (e.g., room temperature) *causes* changes in another variable (e.g., aggression). Other methods, such as correlational or observational studies, cannot tell you that one thing causes another—only an experiment has such power.

However, there are also drawbacks to experiments. Their foremost limitation is the artificial settings in which they occur. Since most experiments require that the researcher establish tight control over the environment in which the research takes place, they are usually conducted in psychological laboratories. These laboratories usually bear little resemblance to any real-world environment that people encounter in their everyday lives. So to examine important questions about social thought and behavior, social psychologists often remove people from their normal social environment and place them in a novel and admittedly artificial laboratory setting. While this may seem like a misguided strategy for studying social thought and behavior, it is important to bear in mind that most experiments in social psychology are not intended to mirror real-world situations. Furthermore, social psychologists acknowledge that experiments are artificial, but still believe them to be powerful and important. How could this be the case? Because experiments are conducted in order to *test theories*, rather than recreate a microcosm of a particular social environment. Because of their power to establish cause and effect among variables, experiments are uniquely suited to test theories and that is why they remain the tool of choice among social psychologists.

To illustrate the value of experiments as a theory-testing tool, consider an experiment from another area of psychology: Ivan Pavlov's (1927) landmark study of classical conditioning. Pavlov was a Russian physiologist who studied the process of digestion in dogs, and he was particularly interested in the role of salivation in digestion. To measure salivation, he placed dogs in a harness in a small, bare, sound-proof room and attached a tube to a dog's cheek that collected saliva. He then sought to demonstrate that the dogs could learn to salivate at the ringing of a bell, by pairing the ringing of the bell with the presentation of food powder. After a series of trials in which the bell and food powder were simultaneously presented, Pavlov then rang the bell without presenting the food powder and discovered that the dogs had learned to salivate at the ringing of the bell alone.

This experimental setting, like many in social psychology that use human participants, is quite strange. It has no real-world counterpart. Outside of Pavlov's laboratory, dogs are rarely placed in small rooms, attached to saliva-collecting devices and then receive food powder after hearing a series of bells. So this experiment is completely artificial—but incredibly important. In fact it is arguably the most famous experiment in the history of psychology and deservedly so. Why is it so important? Because it demonstrated the process now known as classical conditioning, which has had innumerable real-world applications. The power of classical conditioning has been used to prevent children from wetting their bed, prevent predators from attacking livestock, and lower blood pressure. Classical conditioning principles have also proven to be remarkably effective in the treatment of phobias, using a procedure known as systematic desensitization; Pavlov's seemingly esoteric and artificial experiment made it possible to provide relief to thousands of individuals who have been crippled by their fear. In short, Pavlov's study was important because it illustrated the process of classical conditioning, and classical conditioning has had a plethora of applications in the real world.

Social psychology experiments are important for similar reasons. Consider the case of Cognitive Dissonance Theory. This influential theory was first tested in an admittedly artificial laboratory experiment conducted by social psychologists Leon Festinger and J. Merrill Carlsmith (1959). In their classic experiment, participants were asked to perform a series of incredibly boring tasks, such as repeatedly rotating a spool of wood. After performing these mind-numbing tasks for a half hour, participants were asked to lie about how much they enjoyed the tasks, and tell another person that the tasks were enjoyable. Without giving too much away about their study, which you read about in Issue 4, the results provided support for Cognitive Dissonance Theory.

Like Pavlov's famous studies, the details of Festinger and Carlsmith's experiment are somewhat strange and bear no resemblance to any real-world situation. Most of us have never been asked to rotate a small spool of wood and then lie to someone else about how enjoyable it was. Yet this is precisely what participants did in this study. And it turned out to be incredibly important, because 45 years later social psychologists still study cognitive dissonance and its potential application to real-world situations. For example, Cognitive Dissonance Theory has been successfully used to improve racial attitudes (Leippe & Eisenstadt, 1994), encourage condom usage among sexually active young people (Stone, Aronson, Crain, Winslow, & Freid, 1994), and promote water conservation (Dickerson, Thibodeau, Aronson, & Miller, 1992). This artificial laboratory experiment eventually resulted in numerous real-world applications. That is what makes Festinger and Carlsmith's study important. As social psychologist Douglas Mook (1983) pointed out, it is not the details of an experiment that must have some real-world counterpart, or generalize to some real-world situation, it is the *theory* that generalizes to the real-world. An artificial laboratory experiment can have very important, but indirect, real-world applications, because it can be used to test and refine an important theory and the theory may have numerous real-world applications. This was certainly the case with Festinger and Carlsmith's famous study, and it is also true of many other social psychology experiments. Just as we should not dismiss Pavlov's study of classical conditioning because it took place in an artificial setting, we should be careful not to dismiss social psychology experiments as artificial and irrelevant, before we consider the importance of the *theory* that the experiment is designed to test.

The Reality of Social Psychology Experiments

Some people who read the results of laboratory experiments in social psychology may believe that the results have little importance because participants do not become engaged in these experiments. Because the situations are artificial and not realistic, they do not involve participants in the same way that "real-life" situations engage us. As a result, one might be tempted to conclude that experiments are unimportant. Social psychologists have thought carefully about this concern and what it means for an experiment to be "realistic." According to Aronson, Ellsworth, Carlsmith, & Gonzales (1990), experiments can be realistic in different ways, and they draw a distinction between mundane realism and experimental realism. Mundane realism is the extent to which the details of an experiment resemble a particular real-world setting. As has already been discussed, most experiments take place in contexts that do not resemble any real-world setting, so most social psychology experiments do not have mundane realism. On the other hand, experimental realism is the extent to which participants become psychologically involved in the experiment and take the experiment seriously. According to Aronson and his colleagues, as long as an experiment has experimental realism it has the potential to yield important results.

To illustrate the importance of the distinction between mundane realism and experimental realism, consider how "real" reality television is. In the vast majority of reality television shows, the contestants find themselves in highly artificial situations, and because of the contrived nature of these shows, many critics contend that they are not real at all. Indeed, after some reality television shows are over, many contestants confess that some aspects of the show seemed quite strange. At the same time, many contestants also testify to the depth of emotion that they felt during the experience. For example, in the reality television program *Big Brother* a group of thirteen strangers are required to live in single house with no outside contact for three months. This situation is completely artificial. There are few real-world situations that would require you to be cooped up with same people for months with no contact with outside world. Nevertheless this program has been an international hit, with dedicated fans in both the United States and Europe. What can account for its popularity? Aside from its voyeuristic appeal, it is an engaging show because the contestants become completely gripped by the situation. Despite the contrived nature of the situation, the way the contestants behave and the emotions they feel are very real to themselves and to the audience.

Many other reality show contestants have had similar experiences. In the case of the program *Survivor*, contestants often freely admit that they were completely immersed in the situation. The friendships and animosity evident on television are quite real despite the artificial nature of the show. As a further testament to the psychological reality of *Survivor*, two contestants were engaged to be married during the last episode of the season. Let's hope their feelings were authentic.

So is reality television real? In one sense of the word, reality television is not real at all, but in another sense it is very real. To use the jargon of social psychology, reality television is extremely high in experimental realism despite a complete lack of Mundane Realism. Because reality television bears little resemblance to the real world, it does not have Mundane Realism. So by that measure it is not real. However because contestants often become totally immersed in the show and experience genuine emotions, reality television appears to be high in Experimental Realism. So in that sense of the word, reality television is quite real. And just as people become totally engrossed in these artificial situations that we see on television, participants can become completely immersed in psychology experiments despite the inauthentic situations that are concocted in psychology laboratories. As a result, the way participants behave and the emotions they feel are real, in the sense that their reactions seem authentic to the participants themselves. This point will be most vividly illustrated when you read Issue 10 and Issue 11, which will describe the controversies surrounding social psychology's two most famous studies—the Obedience Experiments and the Stanford Prison Experiment. While both of these experiments are unusual by the standards of social psychology, they clearly demonstrate that participants can become totally immersed in an artificial environment. Despite their lack of mundane realism, these studies seemed very real to the participants—and as you will see, they became *too* absorbed in these situations.

Applying Social Psychology

Evident in the discussion of Cognitive Dissonance Theory is the notion that the results of social psychological research should be employed to address serious social issues. The list of social problems that social psychologists have tackled is impressive and include (to name a few) prejudice, hypocrisy, destructive obedience, violence, intergroup conflict, depression, physical illnesses, prison strife, and brainwashing. The list could go on and on.

Social psychologists have not been satisfied to simply study these issues and then hope that the results of the research are useful in some way. Social psychologists have actively sought to apply their research to real-world circumstances and have lobbied to make their voices heard. Some social psychologists have engaged in this kind of work on an individual basis and conducted their own research examining the usefulness of their ideas in the real-world. Other social psychologists have also attempted to put their research to good use on a collective level, through their involvement in various organizations. The most prominent of these organizations is the Society for the Psychological Study of Social Issues (SPSSI), which is devoted to ameliorating social problems through the application of psychological research. This group, which was originally founded in 1937, is comprised of thousands of social scientists including many social psychologists. SPSSI actively lobbies to influence policy decisions, to ensure that policy is informed by the results of the relevant social psychological research. This means that social psychologists, and the organizations to which they belong, are sometimes involved in politics. While some have questioned the wisdom of entering the political fray (see Issue 2), the vast majority of social psychologists enthusiastically agree that social psychological research should play a prominent role in policy decisions. These efforts have proven useful in a number of instances. For example, SPSSI hold congressional briefings on a fairly regular basis. At these briefings, members of the U.S. Congress listen to presentations given by prominent social scientists who describe the results of their research and how it is relevant to social policies, such as affirmative action and hate crime legislation. It is through efforts like this that social psychologists hope to apply the results of their research and promote positive social change.

References

Aronson, E., Ellsworth, P., Carlsmith, J. M., & Gonzales, M. H. (1990). *Methods of Research in Social Psychology* (2nd ed.). New York: McGraw-Hill.

Dickerson, C. A., Thibodeau, R., Aronson, E., & Miller, D. (1992). Using cognitive dissonance to encourage water conservation. *Journal of Applied Social Psychology, 22*, 841–854.

Festinger, L., & Carlsmith, J. M. (1959). The cognitive consequences of forced compliance. *Journal of Abnormal and Social Psychology, 58*, 203–210.

Kravitz, D. A., & Martin, B. (1986). Ringlemann rediscovered: The original article. *Journal of Personality and Social Psychology, 50*, 936–941.

Leippe, M. R., & Eisenstadt, D. (1994). Generalization of dissonance reduction: Decreasing prejudice through induced compliance. *Journal of Personality and Social Psychology, 67*, 395–413.

Mook, D. G. (1983). In defense of external invalidity. *American Psychologist 38*, 37–387.

Pavlov, I. P. (1927). *Conditioned Reflexes*. London: Oxford University Press.

Stone, J., Aronson, E., Crain, A. L., Winslow, M. P., & Freid, C. (1994). Inducing hypocrisy as a means of encouraging young adults to use condoms. *Personality & Social Psychology Bulletin, 20*, 116–128.

On the Internet . . .

The Social Psychology Network

This Web site is an excellent resource that contains an extensive amount of information that is useful to those interested in social psychology. It includes a number of Web pages devoted to prominent social psychologists.

http://www.socialpsychology.org/

Society for Personality and Social Psychology

This Web site is the homepage for the Society for Personality and Social Psychology. Many social psychologists are members of this group, which is part of the American Psychological Association.

http://www.spsp.org/

The Ethics Office for the American Psychological Association

The American Psychological Association publishes a code of ethics that all psychologists are expected to honor. This Web site contains the code of ethics in its entirety.

http://www.apa.org/ethics/

The Society for the Psychological Study of Social Issues

This is the home page for the Society for the Psychological Study of Social Issues, an organization comprised of 3,500 social scientists that is dedicated to applying psychological research to address social problems and inform public policy.

http://www.spssi.org/

PART 1

Ethical Issues in Social Psychology

*E*ver since Stanley Milgram's controversial obedience experiments, psychologists have thought carefully about the ethical issues that confront them when they conduct their research. The most enduring ethical debate revolves around the use of deception, which is used relatively frequently in social psychological research. Additionally the role of social psychological research in promoting social change will also be debated in this section.

- Is Deception of Human Participants Ethical?
- Should Social Psychologists Try to Solve Social Problems?

ISSUE 1

Is Deception of Human Participants Ethical?

YES: Alan C. Elms from "Keeping Deception Honest: Justifying Conditions for Social Scientific Research Stratagems," *Ethical Issues in Social Science Research* (Johns Hopkins University Press, 1982)

NO: Diana Baumrind from "Research Using Intentional Deception," *American Psychologist* (*40*, 1985)

ISSUE SUMMARY

YES: Social Psychologist Alan Elms argues that deception is usually justified when the benefits of research outweigh the ethical costs of the deception.

NO: Psychologist Diana Baumrind believes that deception is never ethically acceptable. The costs of deception seem to be greater than most social psychologists believe.

All social psychologists are obligated to conduct their research in a manner that protects the dignity and welfare of those individuals who participate in their research. The *Ethical Principles of Psychologists and Code of Conduct*, published by the American Psychological Association (APA), spells out exactly how psychologists must treat their participants. These guidelines are enforced by institutional review boards (IRBs), which review proposed research to ensure that psychologists treat their participants ethically. Furthermore, most journals that publish the results of social psychological research require that the data be gathered in accordance with the APA code of ethics.

Most aspects of the APA ethics code are uncontroversial, and psychologists closely adhere to these guidelines. However, one aspect of the APA ethics code has generated considerable controversy among social psychologists—the role of deception in psychological research. Across all sub-disciplines of psychology, only a relatively small proportion of all studies involve some form of deception, so the question of deception is of little importance to the bulk of psychologists. However, within the domain of social psychology a large percentage of studies do, in fact, involve deception. Is this widespread use of deception appropriate? The APA ethics code does permit deception, but only under a limited range of circumstances. Below is the section of the code that delineates the appropriate role of deception:

a. *Psychologists do not conduct a study involving deception unless they have determined that the use of deceptive techniques is justified by the study's significant prospective scientific, educational, or applied value and that effective nondeceptive alternative procedures are not feasible.*

b. *Psychologists do not deceive prospective participants about research that is reasonably expected to cause physical pain or severe emotional distress.*

c. *Psychologists explain any deception that is an integral feature of the design and conduct of an experiment to participants as early as is feasible, preferably at the conclusion of their participation, but no later than at the conclusion of the data collection, and permit participants to withdraw their data.*

So according to the APA, deception is appropriate under some circumstances. In the first selection, Alan Elms will defend a position that is very similar to the official position of the APA, that deception is justified only when there is substantial value in the research project and when alternative techniques are not feasible. However, not all psychologists agree with this position. Diana Baumrind, who has been an outspoken opponent of deception since the 1960s, argues that nearly all deception in psychological research is inherently unethical, and calls for an end to this practice.

POINT	COUNTERPOINT
• Deception is ethical under certain circumstances.	• Deception can never be ethically justified.
• Many important questions about human nature cannot be answered unless deception is used.	• Other techniques besides deception are always available to researchers.
• The harm done by deception is usually minimal.	• Deception has substantial negative consequences.

Alan C. Elms

→ **YES**

Keeping Deception Honest: Justifying Conditions for Social Scientific Research Stratagems

The Problem of Deception: A Consequentialist Middle Ground

Deception is a word used to end arguments, not to begin them. To accuse researchers of deception is to remove them from the ranks of those with whom legitimate human relationships can be pursued. The term is so sweeping that it includes Satin's lures for lost souls, the traitor's treachery, the false lover's violation of a pure heart. How could any deception ever be considered ethically justifiable if it keeps such company?

The use of so broad a term as *deception* is itself deceptive when applied without qualification to certain common procedures in social scientific research. It muddies issues, biases ethical debates, lumps together a vast array of practices that differ in intent, execution, and outcome. Because of such radical differences among various practices labeled "deception," social scientists have suggested other terms for the kinds of stratagems used in their research, such as "staging" or "technical illusions."[1]

But stage plays and magic tricks are not quite on the same order as our research stratagems, either. The researcher hopes that subjects will not realize an illusion is being created. If the experiment is to work, they should perceive the stage scenery through which they are walking, the memorized speeches of the actors around them, as genuine. When the curtain falls, they are not likely to break into spontaneous applause—any more than they are likely to call the Bunco Squad or the Consumer Fraud Division. So "staging" and similar terms are as problematic as "deception." In lieu of a better word, I will continue to use "deception" for the practice of misleading research subjects, even though it obliterates important distinctions among forms of deception.

Certain ethicists refuse to differentiate social scientists' attempts to mislead subjects from any other kind of deception, conceptually as well as terminologically. For them, the argument is already over: there are no circumstances under which social scientific deception is ethically permissible. Non-absolutists

Beauchamp, Tom L., Ruth Faden, R. Jay Wallace Jr., and LeRoy Walters, eds. Ethical Issues in Social Science Research, pp. 232–245. Copyright © 1982 by The John Hopkins University Press. Reprinted with permission of The Johns Hopkins University.

are likely to find such an absolutist stance worth little attention, and I do not have the space to examine it closely here. For those who are interested, Sissela Bok has summarized the basic philosophical arguments against it.[2]

Certain others—I hesitate to call them ethicists, though they do hold down the other end of the ethical scale from the moral absolutists—insist that normal rules do not apply to science, that the end knowledge fully justifies the deceptive means. In extreme form, these people appear to us as Nazi eugenicists or as the mad scientists of Hollywood—much beloved by the moral absolutists, who need such opponents to justify their own extremist stance. In milder form, they include simple corner-cutters, Machiavellian careerists, and earnest believers in the primacy of scientific truth.

The position in the middle of the scale is the hard one to hold. Here are those who see life as filled with moral conflicts, rarely easy to resolve, and who see social scientific research as a necessary part of their ethical life. They see such research as the best route to certain ethical goals, and an element of deception as essential to certain kinds of research. They do not accept deception easily, and so they are the ones who might ask, and who need to know, what conditions make deceptions sometimes ethically tolerable in social scientific research. They are the ones to whom I am mainly speaking, and whom at the same time I am trying to represent.

In so doing, I am taking what is variously called a consequentialist, risk-benefit, or cost-benefit position. Shakespeare neatly dramatized the classic case for this position in *Measure for Measure,* where he presented a novice nun with a moral dilemma: should she yield her virginity to a rapacious judge in order to save her brother's life, or should she deceive the judge and thereby save both her brother and her sexual virtue? The Duke of Vienna, apparently voicing Shakespeare's own sentiments, counsels her to deceive the judge. He assures her that "the doubleness of the benefit defends the deceit from reproof."[3] The Duke and Shakespeare are making a cost-benefit analysis, and they conclude that in this instance the benefits of deception considerably outweigh the costs. Most people other than the strictest moral absolutists would agree: when the value of honesty conflicts with other values, certain circumstances may make those other values more important than honesty, and deception then becomes tolerable.

"Tolerable" does not mean "ethically neutral." Deception is, as Bok argues, never a neutral practice.[4]stop It always carries potential harm to the interests of the deceived, in this case to the research subjects who might have chosen to avoid research participation had they been fully and accurately informed. It always carries potential harm to the deceivers, in this case the researchers and their assistants, whose reputation for veracity may be harmed and whose own character may be affected negatively by repeated deceptive practices. It carries potential harm to the deceivers' profession, since social scientists in general may become less trusted as the deceptive practices of part of the profession become well known. And it carries potential harm to society, in that it may contribute to a general lack of trust and to the willingness of nonprofessionals to act deceptively themselves. Perhaps none of these potential harms will be realized, if social scientific deception remains on a small scale and is surrounded by various kinds of constraints and counteractive efforts. But given the potential for harm, deception is social scientific research is not something to be employed casually. It must be carefully justified and any negative effects must be offset as much as possible.

What, then, are the boundary conditions under which deception can be considered ethically justifiable in social scientific research? I will state the major conditions in a single sentence, and then expound upon each term: *deception is justifiable in social scientific research when* (1) *there is no other feasible way to obtain the desired information,* (2) *the likely benefits substantially outweigh the likely harms,* (3) *subjects are given the option to withdraw from participation at any time without penalty,* (4) *any physical or psychological harm to subjects is temporary,* and (5) *subjects are debriefed as to all substantial deceptions and the research procedures are made available for public review.* All of these conditions are by now familiar to researchers and ethicists; some have already been built into federal law. Most social scientists who use deception have accepted the conditions as reasonable and even necessary components of their own ethical decision-making processes. But not all ethicists have accepted the conditions as *sufficient* justification. I would like to argue that these five conditions are both necessary *and* sufficient justifications for the use of deception in social scientific research.

Lack of Feasible Alternatives

...Deception is at times necessary, ... in order to create a laboratory situation that will seem life-like rather than artificial, since situations that strike the subject as artificial will tell us little about human behavior and may even mislead us. We need experimental control over relevant variables because neither naturalistic observation nor the subtlest statistical manipulations of available data will in all cases allow us to sort out the crucial psychological variables; but, paradoxically, we must sometimes use deception to make an experimentally created situation *seem* real, so that subjects will give genuine, generalizable responses....

But what of alternative routes? Why not, for instance, simply approach people honestly and ask them to tell us about themselves? This is in some circumstances the best procedure to follow, and I certainly find it a more *comfortable* procedure than deceptive experimentation. But Murray points out its weakness as an exclusive approach, in his Principle B. Wittingly or unwittingly, a subject's knowledge that particular aspects of his or her behavior are under study will almost certainly lead to modifications of that behavior. Enough data are available on the powerful effects of "demand characteristics," the subtle and unintended cues from researchers concerning their intentions and expectations, to indicate that explicit acknowledgement of such intentions and expectations could seriously disrupt normal behavior patterns. Further, subjects may have less than admirable reasons for trying intentionally to mislead researchers about their behavior—particularly about those aspects of behavior that society might have a strong interest in understanding and perhaps in working to modify. Destructive obedience, child abuse, racial and sexual prejudice, authoritarianism—the list could easily be extended of important psychological patterns that many people would be reluctant to admit, but that we need to understand much better if we wish to build a more satisfying society for all. If individuals will not talk about such matters honestly when they are asked straightforwardly, some form of research deception may be essential in order to gain the information we need.

Moreover, people may simply not know how they would behave in certain socially important but seldom encountered situations. Concerning such matters, it may be useless to ask people what they would probably do, and impossible to observe them in relevant real-life situations where the major variables are sufficiently unconfounded to let us make sense of the psychological processes at work. Once again, some use of deception to create an experimental reality may be the only effective means to collect essential knowledge.

But what about simulations? The word here refers not to creating an experimental reality by artificial means, but to asking research subjects to *pretend* they are participating in a realistic experiment and having them report how they think they would behave if they really were in such an experiment. This kind of simulation has often been recommended by people who do not wish to abandon the strengths of experimental research but who find deception to be an unacceptable aspect of such research. Unfortunately, simulation has proven to be an inadequate alternative both methodologically and ethically. If the simulation is relatively undetailed, it is not much different from simply asking people directly to describe how they would behave in various circumstances in the real world, and it has the same flaws as that approach—people often don't know, or don't want to tell, how they would behave.[5] If the simulation closely reproduces each step of a genuine experiment, however—if for instance, as in Don Mixon's[6] or Daniel Geller's[7] simulations of the Milgram obedience studies, subjects are walked through every stage of the experiment, being given only the information available to genuine experimental subjects at each stage—it may gain in accuracy of subjects' self-reports at the expense of ethical losses. Simulation subjects may undergo stresses similar in quality if not in intensity to those experienced by genuine subjects, and at the end they may feel similarly misled as to the actual scope or intent of the experiment they have helped to simulate. Using another example, the fact that Philip Zimbardo's prison study[8] was a simulation does not divest it of the ethical dilemmas originally confronted in nonsimulation experiments. Further, even though simulation studies rendered sufficiently close in detail to the original experiment may yield similar data from their "as-if" subjects, serious doubt would always remain about the validity of a simulation study if no "real" experiment were available for comparison. The substitution of simulation studies for experiments experienced by their participants as real thus appears to be a commendable but unrealizable dream.

The Harm-Benefit Calculus

...Remarkably little direct harm has ever come to subjects from academic social scientific research. I say "academic" because I am not willing to attempt any general ethical justification for the research programs of the CIA, General Mills, or the Church of Scientology, social scientific though they may be at times. They are not subject to the same kinds of regulations as academic research, and they are not open to free discussion or to the informal influence of scientific peer pressure. In terms of *academic* research, a potential subject is in far less physical danger during virtually any kind of research participation than in driving across town to an experimental session, or in spending the research hour playing tennis instead. Psychologically, as researchers have often pointed out to institutional review boards, the principal danger to the typical subject is boredom. The individual is at much greater psychological risk in deciding to get married, to have a baby, or to enroll as a college student—all activities typically entered without truly informed consent—than in participating in practically any academic research study ever carried out by a social scientist.

But what of the more notorious examples of psychologically stressful research? I worked behind the scenes of the most notorious of all, the Milgram obedience studies,[9] and I interviewed a substantial sample of the participants later,[10] as did (independently) a psychiatrist.[11] The remarkable thing about the Milgram subjects was not that they suffered great persisting harm, but that they suffered so little, given the intensity of their emotional reactions during the experiment itself. Through a combination of careful debriefing and their own standard coping mechanisms, nearly all subjects were able to process the Milgram experience as interesting but as basically irrelevant to their long-term psychological comfort. Though some commentators refuse to believe this, they must ignore not only the data on the Milgram subjects but also a great deal of evidence about human psychological resilience under much more traumatic conditions—from birth, through adolescence, to terminal illness. It may be possible to find an occasional individual who suffers some kind of lasting distress from an encounter with an inept experimenter, or from some unwanted self-insight induced by research participation.[12] But a botched debriefing cannot be held against the bulk of responsibly conducted studies, and a psychologically fragile individual's reactions to carefully managed research participation are unlikely to be any worse than to an emotionally involving movie, a fire-and-brimstone sermon, or a disappointing job interview....

Given the generally minor harms of properly conducted social scientific research, what are the benefits? It must be acknowledged that few social scientific research studies will produce any *immediate* major benefits to participants or to society. Unless the researcher is testing a specific aspect of a carefully formulated social program, itself derived from earlier and more basic research, the findings are likely to be useful only in terms of adding to the broad body of social scientific knowledge, much of it tentative and even contradictory....

Research projects do differ, however, in their degree of potential benefits, and the differences may be important for our ethical decision making. How do we decide whether a proposed study has enough potential benefits to outweigh its potential harms—given that both are potential rather than actual? If there were easy answers to this question, we would not still be debating it. Our estimates of potential harms and benefits must be very crude at best, informed to some extent by previous experience but retaining a greater margin for error than any of us would like. Unless we decide simply to close down large areas of social scientific research, we must continue making such crude estimates and acting upon them, as individual researchers or as peer reviewers of research by others. Some kind of peer review is essential in assessing potential benefits, though it need not always be as extensive or as formal as certain government agencies now insist. If, by rough estimate, a piece of proposed research may potentially yield minor harms offset by minor benefits, it is not worth much ethical agonizing by anyone. If the rough estimate suggests minor benefits and major harms, we can easily reject the research as ethically unacceptable. If the estimate suggests minor harms and major benefits, most of us would be willing to approve the research, though we might wish to assess its actual harms and benefits later and to revise our judgmental criteria accordingly. It is only when our rough estimates suggest major potential harms *and* major potential benefits that we really begin to worry about the crudity of our estimates—and about what specific meaning to invest in such admittedly ambiguous terms as "major potential benefit."

We have already considered the question of harm with regard to the specific example of the Milgram obedience studies. Let us look at the question of benefit in the same context, since estimates of "major benefit" have been more disputed there than in perhaps any other example. Several of Stanley Milgram's critics appear to assume that his claims for the social value of his research were post-hoc justifications intended to quiet criticisms of his deceptive and stressful experimental practices. But Milgram had made a rather detailed case for substantial potential benefit in his original research proposals, and his research was funded on that basis. He had read widely concerning the events of the Holocaust and the various attempts to explain its origins. He did not propose yet another intellectual analysis, or a psychological study of some phenomenon previously much studied and perhaps vaguely related to the Holocaust, such as conformity to peer pressures. Instead, he proposed a series of studies that would examine specific contextual variables associated with greater or lesser obedience to a realistic command to administer severe physical pain to another individual. Doubtless there are many steps between such displays of individual obedience and the occurrence of a social phenomenon as broad and intense as the Holocaust. But it is reasonable to assume that laboratory research on destructive obedience could make a useful contribution to the understanding of destructive obedience on a large scale, even though it might not be the only way or even the single best way to proceed in elucidating the genesis of Holocaust-like phenomena. Further, it is reasonable to assume that better and wider public understanding of the conditions most likely to promote destructive obedience on a small scale could have a prophylactic effect with regard to destructive obedience on a large scale—although, again, there are surely many forces working in a complex society to strengthen or weaken tendencies toward genocidal Final Solutions. Thus, I think Milgram made a good case concerning potential benefit, on the basis of the issues involved and the means by which he proposed to study them. It is hard to conceive how anyone could make a better case, before the fact, for major benefits from basic social scientific research.

Furthermore, I think a case can now be made that the Milgram research has actually yielded substantial benefits in the years since its publication. Most ethical discussions of deceptive social scientific research heavily stress harm and lightly sketch benefits, as if any negative effects would reverberate through all of human society, while any positive effects would hardly resound beyond laboratory walls. That is not the way the diffusion of knowledge works in our society. I would suggest that Solomon Asch's deception-based research on social conformity helped sensitize a generation of college students to the dangers of conformism. I would suggest that Asch's student, Stanley Milgram, has helped to sensitize another generation, well beyond campus boundaries, to the possibility that they themselves could under certain circumstances be as obedient as the sternest Nazis. As much as Milgarm's research offends certain moral sensibilities, it has also dramatized serious ethical choices so provocatively that virtually every introductory psychology and social psychology textbook of the past decade has prominently featured Milgram's findings.[15] Some social scientists and ethicists find it implausible that laboratory studies of individual psychological phenomena could yield any useful understanding of the dynamics of a Holocaust. I find it even more implausible to assume that research with the broad dissemination and emotional impact of Milgram's studies has not already generated enough introspection and discussion to diminish significantly the likelihood of another Holocaust like phenomenon, at least in this country.

Few social scientific studies are likely to have the individual force of Milgram's obedience research. But judgments about their potential benefit can be made in similar fashion, on the basis of the researcher's serious consideration of factors likely to play a role in major social phenomena, the choice of apt research strategies, and the social implications of anticipated (or unanticipated but possible) research findings. At no time can these judgments be so definitive or so overwhelming as to outweigh certain kinds of research harm. But in combination with the remaining criteria, they may lead to a reasoned decision that limited potential harm deriving from deception and other aspects of the research design are outweighed by the likely long-term benefits of a particular research project as a part of the ongoing social scientific research enterprise.

The Option to Withdraw

One of the objections most often raised against research deception is that it prevents subjects from deciding whether to give their fully informed consent to research participation. "Informed consent" is a concept that grew out of medical experimentation, where the only way for patients to make an effective decision about research participation is to know well in advance what kinds of physical interventions might be imposed upon them. Many medical interventions have potentially serious and virtually irrevocable consequences, and if the patient fails to say "No" before being anesthetized, cut open, injected with cancer cells, infected with bacteria, etc., there may be no way of effectively saying "No" later. The situation is usually very different in social scientific research. As already suggested, the intervention is most often minor and the consequences are temporary or reversible (as by post-research debriefing). Perhaps even more important in an ethical sense is the possibility of an ongoing process of informed consent. Even if, for purposes of conducting a study, subjects must be asked to give their consent to participation partly on the basis of misleading or incomplete information, they can continue their assessment of the study's costs to them as it proceeds, and can be guaranteed the right to quit at any point where they decide that the costs are becoming greater than they wish to bear. This process of "ongoing informed consent" is implicit in many research situations, including interviews and questionnaires where the subject is fully in control of the information he or she supplies. In circumstances where the possible harms are greater—as when a questionnaire deals with particularly sensitive issues, or when an experiment manipulates social or other pressures to continue participation beyond normally tolerable limits of stress—the subject should clearly and emphatically be informed in advance of the right to stop participating at any time without penalty.

In some instances, a research procedure may have the potential to impose upon a subject a psychological harm well outside those encountered in normal social interactions, under circumstances where the subject is misled as to what is about to happen and is unable to withdraw his ongoing consent in time to avoid the harm. Such instances more closely resemble physical intervention without informed consent in medical research than does the usual social scientific study, and they should be placed under the same constraints as medical interventions. I am thinking here of such studies as those in which a subject fills out a personality questionnaire, then is suddenly and falsely told that the questionnaire reveals hidden homosexual tendencies or other characteristics that are highly discrepant from the subject's own self-image. Most subjects appear to accept rather easily, during debriefing, the information that an apparently realistic experimental situation has been fabricated or that a recently introduced stranger is not nearly as bad a person as the experimenter has made him out to be. But I suspect that a false imputation of homosexuality or neurosis, made by a psychologist, may continue to raise self-doubts well after the psychologist has changed stories. The characerization is not a consequence of the subject's own behavior, and its sudden attribution to the subject is made without an opportunity for ongoing informed consent.

The Milgram obedience studies have been criticized on somewhat similar grounds. But I do not see the Milgram studies as falling in the same category, since subjects in those studies were never falsely characterized. Subjects who shocked the "victim" unmercifully did so with little persuasion from the experimenter and much resistance from the "victim." They had the choice throughout the experiment of quitting at any time, and in fact a substantial portion of subjects did quit. A continuing opportunity was provided [to] subjects to make a moral decision, and no force or unusual psychological technique was brought to bear to interfere with that choice. In such instances, where research participation brings unsought self-knowledge, I do feel that the researcher has a responsibility to help the subject cope with such self-knowledge and to give the subject some guidance in integrating it satisfactorily into his or her self-concept over the long run. Milgram's debriefing procedures were designed to do that, and the follow-up research suggests that they were effective in that regard. Self-knowledge in itself, even unsought self-knowledge, does not seem to me an ethically negative "risk." Ethically concerned individuals of many persuasions and cultural roles, including preachers, teachers, novelists, and charismatic leaders, have attempted throughout history to induce such knowledge in anyone whose attention they could momentarily catch, even by deceptive devices (such as embedding lessons about human nature within an apparently innocuous entertainment). The induction of unsought self-knowledge need not be seen as a major mission of social scientists, but neither should it be seen as an evil from which research subjects must be protected at all costs.

Temporary versus Lasting Harm

Though I am primarily a consequentialist rather than a deontologist, I am unwilling to balance the certainty of lasting harm to a misinformed subject against the possibility of general benefits as a result of a particular study. But temporary discomfort, anxiety, or even pain may fairly be weighed among the harms in a harm-benefit ratio, as long as the subject is permitted to cease participation whenever the distress becomes personally intolerable and as long as no lasting scars (physical or psychological) result. The generation of temporarily intense anxiety or pain should not be employed casually, even if these terms are met; it must be more than offset by the potential value of the research. Furthermore, as with unsought self-insight in the previous section, the researcher is obligated to take an active role in restoring the anxious or agitated subject to his or her normal emotional state. The debriefing period is usually the opportune time to do this.

Debriefing and Publicity

The debriefing period, properly used, is a time for limiting or eliminating several potential harms of deceptive research practices. First, it provides the occasion to diminish anxiety and other unpleasant emotional reactions, and to give the subject a sense of the true value of his or her participation as a research subject. Instead of leaving the subject with a sense of having been tricked, the researcher should honestly communicate the difficulty or impossibility of doing research on the topic at hand with full subject foreknowledge, and should describe the efforts necessary to give subjects a realistic—if deceptive—experience in a controlled setting. Second, the debriefing process restores a sense of honesty to the researcher, and by interrupting the role of arch-manipulator, it brings him or her back toward the human level of the subjects. Third, it provides an ethical model to researchers, subjects, and others of how a necessary deception can be limited in its consequences, how deceptions can be used without destroying the integrity of human social contacts or the autonomy and self-esteem of the individuals involved. Given the vast amounts of deception which occur in ordinary social life *without* any intentional debriefing, the use of deception linked with debriefing might even have a salutary effect upon the public sense of ethical standards, as already suggested, rather than producing the invidious effects predicted by certain critics of deceptive practices.

Finally, the requirement of debriefing is ethically advantageous in that it increases the level of publicity connected with the research. I am not referring to publicity in the usual sense of newspaper headlines and talk-show appearances, but to publicity as the term has been used by John Rawls and subsequently by Sissela Bok. As Bok puts it, "According to such a constraint, a moral principle must be capable of public statement and defense."[13] The general requirement of debriefing means that a researcher must at some reasonable point publicize his or her deceptive research procedures to the individuals most likely to be at risk as a result, namely, the subjects, and must therefore be able to justify the deceptions to them or risk some kind of retaliation from them. But publicity must involve more than the researcher's interactions with the subject, as the latter part of boundary condition 5 suggests.

Peer review and reviews by institutional review boards mean more publicity, more occasions when the researcher must be able to offer an acceptable ethical defense of any deceptive practices he or she feels to be required in the chosen research area. Still other professional practices common in the social sciences involve further publicity: peer reviews for academic promotions; peer reviews by granting agencies, in addition to IRB reviews; presentations of research procedures and findings at professional meetings; journal review and publication of research papers.

Conclusion: The Salutary Consequences of Publicity

Several years ago I wrote a short piece for *Psychology Today* in which I compared and contrasted experimental social psychologists with professional con artists.[14] The similarities, which were considerable, mainly concerned the practice of deception. The differences, which were also considerable, included such things as the principal motivations of psychologists vs. those of con artists and the attitudes of the two groups toward "subjects" or "marks." The *major* difference concerned the matter of publicity. Con artists avoid publicity as much as possible, and thus their deceptive practices can grow unchecked except by sheer force of law. Social psychologists, however, ordinarily seek publicity in the form of professional presentations, and have also by and large accepted its necessity in such forms as debriefing. Publicity of a perfectly ordinary professional sort was how the Milgram studies and others became the focus of a great deal of professional discussion of ethics, eventually widening to include discussion in the news media, on television drama programs, and in various circles of government. I say "publicity of a perfectly ordinary professional sort" because no scandal was involved, no hidden deceits were dramatically revealed, no damage suits came to court. Milgram talked and wrote about his research, and other people responded with their views on the ethical considerations involved, and Milgram responded in turn with his, and the dialogue continues.

The dialogue has by no means been a useless one. Deception in social science research has become much more constrained over the past fifteen years, in large part as the result of such voluntary publicity rather than through the coercion of federal regulations and financial threats. The federal government may ultimately outlaw deception in social scientific research altogether, in response to political pressures stronger than social scientists can muster—in which case I would not be surprised to see the spread of bootleg deception research on and off university campuses, conducted by researchers who feel they cannot study certain major issues effectively by any other means. That would be the ultimate ethical disaster for deception research, since in secret it would be hardly more constrained than the con artist's trade. The ultimate condition under which deception research is ethically justifiable is *out in the open,* where its practitioners are continually forced to present their justifications to others and where their critics must resort to reason rather than coercion. Ethical decision making is not a closed system in which a set of rules can be ordained once and applied to all situations forever after. I do not have all the answers about deception, its effects, and its reasonable limits; nor does anyone else. Continuing publicity about the kinds of deception social scientists see as necessary, and about the controlled conditions under which deception should be tolerated in research, will feed the ongoing dialogue about deception in such a way as to make our decisions about it increasingly more realistic, more sophisticated, and more ethical.

Notes

1. Stanley Milgram, "Subject Reaction: The Neglected Factor in the Ethics of Experimentation," *Hastings Center Report* 7, no. 5 (1977): 19.
2. Sissela Bok, *Lying: Moral Choice in Public and Private Life* (New York: Vintage Books, 1979), pp. 34–49.
3. *Measure for Measure,* act 3, scene 1. In William Shakespeare, *The Comedies* (New York: Heritage Press, 1958), p. 267.
4. Bok, *Lying,* pp. 32–33.
5. Jonathan L. Freedman, "Roleplaying: Psychology by Consensus," *Journal of Personality and Social Psychology* 13 (1969): 107–14.
6. Don Mixon, "Instead of Deception," *Journal for the Theory of Social Behavior* 2 (1972): 145–77.
7. Daniel M. Geller, "Involvement in Role-Playing Simulations: A Demonstration with Studies on Obedience," *Journal of Personality and Social Psychology* 36 (1978): 219–35.
8. Philip G. Zimbardo, "Pathology of Imprisonment," *Society* 9, no. 4 (1972): 4–6.
9. Stanley Milgram, *Obedience to Authority* (New York: Harper & Row, 1974).
10. Alan C. Elms, *Social Psychology and Social Relevance* (Boston: Little, Brown, 1972), pp. 153–54.
11. Stanley Milgram, "Issues in the Study of Obedience: A Reply to Baumrind," *American Psychologist* 19 (1964): 848–52.
12. Diana Baumrind, "Metaethical and Normative Considerations Covering the Treatment of Human Subjects in the Behavioral Sciences," in E. C. Kennedy, ed., *Human Rights and Psychological Research* (New York: Crowell, 1975), pp. 37–68.
13. Bok, *Lying,* pp. 97–112.
14. Alan C. Elms, "Alias Johnny Hooker," *Psychology Today* 10, no. 9 (1977): 19.

NO ⤶

Research Using Intentional Deception: Ethical Issues Revisited

In a series of articles (Baumrind, 1964, 1971, 1975a, 1975b, 1978, 1979), beginning with a critique of the Milgram (1964) paradigm, I argue that the use of
intentional deception in the research setting is unethical, imprudent, and
unwarranted scientifically. In response to my latest article (Baumrind, 1979),
Baron (1981) offered "an openly optimistic rejoinder." He claimed that deception research is necessary to accomplish beneficial scientific ends and that as a
result of the guidelines researchers now use informed consent and thorough
debriefing. Two respondents took exception to Baron's optimistic rejoinder.
Dresser (1981) pointed out that in distorting a study's true purpose the investigator necessarily grounds participants' willingness to cooperate on misinformed consent. Goldstein (1981) argued that participants' rights to
autonomy, dignity, and privacy are necessarily violated by deceptive research
practices and rejected Baron's assurance that experimenters were now sensi-
tized to ethical issues. Surveys of the major social psychological journals suggest that Goldstein is correct and Baron's optimism is unwarranted. Ten years
after publication of the *Ethical Principles in the Conduct of Research With
Human Participants* (American Psychological Association, 1973), I was invited
to revisit these issues in the context of a symposium on ethics of deception
research delivered to the International Society for Research on Aggression.

By intentional deception I mean withholding information in order to
obtain participation that the participant might otherwise decline, using
deceptive instructions and confederate manipulations in laboratory research,
and employing concealment and staged manipulations in field settings.
Because perfect communication between human beings is impossible to
achieve, there will always be some degree of misunderstanding in the contract
between researcher and subject. Full disclosure of everything that could possibly affect a given subject's decision to participate is not possible, and therefore cannot be ethically required. Provided that participants agree to
postponement of full disclosure of the purposes of the research, absence of
full disclosure does not constitute intentional deception. The investigator
whose purpose is "to take the person unaware by trickery" or to "cause the
person to believe the false" in order to minimize ambiguity about causal

From *American Psychologist*, vol. 40, no. 2, 1985, pp. 165–175. Copyright © 1985 by American
Psychological Association. Reprinted with permission.

inference is intentionally deceiving subject-participants to further the investigator's scientific ends or career goals.

Investigators continue to use intentional deception and to justify its use. Epistemological superiority is accorded to deceptive methods as a means of controlling the demand characteristics of the setting by assuring that all subjects believe the situation to be realistic and perceive it in the same way. If intentional deception does not accomplish this objective, its epistemological superiority is doubtful, which in turn casts doubt on the benefits of intentional deception and thus on the justification for its use. Although the examples I offer are drawn largely from aggression research, the justification for deceptive practices arises from the research paradigm that guides experimental social psychology as a whole. It is necessary, therefore, to examine that paradigm.

Present Status of Deception Research

If deceit is used to obtain consent, by definition it cannot be informed. Deceptive instructions logically contradict the informed consent provision contained in all federal and professional ethical guidelines. Yet these guidelines do permit each of the provisions guaranteeing informed consent to be waived provided that some or all considerations such as the following pertain:

> (a) The research objective is of great importance and cannot be achieved without the use of deception; (b) on being fully informed later (Principle E), participants are expected to find the procedures reasonable and to suffer no loss of confidence in the integrity of the investigator or of others involved; (c) research participants are allowed to withdraw from the study at any time (Principle F), and are free to withdraw their data when the concealment or misrepresentation is revealed (Principle H); and (e) investigators take full responsibility for detecting and removing stressful aftereffects of the experience (Principle I). (American Psychological Association, 1982, p. 41)

No strategic guidelines are included to assure that these considerations pertain. Institutional review boards (IRBs), as well as investigators, are at liberty to set their own.

Neither the incidence nor the magnitude of deception reported in social psychological research appears to have decreased since 1973. Thus, the APA guidelines appear to serve an expressive rather than a deterrent function. McNamara and Woods (1977) reported a rise to 57% in a survey covering the years 1971 to 1974. In the most recent study (Smith & Richardson, 1983), approximately half of the 464 psychology undergraduates surveyed reported that the experiment in which they had participated used deception. Both figures exceed Seeman's (1969) figures of 18% in 1948 and 37% in 1963. The maximum magnitude of reported deception has not decreased as four exemplars published since the 1973 APA guidelines will illustrate: (a) Milgram's paradigm was duplicated by Shanab and Yahya (1977) with children as young as six; graphic reports of the children's reactions document trembling, lip biting, and nervous laughter; (b) White (1979) used a typical aggression paradigm in which a confederate angered real subjects by evaluating them personally in a highly negative and insulting manner; subjects were then asked to administer shocks to the confederate, after being given a false cover story as to the purpose of the experiment; (c) Zimbardo, Andersen, and Kabat (1981) induced partial deafness through posthypnotic suggestion to study the effect of unrecognized hearing deficit on the development of paranoia; Zimbardo et al. then misinformed subjects as the purpose of the experiment and what experiences they would undergo and recruited subjects with the promise that they would continue to play part in his research, a promise that was not kept; and (d) Marshall and Zimbardo (1979) used multiple high-magnitude deceptions to study the affective consequences of inadequately explained physiological arousal; they misinformed subjects about the purpose of the experiment; they manipulated physiological arousal via injection of epinephrine or placebo after telling subjects that they would receive a vitamin injection; and they misled subjects into thinking their responses were not being monitored when they were. They then postponed debriefing for six weeks until all subjects had been tested. The IRB permitted all of the above manipulations, balking only at a planned "angry" condition on the basis that it was unethical to induce anger in unsuspecting subjects....

Costs of Deception Research

The costs of deceptive research practices accrue to the participants, to the scientific enterprise, and to society.

Harm Done to the Subject

A brief excerpt from an autobiographical account of a former secretary who typed my earlier articles illustrates the subtle but serious harm that can be done to subjects by undermining their trust in their own judgment and in fiduciaries as well as the reluctance many have to admit, even to themselves, that they have been duped.

> This experiment [involving deceptive feedback about quality of performance relative to peers] confirmed my conviction that standards were completely arbitrary ... because the devastating blow was struck by a psychologist, whose competence to judge behavior I had never doubted before....It is not a matter of "belief" but of fact that I found the experience devastating.
>
> I was harmed in an area of my thinking which was central to my personal development at that time. Many of us who volunteered for the experiment were hoping to learn something about ourselves that would help us to gauge our own strengths and weaknesses, and formulate rules for living that took them into account. When, instead, I learned that I did not have any trustworthy way of knowing myself—or anything else—and hence could have no confidence in any lifestyle I formed on the basis of my knowledge, I was not only disappointed, but felt that I had somehow been cheated into learning, not what I needed to learn, but something which

stymied my very efforts to learn. I told literally no one about it for eight years because of a vague feeling of shame over having let myself be tricked and duped. It was only when I realized that I was not peculiar but had, on the contrary, had a *typical* experience that I first recounted it publicly. (Baumrind, 1978, pp. 22–23)

Anecdotal evidence such as this has been challenged as hearsay. A number of studies have been undertaken to establish whether subjects are harmed by deception experiments. The results are equivocal. However, most of these studies rely on self-report rather than behavioral evidence. About 80% of subjects, when asked, say that they were glad to have participated in the experiment. This is used illogically to establish that subjects suffered no harm. Thus, Milgram (1974, p. 195) justified his shocking procedure by citing results of a follow-up questionnaire in which 84% of subjects said they were glad to have participated in the experiment. However, as Patten (1977) pointed out, it is logically inconsistent for Milgram to use the self-reported judgments of overly acquiescent ("destructively obedient") subjects to establish the ethical propriety of his experiments. Similarly, Marshall and Zimbardo's (1979) subjects were chosen for their hypnotic suggestibility and would be expected to defer compliantly to the experimenter's expertise. After all, if self-reports could be regarded as accurate measures of the impact of experimental conditions, we could dispense entirely with experimental manipulation and behavioral measures, substituting instead vivid descriptions of environmental stimuli to which subjects would be instructed to report how they would act.

Self-report questionnaires used to assess participants' reactions are tacked on as an afterthought and generally lack psychometric sophistication. Subjects' self-reported gladness to be stressed and deceived may be explained by a variety of psychological mechanisms in addition to deferential compliance discussed above. These mechanisms include reduction of cognitive dissonance, identification with the aggressor, and masochistic obedience. It takes well-trained clinical interviewers to uncover true feeling of anger, shame, or altered self-image in participants who believe that what they say should conform with their image of a "good subject." Ring, Wallston, and Corey (1970), in their follow-up interview exploring subjective reactions to a Milgram-type obedience experiment, reported that many subjects stated that they were experiencing difficulty in trusting adult authorities. In a recently reported study of the effects of debriefing (Smith & Richardson, 1983), about 20% of 464 introductory psychology undergraduates reported experiencing harm. In the harm group, 61% had participated in a deception experiment as compared to 38% in the no-harm group. Students who had participated in deception experiments tended to perceive psychologists as less trustworthy than did nondeceived participants. Even subjects who deny other harmful effects do report decreased trust in social scientists following deception research. For example, citing instances of experimental deception:

Fillenbaum (1966) found that deception led to increased suspiciousness (even though subjects tended not to act on their suspicions), and Keisner

(1971) found that deceived and debriefed subjects were "less inclined to trust experimenters to tell the truth" (p. 7). Other authors (Silverman, Shulman, & Wiesenthal, 1970; Fine & Lindskold, 1971) have noted that deception decreases compliance with demand characteristics and increases negativistic behavior. (In Wahl, 1972, p. 12)

Decreased trust in fiduciaries then is a generally acknowledged cost of deception itself. Even if we choose to accept self-report data as veridical, 20% of subjects report such harm and the proportion is highest for deception research. From an ethical and legal perspective, harm is done to *each* individual. The harm the minority of subjects report they have suffered is not nullified by the majority of subjects who claim to have escaped unscathed, any more than the harm done victims of drunk drivers can be excused by the disproportionate number of pedestrians with sufficient alacrity to avoid being run over by them.

From a rule-utilitarian perspective, the procedural issue concerns where the locus of control should rightly reside. The generally accepted principle of respect for self-determination dictates that the locus of control should reside with each participant. The subject, like the investigator, retains the right to decide whether the likely benefits to self and society outweigh the likely costs to self and society. The investigator is not privileged to weigh the costs to the subjects against the benefits to society. The principle of informed consent allows the subject to decide how to dispose of his or her person. The subject acting as sovereign agent may freely agree to incur risk, inconvenience, or pain. But a subject whose consent has been obtained by deceitful and fraudulent means has become an object for the investigator to manipulate. A subject can only regain sovereignty by claiming to have been a subject all along and not an object. Not surprisingly, subjects tend to affirm their agency by denying that they have allowed themselves to be treated as objects, and when queried by an experimenter, most will say that they were glad to have been subjects.

Harm Done to the Profession

The harm done by deception researchers accrues to the profession and to the larger society as well as to the individual. The scientific costs of deception in research are considerable. These costs include (a) exhausting the pool of naive subjects, (b) jeopardizing community support for the research enterprise, and (c) undermining the commitment to truth of the researchers themselves.

The power of the scientific community is conferred by the larger community. Social support for behavioral science research is jeopardized when investigators promote parochial values that conflict with more universal principles of moral judgment and moral conduct. The use of the pursuit of truth to justify deceit risks the probable effect of undermining confidence in the scientific enterprise and in the credibility of those who engage in it. As a result of widespread use of deception, psychologists are suspected of being tricksters. Suspicious subjects may respond by role-playing the part they think the investigator expects, doing what they think the investigator wants them to do (Orne, 1962), or pretending to be naive. The *practice* of deceiving participants and of justifying such deception undermines the investigators' own integrity and commitment to truth. Short-term gains are traded for the cumulative costs of long-term deterioration of investigators' ethical sensibilities and integrity and damage to their credibility.

Harm Done to Society

The moral norm of reciprocity proscribing deceitful social relations both acknowledges and places a positive value on the fact that the elements of social reality are reciprocally determined. The inherent cost of behaving deceitfully in the research setting is to undermine trust in expert authorities. If conduct in the laboratory or natural setting cannot be isolated from conduct in daily life, the implications are far-reaching. In a popular article entitled "Snoopology," John Jung (1975) discussed some probable effects of experimentation in real-life situations with persons who did not know they were serving as experimental subjects. These included increased self-consciousness in public places, broadening of the aura of mistrust and suspicion that pervades daily life, inconveniencing and irritating persons by contrived situations, and desensitizing individuals to the needs of others by "boy-who-cried-wolf" effects so that unusual public events are suspected of being part of a research project.

Truth telling and promise keeping serve the function in social relations that physical laws do in the natural world; these practices promote order and regularity in social relations, without which intentional actions would be very nearly impossible. By acting in accord with agreed-upon rules, keeping promises, acting honorably, and following the rules of the game, human beings construct for themselves a coherent consistent environment in which purposive behavior becomes possible.

Benefits of Deception

Even if a simple cost-benefit calculus consistent with act-utilitarianism is adopted and we agree to weigh the costs to subjects against the benefits to humankind, we must still inquire as to what these benefits might be. Consideration of the benefits of a proposed investigation within the context of a cost-benefit ethical analysis requires more stringent standards for what constitutes scientifically and socially valid research than in a purely empirical context. I will argue that the scientific and social benefits of deception research cannot be established with sufficient certitude to tip the scale in favor of procedures that wrong subjects. The deception paradigms employed by experimental social psychologists do not and cannot deliver the reduction in ambiguity that could justify what would otherwise be regarded as ethically unacceptable research practices. Deceptive practices do not succeed in accomplishing the scientific objectives that are used to justify such deception, any better than methods that do not require deception. If the phenomenon being studied is socially important it can be studied in natural or clinical contexts that do not require laboratory manipulation to produce. If laboratory controls are required to create a counterfactual condition that exists nowhere, then in order to claim benefits, it must first be shown that the counterfactual conditions are possible to create in situ and that the common good would be enhanced by doing so.

The claim is made that deceptive manipulations are required to create a psychological reality under experimental conditions that permit valid inference. This claim is based on two assumptions: (a) deceptive instructions create a uniform psychological reality; and (b) causal inference in the social sciences can be achieved with a high level of certitude. But neither of these assumptions has gone unchallenged by critics of experimental social psychological methods.

Deception does not create a uniform psychological reality when subjects in an experiment differ in their level of naivete or in their responses to the possibility of experimental manipulation. It is now common knowledge among many kinds of prospective subjects that deception is employed routinely in social psychological experiments. The tendency of some subjects to assign idiosyncratic meaning rather than to buy the experimenter's cover story, even when it is true, defeats the purpose of deceptive instructions, which is to control subject set. There is evidence that investigators untrained in phenomenological assessment methodology will fail to detect subject suspiciousness. Page (1973) has shown that asking subjects fewer than four questions will classify only 5% of subjects as suspicious, whereas extended questionnaires will yield about 40% suspicious subjects, and the behaviors of suspicious subjects in the experimental situation are generally found to differ from those who are not. Referring to laboratory research, Seeman (1969) concluded, "In view of the frequency with which deception is used in research we may soon be reaching a point where we no longer have naive subjects, but only naive experimenters" (p. 1026).

The traditional experimental social psychologist justifies deception research on the logical positivist presupposition that laboratory observations *could* provide unassailable knowledge if only we were able to produce a uniform psychological reality and do away with error variance. The objective of the traditional social psychology experiment is to enable the experimenter to infer unambiguously the existence and direction of causal relations by ruling out alternative causal explanations. Controls requiring deceptive instructions are introduced with the implicit expectation that their use can provide such unassailable knowledge. But the claim that observations can provide value-free, objective knowledge has been challenged by philosophers and scientists at least since Heisenberg's (1958) principle was enunciated. From the perspective of their critics, experimental controls distort by controlling the phenomena the investigator is attempting to explain. The meaning subjects assign to a situation depends upon the characteristics of that situation, as well as upon subject characteristics. A psychological mechanism observed to operate under one set of experimental conditions often fails to replicate under a somewhat different set of experimental conditions because the meaning persons give a situation is contextual and purposive and dependent upon factors that the experimenter may not even be aware of, such as the strangeness of the situation from the perspective of the subject. Typically the conjunction of events in a laboratory situation is atypical, and the effect of constraining the options a subject has is itself a factor that distorts the responses given and the behavior observed. Whereas laboratory methods construct situations and contexts for persons and then assess how they respond to these extrinsically constructed situations, persons in their natural settings typically construct or select their own social worlds among the options available. Bronfenbrenner (1977) called for an ecological perspective in developmental and social research precisely because he disputed the possibility that subjects *could* assign the same meaning to their behavior in the natural setting as they did in the highly artificial laboratory setting.

Thus, it can be argued that laboratory conditions create the very ambiguity they are intended to dispel. For example, Gardner (1978) could not replicate Glass and Singer's (1972) findings of negative aftereffects of noise when subjects knew that they had the option of discontinuing participation. Assurance of freedom to withdraw removed the effect of the noise stressor. If Glass and Singer intended to study the negative aftereffects of noise per se, their experimental manipulation was inappropriate. If, on the other hand, they intended to study the effects of *inescapable* noise, their experimental situation was highly relevant, but clearly violated participants' right to withdraw. Similarly, the experimental condition created by Milgram in his studies of "destructive obedience" exemplifies a highly ambiguous control that seriously compromises the generalizability of his findings. Because subjects were paid for their participation and recruited on that basis, obedience in Milgram's setting for some subjects might have reflected a sense of fair play and employee loyalty rather than, as for other subjects, shocking obedience. Moreover, Milgram's experimental directives were incongruous and bizarre, thus confusing and distressing the subject. Furthermore, the experimenter's orders were legitimized by the laboratory setting, thus permitting subjects to resolve their sense of incongruity by trusting the good will of the investigator toward both subject and confederate. Far from illuminating real life, as he claimed, Milgram in fact appeared to have constructed a set of conditions so internally inconsistent that they could not occur in real life. His application of his results to destructive obedience in military settings or Nazi Germany (Milgram, 1974) is metaphoric rather than scientific.

Not only was the situation artificial in Milgram's experiment, but all the necessary data were provided by the graduate student confederates who demonstrated conclusively by obeying Milgram's instructions to inflict suffering upon the subjects that normal, well-intentioned people will hurt others who are innocent. The confederates justified their actions on the same bases as the subjects justified theirs, that they were inflicting no real harm. Because subjects' motives could not unambiguously be called destructive obedience and the behavior of his graduate student confederates could, Milgram's deceitful manipulation was neither necessary nor could it permit valid inference to the real-life situations to which Milgram generalized his results.

Defenders of laboratory manipulations have attempted to rebut the criticism that laboratory experiments lack external validity and therefore do not produce knowledge of benefit to society that could justify misinforming subjects. Berkowitz and Donnerstein (1982) argued that laboratory experiments are oriented mainly toward testing causal hypotheses concerning mediational processes and are not carried out to determine the probability that a certain event will occur in a particular population. They claimed that, in theoretically oriented investigations, the specific manipulations and measures are merely arbitrary operational definitions of general theoretical constructs and the subject sample is merely an arbitrary group from the general universe of all humans to which the hypothesis is assumed to apply.

> We have now come to our central thesis: The meaning the subjects assign to the situation they are in and the behavior they are carrying out plays a greater part in determining the generalizability of an experiment's outcome than does the sample's demographic representativeness or the setting's surface realism. (Berkowitz & Donnerstein, 1982, p. 249)

But if the specific operations were interchangeable as Berkowitz and Donnerstein claimed, the context and subject populations could be altered without changing the results. However, failure to replicate social psychological findings when probed by a critical investigator is more the rule than the exception in social psychology, and the failure to replicate can seldom be attributed unambiguously to a controlled change in experimental conditions. Results do not survive even minor changes in the experimental conditions, such as notifying subjects that they may withdraw from an experiment. Therefore, Berkowitz and Donnerstein were incorrect in claiming that the specific operations typically employed in social psychological experiments are interchangeable. In the event that the variables that are untied and independently manipulated in the laboratory setting are necessarily or typically confounded in the natural setting, conditions in the laboratory cannot or will not be replicable. Psychological processes do not occur in a psychosocial vacuum. When the task, variables, and setting can have no real-world counterparts, the processes dissected in the laboratory also cannot operate in the real world. In that case, deceptive research practices cannot be justified by their benefits to science and society.

Furthermore, deceptive practices cannot be justified unless they result in findings that are controversial because the benefit to society of noncontroversial, that is, trivial, findings is minimal. Berkowitz and Donnerstein markedly attenuated the importance of causal hypotheses by claiming that experimenters ask only, *can* "alterations in Variable X lead to changes in Variable Y?" This is generally a trivial question because we almost always know prior to conducting the experiment that the answer is yes. Generally, the phenomenon has already been shown to occur in real life. For example, did Zimbardo and his colleagues (1981) really need to induce partial deafness through posthypnotic suggestion to confirm what is a generally acknowledged clinical observation that unexplained deafness in older people induces suspiciousness? The mechanistic model of development implied by experimental social psychological procedures is not really applicable to social psychological phenomena. If the Cartesian, mechanistic world view is insufficient to explain the physical world, then it is certainly not adequate to explain biosocial and psychosocial phenomena. If physical reality is subject to indeterminacy introduced by the observer, as Heisenberg (1958) assured us it is, how much more true is this of human behavior? The level of complexity of social phenomena and the implausibility of treating human beings as interchangeable or even as identical with themselves over time sharply limit the level of certitude that can accompany any empirical generalization in the sociobehavioral sciences.

A little ingenuity may well yield fruitful alternatives to deception (see Geller, 1982, for a systematic review of such alternatives). If a phenomenon is socially significant it can frequently be observed in situ, making experimental manipulation unnecessary. Alternatively, experimenters could act as subjects in their own experiments and employ introspection. Aggression can certainly be studied in situ. Aggression researchers can study acts intended to harm others in such naturalistic situations as organized sports, which vary along relevant parameters such as rules and normative expectations. Investigators interested in studying how people justify intentionally causing others to suffer in real life have the option of introspective examination of their own behavior as participants in the research process. Thus, in lieu of the familiar teacher–learner aggression paradigm (Berkowitz & Geen, 1966) in which a confederate makes a series of preplanned errors on a word-association task and subjects deliver shocks to the confederate, investigators and their confederates could introspect. It turns out that subjects believe that they are benefiting the learner and therefore are not behaving aggressively in the sense of intending to inflict harm (Kane, Joseph, & Tedeschi, 1976). Experimenters and their confederates argue just as research subjects do that their motives in inflicting emotionally painful discomfort are altruistic or justified by role expectations, even though an objective observer might regard the behavior of confederates and subjects as equally aggressive. For example, Milgram justified his deceptive procedure by suggesting that many subjects were grateful for the insight into their own destructively obedient tendencies that the experiment and debriefing afforded. Investigators could also study retaliative aggression without using deception by introducing certain nondeceptive experimental conditions in which they acted as real, rather than confederate, subjects. Immediately after the usual perfunctory debriefing in deception research, subjects would be instructed to demonstrate behaviorally how they feel about their participation by delivering 0 to 20 mild but genuine electric shocks to the forearm of the experimenter who designed the research. In addition to providing data on subjects' response to deception and some data on retaliative aggression, this aversive reinforcement coda might have the added advantage of rendering superfluous any need for extrinsically imposed codes mandating ethical practices in the conduct of research with human participants.

The suggestion that psychologists serve as their own subjects and introspect was made before me by the investigators whose work Marshall and Zimbardo (1979) failed to replicate:

> In these days of ethical guidelines and human subjects committees, this may very well be the end of the matter, for it is unlikely that anyone will do experiments such as ours or Marshall and Zimbardo's for quite a while, if ever again. On the particular issue at stake, however, this is probably of little moment, for this is one issue on which the readers can serve as their own subjects. If they will do a thorough introspective job after convincing a physician to inject them with .5 cc of a 1:1000 solution of epinephrine, they can decide which of us is right. (Schachter & Singer, 1979, p. 995)

Debriefing

Effective debriefing does not nullify the wrong done participants by deceiving them and may not even repair their damaged self-image or ability to trust adult authorities. Subjects did, after all, commit acts that they believed at the time could be harmful to others, and they were in fact, entrapped into committing those acts by an authority whom they had reason to trust. And if the participants (subjects and confederates) are students, they have, in fact, been provided with a model of behavior in which scientific ends are used to justify deceitful means.

However, if an investigator does elect to use deception, he or she must include an effective debriefing procedure in order to reduce the long-range costs of deception and offer partial reparation to subjects. Sieber (1983) offered carefully considered recommendations for debriefing when deception is used. She argued convincingly that deceptive debriefing is especially unethical and that debriefing in deception research should be undertaken only by a skilled and sympathetic professional, or it may do more harm than good. For example, Mills (1976) presented in detail a debriefing scenario that he developed over 20 years of debriefing, and that provides the participant with an educational experience as well as a truthful account of the experiment's actual nature. The experiment is explained very gradually and every point reviewed until the subject understands. Subjects are given time to reorganize their perceptions of the experiment and their responses to it, from possible humiliation and discomfort to self-acceptance and, it is to be hoped, sympathetic understanding of the researcher's perspective. Subjects are offered a genuine opportunity to withdraw their data after having received a full explanation of the purposes of the experiment. Moreover, by adding to the investigators' emotional and fiscal costs, painstaking and effective debriefing procedures introduce a noncoercive but persuasive deterrent to investigators who are contemplating deception research.

References

American Psychological Association, Committee for the Protection of Human Participants in Research. (1973). *Ethical principles in the conduct of research with human participants.* Washington, DC: Author.

Baron, R. A. (1981). The "Costs of deception" revisited: An openly optimistic rejoinder. *IRB: A Review of Human Subjects Research, 3*(1), 8–10.

Baumrind, D. (1964). Some thoughts on ethics of research: After reading Milgram's "Behavioral study of obedience." *American Psychologist, 19,* 421–423.

Baumrind, D. (1972). Reactions to the May 1972 draft report of the Ad Hoc Committee on Ethical Standards in Psychological Research. *American Psychologist, 27,* 1082–1086.

Berkowitz, L., & Donnerstein, E. (1982). External validity is more than skin deep: Some answers to criticisms of laboratory experiments. *American Psychologist, 37,* 245–257.

Berkowitz, L., & Geen, R. G. (1966). Film violence and the cue properties of available targets. *Journal of Personality and Social Psychology, 3,* 525–530.

Dresser, R. S. (1981). Deception research and the HHS final regulations. *IRE: A Review of Human Subjects Research, 3*(4), 3–4.

Fillenbaum, S. (1966). Prior deception and subsequent experimental performance: The "faithful" subject. *Journal of Personality and Social Psychology, 4*, 532–537.

Gardner, G. T. (1978). Effects of federal human subjects regulations on data obtained in environmental stressor research. *Journal of Personality and Social Psychology, 36*, 628–634.

Glass, D. C., & Singer, J. E. (1972). *Urban stress: Experiments on noise and social stressors.* New York: Academic Press.

Heisenberg, W. K. (1958). *Physics and philosophy.* New York: Harper & Row.

Jung, J. (1975). Snoopology. *Human Behavior, 4*(10), 56–59.

Keisner, R. (1971). *Debriefing and responsiveness to overt experimenter expectancy cues.* Unpublished manuscript, Long Island University, Long Island, NY.

McNamara, J. R., & Woods, K. M. (1977). Ethical considerations in psychological research: A comparative review. *Behavior Therapy, 8*, 703–708.

Milgram, S. (1974). *Obedience to authority.* New York: Harper & Row.

Mills, J. (1976). A procedure for explaining experiments involving deception. *Personality and Social Psychology Bulletin, 2*, 3–13.

Orne, M. T. (1962). On the social psychology of the psychological experiment: With particular reference to demand characteristics and their implications. *American Psychologist, 17*, 776–783.

Page, M. M. (1973). On detecting demand awareness by post-experimental questionnaire. *Journal of Social Psychology, 91*, 305–323.

Patten, S. C. (1977). Milgram's shocking experiments. *Philosophy, 52*, 425–440.

Schachter, S., & Singer J. (1979). Comments on the Maslach and Marshall-Zimbardo experiments. *American Psychologist, 37*, 989–995.

Seeman, J. (1969). Deception in psychological research. *American Psychologist, 24*, 1025–1028.

Sieber, J. E. (1983). Deception in social research III: The nature and limits of debriefing. *IRB: A Review of Human Subjects Research, 5*(3), 1–4.

Smith, S. S., & Richardson, D. (1983). Amelioration of deception and harm in psychological research: The important role of debriefing. *Journal of Personality and Social Psychology, 44*, 1075–1082.

Wahl, J. M. (1972, April). The utility of deception: An empirical analysis. In *Symposium on Ethical Issues in the Experimental Manipulation of Human Beings.* Western Psychological Association, Portland, Oregon.

Zimbardo, P. G., Andersen, S. M., & Kabat, L. G. (1981, June). Induced hearing deficit generates experimental paranoia. *Science, 212*, 1529–1531.

CHALLENGE QUESTIONS

Is Deception of Human Participants Ethical?

1. Have you ever participated in a study that involved deception? If so, how did you feel after the deception was revealed? If you have not been deceived in a psychology experiment, how do you think you would react to the use of deception?
2. Under what conditions do you personally believe that deception is ethical, if ever?
3. How would research in social psychology change if deception were never allowed?
4. Is it possible to accurately weigh the costs and benefits of study involving deception? In other words, do you agree with Elms that such a calculation is possible to perform, or do you believe that such an analysis is usually impossible?

ISSUE 2

Should Social Psychologists
Try to Solve Social Problems?

YES: Arthur Aron and Elaine Aron from "Chutzpah: Social Psychology Takes on the Big Issues," *The Heart of Social Psychology* (Lexington Books, 1989)

NO: David Kipnis from "Accounting for the Use of Behavior Technologies in Social Psychology," *American Psychologist* (*49*, 1994)

ISSUE SUMMARY

YES: Arthur and Elaine Aron believe that social psychologists are passionately devoted to promoting positive social change.

NO: David Kipnis argues that social psychological research benefits those with power and serves to perpetuate the status quo.

Most social psychologists believe that their research should have some positive impact on the field or on society as a whole. If fact, one could argue that should be the reason for conducting any kind of scientific research—ultimately, science should benefit humanity in some way. However, who usually benefits from the technologies that are developed as a result of scientific research?

According to Arthur and Elaine Aron, social psychologists are clearly dedicated to promoting positive social change. To illustrate this point, they describe the research of two prominent figures in the early history of social psychology—Kurt Lewin and Muzafer Sherif. Lewin, who is generally regarded as the founder of modern social psychology, was also the person who uttered the famous phrase "There is nothing so practical as a good theory." This quote illustrates Lewin's belief that theory and research in social psychology should ultimately have some practical and positive impact. The research of Muzafer Sherif will also be discussed. Sherif was one of the first social psychologists to address serious social issues, such as prejudice and conformity, using modern social psychological techniques.

Contrary to the optimistic tone of the first selection, David Kipnis has a dim view of social psychology. He believes that the progressive founders of social psychology were well intentioned and genuinely concerned about promoting positive social change. However, Kipnis contends that the original vision of people like Lewin and Sherif has since been clouded by subsequent generations of social psychologists. Rather than focus on promoting social change like Lewin and others advocated, most contemporary social psychology is aimed at promoting social technologies. According to Kipnis, these technologies—like most technologies developed in other areas of science—are developed to serve those with power and thereby preserve the status quo rather than promote social change.

Before you read the second selection, you should bear in mind that most social psychologists vehemently reject this argument and believe that they honor the tradition of Lewin and the other founders of the field. In fact, many social psychologists are part of an organization called the Society for the Psychological Study of Social Issues (SPSSI), which is devoted to ameliorating social problems through psychological research. But according to Kipnis, even these well-intentioned efforts are misguided.

POINT

- The founders of social psychology, such as Kurt Lewin, were dedicated to addressing serious social issues.
- Contemporary social psychologists continue the tradition that Lewin established.
- Social psychological research can be used to promote positive social change.

COUNTERPOINT

- Subsequent generations of social psychologists have not emphasized the role of research in promoting positive social change.
- Contemporary social psychologists develop behavior technologies that are used to preserve the status quo. Social psychological research benefits those with power.

**Arthur Aron and
Elaine Aron**

Chutzpah: Social Psychology
Takes on the Big Issues

Chutzpah is a Yiddish word meaning the guts to stick your neck out; perhaps even a little *too* far out, and take on something really big. Social psychologists abound in chutzpah, confidently believing that any social question worth debating is worth testing rigorously, if possible with an experiment that sorts out the underlying causes. No area of human concern, from the most pressing practical problems to the most long-standing philosophical issues, is beyond the reach of some determined social psychologist.

A prime example (among hundreds) is Stanley Schachter. So far in his prolific and audacious career, he has studied why people want to be with others, how people know what they feel, what makes people overweight, why people commit crimes, and why people smoke. All these areas have stymied other researchers and the public for years. But whatever the project, in each case Schachter quickly makes breakthroughs. "There's no such thing as a tough area," Schachter has said. "An area's only tough if you don't have an idea."... When pressed, Schachter admitted that

> It's hard to talk about some of these things without sounding pompous. But if I were forced to give advice, I'd say, get problem-oriented, follow your nose and go where problems lead you. Then if something opens up that's interesting and that requires techniques and knowledge with which you're unfamiliar, learn them.

It's that simple when you have chutzpah.

The same sentiment was expressed by Robert Zajonc—an eminent social psychologist especially admired for his gutsiness by many of the social psychologists we interviewed for this book. Over the years; Zajonc has been responsible for a series of breakthrough theories and unexpected experimental results, ranging from the arousing effects on the individual of working in the presence of others to long-term changes in the appearance of married partners.

When we asked Zajonc about social psychology, his attitude was like Schachter's. Zajonc said:

> All problems are solvable. It is simply a matter of finding the methods.... Two weeks before the Wright brothers took off from Kitty Hawk, a man named Simon Newcomb published in *Science* a definitive article showing that it's absolutely impossible to build a machine heavier than air that would fly. So if you did a meta-analysis of all empirical research done before the Wright Brothers, the conclusion would be it's pointless. Give up.... [But with any problem,] it's just a matter of being clever enough, or lucky enough, to formulate it in a way that makes it solvable.

Kurt Lewin—Chutzpah versus Hitler

Stanley Schachter was first a student of Kurt Lewin, whom many consider the founder of modern social psychology. Later Schachter was a student of one of Lewin's famous students, Leon Festinger. Robert Zajonc was a student of Lewin's heir apparent, Desmond Cartwright. Through Schachter, Festinger, Cartwright, and numerous others, Kurt Lewin was the single greatest influence on social psychology—"the giant," according to another eminent pioneer in the field, Theodore Newcomb.... Nearly every major trend in social psychology—group dynamics, cognitive dissonance, attribution theory—has been primarily developed by a student or close associate of Kurt Lewin. After Lewin's death in 1947, the great learning psychologist Edward Tolman wrote:

> Freud, the clinician, and Lewin, the experimentalist, these are the two men who will always be remembered because of the fact that their contrasting but complementary insights first made of psychology a science which was applicable both to real individuals and to real society.

Yet Lewin has hardly achieved the psychic demigod status of Freud. Lewin's theory is no longer widely used in social psychology, and his name appears on only a few research studies. So what was his great influence?

Lewin role-modeled chutzpah (and most of the other qualities of social psychology discussed in this book).

And when Lewin role-modeled something, it stuck. He has been described as "the most charismatic psychologist of his generation."... Or, as Brewster Smith put it, "he had this knack of catalyzing excitement around himself."

Lewin came to America—to Iowa, the heartland—in the mid-1930s. He was fleeing Hitler, and while Lewin was a gentle person, he could also be stubborn. Loving democracy deeply, he set out to attack tyranny the best way he knew, through the new science of social psychology.

Lewin's commitment to democracy was more than abstract political ideology. In contrast to Freud, his very style of *doing* science was democratic. As we said, Lewin's influence was not mainly from his own personal theories or research. It wasn't even from his lectures. It was from his Quasselstrippe (a German word roughly meaning "bull session"), where he sat around chatting with his students and playing with ideas. As their organizer and informal leader, he showed consistent respect and warmth. Whether he was listening to an undergraduate or an eminent colleague, everyone's ideas received a hearing. Lewin was enormously creative, but most important he facilitated creativity in those around him, through his enthusiastic and democratic intellectual leadership.[1]

While Lewin was noted for his good humor, he was vehement on one subject. That, of course, was democracy. Robert Sears, a well-known developmental theorist and colleague of Lewin's at the University of Iowa, commented about Lewin, "The autocratic way he insisted on democracy was a little spectacular.... There was nothing to criticize—but one could not help noticing the fire and the emphasis."

With such fire, it was not surprising that when one of Lewin's new graduate students, Ronald Lippitt, asked about studying the effect of different kinds of leadership structures, Lewin immediately abandoned his other research plans and plunged into the idea.[2] Together with Lippitt, Lewin constructed an ingenious series of experiments to compare scientifically the effects of autocratic versus democratic leadership.

It was a revolutionary idea to take this age-old question of practical affairs and social philosophy and subject it to rigorous scientific scrutiny. Lewin was adamant, however, that all life was the domain of the new science of social psychology. Nothing need be left to speculation and argument. Experimental research would solve the perennial problems of humankind.

The experiment itself was elegantly simple. The subjects were eleven-year-old boys who had volunteered to participate. The researchers organized them into several "clubs" of five boys each, each group a similar composite of personalities (based on teachers' assessments). The clubs chose such names as "Sherlock Holmes," "Dick Tracy," "Secret Agents," and "Charlie Chan." Each club was assigned an adult leader to help it carry out its crafts, games, and so forth over the next twenty weeks of meetings. To assess what went on in the groups, during each meeting several researchers observed. The boys and their parents were also interviewed later about the groups. The groups differed in only one respect—the behavior of the adult leaders.

Initially the leaders adopted one of two styles. One was *autocratic*, in which the leader took charge of every aspect of the tasks, kept the boys in the dark about the next step, and generally maintained complete authority at all times. The other was *democratic*, in which the leader encouraged group discussion and decision making and saw that during each step of an activity the boys were aware of that step's purpose in achieving the activity's overall goal.

Later, when Ralph White came to Iowa as a postdoctoral fellow in political science, he could not resist joining the social psychologists' research team. When White attempted to play the democratic leader, however, Lippitt and Lewin noted that his version of the democratic leader was quite different from the others'. Rather than changing White's approach to the role, Lewin realized that White was really demonstrating a third important leader type: *laissez-faire*, in which the leader plays a completely passive role, allowing members to do as they please and interfering as little as possible.

Thus, in its final form the study compared three leadership styles and the social climates surrounding them.... Great care was taken to make the leaders' behaviors similar in all other ways—for example, in how much joking and kindness they expressed. Each club experienced more than one kind of leader, in a systematic rotation.

The result was clear. Under autocratic leadership, the groups' behaviors fell into one of two general styles: passive and dependent or hostile and resistant. Either way, the autocratic groups' members were less satisfied and less friendly with one another in and out of the groups.

With democratic leadership, there was the greatest independence, the least discontent, and the most friendliness in and out of the group. Moreover, during activities members cooperated more and concentrated more on getting their task done.

The laissez-faire groups were closer to the democratic than the autocratic groups in many ways, except that the members were considerably more apathetic and less work-oriented.

Perhaps the most interesting differences emerged during "test episodes." In one, the experimenters arranged for the leader to come late. On their own, the democratic groups worked well; the authoritarian groups simply stopped doing much of anything; and the laissez-faire groups were active but not very effective in their activities.

In another test episode the experimenters sent in a stranger (a "janitor" or "electrician") while the leader was out, to criticize the group and its members. The authoritarian groups responded with much more hostility, perhaps showing a scapegoating effect.

Almost all the boys preferred the periods in which they had a democratic leader, but the transitions were difficult for most, especially from autocratic to democratic or laissez-faire.

Lewin was not shy about drawing conclusions:

> On the whole, I think that there is ample proof that the difference in behavior in autocratic and democratic situations is not a result of differences in the individuals. There have been few experiences for me as impressive as seeing the expression on children's faces during the first day under an autocratic leader. The group that had formerly been friendly, open, cooperative, and full of life, became within a short half-hour a rather apathetic-looking gathering without initiative. The change from autocracy to democracy seemed to take somewhat more time than that from democracy to autocracy. Autocracy is imposed on the individual. Democracy he has to learn!

Muzafer Sherif Tackles the Problem of War and Peace

Of course, Lewin was not the only source of chutzpah for social psychology. Another pioneer was Muzafer Sherif, who studied under Gardner Murphy at Columbia University. Murphy was a contemporary of Lewin's; in 1935 he wrote (with Lois Murphy) the first modern social psychology text. Later, Gardner Murphy said that social psychology started out as a "relatively well-behaved junior sib among the big boys and girls [of mainstream psychology] who had been around longer and knew better how to accommodate to the academic giants."... But, he noted, "Some of the creative people refused to work within the psychology that was standard for their era. Think of the rebels like Lewin, Sherif, and Moreno."

One must also think of Murphy himself, who was just as confident as Lewin that no human folly would dare to persist once psychology had identified what needed to be done. And so Murphy passed all this social psychology chutzpah on to his students, including Muzafer Sherif, a young graduates student from Turkey who had come to America to study psychology.[3]...

Sherif challenged the conventional methods of measuring attitudes and then conducted one of the first studies experimentally delineating the process of the formation of social norms.... But of all his contributions, the chutzpahs shows through most in a series of three "summer camp" studies...culminating in the study subtitled *The Robber's Cave Experiment*. This is the study that Sherif told us was, among all his works, "closest to my heart."

At Robber's Cave, Oklahoma, Sherif and his students, O.J. Harvey, B.J. White, and W.E. Hood, modestly set out to study the formation of culture, the causes of intergroup conflict, and the resolution of intergroup enmity. (The results were then written up by Sherif's wife, the independently famous social psychologist Carolyn Wood Sherif.) Thus, in a single study, Sherif and company attacked the issues of what creates a society and what causes war and peace.

During the summer of 1954, a number of upper-middle-class, eleven- and twelve-year-old boys were invited to attend "a special summer camp" at Robber's Cave.[4] When they arrived, before they even saw each other, they were randomly divided into two groups and sent to different parts of the large campground. For the first few days, each group was not even aware of the other's existence. Nevertheless, by the second week loyalties were strong. Each group had named itself, and both the Eagles and the Rattlers had developed leaders and informal social rules.

As soon as the two groups did hear about each other, each began to challenge the other to competitions. The researchers added fuel to this inherent competitive spark by bringing the two groups together to play team games, including very hard fought tugs-of-war. In all these competitions the winning group received a prize and the loser nothing.

The researchers used every opportunity to increase the losers' frustration. One technique, developed at a similar camp a previous summer, was to give a party after a competition to "let bygones be bygones." The experimenters deliberately arranged for half the refreshments to be "delectable and whole," while the other half were "crushed and unappetizing." One group was brought to the party just earlier enough to allow its members to select, naturally, all the delectable appetizers. When the other group arrived, they were faced with the unappealing leftovers and the spectacle of plates full of good stuff on the laps of their enemies. The late group was hardly pacified by this turn of events.

Even without this encouragement, the groups had developed an "in- group versus out-group" mentality. Each group called the members of the other group names and considered them inferior. On a questionnaire, the vast majority of both groups rated their own members as "brave," "tough," and "friendly" and rated the other group's as "sneaky," "smart-alecks," and "stinkers."

But now came the next, too-human stage: war. Fights broke out, flags were stolen, raids undertaken, green apples hoarded for "ammunition." The group structures themselves became all too reminiscent of societies at war, with leadership assigned by the group to the toughest kids and with a great focus on attacks and the "enemy." In fact, the researchers had to intervene several times to avoid bloodshed.

Then began the most challenging part of the study. Having created this microcosm of an intolerant and warring world, Sherif and company set out to create peace. First they tried bringing opposing factions together to share pleasant activities. It didn't work; a joint banquet turned into a food fight.

Another idea was religious services emphasizing peace, making:

> The topics were brotherly love, forgiveness of enemies, and cooperation. The boys arranged the services and were enthusiastic about the sermon. Upon solemnly departing from the ceremony, they returned within minutes to their concerns to defeat, avoid, or retaliate against the detested out-group....

Yet another idea was conferences between the group leaders. But the staff didn't even try to arrange them, given the outcome of a spontaneous attempt of this kind during one of the early experiments:

> A high status [member of one group] went on his own initiative to the [other group's] cabin with the aim of negotiating better relationships. He was greeted by a hail of green apples, chased down the path, and derided. Upon returning to his own group, he received no sympathy. Despite his high status, he was rebuked for making the attempt, which was doomed to failure in the opinion of his fellow members.

So much for negotiations. In fact, with every attempt to resolve the conflict, whether initiated by the experimenters or the boys themselves, the hostility seemed only to increase. Indeed, in the first two summer-camp studies, the boys went home harboring a good deal of bad feeling against the opposing groups.

Fortunately for everyone, however, during the 1954 camping session at Robber's Cave the experimenters finally found a strategy that worked: They introduced *superordinate goals*. This was done by setting up a series of situations in which the two groups had to cooperate to attain a joint objective. For example, the camp food truck would not start (thanks to the researchers' surreptitious efforts) and all the boys had to pull together, literally, to get the truck going. Another time the water supply "accidentally" broke down and the boys had to work together to locate the problem along a mile of pipe.

Gradually the war ended. By the time camp was over, the two groups actually asked to go home on the same bus. And when the bus stopped for a rest break, the groups decided to pool their prize money so that everyone could buy malts.

Sherif and his colleagues were entirely aware of the larger implications of their research. In their various reports of the experimental results, they emphasized that nations can coexist peacefully only if they develop meaningful joint goals. On the basis of these studies, Sherif made an impassioned plea:

> The broadening of human bonds is the prerequisite for morality in dealing with peoples outside the narrow in-group bounds, for creation of a widening sense of "we-ness."...
>
> The trend is towards larger and larger dependence between peoples and toward the formation of organizations encompassing them. Historical evidence and empirical data of social science support this trend, even though they also show great human wear and tear, suffering, and reverses for intervals of time.
>
> The great question is whether the trend toward interdependence will be permitted to culminate in the standards of conduct required from all, despite stubborn, last-ditch opposition by islands of resistance, or whether the trend will collapse in the world wide holocaust of a thermonuclear showdown. (Sherif, 1966, p. 174)

What other discipline stands ready to conduct research on how to rescue *Homo sapiens* from self-extinction? What other discipline would have the chutzpah to draw conclusions about war and peace from research at a summer camp for boys? It may be presumptuous, but it is also fortunate that some science is trying. Indeed, most psychologists would agree that Sherif's study remains one of our most important sources of scientific knowledge about the causes and cures of group hatred....

In Conclusion: Where Chutzpah Comes from and Where It Goes

Now that we have sampled the broad range of audacious topics social psychologists have taken on, perhaps we can see this chutzpah in a clearer light. To a certain extent it comes from the nature of the field—the study of the interaction between individuals and social forces. In this arena significant conflicts occur; intense influences push and shove; outcomes dramatically affect everyday life. It would almost be hard to plan a social psychology study that would *not* be a potential conversation piece.

Still, other fields of psychology are potentially as relevant and riveting, yet they generally lack this bold approach. That seems to be simply because chutzpah has not been part of their historical development, whereas in social psychology a generous display of chutzpah has been a social norm from the beginning. Idealistic graduate students with unusual ideas to test were sought and encouraged by their departments. Bold studies of real-life situations were more likely to be accepted for publication by the editors of social psychology journals. And within certain limits, the more difficult and controversial a topic, the more admiration its researchers received when they made scientific sense out of it.

Most of the social psychologists we spoke with were proud of this aspect of their field. For example, when we asked Bob Zajonc about chutzpah, he explained:

> I think that I would call that aspect taking risks. You don't do interesting research if you don't take risks. Period. If you just prove the obvious, that's

not interesting research: The risks may come because the problem is socially delicate, or the risks may come because the problem is intellectually difficult. But usually problems that involve some risks are problems that involve some payoff.

Every discipline has its own history, culture, and social norms. They decide what is worth studying, what methods are appropriate, and what assumptions can be made. These attitudes are passed on from teacher to student and maintained also by journal editors and the hiring practices of academic departments. One can (and probably should, to a certain extent) think of these as limits or blinders placed on the researchers by their field's culture. But as in any culture, these limits also have value: They save the time of those who come after. They don't "reinvent the wheel" or "go down blind alleys." Instead, those who follow are encouraged to build on those who came before. Finally, if it happens that one of a science's norms is *not* to be conservative but to attack new problems with new methods, then its culture is encouraging its own continual regeneration by more or less protecting its own members from itself. Now that's real chutzpah!

Notes

1. Everyone we have spoken with who knew Lewin remarked on his enthusiasm: "He sparkled," as one put it. This enthusiasm was so contagious that when Lewin first visited the United States in 1929, when he still could speak only German, he developed a following that included some who could not understand a word of his talks. They were just taken by the man!
2. Lewin had a warm, easy relationship with everyone around him, including his graduate students. They, in the great American tradition, returned his affection in a variety of ways—including practical jokes. Lippitt told Brewster Smith (an eminent social psychologist, of a later era) the following story: At Iowa, Lewin's graduate students were helping him to get acculturated to the strange ways of America, and they also liked to tease him. So in the process of teaching him American slang, they explained to him that when you really agree with something a person has said, you say, "You sure slobbered a bibful"—a compliment the innocent Lewin proceeded to pay an important colleague during a major scientific presentation.
3. Murphy continued to be an important figure in psychology but mainly in the area of personality theory and research.
4. One commentator...pointed out that Lewin, and presumably Sherif, worked with children for the same reason that learning psychologists work with rats: They are simpler organisms. (One wonders how many children these researchers knew intimately.) That is, one can see the deeper principles without adult complications. But no doubt another reason was the one which now explains the use of sophomore college students: The kids were available, and they were willing or obliged to do what they were told.

NO ←

David Kipnis

Accounting for the Use of Behavior Technologies in Social Psychology

Social psychology shares with all disciplines in the social sciences the task of describing and predicting behavior. Over the past five to six decades, social psychology has taken on the task of changing social behavior. Even in a cursory examination of present-day social psychological journals and textbooks, one finds considerable scholarly effort devoted to the development of systematic techniques for shaping how people think and behave toward each other—that is, the development of behavior technologies.

The purpose of this article is twofold. The first is to analyze the social and scientific reasons that promote the development of behavior technologies in social psychology. The second is to review social issues associated with the use of technology in society at large and to suggest that similar issues may arise in particular settings that use psychological knowledge for practical purposes. Although the article focuses on social psychology, the issues discussed apply, I believe, to all areas of psychology that have developed and use systematic techniques for solving practical problems of human behavior.

Why Do We Want to Change Behavior?

We begin by asking why social psychology has taken on the task of developing systematic procedures for changing peoples' behavior. Other social science disciplines, such as political science, seem content to describe and predict events, not to change them.

Perhaps the simplest answer is that social psychology has available a methodology to change behavior. From the 1870s on, psychologists have offered as proof of their ideas the fact that they could experimentally change human activities in predictable ways. Recall, for instance, John B. Watson's boast about his ability to control people's lives using the methods of classical conditioning:

> Give me a dozen healthy infants, well formed, and my own specified world
> to bring them up in, and I will guarantee to take any one at random and

From *American Psychology*, vol. 49, no. 3, March 1994, pp. 165–172. Copyright © 1994 by the American Psychological Association. Reprinted with permission.

train him to become any type of specialist I select—doctor, lawyer, artist, merchant, and yes, even beggarman and thief, regardless of his talents, penchants, tendencies, abilities, vocation, and race of his ancestors. (Watson, 1925, p.82)

Clinical psychology and organizational psychology also serve as models for social psychology. Unlike experimental psychology, however, in which people are changed to demonstrate an experimental principle, behavioral changes produced by clinical and organizational psychologists are designed to solve practical problems.

If one is not satisfied with methodology as an answer and want to pursue further the question of why social psychology has developed techniques for changing behavior, then one must look at the goals that are set for people by Western culture, not only in their roles as, say, parents or citizens but as scientists.

In this regard, the philosopher Raimundo Panikkar (1986) observed that in Western societies the goal of science is to make practical contributions. Scientists are not educated simply to contemplate knowledge but to use it. The first and foremost question asked about new knowledge is "how can it be used?" Discoveries in chemistry and physics are rapidly applied to engineering, and discoveries in biology and biochemistry to medicine. Similar instances of the wedding of basic research with application can be found in the behavioral sciences. Ideas about intelligence produced the IQ test, the social psychology of leadership produced contingency leadership training, and theories of learning produced programmed instruction, to name but a few of the ways in which social science knowledge is used to solve practical problems.

The Purpose of Change

Given that social psychologists can change behavior, are there particular end states toward which these changes are directed? Is it to make people more altruistic, less aggressive, and more loving? Or is it, as Herman and Chomsky (1988) suggested in *Manufacturing Consent*, to make people more compliant to authority? Perhaps, it is simply to demonstrate that social psychology's knowledge base has matured to the point at which it can, if it chooses, change behavior.

A survey of contemporary applications of social psychology would suggest no simple answer. Some social psychologists apply psychological knowledge to reduce racial prejudice, others to help win elections, and still others to attract consumers to particular products. In the 1940s and 1950s, however, the first and second generations of social psychologists were in agreement about the uses of behavior change techniques. These social psychologists wanted to use them to produce a better world.

Gordon W. Allport (1947), in his inaugural speech as first president of the newly formed Division of Personality and Social Psychology of the American Psychological Association (APA), urged that social psychological knowledge be used to solve the many social problems facing society.

> In forming this Division we are...announcing, in effect, that as a group of scientists we believe we have a contribution to make in interpreting and in remedying some of the serious social dislocations of today.... The test of our fitness to exist and to prosper will be our ability to contribute substantially in the near future to the diagnosis and treatment of the outstanding malady of our time...the fact that man's moral sense is not able to assimilate his technology. (p. 82)

Allport (1947) went on to say that the problems spawned by modern technology—unemployment, wars, and more—problems that were produced by the physical sciences and that have overwhelmed society were not being addressed by the mental and moral sciences (i.e., social psychology). "What public officials want from social psychology is instant help...in the improvement and enlargement of man's moral sense and betterment of human relationships on an international scale" (p. 183).

Allport's (1947) address also called attention to the fact that until the early 1900s, psychology was commonly classified as a moral science. The goals of psychology, he argued, should be "to devise means to redirect human actions to be consistent with these moral roots" (p. 184).

In essence, Allport was calling for the use of psychological knowledge to reduce people's inhumanity toward each other. Although Allport was not specific about how social psychologists were to cure the social woes created by technology, his use of terms such as *treatment and means to redirect human actions* suggest some kind of engineering of human behavior to solve these problems. These engineering treatments, based on social psychological knowledge, would solve the many social problems created by technologies based on knowledge from the physical sciences. In other words, social psychology would provide technological "fixes" to undo the problems created by a technology based on the physical sciences.

Allport's address is remarkable on several counts. First, it is optimistic about what social psychology could do to solve social problems. If by social dislocations, Allport meant that social psychologists should devise remedies for the modern social plagues of poverty, discrimination, delinquency, violence, and loss of hope, he was, showing great faith in the theories of social psychology. Underlying this optimism was the commonly shared belief of most people that technology, if properly used, could solve common human problems and so create a utopia.

Second, Allport showed great temerity in suggesting that social psychology should espouse what today would be labeled mildly liberal views. In the mid-1940s, the Cold War was just beginning, and conservative legislators in Congress perceived such action-oriented speeches as reflecting a Marxist or socialist ideology in psychology. As Johnson (1992) pointed out, congressional opinion in the late 1940s was that the social sciences were radical. This view helped block, for 10 years, psychologists' attempts to receive federal research support.

Finally, Allport's address is remarkable for its bland assumption that psychologists had the right to change social behavior without the consent of the people whose behavior was to be changed.[1] Like the physicians in Ivan Illich's (1976) *Medical Nemesis*, Allport assumed that psychologists know what is best for society. That is, they have the right to decide what constitutes social diseases and how best to eliminate them.

Curing Social Ills

From the 1930s through the 1950s, much of the important research in social psychology was consistent with Allport's call to help humankind regain its moral roots and use knowledge to solve social problems. Systematic techniques were designed that sought, in President Franklin Roosevelt's words, "to cultivate the ability of all people, of all kinds, to live together and work together, in the same world, at peace" (quoted in Allport, 1947, p. 183).

Thus, Krech and Crutchfield (1948), in their innovative social psychology text, reported on means for reducing prejudice through educational techniques. Sherif, Harvey, White, Hood, and Sherif (1961) described techniques for eliminating intergroup conflict by creating crises that required the cooperative actions of previously conflicted groups. Kurt Lewin (1948) demonstrated the value of democratic, rather than autocratic, leadership. He also provided a theoretical rationale and accompanying procedures for reducing resistance of people to change. Chein, Cook, and Harding (1948) were involved in the development of action research techniques that would allow social psychologists to actively intervene in social problems, while still using the methods of science.

These were but a few of the many attempts to "redirect human actions so as to be consistent with their moral roots." Deutsch and Collins (1951) studied interracial housing as a means of reducing racial prejudice. Social psychologists' testimony before the U.S. Supreme Court contributed to overturning the country's segregated school system. During this time, the Society for the Psychological Study of Social Issues was formed to encourage research on moral issues, ranging from poverty to studies of inequality and injustice.

To this day, many social psychologists define social psychological theory in terms of wrongs that need to be righted. This tradition is reflected in chapters in modem social psychological textbooks that address problems of conflict, sexism, prejudice, cultural diversity, and inequality. And, as I discuss in the following section, the failure to maintain this tradition is a source of continuous criticism and debate among psychologists (e.g., Kidder & Fine, 1986; Prilleltensky, 1989; Sampson, 1978).

Social Psychology Redefined

Beginning in the 1950s, one could also find an ever-increasing number of research studies in social psychology that were not directly concerned with the pursuit of Allport's moral goals. Theoretical rather than practical studies became the vogue. These studies were concerned with understanding the psychological basis for social behavior. Practical studies that were reported focused on helping persons who could already help themselves (e.g., advertisers, managers, psychotherapists, labor mediators). The only constant trend from the 1930s to the 1960s, and later, was that most persons whose behavior was changed were not consulted.

In essence, beginning in the 1950s, social psychologists developed a new agenda for social psychology, in which solving social ills played a lesser role. Although I have no certain explanation for this shift, several related events may have contributed. For one, social psychological knowledge is probably inadequate, by itself, to unravel the complex causes of social ills. Second, many psychologists identify with a general model of science that is objective and value free. Allport's call for social psychological research that had a moral basis appears inconsistent with this value-free model of science. Third, the hostility of federal funding agencies to social science research suspected of being "politically left," and not "methodologically rigorous, objective...and important for national welfare and defense" (Johnson, 1992, p. 146), no doubt, encouraged social psychologists to alter their research agendas and their strategies of research. Finally, it is probable that many social psychologists did not share Allport's views.

For these reasons, and perhaps others, the times were right for the exciting theoretical explanations of social behavior offered from the late 1930s through the 1950s by Kurt Lewin. Lewin's ideas about how people perceived their worlds was the point of departure for a "new look" in social psychology. Behavior was explained in Lewin's scheme by tension systems, valences, and other hypothetical constructs that guided social behavior. Although Lewin stressed the impact of the environment on these psychological systems, in practice, real-world events became less important than how these events were perceived and then acted on. In essence, Lewin helped move social psychology from what in philosophy can be labeled a materialistic view of the world to an idealistic view (Fromm, 1969).

Subsequently, students and colleagues of Lewin used these ideas, along with their own, to explain social behavior. Such psychological constructs as dissonance, balance theory, attributions, expectations, cognitions, and beliefs about inequity soon competed with or complemented Lewin's explanations. Today, social psychologists are even seeking explanations of social behavior in evolutionary processes (Buss, 1990) and physiology (i.e., brain functioning and hormonal activity).

Thus, from a discipline oriented by its early leaders toward the solution of social problems, social psychology transformed itself into a discipline oriented toward explaining the psychological causes of social behavior. With this new orientation, the real world and events in it took second stage. Explanations of changes in social behavior were now in terms of the individual's psychology, rather than in terms of changes in society. Events such as unemployment, city crowding, crime, environmental events, and technology were only important to the extent that individuals responded to these events. To be sure, there was and is an active group of environmental social psychologists (e.g., Altman, 1975) who take into account the interplay between world events and individual psychology, but this group remains a minority.

The Experimental Study of Social Behavior

Along with the emphasis on social theory, social psychologists developed a range of sophisticated methodologies for testing their theories. Of all the methods that were developed, the experiment was (and still is) given priority as the way to demonstrate the validity of social psychological ideas.

The successful use of the experiment in learning and perception, no doubt, served as a model for social psychology. Also, leaders of social psychology, such as Kurt Lewin and Leon Festinger, vigorously championed the experiment as the means to clarify and test ideas about social behavior (Deutsch, 1992). In the laboratory, complex social behaviors could be turned on and off at will. One could examine, for example, whether people become more or less aggressive as they experience cognitive dissonance or whether they become more or less altruistic when they are paired with people who are similar or dissimilar to themselves. In short, the use of laboratory techniques allowed social psychologists to progress from simply observing life to controlling it.

It is not surprising that the use of the laboratory study also complements and reinforces social psychology's focus on the perception of events, rather than on the events themselves. This occurs because performing laboratory research requires investigators to spend most of their time in activities such as developing scenarios that selectively mimic events in larger society; making sure that psychological feelings, presumed to mediate responses to these events, are created (e.g., dissonance, expectancies); observing the reactions of college students to these events; and writing articles that describe the findings of these studies. These research activities leave little time to study social behavior outside of the laboratory.

Developing Behavior Technologies

From the 1950s on, it was apparent that the findings of social psychology could be used to solve practical problems. In Laudan's (1977) and Panikkar's (1986) terms, social psychology had become a useful science. By 1971, applications of social psychological knowledge had increased to the point that Jacobo Varela could summarize these efforts in his book *Psychological Solutions to Social Problems: An Introduction to Social Technology*. The book taught people how to use laboratory-validated techniques to persuade others, to resolve conflicts, to control people by Skinnerian conditioning techniques, to become an effective leader, and more.

Although Varela's (1971) book promised to solve social problems, the problems discussed were not Allport's social problems of society. Rather, the focus was on social problems caused by one person refusing or being unable to do what a second person wanted.

The book was only the beginning. Since its publication, behavior technologies have been developed that cause people to change their attitudes, be more persuasive, learn how to make friends, be better salespersons, communicate persuasively, be more restrained and less impulsive, be effective leaders, win elections, obey, or work effectively. Other behavior technologies have been developed to help management decide whom to hire, whom to fire, whom to promote, and what people like or dislike about their business firms or their products. Still other technologies have been developed with a more sinister bent, as for example, helping government agencies break down the beliefs of hostile people by using esoteric, mind-altering drugs and sensory deprivation.

In short, in almost all realms of human activities, behavior technologies have been developed to change social behavior, either with or without people's consent. Although some of these techniques were developed by clinical or organizational psychologists rather than social psychologists, I have listed them because they are used to change social behavior.

Power and Behavior Technology

Robert Dahl (1957) included among the elements of a power act that Person A causes Person B to do something that B would ordinarily not do. Substitute for Person A the term *behavior technology*, and we have a description of what behavior technologies do. In essence, behavior technologies are simply influence tactics developed through science, which agents use to give new direction to people's behavior.

At the beginning of this article I suggested that there are problems associated with the use of technology in society at large that may also arise with the use of behavior technology. These problems arise because of the close relation between technologies of all kinds and social power. I will discuss three related problems. The first concerns who decides what technologies should be developed and what technologies should not be developed, the second concerns the relation between technology and individual autonomy, and the third concerns the ethical neutrality of technology.

Why Some Technologies But Not Others

Earlier I listed many of the behavior technologies that are currently in use. In this section, the questions are why were these diverse technologies developed and why were other equally useful technologies, such as those that might have solved Allport's "serious dislocations of today," not developed.

One explanation is that technologies are ways of building order in our worlds. The particular order that technology builds depends on the distribution of power and the exercise of control in society (Dickson, 1974; Mumford, 1967). Before time, money, and effort are invested in developing a new technology, be it new life-sustaining drugs, new computers, or new weapons, someone must decide that this development is to their benefit—not to the advantage of people in general but to the advantage of some specific person or group of persons.

Quite simply, most technologies are developed to sustain and promote the interests of the dominant social groups. The water mill was developed to increase the capacity of millers, the steam loom to improve the profitability of English manufacturers, and new drugs to increase the profits of drug firms. In other words, technologies are developed because people with power are experiencing problems that they want to solve. Although these technologies may benefit everyone over the long run, it is incorrect to believe that they are developed to increase the good life for all people. The actual uses of pure knowledge mainly reflect the interests of people whose opinions count.

These observations about power can be applied to the development of behavior technologies. Most are developed to strengthen existing social institutions, not to change them. Behavior technologies in such core areas of social psychology as leadership, motivation, social influence, persuasion, conformity, and conflict negotiation are used to help schools, businesses, and government agencies guide individual behavior in ways acceptable to those sponsoring institutions. For example, since the 1950s, the military establishment, research foundations, and businesses have generously funded the study of leadership. The findings of this research have spawned numerous behavior technologies that provide managers and military leaders with guidelines for maintaining the productivity of subordinates.

To be sure, the application of social psychological knowledge is not completely one-sided. The tradition of using psychological knowledge to solve Allport's "serious dislocations of our times" by working for the powerless still lives. McGuire's (1964) attempts to teach soldiers to resist brainwashing; Cialdini's (1985) techniques to help individuals recognize and resist persuasion tactics; and Aronson, Blaney, Stephan, Sikes, and Snapp's (1978) use of systematic procedures to reduce prejudice in classrooms typify the genuine concern of social psychologists for the well-being of people. However, I would describe these efforts as modest compared with the widespread use of social psychological knowledge to support rather than change existing institutions. Moreover, many technologies designed to help the powerless eventually are used by persons with power.[2]

Foucault (1980) remarked that all societies suppress knowledge and sentiments that do not support the existing social order. He argued that what the underclass knows, values, believes, and wants threatens the stability of the existing society. Approaching this issue from a psychological perspective, Kidder and Fine (1986) also described the reluctance of social researchers to conduct research supportive of the views of persons "outside" the system. I believe it is fair to say that no foundation would support, for instance, the development of behavior technologies that could be used by homeless people to gain admittance to our homes as guests or that workers could use to give the appearance of work without actually working. In other words, the research that we do not do, the behavior technologies that we do not build, are concerned with Foucault's suppressed knowledge. For the most part, research applications that validate the existing social order are supported.

I have already listed several reasons for the failure of Allport's plea that social psychologists should use their knowledge to reduce social ills. I now add what is perhaps the most important: That is, Allport did not take into account the realities of power and politics. The belief that research is directed to areas in which the needs are strongest is in the same class as the belief that Santa Claus comes at Christmas time. Allport failed to take into account the social class of the people who were hurting. He failed to reckon that when the parties who are hurting are without power, money, status, and clout, there is limited interest in supporting research to find solutions for their problems.

The point that social power guides the development of social theory and practice is hardly new. In one form or another, critics have suggested that psychology is the guardian of the status quo (e.g., Prilleltensky 1989; Sampson 1978; Sarason, 1981). What may be annoying in my discussion is the implication that psychologists are simply servants of power, eager to trade knowledge for money, perks, and status. This is not my intent. As I have written elsewhere (Kipnis, 1976), most people in Western society lead comfortable lives. As a result, the goal of persons in society, including behavioral scientists, is to maintain and improve this state of affairs. Accordingly, our efforts are directed toward binding people to society, rather than tearing society apart.

My intent in this section has been to make explicit the social and political forces that guide the development of behavior technologies. This leads to the next item for discussion: the circumstances under which behavior technology restrains or enhances individual freedom.

The Issue of Control

The question of how much freedom and how much control is best for people has been debated by social philosophers, by politicians, by psychologists (e.g., Brehm, 1966; Deci, 1992; Fromm, 1941; Rogers & Skinner, 1956; Seligman, 1975), and by people in general. Are people happier when they are told what to do or when they can decide for themselves? Is society better off when people are told what to do?

When the issue of control is examined in relation to behavior technology, we find that it provides increased freedom and choice for some but takes freedom and choice away from others.

The Winners

It is not surprising that behavior technology enriches the lives of people with power. It provides its sponsors and users with the significant advantage of being able to cause behavior in other people. Argyris (1975) reached a similar conclusion in his analysis of the research and theory of major social psychologists. He concluded that research in areas such as conformity, persuasion, and interpersonal attraction is designed to reduce free choice. Similarly, Zimbardo (1969) observed, "Control. That's what current psychology is all about.... It has become the all-consuming task of most psychologists to learn how to bring behavior under stimulus control" (pp. 237–238).

Neither Argyris nor Zimbardo considered who benefits from psychology's focus, although it is perhaps obvious. Technologies, such as management by objectives, contingency leadership, psychological tests to select and promote employees, and self-managed work teams, provide managers with a range of techniques for producing satisfied and productive employees. The newer techniques of psychotherapy, such as flooding, desensitization, and cognitive restructuring, have increased the range of treatment options for therapists. By providing greater control of clients, these newer techniques allow therapists to treat more patients more effectively and in a shorter period of time than was possible using the earlier psychodynamic techniques of therapy.

Similar benefits are found in marketing, in which systematic techniques of persuasion and attitude change have facilitated the sale of products by advertisers and sales personnel. Politicians and government agencies also have benefited from the use of behavior technologies. In the political realm, systematic techniques have been used to persuade voters and to promote support for government policies.

In short, behavior technologies provide people in positions of power with the ability to solve problems involving the exercise of influence. Using these techniques, target persons can be influenced to vote, buy products, work harder, feel better about themselves, and be more compliant, to name but a few of the many behaviors controlled by technology.

The Losers

From Karl Marx in the 19th century to Jacques Ellul (1964) today, a consistent criticism of technology has been that it deprives the ordinary citizen of the ability to behave as he or she might want. Sometimes this loss of freedom is the direct goal of the technology; at other times, the loss of freedom is simply an inadvertent by-product of using the technology (Crabb, 1992).

The reason why the targets of behavior technology lose freedom is because the easiest way to change behavior is to control it. To illustrate: Attitude-change technology works by restricting the alternatives that are available for people to consider when forming opinions, programmed instructions control the numbers of incorrect responses that trainees can make, operant conditioning ties desired rewards to compliance, and leadership technology teaches leaders to select the influence tactics most likely to control their subordinates. In short, a target person's freedom of choice is diminished by such means as disguising the influence attempt, reducing the options available to him or her, manipulating his or her psychological state, or increasing the costs of refusal....

Concluding Observations

The working assumptions of an earlier generation of social psychologists have conspired to create a science whose underlying text is the study of power. These assumptions include the belief that psychological constructs are sufficient to explain social behavior; that social behavior can be controlled, both in the laboratory and in natural settings; and that social psychology should use its science to resolve social ills. Although this last assumption has not been universally accepted, the idea of changing social behavior to solve practical problems has become woven firmly into the assumptions of social psychology.

In this article, I have described some of the ethical and psychological problems inherent in the use of psychological knowledge to change behavior. One might argue that these problems simply reflect the workings of a conservative social psychology; that is, these problems would not occur if the goals of social psychology were directed toward remedying Allport's "serious dislocations of society." I do not agree. The problems I have described are just as likely to occur in a social psychology committed to the elimination of injustice as in a social psychology committed to maintaining the status quo. In other words, political ideology is not the cause of these problems; rather, the exercise of power is the cause....

Notes

1. Morton Deutsch (1975) has discussed the ethical dilemmas involved in using social-psychological knowledge to influence people.
2. For example, in a late 1960s civil rights trial, Richard Christie and colleagues (Schulman, Shaver, Colman, Emrick & Christie, 1973) developed a technique for identifying jurors likely to acquit a defendant charged with murder. Since then, techniques to identify friendly jurors have mainly been used by lawyers whose clients can afford the costs of using the technology.

References

Allport, G. (1947). The emphasis on molar problems. *Psychological Review, 54*, 182–192.

Altman, I. (1975). *The environment and social behavior*. Monterey, CA: Brooks/Cole.

Buss, D. M. (1990). Evolutionary social psychology: Prospects and pitfalls. *Motivation and Emotions, 14*, 265–286.

Chein, I., Cook, S. W., & Harding, J. (1948). The field of action research. *American Psychologist, 3*, 43–50.

Cialdini, R. B. (1985). *Influence: Science and practice*. Glenview, IL: Scott, Foresman.

Deutsch, M. (1975). Introduction. In M. Deutsch & H. A. Hornstein (Eds.), *Applying social psychology* (pp. 1–27). Hillsdale, NJ: Erlbaum.

Deutsch, M., & Collins, M. E. (1951). *Interracial housing: A psychological evaluation of a social experiment*. Minneapolis: University of Minnesota Press.

Fromm, E. (1969). *Marx's concept of man*. New York: Ungar.

Herman, E., & Chomsky, N. (1988). *Manufacturing consent*. New York: Pantheon.

Illich, I. (1976). *Medical nemesis*. New York: Random House.

Johnson, D. (1992). Psychology in Washington: Next to nothingness and being at the National Science Foundation. *Psychological Science, 3*, 145–149.

Mumford, L. (1967). *The myth of the machine*. London: Seeker & Warburg.

Panikkar, R. (1986). Some theses on technology. Logos, 7, 115–25.

Sampson, E. E. (1978). Scientific paradigms and social values: Wanted a scientific revolution. *Journal of Personality and Social Psychology, 36*, 1332–1343.

Sherif, M., Harvey, O., White, B., Hood, W., & Sherif, C. (1961). *Intergroup conflict and cooperation: The Robber's Cove experiment*. Norman, OK: Institute of Group Relations.

CHALLENGE QUESTIONS

Should Social Psychologists Try to Solve Social Problems?

1. For argument's sake, assume for a moment that Kipnis is correct and social psychologists should not attempt to use the results of their research to address social problems. Would there still be any reason for conducting social psychological research?
2. Who decides what kinds of behaviors should be changed by social psychologists? In what way do values seem to influence the kinds of behaviors that social psychologists attempt to change?
3. How would you feel if you took part in an experiment that was designed to change your behavior? Do you think it would bother you? Why, or why not?

On the Internet . . .

The Social Cognition Paper Archive

Eliot Smith, one of the most prominent social cognition researchers, hosts a variety of social cognition resources at this Web site. It was one of the first extensive social psychology sites on the World Wide Web.

`http://www.indiana.edu/~soccog/scarch.html`

Interpersonal Perception

This site is a useful primer on social psychologist David Kenny's approach to understanding interpersonal perception. It describes his Social Relations Model of perception in a fair amount of detail.

`http://users.rcn.com/dakenny/interp.htm`

Implicit Attitudes

This Web site is the home page for Project Implicit, one of the most ambitious online psychology experiments ever conducted. The site allows you to test your own implicit attitudes on a variety of different issues.

`https://implicit.harvard.edu/implicit/`

Self-Esteem

The self-esteem movement has a substantial following on the internet, and the National Association of Self-Esteem, one of the leading organizations in the self-esteem movement, hosts this Web page.

`http://www.self-esteem-nase.org/`

Nonverbal Behavior & Communication

This site has an extensive list of resources for those who may be interested in the psychology of non-verbal behavior.

`http://www3.usal.es/~nonverbal/introduction.htm`

Paul Ekman's Web Site

Paul Ekman is one of the world's foremost authorities on the study of emotion, deception, and non-verbal behavior. This Web page contains many useful resources for learning more about his research.

`http://www.paulekman.com/`

PART 2

Social Cognition

Social cognition is the area of social psychological research that is devoted to understanding the nature of social thought. How do we perceive our social environment? What do we think about other people? What do we think about ourselves? These are the kinds of questions that social cognition researchers seek to answer.

- Are Our Perceptions Often Inaccurate?
- Does Cognitive Dissonance Explain Why Behavior Can Change Attitudes?
- Are Self-Esteem Improvement Programs Misguided?
- Do Positive Illusions Promote Mental Health?
- Can People Accurately Detect Lies?
- Are Repressed Memories Real?

ISSUE 3

Are Our Social Perceptions Often Inaccurate?

YES: Lee Ross and Richard Nisbett from *The Person and the Situation* (McGraw-Hill, 1991)

NO: David C. Funder from "Errors and Mistakes: Evaluating the Accuracy of Social Judgment," *Psychological Bulletin* (*101*, 1987)

ISSUE SUMMARY

YES: Social psychologists Lee Ross and Richard Nisbett believe that people's perceptions of others are often inaccurate because of the dispositionalist bias—the tendency for people to mistakenly believe that the behavior of others is due largely to their personality or disposition.

NO: David C. Funder, a personality psychologist, believes that the artificial laboratory experiments cited by Ross and Nisbett do not necessarily indicate that people's perceptions in the real world are often mistaken. In the real world people's behavior is often due to their disposition.

Having accurate perceptions of other people is important. For example, imagine that you want to ask someone out on a date. Being able to accurately predict the response of the object of your affection would be important. If you correctly believe that he or she would say yes, then you are likely to ask that person out. However, if you incorrectly believe that he or she would say yes, you would likely react with disappointment and frustration when you are rejected. So being able to accurately understand and predict the behavior of others is an important skill to have. But do most of us have that skill? Is it possible that a great many of our social perceptions are mistaken, despite the fact that most of us would benefit from having accurate perceptions of others?

Citing numerous experiments and decades of research, Lee Ross and Richard Nisbett contend that our social perceptions are far more inaccurate than we believe them to be. The most profound error that people make, according to Ross and Nisbett, is the dispositionalist bias. This phenomenon, which is sometimes called the Fundamental Attribution Error, leads us to make inaccurate judgments about other people in a variety of contexts. According to their argument, people are predisposed to believe that the behavior of others is due to their disposition—rather than a particular situation or circumstance. For example, if someone is rude to us, we tend to assume it's because that individual is a generally rude person, instead of assuming that he or she is having a particularly bad day. This frequently leads people to draw erroneous conclusions about others because in actuality, the behavior of people is influenced by situations to a far greater degree than is commonly believed. As a result, people are too quick to assume that people's actions correspond to their true disposition.

David Funder argues that there are profound differences between errors made in social psychology experiments, like those discussed by Ross and Nisbett, and the kind of mistakes that people make when judging others in the real world. For example, people do in fact commit the Fundamental Attribution Error when they take part in psychology experiments, and sometimes believe that a person's behavior corresponds to the disposition, even when it may not. However, in the real world, where people's behavior usually *does* correspond to their disposition, people are usually not misken if they believe the behavior of others is due to their internal disposition. For example, when someone is rude to you, there is a pretty good chance that he or she is generally a rude person, and may not just be having a particularly bad day—as a result, you probably would not be mistaken if you attribute that person's behavior to his or her disposition.

POINT	COUNTERPOINT
• The results of numerous experiments indicate that people's perceptions of others are often inaccurate.	• Research has not demonstrated that people's perceptions of others are usually mistaken.
• As social perceivers, we are usually too quick to assume that people's actions correspond to their dispositions.	• In the real world, people's actions usually do correspond to their disposition.
• Numerous experiments have demonstrated that the dispositionalist bias is one of the major reasons why people make mistakes when explaining the behavior of others.	• The experiments cited by Ross and Nisbett are not indicative of real-world perception and behavior. As a result, people's perceptions of others are often accurate.

Lee Ross and
Richard E. Nisbett

 **YES**

The Person and the Situation

Introduction

Undergraduates taking their first course in social psychology generally are in search of an interesting and enjoyable experience, and they rarely are disappointed. They find out many fascinating things about human behavior, some of which validate common sense and some of which contradict it. The inherent interest value of the material, amounting to high-level gossip about people and social situations, usually ensures that the students are satisfied consumers.

The experience of serious graduate students, who, over the course of four or five years, are immersed in the problems and the orientation of the field, is rather different. For them, the experience is an intellectually wrenching one. Their most basic assumptions about the nature and the causes of human behavior, and about the very predictability of the social world, are challenged. At the end of the process, their views of human behavior and society will differ profoundly from the views held by most other people in their culture. Some of their new insights and beliefs will be held rather tentatively and applied inconsistently to the social events that unfold around them. Others will be held with great conviction, and will be applied confidently. But ironically, even the new insights that they are most confident about will tend to have the effect of making them less certain than their peers about predicting social behavior and making inferences about particular individuals or groups. Social psychology rivals philosophy in its ability to teach people that they do not truly understand the nature of the world....

The Lessons and Challenges of Social Psychology

As graduate students at Columbia University in the 1960s, working primarily with Stanley Schachter, we underwent the experience typical of students exposed to the experimental tradition in social psychology. That is, many of our most fundamental beliefs about human behavior, beliefs that we shared with most other people in our culture and that had remained intact or even been strengthened by our undergraduate courses in the humanities, were abruptly challenged in ways that have shaped our subsequent careers. An introduction to these challenges, which we offer below, provides a departure point for our discussion of the contributions of our discipline. Indeed, the remainder of our book represents an attempt to reconcile common sense and

From PERSPECTIVES OF SOCIAL PSYCHOLOGY, 1991, 1-4, 125-128, 143-144. Copyright © 1991 by McGraw-Hill Companies. Reprinted with permission.

common experience with the empirical lessons and challenges that lie at the core of social psychology....

The Weakness of Individual Differences

Consider the following scenario: While walking briskly to a meeting some distance across a college campus, John comes across a man slumped in a doorway, asking him for help. Will John offer it, or will he continue on his way? Before answering such a question, most people would want to know more about John. Is he someone known to be callous and unfeeling, or is he renowned for his kindness and concern? Is he a stalwart member of the Campus Outreach Organization, or a mainstay of the Conservative Coalition Against Welfare Abuse? In short, what kind of person is John and how has he behaved when his altruism has been tested in the past? Only with such information in hand, most people would agree, could one make a sensible and confident prediction.

In fact, however, nothing one is likely to know or learn about John would be of much use in helping predict John's behavior in the situation we've described. In particular, the type of information about personality that most laypeople would want to have before making a prediction would prove to be of relatively little value. A half century of research has taught us that in this situation, and in most other novel situations, one cannot predict with any accuracy how particular people will respond. At least one cannot do so using information about an individual's personal dispositions or even about that individual's past behavior.

Even scientists who are most concerned with assessing individual differences in personality would concede that our ability to predict how particular people will respond in particular situations is very limited. This "predictability ceiling" is typically reflected in a maximum statistical correlation of .30 between measured individual differences on a given trait dimension and behavior in a novel situation that plausibly tests that dimension. This ceiling, for example, would characterize our ability to predict on the basis of a personality test of honesty how likely different people will be to cheat in a game or on an exam, or to predict on the basis of a test of friendliness or extroversion how much sociability different individuals will show at a particular social gathering. Now a correlation of .30, as we will emphasize later, is by no means trivial. Correlations of this magnitude can be quite important for many prediction purposes. But a correlation of .30 still leaves the great bulk of variance in people's behavior unaccounted for. More importantly, a correlation of this magnitude is a good deal lower than it would have to be to provide the type of predictability that most laypeople anticipate when they make predictions about each other's behavior or make inferences about others' personal attributes. Moreover, the .30 value is an upper limit. For most novel behaviors in most domains, psychologists cannot come close to that. Certainly, as we will see, neither the professional nor the layperson can do that well when obliged to predict behavior in one particular new situation on the basis of actions in one particular prior situation.

Despite such evidence, however, most people staunchly believe that individual differences or traits can be used to predict how people will behave in new situations. Such "dispositionism" is widespread in our culture. What is more, most of us, scientists and laypeople alike, seem to find our dispositionism affirmed by our everyday social experience. The challenge of accounting for this discrepancy between beliefs about everyday experience on the one hand and empirical evidence on the other hand is one of the most important faced by psychologists....

The Power of Situations

While knowledge about John is of surprisingly little value in predicting whether he will help the person slumped in the doorway, details concerning the specifics of the situation would be invaluable. For example, what was the appearance of the person in the doorway? Was he clearly ill, or might he have been a drunk or, even worse, a nodding dope addict? Did his clothing make him look respectably middle class or decently working class, or did he look like a homeless derelict?

Such considerations are fairly obvious once they are mentioned, and the layperson, upon reflection, will generally concede their importance. But few laypeople would concede, much less anticipate, the relevance of some other, subtler, contextual details that empirical research has shown to be important factors influencing bystander intervention. Darley and Batson actually confronted people with a version of the situation we've described and found what some of these factors are. Their subjects were students in a religious seminary who were on their way to deliver a practice sermon. If the subjects were in a hurry (because they thought they were late to give a practice sermon), only about 10 percent helped. By contrast, if they were not in a hurry (because they had plenty of time before giving their sermon), about 63 percent of them helped.

Social psychology has by now amassed a vast store of such empirical parables. The tradition here is simple. Pick a generic situation; then identify and manipulate a situational or contextual variable that intuition or past research leads you to believe will make a difference (ideally, a variable whose impact you think most laypeople, or even most of your peers, somehow fail to appreciate), and see what happens, Sometimes, of course, you will be wrong and your manipulation won't "work." But often the situational variable makes quite a bit of difference. Occasionally, in fact, it makes nearly all the difference, and information about traits and individual differences that other people thought all-important proves all but trivial. If so, you have contributed a situationist classic destined to become part of our field's intellectual legacy. Such empirical parables are important because they illustrate the degree to which ordinary men and women are apt to be mistaken about the power of the situation—the power of particular situational features, and the power of situations in general.

People's inflated belief in the importance of personality traits and dispositions, together with their failure to recognize the importance of situational factors in affecting behavior, has been termed the "fundamental attribution error."... Together with many other social psychologists, we have directed our attention to documenting this conjoint error and attempting to track down its origins....

Lay Personology and Lay Social Psychology

Lay Dispositionism and the Fundamental Attribution Error

...[The] evidence that people are inclined to offer dispositional explanations for behavior instead of situational ones, and that they make inferences about the characteristics of actors when they would do well to make inferences instead about the characteristics of situations is far from new. It has been the subject of intense critical scrutiny. It is appropriate to review this literature now, including some recent and unpublished data. The evidence indicates that laypeople's vigorous personality theories are matched by only the most rudimentary and vestigial of social psychological perspectives. We will show that people (1) infer dispositions from behavior that is manifestly situationally produced [and] (2) overlook situational context factors of substantial importance...

Inferring Dispositions from Situationally Produced Behavior

Failing to discount the implications of behavior in view of the constraints on it.   The classic study demonstrating that lay perceivers fail to be appropriately sensitive to situational constraints was one conducted by Jones and Harris (1967). The study, ironically, was intended initially to show that subjects could make appropriate inferential use of information about situational constraints. Jones and Harris asked their college-student subjects to read essays or listen to speeches presumably written or spoken by fellow students. Subjects were told that the communicator had been assigned one side of the issue. For example, they were informed that the essay was produced by a political science student assigned to write an essay defending Castro's Cuba or that it was produced by a debater required to attack the proposition that marijuana should be legalized. Despite the fact that subjects clearly perceived the heavy constraints on the communicator in these no-choice conditions, their estimates of the true opinions of the communicator were markedly affected by the particular position the communicator had espoused. Subjects assumed that the target was sympathetic to Castro, or opposed to legalization of marijuana, if that was the position in the essay. The study indicates that observers are too willing to take behavior at face value, as reflecting a stable disposition (in this case, an attitudinal disposition), even when it is made abundantly clear that the actor's behavior is under severe external constraints.

Attributing volunteering to a disposition rather than to the compensation offered.   A study by Nisbett, Caputo, Legant, and Marecek (1973) showed that even such an obvious, widely appreciated situational factor as financial incentive can be slighted in explanation and prediction if there is a possibility of explaining behavior in dispositional terms. The investigators allowed observer subjects to watch actor subjects participate in what all were told was a study on decision making; Subjects were female undergraduates. The experimenter announced, "Before we begin the study, I happen to have sort of a real decision for you to make." He explained that the campus "Human Development Institute" would be sponsoring a weekend for the corporate board and some of its prospective financial backers. The spouses of these people would need entertainment and campus tours for the weekend. If the subject could see her way clear to volunteering, she would be paid by the hour. Some subjects were offered $.50 per hour and some were offered $1.50. (Apply a multiplier of approximately 3 or 4 to make the values comprehensible for the 90s.) Only a fifth of the low-payment actors volunteered, while two-thirds of the high-payment actors volunteered. Volunteering was thus largely due to the sheer amount of money offered for doing so.

Both actors and observers were asked about their perceptions of the actor's reasons for volunteering or not volunteering. One item probed the extent to which the actor's behavior was considered an expression of a general disposition to volunteer or not volunteer for worthy activities: "How likely do you think it is that you (or the subject) would also volunteer to canvass for the United Fund?" Observers thought that volunteering actors would be substantially more likely to volunteer to canvass for the United Fund than nonvolunteering actors regardless of whether they had been offered $.50 or $1.50 for doing so. Observers were apparently misled by the actor's behavior, assuming it reflected a dispositional tendency to volunteer rather than a response to a suitably compensated "job opportunity."

Ignoring role determinants in favor of dispositional inferences.   If people can fail to perceive the extent to which financial incentives rather than personal dispositions are determinative of behavior, then it is scarcely surprising to learn that they can also fail to perceive the extent to which subtler factors such as role relations can determine the nature of behavior. A deceptively simple demonstration of this point was made by Ross, Amabile, and Steinmet.... They asked their subjects to play a brief "College Bowl" type of quiz game, in which one subject, selected at random, was to ask the questions and the other was to answer them. The questioner's role was to generate 10 "challenging but not impossible questions," to which the contestant was supposed to provide answers out loud. Questioners, again and again, took advantage of their role to display esoteric knowledge in the questions they posed (for example, "What is the sweet-smelling liquid that comes from whales and is used as a base for perfume?") and in the answers they supplied (in this case ambergris) when contestants failed to answer correctly.

At the end of the session, both of the participants, and, in a subsequent reenactment, observers as well, were required to rate the questioner's and contestant's general knowledge. One might expect that it would have been clear to subjects and observers alike that the questioners' role advantage had been quite substantial. That is, the questioners' role guaranteed that they would reveal no area of ignorance, while the contestants' role gave no opportunity for such selective, self-serving displays. But the role advantage of the questioner did not prove to be sufficiently obvious either to the contestants or to the observers to prevent them from judging the questioners as being unusually knowledgeable. Both contestants: and observers rated the questioner as far more knowledgeable than either the contestant or the "average" student in the university.

Can we generalize from subjects' blindness to the importance of questioner versus contestant "roles" in this study and assume that people will be comparably blind to the importance of more familiar social roles as well? That would be risky, but fortunately, a clever study by Humphrey...allows us to do so. Humphrey set up a laboratory microcosm of a business office. Subjects were told that he was interested in studying "how people work together in an office setting." Some of the subjects were selected, by an ostentatiously random procedure, to be "managers" and to assume supervisory responsibilities, and some were selected to be mere "clerks" who followed orders. Managers were given time to study manuals describing their tasks. While they were studying them, the experimenter showed the clerks the mailboxes, filing system, and so on. The newly constructed office team then went about their business for two hours. The managers, as in a real office, performed reasonably high-skill-level tasks and directed the activity of the clerks, while the clerks were assigned to work on a variety of low-skilled, repetitive jobs and were given little autonomy.

At the end of the work period, managers and clerks rated themselves and each other on a variety of role-related traits. These included leadership, intelligence, motivation for hard work, assertiveness, and supportiveness. In addition, they rated the leadership and motivation for hard work they would be likely to display in a future job of a specific type. On all these traits, managers rated their fellow managers more highly than they rated their clerks. On all but hardworkingness, clerks rated their managers more highly than they rated their fellow clerks.

The parallel of Humphrey's study to the simple demonstration by Ross and his colleagues is therefore complete and its generalizability to real-world settings and concerns is far greater. People find it hard to penetrate beyond appearances to the role determinants of behavior, even when the random basis of role assignment and the particular prerogatives of particular roles are made abundantly clear. (Presumably, in everyday life, where such matters are more ambiguous, even *less* allowance would be made, and the behavior in question would even more willingly be taken at face value.)...

How Could We Be So Wrong?

How could we make such serious errors about such important matters? The question here is often phrased in the terms of evolutionary theory: Judgments about other people are often important to survival and therefore we could not be expected to be terribly wrong about them. Such evolutionary arguments are extremely dangerous in psychology, as Einhorn and Hogarth...have pointed out. The mere fact that some ability manifestly would be of great value to survival does not serve to establish that an organism must have it.

The vervet monkey, for example, is constantly imperiled by leopards and pythons, yet experimental tests have shown that the most seemingly obvious signs indicating the nearness of leopards (such as the presence of a dead gazelle in a tree) do not alarm the vervet monkey. Similarly, the vervet monkey does not recognize the trail of a python, either by its sight or its smell.

And there is the question of whether personality judgments of the sort we have been discussing are really all that important to humans in the conditions under which they evolved. A critic of the social perception tradition has characterized it as "the social psychology of strangers" and has asserted that the errors that characterize our judgments about strangers may have nothing to do with judgments about intimates. It seems to us that there is a distinct possibility that both the characterization and the assertion are correct, or largely so. The lay personality theory discussed in this chapter may apply mostly to judgments about people we do not know well. Evolutionary pressures are more likely to have been applied to judgments about intimates in the early hominid and human troop than to judgments about strangers. Thus a simple reading of base rates for the individual for the particular, familiar situation would have been about all that was needed for quite accurate prediction in daily life. Most sophisticated analyses probably did not become important until people began to trade and travel and thus to meet individuals with unfamiliar behavior and construals.

Of course, many of us today spend most of our time with non-intimates and must constantly make judgments of some importance about near-strangers. So the errors of lay personality theory we have been describing are not mere foibles....

NO ↵

Errors and Mistakes: Evaluating the Accuracy of Social Judgment

The accuracy of human social judgment is a topic of obvious interest and importance. It is only natural to wonder to what degree the judgments we make of the personalities of ourselves and others might be right or wrong, and to desire to improve our accuracy. Nonpsychologists are often surprised and disappointed, therefore, when they begin to take psychology courses and discover that the field has largely foresworn interest in the accuracy issue. The discipline's early, direct interest in accuracy (e.g., Estes, 1938; Taft, 1955; Vernon, 1933) was all but completely stifled some years ago by the publication of a series of methodological critiques by Cronbach (1955), Hastorf and Bender (1952), and others. As a result, according to one authoritative textbook:

> The accuracy issue has all but faded from view in recent years, at least for personality judgments. There is not much present interest in questions about whether people are accurate.... There is, in short, almost no concern with normative questions of accuracy. On the other hand, in recent years there has been a renewed interest in how, why, and in what circumstances people are inaccurate. (Schneider, Hastorf, & Ellsworth, 1979, p. 224; see also Cook, 1984)

Specifically, the psychology of social judgment has been dominated in recent years by a flood of research on the subject of "error." Studies of error appear in the literature at a prodigious rate, are disproportionately likely to be cited (Christensen-Szalanski & Beach, 1984), and fill whole books (Kahneman, Slovic, & Tversky, 1982; Nisbett & Ross, 1980). Psychology instructors have found that the various experimental demonstrations of error, like other counterintuitive phenomena, provide a sure way to spice up an undergraduate lecture in introductory or social psychology.

The study of error is a "hot topic," therefore, and justifiably so. Errors are an indispensable tool for studying the processes of human judgment. They can provide valuable insights into how the cognitive system transforms, augments, and distorts an initial stimulus "input" on the way to a final judgment "output."

From *Psychological Bulletin*, vol.101, no. 1, 1987, pp. 75–76, 78–73, 86–90. Copyright © 1987 by American Psychological Association. Reprinted with permission.

However, there is another, perhaps more important reason why the new research on error is so fashionable. Crandall (1984) writes

> Mistakes are fun! Errors in judgment make humorous anecdotes, but good performance does not. It is fun to lean back in our chairs and chuckle about our goofs. (p. 1499)

More seriously, Evans (1984) writes

> Although it is nice to know that people are reasoning well or making good decisions in some contexts, it is much more important to know when they are not.... Surely, the imperative message for us to impart to decision makers is that of their proneness to error. (pp. 1500–1501)

These quotations exemplify how, in a subtle but unmistakable way, error research has moved well beyond study of the judgment process. Studies of error are equated with studies of whether people "reason well" or "make good decisions." Errors are usually treated as "shortcomings" of judgment, as the title of more than one major work on the subject clearly reflects, and the existence of so many errors is taken to indicate that many if not most of the judgments people make about each other are wrong. In this way, by another name, and through the back door, the accuracy issue has reentered social psychology.

This reentry has occurred even though some investigators have occasionally acknowledged that error in the laboratory and inaccuracy in a larger sense may not be the same thing. Some years ago, D. T. Campbell (1959) wrote, "[many] errors ... will be found to be part-and-parcel of psychological processes of general adaptive usefulness" (p. 340), and Tversky and Kahneman (1983) stated more recently that "the focus on bias and illusion ... neither assumes nor entails that people are perceptually or cognitively inept" (p. 313).

Such disclaimers have had little impact over the years. Psychology's widespread fascination with error research continues to stem primarily from its apparently dramatic implications for accuracy in daily life (e.g., Crandall, 1984; Evans, 1984), *not* from its value for understanding the mechanisms of judgment. This is unfortunate because, according to the thesis of the present article, research on error is almost completely irrelevant to the accuracy of social judgment, and to the extent that the popularity of error research is due to its apparent implications for accuracy, the emphasis on it has been misplaced. The reason is that an error is not the same thing as a mistake.

An "error" is a judgment of a laboratory stimulus that deviates from a model of how that judgment should be made. When this model is normative and rational, the error represents an incorrect judgment. A "mistake," by contrast, is an incorrect judgment in the real world, such as a misjudgment of a real person, and so must be determined by different criteria. Detection of an error implies the existence of a mistake *only* when the process that produces the error also produces incorrect judgments in real life. Unfortunately, this cannot be determined by merely demonstrating the error itself, because the same judgment that is wrong in relation to a laboratory stimulus, taken literally, may be right in terms of a wider, more broadly defined social context, and reflect processes that lead to accurate judgments under ordinary circumstances. Most areas of psychology other than the study of social judgment, for example, the study of visual perception, generally assume that errors in the laboratory are the result of mechanisms that produce correct and adaptive judgments in real life. A different sort of research is needed to assess accuracy, therefore. Such research must let subjects judge real people in authentic social contexts, and use realistic, external criteria for determining when these judgments are right or wrong.

The purposes of this article are to summarize the current state of research on accuracy and error in social judgment, to demonstrate how the two kinds of research are not equivalent, and to propose an agenda for research relevant to accuracy issues. The presentation is in several sections.... The [first] section covers the difference between errors and mistakes, and illuminates the distinction with reference to research on visual perception. The [next] section demonstrates the consequences of failing to distinguish between errors and mistakes in the context of ... specific examples from the social psychological literature, then outlines some general implications of the distinction for interpreting research on error in social judgment. The [last] section describes in general terms the sort of content-oriented research that *could* address accuracy issues.

Two Meanings of "Error"

Like so many other common words (e.g., "reliability," "significance") that psychological jargon has borrowed from ordinary English, the word *error* appears deceptively simple, because its psychological usage is different. In psychology, proper use of the term is technical, not evaluative. An error is any deviation of an individual observation from a standard, such as a sample of population mean, or the output from a predictive model (e.g., a regression). Psychologists attach no negative connotations whatsoever, therefore, to phrases that refer to this sort of deviation, such as "standard error of estimate," "error variance," and "error term."

Still, these phrases can confuse students, because to the nonpsychologist an error is simply a bad thing. The distinction between the two usages is nicely demonstrated in *Funk & Wagnall's Standard College Dictionary* (1963, p. 450), in which the first definition of error is "Something done, said or believed incorrectly; *a mistake*" [emphasis added]. The technical sense is in the fifth definition: "The difference between the observed value of a magnitude and the true or mean value." (Of course, in this context "true" also has a technical meaning.) Errors demonstrated in the laboratory have this second meaning; they represent departures from the experimenter's standard for a "true" response that directly reflects the stimulus. Yet even some psychologists seem to be less aware than they should be of the subtle difference between this sort of error and a mistake.

The difference is subtle because, rather than being discretely different, errors and mistakes anchor opposite ends of a conceptual continuum. At the error end are misjudgments of narrowly defined, artificial stimuli, which represent departures from a normative model. These misjudgments are of no *intrinsic* interest, but can be highly informative about whether the model accurately depicts the process of judgment. Near the other end, labeled "mistake," are misjudgments of more poorly defined, real-life stimuli. These misjudgments are important because of their potentially dangerous consequences. Although it is relatively easy to detect an error, because the nature of the stimulus is precisely known and the normative judgment of it can be modeled with some certainty, it is much more difficult to determine that a judgment, perhaps even the same judgment, is also a mistake, because the criteria must be much broader, and located in the real world. In theory, errors and mistakes shade into each other, but in practice, as several examples later in this article show, errors and mistakes are often clearly distinguishable.

Errors in the Study of Visual Perception

One domain in which the distinction between errors and mistakes usually is kept clear is the study of visual perception. Illusions and misperceptions are seldom discussed as if they revealed "shortcomings" in the visual system.

A classic example, often seen in introductory psychology textbooks, is a drawing of two lines that converge upward, as if toward a horizon (Figure 1). A line segment is drawn near the bottom, and a second segment of equal length is drawn near the top. The second segment appears, incorrectly, to be longer than the first (This is the Ponzo or "railroad lines" illusion; Gregory, 1971.) Although the subject's perception is wrong, notice that in nearly every situation *outside* the laboratory it would be correct. Objects near the horizon that leave equivalent retinal images to nearby objects generally *are* larger. Another famous example is the Müller-Lyer illusion, which is that reversed arrowheads seem to lengthen their connecting shaft, whereas normal arrowheads seem to shrink the shaft (Figure 2). As Gregory (1971) points out, the only place in real life in which shapes like the Müller-Lyer figures appear is on the inside or outside edges of a box (or room), contexts in which a near edge *is* smaller than a far edge that leaves the same retinal image.

Figure 1

The Ponzo or "railroad lines" illusion: The upper segment appears longer, apparently because interpreted in three dimensions, the more usual perceptual situation, it is nearer the horizon and is in fact longer.

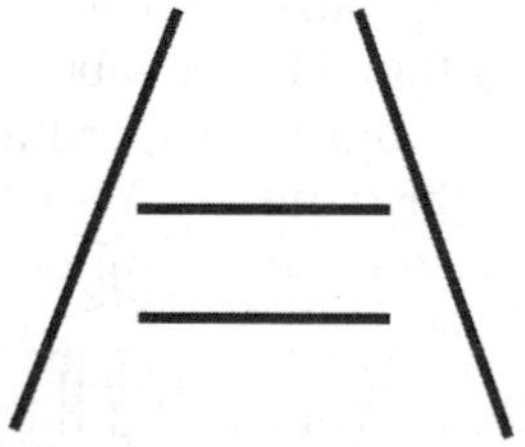

Figure 2

The Müller-Lyer illusion: The left-hand segment appears longer than the right-hand segment, because the arrowheads imply it is a far, inside edge, whereas the arrowheads on the right imply that segment is a nearer, outside edge. (In three-dimensional, real-life settings the processes underlying this illusion generally lead to correct perception.)

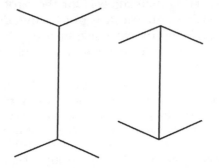

According to Gregory (1971), an early interpretation of the illusion in Figure 2 was that it reflects a general tendency to overestimate acute angles and underestimate obtuse ones, although no reason for such a strange tendency was ever provided. Yet in 1896 a psychologist named A. Thiery proposed that the illusion is related to the way people correctly use perspective in real life, and this interpretation eventually became predominant. Unlike their colleagues in social psychology, modern psychologists who study vision no longer treat illusions as flaws of judgment (Over, 1968). Rather they assume that these illusions reveal "information-processing mechanisms that under normal circumstances make the visual world easier to comprehend" (Gregory, 1971, p. 167; cf. Helmholtz, 1903; Dember & Warm, 1979).[1]

Production of Errors and Illusions

Gregory (1971) points out one reason why the usually effective visual system can be fooled by experimental illusions:

> Pictures [such as Figures 1 and 2] are highly artificial, and present special problems to the perceiving brain. In a sense all pictures are impossible because they have a dual reality. They are seen both as patterns of liens lying on a flat background and as objects depicted in a quite different three-dimensional space. (p. 171)

This dual reality is what keeps visual errors from being visual mistakes. The pairs of stimulus lines in Figures 1 and 2 really are the same length and any judgment otherwise is wrong, so long as the criterion for accuracy is taken very literally as constituting the length of the ink lines on the page. Yet if the figures are considered not as two-dimensional but as representations of three-dimensional stimuli (e.g., as if they were photographs or retinal images), the situation becomes very different—the two lines could in fact be of different lengths. If the figures really represent corners or outside edges, or railroad tracks against a horizon, then the two lines *definitely* are of different length, and the perceiver is not wrong. Perceptual psychologists recognize that the three-dimensional case more realistically approximates the usual situation for visual perceivers. Therefore, they waste no time berating their subjects for the error and instead concentrate on the way it reveals how cues are ordinarily combined into correct three-dimensional judgments of distance and size.

Lindsay and Norman (1972) describe another aspect of the difference between experimental illusions and visual reality:

> Normally, all contextual information fits together. As objects move away, their image size changes by just the right amount. The relative sizes and distances are what they should be. Neither the artist nor the psychologist, however, is constrained to studying real-life situations. The surrealist delights in discovering and intentionally violating the rules for constructing logical perceptions. (pp. 29–30; cf. Hammond, 1966)

In other words, experimental stimuli in perceptual research can be constructed so as to be not only artificial, but impossible—not in terms of the laboratory, of course (nothing is impossible in a laboratory), but in terms of their extrapolation to wider visual reality. A subject will typically be "fooled" by such stimuli, but there is even less reason than in the three-dimensional case to consider his or her error a mistake. A subject's response to "impossible" stimuli cannot reasonably be taken to imply perceptual incapacity in real life. If such incapacities exist, they will have to be demonstrated in other ways.

Visual psychologists understand these two principles well, but their relevance to social psychology is less often appreciated. First, in the same way that every picture has a dual reality, a social psychological experiment exists to the subject both as a two-dimensional, contrived array of stimuli *and* as a three-dimensional, real situation involving interaction among the subject, the experimenter, and even the institution in which the research takes place (cf. Orne, 1962). Thus, a subject's judgment might be an error in terms of the stimuli with which he or she is explicitly presented, but still correct (or at least defensible) in the wider context of the social situation in which the judgment is being made. Second, depending on one's interests (and, perhaps, one's surrealistic inclinations), a researcher can arbitrarily create patterns of social information or even entire social situations that are strange, unusual, or even impossible. A subject's response to such a situation is more likely to represent a (perhaps desperate) "best guess" under bizarre circumstances than a reflection of his or her basic judgmental capacity. The point is that errors can be defined very literally in terms of the immediate concrete stimulus, but before calling that judgment a mistake one needs to take into account the subject's wider social situation and more usual social experience. The next section begins with a detailed consideration of ... representative examples.

Social Errors in a Wider Context

The implications of the principles underlying the production of illusions, just outlined, for research on social judgment can be illustrated by closely considering ... well-known, more or less representative studies. Each, in a different way, shows how an error might be confused with a mistake. Yet these studies are not exceptionally flawed, and most of the comments made about them also apply to many others of the same general type. The purpose of discussing these particular studies is to make a general point in the context of some specific examples, and to survey the recent literature on social judgment in a representative rather than exhaustive manner.

Overattribution

In a classic study of the overattribution effect, Jones and Harris (1967) showed subjects essays favoring Castro that were purportedly written by people who had no choice in what to write. This study revealed a tendency for subjects to see such essays as reflecting their authors' true positions anyway. Subjects assumed that pro-Castro essays were written by pro-Castro authors, despite the situational constraint, and thereby committed an attribution error. A large literature has subsequently demonstrated this effect in a variety of ways (for a review see Jones, 1979), and it is usually interpreted as a judgmental flaw. For example, Nisbett and Ross (1980) describe the effect as demonstrating peoples' [general] overwillingness to ascribe behavior to enduring dispositions" (p. 131).

In their own terms overattribution experiments are perfectly straightforward and the error that subjects make is clear. However, considered in a larger frame, as a social interaction between subject and experimenter, many of these experiments have a curious aspect. The experimenter provides the subject with information that is normatively irrelevant to a judgment, then asks him or her to make that very judgment. In Jones and Harris's (1967) and many subsequent studies, subjects are given an essay and then asked to judge the writer's true attitude. The only clues available to the subjects' judgment are (a) their experience with attitudinal baserates and (b) the essay's content. Because subjects were told that the writer was instructed what to write, experimenters presume that the most rational course would be for subjects to judge the writer's true attitude solely from the baserates. They are deemed in error precisely to the degree that they base their judgments on the essay's content instead. However, subjects have a third piece of information, one that is not "officially" part of the experimental stimulus: (c) the experimenter gave them the essay, for their use (cf. Miller & Rorer, 1982).

As subjects implicitly know, and psycholinguists and sociologists have documented, normal (i.e., extraexperimental) social discourse proceeds according to various rules or "contracts." One of the most important of these rules is that the speaker tell the listener what he or she thinks the listener needs to know. The speaker should not give information that he or she thinks the listener already knows or that he or she believes has no relevance to the situation at hand. Moreover, he or she should not ask questions that the listener has no basis for answering. (For a discussion of these rules, see Clark & Clark's [1980] "given-new contract"; or Goffman, 1974; Grice, 1975; Swann, Giuliano, & Wegner, 1982). As social communicators, experimenters in studies of overattribution routinely violate this contract. Subjects are given information that in one way of thinking, is irrelevant to the judgment they must make. Yet they are given the information in precisely the way that in ordinary discourse, relevant information is provided. Furthermore, they are asked a question ("What is the author's true attitude?") that they cannot answer *unless* they assume the essay to be diagnostic. All of this happens to them while they are subjects in an experiment, under the close scrutiny of psychologists. In terms of the experimental stimuli taken very literally, the subject's response is wrong, an error, just like the perception of someone who looks at Figure 1. However, just as one's perception of Figure 1 is not an error if it is taken as three-dimensional, a subject's response to the total social situation of an overattribution experiment seems to make perfect sense. In this wider context, it seems only natural for subjects to make the "error" of basing their judgments on the information they have been given (cf. Adler, 1984), and inappropriate to construe this error as a mistake.

Moreover, although the overattribution effect is usually cited as deriving from the fundamental attribution error (e.g., Nisbett & Ross, 1980), Quattrone (1982) has shown that a similar experiment will lead subjects to "overattribute" to the *situation* if the experimenter merely asks them to use the essay to estimate situational forces that might be present, instead of the writer's "true" attitude. Thus, the direction of overattribution, that is, to the person or situation, seems to depend more on the specific question the experimenter asks than on any more "fundamental" tendency....

Social Roles

One of the most interesting studies of attribution error is by L. Ross, Amabile, and Steinmetz (1977). Compared to most research in this area, the situation it created for subjects was unusually realistic. Pairs of subjects were randomly assigned to the roles of "questioner" and "contestant" and, in a quiz show-like format, the latter tried to answer questions made up by the former. Afterward, the contestant consistently rated himself or herself as inferior to the questioner in general knowledge. In a second study, uninvolved observers watched a realistic reenactment of the same situation, and manifested the same strong tendency to attribute more general knowledge to the arbitrarily assigned occupant of the questioner role. L. Ross et al.'s discussion of this phenomenon was unrelievedly pessimistic, emphasizing how perceivers "fail" (p. 485), because they "consistently underestimate, and/or make inadequate allowance for, the biasing effects of the questioners' and contestants' roles upon their ability to display general knowledge advantageously" (p. 486). They further claimed that "the phenomenon demonstrated in the ... present experiment has clear implications for the role constrained encounters outside the laboratory" (p. 493).

The unfairness of evaluating the questioner and contestant solely on the basis of their role-constrained performance seems obvious. Yet it may be misleading to regard this "attribution error" in a wholly negative light. The social error of overattribution must, it seems, be preceded by development of a prior and general social *competence,* the ability to recognize and make appropriate attributions for differential task performance in the first place. Overextension of a rule first requires that the rule be acquired; a recognition of how better performance ordinarily implies greater ability must precede any tendency to draw this implication too broadly. A similar developmental sequence is found in many areas of psychology (e.g., language acquisition; see Brown, 1973): Initially, behavior occurs without reference to a rule, then the rule is learned but applied too broadly, then finally the exceptions to the rule are learned. The social roles effect studied by L. Ross et al. seems to involve a failure to recognize an exceptional (and artificial) case, but also seems to require acquisition and application of the rule itself.

This approach has important implications for how we might interpret differences between individuals who do and do not manifest this attribution error. For example, when someone immune to the social roles effect watches the two individuals interact and then concludes they "look about the same" in ability, is this because he or she is the rare individual able to adjust appropriately for the clever way the experimenter rigged the situation, or does he or she simply fail to infer differential ability from the differential performance in the first place? Recently, J. Block and Funder (1986) have obtained relevant data, examining the personality correlates of individual differences in the role effect among 14-year-old subjects. They found that far from being exceptionally sophisticated, those males (and, to a lesser extent, females) who were least vulnerable to the role effect were independently characterized as the least socially competent and least well adjusted. Moreover, individual differences in the role effect correlated positively with self-esteem, and females exhibited the role effect to a significantly greater degree than males, a finding consistent with evidence elsewhere that adolescent females tend to be better attuned socially than males (J. H. Block, 1973; Huston, 1983).

Thus, manifestation of this attribution "error," far from being a symptom of social maladjustment, actually seems associated with a degree of competence, at least in adolescents. To be sure, in Ross et al.'s experiment there was no valid reason for subjects to regard the questioner as any more knowledgeable than the contestant. Yet it also seems likely that in the overwhelming majority of wider, real-life contexts, such differences in apparent performance in fact do reflect differences in ability. Performance may not ordinarily be so constrained by social role, after all, and social roles themselves are not usually conferred quite as arbitrarily as in this experiment. The relation that ordinarily obtains between performance and ability in real life may mean that it is generally more efficient and functional to infer ability directly from performance than to try to adjust for the specific constraints that may be present in every situation encountered.[2] ...

Getting a Fix on Accuracy

If research on the process of social judgment does not address the difference between errors and mistakes, we are left to wonder what sort of empirical research can address the accuracy issue: How accurate is social judgment, anyway?

Phrased this way, the question is probably unanswerable. It can only have meaning in relation to a second question: Compared to what? Some authors (e.g., Nisbett & Ross, 1980), have proposed that people are less accurate than they think they are. Others (e.g., Swann, 1984) have suggested that people are more accurate than some psychologists think they are. If one accepts that people are neither infallibly accurate nor wrong all the time, such discussions seem to lose much of their interest, and reduce to an analysis of the difference between a half-full and a half-empty glass (Loftus & Beach, 1982)....

This article has been highly critical of the currently dominant paradigm that studies error in social judgment. Errors are not necessarily mistakes, I have argued, because judgments (and judgment processes) that are incorrect in terms of a limited experimental context may be correct when applied to a wider more realistic context—a context, in other words, in which judgments are usually made and have real-life consequences. Or, of course, they also may not be correct in a wider context. Yet research on error cannot settle the question. For that reason it is not relevant to the accuracy of human judgment in real life....

Still, the study of error, in social judgment and in judgment generally, is an important and valuable part of psychology. Along with the study of reaction time, error analysis is one of the two most useful tools for learning about how people think. Ironically, however, its great usefulness for studying process is not what has led this research to be so extraordinarily popular. Rather, its popularity is largely if not exclusively due to its apparent and, it turns out, illusory implications for accuracy. That is why the first half of this article had to be so negative. Only when psychologists understand what error research *cannot* deliver, will they fully appreciate what it can....

Notes

1. This difference may arise because the visual system is generally well regarded; visual psychologists are willing to grant that it works well in ordinary circumstances, and so they take errors as clues about how it works rather than as evidence that it works badly. Some social psychologists, by contrast, seem more pessimistic. If one's overall evaluation of human social perception is that it is badly flawed, then it is more natural (if no more justified) to regard errors as manifestations of these flaws.
2. For the observer subjects in such an experiment, a second consideration is also operative. These observers are literally given no information on which to base their attributions of ability, except the role-constrained performances of actor and observers. As in other experiments with overattribution, the very provision of this information itself may well-imply that it is intended to be diagnostic of the judgments to be made and should be used.

References

Adler, J. E. (1984). Abstraction is uncooperative. *Journal for the Theory of Social Behaviour, 14,* 165–181.

Block, J., & Funder, D. C. (1986). Social roles and social perception: Individual differences in attribution and "error." *Journal of Personality and Social Psychology, 51,* 1200–1207.

Block, J. H. (1973). Conceptions of sex role: Some Cross-cultural and longitudinal perspectives. *American Psychologist, 28,* 512–526.

Brown, R. (1973). *A first language: The early stages.* Cambridge, MA: Harvard University Press.

Campbell, D. T. (1959). Systematic error on the part of human links in communication systems. *Information and Control, 1,* 334–369.

Christensen-Szalanski, J. J. J., & Beach, L. R. (1984). The citation bias: Fad and fashion in the judgment and decision literature [Comment]. *American Psychologist, 39,* 75–78.

Clark, H. H., & Clark, E. V. (1977). *Psychology and Language.* New York: Harcourt Brace Jovanovich.

Cook, M. (1984). *Issues in person perception.* London: Methuen.

Crandall, C. S. (1984). The overcitation of examples of poor performance: Fad, fashion, or fun [Comment]? *American Psychologist, 39,* 1499–1500.

Cronbach, L. J. (1955). Processes affecting scores on "understanding of others" and "assumed similarity." *Psychological Bulletin, 52,* 177–193.

Dember, W. N., & Warm, J. S. (1979). *Psychology of perception* (2nd ed.). New York: Holt, Rinehart & Winston.

Estes, S. G. (1938). Judging personality from expressive behavior. *Journal of Abnormal and Social Psychology, 33,* 217–236.

Evans, J. St. B. T. (1984). In defense of the citation bias in the judgment literature [Comment]. *American Psychologist, 39,* 1500–1501.

Funk & Wagnall's standard college dictionary: Text edition. (1963). New York: Harcourt, Brace & World.

Goffman, E. (1974). *Frame analysis.* New York: Harper & Row.

Gregory, R. L. (1971). Visual illusions. In R. C. Atkinson (Ed.), *Contemporary psychology* (pp. 167-177). San Francisco: Freeman.

Grice, H. P. (1975). Logic in conversation. In P. Cole & J. L. Morgan (Eds.), *Syntax and semantics* (Vol. 3, pp. 41–58). New York: Academic Press.

Hammond, K. R. (1966) Probabilistic functionalism: Egon Brunswik's integration of the history, theory, and method of psychology. In K.R. Hammond (Ed.), *The psychology of Egon-Brunswik* (pp. 15–80). New York: Hold, Rinehart & Winston.

Hastorf, A. H., & Bender, I. E. (1952). A caution respecting the measurement of empathic ability. *Journal of Abnormal and Social Psychology: 47,* 574–576.

Helmholtz, H. von (1903). *Popular lectures on scientific subjects* (E. Atkinson, Trans.). New York: Green. (Original work published 1881)

Huston, A. C. (1983). Sex-typing. In E. M. Hetherington (Ed.), *Handbook of child psychology: Vol. 4. Socialization, personality and social development* (pp. 387–467). New York: Wiley.

Jones, E. E. (1979). The rocky road from acts to dispositions. *American Psychologist, 34,* 107–117.

Jones, E. E., & Harris, V. A. (1967). The attribution of attitudes. *Journal of Experimental Social Psychology, 3,* 1–24.

Kahneman, D., Slovic, P., & Tversky, A. (1982). *Judgment under uncertainty: Heuristics and biases.* New York: Cambridge University Press.

Lindsay, P. H., & Norman, D. A. (1972). *Human information processing.* New York: Academic Press.

Loftus, E. F., & Beach, L. R. (1982). Human inference and judgment: Is the glass half empty or half full? *Stanford Law Review, 34,* 939–956.

Nisbett, R., & Ross, L. (1980). *Human inference: Strategies and shortcomings of social judgment.* New York: Prentice Hall.

Orne, M. T. (1962). On the social psychology of the psychological experiment: With particular reference to demand characteristics and their implications. *American Psychologist, 17,* 776–783.

Over, R. (1968). Explanations of visual illusions. *Psychological Bulletin, 70,* 545–562.

Quattrone, G. A. (1982). Overattribution and unit formation: When behavior engulfs the person. *Journal of Personality and Social Psychology: 43,* 593–607.

Ross, L., Amabile, T. M., & Steinmetz, J. L. (1977). Social roles, social control, and biases in social-perception processes. *Journal of Personality and Social Psychology: 35,* 485–494.

Schneider, D. J., Hastorf, A. H., & Ellsworth, P. C. (1979). *Person perception* (2nd ed.). Reading, MA: Addison-Wesley.

Swann, W. B., Jr. (1984). Quest for accuracy in person perception: A matter of pragmatics. *Psychological Review: 91,* 457–477.

Swann, W. B., Jr., Giuliano, T., & Wegner, D. M. (1982). Where leading questions can lead: The power of conjecture in social interaction. *Journal of Personality and Social Psychology, 42,* 1025–1035.

Taft, R. (1955). The ability to judge people. *Psychological Bulletin, 52,* 1–23.

Tversky, A., & Kahneman, D. (1983). Extensional versus intuitive reasoning: The conjunction fallacy in probability judgment. *Psychological Review, 90,* 293–315.

Vernon, P. E. (1933). Some characteristics of the good judge of personality. *Journal of Social Psychology: 4,* 42–58.

CHALLENGE QUESTIONS

Are Our Social Perceptions Often Inaccurate?

1. Can you think of a time that you may have succumbed to the dispositionalist bias? Describe the mistake you made in explaining the behavior of someone and how this instance demonstrated the dispositionalist bias.
2. One of the key elements of Funder's argument is that people's actions usually do correspond to their dispositions. In your experience, have you found this to be the case? Or have you noticed that people often act in a way that is not necessarily consistent with the types of people they are?
3. Assume for a moment that Ross and Nisbett are correct, and that the dispositionalist bias leads people to make incorrect explanations for the behavior of other. What would be the potential harm in making these kinds of mistakes?

ISSUE 4

Does Cognitive Dissonance Explain Why Behavior Can Change Attitudes?

YES: Leon Festinger and James M. Carlsmith from "Cognitive Consequences of Forced Compliance," *Journal of Abnormal and Social Psychology* (58, 1959)

NO: Daryl J. Bem from "Self-Perception: An Alternative Interpretation of Cognitive Dissonance Phenomena," *Psychological Review* (74, 1967)

ISSUE SUMMARY

YES: Social psychologists Leon Festinger and James M. Carlsmith propose their theory of cognitive dissonance to explain why people's attitudes may change after they have acted in a way that is inconsistent with their true attitudes.

NO: Social psychologist Daryl J. Bem proposes a theory of self-perception, which he believes can explain Festinger and Carlsmith's results better than cognitive dissonance theory.

Cognitive dissonance theory is one of the best-known theories in social psychology. Originally proposed by Leon Festinger in 1957, the theory suggests that we strive to maintain consistency in our attitudes and actions. As a result, when there is a contradiction between our attitudes and actions we experience psychological tension. For example, if someone knows that cigarette smoking is dangerous, yet continues to smoke, the smoker would experience psychological tension (called cognitive dissonance) as a result of the seeming contradiction between his or her attitudes and actions. In order to reduce this tension, people can either change their attitudes or change their actual behavior so that they no longer contradict one another. In the case of someone who smokes, this could mean that the smoker can either quit smoking or could change his or her attitudes by downplaying the risks that smoking poses to one's health, in order to reduce the tension that might otherwise occur. In the first selection, Festinger and Carlsmith describe their classic study that demonstrated people may, in fact, change their attitudes when they experience a contradiction between their attitudes and behavior. In their study, participants were asked to perform a variety of boring tasks, such as repeatedly rotating a set of wooden pegs. Afterwards participants were asked to lie about how enjoyable the experiment was, by telling another person that they actually liked the experiment. Some participants were paid $20 dollars to lie, while others were only paid $1 to tell the same lie. According to Festinger and Carlsmith, participants who were only paid $1 to tell the lie experienced psychological tension as a result of performing a behavior (saying that they like the experiment) that conflicted with their true attitudes (the experiment was really boring). They argue that their results provide substantial support for cognitive dissonance theory.

Daryl Bem believes that Festinger and Carlsmith's results do not necessarily demonstrate the importance of cognitive dissonance theory and proposes his own theory, called self-perception theory, to account for the results. According to self-perception theory, when people are unsure of their attitudes, they examine their behavior to determine their attitude. For example, if you are unsure whether you like a particular student in your class, you might examine how you have treated that person. If you've been particularly nice to that person, you would conclude that you like him or her. If you've treated that person poorly, you would conclude that you dislike him or her. In other words, you might infer your attitude toward your classmate based on your behavior.

While this idea may seem counterintuitive, consider the Festinger and Carlsmith study. Participants who were paid $1 to lie, and tell someone that the boring experiment was enjoyable, reported liking the experiment more, compared to those who were paid $20 to tell the same lie. According to self-perception theory, participants who were only paid $1 to tell the lie conclude that they must have liked the experiment if they told someone they liked it, since they had so little financial incentive to tell the lie. They reason "The experiment must not have been that bad if I told someone I liked it for only $1." Thus, people infer their attitudes based on their actions, rather than changing their attitudes as a result of the psychological tension called cognitive dissonance. In order to examine self-perception theory, the second selection will describe a study that partially replicates Festinger and Carlsmith's original experiment. However, this study was designed so that psychological tension (i.e., cognitive dissonance) could not be a plausible explanation for the results. Instead the results of this experiment are more easily explained by self- perception theory.

POINT

- When people behave in a way that contradicts their attitudes, they experience psychological tension called cognitive dissonance.
- People sometimes change their attitudes in order to reduce the psychological tension that is produced by the contradiction between their actions and attitudes.
- Experimental evidence supports cognitive dissonance theory.

COUNTERPOINT

- Psychological tension is not necessarily a consequence of a contradiction between one's attitudes and actions.
- The attitude change that occurs can be explained by self-perception theory.
- Additional research indicates that self-perception theory can account for the results of these experiments.

Leon Festinger and
James M. Carlsmith

 **YES**

Cognitive Consequences of
Forced Compliance

What happens to a person's private opinion if he is forced to do or say something contrary to that opinion? Only recently has there been any experimental work related to this question. Two studies reported by Janis and King (1954; 1956) clearly showed that, at least under some conditions, the private opinion changes so as to bring it into closer correspondence with the overt behavior the person was forced to perform. Specifically, they showed that if a person is forced to improvise a speech supporting a point of view with which he disagrees, his private opinion moves toward the postion advocated in the speech. The observed opinion change is greater than for persons who only hear the speech or for persons who read a prepared speech with emphasis solely on elocution and manner of delivery. The authors of these two studies explain their results mainly in terms of mental rehearsal and thinking up new arguments. In this way, they propose, the person who is forced to improvise a speech convinces himself. They present some evidence, which is not altogether conclusive, in support of this explanation. We will have more to say concerning this explanation in discussing the results of our experiment....

Recently, Festinger (1957) proposed a theory concerning cognitive dissonance from which come a number of derivations about opinion change following forced compliance. Since these derivations are stated in detail by Festinger (1957, Ch. 4), we will here give only a brief outline of the reasoning.

Let us consider a person who privately holds opinion "X" but has, as a result of pressure brought to bear on him, publicly stated that he believes "not X."

1. This person has two cognitions which, psychologically, do not fit together: one of these is the knowledge that he believes "X," the other the knowledge that he has publicly stated that he believes "not X." If no factors other than his private opinion are considered, it would follow, at least in our culture, that if he believes "X" he would publicly state "X." Hence, his cognition of his private belief is dissonant with his cognition concerning his actual public statement.
2. Similarly, the knowledge that he has said "not X" is consonant with (does fit together with) those cognitive elements corresponding to the reasons, pressures, promises of rewards and/or threats of punishment which induced him to say "not X."

From *The Journal of Abnormal and Social Psychology*, vol. 58, 1959, pp. 203–210.

3. In evaluating the total magnitude of dissonance, one must take account of both dissonances and consonances. Let us think of the sum of all the dissonances involving some particular cognition as "D" and the sum of all the consonances as "C." Then we might think of the total magnitude of dissonance as being a function of "D" divided by "D" plus "C."

Let us then see what can be said about the total magnitude of dissonance in a person created by the knowledge that he said "not X" and really believes "X." With everything else held constant, this total magnitude of dissonance would decrease as the number and importance of the pressures which induced him to say "not X" increased. Thus, if the overt behavior was brought about by, say, offers of reward or threats of punishment, the magnitude of dissonance is maximal if these promised rewards or threatened punishments were just barely sufficient to induce the person to say "not X." From this point on, as the promised rewards or threatened punishment become larger, the magnitude of dissonance becomes smaller.

4. One way in which the dissonance can be reduced is for the person to change his private opinion so as to bring it into correspondence with what he has said. One would consequently expect to observe such opinion change after a person has been forced or induced to say something contrary to his private opinion. Furthermore, since the pressure to reduce dissonance will be a function of the magnitude of the dissonance, the observed opinion change should be greatest when the pressure used to elicit the overt behavior is just sufficient to do it.

The present experiment was designed to test this derivation under controlled, laboratory conditions. In the experiment we varied the amount of reward used to force persons to make a statement contrary to their private views. The prediction [from 3 and 4 above] is that the larger the reward given to the subject, the smaller will be the subsequent opinion change.

Procedure

Seventy-one male students in the introductory psychology course at Stanford University were used in the experiment...

When the *S* [the subject] arrived for the experiment on "Measures of Performance" he had to wait for a few minutes in the secretary's office. The experimenter (*E*) then came in, introduced himself to the *S* and, together, they walked into the laboratory room where the *E* said:

This experiment usually takes a little over an hour but, of course, we had to schedule it for two hours. Since we have that extra time, the introductory psychology people asked if they could interview some of our subjects. [Offhand and conversationally.] Did they announce that in class? I gather that they're interviewing some people who have been in experiments. I don't know much about it. Anyhow, they may want to interview you when you're through here.

With no further introduction or explanation the *S* was shown the first task, which involved putting 12 spools onto a tray, emptying the tray, refilling it with spools, and so on. He was told to use one hand and to work at his own speed. He did this for one-half hour. The *E* then removed the tray and spools and placed in front of the *S* a board containing 48 square pegs. His task was to turn each peg a quarter turn clockwise, then another quarter turn, and so on. He was told again to use one hand and to work at his own speed. The *S* worked at this task for another half hour.

While the *S* was working on these tasks, the *E* sat, with a stop watch in his hand, busily making notations on a sheet of paper. He did so in order to make it convincing that this was what the *E* was interested in and that these tasks, and how the *S* worked on them, was the total experiment. From our point of view the experiment had hardly started. The hour which the *S* spent working on the repetitive, monotonous tasks was intended to provide, for each *S* uniformly, an experience about which he would have a somewhat negative opinion.

After the half hour on the second task was over, the *E* conspicuously set the stopwatch back to zero, put it away, pushed his chair back, lit a cigarette, and said:

> O.K. Well, that's all we have in the experiment itself. I'd like to explain what this has been all about so you'll have some idea of why you were doing this. [*E* pauses.] Well, the way the experiment is set up is this. There are actually two groups in the experiment. In one, the group you were in, we bring the subject in and give him essentially no introduction to the experiment. That is, all we tell him is what he needs to know in order to do the tasks, and he has no idea of what the experiment is all about, or what it's going to be like, or anything like that. But in the other group, we have a student that we've hired that works for us regularly, and what I do is take him into the next room where the subject is waiting—the same room you were waiting in before—and I introduce him as if he had just finished being a subject in the experiment. That is, I say: "This is so-and-so, who's just finished the experiment, and I've asked him to tell you a little of what it's about before you start." The fellow who works for us then, in conversation with the next subject, makes these points: [The *E* then produced a sheet headed "For Group B" which had written on it: It was very enjoyable, I had a lot of fun, I enjoyed myself, it was very interesting, it was intriguing, it was exciting. The *E* showed this to the *S* and then proceeded with his false explanation of the purpose of the experiment.] Now, of course, we have this student do this, because if the experimenter does it, it doesn't look realistic, and what we're interested in doing is comparing how these two groups do on the experiment—the one with this previous expectation about the experiment, and the other, like yourself, with essentially none.

Up to this point the procedure was identical for *Ss* in all conditions. From this point on they diverged somewhat. Three conditions were run, Control, One Dollar, and Twenty Dollars, as follows:

Control Condition

The *E* continued:

> Is that fairly clear? [Pause.] Look, that fellow [looks at watch] I was telling you about from the introductory psychology class said he would get here a

couple of minutes from now. Would you mind waiting to see if he wants to talk to you? Fine. Why don't we go into the other room to wait? [The E left the S in the secretary's office for four minutes. He then returned and said:] O.K. Let's check and see if he does want to talk to you.

One and Twenty Dollar Conditions

The E continued:

Is that fairly clear how it is set up and what we're trying to do? [Pause.] Now, I also have a sort of strange thing to ask you. The thing is this. [Long pause, some confusion and uncertainty in the following, with a degree of embarrassment on the part of the E. The manner of the E contrasted strongly with the preceding unhesitant and assured false explanation of the experiment. The point was to make it seem to the S that this was the first time the E had done this and that he felt unsure of himself.] The fellow who normally does this for us couldn't do it today—he just phoned in, and something or other came up for him—so we've been looking around for someone that we could hire to do it for us. You see, we've got another subject waiting [looks at watch] who is supposed to be in that other condition. Now Professor_____, who is in charge of this experiment, suggested that perhaps we could take a chance on your doing it for us. I'll tell you what we had in mind: the thing is, if you could do it for us now, then of course you would know how to do it, and if something like this should ever come up again, that is, the regular fellow couldn't make it, and we had a subject scheduled, it would be very reassuring to us to know that we had somebody else we could call on who knew how to do it. So, if you would be willing to do this for us, we'd like to hire you to do it now and then be on call in the future, if something like this should ever happen again. We can pay you a dollar (twenty dollars) for doing this for us, that is, for doing it now and then being on call. Do you think you could do that for us?

If the S hesitated, the E said things like, "It will only take a few minutes," "The regular person is pretty reliable; this is the first time he has missed," or "If we needed you we could phone you a day or two in advance; if you couldn't make it, of course, we wouldn't expect you to come." After the S agreed to do it, the E gave him the previously mentioned sheet of paper headed "For Group B" and asked him to read it through again. The E then paid the S one dollar (twenty dollars), made out a hand-written receipt form, and asked the S to sign it. He then said:

O.K., the way we'll do it is this. As I said, the next subject should be here by now. I think the next one is a girl. I'll take you into the next room and introduce you to her, saying that you've just finished the experiment and that we've asked you to tell her a little about it. And what we want you to do is just sit down and get into a conversation with her and try to get across the points on that sheet of paper. I'll leave you alone and come back after a couple of minutes. O.K.?

The E then took the S into the secretary's office where he had previously waited and where the next S was waiting. (The secretary had left the office.) He introduced the girl and the S to one another saying that the S had just finished the experiment and would tell her something about it. He then left saying he would return in a couple of minutes. The girl, an undergraduate hired for this role, said little until the S made some positive remarks about the experiment and then said that she was surprised because a friend of hers had taken the experiment the week before and had told her that it was boring and that she ought to try to get out of it. Most Ss responded by saying something like "Oh, no, it's really very interesting. I'm sure you'll enjoy it." The girl, after this listened quietly, accepting and agreeing to everything the S told her. The discussion between the S and the girl was recorded on a hidden tape recorder.

After two minutes the E returned, asked the girl to go into the experimental room, thanked the S for talking to the girl, wrote down his phone number to continue the fiction that we might call on him again in the future and then said: "Look, could we check and see if that fellow from introductory psychology wants to talk to you?"

From this point on, the procedure for all three conditions was once more identical. As the E and the S started to walk to the office where the interviewer was, the E said: "Thanks very much for working on those tasks for us. I hope you did enjoy it. Most of our subjects tell us afterward that they found it quite interesting. You get a chance to see how you react to the tasks and so forth." This short persuasive communication was made in all conditions in exactly the same way. The reason for doing it, theoretically, was to make it easier for anyone who wanted to persuade himself that the tasks had been, indeed, enjoyable.

When they arrived at the interviewer's office, the E asked the interviewer whether or not he wanted to talk to the S. The interviewer said yes, the E shook hands with the S, said good-bye, and left. The interviewer, of course, was always kept in complete ignorance of which condition the S was in. The interview consisted of four questions, on each of which the S was first encouraged to talk about the matter and was then asked to rate his opinion or reaction on an 11-point scale. The questions are as follows:

1. Were the tasks interesting and enjoyable? In what way? In what way were they not? Would you rate how you feel about them on a scale from –5 to +5 where –5 means they were extremely dull and boring, +5 means they were extremely interesting and enjoyable, and zero means they were neutral, neither interesting nor uninteresting.
2. Did the experiment give you an opportunity to learn about your own ability to perform these tasks? In what way? In what way not? Would you rate how you feel about this on a scale from 0 to 10 where 0 means you learned nothing and 10 means you learned a great deal.
3. From what you know about the experiment and the tasks involved in it, would you say the experiment was measuring anything important? That is, do you think the results may have scientific value? In what way? In what way not? Would you rate your opinion on this matter on a scale from 0 to 10 where 0 means the results have no sci-

entific value or importance and 10 means they have a great deal of value and importance.
4. Would you have any desire to participate in another similar experiment? Why? Why not? Would you rate your desire to participate in a similar experiment again on a scale from –5 to +5, where –5 means you would definitely dislike to participate, +5 means you would definitely like to participate, and 0 means you have no particular feeling about it one way or the other.

As may be seen, the questions varied in how directly relevant they were to what the S had told the girl. This point will be discussed further in connection with the results.

At the close of the interview the S was asked what he thought the experiment was about and, following this, was asked directly whether or not he was suspicious of anything and, if so, what he was suspicious of. When the interview was over, the interviewer brought the S back to the experimental room where the E was waiting together with the girl who had posed as the waiting S. (In the control condition, of course, the girl was not there.) The true purpose of the experiment was then explained to the S in detail, and the reasons for each of the various steps in the experiment were explained carefully in relation to the true purpose. All experimental Ss in both One Dollar and Twenty Dollar conditions were asked, after this explanation, to return the money they had been given. All Ss, without exception, were quite willing to return the money.

The data from 11 of the 71 Ss in the experiment had to be discarded for the following reasons:

1. Five Ss (three in the One Dollar and two in the Twenty Dollar condition) indicated in the interview that they were suspicious about having been paid to tell the girl the experiment was fun and suspected that that was the real purpose of the experiment.
2. Two Ss (both in the One Dollar condition) told the girl that they had been hired, that the experiment was really boring but they were supposed to say it was fun.
3. Three Ss (one in the One Dollar and two in the Twenty Dollar condition) refused to take the money and refused to be hired.
4. One S (in the One Dollar condition), immediately after having talked to the girl, demanded her phone number saying he would call her and explain things, and also told the E he wanted to wait until she was finished so he could tell her about it.

These 11 Ss were, of course, run through the total experiment anyhow and the experiment was explained to them afterwards. Their data, however, are not included in the analysis.

Summary of Design

There remain, for analysis, 20 Ss in each of the three conditions. Let us review these briefly: 1. *Control condition.* These Ss were treated identically in all respects to the Ss in the experimental conditions, except that they were never asked to, and never did, tell the waiting girl that the experimental tasks were enjoyable and lots of fun. 2. *One Dollar condition.* These *Ss* were hired for one dollar to tell a waiting *S* that tasks, which were really rather dull and boring, were interesting, enjoyable, and lots of fun. 3. *Twenty Dollar condition.* These *Ss* were hired for twenty dollars to do the same thing.

Results

The major results of the experiment are summarized in Table 1 which lists, separately for each of the three experimental conditions, the average rating which the *Ss* gave at the end of each question on the interview. We will discuss each of the questions on the interview separately, because they were intended to measure different things. One other point before we proceed to examine the data. In all the comparisons, the Control condition should be regarded as a baseline from which to evaluate the results in the other two conditions. The Control condition gives us, essentially, the reactions of *Ss* to the tasks and their opinions about the experiment as falsely explained to them, without the experimental introduction of dissonance. The data from the other conditions may be viewed, in a sense, as changes from this baseline.

Table 1:

Average Ratings on Interview Questions for Each Condition

Question on Interview	Control (N = 20)	One Dollar (N = 20)	Twenty Dollars (N = 20)
		Experimental Condition	
How enjoyable tasks were (rated from -5 to +5)	-.45	+1.35	-.05
How much they learned (rated from 0 to 10)	3.08	2.80	3.15
Scientific importance (rated from 0 to 10)	5.60	6.45	5.18
Participate in similar exp. (rated from -5 to +5)	-.62	+1.20	-.25

How Enjoyable the Tasks Were

The average ratings on this question, presented in the first row of figures in Table 1, are the results most important to the experiment. These results are the ones most directly relevant to the specific dissonance which was experimentally created. It will be recalled that the tasks were purposely arranged to be rather boring and monotonous. And, indeed, in the Control condition the average rating was –.45, somewhat on the negative side of the neutral point.

In the other two conditions, however, the *Ss* told someone that these tasks were interesting and enjoyable. The resulting dissonance could, of course, most directly be reduced by persuading themselves that the tasks were, indeed, interesting and enjoyable. In the One Dollar condition, since the magnitude of dissonance was high, the pressure to reduce this dissonance would also be high. In this condition, the average rating was +1.35, considerably on the positive side and significantly different from the Control condition at the .02 level[1] (t = 2.48).

In the Twenty Dollar condition, where less dissonance was created experimentally because of the greater importance of the consonant relations, there is correspondingly less evidence of dissonance reduction. The average rating in this condition is only –.05, slightly and not significantly higher than the Control condition. The difference between the One Dollar and Twenty Dollar conditions is significant at the .03 level ($t = 2.22$). In short, when an S was induced, by offer of reward, to say something contrary to his private opinion, this private opinion tended to change so as to correspond more closely with what he had said. The greater the reward offered (beyond what was necessary to elicit the behavior) the smaller was the effect.

Desire to Participate in a Similar Experiment

The results from this question are shown in the last row of Table 1. This question is less directly related to the dissonance that was experimentally created for the Ss. Certainly, the more interesting and enjoyable they felt the tasks were, the greater would be their desire to participate in a similar experiment. But other factors would enter also. Hence, one would expect the results on this question to be very similar to the results on "how enjoyable the tasks were" but weaker. Actually, the result, as may be seen in the table, are in exactly the same direction, and the magnitude of the mean differences is fully as large as on the first question. The variability is greater, however, and the differences do not yield high levels of statistical significance. The difference between the One Dollar condition (+1.20) and the Control condition (–.62) is significant at the .08 level ($t = 1.78$). The difference between the One Dollar condition and the Twenty Dollar condition (–.25) reaches only the .15 level of significance ($t = 1.46$).

The Scientific Importance of the Experiment

This question was included because there was a chance that differences might emerge. There are, after all, other ways in which the experimentally created dissonance could be reduced. For example, one way would be for the S to magnify for himself the value of the reward he obtained. This, however, was unlikely in this experiment because money was used for the reward and it is undoubtedly difficult to convince oneself that one dollar is more than it really is. There is another possible way, however. The Ss were given a very good reason, in addition to being paid, for saying what they did to the waiting girl. The Ss were told it was necessary for the experiment. The dissonance could, consequently, be reduced by magnifying the importance of this cognition. The more scientifically important they considered the experiment to be, the less was the total magnitude of dissonance. It is possible, then, that the results on this question, shown in the third row of figures in Table 1, might reflect dissonance reduction.

The results are weakly in line with what one would expect if the dissonance were somewhat reduced in this manner. The One Dollar condition is higher than the other two. The difference between the One and Twenty Dollar conditions reaches the .08 level of significance on a two-tailed test ($t = 1.79$). The difference between the One Dollar and Control conditions is not impressive at all ($t = 1.21$).

The result that the Twenty Dollar condition is actually lower than the Control condition is undoubtedly a matter of chance ($t = 0.58$).

How Much They Learned from the Experiment

The results on this question are shown in the second row of figures in Table 1. The question was included because, as far as we could see, it had nothing to do with the dissonance that was experimentally created and could not be used for dissonance reduction. One would then expect no differences at all among the three conditions. We felt it was important to show that the effect was not a completely general one but was specific to the content of the dissonance which was created. As can be readily seen in Table 1, there are only negligible differences among conditions. The highest t value for any of these differences is only 0.48....

Summary

Recently, Festinger (1957) has proposed a theory concerning cognitive dissonance. Two derivations from this theory are tested here. These are:

1. If a person is induced to do or say something which is contrary to his private opinion, there will be a tendency for him to change his opinion so as to bring it into correspondence with what he has done or said.
2. The larger the pressure used to elicit the overt behavior (beyond the minimum needed to elicit it) the weaker will be the above-mentioned tendency.

A laboratory experiment was designed to test these derivations. Subjects were subjected to a boring experience and then paid to tell someone that the experience had been interesting and enjoyable. The amount of money paid the subject was varied. The private opinions of the subjects concerning the experiences were then determined.

The results strongly corroborate the theory that was tested.

Note

1. All statistical tests referred to in this paper are two-tailed.

References

Festinger, L. *A theory of cognitive dissonance.* Evanston, Ill.: Row Peterson, 1957.

Janis, I. L., & King, B. F. The influence of role-playing on opinion change. *Journal of Abnormal and Social Psychology, 1954, 49*, 211–218.

King, B. T., & Janis, I. L. Comparison of the effectiveness of improvised versus non-improvised role-playing in producing opinion changes. *Human Relations, 1956, 9*, 177–186.

NO ↵

Self-Perception: An Alternative Interpretation of Cognitive Dissonance Phenomena[1]

If a person holds two cognitions that are inconsistent with one another, he will experience the pressure of an aversive motivational state called cognitive dissonance, a pressure which he will seek to remove, among other ways, by altering one of the two "dissonant" cognitions. This proposition is the heart of Festinger's (1957) theory of cognitive dissonance, a theory which has received more widespread attention from personality and social psychologists in the past 10 years than any other contemporary statement about human behavior. Only 5 years after its introduction, Brehm and Cohen (1962) could review over 50 studies conducted within the framework of dissonance theory; and, in the 5 years since the appearance of their book, every major social-psychological journal has averaged at least one article per issue probing some prediction "derived" from the basic propositions of dissonance theory. In popularity, even the empirical law of effect now appears to be running a poor second.

The theory has also had its critics. Reservations about various aspects of the theory have ranged from mild (e.g., Asch, 1958; Bruner, 1957; Kelly, 1962; Osgood, 1960; Zajonc, 1960) to severe (Chapanis & Chapanis, 1964), and alternative interpretations have been offered to account for the results of particular studies (e.g., Chapanis & Chapanis, 1964; Janis & Gilmore, 1956; Lott, 1963; Rosenberg, 1965). No theoretical alternative to dissonance theory has been proposed, however, which attempts both to embrace its major phenomena and to account for some of the secondary patterns of results which have appeared in the supporting experiments but which were not predicted by the theory. This article proposes such an alternative....

The Forced-Compliance Studies

The most frequently cited evidence for dissonance theory comes from an experimental procedure known as the forced-compliance paradigm. In these experiments, an individual is induced to engage in some behavior that would

From *Psychological Review*, vol.57, no.3, 1967, pp. 183–184, 187–190, 199–200. Copyright © 1967 by American Psychological Association. Reprinted with permission.

imply his endorsement of a particular set of beliefs or attitudes. Following his behavior, his "actual" attitude on belief is assessed to see if it is a function of the behavior in which he has engaged and of the manipulated stimulus conditions under which it was evoked. The best known and most widely quoted study of this type was conducted by Festinger and Carlsmith (1959). In their experiment, 60 undergraduates were randomly assigned to one of three experimental conditions. In the $1 condition, S was first required to perform long repetitive laboratory tasks in an individual experimental session. He was then hired by the experimenter as an "assistant" and paid $1 to tell a waiting fellow student (a stooge) that the tasks were enjoyable and interesting. In the $20 condition, each S was hired for $20 to do the same thing. Control Ss simply engaged in the repetitive tasks. After the experiment, each S indicated how much he had enjoyed the tasks. The results show that Ss paid $1 evaluated the tasks as significantly more enjoyable than did Ss who had been paid $20. The $20 Ss did not express attitude significantly different from those expressed by the control Ss.

Dissonance theory interprets these findings by noting that all Ss initially hold the cognition that the tasks are dull and boring. In addition, however, the experimental Ss have the cognition that they have expressed favorable attitudes toward the tasks to a fellow student. These two cognitions are dissonant for Ss in the $1 condition because their overt behavior does not "follow from" their cognition about the task, nor does it follow from the small compensation they are receiving. To reduce the resulting dissonance pressure, they change their cognition about the task so that it is consistent with their overt behavior: they become more favorable toward the tasks. The Ss in the $20 condition, however, experience little or no dissonance because engaging in such behavior "follows from" the large compensation they are receiving. Hence, their final attitude ratings do not differ from those of the control group.

In contrast with this explanation, the present analysis views these results as a case of self-perception. Consider the viewpoint of an outside observer who hears the individual making favorable statements about the tasks to a fellow student, and who further knows that the individual was paid $1 ($20) to do so. This hypothetical observer is then asked to state the actual attitude of the individual he has heard. An outside observer would almost certainly judge a $20 communicator to be "manding" reinforcement (Skinner, 1957); that is, his behavior appears to be under the control of the reinforcement contingencies of the money and not at all under the discriminative control of the tasks he appears to be describing. The $20 communicator is not credible in that his statements cannot be used as a guide for inferring his actual attitudes. Hence, the observer could conclude that the individual found such repetitive tasks dull and boring in spite of what he had said. Although the behavior of a $1 communicator also has some mand properties, an outside observer would be more likely to judge him to be expressing his actual attitudes and, hence, would infer the communicator's attitude from the content of the communication itself. He would thus judge this individual to be favorable toward the tasks. If one now places the hypothetical observer and the communicator into the same skin, the findings obtained by Festinger and Carlsmith are the result.

There is no aversive motivational pressure postulated; the dependent variable is viewed simply as a self-judgment based on the available evidence, evidence that includes the apparent controlling variables of the observed behavior.

If this analysis of the findings is correct, then it should be possible to replicate the inverse functional relation between amount of compensation and the final attitude statement by actually letting an outside observer try to infer the attitude of an *S* in the original study. Conceptually, this replicates the Festinger-Carlsmith experiment with the single exception that the observer and the observed are no longer the same individual.

An Interpersonal Replication of the Festinger-Carlsmith Experiment

Seventy-five college undergraduates participated in an experiment designed to "determine how accurately people can judge another person." Twenty-five *Ss* each served in a $1, a $20, or a control condition. All *Ss* listened to a tape recording which described a college sophomore named Bob Downing, who had participated in an experiment involving two motor tasks. The tasks were described in detail, but nonevaluatively; the alleged purpose of the experiment was also described. At this point, the control *Ss* were asked to evaluate Bob's attitudes toward the tasks. The experimental *Ss* were further told that Bob had accepted an offer of $1 ($20) to go into the waiting room, tell the next *S* that the tasks were fun, and to be prepared to do this again in the future if they needed him. The *Ss* then listened to a brief conversation which they were told was an actual recording of Bob and the girl who was in the waiting room. Bob was heard to argue rather imaginatively that the tasks were fun and enjoyable, while the girl responded very little except for the comments that Festinger and Carlsmith's stooge was instructed to make. The recorded conversation was identical for both experimental conditions in order to remain true to the original study in which no differences in persuasiveness were found between the $1 and the $20 communications. In sum, the situation attempted to duplicate on tape the situation actually experienced by Festinger and Carlsmith's *Ss*.

All *Ss* estimated Bob's responses to the same set of questions employed in the original study. The key question required *Ss* to rate the tasks (or for Bob's attitude toward them) on a scale from –5 to +5, where –5 means that the tasks were extremely dull and boring, +5 means they were extremely interesting and enjoyable, and 0 means they were neutral, neither interesting nor uninteresting.

Results

Table 1 shows the mean ratings for the key question given by *Ss* in all three conditions of both the original experiment and the present replication.

The results show that in both studies the $1 and control conditions are on different sides of the neutral point and are significantly different from one another at the .02 level of significance ($t = 2.48$ in the original study; $i—2.60$ in the replication).[2] In both studies, the $1 condition produced significantly more favorable ratings toward the tasks than did the $20 condition ($t = 2.22$, $p < .03$ in the original study; $t = 3.52$, $p < .001$ in the replication). In neither study is the $20 condition significantly different from the control condition; and, finally, in neither study were there any significant differences between conditions on the other questions asked of Ss about the experiment. Thus, the inverse relation between amount of compensation and the final attitude rating is clearly replicated; and, even though the present analysis does not require the attitude judgments themselves of the interpersonal observers to duplicate those of Ss in the original experiment, it is seen that the two sets of ratings are quite comparable on the 10-point scales.

Since the above replication was conducted, Jones (1966) has reported a study in which Ss' attitudes and observers' judgments were compared directly in the same experiment. Again, the observers' judgments not only replicated the inverse functional relation displayed by the attitude statements of Ss themselves, but the actual scale positions of observers and Ss were again similar.

These successful replications of the functional relation reported by Festinger and Carlsmith provide support for the self-perception analysis. The original Ss may be viewed as simply making self-judgments based on the same kinds of public evidence that the community originally employed in training them to infer the attitudes of any communicator, themselves included. It is not necessary to postulate an aversive motivational drive toward consistency.

Table 1

Attitude Ratings on Interpersonal Estimates of Attitude Ratings Toward the Tasks for Each Condition

Study	Experimental condition		
	Control	$1 compensation	$20 compensation
Festinger-Carlsmith	−0.45	+1.35	−0.05
Interpersonal replication	−1.56	+0.52	−1.96

Note. For the Festinger-Carlsmith study, $N = 20$ in each condition; for the Interpersonal replication study, $N = 25$ in each condition.

These interpersonal replications are illustrative of others which have been reported elsewhere (Bem, 1965). It has been shown that the present analysis applies as well to forced-compliance experiments which utilize compensations much smaller than $20, to studies which manipulate variables other than the amount of compensation, and to studies which evoke different behaviors from S. Alternative dependent variables have also been considered. For example, Brehm and Cohen show that S's rating of how hungry he is can be manipulated by inducing him to volunteer to go without food for different amounts of compensation (1962, pp. 132–137), and a successful interpersonal replication of that experiment again supports the present self-perception analysis of these forced-compliance phenomena (Bem, 1965)....

Notes

1. This research was supported in part by Ford Foundation Grant 140055 to Carnegie Institute of Technology and in part by the Center for Research on Language and Language Behavior, University of Michigan, with funds from the Bureau of Higher Education Research, United States Office of Education. The author is grateful to George R. Madaras and Kenneth M. Peterson for aid in conducting the research and to Sandra L. Bem for critical comments on the manuscript.
2. All significance levels in this article are based on two-tailed tests.

References

ASCH, S. E. Review of L. Festinger, *A theory of cognitive dissonance. Contemporary Psychology,* 1958, 3, 194–195.

BEM, D. J. An experimental analysis of self-persuasion. *Journal of Experimental Social Psychology,* 1965, 1, 199–218.

BREHM, J. W., & Cohen, A. R. *Explorations in cognitive dissonance.* New York: Wiley, 1962.

BRUNER, J. S. Discussion of L. Festinger, The relationship between behavior and cognition. In J. S. Bruner (Ed.), *Contemporary approaches to cognition.* Cambridge: Harvard University Press, 1957. Pp. 151–156.

CHAPANIS, N. P., & CHAPANIS, A. Cognitive dissonance: Five years later. *Psychological Bulletin,* 1964, 61, 1–22.

FESTINGER, L. *A theory of cognitive dissonance.* Stanford: Stanford University Press, 1957.

JANIS, I. L., & GILMORE, J. B. The influence of incentive conditions on the success of role playing in modifying attitudes. *Journal of Personality and Social Psychology,* 1965, 1, 17–27.

JONES, R. G. Forced compliance dissonance predictions: obvious, non-obvious, or nonsense? Paper read at American Psychological Association, New York, September 1966.

KELLY, G. Comments on J. Brehm, Motivational effects of cognitive dissonance. In M. R. Jones (Ed.), *Nebraska symposium on motivation: 1962.* Lincoln: University of Nebraska Press, 1962. Pp. 78–81.

LOTT, B. E. Secondary reinforcement and effort: Comment on Aronson's "The effect of effort on the attractiveness of rewarded and unrewarded stimuli." *Journal of Abnormal and Social Psychology,* 1963, 67, 520–522.

OSGOOD, C. E. Cognitive dynamics in human affairs. *Public Opinion Quarterly,* 1960, 24, 341–365.

ROSENBERG, M. J. When dissonance fails: On eliminating evaluation apprehension from attitude measurement. *Journal of Personality and Social Psychology,* 1965, 1, 28–42.

SKINNER, B. F. *Science and human behavior.* New York: Macmillan, 1953.

ZAJONC, R. B. The concepts of balance, congruity, and dissonance. *Public Opinion Quarterly,* 1960, 24, 280–296.

CHALLENGE QUESTIONS

Does Cognitive Dissonance Explain Why Behavior Can Change Attitudes?

1. Can you think of any practical applications for cognitive dissonance theory? How could the theory be used to eliminate undesirable or unhealthy behavior?
2. Think of a time when you felt psychological tension or discomfort when there was a discrepancy between your attitudes and your actions. Explain the situation and how it made you feel. Did you change either your behavior or attitudes in order to reduce this tension?
3. Do you think self-perception theory applies to you? In other words, can you remember an instance in which you examined your behavior in order to determine your attitude?

ISSUE 5

Applying Social Psychology:
Are Self-Esteem Programs Misguided?

YES: Roy F. Baumeister from "Should Schools Try to Boost Self-Esteem?" *American Educator* (*20*, Summer 1996)

NO: David L. DuBois and Heather D. Tevendale from "Self-Esteem in Childhood and Adolescence: Vaccine or Epiphenomenon?" *Applied & Preventive Psychology* (*8*, 1999)

ISSUE SUMMARY

YES: Social psychologist Roy F. Baumeister argues that self-esteem generally has little or no influence on most important outcomes and that excessively high self-esteem can sometimes have negative consequences.

NO: Psychologists David L. Dubois and Heather D. Tevendale argue that self-esteem is an important factor in adolescent development. Although some advocates of self-esteem improvement programs have overstated the importance of having a positive self-image, programs designed to raise self-esteem still appear to have beneficial effects.

Carl Rogers, one of the most influential figures in the history of psychotherapy, once famously stated that most people "despise themselves, regard themselves as worthless and unlovable." The idea that self-loathing and feelings of low self-worth are commonplace has been tremendously influential in psychotherapy and in popular culture as a whole. If you visit the psychology section of your local bookstore, you will witness the proliferation of self-help books that tout the importance of self-esteem. The widely accepted importance of self-esteem eventually resulted in the emergence of the self-esteem movement. The primary goal of this loosely affiliated band of self-esteem advocates is to raise people's self-esteem through a variety of means, including self-esteem building programs in public schools. Despite the great enthusiasm of the self-esteem movement, a number of social scientists have argued that programs that attempt to build self-esteem are misguided. One of the most outspoken opponents of self-esteem programs is social psychologist

Roy Baumeister. According to Baumeister, not only does low self-esteem have little relationship to negative outcomes and behavior (such as poor academic performance and delinquency) but unrealistically high-self esteem can sometimes have dangerous consequences. Baumeister is not alone in his outlook. For example, Time magazine recently reported that American high school students have high self-esteem compared to their Japanese, Chinese, and Taiwanese counterparts. Yet these students routinely outperform American students, suggesting that raising self-esteem may not be a cure-all. The New York Times even weighed in on the issue with an article that questioned the wisdom of raising self-esteem.

Nonetheless self-esteem improvement programs are still fairly commonplace and are defended vehemently by many in the self-esteem movement. Still, even proponents of self-esteem programs concede that self-esteem is not the major cause of most social problems and that some in the self-esteem movement have irresponsibly inflated the importance of self-esteem. In our second selection, David Dubois and Heather Tevendale argue that self-esteem is a crucial factor for several important outcomes, even if its importance has been overblown by the self-esteem movement. And as a result, efforts to build self-esteem still have great value to individuals and society as a whole.

POINT

- Low self-esteem is not a major cause of social or psychological problems.
- An inflated view of the self can sometimes lead to negative outcomes, like aggression and violence
- Since the benefits of self-esteem are minor, programs designed to raise self-esteem are unlikely to have a major beneficial impact.

COUNTERPOINT

- Self-esteem plays an important role in some important psychological outcomes.
- The bulk of the evidence suggests that high self-esteem has positive effects.
- While some self-esteem programs may be of limited value, a properly designed program can have a substantial positive impact on the lives of young people.

Should Schools Try to Boost Self-Esteem?
Beware the Dark Side

We must raise children's self-esteem!" How often has this sentiment been expressed in recent years in schools, homes, and meeting rooms around the United States? The sentiment reflects the widespread, well-intentioned, earnest, and yet rather pathetic hope that if we can only persuade our kids to love themselves more, they will stop dropping out, getting pregnant, carrying weapons, taking drugs, and getting into trouble, and instead will start achieving great things in school and out.

Unfortunately, the large mass of knowledge that research psychologists have built up around self-esteem does not justify that hope. At best, high self-esteem is a mixed blessing whose total effects are likely to be small and minor. At worst, the pursuit of high self-esteem is a foolish, wasteful, and self-destructive enterprise that may end up doing more harm than good.

Writers on controversial topics should acknowledge their biases, and so let me confess mine: I have a strong bias in favor of self-esteem. I have been excited about self-esteem ever since my student days at Princeton, when I first heard that it was a topic of study. Over the past two decades I have probably published more studies on self-esteem than anybody else in the United States (or elsewhere). It would be great for my career if self-esteem could do everything its boosters hope: I'd be dining frequently at the White House and advising policymakers on how to fix the country's problems.

It is therefore with considerable personal disappointment that I must report that the enthusiastic claims of the self-esteem movement mostly range from fantasy to hogwash. The effects of self-esteem are small, limited, and not all good. Yes, a few people here and there end up worse off because their self-esteem was too low. Then again, other people end up worse off because their self-esteem was too high. And most of the time self-esteem makes surprisingly little difference.

Self-esteem is, literally, how favorably a person regards himself or herself. It is perception (and evaluation), not reality. For example, I think the world would be a better place if we could all manage to be a little nicer to each other. But that's hard: We'd all have to discipline ourselves to change. The self-esteem approach, in contrast, is to skip over the hard work of changing our actions and instead just let us all *think* we're nicer. That won't make

Reprinted with permission from the Summer 1996 issue of the *American Educator*, the quarterly journal of the American Federation of Teachers, AFL-CIO.

the world any better. People with high self-esteem are not in fact any nicer than people with low self-esteem—in fact, the opposite is closer to the truth.

High self-esteem means thinking well of oneself, regardless of whether that perception is based on substantive achievement or mere wishful thinking and self-deception. High self-esteem can mean *confident* and *secure*—but it can also mean *conceited, arrogant, narcissistic,* and *egotistical.*

A recent, widely publicized study dramatized the fact that self-esteem consists of perception and is not necessarily based on reality. In an international scholastic competition, American students achieved the lowest average scores among all participating nationalities. But the American kids rated themselves and their performance the highest. This is precisely what comes of focusing on self-esteem: poor performance accompanied by plenty of empty self-congratulation. Put another way, we get high self-esteem as inflated perceptions covering over a rather dismal reality.

Looking ahead, it is alarming to think what will happen when this generation of schoolchildren grows up into adults who may continue thinking they are smarter than the rest of the world—while actually being dumber. America will be a land of conceited fools.

All of this might fairly be discounted if America were really suffering from an epidemic of low self-esteem, such as if most American schoolchildren generally had such negative views of themselves that they were unable to tackle their homework. But that's not the case. On the contrary, as I'll explain shortly, self-esteem is already inflated throughout the United States. The average American already regards himself or herself as above average. At this point, any further boosting of self-esteem is likely to approach the level of grandiose, egotistical delusions.

Benefits of Self-Esteem

Let us begin with the positive consequences of high self-esteem. Much has been claimed, but very little has been proven. Some years ago California formed a task force to promote self-esteem, and its manifesto was filled with optimistic assertions about how raising self-esteem would help solve most of the personal and social problems in the state. Here is a sample of its rhetoric: "the lack of self-esteem is central to most personal and social ills plaguing our state and nation," and indeed self-esteem was touted as a social vaccine that might inoculate people "against the lures of crime, violence, substance abuse, teen pregnancy, child abuse, chronic welfare dependency, and educational failure."[1]

Such rhetoric is especially remarkable in light of another fact. That same task force commissioned a group of researchers to assemble the relevant facts and findings about self-esteem. Here is what the experts in charge of the project concluded from all the information they gathered: "The news most consistently reported, however, is that the associations between self-esteem and its expected consequences are mixed, insignificant, or absent."[2] In short, self-esteem doesn't have much impact.

Even when the occasional study does link low self-esteem to some problem pattern, there is often a serious chicken-and-egg ambiguity about which comes first. For example, if someone showed that drug-addicted pregnant unmarried school-dropout teenagers with criminal records have low self-esteem, this might mean only that people stop bragging after they mess up their lives. It would not prove that low self-esteem caused the problems. The few researchers who have tried to establish causality have usually concluded that self-esteem is mainly an outcome, not a cause. At best there is a mutual influence of spiraling effects.

To be sure, there are some benefits of high self-esteem. It helps people bounce back after failure and try again. It helps them recover from trauma and misfortune. In general, high self-esteem makes people feel good. Low self-esteem accompanies various emotional vulnerabilities, including depression and anxiety. (Again, though, there is no proof that low self-esteem causes these problems, or that raising self-esteem will prevent them.)

Children who do well in school have slightly higher self-esteem than those who do poorly. Unfortunately the effect is small, and in fact anyone who believes in the value of education should wish for a stronger effect simply on the basis that successful students *deserve* higher self-esteem. Across multiple studies, the average correlation between grades and self-esteem is .24, which means about 6 percent of the variance.[3] In other words, moving from the very highest self-esteem scores to the very lowest would yield about a 6 percent difference in school performance. A small increase in self-esteem, such as might be produced by a school program aimed at boosting self-esteem, would probably make only a 1 percent difference or less. And even that assumes that self-esteem is the cause, not the effect, contrary to many indications. To the extent that it is school success or failure that alters self-esteem, and not the other way around, any independent effort to raise self-esteem would have no effect at all on school performance.

Once again I must say how disappointing I've found these facts to be. Self-esteem is not altogether useless, but its benefits are isolated and minor, except for the fact that it feels good. When I embarked on a career of research on self-esteem, I had hoped for a great deal more.

The Dark Side of High Self-Esteem

The very idea that high self-esteem could have bad consequences strikes some people as startling. The self-esteem movement wants to present self-esteem as having many good and no bad effects. But very few psychological traits are one-sidedly good, and those few are mostly abilities (like intelligence or self-control). High self-esteem can certainly cause its share of problems. If you pause to recall that the category of high self-esteem includes people who think they are great without necessarily *being* great, this conclusion may seem less startling.

A large, important study recently adopted a novel approach to separating self-esteem from all its causes and correlates.[4] The researchers measured how each individual rated himself or herself compared to how that person was rated by others who knew him or her. They were particularly interested in the category of people with inflated self-esteem—the ones who rated themselves higher than their friends rated them. This, after all, is where the self-esteem movement leads: Concentrate on getting kids to think well of themselves, regardless of actual accomplishments. The researchers had no difficulty finding plenty of students who fit that category. They are, in a sense, the star products and poster children of the self-esteem movement.

And what were they like? The researchers' conclusions did not paint an encouraging picture of health, adjustment, or success. On the contrary, the long-term outcomes of these people's lives found above average rates of interpersonal and psychological problems. A second study, with laboratory observations of live interactions, showed these people to be rather obnoxious. They were more likely than others to interrupt when someone else was speaking. They were more prone to disrupt the conversation with angry and hostile remarks. They tended to talk *at* people instead of talking *to* or *with* them. In general, they irritated the other people present. Does any of this sound familiar? This is what comes of inflated self-esteem.

The picture is one of a self-centered, conceited person who is quick to assert his or her own wants but lacks genuine regard for others. That may not be what the self-esteem movement has in mind, but it is what it is likely to produce. In practice, high self-esteem usually amounts to a person thinking that he or she is better than other people. If you think you're better than others, why should you listen to them, be considerate, or keep still when you want to do or say something?

Over the past several years, I have been writing a book on evil and violence (*Evil: Inside Human Violence and Cruelty*, to be published by Freeman this fall). Given my longstanding interest in self-esteem, I naturally wanted to acknowledge any part that it plays. Various pundits and so-called experts have long asserted that low self-esteem causes violence, but I've had enough experience with self-esteem to know that I'd better check the data rather than relying on vague generalizations and ostensibly "common" knowledge.

Two graduate students and I reviewed literally hundreds of studies on the topic. What we found was so surprising that, in addition to my book, we recently published a lengthy article in psychology's most eminent journal, the *Psychological Review*.[5] We combined evidence from all spheres of violence we could find: murder, assault, rape, terrorism, bullies, youth gangs, repressive governments, tyranny, family violence, warfare, oppression, genocide, and more.

We concluded that the idea that low self-esteem causes violence is simply and thoroughly wrong. It is contradicted by a huge mass of information and evidence. People with low self-esteem are generally shy, humble, modest, self-effacing individuals. Violent perpetrators—from Hitler, Hussein, and Amin, down to the common wife-beater or playground bully—are decidedly not like that.

If anything, high self-esteem is closer to the violent personality. Most perpetrators of violence are acting out of some sense of personal superiority, especially one that has been threatened or questioned in some way. I am not saying that high self-esteem, per se, directly causes violence. Not all people with high self-esteem become violent. But violent people are a subset of people with high self-esteem. The main recipe for violence is *threatened egotism*—that is, a belief in personal superiority that is challenged, questioned, or "dissed" by somebody else. Inflated self-esteem often leads to that pattern.

Consider some of the evidence. In the first place, whenever there are two groups with different levels of self-esteem, the more egotistical group is nearly always the more violent one. The most familiar example is gender: Men have higher self-esteem and higher rates of violence. When self-esteem fluctuates, the risk of violence rises with the favorable views of self, such as in manic-depressive illness. Indeed, people who are intoxicated with alcohol show increases in self-esteem and increases in violent tendencies.

A recent study[6] found that nowadays many homicides occur in connection with other crimes such as robbery, but in the remaining cases the homicide is often the result of an altercation that begins with challenges and insults, in which someone's favorable self-opinion is disputed by the other person. The person who feels he (or less often she) is losing face in the argument may resort to violence and murder.

Even within samples of offenders, it appears that indicators of egotism can discriminate violent and troublesome tendencies, and it is the favorable views of self that are linked to the worse actions. A group of researchers administered the California Psychological Inventory to young men (in their late teens) on parole.[7] The researchers were able to predict future parole violations (recidivism) better than previous attempts. Among the traits that predicted high recidivism were being egotistical and outspoken (as well as "touchy," which suggests being easily offended). Meanwhile, being modest and unassuming (associated with low self-esteem) were among the traits linked to being least likely to violate parole. These results all seem to fit the view linking favorable views of self to violent tendencies.

Aggression starts in childhood, and bullies are the most notable examples. They are of particular importance because childhood bullies have been found to be four times more likely than other children to engage in serious criminal behavior during their subsequent adult life. Dan Olweus is an expert who has studied bullies for years, and he recently summarized the conclusions that his program of research has yielded. Unlike victims of bullying (who show multiple indications of low self-esteem), the bullies themselves seemed relatively secure and free from anxiety. "In contrast to a fairly common assumption among psychologists and psychiatrists, we have found no indicators that the aggressive bullies (boys) are anxious and insecure under a tough surface," said Olweus, adding that multiple samples and methods had confirmed this conclusion, and concluding that bullies "do not suffer from poor self-esteem."[8]

One of the most earnest and empathic efforts to understand the subjective experience of committing crimes was that of sociologist Jack Katz.[9] Homicide as well as assault emerged in his study as typically caused by threats to the offender's public image. In Katz's view, the offender privately holds a positive view of self, but the eventual victim impugns that view and implicitly humiliates the offender, often in front of an audience. The response is unplanned violence resulting in injury or death. Katz insisted that feelings of being humiliated are quickly transformed into rage. He argued that many men feel that almost anyone can judge them and impugn their esteem, whereas for women self-esteem is most heavily invested in their intimate relationships— with the result that men will attack strangers while women mainly just murder their intimate partners, because only the partners can threaten their self-esteem to a sufficient degree to provoke such a violent response.

Another example of the relationship between inflated self-esteem and violence focuses on juvenile delinquency. The classic study by Glueck and Glueck compared juvenile delinquents against a matched sample of nondelinquent boys.[10] Although the study was an early one and has been criticized on methodological grounds, it benefited from a large sample and extensive work, and nearly all of their findings have been replicated by subsequent studies. The Glueck and Glueck study did not measure self-esteem directly (indeed it antedated most modern self-esteem scales), but there were plenty of related variables. The pattern of findings offers little to support the hypothesis that low self-esteem causes delinquency. Delinquent boys were more likely than controls to be characterized as self-assertive, socially assertive, defiant, and narcissistic, none of which seems compatible with low self-esteem. Meanwhile, the delinquents were less likely than the comparison group to be marked by the factors that do indicate low self-esteem, including severe insecurity, feelings of helplessness, feelings of being unloved, general anxiety (a frequent correlate of low self-esteem), submissiveness, and fear of failure. Thus, the thoughts and actions of juvenile delinquents suggested that they held quite favorable opinions of themselves.

It is useful to look for convergences between the Gluecks' study and more recent studies of youthful violence, not only because of the seminal nature of the Gluecks' work, but also because their data were collected several decades ago and on an almost entirely white sample, unlike more recent studies. Converging findings thus confer especially high confidence in conclusions that can be supported across time and ethnicity.

One of the most thorough research projects on youth gangs was that of Martin Sanchez Jankowski, whose work involved 10 years, several cities, and 37 gangs.[11] Although as a sociologist he was disinclined to use self-esteem or personality factors as explanatory constructs, his study did furnish several important observations. Jankowski specifically rejected the notion that acting tough is a result of low self-esteem or feelings of inadequacy. In his words, "There have been some studies of gangs that suggest that many gang members have tough exteriors but are insecure on the inside. This is a mistaken observation" (p. 27). He said that for many members, the appeal of the gang is the positive respect it enjoys in the community as well as the respectful treatment from other gang members, which he found to be an important norm in nearly all gangs he studied. He said most gang members "expressed a strong sense of self-competence and a drive to compete with others" (p. 102). When they failed, they always blamed something external rather than personal inadequacy or error. This last observation is especially relevant because several controlled studies have shown that it is characteristic of high self-esteem and contrary to the typical responses of people with low self-esteem.

Recently I appeared on a radio talk show. The hostess seemed to have difficulty accepting the conclusion that low self-esteem is not a cause of violence, possibly because she had swallowed the propaganda line that all good
things come from high self-esteem. To explain our findings, I offered the
example of the Ku Klux Klan. The KKK has long advocated beliefs in white
superiority and has turned violent in response to efforts to extend full equality to black citizens (thereby eroding the superior status of whites). I thought
KKK violence was a good, clear example of threatened egotism.

For a moment the hostess seemed to see the point, but then she jumped
back on the self-esteem bandwagon. "What about deep down inside?" she
asked. I inquired whether she thought that Klansmen believed that they, as
whites were inferior to blacks, which would fit the low self-esteem view. She
balked at the word "inferior" but offered that the violent Klansmen believe
deep down inside that they are "not superior"—in other words, equal—to
blacks.

I didn't know what to say to this basically loony argument. Her theory
that Klan violence could be traced to a "deep down" inner belief that blacks
are equal to whites has two parts, both of which are bizarre: first, that members
of the KKK truly believe in racial equality, and second, that belief in racial equality causes violence. It struck me that attempts to defend the self-esteem movement against the facts end up having to make such preposterous assertions.

Although this particular hostess's idea was absurd, she was invoking a
point that the proponents of self-esteem have on occasion raised as a possibly
valid defense. When obnoxious or socially undesirable acts are performed by
egotistical people, thus contradicting the belief that high self-esteem is generally good, some propose that these obnoxious individuals must secretly have
low self-esteem. Indeed, the editorial reviewers who evaluated our article on
violence for the *Psychological Review* insisted that we tackle this theoretical
question head-on in the final published version of the paper.

There are two main reasons to reject the "hidden low self-esteem" view.
The first is that plenty of researchers have tried and failed to find any indications of this allegedly hidden low self-esteem. It's not for lack of trying, and
indeed it would be quite a feather in any researcher's cap to show that actions
are caused by low self-esteem hidden under a veneer of high self-esteem. Studies of childhood bullies, teen gang members, adult criminals, and various
obnoxious narcissists keep coming to the same conclusion: "We've heard the
theory that these people have low self-esteem or a negative self-image under-
neath, but we sure can't find any sign of it."

The other reason is even more compelling. Suppose it were true (which
it does not seem to be) that some violent people have high self-esteem on the
surface but low self-esteem inside. Which view of self (the surface veneer or
the hidden one) would be the one responsible for violence? We already know
that genuine low self-esteem, when *not* hidden, does not cause violence.
Hence one would have to say that low self-esteem is only linked to violence
when it is hidden. That means that the crucial cause of violence is what is *hid-
ing* the secret insecurity—which means that the "veneer" of high self-esteem is
the cause, and so we are back anyway to the position that egotism is the cause.

There isn't space here to exhaust the dark side of high self-esteem, but let me touch on a few other features. People with high self-esteem are less willing than others to heed advice, for obvious reasons—they usually think they know better. (Whether children with inflated self-esteem are less willing to listen to teachers is one possible implication of this, but to my knowledge this has not yet been studied.) They respond to failure by blaming everyone and everything but themselves, such as a flawed test, a biased or unfair teacher, or an incompetent partner. They sometimes extend their favorable self-opinion to encompass people close to or similar to themselves, but unfortunately this often translates into prejudice and condescension toward people who differ from them. (High self-esteem is in fact linked to prejudice against outgroups.) Finally, when their egotism is threatened, they tend to react irrationally in ways that have been shown to be risky, self-defeating, and even self-destructive.

Boosting Self-Esteem: The Problem of Inflation

Most (though not all) of the problems linked to high self-esteem involve inflated self-esteem, in the sense of overestimating oneself. Based on the research findings produced in laboratories all over North America, I have no objection to people forming a sober, accurate recognition of their actual talents and accomplishments. The violence, the self-defeating behaviors, and the other problems tend to be most acute under conditions of threatened egotism, and inflated self-esteem increases that risk. After all, if you really are smart, your experiences will tend to confirm that fact, and so there's not much danger in high self-esteem that is based on accurate recognition of your intelligence. On the other hand, if you overestimate your abilities, reality will be constantly showing you up and bursting your bubble, and so your (inflated) self-opinion will be bumping up against threats—and those encounters lead to destructive responses.

Unfortunately, a school system that seeks to boost self-esteem in general is likely to produce the more dangerous (inflated) form of self-esteem. It would be fine, for example, to give a hard test and then announce the top few scores for general applause. Such a system recognizes the successful ones, and it shows the rest what the important criteria are (and how much they may need to improve). What is dangerous and worrisome is any procedure that would allow the other students to think that they are just as accomplished as the top scorers even though they did not perform as well. Unfortunately, the self-esteem movement often works in precisely this wrong-headed fashion.

Some students will inevitably be smarter, work harder, learn more, and perform better than others. There is no harm (and in fact probably some positive value) in helping these individuals recognize their superior accomplishments and talents. Such self-esteem is linked to reality and hence less prone to causing dangers and problems.

On the other hand, there is considerable danger and harm in falsely boosting the self-esteem of the other students. It is fine to encourage them to work harder and try to gain an accurate appraisal of their strengths and weaknesses, and it is also fine to recognize their talents and accomplishments in other (including nonacademic) spheres, but don't give them positive feedback that they have not earned. (Also, don't downplay the importance of academic achievement as the central goal of school, such as by suggesting that success at sports or crafts is just as good.) To encourage the lower-performing students to regard their performance just as favorably as the top learners—a strategy all too popular with the self-esteem movement—is a tragic mistake. If successful, it results only in inflated self-esteem, which is the recipe for a host of problems and destructive patterns.

The logical implications of this argument show exactly when self-esteem should be boosted. When people seriously underestimate their abilities and accomplishments, they need boosting. For example, a student who falsely believes she can't succeed at math may end up short-changing herself and failing to fulfill her potential unless she can be helped to realize that yes, she does have the ability to master math.

In contrast, self-esteem should not be boosted when it is already in the accurate range (or higher). A student who correctly believes that math is not his strong point should not be given exaggerated notions of what he can accomplish. Otherwise, the eventual result will be failure and heartbreak. Along the way he's likely to be angry, troublesome, and prone to blame everybody else when something goes wrong.

In my years as an educator I have seen both patterns. But which is more common? Whether boosting self-esteem in general will be helpful or harmful depends on the answer. And the answer is overwhelmingly clear. Far, far more Americans of all ages have accurate or inflated views of themselves than underestimate themselves. They don't need boosting.

Dozens of studies have documented how inflated self-esteem is.[12] Research interest was sparked some years ago by a survey in which 90 percent of adults rated themselves "above average" in driving ability. After all, only half can really be above average. Similar patterns are found with almost all good qualities. A survey about leadership ability found that only 2 percent of high school students rated themselves as below average. Meanwhile, a whopping 25 percent claimed to be in the top 1 percent! Similarly, when asked about ability to get along with others, no students at all said they were below average.[13]

Responses to scales designed to measure self-esteem show the same pattern. There are always plenty of scores at the high end and plenty in the middle, but only a few straggle down toward the low end. This seems to be true no matter which of the many self-esteem scales is used. Moreover, the few individuals who do show the truly low self-esteem scores probably suffer from multiple problems that need professional therapy. Self-esteem boosting from schools would not cure them.

Obviously there's precious little evidence of low self-esteem in such numbers. By definition, plenty of people are in reality below average, but most of them refuse to acknowledge it. Meanwhile large numbers of people clearly overestimate themselves. The top 1 percent can really only contain 1 percent, not the 25 percent who claim to belong there. Meanwhile, the problem that would justify programs aimed at boosting self-esteem—people who significantly underestimate themselves—is extremely rare.

Conclusion

What is to be done? In response to the question about whether schools should boost self-esteem, my answer is: Don't bother. Efforts at boosting self-esteem probably feel good both for students and for teachers, but the real benefits and positive consequences are likely to be minor. Meanwhile, inflated self-esteem carries an assortment of risks and dangers, and so efforts to boost self-esteem may do as much harm as good, or possibly even more. The time, effort, and resources that schools put into self-esteem will not be justified by any palpable improvements in school performance, citizenship, or other outcomes.

There is one psychological trait that schools could help instill and that is likely to payoff much better than self-esteem. That trait is self-control (including self-discipline). Unlike self-esteem, self-control (or lack thereof) is directly and causally involved in a large set of social and personal problems.[14] Addiction, crime, violence, unwanted pregnancy, venereal disease, poor school performance, and many other problems have self-control failure as a core cause. Also unlike self-esteem, self-control brings benefits to both the individual and society. People with better self-control are more successful (socially and academically), happier, and better adjusted, than others. They also make better parents, spouses, colleagues, and employees. In other words, their self-control benefits the people close to them.

Indeed, I am convinced that weak self-control is a crucial link between family breakdown and many social problems. Study after study has shown that children of single parents show up worse than average on almost every measure, ranging from math achievement tests to criminal convictions. Most single parents I know are loving, dedicated, hard-working individuals, but all their energy goes toward providing food and shelter and their children's other basic needs. It seems to take a second parent to provide the supervision and consistent rule enforcement that foster self-control in the child.

How much the schools can do to build self-control is unclear. Still, just recognizing the priority and value of self-control will help. Obviously, self-control is not something that is instilled directly (as in a "self-control class") but rather should be cultivated like a cluster of good habits in connection with regular academic work, especially in the context of clear, consistent enforcement of academic and behavioral standards. The disciplinary and academic culture of a school should be aimed at recognizing and encouraging the self-control of individual students, including rewarding good self-control and punishing its failures or absences. With each new plan, policy, or procedure, school officials might pause to ask "Will this help strengthen self-control?" instead of "Might this hurt anybody's self-esteem?"

In the long run, self-control will do far more for the individuals and for society as a whole than will self-esteem. Moreover, self-control gives people the ability to change and improve themselves, and so it can bring about changes in substantive reality, not just in perception. And if one can make oneself into a better person, self-esteem is likely to increase too. Raising self-control may thus end up boosting self-esteem—but not in the dangerous or superficial ways that flourish now.

My final message to all the people working in today's schools and seeking to help the next generation get a good start is, therefore, as follows: Forget about self-esteem, and concentrate on self-control.

References

1.   California Task Force (1990), *Toward a State of Self-Esteem*, p. 4.

2.   Mecca, Smelser, & Vasconcellos, 1989, *The Social Importance of Self-Esteem*, p. 15.

3.   Hattie & Hansford (1982), in the *Australian Journal of Education*. Note that percent of variance is calculated by squaring the correlation coefficient.

4.   Colvin, Block, & Funder (1995), in the *Journal of Personality and Social Psychology*.

5.   Baumeister, Smart, & Boden, 1996, in *Psychological Review*, Vol. 103, No. 1. Interested readers may wish to consult that article for the full details and findings.

6.   Polk; 1993, in *Journal of Criminal Justice*.

7.   Gough, Wenk, and Rozynko (1965), in *Journal of Abnormal Psychology*.

8.   Olweus, 1994, p. 100. In R. Huesmann (Ed.), *Aggressive Behavior*.

9.   Katz, 1988, *Seductions of crime*.

10.   Glueck & Glueck, 1950, *Unraveling Juvenile Delinquency*.

11.   Jankowski, 1991, *Islands in the Street*.

12.   For reviews, see Taylor & Brown, 1988, in *Psychological Bulletin*; Taylor, 1989, *Positive Illusions*.

13.   These findings are covered in Gilovich's book. A rare exception to this general inflation is that American females are dissatisfied with their bodies and in particular think they are overweight.

14.   For review, see Baumeister, Heatherton, & Tice (1994), *Losing Control*.

NO ⬅

David L. DuBois and
Heather D. Tevendale

Self-Esteem in Childhood and Adolescence: Vaccine or Epiphenomenon?

Positive feelings about the self are widely assumed to be important to healthy developmental outcomes. Theoretically, high levels of self-esteem promote emotional well-being and stability (Harter, 1993), social and behavioral adaptation (Bromley, 1978), academic achievement (Purkey, 1970), and even resilience to the emergence of disorder (Rutter, 1987; Werner & Smith, 1982). The final report of the widely publicized California Task Force to Promote Self-Esteem and Personal and Social Responsibility (1990) went still farther in recent years to propose that self-esteem is "the likeliest candidate for a *social vaccine*, something that inoculates [youth] against the lures of crime, violence, substance abuse, teen pregnancy ... and educational failure" (p. 4). The enthusiastic acceptance of such possibilities by educators and others during the past several decades has led to a remarkable proliferation of practices to promote the self-esteem of children and adolescents (Kohn, 1994). Consequently, we now live in a society in which all youth are likely to be exposed at different points in their development to programs and policies that are directed toward the goal of self-esteem enhancement.

The Self-Esteem Debate

Although considerable public, and private resources continue to be expended on esteem-enhancement activities, the assumptions underlying such practices have become the subject of increased scrutiny and criticism. Several scholars have adopted a highly skeptical stance toward the presumed importance of self-esteem and instead argued that it is likely to be of little or no consequence for healthy developmental outcomes (Damon, 1995; Kohn, 1994; Seligman, 1993). In terms that are no less provocative than the competing metaphor of self-esteem as "social vaccine," Seligman (1993) asserted that "low [or high] self-esteem is an *epiphenomenon*, a mere reflection that your commerce with the world is going badly [or well]. It has no power in itself" (p. 241). At the same time, the contrasting perspective that self-esteem makes a significant contribution to the adaptive outcomes of children and adolescents continues to be well represented in the literature (Harter, 1993; Smelser, 1989).

These disparate viewpoints are referred to in the present article as the "self-esteem debate" (cf. Edwards, 1995). An overview of empirical support for each side of the debate is presented, followed by a review of recent findings indicating a more complex, differential relationship between self-esteem and adaptive outcomes during development. In a concluding section, the self-esteem debate is revisited and recommendations are offered for both future research and intervention.

Self-Esteem As "Vaccine"

Empirical support for views emphasizing the adaptive significance of self-esteem during childhood and adolescence can be found in the literatures of psychology and related fields such as education, medicine, and sociology. High levels of self-esteem among youth have been linked to a variety of favorable outcomes, including positive mood and happiness (M. Rosenberg, 1985), life satisfaction (Huebner, 1991), physical fitness and desirable health practices (Doan & Scherman, 1987; Yarcheski & Mahon, 1989), adaptive classroom behavior (Lerner et al., 1991), and academic achievement (Hattie, 1992). Conversely, children and adolescents lacking in self-esteem have been indicated to be more prone to symptoms of depression and anxiety (Ohannessian, Lerner, Lerner, & von Eye, 1994; Rosenberg, 1985; Towbes, Cohen, & Glyshaw, 1989), interpersonal difficulties such as loneliness (Ammerman, Kazdin, & Van Hasselt, 1993) and rejection by peers (East, Hess, & Lerner, 1987), conduct problems/delinquent behavior (Cole, Chan, & Lytton, 1989; Hinde, Tamplin, & Barrett, 1993; F. R. Rosenberg & M. Rosenberg, 1978), and a wide range of health-risk behaviors and outcomes, including substance use (Schroeder, Laflin, & Weis, 1993), gang membership (Wang, 1994), teen pregnancy (Crockenberg & Soby, 1989), obesity (Jarvie, Lahey, Graziano, & Framer, 1983), eating-disorder symptomatology (Brooks-Gunn, Rock, & Warren, 1989), and suicidal tendencies (Lewinsohn, Rohde, & Seeley, 1993).

Longitudinal studies, although relatively few in number, are particularly noteworthy because of their potential to shed light on the degree to which the levels of self-esteem experienced by youth influence adaptive outcomes at later points in development. The methodologically strongest of the investigations have controlled for initial or "baseline" levels of functioning in analyses and thus are prospective in design. Several of these studies have found evidence of hypothesized adaptive benefits for high levels of self-esteem among developing youth, including facilitation of favorable outcomes in domains such as academic performance and health behavior and, conversely, when absent (e.g., feelings of self-derogation) increased susceptibility to negative outcomes such as depression, eating disorders, substance use, and suicidal behavior several investigations also have found levels of self-esteem assessed during childhood and adolescence to have utility in the prediction of functioning during adulthood (Hauser, 1998; Kaplan, Robbins, & Martin, 1983; R. E. L. Roberts & Bengston, 1993; Slomkowski, Klein, & Mannuzza, 1995; Werner & Smith, 1992; Zuroff, Koestner, & Powers, 1994).

Self-Esteem As "Epiphenomenon"

It is nonetheless equally possible to discern support from the literature for views that question the adaptive significance of self-esteem for developing youth. Thus, although the adaptive correlates of self-esteem during childhood and adolescence have been demonstrated to be quite wide ranging, the magnitude of these relationships is so weak in many instances as to raise concerns regarding their practical significance (Kohn, 1994). Despite the popularity of views linking self-esteem with academic achievement, for example, an average correlation of only .22 was found between the two types of measures across studies (Hattie, 1992). In other words, the associations reported typically have accounted for less than 5% of the variance in criterion measures of school performance. Similar results have been obtained in research examining the relationship of self-esteem to various other aspects of youth behavior and health (Giblin, Poland, & Ager, 1988), including substance use (Schroeder et al., 1993) and teenage pregnancy (Crockenberg & Soby, 1989).

According to the "epiphenomenon" viewpoint (Seligman, 1993), it is also the case that the associations observed in prior research may be attributable entirely to the self-esteem of youth rising and falling in response to varying degrees of adaptive success or failure rather than to any effects of self-esteem on levels of functioning. The significant findings of the prospective studies referred to previously argue against this perspective. Nevertheless, numerous other investigations with this type of design have failed to detect any appreciable influence of self-esteem on similar outcomes. The overall pattern of findings across prospective studies is thus inconsistent and in many instances indicative of a lack of hypothesized effects of self-esteem.

Of further note are several investigations in which findings have implicated high levels of self-esteem in maladaptive patterns of functioning, including greater use of alcohol and drugs (DeSimone, Murray, & Lester, 1994; Olmstead, Guy, O'Malley, & Bentler, 1991), initiation of sexual intercourse at earlier ages (Crockett, Bingham, Chopak, & Vicary, 1996; Jessor & Jessor, 1975), delinquent behavior and gang involvement (Baumeister, Smart, & Boden, 1996), and poorer academic performance (Skaalvik & Hagtvet, 1990). Interestingly, this possibility that high levels of self-esteem may contribute to maladaptive patterns of functioning for youth under certain sets of circumstances is not addressed by views on *either* side of the debate concerning the role of self-esteem in child and adolescent development.

Beyond the Self-Esteem Debate

When taking all available findings into account, it must be acknowledged that neither the "vaccine" or "epiphenomenon" views of self-esteem enjoys particularly strong or convincing support. There are, however, several promising trends in research that move beyond these relatively simplistic, one-sided views regarding the adaptive significance of self-esteem during development.

Adaptive Significance of Multiple Facets of Self-Esteem

In the vast majority of studies, self-esteem has been assessed simply by having youth rate themselves on a series of generally phrased items that pertain to their overall feelings of self-worth (e.g., "On the whole, I am satisfied with myself"). In contrast to the relatively global and undifferentiated nature of such measures, recent research reflects a growing interest in more refined assessments that target multiple, distinct facets of the self-esteem of youth. The facets of self-esteem investigated include (a) domain-specific evaluations of the self, (b) separate positive and negative dimensions of self-evaluation, (c) presented feelings of self-worth evident in observable behavior, and (d) stability of self-esteem.

Domain-specific self-evaluations. Research provides strong support for multidimensional frameworks of self-esteem and, relatedly, self-concept among school-age children and adolescents in which multiple, distinct aspects of self-evaluation are distinguished from one another and viewed as potentially significant influences on adaptation (DuBois, Felner, Brand, Phillips, & Lease, 1996; Harter, 1983, 1990; Hattie, 1992; Marsh, Byrne, & Shavelson, 1992). In accordance with this work, there is a substantial accumulation of findings pertaining to the adaptive significance of different domains of self-evaluation for children and adolescents. Favorable evaluations by youth of their academic skills and abilities, for example, have been found to be a robust correlate of higher levels of academic achievement (Hattie, 1992) and in longitudinal research have been indicated to have positive effects on future levels of achievement (Marsh & Yeung, 1997; M. Rosenberg, Schooler, Schoenbach, & Rosenberg, 1995; Skaalvik & Hagtvet, 1990), even when controlling for objective levels of ability (Marsh, 1990). In other research, negative evaluations of body image have been implicated as contributing not only to both eating-disorder symptomatology (Attie & Brooks-Gunn, 1989; Brooks-Gunn et al., 1989) and obesity (Klesges et al., 1992; Kolody & Sallis, 1995), but also depressive symptoms (Allgood-Merten, Lewinsohn, & Hops, 1990), whereas less positive views of the self relating to school and family relations have been linked differentially to both conduct problems (Cole et al., 1989) and substance use (Young, Werch, & Bakema, 1989). Profiles of self-evaluations across multiple domains also have been found to exhibit significant relationships with youth adjustment in several investigations (Harter & Whitesell, 1996; Koenig, Howard, Offer, & Cremerius, 1984; Lenerz & Gamble, 1986), even when controlling for levels of global self-esteem associated with differing profiles (DuBois, Bull, Sherman, & Roberts, 1998; DuBois, Felner, & Brand, 1997). Findings from this research indicate, for example, that a pervasive pattern of unfavorable appraisals of the self across multiple domains may significantly increase risk for a wide range of adaptive difficulties (DuBois et al., 1997, 1998; Harter & Whitesell, 1996; Koenig et al., 1984). It also appears that more variable patterns of self-evaluation may promote certain aspects of adjustment but interfere with others. Illustratively, a profile reflecting relatively more favorable views of the self pertaining to school and family in comparison to peer relations and associated domains (e.g., body image) has been linked to positive patterns of conduct and academic achievement but also implicated in greater risk for emotional difficulties during early adolescence when peer-oriented concerns are likely to be important for the overall well-being of many youth (DuBois et al., 1997, 1998). Cumulatively, results indicate that domain-specific aspects of self-evaluation are important to consider during development both separately and in combination with one another. Significant increases in understanding and prediction of the adaptive correlates of self-esteem seem likely to occur with greater usage of relevant, multidimensional assessment instruments (Harter, 1990).

Negative and positive dimensions of self-evaluation. Another concern receiving attention is the possibility that negative and positive dimensions of self-evaluation have distinct influences on youth adjustment. In a recent study investigating this issue (Owens, 1994), longitudinal analyses of data for a large, national sample of adolescent boys indicated independent (i.e., nonoverlapping) effects of both negative and positive dimensions of self-evaluation on grades as well as levels of delinquent behavior. Effects on depression also were evident, but limited to negative self-evaluations (i.e., self-depreciation). Owens (1994) concluded that future researchers should "closely examine the relations between *positive* and *negative* dimensions of self-esteem and relevant outcomes or correlates and not simply assume that self-esteem is a unidimensional construct measured by indicators that all have the same relations with external variables" (p. 405). This conclusion is similar to that reached in more extensive research that has investigated the adaptive correlates of positive and negative dimensions of self-evaluation among adult samples (Brown, Andrews, Bifulco, & Veiel, 1990). As further investigations with children and adolescents include separate measures of positive and negative dimensions of self-esteem (e.g., Patterson 1997), outcomes in different areas may be able to be identified that are particularly sensitive to one or the other aspect of self-evaluation

Presented self-esteem. Aspects of self-esteem evident in the observable behavior of children and adolescents also have received consideration (Demo, 1985; Harter, 1990). Dimensions of self-esteem corresponding to the experienced and presented self have been distinguished in this regard (Savin-Williams & Demo, 1983a) with the former encompassing "the self as evaluated by the individual" (p. 124) and the latter "that dimension which an individual verbally and non-verbally reveals to the social world" (p. 123). Based on the findings of a series of studies that included measures of both experienced self-esteem (i.e., self-report and interview assessments) and presented self-esteem (i.e., observer and peer ratings), Savin-Williams and Demo (Demo, 1985; Savin-Williams & Demo, 1983a, 1984; Savin-Williams & Jacquish, 1981) concluded that the two could be reliably distinguished with their estimated degree of correlation ranging from moderately strong ($r = .57$) to weak ($r = .12$) across different groups. Because of the nearly exclusive reliance on self-report measures of self-esteem in research investigating its adaptive correlates, available findings primarily address experienced aspects of self-esteem rather than presented aspects, such as those that may be evident to observers such as parents or teachers. This is a significant concern given that the two types of measures could reveal differential patterns of relationship between self-esteem and criterion indices of adjustment. Illustrative in this regard are the findings of a study in which both self-report and teacher ratings of self-esteem were examined along with several other measures in relationship to discrepancies between elementary school children's self-perceptions of their academic competence and more objective measures obtained from teachers and standardized tests (Connell & Ilardi, 1987). Analyses comparing children who either underrated or overrated their competence relative to the views of teachers revealed a problematic pattern of adjustment for overraters. Overraters had greater self-reported and teacher-reported anxiety and, according to teacher ratings, lower self-esteem, poorer coping strategies (e.g., greater use of denial), and less internalized self-regulatory styles. Interestingly, however, these youth nevertheless self-reported significantly *higher* self-esteem than underraters (Connell & Ilardi, 1987). Thus, it appears that even when self-reported high levels of self-esteem are linked to unfavorable patterns of adjustment among children and adolescents, relationships in more expected directions may be revealed upon consideration of observer ratings of self-esteem. Observational measures may be particularly useful in this regard for detecting low levels of self-esteem that youth are unwilling or unable to acknowledge directly themselves because of defensive or self-enhancing tendencies.

Self-esteem stability. Prior research has concerned itself almost entirely with the adaptive implications of the levels of self-esteem that youth are experiencing at particular points in time. This approach is limited, however, because it fails to consider the significance of change or fluctuation that may be evident in the self-esteem of children and adolescents across time and situations (M. Rosenberg, 1985). Correlational estimates have indicated considerable overall stability in levels of self-esteem during development across periods ranging from a few months to several years (Alsaker & Olweus, 1992; Block & Robins, 1993; Simmons & Blyth, 1987), but have been criticized as masking potentially important patterns of differential change and stability across subgroups of youth within samples (Hirsch & DuBois, 1991). In accordance with this latter concern, several recent investigations have documented contrasting longitudinal trajectories of change in self-esteem during the period of transition from childhood to adolescence (Hirsch & DuBois, 1991; Seidman & Hsueh, 1997; Zimmerman, Copeland, Shope, & Dielman, 1997). Noteworthy among the trajectories identified is a pattern of markedly declining self-esteem for as many as 1 in 5 youth in each sample. Significant differences have been found on measures of adaptive outcomes associated with trajectories, including a pattern of notably greater impairment across a wide range of areas of functioning for the trajectory involving a steep decline in self-esteem overtime (Hirsch & DuBois, 1991; Seidman & Hsueh, 1997; Zimmerman et al., 1997).

Many youth also report more short-term, day-to-day fluctuations in their feelings about themselves (M. Rosenberg, 1985; Savin-Williams & Demo, 1983b; Verkuyten, 1995). This type of lack of stability in self-esteem has been suggested to be indicative of fragile or vulnerable feelings of self-worth and thus increased susceptibility to adaptive difficulties (Kernis, 1993; J. E. Roberts & Monroe, 1994). In accordance with this perspective, short-term fluctuations in the self-esteem of children and adolescents have been implicated in less favorable patterns of functioning in several investigations (M. Rosenberg, 1985; Tevendale, DuBois, Lopez, & Prindiville, 1996; Verkuyten 1992, cited in Verkuyten, 1995; Waschull & Kernis, 1996). Waschull and Kernis (1996), for example, found that instability in self-esteem among elementary school children was associated with lower reported levels of intrinsic motivation for classroom learning as well as a greater tendency to report reasons for becoming angry that reflected threats to self-esteem. Findings in most instances have remained significant even when controlling for scores on more commonly used measures that are oriented toward assessing the typical or "baseline" levels of self-esteem that children and adolescents experience. It appears therefore that short-term stability in self-esteem may be an influential factor in adaptive outcomes during development independent of the levels of self-esteem that are most characteristic or representative of youth....

Implications for Intervention

Pending further research in the directions indicated, what implications do current findings have for interventions focusing on the enhancement of self-esteem among children and adolescents? As noted previously, there has been increased criticism of such programs in recent years (Damon, 1995; Kohn, 1994). In accordance with these concerns, evaluation outcome data indicate only modest, short-lived increases in self-esteem for youth participating in most programs (Hattie, 1992) and even fewer, if any effects on targeted aspects of adjustment such as academic achievement (Scheirer & Kraut, 1979) or problem behavior (Dryfoos, 1990).[1] To date, however, programs have not reflected an adequate appreciation of the relatively complex, differentiated relationship between self-esteem and youth adjustment that is suggested by empirical research. Greater attention to this concern in both the design and evaluation of esteem-enhancement interventions for youth could yield substantially more positive results.

1. *Design interventions to enhance multiple facets of self-esteem and relevant other self-system components.* Esteem-enhancement programs for youth have focused primarily on increasing global or overall feelings of self-worth. This is a significant limitation given the potential that a more multifaceted and differentiated approach to esteem enhancement would seem to offer for insuring positive youth outcomes. One promising avenue to pursue is the design of interventions to address specific domains of self-evaluation that are most relevant to program goals. Thus, it may be that intervention components focusing on body image are especially important for the prevention of eating disorders, whereas strategies directed toward academic components of self-esteem are of greatest value when seeking to promote school performance. Profiles of self-evaluation across multiple domains also seem useful to consider in the design of programs as a means of facilitating the attainment of overall configurations of views of the self that are likely to contribute to posi-

tive outcomes. Further possible innovations that could be geared toward other facets of self-esteem include training in coping strategies to minimize short-term fluctuations in feelings of self-worth, practices to allow youth to achieve greater consistency between experienced and presented aspects of self-esteem, and activities tailored specifically toward either positive or negative dimensions of self-evaluation. Corresponding, multifaceted assessments of self-esteem incorporated into evaluation protocols for programs would allow for increased sensitivity to possible influences on diverse aspects of youth self-esteem. It also may be of significant value for interventions to both address and measure other relevant components of the developing self-system (e.g., self-efficacy beliefs). This type of further broadening of the scope of esteem-enhancement programs would allow for a more integrative and comprehensive approach and thus potentially yield stronger results.

2. *Focus programs on realistic, normative sources of self-esteem with adequate fit to the surrounding environment.* The sources of self-esteem emphasized in programs constitute a further area of concern. Most programs are curricular in format and consist of exercises in which youth are encouraged to appreciate their strengths and inherent worth as persons (e.g., selectively identifying positive personal characteristics). A significant limitation with this approach is that youth may adopt positive views of themselves even in instances when such views are neither realistic nor adequately supported by relevant personal behavior or accomplishments (cf. Damon, 1995). Available research, it will be recalled, suggests that gains in self-esteem that accrue in this manner may offer relatively few, if any, adaptive benefits. To address this concern, the scope of esteem-enhancement interventions should be expanded to incorporate elements focused more on normative developmental sources of feelings of self-worth (cf. Crockenberg & Soby, 1989). These types of programs might include skill-development and goal-setting components as well as an emphasis on increasing opportunities for success and positive recognition in meaningful pursuits (e.g., extracurricular activities). In view of the possibly enhanced adaptive value of efficacy-linked feelings of self-worth (Rutter, 1987), esteem-enhancement interventions with this latter type of orientation could turn out to be a particularly effective means of facilitating the attainment of desired outcomes in programs. In pursuing such an approach it may be important to include provisions to ensure that the bases for self-esteem fostered not only represent an adequate fit with the youth's surrounding environment (DuBois et al., 1998), but also allow for expression of distinctive attributes of the emerging self (Harter, 1997).

3. *Target programs to specific populations.* Most esteem-enhancement interventions have been designed in a relatively generic manner and have been evaluated only in terms of their effects on relatively narrowly defined groups of youth (e.g., White, middle class). Consequently, there has not been a systematic effort to adapt program aims and materials to the needs of youth from diverse backgrounds or to examine variability in outcomes across such groups. The need for greater attention to this concern is underscored by the manner in which various characteristics of youth (e.g., race/ethnicity) have been indicated to moderate the relationship of self-esteem to adjustment out-

comes during development. Illustratively, in order to ensure that interventions are optimally sensitive to issues confronting youth who belong to racial and ethnic minority groups, it may be necessary to incorporate components that focus specifically on concerns that are relevant for such youth (e.g., development of a positive racial/ethnic identity). Children and adolescents from backgrounds of environmental stress and disadvantage are also clearly deserving of increased consideration. Protective benefits of self-esteem for such youth could translate into differentially strong program outcomes, thus helping to establish esteem enhancement as an effective intervention strategy for youth from high-risk backgrounds. Evaluating and attempting to facilitate the role of self-esteem in mediating the effects of other types of interventions with populations of youth at risk seems a further promising avenue to explore.

 4. Intervene to directly promote adaptive functioning. With few exceptions, esteem-enhancement interventions have sought to produce gains in focal areas of adjustment (e.g., academic achievement) indirectly via strategies designed to increase feelings of self-worth. In view of the evidence for bidirectional, recursive patterns of influence between self-esteem and adaptive outcomes, it may be useful to expand programs to also include elements that are intended to directly facilitate targeted aspects of functioning (e.g., tutoring to improve performance in school). This approach would offer the opportunity to initiate mutually reinforcing linkages between self-esteem and youth adjustment and thus facilitate the attainment of more lasting and substantial program outcomes.

Concluding Comments

Several noteworthy leads are available for researchers to pursue in their efforts to better understand the adaptive significance of self-esteem during development. The overall picture that is conveyed, however, is much less straightforward than typically has been assumed. This state of affairs may be dissatisfying to those who are heavily invested in supporting views associated with either side of the self-esteem debate and perhaps even overwhelming to others who are faced with the task of developing esteem-enhancement interventions for youth that are adequately informed by the existing base of empirical knowledge. Alternatively, research and interventions focused on self-esteem and its implications for child and adolescent adjustment could either be continued largely along past lines or, as some have suggested (e.g., Kohn, 1994), abandoned altogether. Neither of these options seems defensible to us. We are reminded in this regard of the observation that, "For every problem there is a simple answer that is wrong."[2] Further investigation of promising developments in recent research and careful consideration of their implications for intervention will be necessary in order to ensure that this admonition does not go unheeded.

Notes

1. More favorable results were found in a recent meta-analysis of the effectiveness of esteem-enhancement programs for children and adolescents (Haney & Durlak, 1998). Significant limitations in available findings, however, continued to be noted (e.g., lack of demonstrated effects at follow-up assessments).
2. Seymour Sarason (1995, p. 62) attributed this quote to H. L. Mencken.

References

Allgood-Merten, B., Lewinsohn, P.M., & Hops, H. (1990). Sex differences and adolescent depression. *Journal of Abnormal Psychology, 99*, 55–63.

Alsaker, F. D., & Olweus, D. (1992). Stability of global self-evaluations in early adolescence: A cohort longitudinal study. *Journal of Research on Adolescence, 2*, 123–145.

Ammerman, R. T., Kazdin, A. E., & Van Hasselt, B. (1993). Correlates of loneliness in nonreferred and psychiatrically hospitalized children. *Journal of Child & Family Studies, 2*, 187–202.

Attie, I., & Brooks-Gunn, J. (1989). Development of eating problems in adolescent girls: A longitudinal study. *Developmental Psychology, 25*, 70–79.

Baumeister, R. E, Smart, L., & Boden, J. M. (1996). Relation of threatened egotism to violence and aggression: The dark side of high self-esteem. *Psychological Review, 103*, 5–33.

Block, J., & Robins, R. W. (1993). A longitudinal study of consistency and change in self-esteem from early adolescence to early adulthood. *Child Development, 64*, 909–923.

Bromley, D. B. (1978). Natural language and the development of the self. In C. B. Keasey (Ed.), *Nebraska symposium on motivation* (Vol. 25, pp. 117–167). Lincoln, NE: University of Nebraska Press.

Brooks-Gunn, J., Rock, D., & Warren, M. P. (1989). Comparability of constructs across the adolescent years. *Developmental Psychology, 25*, 51–60.

Brown, G. W., Andrews, B., Bifulco, A., & Veiel, H. (1990). Self-esteem and depression: I. Measurement issues and prediction of onset. *Social Psychiatry and Psychiatric Epidemiology, 25*, 200–209.

California Task Force to Promote Self-Esteem and Personal and Social Responsibility. (1990). *Toward a state of esteem.* Sacramento, CA: California State Department of Education.

Cole, P. G., Chan, L. K. S., & Lytton, L. (1989). Perceived competence of juvenile delinquents and nondelinquents. *Journal of Special Education, 23*, 294–302.

Connell, J. P., & Ilardi, B. C. (1987). Self-system concomitants of discrepancies between children's and teachers' evaluations of academic competence. *Child Development, 58*, 1297–1307.

Crockenberg, S. B., & Soby, B. A. (1989). Self-esteem and teenage pregnancy. In A. M. Mecca, N. J. Smelser, & J. Vasconcellos (Eds.), *The social importance of self-esteem* (pp. 125–164). Berkeley, CA: University of California Press.

Crockett, L. J., Bingham, R., Chopak, J. S., & Vicary, J. R. (1996). Timing of first sexual intercourse: The role of social control, social learning, and problem behavior. *Journal of Youth and Adolescence, 25*, 89–111.

Damon, W. (1995). Greater expectations: *Overcoming the culture of indulgence in America's homes and schools.* New York: Free Press.

Demo, D. H. (1985). The measurement of self-esteem: Refining our methods." *Journal of Personality and Social Psychology, 48*, 1490–1502.

DeSimone, A., Murray, P., & Lester, D. (1994). Alcohol use, self-esteem, depression and suicidality in high school students. *Adolescence, 29*, 939–942.

Doan, R. E., & Scherman, A. (1987). The therapeutic effect of physical fitness on measures of personality: A literature review. *Journal of Counseling and Development, 66*, 28–36.

Dryfoos, J. G. (1990). *Adolescents at risk: Prevalence and prevention*. New York: Oxford University Press.

DuBois, D. L., Bull, C. A., Sherman, M. D., & Roberts, M. (1998). Self-esteem and adjustment in early adolescence: A social-contextual perspective. *Journal of Youth and Adolescence, 27*, 557–583.

DuBois, D. L., Felner, R. D., & Brand, S. (1997, April). Self-esteem profiles and adjustment in early adolescence: A two-year longitudinal study. In D. L. DuBois (Chair), *Trajectories and profiles of self-esteem in adolescence: Identification and implications for adjustment*. Symposium conducted at the biennial meeting of the Society for Research on Child Development, Washington, DC.

DuBois, D. L., Felner, R. D., Brand, S., Phillips, R. S. C., & Lease, A. M. (1996). Early adolescent self-esteem: A developmental-ecological framework and assessment strategy. *Journal of Research on Adolescence, 6*, 541–578.

East, P. L., Hess, L. E., & Lerner, R. M. (1987). Peer social support and adjustment of early adolescent peer groups. *Journal of Early Adolescence, 7*,153–163.

Edwards, R. (1995, May). Is self-esteem really all that important? *APA Monitor*, pp. 43–44.

Giblin, P. T., Poland, M. L., & Ager, J. W. (1988). Clinical applications of self-esteem and locus of control to adolescent health. *Journal of Adolescent Health Care, 9*, 1–14.

Haney, P., & Durlak, J. A. (1998). Changing self-esteem in children and adolescents: A meta-analysis review. *Journal of Clinical Child Psychology, 27*, 423–433.

Harter, S. (1983). Developmental perspectives on the self-system. In P. H. Mussen (Series Ed.) & E. M. Hetherington (Vol. Ed.), *Handbook of child psychology: Vol. 4. Socialization, personality, and social development* (4th ed., pp. 275–386). New York: Wiley.

Harter, S. (1990). Causes, correlates, and the functional role of global self-worth: A life-span perspective. In R. J. Sternberg & J. Kolligan, Jr. (Eds.), *Competence considered* (pp. 67–97). New Haven, CT: Yale University Press.

Harter, S. (1993). Causes and consequences of low self-esteem in children and adolescents. In R. F. Baumeister (Ed.), *Self-esteem: The puzzle of low self-regard* (pp. 87–116). New York: Plenum Press.

Harter, S. (1997). The personal self in social context: Barriers to authenticity. In R. D. Ashmore & L. J. Jussim (Eds.), *Self and identity: Fundamental issues* (pp. 81–105). New York: Oxford University Press.

Harter, S., & Whitesell, N. R. (1996). Multiple pathways to self-reported depression and self-reported psychological adjustment among adolescents. *Development & Psychopathology, 8*, 761–77.

Hattie, J. (1992). *Self-concept*. Hillsdale, NJ: Lawrence Erlbaum.

Hauser, S. T. (1998, March). *Understanding resilient outcomes: Adolescent lives across time and generations*. Paper presented at the biennial meeting of the Society for Research on Adolescence, San Diego, CA.

Hinde, R. A., Tamplin, A., & Barrett, J. (1993). Home correlates of aggression in preschool. *Aggressive Behavior, 19*, 85–105.

Hirsch, B. J., & DuBois, D. L. (1991). Self-esteem in early adolescence: The identification and prediction of contrasting longitudinal trajectories. *Journal of Youth and Adolescence, 20,* 53–72.

Huebner, E. S. (1991). Correlates of life satisfaction in children. *Social Psychology Quarterly, 6,* 103–111.

Jarvie, G. J., Lahey, B., Graziano, W., & Framer, E. (1983). Childhood obesity and social stigma: What we know and what we don't know. *Developmental Review, 3,* 237–273.

Jessor, S. L., & Jessor, R. (1975). Transition from virginity to nonvirginity among youth: A social-psychological study over time. *Developmental Psychology, 11,* 473–484.

Kaplan, H. B., Robbins, C., & Martin, S. S. (1983). Antecedents of psychological distress in young adults: Self-rejection, deprivation of social support, and life events. *Journal of Health and Social Behavior, 24,* 230–244.

Kernis, M. H. (1993). The roles of stability and level of self-esteem in psychological functioning. In R. Baumeister (Ed.), *Self-esteem: The puzzle of low self-regard* (pp. 167–182). New York: Plenum Press.

Klesges, R. C., Haddock, C. K., Stein, R. J., Klesges, L. M., Eck, L. H., & Hanson, C. L. (1992). Relationship between psychological functioning and body fat in preschool children: A longitudinal investigation. *Journal of Consulting and Clinical Psychology, 60,* 793–796.

Koenig, L., Howard, K. I., Offer, D., & Cremerius, M. (1984). Psychopathology and adolescent self-image. In D. Offer, E. Ostrov, & K. I. Howard (Eds.), *Patterns of adolescent self-image* (pp. 57–71). San Francisco: Jossey-Bass.

Kohn, A. (1994, December). The truth about self-esteem. *Phi Delta Kappan,* pp. 272–283.

Kolody, B., & Sallis, J. F. (1995). A prospective study of ponderosity, body image, self-concept, and psychological variables in children. *Developmental and Behavioral Pediatrics, 16,* 1–5.

Lenerz, K., & Gamble, W. (1986, March). Domains of self-perception in early adolescence: Relations to psychosocial functioning. In R. M. Lerner (Chair), *Transitions in early adolescence: Findings from the Pennsylvania Early Adolescent Transitions Study (PEATS).* Symposium conducted at the First Biennial Meeting of the Society for Research on Adolescence, Madison, WI.

Lerner, R. M., Lerner, J. V., Hess, L. E., Schwab, J., Jovanovic, J., Talwar, R., & Kucher, J. S. (1991). Physical attractiveness and psychosocial functioning among early adolescents. *Journal of Early Adolescence, 11,* 300–320.

Lewinsohn, P. M., Rohde, P., & Seeley, J. R. (1993). Psychosocial characteristics of adolescents with a history of suicide attempt. *Journal of the American Academy of Child and Adolescent Psychiatry, 32,* 60–68.

Marsh, H. W., Byrne, B. M., & Shavelson, R. J. (1992). A multidimensional, hierarchical self-concept. In T. M. Brinthaupt & R. P. Lipka (Eds.), *The self: Definitional and methodological issues* (pp. 44–95). Albany, NY: State University of New York Press.

Marsh, H. W., & Yeung, A. S. (1997). Causal effects of academic self-concept on academic achievement: Structural equation models of longitudinal data. *Journal of Educational Psychology, 89,* 41–54.

Ohannessian, C. M., Lerner, R. M., Lerner, J. V., & von Eye, A. (1994). A longitudinal study of perceived family adjustment and emotional adjustment in early adolescence. *Journal of Early Adolescence, 14,* 371–390.

Olmstead, R. E., Guy, S. M., O'Malley, P. M., & Bentler, P. M. (1991). Longitudinal assessment of the relationship between self-esteem, fatalism, loneliness, and substance use. *Journal of Social Behavior and Personality, 6,* 749–770.

Owens, T. J. (1994). Two dimensions of self-esteem: Reciprocal effects of positive self-worth and self-depreciation on adolescent problems. *American Sociological Review, 59,* 391–407.

Patterson, L. J. M. (1997). Long-term unemployment amongst adolescents: A longitudinal study. *Journal of Adolescence, 20,* 261–280.

Purkey, W. W. (1970). *Self concept and school achievement.* Englewood Cliffs, NJ: Prentice-Hall.

Roberts, J. E., & Monroe, S. M. (1994). A multidimensional model of self-esteem in depression. *Clinical Psychology Review, 14,* 161–181.

Roberts, R. E. L., & Bengtson, V. L. (1993). Relationships with parents, self-esteem, and psychological well-being in young adulthood. *Social Psychology Quarterly, 56,* 263–277.

Rosenberg, F. R., & Rosenberg, M. (1978). Self-esteem and delinquency. *Journal of Youth and Adolescence, 7,* 279–294.

Rosenberg, M. (1985). Self-concept and psychological well-being in adolescence. In R. L. Leahy (Ed.), *The development of the self* (pp. 205–246). Orlando, FL: Academic Press.

Rosenberg, M., Schooler, C, Schoenbach, C., & Rosenberg, F. (1995). Global self-esteem and specific self-esteem: Different concepts, different outcomes. *American Sociological Review, 60,* 141–156.

Rutter, M. (1987). Psychosocial resilience and protective mechanisms. *American Journal of Orthopsychiatry, 57,* 316–331.

Sarason, S. B. (1995). *Parental involvement and the political principle: Why the existing governance structure of schools should be abolished.* San Francisco: Jossey-Bass.

Savin-Williams, R. C., & Demo, D. H. (1983a). Conceiving or misconceiving the self: Issues in adolescent self-esteem. *Journal of Early Adolescence, 3,* 121–140.

Savin-Williams, R. C., & Demo, D. H. (1983b). Situational and transituational determinants of adolescent self-feelings. *Journal of Personality and Social Psychology, 44,* 824–833.

Savin-Williams, R. C., & Demo, D. H. (1984). Developmental change and stability in adolescent self-concept. *Developmental Psychology, 20,* 1100–1110.

Savin-Williams, R. C., & Jaquish, G. A. (1981). The assessment of adolescent self-esteem: A comparison of methods. *Journal of Personality, 49,* 324–336.

Scheirer, M. A., & Kraut, R. E. (1979). Increasing educational achievement via self concept change. *Review of Educational Research, 49,* 131–149.

Schroeder, D. S., Laflin, M. T., & Weis, D. L. (1993). Is there a relationship between self-esteem and drug use? Methodological and statistical limitations of the research. *Journal of Drug Issues, 23,* 645–665.

Seidman, E., & Hsueh, J. (1997, April). Self-esteem trajectories across the transitions to junior and senior high school. In D. L. DuBois (Chair), *Trajectories and profiles of self-esteem in adolescence: Identification and implications for adjustment.* Symposium conducted at the biennial meeting of the Society for Research on Child Development, Washington, DC.

Seligman, M. E. P. (1993). *What you can change and what you can't: The complete guide to successful self-improvement.* New York: Fawcett.

Simmons, R. G., & Blyth, D. A. (1987). *Moving into adolescence: The impact of pubertal change and school context.* New York: Aldine de Gruyter.

Skaalvik, E. M., & Hagtvet, K. A. (1990). Academic achievement and self-concept: An analysis of causal predominance in a developmental perspective. *Journal of Personality and Social Psychology, 58,* 292–307.

Slomkowski, C., Klein, R. G., & Mannuzza, S. (1995). Is self-esteem an important outcome in hyperactive children? *Journal of Abnormal Child Psychology, 23,* 303–315.

Smelser, N. J. (1989). Self-esteem and social problems: An introduction. In A. M. Mecca, N. J. Smelser, & J. Vasconcellos (Eds.), *The social importance of self-esteem* (pp. 1–23). Berkeley, CA: University of California Press.

Tevendale, H. D., DuBois, D. L., Lopez, C., & Prindiville, S. L. (1997). Self-esteem stability and early adolescent adjustment: An exploratory study. *Journal of Early Adolescence, 17,* 216–237.

Towbes, L., Cohen, L., & Glyshaw, K. (1989). Instrumentality as a life-stress moderator for early versus middle adolescents. *Journal of Personality and Social Psychology, 57,* 109–119.

Verkuyten, M. (1995). Self-esteem, self-concept stability, and aspects of ethnic identity among minority and majority youth in the Netherlands. *Journal of Youth and Adolescence, 24,* 155–175.

Wang, A. Y. (1994). Pride and prejudice in high school gang members. *Adolescence, 29,* 279–291.

Waschull, S. B., & Kernis, M. H. (1996). Level and stability of self-esteem as predictors of children's intrinsic motivation and reasons for anger. *Personality and Social Psychology Bulletin, 22,* 4–13.

Werner, E. E., & Smith, R. S. (1982). *Vulnerable but invincible: A longitudinal study of resilient children and youth.* New York: McGraw-Hill.

Werner, E. E., & Smith, R. S. (1992). *Overcoming the odds: High risk children from birth to adulthood.* Ithaca. NY: Cornell University Press.

Yarcheski, A., & Mahon, N. E. (1989). A causal model of positive health practices: The relationship between approach and replication. *Nursing Research, 38,* 88–93.

Young, M., Werch, C. E., & Bakema, D. (1989). Area specific self-esteem scales and substance use among elementary and middle school children. *Journal of School Health, 59,* 251–254.

Zimmennan, M. A., Copeland, L. A., Shope, J. T., & Dielman, T. E. (1997). A longitudinal study of self-esteem: Implications for adolescent development. *Journal of Youth and Adolescence, 26,* 117–141.

Zuroff, D. C., Koesmer, R., & Powers, T. A. (1994). Self-criticism at age 12: A longitudinal study of adjustment. *Cognitive Therapy and Research, 18,* 367–385.

CHALLENGE QUESTIONS

Applying Social Psychology:
Are Self-Esteem Programs Misguided?

1. If excessively high self-esteem is linked to problematic behaviors, such as aggression, how could advocates of the self-esteem improvement programs tailor their approach, so that individuals' self-esteem does not become unrealistically inflated?
2. Assume for a moment that self-esteem is not an important cause of positive outcomes, such as academic achievement. Could you still make a case that it is important to have high self-esteem? In other words, is having a positive self-image important regardless of its impact on adaptive functioning?
3. If self-esteem programs are not the "cure-all" that they were once promised to be, can you think of other interventions that could be designed to reduce problem behaviors among adolsencents, such as delinquency and poor academic achievement?

ISSUE 6

Do Positive Illusions Promote Mental Health?

YES: Shelley E. Taylor and Jonathon D. Brown, from "Illusion and Well-Being: A Social Psychological Perspective on Mental Health," *Psychological Bulletin* (*103*, 1988)

NO: Randall Colvin, Jack Block, and David D. Funder, from "Overly Positive Self-Evaluations and Personality: Negative Implications for Mental Health," *Journal of Personality and Social Psychology* (*68*, 1995)

ISSUE SUMMARY

YES: Shelley Taylor and Jonathon Brown argue that people have unrealistically positive views of themselves. These "positive illusions" promote psychological well-being.

NO: C. Randall Colvin, Jack Block, and David Funder agree that many people have positive views of themselves. However, these positive self-views should not necessarily be considered illusory.

Health psychology is an interdisciplinary field of psychology that is devoted to understanding how human thought and behavior may contribute to our well-being. Many prominent researchers in health psychology are social psychologists. One of the best-known social psychologists in the field is Shelley Taylor. Along with her colleagues, Taylor has examined the link between our self-perceptions are our physical and psychological health. The results of Taylor's research indicate that our self-perceptions are not always accurate. Contrary to the old saying "I am my own worst critic," our self-perceptions tend to be very positive and in some cases these perceptions appear to be unrealistically positive. Shelley Taylor and Jonathon Brown refer to these unrealistically positive self-perceptions as "positive illusions." Are such unrealistically positive self-views healthy? There is some reason to think that such an optimistic outlook should be helpful. According to Taylor and Brown, people who are depressed tend to have fewer positive illusions, compared to people who are not depressed. This suggests that the absence of positive illusions predisposes people to depression. Thus positive self-views may be linked to mental health, even if these self-views are unrealistic. This notion flies in the face of the conventional wisdom in clinical psychology, which has traditionally linked mental health with accurate self-perceptions. Those who have inaccurate perceptions of themselves have traditionally been regarded as mentally unhealthy and out of touch with reality. Taylor and Brown concluded this traditional view may be mistaken.

C. Randall Colvin, Jack Block, and David Funder agree with the traditional view that realistic self-perceptions are healthier than unrealistic perceptions. They believe that the evidence supposedly documenting the widespread existence of "positive illusions" is not very strong. While the evidence does indicate that people generally think highly of themselves, it does not necessarily indicate that most people's self-perceptions are illusory or inaccurate. Furthermore, Colvin, Block, and Funder argue that those who have unrealistically positive self-perceptions—whom they refer to as "self-enhancers"—are not necessarily more mentally healthy than those with more realistic views of themselves.

POINT

- Many people have unrealistically positive self-images.
- Positive self-perceptions, even when they are illusory, are usually healthy.
- Traditional conceptions of mental health, which link mental health with accurate self-perceptions, may be mistaken.

COUNTERPOINT

- The available evidence does not necessarily indicate that positive self-views are usually illusory.
- The evidence does not indicate that people with unrealistically positive views of the self are healthier than others.
- The evidence does not indicate that the traditional view is mistaken.

Shelley E. Taylor and
Jonathon D. Brown

 **YES**

Illusion and Well-Being: A Social Psychological Perspective on Mental Health

Decades of psychological wisdom have established contact with reality as a hallmark of mental health. In this view, the well-adjusted person is thought to engage in accurate reality testing, whereas the individual whose vision is clouded by illusion is regarded as vulnerable to, if not already a victim of, mental illness. Despite its plausibility, this viewpoint is increasingly difficult to maintain (cf. Lazarus, 1983). A substantial amount of research testifies to the prevalence of illusion in normal human cognition (see Fiske & Taylor, 1984; Greenwald, 1980; Nisbett & Ross, 1980; Sackeim, 1983; Taylor, 1983). Moreover these illusions often involve central aspects of the self and the environment and, therefore, cannot be dismissed as inconsequential.

In this article, we review research suggesting that certain illusions may be adaptive for mental health and well-being. In particular; we examine evidence that a set of interrelated positive illusions—namely, unrealistically positive self-evaluations, exaggerated perceptions of control or mastery, and unrealistic optimism—can serve a wide variety of cognitive, affective, and social functions. We also attempt to resolve the following paradox: How can positive misperceptions of one's self and the environment be adaptive when accurate information processing seems to be essential for learning and successful functioning in the world? Our primary goal is to weave a theoretical context for thinking about mental health. A secondary goal is to create an integrative framework for a voluminous literature in social cognition concerning perceptions of the self and the environment.

Mental Health as Contact with Reality

Throughout psychological history, a variety of views of mental health have been proffered, some idiosyncratic and others widely shared. Within this theoretical diversity, a dominant position has maintained that the psychologically healthy person is one who maintains close contact with reality. For example, in her distillation of the dominant views of mental health at the

From *Psychological Bulletin*, vol. 103, no. 2, 1988, pp. 193–210. Copyright © 1988 by American Psychological Association. Reprinted with permission.

time, Jahoda (1958) noted that the majority of theories considered contact with reality to be a critical component of mental health. This theme is prominent in the writings of Allport (1943), Erikson (1950), Menninger (1930), and Fromm (1955), among others. For example, concerning his self-actualized individuals, Maslow (1950) wrote,

> Our healthy individuals find it possible to accept themselves and their own nature without chagrin or complaint.... They can accept their own human nature with all of its discrepancies from the ideal image without feeling real concern. It would convey the wrong impression to say that they are self-satisfied. What we must rather say is that they can take the frailties and sins, weaknesses and evils of human nature in the same unquestioning spirit that one takes or accepts the characteristics of nature. (p. 54)

On the basis of her review, Jahode concluded,

> The perception of reality is called mentally healthy when what the individual sees corresponds to what is actually there. (1958, p. 6)

> Mentally healthy perception means a process of viewing the world so that one is able to take in matters one wishes were different without distorting them to fit these wishes. (1953, p. 349)

Since Jahoda's report, the position that the mentally healthy person perceives reality accurately has been put forth in major works by Haan (1977) and Vaillant (1977), and it has also been incorporated into textbooks on adjustment (e.g., Jourard & Landsman, 1980; Schulz, 1977). For example, after reviewing a large number of theories of the healthy personality, Jourard and Landsman (1980) noted, "The ability to perceive reality as it 'really is' is fundamental to effective functioning. It is considered one of the two preconditions to the development of [the healthy personality]" (p. 75).

To summarize, then, although it is not the only theoretical perspective on the mentally healthy person, the view that psychological health depends on accurate perceptions of reality has been widely promulgated and widely shared in the literature on mental health.

Social Cognition, Reality, and Illusion

Early theorists in social cognition adopted a view of the person's information-processing capabilities that is quite similar to the viewpoint just described. These theorists maintained that the social perceiver monitors and interacts with the world like a naive scientist (see Fischhoff, 1976; Fiske & Taylor; 1984; Nisbett & Ross, 1980, for discussions). According to this view, the person gathers data in an unbiased manner; combines it in some logical, identifiable fashion; and reaches generally good, accurate inferences and decisions. Theories of the causal attribution process (e.g., Kelley, 1967), prediction (see Kahneman & Tversky, 1973), judgments of covariation, and other tasks of social inference (see Fiske & Taylor, 1984; Nisbett & Ross, 1980) incorporated the assumptions of the naive scientist as normative guidelines with which actual behavior could be compared.

It rapidly became evident, however, that the social perceiver's actual inferential work and decision making looked little like these normative models. Rather, information processing is full of incomplete data gathering, shortcuts, errors, and biases (see Fiske & Taylor, 1984; Nisbett & Ross, 1980, for reviews). In particular, prior expectations and self-serving interpretations weigh heavily into the social judgment process. In summarizing this work, Fiske and Taylor (1984) noted, "Instead of a naive scientist entering the environment in search of the truth, we find the rather unflattering picture of a charlatan trying to make the data come out in a manner most advantageous to his or her already-held theories" (p. 88). The implications of these conclusions for cognitive functioning have been widely debated and discussed (see Fiske & Taylor, 1984; Greenwald, 1980; Nisbett & Ross, 1980). But these findings also seem to have implications for the understanding of mental health, inasmuch as they appear to contradict a dominant conception of its attributes: How can the normal, healthy individual perceive reality accurately if his or her perceptions are so evidently biased and self-serving? Before considering this issue, a note concerning terminology is required.

At this point, we exchange the terms *error* and *bias* for a broader term, *illusion*. There are several reasons for this change in terminology. *Error and bias* imply short-term mistakes and distortions, respectively, that might be caused by careless oversight or other temporary negligences (cf. Funder, 1987). *Illusion*, in contrast, implies a more general, enduring pattern of error, bias, or both that assumes a particular direction or shape. As the evidence will show, the illusions to be considered (unrealistically positive self-evaluations, exaggerated perceptions of control, and unrealistic optimism) do indeed seem to be pervasive, enduring, and systematic. Illusion is defined as

> a perception that represents what is perceived in a way different from the
> way it is in reality. An illusion is a false mental image or conception which
> may be a misinterpretation of a real appearance or may be something imagined. It may be pleasing, harmless, or even useful (Stein, 1982, p. 662).

The definition of an illusion as a belief that departs from reality presupposes an objective grasp of reality. This point puts us on the perilous brink of philosophical debate concerning whether one can ever know reality. Fortunately, at least to some degree, the methodologies of social psychology spare us this frustrating conundrum by providing operational definitions. In some cases, evidence for illusions comes from experimental work that manipulates feedback provided to a person (e.g., whether the person succeeded or failed on a task) and measures the individual's perceptions or recall of that feedback; this paradigm can provide estimates of an individual's accuracy as well as information about the direction (positive or negative) of any distortions. As will be seen, people typically distort such feedback in a self-serving manner. More subjective self-evaluations (e.g., how happy or well-adjusted one is) do not have these same objective standards of comparison. In such cases, an illusion is implied if the majority of people report that they are more (or less) likely than the majority of people to hold a particular belief. For example, if most people believe that they are happier; better adjusted, and more skilled on a variety of tasks than most other people, such perceptions provide evidence suggestive of an illusion. Illusions about the future are operationally difficult to establish because no one knows what the future will bring. If it can be shown, however, that most people believe that their future is more positive than that of most other people or more positive than objective baserate data can support, then evidence suggestive of illusions about the future is provided. We now turn to the evidence for these illusions.

Positive Illusions and Social Cognition

Any taxonomy of illusions is, to some extent, arbitrary. Many researchers have studied biases in the processing of self-relevant information and have given their similar phenomena different names. There is, however, considerable overlap in findings, and three that consistently emerge can be labeled *unrealistically positive views of the self, exaggerated perceptions of personal control, and unrealistic optimism.* Those familiar with the research evidence will recognize that much of the evidence for these positive illusions comes from experimental studies and from research with college students. We will have more to say about potential biases in the experimental literature later in this article. At present, it is important to note that all three of the illusions to be discussed have been documented in noncollege populations as well.

Unrealistically Positive Views of the Self

As indicated earlier, a traditional conception of mental health asserts that the well-adjusted individual possesses a view of the self that includes an awareness and acceptance of both the positive and negative aspects of self. In contrast to this portrayal, evidence indicates that most individuals possess a very positive view of the self (see Greenwald, 1980, for a review). When asked to indicate how accurately positive and negative personality adjectives describe the self, normal subjects judged positive traits to be overwhelmingly more characteristic of self than negative attributes (Alicke, 1985; Brown, 1986). Additionally, for most individuals, positive personality information is efficiently processed and easily recalled, whereas negative personality information is poorly processed and difficult to recall (Kuiper & Derry, 1982; Kuiper & MacDonald, 1982; Kuiper; Olinger, MacDonald, & Shaw, 1985). Most individuals also show poorer recall for information related to failure than to success (Silverman, 1964) and tend to recall their task performance as more positive than it actually was (Crary, 1966). Research on the self-serving bias in causal attribution documents that most individuals are more likely to attribute positive than negative outcomes to the self (see Bradley, 1978; Miller & Ross, 1975; Ross & Fletcher, 1985; Zuckerman, 1979, for reviews).[1]

Even when negative aspects of the self are acknowledged, they tend to be dismissed as inconsequential. One's poor abilities tend to be perceived as common, but one's favored abilities are seen as rare and distinctive (Campbell, 1986; G. Marks, 1984). Furthermore, the things that people are not proficient at are perceived as less important than the things that they are proficient at (e.g., Campbell, 1986, Harackiewicz, Sansone, & Manderlink, 1985; Lewicki, 1984; Rosenberg, 1979). And people perceive that they have improved on abilities that are important to them even when their performance has remained unchanged (Conway & Ross, 1984).

In sum, far from being balanced between the positive and the negative, the perception of self that most individuals hold is heavily weighted toward the positive end of the scale. Of course, this imbalance does not in and of itself provide evidence that such views are unrealistic or illusory. Evidence of this nature is, however, available.

First, there exists a pervasive tendency to see the self as better than others. Individuals judge positive personality attributes to be more descriptive of themselves than of the average person but see negative personality attributes as less descriptive of themselves than of the average person (Alicke, 1985; Brown, 1986). This effect has been documented for a wide range of traits (Brown, 1986) and abilities (Campbell, 1986; Larwood & Whittaker, 1977); individuals even believe that their driving ability is superior to others' (Svenson, 1981). Because it is logically impossible for most people to be better than the average person, these highly skewed, positive views of the self can be regarded as evidence for their unrealistic and illusory nature. People also tend to use their positive qualities when appraising others, thereby virtually assuring a favorable self other comparison (Lewicki, 1983). And people give others less credit for success and more blame for failure than they ascribe to themselves (Forsyth & Schlenker, 1977; Green & Gross, 1979; Mirels, 1980; Schlenker & Miller, 1977; Taylor & Koivumaki, 1976).

Although the tendency to see the self as better than others is attenuated somewhat when the others being evaluated are close friends or relatives (Brown, 1986), a corresponding tendency exists for individuals to see their intimates as better than average. One's friends are evaluated more positively and less negatively than the average person (Brown, 1986), and, compared with others, close friends and relatives receive more credit for success and less blame for failure (Hall & Taylor; 1976; Taylor & Koivumaki, 1976). Moreover, these effects at the individual level also occur at the group level: Research using the minimal intergroup paradigm has established that even under the most minimal of social conditions, a pervasive tendency exists for individuals to see their own group as better than other groups (see Tajfel & Turner, 1986, for a review). Thus, although research demonstrates a general person-positivity bias (Schneider, Hastorf, & Ellsworth, 1979; Sears, 1983), individuals are inclined to appraise themselves and their close associates in far more positive and less negative terms than they appraise most other people.

A second source of evidence pertaining to the illusory quality of positive self-perceptions comes from investigations in which self-ratings have been compared with judgments made by observers. Lewinsohn, Mischel, Chaplin, and Barton (1980) had observers watch college-student subjects complete a group-interaction task. Observers then rated each subject along a number of personality dimensions (e.g., friendly, warm, and assertive). Subjects also rated themselves on each attribute. The results showed that self-ratings were significantly more positive than the observers' ratings. In other words, individuals saw themselves in more flattering terms than they were seen in by others.

In sum, the perception of self that most individuals hold is not as well-balanced as traditional models of mental health suggest. Rather than being attentive to both the favorable and unfavorable aspects of self, normal individuals appear to be very cognizant of their strengths and assets and considerably less aware of their weaknesses and faults. Evidence that these flattering self-portrayals are illusory comes from studies in which researchers have found that (a) most individuals see themselves as better than the average person and (b) most individuals see themselves as better than others see them. For these reasons, overly positive views of the self appear to be illusory. [2]

Does there exist a group of individuals that is accepting of both the good and the bad aspects of themselves as many views of mental health maintain the normal person is? Suggestive evidence indicates that individuals who are low in self-esteem, moderately depressed, or both are more balanced in self-perceptions (see Coyne & Gotlieb, 1983; Ruehlman, West, & Pasahow, 1985; Watson & Clark, 1984, for reviews). These individuals tend to (a) recall positive and negative self-relevant information with equal frequency (e.g., Kuiper & Derry, 1982; Kuiper & MacDonald, 1982), (b) show greater evenhandedness in their attributions of responsibility for valenced outcomes (e.g., Campbell & Fairey, 1985; Kuiper, 1978; Rizley, 1978), (c) display greater congruence between self-evaluations and evaluations of others (e.g., Brown, 1986), and (d) offer self-appraisals that coincide more closely with appraisals by objective observers (e.g., Lewinsohn et al., 1980). In short, it appears to be not the well-adjusted individual but the individual who experiences subjective distress who is more likely to process self-relevant information in a relatively unbiased and balanced fashion. These findings are inconsistent with the notion that realistic and even-handed perceptions of self are characteristic of mental health.

Illusions of Control

A second domain in which most individuals' perceptions appear to be less than realistic concerns beliefs about personal control over environmental occurrences. Many theorists, including social psychologists (e.g., Heider, 1958), developmental psychologists (e.g., White, 1959), learning theorists (Bandura, 1977; deCharms, 1968), and psychoanalytic theorists (Fenichel, 1945; Hendrick, 1942), have maintained that a sense of personal control is integral to the self-concept and self-esteem. Research evidence, however, suggests that people's beliefs in personal control are sometimes greater than can be justified.

In a series of studies adopting gambling formats, Langer and her associates (Langer, 1975; Langer & Roth, 1975) found that people often act as if they have control in situations that are actually determined by chance. When manipulations suggestive of skill, such as competition, choice, familiarity, and involvement, are introduced into chance situations, people behave as if the situations were determined by skill and, thus, were ones over which they could exert some control (see also Goffman, 1967). For example, people infer that they have greater control if they personally throw dice than if someone else does it for them (Fleming & Darley, 1986; Langer, 1975). Similarly, a large literature on covariation estimation indicates that people substantially overestimate their degree of control over heavily chance-determined events (see Crocker, 1982, for a review). When people expect to produce a certain outcome and the outcome then occurs, they often overestimate the degree to which they were instrumental in bringing it about (see Miller & Ross, 1975).

Is there any group in which this illusion of control appears to be absent? Mildly and severely depressed individuals appear to be less vulnerable to the illusion of control (Abramson & Alloy, 1981; Golin, Terrell, & Johnson, 1977; Gelin, Terrell, Weitz, & Drost, 1979; M. S. Greenberg & Alloy, 1988). When skill cues are introduced into a chance-related task or when outcomes occur as predicted, depressed individuals provide more accurate estimates of their degree of personal control than do nondepressed people. Similarly, relative to nondepressed people, those in whom a negative mood has been induced show more realistic perceptions of personal control (Alloy, Abramson, & Yiscusi, 1981; see also Shrauger & Terbovic, 1976). This is not to suggest that depressed people or those in whom a negative mood has been induced are always more accurate than nondepressed subjects in their estimates of personal control (e.g., Abramson, Alloy, & Rosoff, 1981; Benassi & Mahler, 1985) but that the preponderance of evidence lies in this direction. Realistic perceptions of personal control thus appear to be more characteristic of individuals in a depressed affective state than individuals in a nondepressed affective state.

Unrealistic Optimism

Research suggests that most people are future oriented. In one survey (Gonzales & Zimbardo, 1985), the majority of respondents rated themselves as oriented toward the present and the future (57%) or primarily toward the future (33%) rather than toward the present only (9%) or toward the past (1%). Optimism pervades people's thinking about the future (Tiger, 1979). Research suggests that most people believe that the present is better than the past and that the future will be even better (Brickman, Coates, & Janoff-Bulman, 1978). Questionnaires that survey Americans about the future have found the majority to be hopeful and confident that things can only improve (Free & Cantril, 1968). When asked what they thought was possible for them in the future, college students reported more than four times as many positive as negative possibilities (Markus & Nurius, 1986).

Is there any evidence, however, that such optimism is actually unrealistic? Although the future may well hold more subjectively positive events than negative ones for most individuals, as with excessively positive views of the self, evidence for the illusory nature of optimism comes from studies comparing judgments of self with judgments of others. The evidence indicates that although the warm and generous vision of the future that individuals entertain extends to all people, it is decidedly more in evidence for the self. People estimate the likelihood that they will experience a wide variety of pleasant events, such as liking their first job, getting a good salary, or having a gifted child, as higher than those of their peers (Weinstein, 1980). Conversely, when asked their chances of experiencing a wide variety of negative events, including having an automobile accident (Robertson, 1977), being a crime victim (Perloff & Fetzer, (1986), having trouble finding a job (Weinstein, 1980), or becoming ill (Perloff & Fetzer, 1986) or depressed (Kuiper, MacDonald, & Derry, 1983), most people believe that they are less likely than their peers to experience such negative events. In effect, most people seem to be saying, "The future will be great, especially for me." Because not everyone's future can be rosier than their peers', the extreme optimism that individuals display appears to be illusory.

Other evidence also suggests that individuals hold unrealistically positive views of the future. Over a wide variety of tasks, subjects' predictions of what will occur correspond closely to what they would like to see happen or to what is socially desirable rather than to what is objectively likely (Cantril, 1938; Lund, 1975; McGuire, 1960; Pruitt & Hoge, 1965; Sherman, 1980). Both children and adults overestimate the degree to which they will do well on future tasks (e.g., Crandall, Solomon, & Kelleway, 1955; Irwin, 1944, 1953; R. W. Marks, 1951), and they are more likely to provide such overestimates the more personally important the task is (Frank, 1953). Unrealistic optimism has even been documented for events that are entirely chance determined (Irwin, 1953; Langer & Roth, 1975; R. W. Marks, 1951).

In contrast to the extremely positive view of the future displayed by normal individuals, mildly depressed people and those with low self-esteem appear to entertain more balanced assessments of their likely future circumstances (see Ruehlman et al., 1985, for a review). Relative to judgments concerning others, these individuals fail to exhibit the self-enhancing tendency to see positive events as more likely for self and negative events as less likely for self (Alloy & Ahrens, 1987; Brown, 1985; Pietromonaco & Markus, 1985; Pyszczynski, Holt, & Greenberg, 1987). Thus, although in some cases such tendencies may reflect pessimism on the part of depressed people, it appears to be individuals who are high, not low, in subjective well-being who evince more biased perceptions of the future.

Summary

To summarize, traditional conceptions of mental health assert that well-adjusted individuals possess relatively accurate perceptions of themselves, their capacity to control important events in their lives, and their future. In contrast to this portrayal, a great deal of research in social, personality, clinical, and developmental psychology documents that normal individuals possess unrealistically positive views of themselves, an exaggerated belief in their ability to control their environment, and a view of the future that maintains that their future will be far better than the average person's. Furthermore, individuals who are moderately depressed or low in self-esteem consistently display an absence of such enhancing illusions. Together, these findings appear inconsistent with the notion that accurate self-knowledge is the hall-mark of mental health....

In conclusion, the overriding implication that we draw from our analysis of this literature is that certain biases in perception that have previously been thought of as amusing peccadillos at best and serious flaws in information processing at worst may actually be highly adaptive under many circum-stances. The individual who responds to negative, ambiguous, or unsupport-ive feedback with a positive sense of self, a belief in personal efficacy, and an optimistic sense of the future will, we maintain, be happier, more caring, and more productive than the individual who perceives this same information accurately and integrates it into his or her view of the self, the world, and the future. In this sense, the capacity to develop and maintain positive illusions may be thought of as a valuable human resource to be nurtured and pro-moted, rather than an error-prone processing system to be corrected. In any case, these illusions help make each individual's world a warmer and more active and beneficent place in which to live.

Notes

1. Despite a general pattern indicating that people accept more respon-sibility for positive outcomes than for negative outcomes, some evi-dence suggests that people may exaggerate their own causal role in the occurrence of highly negative events (e.g., Bulman & Wortman, 1977; Janoff-Bulman, 1979; Taylor, Lichtman, & Wood, 1984). These data might appear to be at odds with a general pattern of self-serving attri-butions, but they may not be. Self-attribution does not imply per-sonal responsibility or self-blame (Shaver & Drown, 1986) and therefore may not produce any blow to self-esteem. Moreover, some have suggested that self-attribution may enable people to begin to achieve mastery over an adverse event, helping to maintain a sense of personal control (Bulman & Wortman, 1977; Taylor, 1983).

2. One might argue that overly positive self-descriptions reflect public posturing rather than privately held beliefs. Several factors, however, argue against the plausibility of a strict self-presentational interpre-tation of this phenomenon. For example, Greenwald and Breckler (1985) reviewed evidence indicating that (a) self-evaluations are at least as favorable under private conditions as they are under public conditions; (b) favorable self-evaluations occur even when strong constraints to be honest are present; (c) favorable self-referent judg-ments are made very rapidly, suggesting that people are not engag-ing in deliberate (time-consuming) fabrication; and (d) self-enhancing judgments are acted on. For these as well as other rea-sons, a consensus is emerging at the theoretical level that individu-als do not offer flattering self-evaluations merely as a means of managing a public impression of competency (see Schlenker, 1980; Tesser & Moore, 1986; Tetlock & Manstead, 1985).

References

Abramson, L. Y., & Alloy, L. B. (1981). Depression, non-depression, and cognitive illusions: A reply to Schwartz. *Journal of Experimental Psychology, 110,* 436–447.

Abramson, L. Y., Alloy, L. B., & Rosoff, R. (1981). Depression and the generation of complex hypotheses in the judgment of contingency. *Behaviour Research and Therapy, 19,* 35–45.

Alicke, M. D. (1985). Global self-evaluation as determined by the desirability and controllability of trait adjectives. *Journal of Personality and Social Psychology, 49,* 1621–1630.

Alloy, L. B., Abramson, L. Y., & Viscusi, D. (1981). Induced mood and the illusion of control. *Journal of Personality and Social Psychology, 41,* 1129–1140.

Alloy, L. B., & Ahrens, A. H. (1987). Depression and pessimism for the future: Biased use of statistically relevant information in predictions for self versus others. *Journal of Personality and Social Psychology, 52,* 366–378.

Allport, G. W. (1943). *Becoming: Basic considerations for a psychology of personality.* New Haven, CT: Yale University Press.

Bandura, A. (1977) *Social learning theory.* Englewood Cliffs, NJ: Prentice-Hall.

Benassi, V. A., & Mahler, H. I. M. (1985). Contingency judgments by depressed college students: Sadder but not always wiser. *Journal of Personality and Social Psychology, 49,* 1323–1329.

Bradley, G. W. (1978). Self-serving biases in the attribution process: A reexamination of the fact or fiction question. *Journal of Personality and Social Psychology, 36,* 56–71.

Brickman, P., Coates, D., & Janoff-Bulman, R. (1978). Lottery winners and accident victims: Is happiness relative? *Journal of Personality and Social Psychology, 35,* 917–927.

Brown, J. D. (1985). [Self-esteem and unrealistic optimism about the future]. Unpublished data, University of California, Los Angeles.

Brown, J. D. (1986). Evaluations of self and others: Self-enhancement biases in social judgments. *Social Cognition, 4,* 353–376.

Bulman, R. J., & Wortman, C. B. (1977). Attributions of blame and coping in the "real world": Severe accident victims react to their lot. *Journal of Personality and Social Psychology, 35,* 351–363.

Campbell, J. D. (1986). Similarity and uniqueness: The effects of attribute type relevance, and individual differences in self-esteem and depression. *Journal of Personality and Social Psychology, 50,* 281–294.

Campbell, J. D., & Fairey, P. J. (1985). Effects of self-esteem, hypothetical explanations, and verbalization of expectancies on future performance. *Journal of Personality and Social Psychology, 48,* 1097–1111.

Cantril, H. (1938). The prediction of social events. *Journal of Abnormal and Social Psychology, 33,* 364–389.

Conway, M., & Ross, M. (1984). Getting what you want by revising what you had. *Journal of Personality and Social Psychology, 47,* 738–748.

Coyne, J. C., & Gotlieb, I. H. (1983). The role of cognition in depression: A critical appraisal. *Psychological Bulletin, 94,* 472–505.

Crandall, V. J., Solomon, D., & Kelleway, R. (1955). Expectancy statements and decision times as functions of objective probabilities and reinforcement values. *Journal of Personality, 24,* 192–203.

Crary, W. G. (1966). Reactions to incongruent self-experiences. *Journal of Consulting Psychology, 30,* 246–252.

Crocker, J. (1982). Biased questions in judgment of covariation studies. *Personality and Social Psychology Bulletin, 8,* 214–220.

deCharms, R. (1968). *Personal causation: The internal affective determinants of behavior.* New York: Academic Press.

Erikson, E. H. (1950). *Childhood and society* (2nd ed.). New York: Norton.

Fenichel, O. (1945). *The psychoanalytic theory of neurosis.* New York: Norton.

Fischhoff, B. (1976). Attribution theory and judgment under uncertainty. In J. H. Harvey, W. J. Ickes, & R. F. Kidd (Eds.), *New directions in attribution research* (Vol. 1, pp. 421–452). Hillsdale, NJ: Erlbaum.

Fiske, S. T., & Taylor, S. E. (1984). *Social cognition.* Reading, MA: Addison-Wesley.

Fleming, J., & Darley, J. M. (1986). *Perceiving intention in constrained behavior: The role of purposeful and constrained action cues in correspondence bias effects.* Unpublished manuscript, Princeton University, Princeton, NJ.

Forsyth, D. R., & Schlenker, B. R. (1977). Attributing the causes of group performance: Effects of performance quality, task importance, and future testing. *Journal of Personality, 45,* 220–236.

Frank, J. D. (1953). Some psychological determinants of the level of aspiration. *American Journal of Psychology, 47,* 285–293.

Free, L. A., & Cantril, H. (1968). *The political beliefs of Americans: A study of public opinion.* New York: Clarion.

Fromm, E. (1955). *The sane society.* New York: Rinehart.

Funder, D. C. (1987). Errors and mistakes: Evaluating the accuracy of social judgment. *Psychological Bulletin, 101,* 75–90.

Goffman, E. (1967). *Interaction ritual.* Newport Beach, CA: Westcliff.

Golin, S.,Terrell, T., & Johnson, B. (1977). Depression and the illusion of control. *Journal of Abnormal Psychology, 86,* 440–442.

Golin, S., Terrell, T., Weitz, J., & Drost, P. L. (1979), The illusion of control among depressed patients. *Journal of Abnormal Psychology, 88,* 454–457.

Gonzales, A., & Zimbardo, P. G. (1985, March). Time in perspective. *Psychology Today,* pp. 21–26.

Green, S. K., & Gross, A. E. (1979). Self-serving biases in implicit evaluations. *Personality and Social Psychology Bulletin, 5,* 214–217.

Greenberg, M. S., & Alloy, L. B. (1988). Depression versus anxiety: Differences in self and other schemata. In L. B. Alloy (Ed.), *Cognitive processes in depression.* New York: Guilford Press.

Greenwald, A. G. (1980). The totalitarian ego: Fabrication and revision of personal history. *American Psychologist, 35,* 603–618.

Greenwald, A. G., & Breckler, S. J. (1985). To whom is the self presented? In B. Schlenker (Ed.), *The self and social life* (pp. 126–145). New York: McGraw-Hill.

Haan, N. (1977). *Coping and defending.* New York: Academic Press.

Hall, J., & Taylor, S. E. (1976). When love is blind. *Human Relations, 29,* 751–761.

Harackiewicz, J. M., Sansone, C., & Manderlink, G. (1985). Competence, achievement orientation, and intrinsic motivation: A process analysis. *Journal of Personality and Social Psychology, 48,* 493–508.

Heider, F. (1958). *The psychology of interpersonal relations.* New York: Wiley.

Hendrick, I. (1942). Instinct and the ego during infancy. *Psychoanalytic Quarterly, 11,* 33–58.

Irwin, F. W., (1944). The realism of expectations. *Psychological Review, 51,* 120–126.

Irwin, F. W. (1953). Stated expectations as functions of probability and desirability of outcomes. *Journal of Personality, 21,* 329–335.

Jahoda, M. (1953). The meaning of psychological health. *Social Casework, 34,* 349.

Jahoda, M. (1958). *Current concepts of positive mental health.* New York: Basic Books.

Janoff-Bulman, R. (1979). Characterological versus behavioral self-blame: Inquiries into depression and rape. *Journal of Personality and Social psychology, 37,* 1798–1809.

Jourard, S. M., & Landsman, T. (1980). *Healthy personality: An approach from the viewpoint of humanistic psychology* (4th ed.). New York: Macmillan.

Kahneman, D., & Tversky, A. (1973). On the psychology of prediction. *Psychological Review, 80,* 237–251.

Kelley, H. H. (1967). Attribution theory in social psychology. In D. Levine (Ed.), *Nebraska Symposium on Motivation* (Vol. 15, pp. 192–240). Lincoln: University of Nebraska Press.

Kuiper, N. A. (1978). Depression and causal attributions for success and failure. *Journal of Personality and Social Psychology, 36,* 236–246.

Kuiper, N. A., & Derry, P. A. (1982). Depressed and nondepressed content self-reference in mild depression. *Journal of Personality, 50,* 67–79.

Kuiper, N. A., & MacDonald, M. R. (1982). Self and other perception in mild depressives. *Social Cognition, 1,* 233–239.

Kuiper, N. A., MacDonald, M. R, & Derry, P. A. (1983). Parameters of a depressive self-schema. In J. Suls & A. G. Greenwald (Eds.), *Psychological perspectives on the self* (Vol. 2, pp. 191–217). Hillsdale, NJ: Erlbaum.

Kuiper, N. A., Olinger, L. J., MacDonald, M. R., & Shaw, B. F. (1985). Self-schema processing of depressed and nondepressed content: The effects of vulnerability on depression. *Social Cognition, 3,* 77–93.

Langer, E. J. (1975). The illusion of control. *Journal of Personality and Social Psychology, 32,* 311–328.

Langer, E. J., & Roth, J. (1975). Heads I win, tails it's chance: The illusion of control as a function of the sequence of outcomes in a purely chance task. *Journal of Personality and Social Psychology, 32,* 951–955.

Larwood, L., & Whittaker, W. (1977). Managerial myopia: Self-serving biases in organizational planning. *Journal of Applied Psychology, 62,* 194–198.

Lazarus, R. S. (1983). The costs and benefits of denial. In S. Breznitz (Ed.), *Denial of stress* (pp. 1–30). New York: International Universities Press.

Lewicki, P. (1983). Self-image bias in person perception. *Journal of Personality and Social Psychology, 45,* 384–393.

Lewicki, P. (1984). Self-schema and social information processing. *Journal of Personality and Social Psychology, 47,* 1177–1190.

Lewinsohn, P. M., Mischel, W., Chaplin, W., & Barton, R. (1980). Social competence and depression: The role of illusory self-perceptions. *Journal of Abnormal Psychology, 89,* 203–212.

Lund, F. H. (1975). The psychology of belief: A study of its emotional and volitional determinants. *Journal of Abnormal and Social Psychology, 20,* 63–81.

Marks, G. (1984). Thinking one's abilities are unique and one's opinions are common. *Personality and Social Psychological Bulletin, 10,* 203–208.

Marks, R. W. (1951). The effect of probability, desirability, and "privilege" on the stated expectations of children. *Journal of Personality, 19*, 332–351.

Markus, H., & Nurius, P. (1986). Possible selves. *American Psychologist, 41*, 954–969.

Maslow, A. H. (1950). Self-actualizing people: A study of psychological health. *Personality*. Symposium No. 1, 11–34.

McGuire, W. (1960). A syllogistic analysis of cognitive relationships. In M. Rosenberg, C. Hovland, W. McGuire, R. Abelson, & J. Brehm (Eds.), *Attitude organization and change* (pp. 65–111). New Haven, CT: Yale University Press.

Menninger, K. A. (1930). What is a healthy mind? In N. A. Crawford & K. A. Menninger (Eds.), *The healthy-minded child*. New York: Coward-McCann.

Miller, D. T., & Ross, M (1975). Self-serving biases in attribution of causality: Fact or fiction? *Psychological Bulletin, 82*, 213–225.

Mirels, H. L. (1980). The avowal of responsibility for good and bad outcomes: The effects of generalized self-serving biases. *Personality and Social Psychology Bulletin, 6*, 299–306.

Nisbett, R. E., & Ross, L. (1980). *Human inference: Strategies and shortcomings of social judgment*. Englewood Cliffs, NJ: Prentice Hall.

Perloff, L. S., & Fetzer, B. K. (1986). Self–other judgments and perceived vulnerability of victimization. *Journal of Personality and Social Psychology, 50*, 502–510.

Pietromonaco, P. R., & Markus, H. (1985). The nature of negative thoughts in depression. *Journal of Personality and Social, 48*, 799–807.

Pruitt, D. G., &. Hoge, R. D. (1965). Strength of the relationship between the value of an event and its subjective probability as a function of method of measurement. *Journal of Experimental Psychology, 5*, 483–489.

Pyszczynski, T., Holt, K., &. Greenberg, J. (1987). Depression, self-focused attention, and expectancies for positive and negative future life events for self and others. *Journal of Personality and Social Psychology, 52*, 994–1001.

Rizley. R. (1978). Depression and distortion in the attribution of causality. *Journal of Abnormal Psychology, 87*, 32–48.

Robertson, L. S. (1977). Car crashes: Perceived vulnerability and willingness to pay for crash protection. *Journal of Community Health, 3*, 136–141.

Rosenberg, M. (1979). *Conceiving the self*. New York: Basic Books.

Ross, M., & Fletcher, G. J. O. (1985). Attribution and social perception. In G. Undzey & E. Aronson. (Eds.), *The handbook of social psychology* (3rd ed., pp. 73–122). Reading, MA: Addison-Wesley.

Ruehlman, L. S., West, S. G., & Pasahow, R. J. (1985). Depression and evaluative schemata. *Journal of Personality, 53*, 46–92.

Sackeim, H. A. (1983). Self-deception, self-esteem, and depression: The adaptive value of lying to oneself. In J. Masling (Ed.), *Empirical studies of psychoanalytical theories* (Vol. I, pp. 101–157). Hillsdale, NJ: Analytic Press.

Schlenker, B. R (1980). *Impression Management*. Monterey, CA: Brooks/Cole.

Schlenker, B. R., & Miller, R. S. (1977). Egocentrism in groups: Self-serving biases or logical information processing? *Journal of Personality and Social Psychology, 35*, 755–764.

Schneider, D. J., Hastorf, A. H., & Ellsworth, P. C. (1979). *Person perception*. Reading, MA: Addison-Wesley.

Schulz, D. (1977). *Growth psychology: Models of the healthy personality*. New York: Van Nostrand Reinhold.

Sears, D. O. (1983). The person-positivity bias. *Journal of Personality and Social Psychology, 44*, 233–250.

Shaver, K. G., & Drown, D. (1986). On causality, responsibility, and self-blame: A theoretical note. *Journal of Personality and Social Psychology, 4*, 697–702.

Sherman, S. J. (1980). On the self-erasing nature of errors of prediction. *Journal of Personality and Social Psychology, 39*, 111–121.

Shrauger, J. S., & Terbovic, M. L. (1976). Self-evaluation and assessments of performance by self and others. *Journal of Consulting and Clinical Psychology, 44*, 564–572.

Silverman, I. (1964). Self-esteem and differential responsiveness to success and failure. *Journal of Abnormal and Social Psychology, 69*, 115–119.

Stein, J. (Ed.). (1982) *The Random House dictionary of the English language* (unabridged ed.). New York: Random House.

Svenson, O. (1981). Are we all less risky and more skillful than our fellow drivers? *Acta Psychological, 47*, 143–148.

Tajfel, H., & Turner, J. C. (1986). The social identity theory of intergroup behavior. In S. Worchel & W. Austin (Eds.), *Psychology of intergroup relations* (pp. 7–24). Chicago: Nelson–Hall.

Taylor, S. E. (1983). Adjustment to threatening events: A theory of cognitive adaptation. *American psychologist, 38*, 1161–1173.

Taylor, S. E., & Koivumaki, J. H. (1976). The perception of self and others: Acquaintanceship; affect, and actor-observer differences. *Journal of Personality and Social Psychology, 33*, 403–408.

Taylor, S. E., Lichtman, R. R., & Wood, J. V. (1984). Attributions, beliefs about control, and adjustment to breast cancer. *Journal of Personality and Social Psychology, 46*, 489–502.

Tesser, A., & Moore, J. (1986). On the convergence of public and private aspects of self. In R. F. Baumeister (Ed.), *Public self and private life* (pp. 99–116). New York: Springer-Verlag.

Tetlock, P. E., & Manstead, A. S. R. (1985). Impression management versus intrapsychic explanations in social psychology: A useful dichotomy? *Psychological Review, 92*, 59–77.

Tiger, L. (1979). *Optimism: The biology of hope*. New York: Simon & Schuster.

Vallant, G. (1977). *Adaptation to life*. Boston: Little, Brown.

Watson, D., & Clark, L. A. (1984). Negative affectivity: The disposition to experience aversive emotional states. *Psychological Bulletin, 96*, 465–490.

Weinstein, N. D. (1980). Unrealistic optimism about future life events, *Journal of Personality and Social Psychology, 39*, 806–820.

White, R. W. (1959). Motivation reconsidered: The concept of competence. *Psychological Review, 66*, 297–335.

Zuckerman, M. (1979). Attribution of success and failure revisited, or: The motivational bias is alive and will in attribution theory. *Journal of Personality, 47*, 245–287.

NO ↵

C. Randall Colvin,
Jack Block, and David C. Funder

Overly Positive Self-Evaluations and Personality: Negative Implications for Mental Health

$\mathbf{T}$raditional conceptions of mental health have held that well-adjusted people perceive relatively accurately the impact and ramifications of their social behavior and possess generally valid information about the self. Jahoda (1958) described the mentally healthy person as someone "able to take in matters one wishes were different, without distorting them to fit these wishes" (p. 51). Allport (1937) also placed great importance on accurate self-knowledge, stating that

> an impartial and objective attitude toward oneself is held to be a primary virtue, basic to the development of all others. There is but a weak case for chronic self-deception with its crippling self-justifications and rationalizations that prevent adaptation and growth. And so it may be said that if any trait of personality is intrinsically desirable, it is the disposition and ability to see oneself in perspective (p. 422)

Despite the long influence of these and related writings, and their obvious accordance with common sense, the reality-based view of mental health recently has undergone serious challenge.

In a highly influential and provocative article, Taylor and Brown (1988) surveyed the then-current social psychological literature and concluded that mentally healthy individuals characteristically manifest three "pervasive, enduring, and systematic" (p. 194) illusions. These illusions are *unrealistically positive self-evaluations, exaggerated perceptions of control or mastery,* and *unrealistic optimism.* They educed this conclusion from studies purportedly demonstrating that depressed and low-self-esteem individuals exhibit more accurate perceptions than persons who are not depressed or who are high in self-esteem. They further argued that individuals who engage in such self-enhancing positive illusions are more disposed to be psychologically healthy. This radically different view of mental health has become widely cited and suddenly popular.

From *Journal of Personality and Social Psychology*, vol. 68, no. 6, 1995, pp. 1152–1162. Copyright © 1995 by American Psychological Association. Reprinted with permission.

Taylor and Brown's influential conclusion hinges on whether the studies they evaluate have used valid, even reasonable, criteria for self-enhancement. Three criteria have been used, prior to and subsequent to the publication of Taylor and Brown's review.

First, several studies reviewed by Taylor and Brown (1988), and other more recent studies, report that participants rate themselves more favorably and less negatively than generalized others (e.g., an unknown hypothetical average college student). These findings have been used to conclude that the perception most people have of themselves is unrealistic and overly positive (e.g., Alicke, 1985; Alloy & Ahrens, 1987; Brinthaupt, Moreland, & Levine, 1991; Brown, 1986; Pyzczynski, Holt, & Greenberg, 1987). Moreover, participants who like themselves and experience relatively high levels of positive affect have been reported to exhibit a greater discrepancy between self-ratings and ratings of a generalized other than participants who feel less positively about themselves and who manifest relatively high levels of negative affect (e.g., Agostinelli, Sherman, Presson, & Chassin, 1992; Brown, 1986). These data have been interpreted as indicating that whereas most people tend to self-enhance, high-self-esteem individuals are more likely to exhibit self-enhancing tendencies than are low-self-esteem individuals.

A second set of studies has demonstrated that when people are asked to rank themselves in comparison to "most other people" on broad personality characteristics or on general abilities, the majority of people rank themselves higher than most other people. Because logically all or most people cannot rank higher than the median rank, it has been concluded that people exaggerate their positive personal characteristics (Buunk & Van Yperen, 1991; Larwood & Whitaker; 1977; Pelham & Swann, 1989; Svenson, 1981; Weinstein, 1980).

A third set of studies has shown that people tend to recall more positive than negative information about the self (Crary, 1966; Kuiper & Derry, 1982; Kuiper & MacDonald, 1982; Kuiper, Olinger, MacDonald, & Shaw, 1985; Silverman, 1964). This finding is particularly pronounced for individuals who have high self-esteem or who experience relatively high levels of positive affect. Persons low in self-esteem or who are moderately dysphoric tend to recall a less imbalanced number of positive and negative characteristics. These results have been interpreted as indicating that well-functioning individuals exhibit distortions in memory and recall that serve to enhance their self-regard (e.g., Kuiper & Derry, 1982; Kuiper & MacDonald, 1982).

However, this evidence and these conclusions recently have undergone critical reevaluation (Colvin & Block, 1994). A key point of Colvin and Block's critique is that these several kinds of studies, just cited, are generally uninformative about the process, meaning, and effect of self-enhancement because they all lack a reasonable operationalization of self-enhancement. To evaluate whether a person accurately views him- or herself, a comparison of the individual's self-description with valid external criteria for that person is required (Colvin & Block, 1994; Cronbach & Meehl, 1955). This minimum standard generally has not been observed. As a result, prior studies investigating self-enhancement have been plagued by ambiguous results permitting alternative explanations.

For example, studies comparing participants' self-descriptions with their descriptions of generalized others are of obscure implication. In an unknown number of instances, when a participant describes him- or herself more favorably than an unknown and hypothetical average person, he or she will be accurate (i.e., some individuals are indeed better off than the average individual). A normative finding that, on average, individuals view themselves as better than average, does not separate the accurate individuals from the inaccurate, self-enhancing individuals. In other cases, the application of valid logic may be responsible for discrepancies between self and other descriptions. College students typically have been the kind of people asked to participate in these experiments. College students know themselves to be relatively intelligent, they also know that intelligence varies greatly across individuals, and therefore it is logical and valid for them to rate themselves as higher in intelligence than an unknown, average person.

There is a further problem with attributing self-enhancement bias to all people who rate themselves "better off than most." Ranking oneself relative to "most others" on a broadly construed dimension is inherently problematic. If people are asked to rank themselves relative to others on happiness, for example, Jeff might rank himself highly because of his ability as a baseball player, Jackie might rank herself highly because of her musical talents, and John might rank himself because of the money he has accumulated. Because these are important and defining characteristics of one's self-concept, they represent appropriate choices on which to compare the self with others. It is thus conceivable that a majority of people can be better off than most when the dimension to be rated is vaguely defined and people are given the latitude to rank themselves on self-selected, often idiosyncratic categories. It has been demonstrated that when a dimension is clearly and precisely defined, thereby limiting private interpretations, the better-off-than-most effect diminishes (Dunning, Meyerowitz, & Holzberg, 1989).

More generally, Robins and John (1997) point out that in fact most people can be better than average on any characteristic, as long as (a) the central tendency is taken to be indicated by the arithmetic mean rather than the median, and (b) even a small number of individuals are much below that mean (i.e., characteristic's distribution is negatively skewed). For example, if the comparison group includes a few pathologically depressed individuals, then nearly everybody else in that group could be above the mean in happiness.

In other studies, the finding of a higher ratio of positive to negative trait descriptors for well-adjusted people than for poorly adjusted people does not imply that mentally healthy individuals exhibit an unrealistic self-enhancement bias, neither does it imply undue self-deprecation on the part of less mentally healthy individuals. Rather, this finding is definitional or tautological: Mentally healthy people should have more positive things to say about themselves than should people who are poorly adjusted, think negatively of themselves, and are dysphoric (J. Block & Thomas, 1955; Gjerde, Block, & Block, 1988; Kendall, Howard, & Hays, 1989; Rosenberg, 1985). Therefore, it is not surprising that when individuals are asked to recall self-defining characteristics, mentally healthy people recall positive traits with greater ease and frequency than do people lacking in mental health (e.g., Kuiper & Derry, 1982; Kuiper & MacDonald, 1982).

An additional limitation of these various approaches to studying overly positive self-evaluations is that, typically, self-reports of personality are used to identify the characteristics of self-enhancing people. A frequent finding from this kind of research has been that people who self-enhance also describe themselves as being high in self-esteem. This result, although robust, is of doubtful import. By definition, individuals who exhibit self-enhancing tendencies should positively distort affect-laden self-evaluations. Therefore, all self-report measures that contain a self-evaluation component may well be positively biased and of questionable validity for individuals with self-enhancing tendencies (J. Block & Thomas, 1955; Shedler, Mayman, & Manis, 1993).

The preceding discussion suggests that the criteria for overly positive self-evaluation used in previous research have been problematic and therefore that the conclusion reached of a relation between positive illusions and mental health may be premature. To advance understanding further in this area will require more and different data from that reported to date....

References

Agostinelli, G., Sherman, S. J., Presson, C. C., & Chassin, L. (1992). Self-protection and self-enhancement biases in estimates of population prevalence. *Personality and Social Psychology Bulletin, 18*, 631–642.

Alicke, M. D. (1985). Global self-evaluation as determined by the desirability and controllability of trait adjectives. *Journal of Personality and Social Psychology, 49*, 1621–1630.

Alloy, L. B., & Ahrens, A. H. (1987). Depression and pessimism for the future: Biased use of statistically relevant information in predictions for self versus others. *Journal of Personality and Social Psychology, 41*, 366–378.

Allport, G. W. (1937). *Personality: A psychological interpretation.* New York: Holt, Rinehart & Winston.

Block, J., & Thomas, H. (1955). Is satisfaction with self a measure of adjustment? *Journal of Abnormal and Social Psychology, 51*, 254–259.

Brinthaupt, T. M., Moreland, R. L., & Levine, J. M. (1991). Sources of optimism among prospective group members. *Personality and Social Psychology Bulletin, 17*, 36–43.

Brown, J. D. (1986). Evaluations of self and others: Self-enhancement biases in social judgments. *Social Cognition, 4*, 353–376.

Buunk, B. P., & Van Yperen, N. W. (1991). Referential comparisons, relational comparisons, and exchange orientation: Their relation to marital satisfaction. *Personality and Social Psychology Bulletin, 17*, 709–717.

Colvin, C. R., & Block, J. (1994). Do positive illusions foster mental health? An examination of the Taylor and Brown formulation. *Psychological Bulletin, 116*, 3–20.

Crary, W. G. (1966). Reactions to incongruent self-experiences. *Journal of Consulting Psychology, 30*, 246–252.

Cronbach, L. J., & Meehl, P. E. (1955). Construct validity in psychological tests. *Psychological Bulletin, 52*, 281–302.

Dunning, D., Meyerowitz, J. A., & Holzberg, A. (1989). Ambiguity and self-evaluation: The role of idiosyncratic trait definitions in self-serving assessments of ability. *Journal of Personality and Social Psychology, 57,* 1082–1090.

Gjerde, P. F, Block, J., & Block, J. H. (1988). Depressive symptoms and personality during late adolescence: Gender differences in the externalization-internalization of symptom expression. *Journal of Abnormal Psychology, 86,* 475–486.

Jahoda, M. (1958). *Current concepts of positive mental health.* New York: Basic Books.

Kendall, P. C., Howard, B. L., & Hays, R. C. (1989). Self-referent speech and psychopathology: The balance of positive and negative thinking. *Cognitive Therapy and Research, 13,* 583–598.

Kuiper, N. A., & Derry, P. A. (1982). Depressed and nondepressed content self-reference in mild depression. *Journal of Personality, 50,* 67–79.

Kuiper, N. A., & MacDonald, M. R. (1982) Self and other perception in mild depressives. *Social Cognition, 1,* 233–239.

Kuiper, N. A., Olinger, L. J., MacDonald, M. R., & Shaw, B. F. (1985). Self-schema processing of depressed and nondepressed content: The effects of vulnerability on depression. *Social Cognition, 3,* 77–93.

Larwood, L., & Whitaker, W. (1977). Managerial myopia: Self-serving biases in organizational planning. *Journal of Applied Psychology, 62,* 194–198.

Pelham, B. W., & Swann, W. B., Jr. (1989). From self-conceptions to self-worth: On the sources and structure of global self-esteem. *Journal of Personality and Social Psychology, 57,* 672–680.

Pyszczynski, T., Holt, K., & Greenberg, J. (1987). Depression, self-focused attention, and expectancies for positive and negative future life events for self and others. *Journal of Personality and Social Psychology, 52,* 994–1001.

Robins, R. W., & John, O. P. (1997). The quest for self-insight: Theory and research on the accuracy of self-perception. In R. Hogan, J. Johnson, & S. Briggs (Eds.), *Handbook of personality psychology.* San Diego, CA: Academic Press.

Rosenberg, M. (1985). Self-concept and psychological well-being in adolescence. In R. Leahy (Ed.), *The development of the self* (pp. 205–246). New York: Academic Press.

Shedler, J., Mayman, M., & Manis, M. (1993). The illusion of mental health. *American Psychologist, 48,* 1117–1131.

Silverman, I. (1964). Self-esteem and differential responsiveness to success and failure. *Journal of Abnormal and Social Psychology, 69,* 115–119.

Svenson, O. (1981). Are we all less risky and more skillful than our fellow drivers? *Acta Psychologica, 47,* 143–148.

Taylor, S. E., & Brown, J. D. (1988). Illusion and well-being: A social psychological perspective on mental health. *Psychological Bulletin, 103,* 193–210.

Weinstein, N. D. (1980). Unrealistic optimism about future life events. *Journal of Personality and Social Psychology, 39,* 806–820.

CHALLENGE QUESTIONS

Do Positive Illusions
Promote Mental Health?

1. Do you have any positive illusions about yourself? Or do you think that your self-perceptions are largely accurate?
2. Could there be any downsides to positive illusions? Could there be any negative consequences to unrealistically positive self-images?
3. If positive illusions really do promote health, should psychologists encourage people to think positively of themselves, regardless of whether those thoughts are accurate? Or should psychologists encourage people to have accurate self-images, even if those self-images might be negative?

ISSUE 7

Can People Accurately Detect Lies?

YES: James Geary from "How to Spot a Liar," *Time Europe* (March 13, 2000)

NO: Bella M. DePaulo from "Spotting Lies: Can Humans Learn to Do Better?" *Current Directions in Psychological Science* (3, June 1994)

ISSUE SUMMARY

YES: Journalist James Geary discusses research that has examined the effectiveness of various lie detection schemes. Although the average person is not very adept at detecting lies, according to the research of psychologist Paul Ekman, people can be trained to detect the cues to deceit and become quite good at detecting lies.

NO: Social psychologist Bella M. DePaulo agrees that the average person is not a very reliable lie detector. However, DePaulo believes that improving people's lie detection skills is not as straightforward as it may seem.

For better or worse, lying is part of our everyday lives. This fact has been documented in studies of lying, which indicate the average person does lie on a daily basis (DePaulo, et al., *Journal of Personality and Social Psychology, 70,* 1996). Many lies that people tell are harmless and seem to make our lives more convenient. For example, when someone asks "How are you doing today?" you are likely to reply "good" or "fine" regardless of your true feelings. Imagine if you replied "Terrible!" You would likely have to take the time and effort necessary to explain, perhaps to a total stranger, exactly why you feel terrible. Telling a white lie allows you to avoid that circumstance. So many of the lies that people tell are adaptive and may make our lives easier.

However, not all of the lies that people tell are so innocuous. Lies sometimes have serious consequences, which are referred to as "high stakes" lies (Frank & Ekman, *Journal of Personality and Social Psychology, 72,* 1997). When a spouse lies about marital infidelity or when a politician lies about a campaign promise, the inability to detect the deception could have serious consequences. For this reason, it would be highly desirable for people to detect these kinds of lies. Unfortunately the average person is not a particularly good lie detector. In controlled studies of lie detection, most people detect deception at a level that is, at best, only slightly better than chance.

Since the average person cannot detect lies with great accuracy, there have been a variety of attempts to improve people's lie detection skills. The first reading will outline some of these lie detection schemes and discuss whether any of the approaches can indeed improve our ability to detect deceit. This selection will discuss the research of Paul Ekman, one of the leading authorities on lying and lie detection. Over the past 30 years, Ekman's research has indicated that deception can be reliably detected by examining the moment-to-moment changes in the facial expressions of others. According to Ekman, people can be trained to recognize these momentary facial expressions and more accurately detect the true feelings that people are experiencing. Another lie detection technique called voice stress analysis, which relies upon detecting deceit through tone of voice, will be addressed as well. In the second selection, Bella DePaulo paints a less optimistic picture than Ekman. She believes that attempts to train people to detect lies have usually been unsuccessful for several reasons. For example, she argues that different liars uses different tactics to conceal their deception. As a result, the ability to detect deceit in one person does not necessarily mean that deception can be reliably detected in a second person. This makes it quite difficult to develop a training program that will significantly increase people's ability to detect deception.

POINT

- Given the right training, most people can become more accurate lie detectors.
- Deceit can-reliably be detected by examining moment-to-moment changes in the facial expression of others.
- Computers that analyze tone of voice may also be useful in detecting deceit.

COUNTERPOINT

- Previous attempts to improve people's lie detection ability have not been particularly successful.
- Different types of liars use different tactics to conceal deceit.
- While tone of voice is a cue that may sometimes indicate deception, there are many instances in which tone of voice does not indicate deceit.

James Geary

 **YES**

How to Spot a Liar

You can tell a lie but you will give yourself away. Your heart will race. Your skin will sweat... I will know. I am the lie detector." Thus began each episode of Lie Detector, a strange cross between a relationship counseling session and an episode of the Jerry Springer Show that ran on British daytime television last year. Against a backdrop of flashing computer screens and eerie blue light, participants—usually feuding couples but sometimes warring neighbors or aggrieved business partners—sat on a couch and were quizzed by the program's host. A frequent topic of discussion was one guest's suspicion that his or her partner had been unfaithful. The person suspected of infidelity denied it, of course, and the object of the show was to find out—through cross-examination and computer analysis—whether that person was telling the truth.

However much we may abhor it, deception comes naturally to all living things. Birds do it by feigning injury to lead hungry predators away from nesting young. Spider crabs do it by disguise: adorning themselves with strips of kelp and other debris, they pretend to be something they are not—and so escape their enemies. Nature amply rewards successful deceivers by allowing them to survive long enough to mate and reproduce. So it may come as no surprise to learn that human beings—who, according to psychologist Gerald Jellison of the University of South California, are lied to about 200 times a day, roughly one untruth every five minutes—often deceive for exactly the same reasons: to save their own skins or to get something they can't get by other means.

But knowing how to catch deceit can be just as important a survival skill as knowing how to tell a lie and get away with it. A person able to spot falsehood quickly is unlikely to be swindled by an unscrupulous business associate or hoodwinked by a devious spouse. Luckily, nature provides more than enough clues to trap dissemblers in their own tangled webs—if you know where to look. By closely observing facial expressions, body language and tone of voice, practically anyone can recognize the telltale signs of lying. Researchers are even programming computers—like those used on Lie Detector—to get at the truth by analyzing the same physical cues available to the naked eye and ear. "With the proper training, many people can learn to reliably detect lies," says Paul Ekman, professor of psychology at the University of California, San Francisco, who has spent the past 15 years studying the secret art of deception.

In order to know what kind of lies work best, successful liars need to accurately assess other people's emotional states. Ekman's research shows that this same emotional intelligence is essential for good lie detectors, too. The emotional state to watch out for is stress, the conflict most liars feel between the truth and what they actually say and do.

Even high-tech lie detectors don't detect lies as such; they merely detect the physical cues of emotions, which may or may not correspond to what the person being tested is saying. Polygraphs, for instance, measure respiration, heart rate and skin conductivity, which tend to increase when people are nervous—as they usually are when lying. Nervous people typically perspire, and the salts contained in perspiration conduct electricity. That's why a sudden leap in skin conductivity indicates nervousness—about getting caught, perhaps?—which might, in turn, suggest that someone is being economical with the truth. On the other hand, it might also mean that the lights in the television studio are too hot—which is one reason polygraph tests are inadmissible in court. "Good lie detectors don't rely on a single sign," Ekman says, "but interpret clusters of verbal and nonverbal clues that suggest someone might be lying."

Those clues are written all over the face. Because the musculature of the face is directly connected to the areas of the brain that process emotion, the countenance can be a window to the soul. Neurological studies even suggest that genuine emotions travel different pathways through the brain than insincere ones. If a patient paralyzed by stroke on one side of the face, for example, is asked to smile deliberately, only the mobile side of the mouth is raised. But tell that same person a funny joke, and the patient breaks into a full and spontaneous smile. Very few people—most notably, actors and politicians—are able to consciously control all of their facial expressions. Lies can often be caught when the liar's true feelings briefly leak through the mask of deception. "We don't think before we feel," Ekman says. "Expressions tend to show up on the face before we're even conscious of experiencing an emotion."

One of the most difficult facial expressions to fake—or conceal, if it is genuinely felt—is sadness. When someone is truly sad, the forehead wrinkles with grief and the inner corners of the eyebrows are pulled up. Fewer than 15% of the people Ekman tested were able to produce this eyebrow movement voluntarily. By contrast, the lowering of the eyebrows associated with an angry scowl can be replicated at will by almost everybody. "If someone claims they are sad and the inner corners of their eyebrows don't go up," Ekman says, "the sadness is probably false."

The smile, on the other hand, is one of the easiest facial expressions to counterfeit. It takes just two muscles—the zygomaticus major muscles that extend from the cheekbones to the corners of the lips—to produce a grin. But there's a catch. A genuine smile affects not only the corners of the lips but also the orbicularis oculi, the muscle around the eye that produces the distinctive "crow's-feet" associated with people who laugh a lot. A counterfeit grin can be unmasked if the lip corners go up, the eyes crinkle but the inner corners of the eyebrows are not lowered, a movement controlled by the orbicularis oculi that is difficult to fake. The absence of lowered eyebrows is one reason why false smiles look so strained and stiff.

Ekman and his colleagues have classified all the muscle movements—ranging from the thin, taut lips of fury to the arched eyebrows of surprise—that underlie the complete repertoire of human facial expressions. In addition to the nervous tics and jitters that can give liars away, Ekman discovered that fibbers often allow the truth to slip through in brief, unguarded facial expressions. Lasting no more than a quarter of a second, these fleeting glimpses of a person's true emotional state—or "microexpressions," as Ekman calls them—are reliable guides to veracity.

In a series of tests, Ekman interviewed and videotaped a group of male American college students about their opinions regarding capital punishment. Some participants were instructed to tell the truth—whether they were for or against the death penalty—and some were instructed to lie. Liars who successfully fooled the interviewer received $50. Ekman then studied the tapes to map the microexpressions of mendacity.

One student, for example, appeared calm and reasonable as he listed the reasons why the death penalty was wrong. But every time he expressed these opinions, he swiftly, almost imperceptibly, shook his head. But the movement is so subtle and quick many people don't even see it until it's pointed out to them. While his words explained the arguments against capital punishment, the quick, involuntary shudder of his head was saying loud and clear, "No, I don't believe this!" He was, in fact, lying, having been for many years a firm supporter of the death penalty.

THE LYIN' KING

Four signs that may indicate deception

1. **AN EMBLEM** is a gesture with a specific meaning, like shrugging the shoulders to say, "I don't know." An emblem may be a sign of deceit if only part of the gesture is performed (a one-shoulder shrug, for example) or if it is performed in a concealed manner.
2. **MANIPULATORS** are repetitive touching motions like scratching the nose, tapping the foot or twisting the hair. They tend to increase when people are nervous, and may be an attempt to conceal incriminating facial expressions.
3. **AN ILLUSTRATOR** is a movement that emphasizes speech. Illustrators increase with emotion, so too few may indicate false feelings while too many may be an attempt to distract attention from signs of deceit on the face.
4. **MICROEXPRESSIONS** flash across the face in less than a quarter of a second—a frown, for example, that is quickly covered up by a grin. Though fleeting, they can reveal subtle clues about the true feelings that a person may wish to repress or conceal.

"With proper training, many people can learn to reliably detect lies."

"It would be an impossible world if no one lied."

James Geary/London
With reporting by Eric Silver/Jerusalem.

Another student also said that he was against the death penalty. But during the interview, he spoke very slowly, paused often, and rarely looked the interrogator in the eye, instead fixing his gaze on some vague point on the floor. Speech that is too slow (or too fast), frequent hesitations, lack of direct eye contact: these are all classic symptoms of lying. But this man was telling the truth. He paused and hesitated because he was shy. After all, even honest and normally composed individuals can become flustered if they believe others suspect them of lying. His lack of eye contact could be explained by the fact that he came from Asia, where an averted gaze is often a sign of deference and respect, not deception. This scenario highlights Ekman's admonition that before branding someone a liar, you must first know that person's normal behavior patterns and discount other explanations, such as cultural differences.

Ekman has used this tape to test hundreds of subjects. His conclusion: most people are lousy lie detectors, with few individuals able to spot duplicity more than 50% of the time. But Ekman's most recent study, published last year in Psychological Science, found that four groups of people did significantly better than chance: members of the U.S. Central Intelligence Agency, other U.S. federal law enforcement officers, a handful of Los Angeles County sheriffs and a group of clinical psychologists. Reassuringly, perhaps, the federal officials performed best, accurately detecting liars 73% of the time. What makes these groups so good at lie catching? According to Ekman, it's training, experience and motivation. The jobs—and in some cases, the lives—of everyone in these groups depend on their ability to pick up deceit.

Ekman has used his findings to assist law enforcement agents—including members of the U.S. Secret Service and Federal Bureau of Investigation, Britain's Scotland Yard and the Israeli police force—in criminal investigations and antiterrorist activities. He refuses to work with politicians. "It is unlikely that judging deception from demeanor alone will ever be admissible in court," Ekman says. "But the research shows that it's possible for some people to make highly accurate judgments about lying without any special aids, such as computers."

But for those who still prefer a bit of technological assistance, there's the Verdicator—a device that, according to its 27-year-old inventor Amir Liberman, enables anyone equipped with a personal computer and a phone or microphone to catch a liar. A person's tone of voice can be just as revealing as the expression on his face. A low tone, for example, can suggest a person is lying or is stressed, while a higher pitch can mean excitement. Liberman claims the Verdicator, a $2,500 piece of software produced by Integritek Technologies in Petah Tikvah near Tel Aviv, is between 85% and 95% accurate in determining whether the person on the other end of the line is lying, an accuracy rate better than that for traditional polygraphs. "Our software knows how to size you up," Liberman boasts.

The Verdicator delivers its results by analyzing voice fluctuations that are usually inaudible to the human ear. When a person is under stress, anxiety may cause muscle tension and reduce blood flow to the vocal cords, producing a distinctive pattern of sound waves. Liberman has catalogued these patterns and programmed the Verdicator to distinguish among tones that indicate excitement, cognitive stress—the difference between what you think and what you say—and outright deceit. Once linked to a communications device and computer, the Verdicator monitors the subtle vocal tremors of your conversational partner and displays an assessment of that person's veracity on the screen. "The system can tell how nervous you are," Liberman explains. "It builds a psychological profile of what you feel and compares it to patterns associated with deception." And the Verdicator has one great advantage over the polygraph: the suspect doesn't need to know he's being tested. To be accurate, though, the Verdicator must pick up changes—which might indicate deceit—in a person's normal voice.

During the Monica Lewinsky scandal, Liberman demonstrated the system on President Clinton's famous disclaimer, "I did not have sexual relations with that woman." After analyzing an audio tape of the statement 100 times, the Verdicator showed that Clinton "was telling the truth," Liberman says, "but he had very high levels of cognitive stress, or 'guilt knowledge.' He didn't have sexual relations, but he did have something else."

Integritek will not name the law enforcement agencies, banks or financial institutions that are using the Verdicator. But company president Naaman Boury says that last year more than 500 Verdicators were sold in North and South America, Australia, Asia and Europe. The Japanese firm Atlus is marketing a consumer version of the Verdicator in Asia. "We get the best results—close to 95% accuracy—in Japan," Liberman reports. "The Japanese feel very uncomfortable when lying. We get the poorest results—nearer 85% accuracy—in Russia, where people seldom seem to say what they really feel."

In moderation, lying is a normal—even necessary—part of life. "It would be an impossible world if no one lied," Ekman says. But by the same token, it would be an intolerable world if we could never tell when someone was lying. For those lies that are morally wrong and potentially harmful, would-be lie detectors can learn a lot from looking and listening very carefully. Cheating partners, snake oil salesmen and scheming politicians, beware! The truth is out there.

NO ⏎

Bella M. DePaulo

Spotting Lies: Can Humans Learn to Do Better?

Though cynicism may seem rampant, the empirical fact is that most people seem to believe most of what they hear most of the time. I have seen this repeatedly in the studies my colleagues and I have conducted on the detection of deception.[1] To determine whether people can separate truths from lies, we show them videotapes we have made of people we know to be lying or telling the truth. The topics of these lies and truths vary widely. For example, sometimes the people on the tape are talking about their feelings about other people they know; other times, the speakers are describing their opinions about controversial issues; in still other studies, they are talking to an artist about their preferences for various paintings, some of which are the artist's own work. When we show people ("judges") these tapes, we ask them to tell us, for each segment that they watch, whether they think the person on the tape (the "speaker") was lying or telling the truth. We also ask them to indicate, on rating scales, just how deceptive or truthful the speaker seemed to be. We might also ask them how they think the speaker really did feel and what impression the speaker was trying to convey about how he or she felt. For example, it might seem that the speaker was politely trying to give the impression that she liked the person she was describing, when in facts he detested that person.

Typically, the tapes that we play for our judges include equal numbers of truths and lies. Yet when judges watch or hear the tapes, they almost always think that many more of the messages are truths than lies. (One of the rare exceptions was a study in which the speakers on the tape were experienced salespersons pitching the kinds of products that they sell; in that study, the judges more often thought that the salespersons were lying.[2]) Similarly, judges typically believe that the speakers really do feel the way they are claiming to feel. When a speaker claims to like a painting, the judges are more inclined to believe that he or she really does like it than to infer that the kind words are a facade to cover genuine loathing.

Despite this compelling inclination to take what other people say at face value, judges are not totally blind to the differences between truths and lies. When we ask them to indicate just how deceptive or truthful the speakers seemed to be, judges reliably rate the lies as somewhat more deceptive than the truths. The ratings of both the lies and the truths are almost always on the truthful end of the scale; still, the lies seem to the judges to be a little less truthful than the truths.[3] When we study humans' ability to detect lies, it is this ability to distinguish truths from lies that we examine.

Would People Be Better Lie Detectors if They Were Less Trusting?

Carol Toris and I did a simple study to see whether people would be better lie detectors it they were forewarned of the possibility that another person might be lying to them.[4] Subjects played the role of interviewers and either were or were not forewarned that the applicants might lie to them. The forewarned interviewers did indeed become less trusting: They thought the applicants were generally more deceptive than did the interviewers whose suspicions had not been aroused. But the suspicious interviewers did not become any more accurate at distinguishing liars from truth tellers. That is,they did not rate the applicants who really were lying as any more deceptive than the ones who were telling the truth.

Robert Rosenthal and I have seen the same pattern in our studies of sex differences in detecting deceit.[5] In the way that they perceive the liars and the truth tellers on our videotapes, men are generally less trusting than women. For example, when judges watch subjects who are talking to an art student about paintings, the male judges are more likely than female judges to think that the subjects are exaggerating their liking for the paintings; the women, in contrast,are more inclined to believe that the liking expressed by the subjects is genuine. Again, though, men and women do not differ in their abilities to distinguish liars from truthtellers, that is, to see the liars as relatively less than the truth tellers.

Would People Be Better Lie Detectors if They Had More Experience at It?

To distinguish truths from lies may require some knowledge or sensitivity about the ways that lies differ from truths. Perhaps this sort of understanding comes with endless practice at trying to detect deceit. Roger Pfeifer and I studied the lie detection skills of federal law enforcement officers who had worked for years at jobs that routinely involved attempts to detect deceit.[6] These officers and undergraduate students who had no special experience or training at detecting deceit both listened to the same audiotapes of students who were lying or telling the truth about their opinions about controversial issues. Across this test of 32 lies and 32 truths, the officers were no more accurate than the students at discriminating truths from lies—they only thought they were. That is, the officers were more confident than the students, and their confidence increased over the course of the test, although their accuracy did not. A study of experienced customs inspectors told the same tale: They were no better than lay persons at discerning which potential "smugglers" to search in a mock customs inspection conducted at an airport.[7] Similarly, in studies of special groups of people who should be especially skilled lie detectors—members of the U.S. Secret Service, federal polygraphers, judges, police, psychiatrists, and special interest groups (e.g., business people and lawyers)—as well as students, Paul Ekman and Maureen O'Sullivan have found generally unimpressive levels of accuracy at detecting deceit.[8] Of those groups, only the Secret Service did particularly well.

Another kind of experience that intuitively might seem to predict skill at knowing when someone is lying is the kind that comes from getting to know someone over the course of a deepening relationship. Should not dating partners, spouses, and close friends be much more perceptive than strangers at spotting each other's lies? Once again, research has shown that experience is no guarantee of sensitivity to deceit. Compared with strangers, relational partners are more trusting of each other's truthfulness and more certain that their impressions of each other's truthfulness or deceptiveness are correct. But unless that trust severed somehow, they are ordinarily not more accurate at detecting each other's deceit.[9]

Perhaps there is still another way in which experience might predict skill at detecting deception. Maybe any special skills that people have at detecting deceit are specific to the kinds of lies they are most experienced at hearing—the "I've heard that one before" phenomenon. My colleagues and I already knew from prior work in our lab that people lie differently to attractive people than to unattractive people. Interestingly, they lie more transparently to the former. We wanted to know whether the lies told to attractive people are especially transparent to judges who are themselves attractive. To test this idea, we asked judges who were themselves either attractive or unattractive to watch tapes of speakers who were lying and telling the truth to attactive and unattractive listeners.[10] The judges, however, could see only the speakers; they did not even know that the listeners varied systematically in attractiveness. Further, the speakers all lied and told the truth about the same topics—their opinions on controversial issues. These were not the stereotypical "gee, what beautiful eyes you have" kinds of lies. We found, once again, that the lies told to attractive listeners were easier to detect than were the lies told to unattractive listeners. More important, the lies told to attractive listerners were especially obvious to the judges who were themselves attractive. The unattractive judges, in contrast, did relatively better at detecting the lies told to the unattractive listeners.

There is other evidence, too, that skill at detecting lies may be specific to particular kinds of lies. For example, we have found that the ability to detect lies when liars are trying to hide their fond feelings is not related to the ability to detect lies when liars are trying to conceal ill will. We have also found that skill detecting women's lies is unrelated to skill at detecting men's lies.[11] There is another interesting bit of evidence or specificity, which comes from a study in which Miron Zuckerman and his colleagues tried to train judges to be more accurate detectors of deceit.[12] The training procedure was very straightforward. Judges watched a segment in which a speaker was lying or telling the truth, and then they recorded their judgment as to whether the speaker was lying. Next, they were told whether the segment was in fact a lie or a truth. This procedure was repeated for several lies and truths told by the same speaker. Judges who were "trained" in this way did indeed become better at detecting deception, but only when watching the speaker they were trained on. Their new and improved deception detection skills did not generalize different liars.

There is even evidence for specificity at a cultural level. Charles Bond and his colleagues have shown that both Americans and Jordanians can distinguish lies from truths when judging members of their own culture; however, they cannot differentiate each other's truths and lies.[13]

How Do Lies Differ from Truths?

Intuitively, it may seem that the best way to train people to detect deceit is to instruct them about the kinds of behaviors that really do distinguish truths from lies and to give them practice at recognizing such behaviors. This approach assumes that there are known differences between truths and lies, and in fact there are.[1]

Meta-analyses of the many studies of cues to deception reported in the literature indicate that when people are lying, they blink more, have more dilated pupils, and show more *adaptors* (self-manipulating gestures, such as rubbing or scratching than they do when they are telling the truth. They also give shorter responses that are more negative, more irrelevant, and more generalized. They speak in a more distancing way (as if they do not really want to commit themselves to what they are saying), and they speak in a higher pitch. Though people who are about to tell a lie take more time to plan what they are about to say than do people who are about to tell the truth, the resulting statements tend to be more internally discrepant and more marred by hesitations, repetitions, grammatical errors, slips of the tongue, and other disfluencies. The lies seem rehearsed and lacking in spontaneity.[14]

There are, then, some important behavioral cues to deception. But for a variety of reasons, I am not optimistic about the prospects of teaching these cues directly, despite the fact that some limited successes have been reported. First, although these findings were obtained across a variety of studios, they are qualified in important ways. For example, it is possible to divide the studies based on whether the liars were more or less motivated to get away with their lies. When this is done, it becomes apparent that the cues to deception differ. When people are more highly motivated to get away with their lies (compared with when they do not care as much), they shift their postures less, move their heads less, show fewer adaptors, gaze less, and even blink less when they are lying than when they are telling the truth. Their answers are also shorter and spoken more slowly. The overall impression they seem to convey is one of inhibition and rigidity, as if they are trying too hard to control their behavior and thereby overcontrolling it. (It may be this dampening of expressiveness that accounts for another counterintuitive finding documented repeatedly in my lab—that is, that people who are most motivated to get away with their lies are ironically, least likely to be successful at doing so when other people can see or hear any of their nonverbal cues.) Degree of liars' motivation is just one of the factors that will qualify conclusions about cues to deceit. There will be many others. For example, cues to deceit should vary with emotional state, The liar who feels guilty about a grave offense, for example, will probably lie in different ways than with a friend bubbling over with glee in an attempt to conceal a surprise birthday celebration.

Second, all these cues are associated with deceit only probabilistically. There is no one cue that always indicates that a person is lying. And each of the cues that is associated with deceit is also associated with other psychological states and conditions. For example, people speak in a higher pitch not only when they are lying but also when they are talking to children.

Third, as suggested by the training study in which improvement did not generalize to different liars, there are important individual differences in the ways that people lie. When Machiavellian people are rightly accused of lying, for example, they look their accusers in the eye while denying they have lied, It is the "low-Mach" types who conform to the cultural stereotype about lying and instead look away. Further, to determine when a person is lying, it is important to understand that person's usual ways of behaving. For instance, although halting and disfluent speech can be a sign of deceit, there are people who characteristically speak haltingly and disfluently; for them, verbal clutter is unlikely to indicate deceit unless it is even more marked than usual. Moreover, some people may be so skilled at lying that it is virtually impossible for anyone to distinguish their lies from their truths. In the study of experienced salespersons, for example, the same kinds of judges (introductory psychology students) who could detect differences between the truths and lies of inexperienced liars could see no differences at all between the truths and lies told by experienced salespersons.[2] Even when the judges were given a hint that improved their lie detection success when they were observing inexperienced liars (namely, to pay special attention to tone or voice), they still could not differentiate the salespersons' lies and truths.

Does this mean that it is hopeless to try to refine people's sensitivity to the differences between truths and lies? Perhaps not. I think people know more about deception than it appears when experimenters ask them directly whether they think someone is lying. Sometimes people who cannot distinguish truths from lies by their ratings of deceptiveness can make a distinction by their ratings of some other attribute, such as ambivalence. Also, when people talk out loud as they try to decide whether someone is lying or not, they sound less confident when the message they are considering is a lie than when it is a truth; further, they are more likely to mention the possibility that the message is a lie when it really is.[15] Interviewers sometimes behave differently toward liars than toward truth tellers; for example, they might ask liars more questions that sound suspicious.[16] I think, then, that people have implicit knowledge about deception that they do not quite know how to access. Just how they can learn to access it is the question my students and I are currently pursuing.

Notes

1. B.M. DePaulo, J.I. Stone, and G.D. Lassiter, Deceiving and detecting deceit, in *The Self and Social Life*, B.R. Schlenker, Ed. (McGraw-Hill, New York, 1985).
2. P.J. DePaulo and B.M. DePaulo, Can attempted deception by salespersons and customers be detected through nonverbal behavior cues? *Journal of Applied Social Psychology*, 19, 1552–1557 (1989).
3. In studies in which judges simply indicate whether they think the speaker was lying or telling the truth, and lies and truths occur equally often, accuracy rarely exceeds 60%. A chance level of accuracy would be 50% in those studies.
4. C. Toris and B.M. DePaulo, Effects of actual deception and suspiciousness of deception on interpersonal perceptions, *Journal of Personality and Social Psychology, 47*, 1063–1073 (1984).
5. R. Rosenthal and B.M. DePaulo, Sex differences in evesdropping on nonverbal cues, *Journal of Personality and Social Psychology, 37*, 273–285 (1979).
6. B.M. DePaulo, and R.L. Pfeifer, On-the-job experience and skill at detecting deception, *Journal of Applied Social Psychology, 16*, 249–267 (1986).
7. R.E. Kraut and D. Poe, Behavioral roots of person perception: The deception judgments of customs inspectors and laypersons, *Journal of Personality and Social Psychology, 39*, 784–798 (1980).
8. P. Ekman and M. O'Sullivan, Who can catch a liar? *American Psychologist, 46*, 913–920 (1991).
9. S.A. McCornack and T.R. Levine, When lovers become leery: The relationship between suspiciousness and accuracy in detecting deception, *Communication Monographs, 57*, 219–230 (1990).
10. B.M. DePaulo, J. Tang, and J.I. Stone, Physical attractiveness and skill at detecting deception, *Personality and Social Psychology Bulletin, 13*, 177–187 (1987).
11. B.M. DePaulo, and R. Rosenthal, Telling lies, *Journal of Personality and Social Psychology, 37*, 1713–1722 (1979).
12. M. Zuckerman, R. Koestner, and A.O. Alton, Learning to detect deception, *Journal of Personality and Social Psychology, 46*, 519–528 (1984).
13. C.F. Bond Jr., A. Omar, A. Mahmoud, and R.N. Bonser, Lie detection across cultures, *Journal of Nonverbal Behavior, 14*, 189–204 (1990).
14. Other behavioral cues to deception have also been documented, but are based on fewer studies. For example, Ekman and his colleagues showed that nurses who were pretending to watch a pleasant film when the film was actually very gory smiled in different ways than the nurses who really were watching a pleasant film and telling the truth about it. The lying nurses were less likely to show smiles of genuine enjoyment ("Duchenne" smiles) and more likely to "masking" smiles in which traces of their negative feelings were discernible. These data were reported in P. Ekman, W.V. Friesen, and M. O'Sullivan, Smiles while lying, *Journal of Personality and Social Psychology, 54*, 414–420 (1988).
15. K. Hurd and P. Noller, Decoding deception: A look at the process, *Journal of Nonverbal Behavior, 12*, 217–233 (1988).
16. D.B. Buller, K.D. Strzyzewski, and J. Comstock, Interpersonal deception: Deceivers' reactions to receivers' suspicions and probing, *Communication Monographs, 58*, 1–24 (1991).

CHALLENGE QUESTIONS

Can People Accurately Detect Lies?

1. Do you think that you are a good lie detector? What strategies do you use to detect deception? How do you know whether these strategies actually work?
2. What strategies do you use when you are trying to deceive someone? Do you think that the lie detection techniques proposed by Ekman would successfully detect your deception?
3. Imagine if everyone were a perfect lie detector and could always detect deception. How would this change the nature of our everyday social interactions?

ISSUE 8

Are Repressed Memories Real?

YES: Richard P. Kluft, from "The Argument for the Reality of Delayed Recall of Trauma," *Trauma and Memory: Clinical and Legal Controversies* (Oxford University Press, 1997)

NO: Elizabeth F. Loftus, from "Creating False Memories," *Scientific American* (*277*, September 1997)

ISSUE SUMMARY

YES: Psychiatrist Richard Kluft believes that repressed and recovered memories are real, and often reflect real instances of trauma and abuse.

NO: Cognitive psychologist Elizabeth Loftus argues that false memories can be created with surprising ease. As a result many repressed and recovered memories many not reflect real traumatic or abusive events.

Traditionally, there has been a significant exchange of ideas among the different areas of psychology such as clinical, cognitive, and social psychology. Insights generated by cognitive psychologists have inspired important social psychological research and vice versa. Similarly, research in both cognitive and social psychology has important implications for clinical psychologists. For example, social psychologists have extensively studied the process of attribution—the way we explain the behavior of others and ourselves. Using the attribution research, clinical psychologists have attempted to understand how attributions may help explain the nature of depression and have linked certain types of attributions with depression. Thus, the results of social psychological research have proven useful for understanding a serious psychological disorder.

The current readings will address another area in which there has been an exchange among the different areas of psychology. Many cognitive psychologists, as well as some social and personality psychologists, study memory. How accurate is our memory? How well do we remember things that have happened to us? Elizabeth Loftus is a cognitive psychologist who was spent decades studying the nature of human memory. Some of her research has examined false memories. In the second reading, Loftus will describe her research that indicates false memories can be created with alarming ease. This work also has a strong social psychological flavor because these memories and false memories usually have a social component to them—they often are memories that involve other people. The most controversial aspect of Loftus' research deals with the debate surrounding repressed memories. Repressed memories are those events that were once forgotten but are subsequently remembered (i.e., recovered), often during the process of therapy. Based on the results of her research, Loftus has suggested that many of these memories are false. Such a finding would have dire importance because the content of repressed memories are often disturbing. They often involve recollections of sexual abuse, and criminal allegations have arisen as a result of the recovery of repressed memories.

In the first selection, psychiatrist Richard Kluft argues that these recovered memories are real. According to Kluft, people repress memories that are particularly distressing in order to shield themselves from the stress of these traumatic events. In support of his case, he cites several confirmed instances in which individuals have repressed their memory of some disturbing event. He also argues that studies conducted by Loftus and others, which seem to suggest that false memories are easily created, do not convincingly demonstrate that recovered memories are false. As a result, we should take memories of abuse that are repressed, and subsequently recovered, very seriously.

POINT

- Experimental research clearly demonstrates that false memories can be easily created.
- The results of the experimental research strongly imply that actual cases of repressed memories, which are subsequently recovered through psychotherapy, may actually be false.
- Many allegations of criminal abuse that may have arisen based on recovered memories are likely to be untrue.

COUNTERPOINT

- This research may not always be relevant to real cases of recovered memories
- Recovered memories are usually real.
- Many allegations of abuse are true.

Richard P. Kluft ➡ **YES**

The Argument for the Reality of Delayed Recall of Trauma

In any debate over the reality of recovered memory, it is useful to clarify the grounds of the debate, that is, to specify the issue that is being debated. If arguments are being proposed to the effect that there is no such thing as recovered memory, so that any apparently recovered memory can be discounted a priori, the premise of the debate can be formulated: resolved, that there is no demonstrable instance in which accurate, once unavailable memories have been recovered. I have avoided the use of the terms *recovered memory* and *repressed memory* in the resolution itself because these terms not only have become politicized, but the former term has no correlation to traditional clinical literature, and the latter represents an overgeneralized use of the term *repression*, which is only one of the processes by which the defensive exclusion of autobiographical experience from available and routinely retrievable memory may occur.

If the affirmative case is proven, then there is no such thing as a recovered memory. Should the negative prevail, such a phenomenon exists. The debate concerns whether there are demonstrable instances of the recovery of repressed, dissociated, or otherwise unavailable memory. Circumspect authorities would observe that since it is impossible to prove a negative, the debate can only be won by the affirmative side's discounting of any and all evidence that repressed and recovered memories exist. This is why vigorous attacks have been launched against virtually every article that appears to document this phenomenon, and efforts have been made to overextend implications that memory not only can be but will be distorted by various forms of suggestion and influence. Another consideration in this debate is that the affirmative side must make its case by advancing falsifiable arguments. Opinions cannot be stated as if they were facts. All recovered memories must be demonstrated to be false by objective data, and by unimpeachable corroborations of their falseness, not simply by allegations or statements of belief. Pope[1] has explored this dilemma very thoughtfully. That is, advancing lines of reasoning that cannot be tested, but permit the infinite, defensive rationalization of one's point of view from a lofty retreat remote from all threat of disconfirmation, falls short of scientific acceptability....

From Richard P. Kluft, THE ARGUMENT FOR THE REALITY OF DELAYED RECALL OF TRAUMA AND MEMORY, in Paul S. Appelbaum, Lisa A. Uyehara, and Mark R. Elin, eds., Trauma and Memory: Clinical and Legal Controversies (Oxford University Press, 1997).

Clinical Experiences Supporting the Recovery of Long-Unavailable Memories

For many years, in addition to conducting a psychiatric practice in Philadelphia, I had the privilege of treating patients in a small city surrounded by farmlands and semirural areas. During that period, that city's population base was stable, with relatively little mobility. For most of that time the area was underserved by mental health professionals and there was relatively little therapist-switching. I had the opportunity to observe the life cycles of many families over a period of 18 years. It was predominantly in this setting that I followed 210 patients with dissociative identity disorder (DID; formerly multiple personality disorder [MPD]) and was able to sketch out the natural history of this disorder.[2] I came to know many patients and their families in a manner that I rarely experienced in my urban practice, and I remained in contact with them over a prolonged period of time. Often information that was unavailable during my patients' treatments came my way a decade later. In this setting I learned that many of the allegations of abuse that were made by my patients (whether always in conscious awareness or recovered in therapy) were in fact true, even allegations that were vehemently denied by their families at the time when I first treated the patients. I also learned that some of the accusations were lies, and that some were based on misperceptions or distorted recall. In 1984 I cautioned that the therapist "must remain aware ... that material influenced by intrusive inquiry or iatrogenic dissociation may be subject to distortion. In a given patient, one may find episodes of photographic recall, confabulation, screen phenomena, confusion between dreams or fantasies and reality, irregular recollection, and willful misrepresentation. One awaits a goodness of fit among several forms of data, and often must be satisfied to remain uncertain."[3] I did not encounter instances in which false accusations were triggered in therapy, but I must acknowledge that the possibility exists.

Here I will focus on several examples of confirmed recovered memories. My files contain hundreds of such confirmations.

In the mid-1970s I was treating a female colleague who seemed unable to sort out her relationships with men. A bright and attractive woman, she had distanced herself from her alcoholic family only after winning her own battles with addiction. As her psychoanalytically oriented psychotherapy proceeded, which was supported by her participation in Alcoholics Anonymous, we both appreciated that she became unable to express herself whenever transference feelings toward me came under exploration. After several months of mutual confusion, we decided to use hypnosis to explore her block. She was an excellent hypnotic subject. While in trance she recovered memories of her first therapy, which was conducted by an addiction counselor. He had encouraged the development of an extremely positive transference and then exploited it to seduce her. Once out of trance she was mortified, but she steeled herself to report that, although she had completely forgotten that particular experience, she had reenacted the same pattern with the leader of a therapy group. She had not felt comfortable enough to admit her growing fears that the same might happen with me. Now her shutting down whenever she began to experience feelings toward me made sense to both of us. Her therapy continued to a successful conclusion, and her relationships with men became satisfactory to her.

A decade later, her former alcoholism counselor came to me for psychotherapy. After several sessions, he revealed what he considered the two worst things he had ever done. While an active alcoholic, he had molested his own daughter. When he became a recovering alcoholic and respected therapist, he had become infatuated with a beautiful young patient and had manipulated her idealization of him to seduce her. "You know her. You treated her. You must think I'm a real bastard." He spoke briefly about his relationship with my other patient, confirming her hypnotically retrieved account in detail. The next day, he left me a message which said that he was too embarrassed to return. He transferred to a therapist who had never known his victim.

In another case, two sisters, who were long estranged, were reunited after twenty years as they attended their dying mother. One sister, who was my patient, had always been aware of sexual abuse by her father and had recovered memories of abuse by a baby-sitter in the course of her therapy. She asked her sister if the sister had any knowledge of such an incident. Her sister not only recalled the event but supplied details that confirmed additional circumstances which my patient had recovered in the course of her treatment but which she had not yet shared with her sister. Each confirmed the other's recollection of father-daughter incest, with reference to several specific instances. Furthermore, their dying mother apologized to my patient for her harsh treatment of her, which my patient had recovered in psychotherapy but had doubted to be true.

Another example of confirmed recovered memories concerns a man who had served in Vietnam as a Marine who maintained in therapy that he and his unit had seen no combat over a particular period. However, also in therapy, he recovered memories of an attack on his base and of his killing several armed Vietnamese attackers. After recovering these memories, he disbelieved them. At a Washington, D.C. commemoration for Vietnam veterans he became irritated when a wartime buddy reminded him of his role in this fire fight. He told the friend that he must be wrong, that he had never fired his weapon in combat. The man was shocked, and shook his head, uncomprehending. "You were a ... hero, man!" The patient's military records reveal that his unit had indeed been in combat and had maintained a defensive perimeter around a supply base that was frequently under attack throughout the period during which the patient maintained that his unit had seen no action. For reasons unrelated to this account, this man had joined the Marines, hoping to be killed. He had repeatedly volunteered for hazardous duty in the effort to bring about his own death. Although he eagerly placed himself at risk, he was passionately opposed to taking another human life. Ultimately, he was able to confront the fact that despite his beliefs and apparent wish to die, when faced with a genuine life-and-death decision, he had methodically and efficiently dispatched several enemy combatants at close range, an act that was witnessed by his buddy. His repugnance and conflict over this action apparently drove it from his memory. It took months to work through his guilt over his having taken the lives of the Vietcong attackers.

A woman with multiple personality disorder underwent hypnosis to access personalities and to explore missing periods of time in her life. During her assessment and treatment, she had denied that she had ever been mistreated by a previous therapist. Fourteen months later, a personality that was contacted through hypnosis indicated that the patient's prior psychiatrist had exploited her sexually. Against my advice, she revealed this information to her prior psychiatrist. When he learned that his former patient was revealing his boundary violations, he telephoned me. He asked me to treat him, he admitted his indiscretions, and he insisted that since he was now my patient, I could not reveal what I knew, due to my duty of confidentiality! He was not pleased when I reminded him that I had never agreed to treat him, and that I was not disposed to accept the constraints he tried to impose. This case was one of several in which alleged therapist abuses, which were often not in patients' conscious awareness at the beginning of the patients' therapy with the author, were later confirmed.[4,5]

A married woman in her late 20s who had been adopted at birth came for a consultation to discuss the pluses and minuses of tracing her birth parents. Now the mother of two toddlers, she was increasingly curious about her own origins. After she located her birth parents, she returned to discuss her reactions. During this interview she spoke at length about the mental illness of her adoptive mother, who ultimately had been institutionalized as a paranoid schizophrenic. While discussing her adoptive mother's suspiciousness and unusual behavior (such as shooting a rifle at aircraft flying over the family farm), she dissociated into an alter personality and began to talk about a psychotic ritual of her mother's, a practice that was repeated over and over again. In it, her mother and she undressed. Her mother made her lie under a blanket on her abdomen and crawl out between her legs to be "born." Then her mother would express delight at her daughter's birth. When the patient switched back to her previous personality, she was amnestic for the above revelations. However, within minutes, she had a flashback of bizarre enematization experiences at her mother's hands.

She decided to enter treatment to explore these phenomena and to better understand herself. Much abuse material emerged under hypnosis. After the third hypnotic session the patient was sure that the recollections were inaccurate, but she appreciated that her long-standing depression was fading. We discussed how to approach the resolution of her uncertainty. Her adoptive parents were deceased. They had raised her on an isolated farm in a wooded rural area with no close neighbors. No close relatives of her parents were available as resources. I asked her to bring in any school and medical records, and any family materials or photo albums in her possession for us to review. I really had no hopes that anything would emerge, but wanted to leave no stone unturned. The next day she called me in tears. Not only had she found albums, she had found her mother's diaries, which described her mother's "experiments on the girl." They included detailed accounts of every abuse the patient had shared with me. Unable to tolerate having this material in her home, she presented me with a box of her mother's diaries and with yearly school pictures of herself, on the backs of which were written her mother's comments and planned experiments (ie., abuses). When I asked her what she thought I should do with these materials, she paused thoughtfully and replied: "Someday you may find people don't believe child abuse happens, and that people can forget their abuse. If you ever need to prove it happens, you have this box." That conversation occurred in 1978. Upon an 18-year follow-up, she is integrated, symptom-free, and well. Several years after the conclusion of her therapy she went to graduate school in psychology. She currently is a practicing mental health professional....

Perspectives on Discrediting the Possible Recovery of Repressed Memory

Limitations of space preclude the possibility of my making a detailed critique of the arguments against the possibility of the recovery of repressed or otherwise unavailable memory. However, I will comment briefly on a small number of the issues that have been raised in that connection.

Often the argument is made that there are no data to sustain the notion of repression, so that any material alleged to have been repressed and then recovered is a priori suspect. Concepts such as repression and the unconscious mind have proven very elusive subjects of study in the experimental setting. Many laboratory models that have been advanced are far from convincing as paradigms.

The work of Holmes[6] is frequently cited in arguments opposing the existence of repression. It is of historical note that this work appears in an important book[7] containing 18 contributions, 17 of which come to different conclusions than that of Holmes. In this publication, Holmes demonstrates that several experimental constructs of repression were subject to plausible alternative explanations. Unfortunately, he uses motivated skepticism[8] adroitly. His dismissal of the possible relevance of criticism of his paradigms and his disregard of anecdotal clinical information is glib and cavalier.

In his 1970 study he tested the hypothesis that the recall of experiences is determined by the intensity of affect associated with the experiences at the time of recall; that the intensity of the affect associated with given experiences declines over time; and that the affect associated with displeasure will decline more rapidly than that associated with pleasant experiences. He had college students keep a diary of their pleasant and unpleasant experiences for a week. They were to score each experience for pleasantness and unpleasantness on a nine-point scale. A week later they were asked unexpectedly to write down the experiences from their diary cards and to score them again. The results indicated that unpleasant experiences showed greater declines than did pleasant ones and were less likely to be recalled. Holmes concluded that recall of unpleasant experiences was due to reduced affective intensity rather than to repression. He speculated that intensity was reduced because unpleasant experiences, such as failing a French test, were found not to matter that much, or remediative actions could alter the nature of the experience. He also proposed that, with further thought, the attitudes toward the events might become more positive, and therefore the intensity of the negativity would be reduced.

I would like to raise the possibility that the nature of the phenomena that Holmes studied is somewhat different from the materials encountered by clinicians working with traumatized populations. An incestuous experience or a gang-rape might be more traumatic than failing a French test. I do not quarrel with Dr. Holmes' experiment per se, but I do think that trauma-related problems of memory may be managed in a different manner and that this different manner may involve repression and dissociation. I do not think his experimental universe was sufficiently diverse to support his conclusions. Although I consider Holmes's work thought-provoking and ingenious, I seriously doubt that his arguments against the possibility of the recovery of memories[9] deal with the phenomena in question. When we turn to the famous lost-in-the-mall scenario ... of Elizabeth Loftus, who is often regarded as a very influential participant in the debate over recovered memory, we encounter another family of difficulties. In her study, 5 young subjects, "all friends and relatives of our research group"[10, 11] were taken through a reflection on early life experiences, most of which were accurate, but one of which—the experimentally suggested one—was not. The subjects were led by siblings and others to believe that they had been lost in a mall, when this had not occurred. Not only was it possible to cause the subjects to report this, but they often confabulated additional details as their stories took on lives of their own. On this basis she argued that it is possible for therapists to implant false memories that will be elaborated further and regarded as credible.[10,11]

I wonder about the generalizability of this experiment, and am troubled by its ethics. Young children were exposed to deliberately mendacious behavior by their siblings and concerned others, and were then told they were duped. I question whether the possible deleterious long-term effects on the relationship of those involved is acceptable. I wonder about the appropriateness of the strategy of teaching children to become involved in systematic deception. I also wonder about the message conveyed about authority figures and the nature of truth that is given to the young subjects. Were I on a human subjects review committee, I would not have passed on this one. When Dr. Loftus has been asked about this, she dismisses such concerns by stating there have been no adverse effects. She offers as proof that when the children understood what had occurred, some of her own subjects took to doing similar deceptions with their friends.[11] To me this is chilling. Perhaps these subjects are only engaging in a benign attempt to achieve mastery, but I would like to raise the possibility that adult authority figures have taught them to think that truth is a malleable commodity that can be distorted at one's convenience or whimsy. These children may be demonstrating the mechanism of identification with the aggressor, a severely pathological defensive adaptation.

I also think the design leaves much to be desired, because it does not narrow the variables in a manner that allows the results to mean anything. It becomes a Rorschach to confirm one's bias. We see a study not of memory but of social persuasion. Whether the implantation of the so-called memory by an older sibling who says he was there as an eye-witness and who has a powerful affective relationship with and position of authority over the child mirrors the position of the therapist is questionable. The therapist was not a first-hand witness to a patient's past, and the therapist is not lying, or trying consciously to systematically direct the patient's perception of the truth, or using techniques verging on the interrogatory. In addition, children are accustomed to the idea of getting lost.[12] It is a normal fear, it is the plot of innumerable fairy tales, and it is the subject of myriad maternal warnings. Children likely have a preexisting schema in mind with regard to getting lost, which can be tapped readily by suggestion because it is already present.[12] With regard to incest, however, the incest fantasies described as universal by Freud are not traumatic in nature, like the ones reported by incest victims. We cannot assume that there is a schema for abrupt anal or oral rape, for example, that is lying dormant and ready to be brought to immediate fruition by a therapist who asks a bland question about whether the patient has had any unwanted sexual experiences.

As a study on social persuasion, however, the lost-in-the-mall scenario demonstrates that when a family has a story about how an event happened, it may drive out the autobiographical memory of those involved. This need not be an instance in which a child is convinced that an event has occurred when it has not. It could just as easily explain how a child is persuaded that an event that did occur has not occurred, a possibility Loftus herself has acknowledged.[11] It is a curious irony that in 1983, a syndrome was described in which the family conspires to deny the reality of a traumatic event, and finally the victim endorses the alternate reality. This, of course, is the child sexual abuse accommodation syndrome, which was explored by Roland Summit-one of the experts frequently attacked by those who believe that recovered memories of childhood sexual abuse should be discredited. Loftus's lost-in-the-mall scenario offers confirmation of Summit's earlier observations: a family determined to distort a child's sense of reality has a good chance of achieving its objectives.

It is possible that insights gained from Loftus's lost-in-the-mall scenario and Summit's child sexual abuse accommodation syndrome may cast some light on a phenomenon that is of great interest in the current false memory controversy. Retractors are individuals who at one time believed that they were abused, but who have come to believe that their memories of abuse are inaccurate. Some retractors change their minds in the context of strong interpersonal pressures that have features in common with those exerted upon individuals in the lost-in-the-mall scenario and the child sexual abuse accommodation syndrome. Could it be that retractors rather than therapy patients demonstrate the forces that Dr. Loftus has studied? This could prove an interesting subject for future research.

Another aspect of the Loftus research that has received little attention is that only a small minority of the subjects who received misdirection cues took the indicated misdirections. Most did not. This research might be cited as evidence that most persons, even those subjected to an intense campaign to distort their memories and induce confabulations, will reject such suggestions. Since the reader of this [selection] may have heard many an attack on the gullibility and ineptitude of clinicians by speakers representing themselves as guardians of science, it may be useful to consider an analysis from the perspective of a clinician who worries that the perfect can be the enemy of the good, and that taking too literally the warnings of researchers can destroy the capacity to render good therapy.

The progress of science is a parade of paradigms[13] that strut their arrogant hour upon the stage, expressing themselves in allegories called experiments, depreciating, belittling, and berating everything the paradigm of choice does not embrace. Paradigms collapse by virtue of their exclusion of or failure to address data they had deemed unimportant within the worldview of that particular paradigm. In the language of Greek tragedy, every paradigm has a tragic flaw, overstates its applicability (overweening pride), and is humiliated by fate (retribution).

By disregarding information, paradigms embrace the same mechanisms that we find in the more familiar processes of dissociation, repression, denial, splitting, and even more primitive mechanisms. Perhaps the excesses of such uses of science so fascinate me as a clinician because it helps me to appreciate that laboratory science that is unanchored in common sense is a primitive character disorder verging on decompensation into psychosis, a term that indicates that there is a major failure to appreciate reality. We mock the mad scientist in a grade-B movie and enjoy his or her downfall precisely because, like an incestuous Greek king or a Shakespearean regicide, the order of the universe is destroyed by his or her arrogance and false attempts to impose his or her self-deceived facsimile of natural order upon reality, and his or her defeat is necessary in order to preserve the true order of the world. It follows that the attempt to conform clinical practice rigidly to scientific findings is doomed to defeat, because it will introduce borderline and/or psychotic features into the thinking of the clinician.

Additional Remarks on the Recollection and the Nonrecollection of Trauma

...Elizabeth Loftus, Ph.D., is a brilliant researcher and scholar. She has described her own experiences of abuse and reflected upon her incomplete recollection of it. Her words are captured in a deposition cited by Whitfield.[14] She both denies she repressed the memory of the abuse, and speaks of her uncertainty about the number of occurrences, and of her memory having taken and destroyed her recollections of her abuser. In the same account we find both recollection and the absence of recollection. This might be understood as either confusing, or expectable. As Whitfield notes, trauma dissociates and confuses memory, and trying to block traumata out with guilt, shame, and/or threats of harm can drive its mental representation out of awareness.

Loftus's experience can be understood as capturing the essence of the intimately intertwined nature of both the memory and the banishing from memory of traumatization. Rather than polarized opposites, they may be understood by analogy with the intrusive and numbing aspects of the posttraumatic response. While there are some instances in which clear and striking memory is retained, and some in which its abolition is virtually complete, more often, the two processes proceed side by side. An example of this may be that often only the central aspect of a traumatic event is recalled. The details may neither be registered not retrieved.

References

1. Pope KS: Memory, abuse, and science: questioning claims about the false memory epidemic. Am Psychol 1996; 51:957–974.
2. Kluft RP: The natural history of multiple personality disorder. *In* RP Kluft (Ed.), Childhood Antecedents of Multiple Personality. Washington, DC: American Psychiatric Press, 1985, pp. 197–238.
3. Kluft RP: Treatment of multiple personality disorders. Psychiatr Clin North Am 1984; 7:121–134a.
4. Kluft RP: Dissociation and subsequent vulnerability: a preliminary study. Dissociation 1990; 3:167–173.
5. Kluft RP: Incest and subsequent revictimization: the case of therapist-patient sexual exploitation, with a description of the sitting duck syndrome. *In* RP Kluft (Ed.), Incest-related Syndromes of Adult Psychopathology. Washington, DC: American Psychiatric Press, 1990, pp. 263–287.
6. Holmes DS: The evidence for repression. *In* JL Singer (Ed.), Repression and Dissociation. Chicago: University of Chicago Press, 1990, pp. 85–102.
7. Singer JL (Ed.): Repression and Dissociation. Chicago: University of Chicago Press, 1990.
8. Ditto PH, Lopez DF: Motivated skepticism: use of differential decision criteria for preferred and non-preferred conclusions. J Pers Soc Psychol 1992; 63:568–584.
9. Holmes DL: Repression: theory versus evidence. Paper presented at the University of Kansas Medical Center's Conference on Childhood Sexual Abuse and Memories: Current Controversies. Kansas City, Kansas, April 1995.
10. Loftus E: The nature of memory: what we know. Paper presented at the University of Kansas Medical Center's Conference on Childhood Sexual Abuse and Memories: Current Controversies. Kansas City, Kansas, April 1995.
11. Loftus E: Eyewitness memory: implications for the dissociative disorders field. Paper presented at the meeting of the International Society for the Study of Dissociation, International Fall Conference. Orlando, FL, September 1995.
12. Pedzek K, Roe C: Memory for childhood events: how suggestible is it? Consciousness Cogn 1994; 3:374–387.
13. Kuhn TS: The Structure of Scientific Revolutions (2nd ed., enlarged). Chicago: University of Chicago Press, 1971.
14. Whitfield CL: Memory and Abuse: Remembering and Healing the Effects of Trauma. Deerfield Beach FL: Heath Communications, Inc., 1995.

NO ⤶

Elizabeth F. Loftus

Creating False Memories

In 1986 Nadean Cool, a nurse's aide in Wisconsin, sought therapy from a psychiatrist to help her cope with her reaction to a traumatic event experienced by her daughter. During therapy, the psychiatrist used hypnosis and other suggestive techniques to dig out buried memories of abuse that Cool herself had allegedly experienced. In the process, Cool became convinced that she had repressed memories of having been in a satanic cult, of eating babies, of being raped, of having sex with animals and of being forced to watch the murder of her eight-year-old friend. She came to believe that she had more than 120 personalities—children, adults, angels and even a duck—all because, Cool was told, she had experienced severe childhood sexual and physical abuse. The psychiatrist also performed exorcisms on her, one of which lasted for five hours and included the sprinkling of holy water and screams for Satan to leave Cool's body.

When Cool finally realized that false memories had been planted, she sued the psychiatrist for malpractice. In March 1997, after five weeks of trial, her case was settled out of court for $2.4 million.

Nadean Cool is not the only patient to develop false memories as a result of questionable therapy. In Missouri in 1992 a church counselor helped Beth Rutherford to remember during therapy that her father, a clergyman, had regularly raped her between the ages of seven and 14 and that her mother sometimes helped him by holding her down. Under her therapist's guidance, Rutherford developed memories of her father twice impregnating her and forcing her to abort the fetus herself with a coat hanger. The father had to resign from his post as a clergyman when the allegations were made public. Later medical examination of the daughter revealed, however, that she was still a virgin at age 22 and had never been pregnant. The daughter sued the therapist and received a $1-million settlement in 1996.

About a year earlier two juries returned verdicts against a Minnesota psychiatrist accused of planting false memories by former patients Vynnette Hamanne and Elizabeth Carlson, who under hypnosis and sodium amytal, and after being fed misinformation about the workings of memory, had come to remember horrific abuse by family members. The juries awarded Hammane $2.67 million and Carlson $2.5 million for their ordeals.

In all four cases, the women developed memories about childhood abuse in therapy and then later denied their authenticity. How can we determine if memories of childhood abuse are true or false? Without corroboration, it is very difficult to differentiate between false memories and true ones. Also, in these cases, some memories were contrary to physical evidence, such as explicit and detailed recollections of rape and abortion when medical examination confirmed virginity. How is it possible for people to acquire elaborate and confident false memories? A growing number of investigations demonstrate that under the right circumstances false memories can be instilled rather easily in some people.

My own research into memory distortion goes back to the early 1970s, when I began studies of the "misinformation effect." These studies show that when people who witness an event are later exposed to new and misleading information about it, their recollections often become distorted. In one example, participants viewed a simulated automobile accident at an intersection with a stop sign. After the viewing, half the participants received a suggestion that the traffic sign was a yield sign. When asked later what traffic sign they remembered seeing at the intersection, those who had been given the suggestion tended to claim that they had seen a yield sign. Those who had not received the phony information were much more accurate in their recollection of the traffic sign.

My students and I have now conducted more than 200 experiments involving over 20,000 individuals that document how exposure to misinformation induces memory distortion. In these studies, people "recalled" a conspicuous barn in a bucolic scene that contained no buildings at all, broken glass and tape recorders that were not in the scenes they viewed, a white instead of a blue vehicle in a crime scene, and Minnie Mouse when they actually saw Mickey Mouse. Taken together, these studies show that misinformation can change an individual's recollection in predictable and sometimes very powerful ways.

Misinformation has the potential for invading our memories when we talk to other people, when we are suggestively interrogated or when we read or view media coverage about some event that we may have experienced ourselves. After more than two decades of exploring the power of misinformation, researchers have learned a great deal about the conditions that make people susceptible to memory modification. Memories are more easily modified, for instance, when the passage of time allows the original memory to fade.

False Childhood Memories

It is one thing to change a detail or two in an otherwise intact memory but quite another to plant a false memory of an event that never happened. To study false memory, my students and I first had to find a way to plant a pseudomemory that would not cause our subjects undue emotional stress, either in the process of creating the false memory or when we revealed that they had been intentionally deceived. Yet we wanted to try to plant a memory that would be at least mildly traumatic, had the experience actually happened.

My research associate, Jacqueline E. Pickrell, and I settled on trying to plant a specific memory of being lost in a shopping mall or large department store at about the age of five. Here's how we did it. We asked our subjects, 24 individuals ranging in age from 18 to 53, to try to remember childhood events that had been recounted to us by a parent, an older sibling or another close relative. We prepared a booklet for each participant containing one-paragraph stories about three events that had actually happened to him or her and one that had not. We constructed the false event using information about a plausible shopping trip provided by a relative, who also verified that the participant had not in fact been lost at about the age of five. The lost-in-the-mall scenario included the following elements: lost for an extended period, crying, aid and comfort by an elderly woman and, finally, reunion with the family.

After reading each story in the booklet, the participants wrote what they remembered about the event. If they did not remember it, they were instructed to write, "I do not remember this." In two follow-up interviews, we told the participants that we were interested in examining how much detail they could remember and how their memories compared with those of their relative. The event paragraphs were not read to them verbatim, but rather parts were provided as retrieval cues. The participants recalled something about 49 of the 72 true events (68 percent) immediately after the initial reading of the booklet and also in each of the two follow-up interviews. After reading the booklet, seven of the 24 participants (29 percent) remembered either partially or fully the false event constructed for them, and in the two follow-up interviews six participants (25 percent) continued to claim that they remembered the fictitious event. Statistically, there were some differences between the true memories and the false ones: participants used more words to describe the true memories, and they rated the true memories as being somewhat more clear. But if an onlooker were to observe many of our participants describe an event, it would be difficult indeed to tell whether the account was of a true or a false memory.

Of course, being lost, however frightening, is not the same as being abused. But the lost-in-the-mall study is not about real experiences of being lost; it is about planting false memories of being lost. The paradigm shows a way of instilling false memories and takes a step toward allowing us to understand how this might happen in real-world settings. Moreover, the study provides evidence that people can be led to remember their past in different ways, and they can even be coaxed into "remembering" entire events that never happened.

Studies in other laboratories using a similar experimental procedure have produced similar results. For instance, Ira Hyman, Troy H. Husband and F. James Billing of Western Washington University asked college students to recall childhood experiences that had been recounted by their parents. The researchers told the students that the study was about how people remember shared experiences differently. In addition to actual events reported by parents, each participant was given one false event—either an overnight hospitalization for a high fever and a possible ear infection, or a birthday party with pizza and a clown—that supposedly happened at about the age of five. The parents confirmed that neither of these events actually took place.

Hyman found that students fully or partially recalled 84 percent of the true events in the first interview and 88 percent in the second interview. None of the participants recalled the false event during the first interview, but 20 percent said they remembered something about the false event in the second interview. One participant who had been exposed to the emergency hospitalization story later remembered a male doctor, a female nurse and a friend from church who came to visit at the hospital.

In another study, along with true events Hyman presented different false events, such as accidentally spilling a bowl of punch on the parents of the bride at a wedding reception or having to evacuate a grocery store when the overhead sprinkler systems erroneously activated. Again, none of the participants recalled the false event during the first interview, but 18 percent remembered something about it in the second interview and 25 percent in the third interview. For example, during the first interview, one participant, when asked about the fictitious wedding event, stated, "I have no clue. I have never heard that one before." In the second interview, the participant said, "It was an outdoor wedding, and I think we were running around and knocked something over like the punch bowl or something and made a big mess and of course got yelled at for it."

Imagination Inflation

The finding that an external suggestion can lead to the construction of false childhood memories helps us understand the process by which false memories arise. It is natural to wonder whether this research is applicable in real situations such as being interrogated by law officers or in psychotherapy. Although strong suggestion may not routinely occur in police questioning or therapy, suggestion in the form of an imagination exercise sometimes does. For instance, when trying to obtain a confession, law officers may ask a suspect to imagine having participated in a criminal act. Some mental health professionals encourage patients to imagine childhood events as a way of recovering supposedly hidden memories.

Surveys of clinical psychologists reveal that 11 percent instruct their clients to "let the imagination run wild," and 22 percent tell their clients to "give free rein to the imagination." Therapist Wendy Maltz, author of a popular book on childhood sexual abuse, advocates telling the parent: "Spend time imagining that you were sexually abused, without worrying about accuracy, proving anything, or having your ideas make sense.... Ask yourself... these questions: What time of day is it? Where are you? Indoors or outdoors? What kind of things are happening? Is there one or more person with you?" Maltz further recommends that therapists continue to ask questions such as "Who would have been likely perpetrators? When were you most vulnerable to sexual abuse in your life?"

The increasing use of such imagination exercises led me and several colleagues to wonder about their consequences. What happens when people imagine childhood experiences that did not happen to them? Does imagining a childhood event increase confidence that it occurred? To explore this, we designed a three-stage procedure. We first asked individuals to indicate the likelihood that certain events happened to them during their childhood. The list contains 40 events, each rated on a scale ranging from "definitely did not happen" to "definitely did happen."" Two weeks later we asked the participants to imagine that they had experienced some of these events. Different subjects were asked to imagine different events. Sometime later the participants again were asked to respond to the original list of 40 childhood events, indicating how likely it was that these events actually happened to them.

Consider one of the imagination exercises. Participants are told to imagine playing inside at home after school, hearing a strange noise outside, running toward the window, tripping, falling, reaching out and breaking the window with their hand. In addition, we asked participants questions such as "What did you trip on? How did you feel?"

In one study 24 percent of the participants who imagined the broken-window scenario later reported an increase in confidence that the event had occurred, whereas only 12 percent of those who were not asked to imagine the incident reported an increase in the likelihood that it had taken place. We found this "imagination inflation" effect in each of the eight events that participants were asked to imagine. A number of possible explanations come to mind. An obvious one is that an act of imagination simply makes the event seem more familiar and that familiarity is mistakenly related to childhood memories rather than to the act of imagination. Such source confusion—when a person does not remember the source of information—can be especially acute for the distant experiences of childhood.

Studies by Lyn Goff and Henry L. Roediger III of Washington University of recent rather than childhood experiences more directly connect imagined actions to the construction of false memory. During the initial session, the researchers instructed participants to perform the stated action, imagine doing it or just listen to the statement and do nothing else. The actions were simple ones: knock on the table, lift the stapler, break the toothpick, cross your fingers, roll your eyes. During the second session, the participants were asked to imagine some of the actions that they had not previously performed. During the final session, they answered questions about what actions they actually performed during the initial session. The investigators found that the more times participants imagined an unperformed action, the more likely they were to remember having performed it.

Impossible Memories

It is highly unlikely that an adult can recall genuine episodic memories from the first year of life, in part because the hippocampus, which plays a key role in the creation of memories, has not matured enough to form and store longlasting memories that can be retrieved in adulthood. A procedure for planting "impossible" memories about experiences that occur shortly after birth has been developed by the late Nicholas Spanos and his collaborators at Carleton University. Individuals are led to believe that they have well-coordinated eye movements and visual exploration skills probably because they were born in hospitals that hung swinging, colored mobiles over infant cribs. To confirm whether they had such an experience, half the participants are hypnotized, age-regressed to the day after birth and asked what they remembered. The other half of the group participates in a "guided mnemonic restructuring" procedure that uses age regression as well as active encouragement to re-create the infant experiences by imagining them.

Spanos and his co-workers found that the vast majority of their subjects were susceptible to these memory-planting procedures. Both the hypnotic and guided participants reported infant memories. Surprisingly, the guided group did so somewhat more (95 versus 70 percent). Both groups remembered the colored mobile at a relatively high rate (56 percent of the guided group and 46 percent of the hypnotic subjects). Many participants who did not remember the mobile did recall other things, such as doctors, nurses, bright lights, cribs and masks. Also, in both groups, of those who reported memories of infancy, 49 percent felt that they were real memories, as opposed to 16 percent who claimed that they were merely fantasies. These findings confirm earlier studies that many individuals can be led to construct complex, vivid and detailed false memories via a rather simple procedure. Hypnosis clearly is not necessary.

How False Memories Form

In the lost-in-the-mall study, implantation of false memory occurred when another person, usually a family member, claimed that the incident happened. Corroboration of an event by another person can be a powerful technique for instilling a false memory. In fact, merely claiming to have seen a person do something can lead that person to make a false confession of wrongdoing.

This effect was demonstrated in a study by Saul M. Kassin and his colleagues at Williams College, who investigated the reactions of individuals falsely accused of damaging a computer by pressing the wrong key. The innocent participants initially denied the charge, but when a confederate said that she had seen them perform the action, many participants signed a confession, internalized guilt for the act and went on to confabulate details that were consistent with that belief. These findings show that false incriminating evidence can induce people to accept guilt for a crime they did not commit and even to develop memories to support their guilty feelings.

Research is beginning to give us an understanding of how false memories of complete, emotional and self-participatory experiences are created in adults. First, there are social demands on individuals to remember; for instance, researchers exert some pressure on participants in a study to come up with memories. Second, memory construction by imagining events can be explicitly encouraged when people are having trouble remembering. And, finally, individuals can be encouraged not to think about whether their constructions are real or not. Creation of false memories is most likely to occur when these external factors are present, whether in an experimental setting, in a therapeutic setting or during everyday activities.

False memories are constructed by combining actual memories with the content of suggestions received from others. During the process, individuals may forget the source of the information. This is a classic example of source confusion, in which the content and the source become dissociated.

Of course, because we can implant false childhood memories in some individuals in no way implies that all memories that arise after suggestion are necessarily false. Put another way, although experimental work on the creation of false memories may raise doubt about the validity of long-buried memories, such as repeated trauma, it in no way disproves them. Without corroboration, there is little that can be done to help even the most experienced evaluator to differentiate true memories from ones that were suggestively planted.

The precise mechanisms by which such false memories are constructed await further research. We still have much to learn about the degree of confidence and the characteristics of false memories created in these ways, and we need to discover what types of individuals are particularly susceptible to these forms of suggestion and who is resistant.

As we continue this work, it is important to heed the cautionary tale in the data we have already obtained: mental health professionals and others must be aware of how greatly they can influence the recollection of events and of the urgent need for maintaining restraint in situations in which imagination is used as an aid in recovering presumably lost memories.

CHALLENGE QUESTIONS

Are Repressed Memories Real?

1. Kluft argues that the studies described by Loftus do not necessarily suggest that recovered memories are false, because the results of the studies do not generalize to real-world cases of recovered memories. How would you design a study involving real cases of recovered memories that would allow you to determine if most cases of recovered memories are false?
2. Were you surprised to read how easily false memories seemed to be created in the studies described by Loftus? Have you ever had a memory that you know, or perhaps just suspect, was false?
3. Should psychotherapists take steps to ensure that false memories are not created through the course of psychotherapy? If so, what steps should be taken? If not, why is action unnecessary?

On the Internet...

The Stanley Milgram Web Site

Dr. Thomas Blass, one of world's foremost authorities on the obedience studies and author of Milgram's biography, hosts this Web site. The site contains some little-known information about Milgram.

> http://www.stanleymilgram.com/

The Stanford Prison Experiment

This site contains information about Philip Zimbardo's famous experiment that cannot be found in any other sources, such as the informed consent documents that participants were asked to sign and the original instructions given to the prison guards.

> http://www.prisonexp.org/

Cult Critics

This Web site is the homepage for noted cult critic, Rick Ross. It contains various readings that highlight the dangers associated with cults. There are also a number of links to the Web sites of other cult critics.

> http://www.rickross.com/

New Religious Movements

The organizations that some critics call "cults" are sometimes referred to as "new religious movements" by others. This Web site is the home for the Center of Study on New Religions, which offers a very different perspective on such organizations, compared to the Web sites of cult critics.

> http://www.cesnur.org/

Persuasion

This Web site describes many social psychological principles of influence and persuasion. It also describes how these principles are relevant to our everyday lives.

> http://www.as.wvu.edu/~sbb/comm221/primer.htm

PART 3

Social Influence

*H*ow does the presence of others, whether real or imagined, influence our own attitudes, beliefs, and behavior? This is the fundamental question in the realm of social influence research. Social psychology's most famous experiments have examined the process of social influence, and you will read about the controversy surrounding some of those landmark studies.

- Do Gender Roles Explain Sex Differences in Social Behavior?
- Do Milgram's Obedience Experiments Help Explain the Nature of the Holocaust?
- Does the Stanford Prison Experiment Help Explain the Effects of Imprisonment?
- Is Subliminal Persuasion a Myth?
- Can People Really Be Brainwashed?

ISSUE 9

Do Gender Roles Explain
Sex Differences in Social Behavior?

YES: Alice H. Eagly and Wendy Wood, from "The Origins of Sex Differences in Social Behavior: Evolved Dispositions versus Social Roles," *American Psychologist* (*54*, June 1999)

NO: David M. Buss, from "Psychological Sex Differences," *American Psychologist* (*50*, March 1995)

ISSUE SUMMARY

YES: Social psychologists Alice Eagly and Wendy Wood argue that gender differences can be explained by the different social roles that women and men occupy in society.

NO: Evolutionary psychologist David Buss believes that gender differences reflect the different adaptive challenges women and men have faced in human evolutionary history.

Common sense seems to tell us that women and men do not always think and act in the same way. This intuitive notion is supported by social psychological research, which demonstrates that women and men do differ in some respects. While there is some debate regarding the magnitude of gender differences, with many psychologists believing that gender differences are smaller than intuition suggests, there is little disagreement that some gender differences are real. But why do these differences exist? What could be the source of gender differences in social behavior?

Alice Eagly and Wendy Wood argue that the primary factors that determine gender differences in social behavior are the different social roles that women and men occupy. For a variety of reasons, women and men are steered into different social roles, and once women and men find themselves occupying these different social roles, they develop different abilities and skills that allow them to succeed in those roles. As Eagly and Wood point out, traditional gender roles dictate that women tend to occupy the child care role while men tend to occupy the employment role. Since these different roles require people to act in different ways, gender differences in behavior are a result of the differential placement of women and men into these very different roles.

David Buss, one of the leading theorists in the evolutionary psychology movement, believes that many gender differences in social behavior can be explained by principles of evolution. According to Buss, gender differences arise, in part, because of different evolutionary challenges that women and men faced in our ancestral past. Women and men have had to evolve differently in order to survive and thrive. So current gender differences in social behavior are an artifact of our evolutionary history.

Furthermore, while the authors ultimately believe that gender differences in social behavior originate from very different sources, both reject the false dichotomy that pits biological forces against social influences, and argue that nature and nurture interact with one another to produce gender differences.

POINT

- Gender differences in social behavior are a result of social roles.
- Current gender differences reflect contemporary social roles that women and men occupy.
- Gender inequality is a product of social structure not evolution.

COUNTERPOINT

- Gender differences in social behavior are a result of our evolutionary history.
- Men and women differ in the domains in which they have faced different evolutionary challenges.
- Reducing gender inequality will be difficult if we do not acknowledge that some gender differences may have an evolutionary basis.

**Alice H. Eagly and
Wendy Wood**

 **YES**

The Origins of Sex Differences in Human Behavior: Evolved Dispositions Versus Social Roles

$\mathbf{A}$s more research psychologists have become willing to acknowledge that some aspects of social behavior, personality, and abilities differ between women and men . . . their attention has begun to focus on the causes of these differences. Debates about causes center, at least in part. on determining what can be considered the basic or ultimate causes of sex differences. Theories of sex differences that address causes at this level are termed in this article *origin theories*. . . . In such theories, causation flows from a basic cause to sex-differentiated behavior, and biological, psychological, and social processes mediate the relation between the basic cause and behavior. In this article, we consider two types of origin theories: One of these implicates evolved psychological dispositions, and the other implicates social structure. Evolutionary psychology. . .thus represents the first type of origin theory, and social psychological theories that emphasize social structure represent the second type of origin theory. . . .

In the origin theory proposed by evolutionary psychologists, the critical causal arrow points from evolutionary adaptations to psychological sex differences. Because women and men possess sex-specific evolved mechanisms, they differ psychologically and tend to occupy different social roles. In contrast, in the social structural origin theory, the critical causal arrow points from social structure to psychological sex differences. Because men and women tend to occupy different social roles, they become psychologically different in ways that adjust them to these roles.

One important feature is shared by these two origin theories: Both offer a functional analysis of behavior that emphasizes adjustment to environmental conditions. However, the two schools of thought differ radically in their analysis of the nature and timing of the adjustments that are most important to sex-differentiated behavior. Evolutionary psychologists believe that females and males faced different pressures in primeval environments and that the sexes' differing reproductive status was the key feature of ancestral life that framed sex-typed adaptive problems. The resolutions of these problems produced sex-specific evolved mechanisms that humans carry with them as a spe-

From *American Psychologist*, June 1999, pp. 408–423. © 1999 by the American Psychological Association. Reprinted by permission.

cies and that are held to be the root cause of sex-differentiated behavior. Although evolutionary psychologists readily acknowledge the abstract principle that environmental conditions can influence the development and expression of evolved dispositions, they have given limited attention to variation of sex differences in response to individual, situational, and cultural conditions. . . . For example, Buss (1998) emphasized "universal or near-universal sex differences (p. 421) in preferences for long-term mates.

Social structuralists maintain that the situations faced by women and men are quite variable across societies and historical periods as social organization changes in response to technological, ecological, and other transformations. From a social structural perspective, a society's division of labor between the sexes is the engine of sex-differentiated behavior, because it summarizes the social constraints under which men and women carry out their lives. Sex differences are viewed as accommodations to the differing restrictions and opportunities that a society maintains for its men and women, and sex-differentiated behavior is held to be contingent on a range of individual, situational, and cultural conditions (see Deaux & LaFrance, 1998). Despite this emphasis on the social environment, social structuralists typically acknowledge the importance of some genetically mediated sex differences. Physical differences between the sexes, particularly men's greater size and strength and women's childbearing and lactation, are very important because they interact with shared cultural beliefs, social organization, and the demands of the economy to influence the role assignments that constitute the sexual division of labor within a society and produce psychological sex differences (Eagly, 1987; Wood & Eagly, 1999). . . .

Social Structural Theory as an Origin Theory of Sex Differences

A respected tradition in the social sciences locates the origins of sex differences, not in evolved psychological dispositions that are built into the human psyche, but in the contrasting social positions of women and men. In contemporary American society, as in many world societies, women have less power and status than men and control fewer resources. This feature of social structure is often labeled gender hierarchy, or in feminist writing it may be called patriarchy. In addition, as the division of labor is realized in the United States and many other nations, women perform more domestic work than men and spend fewer hours in paid employment (Shelton, 1992). Although most women in the United States are employed in the paid workforce, they have lower wages than men, are concentrated in different occupations, and are thinly represented at the highest levels of organizational hierarchies (Jacobs, 1989; Reskin & Padavic, 1994; Tomaskovic-Devey, 1995). From a social structural perspective, the underlying cause of sex-differentiated behavior is this concentration of men and women in differing roles.

The determinants of the distribution of men and women into social roles are many and include the biological endowment of women and men. The sex-differentiated physical attributes that influence role occupancy include men's greater size and strength, which gives them priority in jobs demanding certain types of strenuous activity, especially activities involving upper body strength. These physical attributes of men are less important in societies in which few occupational roles require these attributes, such as post-industrial societies. Also important in relation to role distributions are women's childbearing and in many societies their activity of suckling infants for long periods of time; these obligations give them priority in roles involving the care of very young children and cause conflict with roles requiring extended absence from home and uninterrupted activity. These reproductive activities of women are less important in societies with low birthrates, less reliance on lactation for feeding infants, and greater reliance on nonmaternal care of young children.

In general, physical sex differences, in interaction with social and ecological conditions, influence the roles held by men and women because certain activities are more efficiently accomplished by one sex. The benefits of this greater efficiency can be realized when women and men are allied in cooperative relationships and establish a division of labor. The particular character of the activities that each sex performs then determines its placement in the social structure (see Wood & Eagly, 1999). As historians and anthropologists have argued (e.g., Ehrenberg, 1989; Harris, 1993; Lerner, 1986; Sanday, 1981), men typically specialized in activities (e.g., warfare, herding) that yielded greater status, wealth, and power, especially as societies became more complex. Thus, when sex differences in status emerged, they tended to favor men.

The differing distributions of men and women into social roles form the basis for a social structural metatheory of sex differences, just as evolutionary theory provides a metatheory. The major portion of this social structural theory follows from the typical features of the roles of men and women. Thus, the first metatheoretical principle derives from the greater power and status that tends to be associated with male-dominated roles and can be succinctly stated as follows: Men's accommodation to roles with greater power and status produces more dominant behavior, and women's accommodation to roles with lesser power and status produces more subordinate behavior (Ridgeway & Diekema, 1992). Dominant behavior is controlling, assertive, relatively directive and autocratic, and may involve sexual control. Subordinate behavior is more compliant to social influence, less overtly aggressive, more cooperative and conciliatory, and may involve a lack of sexual autonomy.

The second metatheoretical principle follows from the differing balance of activities associated with the typical roles of each sex. Women and men seek to accommodate sex-typical roles by acquiring the specific skills and resources linked to successful role performance and by adapting their social behavior to role requirements. A variety of sex-specific skills and beliefs arise from the typical family and economic roles of men and women, which in many societies can be described as resource provider and homemaker. Women and men seek to accommodate to these roles by acquiring role-related skills. for example, women learning domestic skills such as cooking and men learning skills that are marketable in the paid economy. The psychological attributes and social behaviors associated with these roles have been characterized in terms of the distinction between communal and agentic characteristics (Bakan, 1966; Eagly, 1987). Thus, women's accommodation to the domestic role and to female-dominated occupations favors a pattern of interpersonally facilitative and friendly behaviors that can be termed communal. In particular, the assignment of the majority of child rearing to women encourages nurturant behaviors that facilitate care for children and other individuals. The importance of close relationships to women's nurturing role favors the acquisition of superior interpersonal skills and the ability to communicate nonverbally. In contrast, men's accommodation to the employment role, especially to male-dominated occupations, favors a pattern of assertive and independent behaviors that can be termed agentic (Eagly & Steffen. 1984), This argument is not to deny that paid occupations show wide variation in the extent to which they favor more masculine or feminine qualities. In support of the idea that sex-differentiated behaviors are shaped by paid occupations are demonstrations that to the extent that occupations are male dominated, they are thought to require agentic personal qualities. In contrast, to the extent that occupations are female dominated, they are thought to require communal personal qualities (Cejka & Eagly, 1999; Glick, 1991).

In social structural theories, differential role occupancy affects behavior through a variety of mediating processes. In social role theory (Eagly, 1987; Eagly et al., 2000), an important mediating process is the formation of gender roles by which people of each sex are expected to have characteristics that equip them for the tasks that they typically carry out. These expectations encompass the preferred or desirable attributes of men and women as well as their typical attributes. Gender roles are emergents from the productive work of the sexes; the characteristics that are required to perform sex-typical tasks become stereotypic of women or men. To the extent that women more than men occupy roles that demand communal behaviors, domestic behaviors, or subordinate behaviors for successful role performance, such tendencies become stereotypic of women and are incorporated into a female gender role. To the extent that men more than women occupy roles that demand agentic behaviors, resource acquisition behaviors, or dominant behaviors for successful role performance, such tendencies become stereotypic of men and are incorporated into a male gender role. Gender roles facilitate the activities typically carried out by people of each sex. For example, the expectation that women be other-oriented and compassionate facilitates their nurturing activities within the family as well as their work in many female-dominated occupations (e.g., teacher, nurse, social worker).

People communicate gender-stereotypic expectations in social interaction and can directly induce the targets of these expectations to engage in behavior that confirms them (e.g., Skrypnek & Snyder, 1982; Wood & Karten, 1986). Such effects of gender roles are congruent with theory and research on the behavioral confirmation of stereotypes and other expectancies (see Olson, Roese, & Zanna, 1996). Gender-stereotypic expectations can also affect behavior by becoming internalized as part of individuals' self-concepts and personalities (Feingold, 1994). Under such circumstances, gender roles affect behavior through self-regulatory processes (Wood, Christensen, Hebl, & Rothgerber, 1997). The individual psychology that underlies these processes is assumed to be the maximization of utilities. People perceive these utilities from the rewards and costs that emerge in social interaction, which takes place within the constraints of organizational and societal arrangements.

Gender roles coexist with specific roles based on factors such as family relationships and occupation. These specific social roles contribute directly to sex-differentiated behavior when women and men are differently distributed into them—for example, women into the homemaker role and men into the provider role. In contrast, when men and women occupy the same specific social role, sex differences would tend to erode because specific roles are constraining (e.g., Eagly & Johnson, 1990). However, gender roles ordinarily continue to have some impact on behavior, even in the presence of specific roles (see Gutek & Morasch, 1983; Moscowitz, Suh, & Desaulniers, 1994; Ridgeway, 1997). Moreover, experimental evidence (e.g., Hembroff, 1982) suggests that people combine or average the expectations associated with specific roles and more diffuse roles such as gender roles in a manner that weights each set of expectations according to its relevance to the task at hand.

The social structural perspective provides a broad theoretical outline within which many social scientific theories of sex-differentiated behavior can be placed. These theories focus on different aspects of the processes by which societies produce sex-differentiated behavior, and many theories have spawned detailed predictions and a substantial body of empirical research (see Beall & Stemberg, 1993; Canary & Dindia, 1998; England & Browne, 1992). For example, developmental psychologists have studied socialization in the family, school, and peer group. Social psychologists have examined the impact of gendered self-schemas, men's greater status, sex-differentiated expectations about behavior, and gendered patterns of social interaction. Sociologists have implicated organizational factors such as discriminatory employment practices, societal factors such as men's greater ownership of capital, and cultural factors such as the ideologies that legitimize gender inequality. Social scientists have thus provided an array of interrelated theories, each of which illuminates certain aspects of the processes by which sex-differentiated behavior is produced.

In summary, in social structural accounts, women and men are differently distributed into social roles, and these differing role assignments can be broadly described in terms of a sexual division of labor and a gender hierarchy. This division of labor and the patriarchal hierarchy that sometimes accompanies it provide the engine of sex-differentiated behavior because they trigger social and psychological processes by which men and women seek somewhat different experiences to maximize their outcomes within the constraints that societies establish for people of their sex. Sex differences in behavior thus reflect contemporaneous social conditions. . . .

REFERENCES

Archer, J. (1996) Sex differences in social behavior: Are the social role and evolutionary explanations compatible? *American Psychologist, 51,* 909–917.

Baken, D. (1966). *The duality of human existence: An essay on psychology and religion.* Chicago: Rand McNally.

Beall, A. E., & Sternberg, R. J. (Eds.). (1963). *The psychology of gender.* New York: Guilford Press.

Buss, D. M. (1995a). Evolutionary psychology: A new paradigm for psychological science. *Psychological Inquiry, 6,* 1–30.

Buss, D. M. (1995b). Psychological sex differences: Origins through sexual selection. *American Psychologist, 50,* 164–168.

Buss, D. M. (1998). The psychology of human mate selection: Exploring the complexity of the strategic repertoire. In C. Crawford & D.L. Krebs (Eds.), *Handbook of evolutionary psychology: Ideas, issues, and applications* (pp. 405–429). Mahwah, NJ: Erlbaum.

Buss, D. M., & Kendrick, D. T. (1998). Evolutionary social psychology. In D.T. Gilbert, S.T. Fiske & G. Lindzey (Eds.). *The handbook of social psycology* (4th ed., Vol.2, pp. 982–1026). Boston: McGraw-Hill.

Canary, D. J., & Dindia. K. (Eds.). (1998). *Sex differences and similarities in communication: Critical essays and empirical investigations of sex and gender in interaction.* Mahwah, NJ: Erlbaum.

Cejka, M. A. & Eagly, A. H. (1999). Gender-stereotypic images of occupations correspond to the sex segegation of employment. *Personality and Social Psychology Bulletin, 25,* 413–423.

Deaux, K., & LaFrance, M. (1998). Gender. In D. T. Gilbert, S. T. Fiske, & G. Lindzey (Eds.), *The handbook of social psychology* (4th ed., Vol. 1, pp. 788–827). Boston: McGraw-Hill.

Eagly, A. H. (1987). *Sex differences in social behavior: A socio-role interpretation.* Hillsdale, NJ: Erlbaum.

Eagly, A. H. (1995). The science and politics of comparing women and men. *Americal Psychologist, 50,* 145–158.

Eagly, A. H., Ashmore, R. D., Makhijani, M. G., & Longo, L. C. (1991). What is beautiful is good, but...: A meta-analytic review of research on the physical attractiveness stereotype. *Psychological Bulletin, 110,* 109–128.

Eagly, A. H., & Johnson, B. T. (1990). Gender and leadership style: A meta-analysis. *Psychological Bulletin, 108,* 233–256.

Eagly, A. H., & Steffen, V. J. (1984). Gender stereotypes stem from the distribution of women and men into social roles. *Journal of Personality and Social Psychology, 46,* 735–754.

Eagly, A. H. Wood, W., & Diekman, A. (2000). Social role theory of sex differences and similarities: A current appraisal. In T. Eckes & H. M. Trautner (Eds.), *The developmental social psychology of gender.* Mahwah, NJ: Erlbaum.

Ehrenberg, M. (1989). *Women in prehistory.* London: British Museum Publications.

England, P., & Browne, I. (1992). Internalization and constraint in women's subordination. In B. Agger (Ed)., *Current perspectives in social theory* (Vol. 12, pp. 97–123). Greenwich, CT: JAI Press.

Feingold A. (1994). Gender differences in personality: A meta-analysis. *Psychological Bulletin, 116,* 429–456.

Ferree, M. M. (1991). The gender division of labor in two-earner marriages: Dimensions of variability and change. *Journal of Family Issues, 12,* 158–180.

Glick, P. (1991). Trait-based and sex-based discrimination in occupational prestige, occupational salary, and hiring, *Sex Roles, 25,* 351–378.

Gutek, B. A., & Morash, B. (1983). Sex-ratios, sex-role spillover, and sexual harassment of women at work. *Journal of Social Issues, 38*(4), 55–74.

Halpern, D. F. (1997) Sex differences in intelligence: Implications for education. *American Psychologist, 52,* 1091–1102.

Harris, M. (1993). The evolution of human gender hierarchies: A trial formulation. In B. D. Miller (Ed.), *Sex and gender hierarchies* (pp. 57–79). New York: Cambridge University Press.

Hembroff, L. A. (1982). Resolving status inconsistency: An expectation states theory and test. *Social Forces, 61,* 183–205.

Jacobs., J. A., (1989). *Revolving doors: Sex segregation and women's careers.* Stanford, CA: Stanford University Press.

Kenrick, D. T., & Keefe, R. C. (1992). Age preferences in mates reflect sex differences in human reproductive strategies. *Behavioral and Brain Sciences, 15,* 75–91.

Lerner, G. (1986). *The creation of patriarchy.* New York: Oxford University Press.

Lorenzi-Cioldi, F. (1998). Group status and perceptions of homogeneity. In W. Stroebe & M. Hewstone (Eds.), *European review of social psychology* (Vol. 9, pp. 31–75). Chichester, England: Wiley.

Moscowitz, D. W., Suh, E. J., & Desaulniers, J. (1994). Situational influences on gender differences in agency and communion. *Journal of Personality and Social Psychology, 66,* 753–761.

Olson, J. M., Roese, N. J., & Zanna, M. P. (1996). Expectancies. In E. T. Higgins & A. W. Kruglanski (Ed.), *Social psychology: Handbook of basic principles* (pp. 211–238). New York: Guilford.

Reskin, B. F., & Padavic, I. (1994). *Women and men at work.* Thousand Oaks, CA: Pine Forge Press.

Ridgeway, C. L. (1991). The social construction of status value: Gender and other nominal characteristics. *Social Forces, 70,* 367–386.

Ridgeway, C. L. (1997). Interaction and the conservation of gender inequality: Considering employment. *American Sociological Review, 62,* 218–235.

Ridgeway, C. L., & Diekema, D. (1992). Are gender differences status differences? In C. L. Ridgeway (Ed.), *Gender, interaction, and inequality* (pp. 157–180). New York: Springer-Verlag.

Sanday, P. R. (1981). *Female power and male dominance: On the origins of sexual inequality.* New York: Cambridge University Press.

Shelton, B. A. (1992). *Women, men and time: Gender differences in paid work, housework, and leisure.* New York: Greenwood Press.

Skrypnek, B. J., & Snyder, M. (1982). On the self-perpetuating nature of stereotypes about women and men. *Journal of Experimental Social Psychology, 18,* 277–291.

Tomaskovic-Devey, D. (1995). Sex composition and gendered earnings inequality: A comparison of job and occupational models. In J. A. Jacobs (Ed.), *Gender inequality at work* (pp. 23–56). Thousand Oaks, CA: Sage.

Tooby, J., & Cosmides, L. (1992). The psychological foundations of culture. In J. H. Barkow, L. Cosmides, & J. Tooby (Eds), *The adapted mind: Evolutionary psychology and the generation of culture* (pp. 19–136). New York: Oxford University Press.

West, C., & Zimmerman, D. H. (1987). Doing gender. *Gender & Society, 1,* 125–151.

Wiley, M. G. (1995). Sex category and gender in social psychology. In K. S. Cook, G. A. Fine, & J. S. House (Eds.), *Sociological perspectives on social psychology* (pp. 362–386). Boston: Allyn & Bacon.

Wood, W., Christensen, P. N., Hebl, M. R., & Rothgerber, H. (1997). Conformity to sex-typed norms, affect, and the self-concept. *Journal of Personality and Social Psychology, 73,* 523–535.

Wood, W., & Eagly, A. H. (1999). *Social structure and the origins of sex differences in social behavior.* Manuscript in preparation.

Wood, W., & Karten, S. J. (1986). Sex differences in interaction style as a product of perceived sex differences in competence. *Journal of Personality and Social Psychology, 50,* 341–347.

NO ↵

David M. Buss

Psychological Sex Differences: Origins Through Sexual Selection

Evolutionary psychology predicts that males and females will be the same or similar in all those domains in which the sexes have faced the same or similar adaptive problems. Both sexes have sweat glands because both sexes have faced the adaptive problem of thermal regulation. Both sexes have similar (although not identical) taste preferences for fat, sugar, salt, and particular amino acids because both sexes have faced similar (although not identical) food consumption problems. Both sexes grow callouses when they experience repeated rubbing on their skin because both sexes have faced the adaptive problem of physical damage from environmental friction.

In other domains, men and women have faced substantially different adaptive problems throughout human evolutionary history. In the physical realm, for example, women have faced the problem of childbirth; men have not. Women, therefore, have evolved particular adaptations that are absent in men, such as a cervix that dilates to 10 centimeters just prior to giving birth, mechanisms for producing labor contractions, and the release of oxytocin in the blood stream during childbirth.

Men and women have also faced different information-processing problems in some adaptive domains. Because fertilization occurs internally within the woman, for example, men have faced the adaptive problem of uncertainty of paternity in putative offspring. Men who failed to solve this problem risked investing resources in children who were not their own. All people descend from a long line of ancestral men whose adaptations (i.e., psychological mechanisms) led them to behave in ways that increased their likelihood of paternity and decreased the odds of investing in children who were putatively theirs but whose genetic fathers were other men. This does not imply, of course, that men were or are consciously aware of the adaptive problem of compromised paternity.

Women faced the problem of securing a reliable or replenishable supply of resources to carry them through pregnancy and lactation, especially when food resources were scarce (e.g., during droughts or harsh winters). All people are descendants of a long and unbroken line of women who successfully solved this adaptive challenge—for example, by preferring mates who showed the ability to accrue resources and the willingness to provide them for partic-

From David M. Buss, "Psychological Sex Differences: Origins Through Sexual Selection," *American Psychologist*, vol. 50, no. 3 (March 1995), pp. 164–168. Copyright © 1995 by the American Psychological Association, Inc. Adapted with permission of the publisher and the author.

ular women (Buss, 1994). Those women who failed to solve this problem failed to survive, imperiled the survival chances of their children, and hence failed to continue their lineage.

Evolutionary psychologists predict that the sexes will differ in precisely those domains in which women and men have faced different sorts of adaptive problems (Buss, 1994). To an evolutionary psychologist, the likelihood that the sexes are psychologically identical in domains in which they have recurrently confronted different adaptive problems over the long expanse of human evolutionary history is essentially zero (Symons, 1992). The key question, therefore, is not whether men and women differ psychologically. Rather, the key questions about sex differences, from an evolutionary psychological perspective, are (a) In what domains have women and men faced different adaptive problems? (b) What are the sex-differentiated psychological mechanisms of women and men that have evolved in response to these sex-differentiated adaptive problems? (c) Which social, cultural, and contextual inputs moderate the magnitude of expressed sex differences?

Sexual Selection Defines the Primary Domains in Which the Sexes Have Faced Different Adaptive Challenges

Although many who are not biologists equate evolution with natural selection or survival selection, Darwin (1871) sculpted what he believed to be a second theory of evolution—the theory of sexual selection. Sexual selection is the causal process of the evolution of characteristics on the basis of reproductive advantage, as opposed to survival advantage. Sexual selection occurs in two forms. First, members of one sex can successfully outcompete members of their own sex in a process of intrasexual competition. Whatever characteristics lead to success in these same-sex competitions—be they greater size, strength, cunning, or social skills—can evolve or increase in frequency by virtue of the reproductive advantage accrued by the winners through increased access to more numerous or more desirable mates.

Second, members of one sex can evolve preferences for desirable qualities in potential mates through the process of intersexual selection. If members of one sex exhibit some consensus about which qualities are desirable in the other sex, then members of the other sex who possess the desirable qualities will gain a preferential mating advantage. Hence, the desirable qualities— be they morphological features such as antlers or plumage or psychological features such as a lower threshold for risk taking to acquire resources—can evolve by virtue of the reproductive advantage attained by those who are preferentially chosen for possessing the desirable qualities. Among humans, both causal processes—preferential mate choice and same-sex competition for access to mates—are prevalent among both sexes, and probably have been throughout human evolutionary history (Buss, 1994).

Hypotheses About Psychological Sex Differences Follow From Sexual Asymmetries in Mate Selection and Intrasexual Competition.

Although a detailed analysis of psychological sex differences is well beyond the scope of this [selection] (see Buss, 1994), a few of the most obvious differences in adaptive problems include the following.

Paternity uncertainty. Because fertilization occurs internally within women, men are always less than 100% certain (again, no conscious awareness implied) that their putative children are genetically their own. Some cultures have phrases to describe this, such as "mama's baby, papa's maybe." Women are always 100% certain that the children they bear are their own.

Identifying reproductively valuable women. Because women's ovulation is concealed and there is no evidence that men can detect when women ovulate, ancestral men had the difficult adaptive challenge of identifying which women were more fertile. Although ancestral women would also have faced the problem of identifying fertile men, the problem is considerably less severe (a) because most men remain fertile throughout their life span, whereas fertility is steeply age graded among women and (b) because women invest more heavily in offspring, making them the more "valuable" sex, competed for more intensely by men seeking sexual access. Thus, there is rarely a shortage of men willing to contribute the sperm necessary for fertilization, whereas from a man's perspective, there is a pervasive shortage of fertile women.

Gaining sexual access to women. Because of the large asymmetry between men and women in their minimum obligatory parental investment—nine months gestation for women versus an act of sex for men—the direct reproductive benefits of gaining sexual access to a variety of mates would have been much higher for men than for women throughout human evolutionary history (Symons, 1979; Trivers, 1972). Therefore, in social contexts in which some short-term mating or polygynous mating were possible, men who succeeded in gaining sexual access to a variety of women, other things being equal, would have experienced greater reproductive success than men who failed to gain such access (see also Greiling, 1993, for adaptive benefits to women of short-term mating).

Identifying men who are able to invest. Because of the tremendous burdens of a nine-month pregnancy and subsequent lactation, women who selected men, who were able to invest resources in them and their offspring would have been at a tremendous advantage in survival and reproductive currencies compared with women who were indifferent to the investment capabilities of the man with whom they chose to mate.

Identifying men who are willing to invest.   Having resources is not enough. Copulating with a man who had resources but who displayed a hasty postcopulatory departure would have been detrimental to the woman, particularly if she became pregnant and faced raising a child without the aid and protection of an investing father. A man with excellent resource-accruing capacities might channel resources to another woman or pursue short-term sexual opportunities with a variety of women. A woman who had the ability to detect a man's willingness to invest in her and her children would have an adaptive advantage compared with women who were oblivious to a man's willingness or unwillingness to invest.

These are just a few of the adaptive problems that women and men have confronted differently or to differing degrees. Other examples of sex-linked adaptive problems include those of coalitional warfare, coalitional defense, hunting, gathering, combating sex-linked forms of reputational damage, embodying sex-linked prestige criteria, and attracting mates by fulfilling the differing desires of the other sex—domains that all have consequences for mating but are sufficiently wide-ranging to span a great deal of social psychology (Buss, 1994). It is in these domains that evolutionary psychologists anticipate the most pronounced sex differences—differences in solutions to sex-linked adaptive problems in the form of evolved psychological mechanisms.

Psychological Sex Differences Are Well Documented Empirically in the Domains Predicted by Theories Anchored in Sexual Selection

When Maccoby and Jacklin (1974) published their classic book on the psychology of sex differences, knowledge was spotty and methods for summarizing the literature were largely subjective and interpretive (Eagly, 1995). Since that time, there has been a veritable explosion of empirical findings, along with quantitative meta-analytic procedures for evaluating them (e.g., Eagly, 1995; Feingold, 1990; Hall, 1978; Hyde, 1996; Oliver & Hyde, 1993; Rosenthal, 1991). Although new domains of sex differences continue to surface, such as the recently documented female advantage in spatial location memory (Silverman & Eals, 1992), the outlines of where researchers find large, medium, small, and no sex differences are starting to emerge more clearly.

A few selected findings illustrate the heuristic power of evolutionary psychology. Cohen (1977) used the widely adopted d statistic as the index of magnitude of effect to propose a rule of thumb for evaluating effect sizes: 0.20 = "small," 0.50 = "medium," and 0.80 = "large." As Hyde (in press) has pointed out in a chapter titled "Where Are the Gender Differences? Where Are the Gender Similarities?," sex differences in the intellectual and cognitive ability domains tend to be small. Women's verbal skills tend to be slightly higher than men's ($d = -0.11$). Sex differences in math also tend to be small ($d = 0.15$). Most tests of general cognitive ability, in short, reveal small sex differences.

The primary exception to the general trend of small sex differences in the cognitive abilities domain occurs with spatial rotation. This ability is essential for successful hunting, in which the trajectory and velocity of a spear must anticipate correctly the trajectory of an animal as each moves with different speeds through space and time. For spatial rotation ability, $d = 0.73$. Other sorts of skills involved in hunting also show large magnitudes of sex differences, such as throwing velocity ($d = 2.18$), throwing distance ($d = 1.98$), and throwing accuracy ($d = 0.96$; Ashmore, 1990). Skilled hunters, as good providers, are known to be sexually attractive to women in current and traditional tribal societies (Hill & Hurtado, 1989; Symons, 1979).

Large sex differences appear reliably for precisely the aspects of sexuality and mating predicted by evolutionary theories of sexual strategies (Buss & Schmitt, 1993). Oliver and Hyde (1993), for example, documented a large sex difference in attitudes toward casual sex ($d = 0.81$). Similar sex differences have been found with other measures of men's desire for casual sex partners, a psychological solution to the problem of seeking sexual access to a variety of partners (Buss & Schmitt, 1993; Symons, 1979). For example, men state that they would ideally like to have more than 18 sex partners in their lifetimes, whereas women state that they would desire only 4 or 5 ($d = 0.87$; Buss & Schmitt, 1993). In another study that has been replicated twice, 75% of the men but 0% of the women approached by an attractive stranger of the opposite sex consented to a request for sex (Clark & Hatfield, 1989).

Women tend to be more exacting than men, as predicted, in their standards for a short-term mate ($d = 0.79$). Women tend to place greater value on good financial prospects in a mate—a finding confirmed in a study of 10,047 individuals residing in 37 cultures located on six continents and five islands from around the world (Buss, 1989a). More so than men, women especially disdain qualities in a potential mate that signal inability to accrue resources, such as lack of ambition ($d = 1.38$) and lack of education ($d = 1.06$). Women desire physical protection abilities more than men, both in short-term mating ($d = 0.94$) and in long-term mating ($d = 0.66$).

Men and women also differ in the weighting given to cues that trigger sexual jealousy. Buss, Larsen, Westen, and Semmelroth (1992) presented men and women with the following dilemma: "What would upset or distress you more: (a) imagining your partner forming a deep emotional attachment to someone else or (b) imagining your partner enjoying passionate sexual intercourse with that other person" (p. 252). Men expressed greater distress about sexual than emotional infidelity, whereas women showed the opposite pattern. The difference between the sexes in which scenario was more distressing was 43% ($d = 0.98$). These sex differences have been replicated by different investigators (Wiederman & Allgeier, 1993) with physiological recording devices (Buss et al., 1992) and have been replicated in other cultures (Buunk, Angleitner, Oubaid, & Buss, 1994).

These sex differences are precisely those predicted by evolutionary psychological theories based on sexual selection. They represent only a sampling from a larger body of supporting evidence. The sexes also differ substantially in wide variety of other ways that are predicted by sexual selection theory, such as in thresholds for physical risk taking (Wilson & Daly, 1985), in frequency of perpetrating homicides (Daly & Wilson, 1988), in thresholds for inferring sexual intent in others (Abby, 1982), in perceptions of the magnitude of upset people experience as the victims of sexual aggression (Buss, 1989b), and in the frequency of committing violent crimes of all sorts (Daly & Wilson, 1988). As noted by Donald Brown (1991), "it will be irresponsible to continue shunting these [findings] aside, fraud to deny that they exist" (p. 156). Evolutionary psychology sheds light on why these differences exist.

Conclusions

Strong sex differences occur reliably in domains closely linked with sex and mating, precisely as predicted by psychological theories based on sexual selection (Buss, 1994). Within these domains, the psychological sex differences are patterned in a manner that maps precisely onto the adaptive problems men and women have faced over human evolutionary history. Indeed, in most cases, the evolutionary hypotheses about sex differences were generated a decade or more before the empirical tests of them were conducted and the sex differences discovered. These models thus have heuristic and predictive power.

The evolutionary psychology perspective also offers several insights into the broader discourse on sex differences. First, neither women nor men can be considered "superior" or "inferior" to the other, any more than a bird's wings can be considered superior or inferior to a fish's fins or a kangaroo's legs. Each sex possesses mechanisms designed to deal with its own adaptive challenges—some similar and some different—and so notions of superiority or inferiority are logically incoherent from the vantage point of evolutionary psychology. The meta-theory of evolutionary psychology is descriptive, not prescriptive—it carries no values in its teeth.

Second, contrary to common misconceptions about evolutionary psychology, finding that sex differences originated through a causal process of sexual selection does not imply that the differences are unchangeable or intractable. On the contrary, understanding their origins provides a powerful heuristic to the contexts in which the sex differences are most likely to be manifested (e.g., in the context of mate competition) and hence provides a guide to effective loci for intervention if change is judged to be desirable.

Third, although some worry that inquiries into the existence and evolutionary origins of sex differences will lead to justification for the status quo, it is hard to believe that attempts to change the status quo can be very effective if they are undertaken in ignorance of sex differences that actually exist. Knowledge is power, and attempts to intervene in the absence of knowledge may resemble a surgeon operating blindfolded—there may be more bloodshed than healing (Tooby & Cosmides, 1992).

The perspective of evolutionary psychology jettisons the outmoded dualistic thinking inherent in much current discourse by getting rid of the false dichotomy between biological and social. It offers a truly interactionist position that specifies the particular features of social context that are especially critical for processing by our evolved psychological mechanisms. No other theory of sex differences has been capable of predicting and explaining the large number of precise, detailed, patterned sex differences discovered by research guided by evolutionary psychology (e.g., Bailey, Gaulin, Agyei, & Gladue, 1994; Buss & Schmitt, 1993; Daly & Wilson, 1988; Ellis & Symons, 1990; Gangestad & Simpson, 1990; Greer & Buss, 1994; Kenrick & Keefe, 1992; Symons, 1979). Evolutionary psychology possesses the heuristic power to guide investigators to the particular domains in which the most pronounced sex differences, as well as similarities, will be found. People grappling with the existence and implications of psychological sex differences cannot afford to ignore their most likely evolutionary origins through sexual selection.

References

Abby, A. (1982). Sex differences in attributions for friendly behavior: Do males misperceive females' friendliness? *Journal of Personality and Social Psychology, 32,* 830–838.

Ashmore, R. D. (1990). Sex, gender, and the individual. In L. A. Pervin (Ed.), *Handbook of personality: Theory and research* (pp. 486–526). New York: Guilford Press.

Bailey, J. M., Gaulin, S., Agyei, Y., & Gladue, B. A. (1994). Effects of gender and sexual orientation on evolutionarily relevant aspects of human mating psychology. *Journal of Personality and Social Psychology, 66,* 1074–1080.

Brown, D. (1991). *Human universals.* Philadelphia: Temple University Press.

Buss, D. M. (1989a). Sex differences in human mate preferences: Evolutionary hypotheses tested in 37 cultures. *Behavioral and Brain Sciences, 12,* 1–49.

Buss, D. M. (1989b). Conflict between the sexes: Strategic interference and the evocation of anger and upset. *Journal of Personality and Social Psychology, 56,*735–747.

Buss, D. M. (1994). *The evolution of desire: Strategies of human mating.* New York: Basic Books.

Buss, D. M., Larsen, R., Westen, D., & Semmelroth, J. (1992). Sex differences in jealousy: Evolution, physiology, and psychology. *Psychological Science, 3,* 251–255.

Buss, D. M., & Schmitt, D. P. (1993). Sexual strategies theory: An evolutionary perspective on human mating. *Psychological Review, 100,* 204–232.

Buunk, B., Angleitner, A., Oubaid, V., & Buss, D. M. (1994). *Sexual and cultural differences in jealousy: Tests from the Netherlands, Germany, and the United States.* Manuscript submitted for publication.

Clark, R. D., & Hatfield, E. (1989). Gender differences in receptivity to sexual offers. *Journal of Psychology and Human Sexuality, 2,* 39–55.

Cohen, J. (1977). *Statistical power analysis for the behavioral sciences.* San Diego, CA: Academic Press.

Daly, M., & Wilson, M. (1988). *Homicide.* New York: Aldine de Gruyter.

Darwin, C. (1871). *The descent of man and selection in relation to sex.* London: Murray.

Eagly, A. H. (1995). The science and politics of comparing women and men. *American Psychologist, 50,* 145–158.

Ellis, B. J., & Symons, D. (1990). Sex differences in sexual fantasy: An evolutionary psychological approach. *Journal of Sex Research, 27,* 527–556.

Feingold, A. (1990). Gender differences in effects of physical attractiveness on romantic attraction: A comparison across five research paradigms. *Journal of Personality and Social Psychology, 59,* 981–993.

Gangestad, S. W., & Simpson, J. A. (1990). Toward an evolutionary history of female sociosexual variation. *Journal of Personality, 58,* 69–96.

Greer, A., & Buss, D. M. (1994). Tactics for promoting sexual encounters. *Journal of Sex Research, 5,* 185–201.

Greiling, H. (1993, June). *Women's short-term sexual strategies.* Paper presented at the Conference on Evolution and the Social Sciences, London School of Economics, London, England.

Hall, J. A. (1978). Gender effects in decoding nonverbal cues. *Psychological Bulletin, 85,* 845–852.

Hill, K., & Hurtado, M. (1989). Hunter-gatherers of the new world. *American Scientist, 77,* 437–443.

Hyde, J. S. (1996). Where are the gender differences? Where are the gender similarities? In D. M. Buss & N. Malamuth (Eds.), *Sex, power, conflict: Feminist and evolutionary perspectives.* New York: Oxford University Press.

Kenrick, D. T., & Keefe, R. C. (1992). Age preferences in mates reflect sex differences in reproductive strategies. *Behavioral and Brain Sciences, 15,* 75–133.

Maccoby, E. E., & Jacklin, C. N. (1974). *The psychology of sex differences.* Stanford, CA: Stanford University Press.

Oliver, M. B., & Hyde, J. S. (1993). Gender differences in sexuality: A meta-analysis. *Psychological Bulletin, 114,* 29–51.

Rosenthal, R. (1991). *Meta-analytic procedures for social research* (rev. ed.). Newbury Park, CA: Sage.

Silverman, I., & Eals, M. (1992). Sex differences in spatial abilities: Evolutionary theory and data. In J. Barkow, L. Cosmides, & J. Tooby (Eds.), *The adapted mind: Evolutionary psychology and the generation of culture* (pp. 539–549). New York: Oxford University Press.

Symons, D. (1979). *The evolution of human sexuality.* New York: Oxford University Press.

Symons, D. (1992). On the use and misuse of Darwinism in the study of human behavior. In J. Barklow, L. Cosmides, & J. Tooby (Eds.), *The adapted mind: Evolutionary psychology and the generation of culture.* (pp. 137–159). New York: Oxford University Press.

Tooby, J., & Cosmides, L. (1992). Psychological foundations of culture. In J. Barkow, L. Cosmides, & J. Tooby (Eds.), *The adapted mind: Evolutionary psychology and the generation of culture* (pp. 119–136). New York: Oxford University Press.

Trivers, R. (1972). Parental investment and sexual selection. In B. Campbell (Ed.), *Sexual selection and the descent of man* (pp. 136–179). New York: Aldine de Gruyter.

Wiederman, M. W., & Allgeier, E. R. (1993). Gender differences in sexual jealousy: Adaptationist or social learning explanation? *Ethology and Sociobiology, 14,* 115–140.

Wilson, M., & Daly, M. (1985). Competitiveness, risk taking, and violence: The young male syndrome. *Ethology and Sociobiology, 6,* 59–73.

CHALLENGE QUESTIONS

Do Gender Roles Explain Sex Differences in Social Behavior?

1. In your opinion, does the evolutionary perspective perpetuate gender inequality as some critics have contended?
2. How should gender differences in social behavior change in the future? What do you think Eagly and Wood would say about changes over time? What would Buss say?
3. If Eagly and Wood are correct and social roles are the primary determinant of gender differences, what strategies should be used to promote gender equality? Would these strategies be effective if Buss is correct and evolution is the primary cause of gender differences?

Do Milgram's Obedience Experiments Help Explain the Nature of the Holocaust?

YES: John P. Sabini and Maury Silver from "Destroying the Innocent with a Clear Conscience: A Sociopsychology of the Holocaust," in *Survivors, Victims and Perpetrators: Essays on the Nazi Holocaust* (Hemisphere Publishing, 1980)

NO: Florence Miale and Michael Selzer from *The Nuremberg Mind*, (Quadrangle/New York Times Book Company, 1975)

ISSUE SUMMARY

YES: Social psychologists John P. Sabini and Maury Silver believe that the Obedience Experiments captured the most important psychological aspects of the Holocaust, by demonstrating that normal people can be made to harm others with alarming ease.

NO: Psychotherapist Florence R. Miale and political scientist Michael Selzer believe that Milgram's results are not as convincing as is often believed. They contend that the findings of these controversial experiments can be explained by individual differences in participants' willingness to inflict pain on others.

Stanley Milgram's Obedience Experiments are undoubtedly the most famous studies in the history of social psychology. Milgram was interested in whether people would obey the immoral commands of an authority figure. To investigate this question, Milgram led people to believe that they would be required to deliver an electrical shock to another person. (In actuality the shocks were fake, and no one was ever harmed.) The results of his experiment were stunning. *Everyone* who participated in his original study complied with the order to shock a total stranger. Even more disturbingly, nearly two-thirds of all those who participated went on to administer the most severe shock possible—a deadly 450 volts. Milgram's findings reverberated throughout the psychological community and continue to generate controversy to this day. But what do his experiments really mean? Milgram believed that his results demonstrated one of the principle reasons why the Holocaust occurred on such a wide scale—ordinary people are likely to obey the orders of authority figures even when they know the order is immoral and unjust.

Was Milgram right? Both of the readings will address this question by discussing a prominent figure in the Holocaust, Adolf Eichmann. Eichmann was largely responsible for the deportation of Jews to the death camps where millions were exterminated. Following Germany's surrender in the Second World War, he eluded capture by the victorious Allies but was eventually arrested by Israeli agents in Argentina in 1960. In the highly publicized war crimes trial that followed, Eichmann maintained that he was simply obeying the orders of his superiors. In his closing statement, Eichmann insisted that "my life's principle, which I was taught very early on, was to desire and to strive to achieve ethical values...however, I was prevented by the State from living according to this principle."

Do Milgram's Obedience Experiments demonstrate that the Nazi State was responsible for transforming decent, ordinary Germans into murderers, as Eichmann contended? John Sabini and Maury Silver reason that the experiments do explain the psychological dynamics of those who committed the atrocities of the Holocaust. Under certain circumstances, psychologically normal individuals, like Eichmann, can be made to harm innocent people with surprising ease. While this does not absolve Eichmann and the thousands of Germans who perpetrated the Holocaust, it was obedience to the authority of the Nazi State that ultimately led so many Germans to commit murderous acts.

Florence Miale and Michael Selzer reject Milgram's conclusion that obedience can lead ordinary people to inflict pain on others. According to their position, Milgram erroneously assumed that *all* individuals are reluctant to harm other people. Miale and Selzer believe that this assumption is incorrect. Some individuals, such as the Nazi leadership, may be quite willing to inflict injury on others when the sanctions against inflicting pain are removed. Thus, some participants in the Obedience Experiments, like many Nazis in the Holocaust, harmed others not out of obedience, but because the situation allowed them to express their desire to harm. Miale and Selzer conclude that Eichmann and many other Nazis participated in the Holocaust not because they were reluctantly following orders, but because the Holocaust afforded them the opportunity to express their desire to murder Jews.

POINT

- Obedience to authority is one of the primary reasons that the Holocaust occurred on such a large scale.
- Instead of being motivated by a hatred of Jews, many people may have participated in the Holocaust because they were part of the bureaucracy of the German state.
- While some Germans did commit atrocities because they were following orders, this does not absolve them of their crimes.

COUNTERPOINT

- The psychology of Nazi leaders can better explain the nature of the Holocaust.
- The Holocaust allowed many Nazis, such as Adolf Eichmann, to express their desire to harm Jews.
- "I was just following orders" was simply an excuse used by Nazis to evade their reasonability for their actions.

John P. Sabini and
Maury Silver

 **YES**

Destroying the Innocent
with a Clear Conscience:
A Sociopsychology of the Holocaust

In Paris on November 7, 1938, Herschl Grynszpan, a 17-year-old Polish Jew, shot and killed Ernst von Rath, third secretary of the German Embassy. In Germany the response was *Kristallnacht*.

During the days of *Kristallnacht*, synagogues were razed, shop windows shattered, thousands of Jewish businesses destroyed, and tens of thousands of Jews attacked, tortured, and humiliated. Nearly 100 Jews were killed. As an outpouring of hatred, vicious anti-Semitism, and unrestrained sadism, *Kristallnacht* appears to display the essence of the Holocaust. To develop an analysis centering on *Kristallnacht*, we would explore such traditional social-psychological issues as the psychology of the mob. (cf. Milgram & Toch, 1969), techniques of propaganda (cf. McGuire, 1969), and the character structure of the anti-Semite and fascist (cf. Adorno, Frenkel-Brunswik, Levinson, & Sanford, 1950).

But *Kristallnacht* cannot be our focus. *Kristallnacht*, a pogrom, an instrument of terror is typical of the long-standing tradition of European anti-Semitism not the new Nazi order, not the systematic, extermination of European Jewry. Mob violence is a primitive, ineffective technique of extermination. It *is* an effective method of terrorizing a population, keeping people in their place, perhaps even of forcing some to abandon their religious or political convictions, but these were never Hitler's aims with regard to the Jews; he meant to destroy them.

Consider the numbers. The German state annihilated approximately six million Jews. At the rate of 100 per day this would have required nearly 200 years. Mob violence rests on the wrong psychological basis, on violent emotion. People can be manipulated into fury, but fury cannot be maintained for 200 years. Emotions, and their biological basis, have a natural time course; lust, even blood lust, is eventually sated. Further, emotions are notoriously fickle, can be turned. A lynch mob is unreliable, it can sometimes be moved to sympathy—say by a child's suffering. To eradicate a "race" it is essential to kill the children.

Thorough, comprehensive, exhaustive murder required the replacement of the mob with a bureaucracy, the replacement of shared rage with obedience to authority. The requisite bureaucracy would be effective whether manned by extreme or tepid anti-Semites, considerably broadening the pool of potential recruits; it would govern the actions of its members not by arousing passions but by organizing routines; it would only make distinctions it was designed to make, not those its members might be moved to make, say, between children and adults, scholar and thief, innocent and guilty; it would be responsive to the will of the ultimate authority through a hierarchy of responsibility—whatever that will might be. It was this bureaucratization of evil, the institutionalization of murder that marked the Third Reich; our focus then will be on the social psychology of individual action within the context of hierarchical institutions. Hence with Eichmann the bureaucrat not *Kristallnacht* is where an answer to the question "How could it have happened?" will be sought.

As Arendt (1965) tells it, Eichmann was a disappointment. Those who expected some passionate, deep-seated evil in the character of an organizer of the German death machine were frustrated, not because Eichmann revealed some nobility of character incompatible with a passion to destroy, but because the utter shallowness of the man was inconsistent with any deep principle. It is not the angry rioter we must understand but Eichmann, the colorless bureaucrat, replicated two million times in those who assembled the trains, dispatched the supplies, manufactured the poison gas, filed the paper work, sent out the death notices, guarded the prisoners, pointed left and right, supervised the loading-unloading of the vans, disposed of the ashes, and performed the countless other tasks that also constituted the Holocaust. An excerpt from the Auschwitz diary of SS Professor Dr. Hans Hermann Kremer illustrates the particular quality of murder as bureaucratized in the Third Reich, its place in the life of its operatives, how distant this murder is from passionate impulse, the distance between the rioter and the functionary.

> *September 6, 1942.* Today, Sunday, excellent lunch: tomato soup, half a hen with potatoes and red cabbage (20g. fat), sweets and marvelous vanilla ice ... in the evening at 8.00 hours outside for a Sonderaktion.[1]
>
> *September 9, 1942.* This morning I got the most pleasant news from my lawyer, Prof. Dr. Hallermann in Münster, that I got divorced from my wife on the first of this month (Note: I see colors again, a black curtain is drawn back from my life!). Later on, present as doctor at a corporal punishment of eight prisoners and an execution by shooting with small-calibre rifles. Got soap flakes and two pieces of soap.... In the evening present at a Sonderaktion, fourth time.[2]

How could a Sonderaktion and soap flakes possibly be mentioned in the same breath? How could someone participate in mass murder without showing some emotion—distress, anger, or perhaps glee? Our account, then, attempts to explain not mass murder but mass murder of this special sort. Brutality, torture, rage, and even sadism in its restricted sexual sense were not missing from the Holocaust, but they were not its special features. They were neither necessary nor sufficient: what was needed was a machine not a beast. What is novel about the psychology of the Holocaust is not murder but the bloodlessness of the murderer. What needs explanation is not so much how the sadist could murder but how murder could come to occupy the same level of importance as soap flakes.

Obedience to Authority

Eichmann has offered an account of this kind of murder; he has explained that he (and by extension the two million others) were merely doing their jobs (cf. Hilberg, 1961). This was a bizarre attempt to *justify* genocide, but could it be part of a correct *explanation*? Is it possible for someone not a sadist or a psychopath to kill innocent individuals just because ordered to do so? Stanley Milgram (1974), in a brilliant series of social psychological experiments, addressed this question.

The logic of his study was simple. An experimenter ordered subjects to deliver increasingly painful punishment to another person within the context of what the experimenter claimed was an important study of the relation between punishment and learning. Milgram was interested in knowing at what point people would refuse to inflict further punishment on a fellow human being.

In Milgram's experiment the individual is faced with a dramatic choice, one apparently involving extreme pain and perhaps injury to another human being. The subjects are recruited to participate in an experiment on memory. When each arrives at the laboratory, the experimenter tells him and another subject, a kindly, pleasant, avuncular, middle-aged gentleman (actually a confederate) that the study concerns the effects of punishment on learning. After a rigged drawing the lucky subject wins the role of teacher and the confederate becomes the "learner." The teacher and learner are taken to an adjacent room, and the learner is strapped into a chair, electrodes attached to his arms, supposedly to prevent excessive movement; the effect was to make it appear impossible to escape. While strapped in the chair the learner diffidently mentions that he has a heart condition. The experimenter replies that while the shocks may be painful, they cause no permanent tissue damage. The teacher is instructed to read to the learner a list of word pairs, to test him on the list, and to administer punishment, an electric shock, whenever the learner errs. The teacher is given a sample shock of 45 volts (the only real shock ever administered). The experimenter instructs the teacher to increase the intensity of the shock one step on the shock generator for each error. The generator has 30 switches labeled from 15 to 450 volts, 10 times the sample shock. Beneath these voltage readings are verbal labels ranging from "SLIGHT SHOCK" to "DANGER: SEVERE SHOCK" and finally "XX."

The experiment starts routinely. By the fifth shock level, however, the confederate grunts in annoyance, and by the eighth shock level he shouts that the shocks are becoming painful. By the tenth level (150 volts) he cries out "Experimenter, get me out of here! I won't be in the experiment any more! I refuse to go on!" This response makes plain the intensity of the pain, and underscores the learner's *right* to be released regardless of the intensity of the pain. By 270 volts the learner's response becomes an agonized scream, and at 300 volts the learner refuses to supply any further answers. From 300 volts to 330 volts he shrieks in pain at each shock and gives no answer (the teacher is told to treat the failure to answer as an erroneous answer and to continue to shock). From 330 volts on the learner is not heard from, and the teacher has no way to know whether the learner is still conscious or, for that matter, alive (the teacher also knew that the experimenter could not tell about the condition of the victim from his position in the same room as the teacher).

Typically the teacher attempts to break off the experiment many times during the session. When he tries to do so, the experimenter instructs him to continue. If he refuses, the experimenter insists, finally telling him, "You must continue; you have no other choice." If the subject still refuses, the experimenter ends the experiment. The question of interest is the point at which the subject will terminate the experiment.

The situation is extremely realistic and tension-provoking. An observer (Milgram, 1963) has related:

> I observed a mature and initially poised businessman enter the laboratory smiling and confident. Within 20 minutes he was reduced to a twitching, stuttering wreck, who was rapidly approaching a point of nervous collapse. He constantly pulled on his earlobe, and twisted his hands. At one point he pushed his fist into his forehead and muttered: "Oh God, let's stop it." And yet he continued to respond to every word of the experimenter, and obeyed to the end. (p. 377)

We would expect that at most a small minority of subjects would continue to shock beyond the point at which the victim screamed in pain and demanded to be released. We certainly would expect that very, very few people would continue to the point of 450 volts. Indeed Milgram asked a sample of undergraduates, a sample of psychiatrists, and a sample of adults of various occupations to predict whether they would obey the orders of the experimenter. Each of these 110 people claimed that he or she would disobey at some point. Milgram, aware of the fact that people would be unwilling to admit that they themselves would obey such an unreasonable and unconscionable order, asked another sample of middle-class adults to predict how far *other people* would go in such a procedure. The average prediction was that perhaps one person in a thousand would continue to the end. This prediction was very far from the mark. In fact 65% (26 out of 40) of the subjects obeyed to the end.

Of course Milgram's subjects were not like Eichmann. Typically they protested, complained, and frequently showed signs of tension while carrying out their task. Arendt's report of Eichmann's prison interviews in Jerusalem shows no corresponding difficulty in carrying out his orders—the Final Solution. But this difference must not obscure the central point: subjects in the experiment *did* continue to shock even though the person they were shocking demanded to be released and withdrew his consent, even though the person they were shocking had ceased responding and might have been unconscious or even dead. Subjects in the experiment were induced to act in ways that we simply would not expect ordinary citizens of no obvious deficit of conscience to act.

In two other variants of the Milgram experiment there was a reduction in the subject's protests and emotional displays and an increase in obedience. In one variation the subject is not himself ordered to pull the switch delivering the shock but rather he performs a different, also essential task, while another person (in reality a confederate) pulls the switch. In this case roughly 90% (37 out of 40) of the subjects continued to perform the subsidiary task through 450 volts. The vast majority of the millions implicated in the Holocaust were involved in analogous subsidiary but essential functions. Further, they performed them distant from the actual gassing, burnings, and shootings. Distance from the victim, Milgram found, also has a profound effect on the level of obedience and on the stress experienced in obeying—from 20% obedience and great stress in a condition in which the subject has to physically press the victim's hand to the shock plate to virtually complete obedience and little stress in a condition in which the subject's information about the victim's suffering is dependent almost entirely on the verbal designations on the shock machine.

The central problem remains: How could the subjects in the Milgram experiments bring themselves to continue shocking the victim? This problem is exacerbated, not relieved, by the fact that some experienced great tension. If they were that upset by what they were doing, why didn't they stop?

Subjects in the Milgram experiment sometimes turned to the experimenter and asked who was responsible for their shocking the learner. The experimenter replied that *he* accepted full responsibility and subjects seemed to accept this and thus continued shocking. Yet how *could* the experimenter take upon himself their responsibility? Responsibility is not property that can be borrowed, shared, loaned, or repossessed. Responsibility is related to the *proper* allocation of moral praise and blame; assessing a person's responsibility involves considerations of what the person intended to do, what he realized or should have realized, what the individual could or could not have done, and so forth, as well as considerations relating to the gravity of the rule transgressed, the priority of competing claims, and the like. How could the experimenter's offer to assume responsibility alter any of these considerations; hence how could his offer alter whether the subjects were or were not responsible?...

As for the behavior or Milgram's subjects, while it is correct to point out that they continued to obey because they *felt* that they were not responsible even though they were responsible, we now are obligated to explain how they could feel not responsible when they in fact were, especially since as people attempting to predict behavior in the experiment, or as jurists considering the crimes of members of the SS, we see quite clearly that they were responsible. Responsibility is not something like personal property that one can divest oneself of, or that even an experimenter or a Führer can give or take away. How then could these subjects be guilty of this misinterpretation? Understanding how responsibility works in a bureaucracy provides a clue. Within an organization a section head, for example, is responsible for planning a job, assigning responsibilities among the workers, and even relieving some workers of responsibilities. A subordinate is only responsible for carrying out the plan. If the subordinate executes the plan according to specifications, then it is not his or her fault if the larger project fails because the plan was misconceived. The boss was responsible for the plan; the subordinate was responsible for only part of the execution. We could say that here responsibility has been partitioned, taken over, and shared. However, if the organization were indicted, it would be queer indeed for the subordinates to offer to the judge, as Eichmann did (and Milgram's subjects might have had it come to that), the excuse that they were not responsible, that their boss had relieved them of responsibility, and further, they had not constructed the plan but had merely carried it out. To offer such an excuse would be to ludicrously confuse the issues of technical and moral (or legal) responsibility.

The question of *technical* responsibility, the question of who is accountable for which part of a larger plan, arises within an institution and is decided by that institution. Questions of *moral* responsibility *cannot* be confined within institutions and resist resolutions by institutional superiors. Obedient subjects in the Milgram experiment who felt reassured by the experimenter's acceptance of responsibility apparently succumbed to a confusion between these two sorts of responsibility. The obedient Eichmann, at least in some of his moods, refused to the death to concede that such a distinction between technical and moral responsibility *can* be drawn.

So long as our institutions are legitimate and act within the limits of our shared morality, we are, as moral actors, free to ignore the broader question of moral responsibility as a matter of convenience. Ordinarily, convinced of the benevolence of the organizations of which we are a part, we do not trouble ourselves with questions of moral responsibility for the routine doing of our job. Eichmann and Milgram's subjects lost the right to be unconcerned with the moral implications of their actions just when the German state and the experimenter's demands became immoral. Milgram's obedient subjects and Hitler's murderers ought to have seen that these institutions were no longer legitimate, could no longer claim their loyalty, and could no longer settle for them the question of moral responsibility. Milgram's subjects, insofar as they accepted the experimenter's explicit or implicit claim to accept responsibility, failed to see what is, from a distance, so obvious.

Morality and the Legitimacy of the Authority

One might suppose that the failure of Eichmann and the millions like him to perceive the patent immorality of the German state bureaucracy must be different from the failure of Milgram's subjects to see what had become of the experiment. After all, the magnitude of the failure in the Eichmann case is so much greater, the responsibility so much greater, that it would seem that we need different principles to explain it. We want to assume that the German bureaucrats acted out of a deep anti-Semitism, or perhaps financial self-interest, or perhaps they just sought to avoid the Russian front. We want to see the German failure as motivated in a way that the moral failure of Milgram's subjects seems not to be. Further variants of the Milgram experiment address the question of whether we need to assume such deep and particular motivation.

In one version the experiment is repeated not for the benefit of pure science, under the auspices of august Yale University, but rather for a firm of private industrial consultants located in a somewhat run-down commercial building in an office which barely managed to appear respectable. Yet in this setting, 19 out of 40 subjects obeyed fully. Although this is fewer than the 26 out of 40 at Yale, it is not significantly so. The rather shabby setting in an institution of vague if not questionable aims was not only sufficient to induce subjects to start the experiment but to keep them going to the end.

A second variant further explores the issue of legitimacy. Subjects in the original condition sometimes reported that the reason they continued was that the experiment was fair—the learner had volunteered to be in the experiment. But as an explanation this implies that the subject would not have obeyed if the experiment had not been fair, at least in this restricted sense. This possible explanation was examined in a condition in which the learner, in the presence of the subject and experimenter, agrees to participate only if the experimenter would agree to stop the experiment if and when he, the learner, wanted it stopped. The experimenter agreed. As in the other conditions the learner demands that the experiment be stopped at 150 volts. Sixteen out of 40 subjects continued to the end, even though this was in clear violation of the prior agreement. If anything ought to have undermined the legitimacy of the enterprise, this violation ought to have done so. It did not. These experiments do not explain *why* institutions keep such a strong presumption of legitimacy, why it is so difficult for people to extract themselves on moral grounds, but it does illustrate that people can treat corrupt institutions as legitimate in cases in which it would not seem possible to do so, even though they have *no* ulterior motive. For people to perceive the Nazi government as legitimate even while it was slaughtering millions, it would seem that it was not necessary to personally profit by, for example, taking over confiscated Jewish businesses.

Participating in a "legitimate" enterprise allowed subjects and bureaucrats to ignore the immoral implications of their actions in two ways. First, the issue of moral responsibility for the goals of the organization just does not come up in legitimate institutions; to do their jobs, people do not have to think about such matters. Second, even if subjects or bureaucrats *had* addressed the question of moral responsibility, bureaucratic structure would have helped them answer the question incorrectly; the relation between an individual's action and the rules and commands of an organization obscures personal responsibility.

Responsibility and Intent

Typically there is a close relation between responsibility and intent—we are responsible for what we intend to do, what we are *trying* to do. If we accidentally cause something that was not our intent, then we have lessened or no responsibility. For example, if we accidentally step on someone's toy poodle, we may be guilty of clumsiness but not cruelty to animals, since we do not intend to hurt the beast. Lack of intent is a quite common ingredient of justifications and excuses in everyday life. An act we do not intend is usually a mistake, an error, an inadvertent consequence, and for these reasons our responsibility for them is usually diminished. In fact the link between responsibility and intent is even tighter: if we were asked what we are doing at a given moment, we would be likely to reply by mentioning the goal of our action, what we are intending. We would not be likely to point out the constituents or consequences aside from our goal or goals. For example, going to the store to get a loaf of bread is also: putting on our coat, going down stairs, walking down the street, wearing down our shoes, passing our friend's house, and, also, contributing to the profits of the grocery store owner, providing employment for the clerks, using up the earth's scarce resources, and so forth. However, of all of these, "going for a loaf of bread" (our goal) is the only one we are likely to see ourselves as "really" doing. The typical Milgram subject was only trying to be a good subject, help the experiment, and, perhaps, contribute to science; one imagines, the German bureaucrat, similarly, as trying only to do his job well, follow the rules, perhaps support his family. In both cases the evil they did was not intended; it was perhaps easy to "feel" that the evil was not their doing, to feel that it had an accidental quality. Moreover, in both cases not only was destroying others not something they were trying to do, but, as in the case of the poodle who was accidentally stepped on, it was something they *would never* try to do. Carrying out the evil may even have been something they despised doing while they did, it. For all these reasons, it was easy for Milgram's subjects, and at least some bureaucrats, to feel so innocent, so lacking in responsibility for the evil they performed. But feelings aside, they were responsible-not because their protestations of innocent intent were necessarily insincere but because in *these* cases the question of intent is irrelevant to the question of responsibility. No matter how much the evil that was a part, say, of dispatching the trains, when those trains went from Warsaw to Auschwitz, *felt* accidental it was not. Eichmann knew what his actions caused. Eichmann may well have been personally indifferent as to whether the Jews were annihilated, sent to Madagascar, or allowed to fulfill the Zionist dream, and in that sense he did not intend the Holocaust, but he was still responsible because people are responsible for all that they *cause* so long as they can or should see that they cause it. We may *feel* responsible only for what we intend; we *are* responsible for all that we do, and we know it.

Because our *feelings* of responsibility are grounded in our intentions, and bureaucracies arrange that everyone need only intend to follow the rules, the result is that bureaucracies have a genius for organizing evil. The bureaucrat knows what the rules of the bureaucracy dictate that he ought to do; if he should find some action contrary to his inclinations, he can still do it with a clear conscience, since he knows the action is contrary to his inclinations, can be divorced from his intentions. Even if he actually does want to bring about the very thing the bureaucracy tells him to do, and he suspects that it is wrong, he can still correctly maintain that even though he wanted to do it, he would have refrained in light of its questionable moral status were it not for the fact that he was ordered to do it. Of course this is germane to the question of *intent* but irrelevant to the issue of *responsibility*. Insofar as these concepts are muddled, morality is lost from the bureaucracy as a whole; each and everyone is allowed to *feel* free of responsibility except, perhaps, the person who put it all together.

An important difference between Eichmann and Milgram's subjects is that Eichmann, unlike the obedient subjects who gave every evidence of detesting their role and resisting it, did not obey orders passively but actively strove to carry them out efficiently, intelligently, creatively, and most important, visibly—after all, his advancement depended on it. And trying to advance was what Eichmann, at least as Arendt tells it, saw himself as doing. Orders from above provided the ready excuse for him to kill millions as his particular pathway to self-advancement. This was why Eichmann was able to complain to his Jewish interrogator of the injustice of his being passed over in his difficult struggle to improve his position. The covering excuse of superior orders allows the individual to pursue personal goals (wealth, status, power, etc.) as well as more altruistic goals (providing for his family).

Doing one's duty is an important virtue, something that might justify actions one would not ordinarily do. A professor might fail a student, for example, keeping him or her out of medical school (inflicting real pain, something ordinarily proscribed), out of a duty to grade fairly, yet we find the teacher virtuous not a sadist. But just as a lack of evil intent does not necessarily absolve one of the responsibility, neither does a virtuous intent. If in pursuit of the virtue of punctuality, we were to jostle an elderly cripple to the ground or refuse to yield the right of way to an ambulance, then we could not offer as an excuse that punctuality was a virtue. Nor can we excuse Eichmann his genocide because he so well exemplified the virtue of adherence to duty....

Conclusion

The thrust of this chapter has been to bring the phenomena of the camps closer to home, to see how this horror, this inhumanity could have been the product not only of deranged individuals but of normal people placed in deranged and degrading circumstances. We have attempted to draw links between what we know the artisans of the Holocaust did and what ordinary, American people have done in laboratory settings. We have tried to show how this behavior that we cannot understand is more comprehensible if we analyze it in terms of the influences of authority and peer support on people's moral judgments.

There is, however, a danger in this. The task of making something understandable *is* to make us see how it could have happened by showing how it is akin to something we can already grasp. There is a common tendency to slide from understanding to excusing. We are accustomed to thinking that once we have understood how someone came to do something, we are then compelled to forgive. In this case we cannot allow understanding to lead to excuse or forgiveness. As scientists examining the phenomenon, we are committed to trying to discover its similarities with things that we know, how it follows from fundamental facts of human nature; only when this is done do we have an adequate grasp of the phenomenon. We, at the same time, must take the position that no matter how well we understand, no matter how clearly we see the behavior as an expression of something basic to human nature, we cannot alter our moral judgment of these actions or the actors who performed them.

There is a precedent for this paradox. Greek tragedy is absorbed with the attempt to make evil understandable, to relate it to common flaws in human nature. Our appreciation of how hard it is to do right when fate and circumstances conspire to trick us cannot obscure the fact that the measure of human nature is our capacity to do what is right and resist what is wrong.

Notes

1. "The most spectacular of the mass atrocities were called *Sonderaktionen* (special actions). One of these, which was practiced particularly in Auschwitz, was the burning of live prisoners, especially children, in pits measuring 20 by 40 to 50 meters, on piles of gasoline-soaked wood" (Alexander, 1949, reported in Cohen, 1953).
2. From *Human Behavior in the Concentration Camp* by Elie A. Cohen. Copyright © 1953 by Grosset & Dunlap, Inc. Reprinted by permission of Grosset & Dunlap, Inc.

References

Adorno, T., Frenkel-Brunswik, E., Levinson, D., & Sanford, N. *The authoritarian personality*. New York: Harper, 1950.

Alexander, L. The molding of personality under dictatorship. *Journal of Criminal Law ad Criminology of Northwestern University*, May–June 1949, *40*.

Arendt, H. *Eichmann in Jerusalem* (2nd ed.). New York: Viking Press, 1965.

Cohen, E. *Human behavior in the concentration camp*. New York: Grosset & Dunlap, 1953.

Hilberg, R. *The destruction of the European Jews*. Chicago: Quadrangle Books, 1961.

McGuire, W. J. The nature of attitudes and attitude change. In G. Lindzey & E. Aronson (Eds.), *Handbook of social psychology* (2nd ed.), Vol. 3. Reading, Mass.: Addison-Wesley, 1969, 136–314.

Milgram, S. Behavioral study of obedience. *Journal of Abnormal and Social Psychology*, 1963, *67*, 371–378.

Milgram, S. *Obedience to authority*. New York: Harper & Row, 1974.

Milgram, S., & Toch, H. Collective behavior: Crowds and social movements. In G. Lindzey & E. Aronson (Eds.), *Handbook of social psychology* (2nd ed.), Vol. 4. Reading, Mass.: Addison-Wesley, 1969. 507–610.

Florence R. Miale
and Michael Selzer

Banality?

We were only obeying orders...

After the end of World War II, thousands of men were brought to trial for the horrendous deeds which they had committed during the twelve years of the Nazi Reich.

Almost invariably, regardless, of the rank that they had held in the Nazi hierarchy or the scope of the crimes of which they were accused, these men pleaded the same case in their defense. "We were only following orders," they claimed, depicting themselves as decent and law-abiding citizens who obeyed legitimate orders from their legitimate superiors just as decent and law-abiding citizens do anywhere else in the world. If what they had done was wrong, they asserted, then not they but the individuals who had issued those orders to them should be tried and punished. From the lowliest soldier in the SS to the highest officials in Hitler's immediate entourage, and with only a few notable exceptions, the indicted pointed the finger of guilt at someone above them. Ultimately, they claimed, only one man in Nazi Germany was really responsible for all the terrible tragedies that had occurred. He was the *Fuehrer*, and the orders which they had obeyed stemmed from his authority.

This spurious and contemptible argument was consistently rejected by international tribunals, military courts, and criminal courts in countries throughout Europe. One element in it, however, raises questions which deserve close consideration.

In support of their contention that they were merely obeying orders, the Nazi criminals insisted that they were not the subhuman beasts, the insatiable sadists, of popular imagination. They claimed, rather, that they were ordinary, normal people, fundamentally similar to you and us. They had not wanted to do the terrible things of which they now stood accused—so they said—and had not enjoyed doing them. Far from being brutal and violent perverts, they were so averse to violence that they would get upset if they had so much as to punish their own children for misbehaving.

At first glance there appears to be no reason why we should pay any attention to this outrageous notion. We *know* that the Nazis were not ordinary, normal people, just as we know that we, as ordinary, normal people, could never do what they did. But a moment's reflection might lead us to think otherwise, or at least to recognize that the problems posed by the Nazis' claims are rather more complex than they initially appear to be.

We assume that ordinary people are basically decent, and this is one of the reasons why we find it so difficult to take seriously the assertion that the Nazis were ordinary people. But what is the evidence for this assumption? Although a belief in human decency is a necessary underpinning for our democratic institutions, it surely rests on an ideological commitment rather than on empirical fact. As such, it flies in the face of other views of human nature. Whoever first remarked that *homo hominis lupus* ("man is a wolf to man"), for example, would by no means have taken it for granted that the Nazis represented a point well beyond the furthest extremes of human normality. Of course, this view is no more capable of empirical demonstration than the one which asserts that human beings are fundamentally decent. Both are assumptions that probably tell us more about the people who hold them, and the societies which institutionalize them, than they do about human nature itself. Depending on how you choose to look at it, history provides ample justification for either view—or for neither, or for both. For our purposes here, however, it is important to establish the arbitrariness of the belief that the Nazis could not have been ordinary people because ordinary people are basically decent.

In its own bizarre way, moreover, the Nazi defense echoes some of the most basic findings of modern social science. These have pointed to the very considerable extent to which the perceptions, values, and behavior of individuals are shaped by social forces beyond our control—and often, indeed, beyond our recognition. Is it not, then, at least possible that under the extraordinary circumstances of Nazi Germany quite ordinary people could indeed have been induced to do the most revolting things? Perhaps the Nazis really were what they claimed to be: normal, ordinary people who acted as they did not because they were sadists or perverts or brutes but because they were powerless to resist the ineluctable logic of the situations in which they found themselves, victims of social forces not of their own making and whose distinctive qualities they did not necessarily endorse or even recognize. If the prime ministers of England and France could believe that Adolf Hitler was a peaceful and honorable man, are ordinary Germans to be considered base perverts for having trusted him? If a Catholic pope and an American president, each in complicitous silence, failed to hinder the destruction of European Jewry, are ordinary Germans to be considered bloodthirsty demons for not having impeded Hitler's genocidal lust? It is not a moral question which we are asking here, but rather a phenomenological one regarding the kind of behavior which, in a highly abnormal context, is compatible with human normality.

In the past thirty years or so, a number of prominent scholars and intellectuals have lent their own authority to this aspect of the Nazi defense. They have suggested, in effect not only that ordinary, normal people can behave like the Nazis, but also that *the Nazi leaders themselves were ordinary, normal people.* Their opinions, we suspect, have been rather more influential than scholars' opinions usually are, and for this reason we wish to examine them carefully. We will focus in particular on the work of... Stanley Milgram,...a leading social psychologist....

At about the time that the Eichmann trial was taking place in Jerusalem, Stanley Milgram, a psychologist at Yale University, launched a study which has often been referred to since as "the Eichmann experiment."

Milgram sought to discover the extent to which human beings will obey commands which come increasingly into conflict with their consciences. The experiment was conducted along the following lines.

Volunteers were invited through an advertisement in a newspaper to participate in an experimental study of memory and learning. Assigned the role of "teacher," they were given a brief explanation of what was expected of them and assured that they could abandon the experiment at any time they chose to, and that they would receive the small fee and bus fare promised in the advertisement regardless of the point at which they did break off. They were then seated in front of an impressive-looking machine called a "shock generator." The control panel of the machine had thirty switches on it whose voltage increased in 15-volt increments from 15 to 450; verbal designations ranging from SLIGHT SHOCK to DANGER—SEVERE SHOCK identified groups of four or more switches.

The "teacher's" task was to administer an electric shock to another person—the "learner," who was strapped into a chair—every time he made a mistake in a simple memory test. The first mistake was punished by a shock of 15 volts, the second by one of 30 volts, and so on. In fact, the "learner" was an actor who in reality received no shock at all. As his "punishment" increased in severity, however, he begin to indicate discomfort. At 75 volts he grunted; at 120 volts he complained verbally; at 150 volts he demanded to be released from the experiment. "At 285 volts," reports Milgram, "his response can only be described as an agonized scream." Shortly thereafter he slumped forward, apparently unconscious—or dead.

In the experiments, the teacher typically experienced intense inner conflict as he administered what he believed to be ever more painful and dangerous shocks. His behavior was carefully supervised by the experimenter himself. When the teacher asked for advice as to whether to continue increasing the punishments, or else indicated that he did not wish to continue the task, the experimenter responded with a series of verbal "prods," the mildest of which was "Please continue" and the most severe, "You have no other choice, you *must* go on."

Sweating, trembling, and in other ways indicating their extreme reluctance to continue administering the punishments, *65 percent of the teachers nevertheless obeyed orders all the way to the end of the scale on the shock generator!* Not a single teacher disobeyed the experimenter's orders before reaching 300 volts—marked INTENSE SHOCK—and only 12.5 percent of them stopped at this point (Milgram, 1974, p. 35). The mean maximum shock level administered by the teachers before refusing to go further was 405 volts, or well within the DANGER—SEVERE SHOCK range.

Using other groups of teachers, Milgram then altered the experimental design. In one version, the experimenter was called away from the laboratory and the teacher was left to continue the shocks on his own; in another, the teacher was supervised by two experimenters who, when appealed to by the teacher, would give contradictory orders, one telling him to discontinue the experiment if he felt that he should, the other insisting that he continue, regardless of his own feelings. In yet another version, the teacher was not instructed to administer the punishments in increasingly severe shocks but was left to select the voltage level by himself.

These variations produced interesting results. Obedience dropped sharply when the experimenter was physically absent from the laboratory and when two experimenters were giving the teacher contradictory instructions. The most dramatic results were obtained when the teachers were left to select the shock level by themselves; in this series of experiments the average shock administered by the teachers was about 55 volts (SLIGHT SHOCK), which elicited no signs of discomfort from the learner....

What do these findings indicate? Milgram's explanation of them is unequivocal. "Whatever leads to shocking the victims at the highest levels cannot be explained by autonomously generated aggression," he declares, "but needs to be explained by the transformation of behavior that comes through obedience to orders...." Indeed, Milgram goes on to suggest that while the teachers in his experiments may have been *upset* about having to administer the shocks, they did not consider their actions *wrong* at the time that they were performing them. And this not only because they did not regard themselves as responsible for their actions (they were merely obeying orders given to them by others), but also because they had transferred to the experimenter the *responsibility for determining whether their actions were immoral or not*. "Although the subject performs the action," Milgram declares, "he allows the authority to define its meaning"....

The human being's ability to obey an order and to avoid considering (or at least being deterred from obedience by) its manifest immorality is, Milgram suggests, rooted in our species' evolutionary struggle for survival. Without this capacity we would not be able to function in a hierarchical social organization. But with it we can, thereby making it possible for an individual to belong to a group whose strength and, therefore, capacity for survival is far greater than his own. Every human being possesses the capacity to function as an individual exercising his own moral judgment and equally, the capacity to relinquish his autonomy and, as a member of a social hierarchy, obey his superior's orders and accept *his* moral judgment.

> When the individual [is] *on his own*, conscience is brought into play. But when he functions in an organizational mode, directions that come from the higher level component are not assessed against the internal standards of moral judgment.... The psychology of obedience does not depend on the placement within the larger hierarchy: the psychological adjustments of an obedient Wehrmacht general to Adolf Hitler parallel those of the lowest infantry man to his superior, and so forth, throughout the system. Only the psychology of the ultimate leader demands a different set of explanatory principles.... The social psychology of this century reveals a major les-

son: often, it is not so much the kind of person a man is as the kind of situation in which he finds himself that determines how he will act.

Eichmann and his fellows, then, were right.... The most vicious act in human history is not to be explained by the viciousness of the human beings who perpetrated it. Rather, the largest slaughter of human beings in history is to be accounted for by a mechanism that has its origins in the human struggle for survival. Obedience rather than aggression is what made the ghastly tragedy possible. Moreover, under the conditions which prevailed in Nazi Germany, any of us decent, normal people could have behaved as the most bestial Nazi did.

This, at least, is what Milgram would have us believe. But are the conclusions which he draws from the results of his experiments warranted?

A close look at the way in which he reached those conclusions reveals that they rest on a surprising measure of arbitrariness and dogmatism. To begin with, let us note how Milgram accounts for the *disobedience* of some of the teachers. "Residues of selfhood," he says of them, "keep personal values alive in the subject and lead to strain which, if sufficiently powerful, can result in disobedience".

Obedient subjects, then, are those who have failed to keep their personal values alive in the situation in which they found themselves, while disobedient ones have managed to do so.

Surely the results could be explained equally well along different lines. It could be argued that the disobedient subjects did not merely keep their personal values alive, as Milgram suggests, but that *they actually had different values to start with.* Milgram tacitly equates "personal values" with "not causing pain to others." But where is the evidence that these were, indeed, the personal values of *all* his subjects? Is it not possible that the disobedient subjects disobeyed because they were more moral, more averse to inflicting pain on other human beings, than the obedient subjects?

Milgram seeks to anticipate this objection by referring to the version,of the experiment in which the teacher is allowed to select the shock level by himself. On these occasions, it will be recalled, very much lower voltages were chosen than were administered under the instructions of the experimenter. With reference to these results, Milgram asks: "If destructive impulses were really pressing for release, and the subject could justify his use of high shock levels in the cause of science, why did they [*sic*] not make the victim suffer?"....

One answer to this question is, indeed, that which Milgram offers. The difference between obedients and disobedients vanishes, to all intents and purposes, in the absence of external authority. From this, Milgram infers that the presence of that external authority is the factor which led many of the subjects to administer inordinately high shocks. Since authority demands obedience, this argument goes, the reason the subjects administered such high shocks was that they were obeying the authority of the experimenter.

But another explanation of the same facts is, at the least, equally plausible. If we assume that the obedients were more aggressive and more violent than the disobedients, it becomes reasonable to see the function of the authority of the experimenter in rather different terms from those suggested by Milgram. The authoritative command of the experimenter to administer the shocks, we may speculate, *gave sanction to and released the aggressive drives of the so-called obedient subjects.*

Those drives....are legitimized, as it were, by the authority of the experimenter.... The manifest tension observed in the teachers as they administered the higher voltage shocks reflects a struggle, not between their "personal values" and their inclination to surrender these to the experimenter (as Milgram argues), but between their aggressive drives and their own internal....restraints on them.

The function of the authority's command, then, is not to say, in effect, "be violent *despite* yourself; let me do the judging for you," but rather, "I won't punish you if you indulge your appetite for violence: indeed, I would really like you to do so." Some people, because of the amount of violence in them.... are more likely to accept this invitation than others. But even in....most violent of Milgram's subjects....were strong enough to put up a good fight *against* that invitation; if it could not prevent the subjects from being violent, it at least made them feel extremely uneasy about what they were doing.

This hypothesis is also consistent with the fact that without external sanction all subjects administered a far lower level of shock. In this situation the potentially obedient subjects are deprived of the invitation to do great violence to another human being. Without such an overt, external stimulus, the potential obedient's aggressive drives are once again brought under.... control....with the result that he behaves in much the same way as the potential disobedient.

The difference between these two groups, then, does not lie in the durability or otherwise of their "personal values" but in the nature of those values. One group is less prone to violence—more moral, more decent—than the other. And the social lesson to be learned from this is not that in a wicked world decent people will act in a wicked way but that in a wicked world people with a penchant for wickedness will freely indulge it, justifying themselves (when called upon to do so) on the grounds that they were merely obeying orders.

Here then is a radically different explanation from the one offered by Milgram. Both explanations are based on the same facts but draw different conclusions from them. More data would, perhaps, enable us to settle the debate one way or another. Unfortunately, those facts are not available, because Milgram chose not to pursue them.

The first group of subjects in his experiment—thirty-four Yale students—were subsequently examined by another psychologist, Lawrence Kohlberg, who has specialized in the study of the development of moral judgment in individuals as they mature. Kohlberg's finding was that the students who broke off were at a higher level of moral development than those who remained obedient to the end (Kohlberg). Reporting this, however, Milgram merely says that "Kohlberg's findings are suggestive, though not very strong".... He does not explain this judgment, and he does not incorporate even the "suggestive" aspects of Kohlberg's work into his own analysis. More important, Milgram makes no attempt to account for his failure to develop independent information on the moral caliber of all of his subjects. Without this information, his hypothesis about their behavior can be neither proven nor disproven.

It is interesting to speculate about what the results would have been if Milgram had run one series of experiments with criminals guilty of repeated crimes of violence. As confirmed disobedients, Milgram would presumably expect them to administer significantly lower levels of shocks than normal, law-abiding citizens.

As the paradigm of the Nazi world which Milgram claims that they are, his experiments suffer from at least one overwhelming defect. It is well known that the Jews were subjected to intense vilification by the Nazi propaganda machine for several years before their actual extermination began. This propaganda gave official sanction to what had always been strong anti-Semitic currents in German life and disposed Germans all the more to regard Jews as sinister, dangerous, hateful, and altogether less than human.

Of the actor—learner in his experiments, on the other hand, Milgram writes: "The victim was played by a 47-year-old accountant, trained for the role; he was of Irish-American descent and most observers found him mild-mannered and likable".... Milgram does not explain why he chose this individual as the learner in preference to some other personality type. The effect, if not the intention, of this selection is to weight the scales in favor of his interpretation of the results. Who would want to vent his aggressive impulses on a mild and likeable middle-aged man? *Therefore*, we have additional reason to believe that the teachers acted out of obedience rather than from aggression. Milgram does not say this, of course, but it is a bias in the implementation of the experimental design which deserves to be noted.

But the Jews whom the Nazis exterminated were not, as we have seen, viewed by their torturers as "mild-mannered and likable"—indeed, quite the opposite. For his experiments to have approximated conditions in Nazi Germany, Milgram would have had to have had members of, shall we say, the Ku Klux Klan as teachers and a black person as learner. He did not do so, of course, and we must conclude therefore, that his experiments are almost as irrelevant to an understanding of the Nazi phenomenon in Germany as his interpretation of the results of those experiments is inconclusive (Wrightsman)....

Milgram....has [not] established a persuasive case in favor of their contention that the Nazi leadership was composed of normal, ordinary people.... The most startling fact established by Milgram is that under the conditions prevailing in his laboratory (which are not quite as representative of Nazi Germany as he claims they are), a surprisingly large proportion of people will inflict a great deal of pain on an innocent and helpless person. Whether this indicates that most people are capable of mindless obedience even to brutal orders, as Milgram suggests, or, alternatively, that many more people than we would like to believe have a terrifyingly great capacity for violence when the restraints against it are removed is, as we have seen, open to question....

CHALLENGE QUESTIONS

Do Milgram's Obedience Experiments Help Explain the Nature of the Holocaust?

1. How do you think you would have behaved if you were a participant in the Obedience Experiments? Do you think you would have disobeyed the orders of the experimenter? If so, at what point do you think you would have disobeyed, and why?
2. Does it seem like Milgram's analysis is useful in explaining other historical examples of genocide? Or do you think that obedience to authority may be irrelevant to our understanding of the other acts of genocide?
3. If Milgram were right, and obedience to authority is one of the primary reasons the Holocaust occurred, what steps should be taken in order to prevent similar events from occurring in the future?

ISSUE 11

Does the Stanford Prison Experiment Help Explain the Effects of Imprisonment?

YES: Craig Haney and Philip Zimbardo from "The Past and Future of U.S. Prison Policy: Twenty-Five Years after the Stanford Prison Experiment," *American Psychologist* (53, July 1998)

NO: David T. Lykken from "Psychology and the Criminal Justice System: A Reply to Haney and Zimbardo," *The General Psychologist* (35, 2000)

ISSUE SUMMARY

YES: Social psychologists Craig Haney and Philip Zimbardo, believe that the results of the Stanford Prison Experiment should inform U.S. prison policy.

NO: Behavioral geneticist David T. Lykken argues that the experiment was not realistic enough to say anything meaningful about real prison life and that personality factors are more important in determining the behavior of prisoners.

With the possible exception of Milgram's obedience studies (see Issue 10), the Stanford Prison Experiment is the most well-known study in the field of social psychology. The infamous experiment has inspired at least one movie (appropriately titled *The Experiment*) with a second big budget movie rumored to be in production. It has been profiled on the venerable television news program "60 Minutes," and a Los Angeles–based punk rock band now calls itself *The Stanford Prison Experiment*. The story that the experiment tells is quite compelling—a group of normal, healthy, and bright college students are placed in a simulated prison as part of a psychology experiment, and the experiment seemingly spins out of control as the "simulation" becomes all too real. Despite its dramatic results and notorious popularity, the Stanford Prison Experiment was an unusual study that bears little resemblance to most social psychological research. What made the Stanford Prison Experiment unique was the painstaking effort to create an environment that truly seemed to mirror a real-life prison. Great lengths were taken to ensure that everyone in the simulation—both prisoners and guards—would feel like they were in a true prison.

This careful attention to detail raises the possibility that the behavior observed throughout the course of the study might truly reflect the type of behavior and psychological transformation that occurs among real prison inmates and real prison guards. Philip Zimbardo and Craig Haney, two of the creators of the Stanford Prison Experiment, will argue that since the experiment did successfully simulate the psychological effects of prisons, the experiment has great relevance not only for what it tells us about human nature in general, but the experiment can also directly inform prison policy. Zimbardo and Haney argue that the Stanford Prison Experiment demonstrates that prisons are inherently dehumanizing institutions and that reform is essential to combat the epidemic of crime and imprisonment in the United States.

David Lykken argues that despite some superficial similarities to real prisons, the Stanford Prison Experiment does not aid our understanding of prison life. In his view, since the study lasted only several days, it bears little resemblances to actual prison life and therefore cannot tell us anything meaningful about the nature or crime and punishment. Furthermore since the simulated prisoners were relatively normal individuals, they bear little resemblance to criminals, at least from a psychological perspective. He argues that the epidemic of imprisonment is due to an epidemic of crime—not vice versa.

POINT

- The Stanford Prison Experiment demonstrated that prisons are an inherently dehumanizing social environment.
- For political reasons, the results of the experiment have not informed prison policy in the United States.
- The dramatic increases in the prison population has not curtailed crime.

COUNTERPOINT

- The experiment was not realistic enough to tell us anything about real prison life.
- Because the experiment was not very realistic, the results should not inform prison policy.
- Increases in the prison population are due to an epidemic in crime—not vice versa.

217

Craig Haney and
Philip Zimbardo

 **YES**

The Past and Future of U.S. Prison Policy: Twenty-Five Years after the Stanford Prison Experiment

Twenty-five years ago, a group of psychologically healthy, normal college students (and several presumably mentally sound experimenters) were temporarily but dramatically transformed in the course of six days spent in a prison-like environment, in research that came to be known as the Stanford Prison Experiment (SPE; Haney, Banks, & Zimbardo, 1973). The outcome of our study was shocking and unexpected to us, our professional colleagues, and the general public. Otherwise emotionally strong college students who were randomly assigned to be mock-prisoners suffered acute psychological trauma and breakdowns. Some of the students begged to be released from the intense pains of less than a week of merely simulated imprisonment, whereas others adapted by becoming blindly obedient to the unjust authority of the guards. The guards, too—who also had been carefully chosen on the basis of their normal–average scores on a variety of personality measures—quickly internalized their randomly assigned role. Many of these seemingly gentle and caring young men, some of whom had described themselves as pacifists or Vietnam War "doves," soon began mistreating their peers and were indifferent to the obvious suffering that their actions produced. Several of them devised sadistically inventive ways to harass and degrade the prisoners, and none of the less actively cruel mock-guards ever intervened or complained about the abuses they witnessed. Most of the worst prisoner treatment came on the night shifts and other occasions when the guards thought they could avoid the surveillance and interference of the research team. Our planned two-week experiment had to be aborted after only six days because the experience dramatically and painfully transformed most of the participants in ways we did not anticipate, prepare for, or predict.

These shocking results attracted an enormous amount of public and media attention and became the focus of much academic writing and commentary. For example, in addition to our own analyses of the outcome of the study itself (e.g., Haney et al., 1973; Haney & Zimbardo, 1977; Zimbardo, 1975; Zimbardo, Haney, Banks, & Jaffe, 1974) and the various methodological and ethical

From *American Psychologist*, vol. 53, No. 7, June 1998, pp. 709–727. (adapted) © 1998 by the American Psychological Association. Reprinted by permission.

issues that it raised (e.g., Haney, 1976; Zimbardo, 1973), the SPE was hailed by former American Psychological Association president George Miller (1980) as an exemplar of the way in which psychological research could and should be "given away" to the public because its important lessons could be readily understood and appreciated by nonprofessionals. On the 25th anniversary of this study, we reflect on its continuing message for contemporary prison policy in light of the quarter century of criminal justice history that has transpired since we concluded the experiment.

When we conceived of the SPE, the discipline of psychology was in the midst of what has been called a "situational revolution." Our study was one of the "host of celebrated laboratory and field studies" that Ross and Nisbett (1991) referred to as having demonstrated the ways in which "the immediate social situation can overwhelm in importance the type of individual differences in personal traits or dispositions that people normally think of as being determinative of social behavior." Along with much other research conducted over the past two and one-half decades illustrating the enormous power of situations, the SPE is often cited in textbooks and journal articles as a demonstration of the way in which social contexts can influence, alter, shape, and transform human behavior.

Our goal in conducting the SPE was to extend that basic perspective—one emphasizing the potency of social situations—into a relatively unexplored area of social psychology. Specifically, our study represented an experimental demonstration of the extraordinary power of *institutional* environments to influence those who passed through them. In contrast to the companion research of Stanley Milgram (1974) that focused on individual compliance in the face of an authority figure's increasingly extreme and unjust demands, the SPE examined the conformity pressures brought to bear on groups of people functioning within the same institutional setting (see Carr 1995). Our "institution" rapidly developed sufficient power to bend and twist human behavior in ways that confounded expert predictions and violated the expectations of those who created and participated in it. And, because the unique design of the study allowed us to minimize the role of personality or dispositional variables, the SPE yielded especially clear psychological insights about the nature and dynamics of social and institutional control.

The behavior of prisoners and guards in our simulated environment bore a remarkable similarity to patterns found in actual prisons. As we wrote, "Despite the fact that guards and prisoners were essentially free to engage in any form of interaction... the characteristic nature of their encounters tended to be negative, hostile, affrontive and dehumanising" (Haney et al., 1973, p. 80). Specifically, verbal interactions were pervaded by threats, insults, and deindividuating references that were most commonly directed by guards against prisoners. The environment we had fashioned in the basement hallway of Stanford University's Department of Psychology became so real for the participants that it completely dominated their day-to-day existence (e.g., 90% of prisoners' in-cell conversations focused on "prison"-related topics), dramatically affected their moods and emotional states (e.g., prisoners expressed three times as much negative affect as did guards), and at least temporarily undermined their sense of self (e.g., both groups expressed increasingly more deprecating self-evaluations over time). Behaviorally, guards most often gave commands and engaged in confrontive or aggressive acts toward prisoners, whereas the prisoners initiated increasingly less behavior; failed to support each other more often than not; negatively evaluated each other in ways that were consistent with the guards' views of them; and as the experiment progressed, more frequently expressed intentions to do harm to others (even as they became increasingly more docile and conforming to the whims of the guards). We concluded,

> The negative, anti-social reactions observed were not the product of an environment created by combining a collection of deviant personalities, but rather the result of an intrinsically pathological situation, which could distort and rechannel the behaviour of essentially normal individuals. The abnormality here resided in the psychological nature of the situation and not in those who passed through it. (Haney et al., 1973, p. 90)

In much of the research and writing we have done since then, the SPE has served as an inspiration and intellectual platform from which to extend the conceptual relevance of situational variables into two very different domains. One of us examined the coercive power of legal institutions in general and prisons in particular (e.g., Haney, 1993a, 1997b, 1997c, 1997d, 1998; Haney & Lynch, 1997), as well as the importance of situational factors in explaining and reducing crime (e.g., Haney, 1983, 1994, 1995, 1997a). The other of us explored the dimensions of intrapsychic "psychological prisons" that constrict human experience and undermine human potential (e.g., Brodt & Zimbardo, 1981; Zimbardo, 1977; Zimbardo, Pilkonis, & Norwood, 1975) and the ways in which "mind-altering" social psychological dynamics can distort individual judgment and negatively influence behavior (e.g., Zimbardo, 1979; Zimbardo & Andersen, 1993). Because the SPE was intended as a critical demonstration of the negative effects of extreme institutional environments, much of the work that grew out of this original study was change-oriented and explored the ways in which social and legal institutions and practices might be transformed to make them more responsive to humane psychological imperatives (e.g., Haney, 1993b; Haney & Pettigrew, 1986; Haney & Zimbardo, 1977; Zimbardo, 1975; Zimbardo et al., 1974).

In this article, we return to the core issue that guided the original study (Haney et al., 1973)—the implications of situational models of behavior for criminal justice institutions. We use the SPE as a point of historical departure to briefly examine the ways in which policies concerning crime and punishment have been transformed over the intervening 25 years. We argue that a series of psychological insights derived from the SPE and related studies, and the broad perspective that they advanced, still can contribute to the resolution of many of the critical problems that currently plague correctional policy in the United States.

Crime and Punishment a Quarter Century Ago

The story of how the nature and purpose of imprisonment have been transformed over the past 25 years is very different from the one that we once hoped and expected we would be able to tell. At the time we conducted the SPE—in 1971—there was widespread concern about the fairness and the efficacy of the criminal justice system. Scholars, politicians, and members of the public wondered aloud whether prisons were too harsh, whether they adequately rehabilitated prisoners, and whether there were alternatives to incarceration that would better serve correctional needs and interests. Many states were already alarmed about increased levels of overcrowding. Indeed, in those days, prisons that operated at close to 90% of capacity were thought to be dangerously overcrowded. It was widely understood by legislators and penologists alike that under such conditions, programming resources were stretched too thin, and prison administrators were left with increasingly fewer degrees of freedom with which to respond to interpersonal conflicts and a range of other inmate problems.

Despite these concerns about overcrowding, there was a functional moratorium on prison construction in place in most parts of the country. Whatever else it represented, the moratorium reflected a genuine skepticism at some of the very highest levels of government about the viability of prison as a solution to the crime problem. Indeed, the report of the National Advisory Commission on Criminal Justice Standards and Goals (1973), published at around the same time we published the results of the SPE, concluded that prisons, juvenile reformatories, and jails had achieved what it characterized as a "shocking record of failure" (p. 597), suggested that these institutions may have been responsible for creating more crime than they prevented, and recommended that the moratorium on prison construction last at least another 10 years. . . .

The Imprisoning of America

The moratorium on new prison construction that was in place at the time of the SPE was ended by the confluence of several separate, powerful forces. For one, legislators continued to vie for the mantle of "toughest on crime" by regularly increasing the lengths of prison sentences. Of course, this meant that prisoners were incarcerated for progressively longer periods of time. In addition, the sentencing discretion of judges was almost completely subjugated to the various aforementioned legislative grids, formulas, and guidelines. Moreover, the advent of determinate sentencing meant that prison administrators had no outlets at the other end of this flow of prisoners to relieve population pressures (which, under indeterminate sentencing, had been discretionary). Finally, federal district court judges began to enter judicial orders that prohibited states from, among other things, cramming two and three or more prisoners into one-person (typically six feet by nine feet) cells (e.g., *Burks v. Walsh*, 1978; *Capps v. Atiyeh*, 1980). Eventually even long-time opponents of new prisons agreed that prisoners could no longer be housed in these shockingly inadequate spaces and reluctantly faced the inevitable: Prison construction began on an unprecedented scale across the country.

Although this rapid prison construction briefly eased the overcrowding problem, prisoner populations continued to grow at unprecedented rates (see Figure 1). It soon became clear that even dramatic increases in the number of new prisons could not keep pace. In fact, almost continuously over the past 25 years, penologists have described U.S. prisons as "in crisis" and have characterized each new level of overcrowding as "unprecedented." As the decade of the 1980s came to a close, the United States was imprisoning more people for longer periods of time than ever before in our history, far surpassing other industrialized democracies in the use of incarceration as a crime control measure (Mauer, 1992, 1995). As of June 1997, the most recent date for which figures are available, the total number of persons incarcerated in the United States exceeded 1.7 million (Bureau of Justice Statistics, 1998), which continues the upward trend of the previous 11 years, from 1985 to 1996, when the number rose from 744,208 to 1,630,940. Indeed, 10 years ago, long before today's record rates were attained, one scholar concluded, "It is easily demonstrable that America's use of prison is excessive to the point of barbarity, with a prison rate several times higher than that of other similarly developed Western countries" (Newman, 1988, p. 346). A year later, a reviewer wrote in the pages of *Contemporary Psychology*:

> American prison and jail populations have reached historically high levels.... It is noteworthy that, although in several recent years the levels of reported crime declined, the prison and jail populations continued to rise. The desire for punishment seems to have taken on a life of its own. (McConville, 1989, p. 928)

The push to higher rates and lengths of incarceration has only intensified since then. Most state and federal prisons now operate well above their rated capacities, with many overcrowded to nearly twice their design limits. At the start of the 1990s, the United States incarcerated more persons per capita than any other modern nation in the world. The international disparities are most striking when the U.S. incarceration rate is contrasted to those of other nations with which the United States is often compared, such as Japan, The Netherlands, Australia, and the United Kingdom; throughout most of the present decade, the U.S. rates have consistently been between four and eight times as high as those of these other nations (e.g., Christie, 1994; Mauer, 1992, 1995). In fact, rates of incarceration have continued to climb in the United States, reaching the unprecedented levels of more than 500 per 100,000 in 1992 and then 600 per 100,000 in 1996. . . .

Remarkably, the radical transformations we have described in the nation's penal policy occurred with almost no input from the discipline of psychology. Correctional administrators, politicians, policymakers, and judicial decision makers not only ignored most of the lessons that emerged from the SPE but also disregarded the insights of a number of psychologists who preceded us and the scores of others who wrote about, extended, and elaborated on the same lessons in empirical studies and theoretical pieces published

Figure 1
Number of Prisoners in the United States, 1970–1995

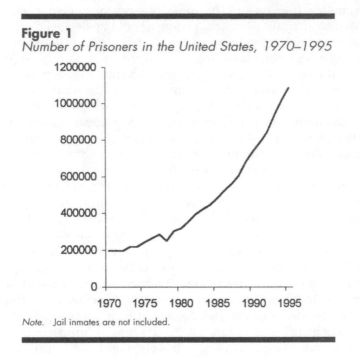

Note. Jail inmates are not included.

over the past several decades. Indeed, there is now a vast social science literature that underscores, in various ways, the critical importance of situation and
context in influencing social behavior, especially in psychologically powerful
situations like prisons. These lessons, insights, and literature deserve to be
taken into account as the nation's prison system moves into the next century.

Here then is a series of propositions derived or closely extrapolated from
the SPE and the large body of related research that underscores the power of
situations and social context to shape and transform human behavior. Each
proposition argues for the creation of a new corrections agenda that would
take us in a fundamentally different direction from the one in which we have
been moving over the past quarter century.

First, the SPE underscored the degree to which prison environments are
themselves powerful, potentially damaging situations whose negative psychological effects must be taken seriously, carefully evaluated, and purposefully
regulated and controlled. When appropriate, these environments must be
changed or (in extreme cases) eliminated. Of course, the SPE demonstrated the
power of situations to overwhelm psychologically normal, healthy people and
to elicit from them unexpectedly cruel, yet "situationally appropriate" behavior. In many instances during our study, the participants' behavior (and our
own) directly contravened personal value systems and deviated dramatically
from past records of conduct. This behavior was elicited by the social context
and roles we created, and it had painful, even traumatic consequences for the
prisoners against whom it was directed.

The policy implications of these observations seem clear. For one, because of their harmful potential, prisons should be deployed very sparingly in the war on crime. Recognition of the tendency of prison environments to become psychologically damaging also provides a strong argument for increased and more realistic legal and governmental oversight of penal institutions in ways that are sensitive to and designed to limit their potentially destructive impact. In addition, it argues in favor of significantly revising the allocation of criminal justice resources to more seriously explore, create, and evaluate humane alternatives to traditional correctional environments.

Second, the SPE also revealed how easily even a minimalist prison could become painful and powerful. By almost any comparative standard, ours was an extraordinarily benign prison. None of the guards at the "Stanford Prison" were armed, and there were obvious limits to the ways in which they could or would react to prisoners' disobedience, rebellion, or even escape. Yet, even in this minimalist prison setting, all of our "guards" participated in one way or another in the pattern of mistreatment that quickly developed. Indeed, some escalated their definition of "role-appropriate" behavior to become highly feared, sadistic tormentors. Although the prisoners' terms of incarceration were extremely abbreviated (corresponding, really, to very short-term pretrial detention in a county jail), half of our prisoner-participants left before the study was terminated because they could not tolerate the pains of this merely simulated imprisonment. The pains were as much psychological—feelings of powerlessness, degradation, frustration, and emotional distress—as physical—sleep deprivation, poor diet, and unhealthy living conditions. Unlike our participants, of course, many experienced prisoners have learned to suppress such outward signs of psychological vulnerability lest they be interpreted as weakness, inviting exploitation by others.

Thus, the SPE and other related studies demonstrating the power of social contexts teach a lesson about the way in which certain situational conditions can interact and work in combination to produce a dehumanizing whole that is more damaging than the sum of its individual institutional parts. Legal doctrines that fail to explicitly take into account and formally consider the totality of these situational conditions miss this psychological point. The effects of situations and social contexts must be assessed from the perspective of those within them. The experiential perspective of prison inmates—the meaning of the prison experience and its effects on them—is the most useful starting point for determining whether a particular set of prison conditions is cruel and unusual. But a macroexperiential perspective does not allow for the parsing of individual factors or aspects of a situation whose psychological consequences can then be separately assessed. Thus, legal regulators and the psychological experts who assist them also must be sensitive to the ways in which different aspects of a particular situation interact and aggregate in the lives of the persons who inhabit total institutions like prisons as well as their capacity to produce significant effects on the basis of seemingly subtle changes and modifications that build up over time. In contexts such as these, there is much more to the "basic necessities of life" than "single, identifiable human need[s] such as food, warmth or exercise" (*Wilson v. Seiter*, 1991, p. 304). Even if this view is "too amorphous" for members of the current Supreme Court to appreciate or apply, it is the only psychologically defensible approach to assessing the effects of a particular prison and gauging its overall impact on those who live within its walls.

In a related vein, recent research has shown how school children can develop maladjusted, aggressive behavior patterns based on initially marginal deviations from other children that get amplified in classroom interactions and aggregated over time until they become manifested as "problem children" (Caprara & Zimbardo, 1996). Evidence of the same processes at work can be found in the life histories of persons accused and convicted of capital crime (Haney, 1995). In similar ways, initially small behavioral problems and dysfunctional social adaptations by individual prisoners may become amplified and aggravated over time in prison settings that require daily interaction with other prisoners and guards.

Recall also that the SPE was purposely populated with young men who were selected on the basis of their initial mental and physical health and normality, both of which, less than a week later, had badly deteriorated. Real prisons use no such selection procedures. Indeed, one of the casualties of severe overcrowding in many prison systems has been that even rudimentary classification decisions based on the psychological makeup of entering cohorts of prisoners are forgone (see Clements, 1979, 1985). Pathology that is inherent in the structure of the prison situation is likely given a boost by the pathology that some prisoners and guards bring with them into the institutions themselves. Thus, although ours was clearly a study of the power of situational characteristics, we certainly acknowledge the value of interactional models of social and institutional behavior. Prison systems should not ignore individual vulnerabilities in attempting to optimize institutional adjustment, minimize behavioral and psychological problems, understand differences in institutional adaptations and capacities to survive, and intelligently allocate treatment and other resources (e.g., Haney & Specter, 2001).

Third, if situations matter and people can be transformed by them when they go into prisons, they matter equally, if not more, when they come out of prison. This suggests very clearly that programs of prisoner change cannot ignore situations and social conditions that prevail after release if they are to have any hope of sustaining whatever positive gains are achieved during periods of imprisonment and lowering distressingly high recidivism rates. Several implications can be drawn from this observation. The first is that prisons must more routinely use transitional or "decompression" programs that gradually reverse the effects of the extreme environments in which convicts have been confined. These programs must be aimed at preparing prisoners for the radically different situations that they will enter in the free world. Otherwise, prisoners who were ill-prepared for job and social situations before they entered prison become more so over time, and the longer they have been imprisoned, the more likely it is that rapid technological and social change will have dramatically transformed the world to which they return.

The SPE and related studies also imply that exclusively individual-centered approaches to crime control (like imprisonment) are self-limiting and doomed to failure in the absence of other approaches that simultaneously and systematically address criminogenic situational and contextual factors. Because traditional models of rehabilitation are person-centered and dispositional in nature (focusing entirely on individual-level change), they typically have ignored the postrelease situational factors that help to account for discouraging rates of recidivism. Yet, the recognition that people can be significantly changed and transformed by immediate situational conditions also implies that certain kinds of situations in the free world can override and negate positive prison change. Thus, correctional and parole resources must be shifted to the transformation of certain criminogenic situations in the larger society if ex-convicts are to meaningfully and effectively adapt. Successful post-release adjustment may depend as much on the criminal justice system's ability to change certain components of an ex-convict's situation *after* imprisonment—helping to get housing, employment, and drug or alcohol counseling for starters—as it does on any of the positive rehabilitative changes made by individual prisoners during confinement itself.

This perspective also underscores the way in which long-term legacies of exposure to powerful and destructive situations, contexts, and structures means that prisons themselves can act as criminogenic agents—in both their primary effects on prisoners and secondary effects on the lives of persons connected to them—thereby serving to increase rather than decrease the amount of crime that occurs within a society. Department of corrections data show that about a fourth of those initially imprisoned for nonviolent crimes are sentenced a second time for committing a violent offense. Whatever else it reflects; this pattern highlights the possibility that prison serves to transmit violent habits and values rather than to reduce them. Moreover, like many of these lessons, this one counsels policymakers to take the full range of the social and economic costs of imprisonment into account in calculations that guide long-term crime control strategies. It also argues in favor of incorporating the deleterious effects of prior terms of incarceration into at least certain models of legal responsibility (e.g., Haney, 1995).

Fourth, despite using several valid personality tests in the SPE, we found that we were unable to predict (or even postdict) who would behave in what ways and why (Haney et al., 1973). This kind of failure underscores the possibility that behavioral prediction and explanation in extreme situations like prisons will be successful only if they are approached with more situationally sensitive models than are typically used. For example, most current personality trait measures ask respondents to report on characteristic ways of responding in familiar situations or scenarios. They do not and cannot tap into reactions that might occur in novel, extreme, or especially potent situations—like the SPE or Milgram's (1974) obedience paradigm—and thus have little predictive value when extrapolated to such extreme cases. More situationally sensitive models would attend less to characteristic ways of behaving in typical situations and more to the characteristics of the particular situations in which behavior occurs. In prison, explanations of disciplinary infractions and violence would focus more on the context in which they transpired and less on the prisoners who engaged in them (e.g., Wenk & Emrich, 1972; Wright, 1991). Similarly, the ability to predict the likelihood of reoffending and the probability of repeated violent behavior should be enhanced by conceptualizing persons as embedded in a social context and rich interpersonal environment, rather than as abstract bundles of traits and proclivities (e.g., Monahan & Klassen, 1982).

This perspective has implications for policies of crime control as well as psychological prediction. Virtually all sophisticated, contemporary accounts of social behavior now acknowledge the empirical and theoretical significance of situation, context, and structure (e.g., Bandura, 1978, 1991; Duke, 1987; Ekehammar, 1974; Georgoudi & Rosnow, 1985; Mischel, 1979; Veroff, 1983). In academic circles at least, the problems of crime and violence—formerly viewed in almost exclusively individualistic terms—are now understood through multi-level analyses that grant equal if not primary significance to situational, community, and structural variables (e.g., Hepburn, 1973; McEwan & Knowles, 1984; Sampson & Lauritsen, 1994; Toch, 1985). Yet, little of this knowledge has made its way into prevailing criminal justice policies. Lessons about the power of extreme situations to shape and transform behavior—independent or in spite of pre-existing dispositions—can be applied to contemporary strategies of crime control that invest more substantial resources in transforming destructive familial and social contexts rather than concentrating exclusively on reactive policies that target only individual lawbreakers (cf. Masten & Garmezy 1985; Patterson, DeBaryshe, & Ramsey, 1989).

Fifth, genuine and meaningful prison and criminal justice reform is unlikely to be advanced by persons who are themselves "captives" of powerful correctional environments. We learned this lesson in a modest but direct way when in the span of six short days in the SPE, our own perspectives were radically altered, our sense of ethics, propriety, and humanity temporarily suspended. Our experience with the SPE underscored the degree to which institutional settings can develop a life of their own, independent of the wishes, intentions, and purposes of those who run them (Haney & Zimbardo, 1977). Like all powerful situations, real prisons transform the worldviews of those who inhabit them, on both sides of the bars. Thus, the SPE also contained the seeds of a basic but important message about prison reform—that good people with good intentions are not enough to create good prisons. Institutional structures themselves must be changed to meaningfully improve the quality of prison life (Haney & Pettigrew, 1986).

Indeed, the SPE was an "irrational" prison whose staff had no legal mandate to punish prisoners who, in turn, had done nothing to deserve their mistreatment. Yet, the "psychologic" of the environment was more powerful than the benign intentions or predispositions of the participants. Routines develop; rules are made and applied, altered and followed without question; policies enacted for short-term convenience become part of the institutional status quo and difficult to alter; and unexpected events and emergencies challenge existing resources and compromise treatment in ways that persist long after the crisis has passed. Prisons are especially vulnerable to these common institutional dynamics because they are so resistant to external pressures for change and even rebuff outside attempts at scrutinizing their daily operating procedures.

These observations certainly imply that the legal mechanisms supposedly designed to control prison excesses should not focus exclusively on the intentions of the staff and administrators who run the institution but would do well to look instead at the effects of the situation or context itself in shaping their behavior (cf. *Farmer v. Brennan*, 1994). Harmful structures do not require ill-intentioned persons to inflict psychological damage on those in their charge and can induce good people with the best of intentions to engage in evil deeds (Haney & Zimbardo, 1977; Zimbardo, 1979). "Mechanisms of moral disengagement" distance people from the ethical ambiguity of their actions and the painful consequences of their deeds, and they may operate with destructive force in many legal and institutional contexts, facilitating cruel and unusual treatment by otherwise caring and law-abiding persons (e.g., Bandura, 1989; Browning, 1993; Gibson, 1991; Haney, 1997c).

In addition, the SPE and the perspective it advanced also suggest that prison change will come about only when those who are outside of this powerful situation are empowered to act on it. A society may be forced to presume the categorical expertise of prison officials to run the institutions with which they have been entrusted, but this presumption is a rebuttable one. Moreover, to depend exclusively on those whose perspectives have been created and maintained by these powerful situations to, in turn, transform or control them is shortsighted and psychologically naive. This task must fall to those with a different logic and point of view, independent of and free from the forces of the situation itself. To be sure, the current legal retreat to hands-off policies in which the courts defer to the presumably greater expertise of correctional officials ignores the potency of prison settings to alter the judgments of those charged with the responsibility of running them. The SPE and much other research on these powerful environments teach that this retreat is terribly ill-advised.

Finally, the SPE implicitly argued for a more activist scholarship in which psychologists engage with the important social and policy questions of the day. The implications we have drawn from the SPE argue in favor of more critically and more realistically evaluating the nature and effect of imprisonment and developing psychologically informed limits to the amount of prison pain one is willing to inflict in the name of social control (Haney, 1997b, 1998). Yet, this would require the participation of social scientists willing to examine these issues, confront the outmoded models and concepts that guide criminal justice practices, and develop meaningful and effective alternatives. Historically, psychologists once contributed significantly to the intellectual framework on which modern corrections was built (Haney, 1982). In the course of the past 25 years, they have relinquished voice and authority in the debates that surround prison policy. Their absence has created an ethical and intellectual void that has undermined both the quality and the legitimacy of correctional practices.

It has helped compromise the amount of social justice our society now dispenses.

REFERENCES

Bandura, A. (1978). The self system in reciprocal determinism. *American Psychologist, 33*, 344–358.

Bandura, A. (1989). Mechanisms of moral disengagement. In W. Reich (Ed.), *Origins of terrorism: Psychologies, ideologies, theologies, states of mind* (pp. 161–191). New York: Cambridge University Press.

Bandura, A. (1991). Social cognitive theory of moral thought and action. In W. Kurtines & J. Gewirtz (Eds.), *Handbook of moral behavior and development: Vol. 1. Theory* (pp. 45–102). Hillsdale, NJ: Erlbaum.

Brodt, S., & Zimbardo, P. (1981). Modifying shyness-related social behavior through symptom misattribution. *Journal of Personality and Social Psychology, 41*, 437–449.

Browning, C. (1993). *Ordinary men: Reserve Police Battalion 101 and the final solution in Poland*. New York: Harper Perennial.

Bureau of Justice Statistics. (1998, January 18). *Nation's prisons and jails hold more than 1.7 million: Up almost 100,000 in a year* [Press release]. Washington, DC: U.S. Department of Justice.

Burks v. Walsh, 461 F. Supp. 934 (W.D. Missouri 1978).

Capps v. Atiyeh, 495 F. Supp. 802 (D. Ore. 1980).

Caprara, G., & Zimbardo, P. (1996). Aggregation and amplification of marginal deviations in the social construction of personality and maladjustment. *European Journal of Personality, 10*, 79–110.

Carr, S. (1995). Demystifying the Stanford Prison Study. *The British Psychological Society Social Psychology Section Newsletter, 33*, 31–34.

Christie, N. (1994). *Crime control as industry: Towards gulags, Western style?* (2nd ed.). London: Routledge.

Clements, C. (1979). Crowded prisons: A review of psychological and environmental effects. *Law and Human Behavior, 3*, 217–225.

Clements, C. (1985). Towards an objective approach to offender classification. *Law & Psychology Review, 9*, 45–55.

Duke, M. (1987). The situational stream hypothesis: A unifying view of behavior with special emphasis on adaptive and maladaptive personality patterns. *Journal of Research in Personality, 21*, 239–263.

Ekehammar, B. (1974). Interactionism in personality from a historical perspective. *Psychological Bulletin, 81*, 1026–1048.

Farmer v. Brennan, 114 S. Ct. 1970 (1994).

Georgoudi, M., & Rosnow, R. (1985). Notes toward a contextualist understanding of social psychology. *Personality and Social Psychology Bulletin, 11*, 5–22.

Gibson, J. (1991). Training good people to inflict pain: State terror and social learning. *Journal of Humanistic Psychology, 31*, 72–87.

Haney, C. (1976). The play's the thing: Methodological notes on social simulations. In P. Golden (Ed.), *The research experience* (pp. 177–190). Itasca, IL: Peacock.

Haney, C. (1983). The good, the bad, and the lawful: An essay on psychological injustice. In W. Laufer & J. Day (Eds.), *Personality theory, moral development, and criminal behavior* (pp. 107–117). Lexington, MA: Lexington Books.

Haney, C. (1993a). Infamous punishment: The psychological effects of isolation. *National Prison Project Journal, 8,* 3–21.

Haney, C. (1994, March 3). Three strikes for Ronnie's kids, now Bill's. *Los Angeles Times,* p. B7.

Haney, C. (1995). The social context of capital murder: Social histories and the logic of mitigation. *Santa Clara Law Review, 35,* 547–609.

Haney, C. (1997a). Psychological secrecy and the death penalty: Observations on "the mere extinguishment of life." *Studies in Law, Politics, and Society, 16,* 3–68.

Haney, C. (1997b). Psychology and the limits to prison pain: Confronting the coming crisis in Eighth Amendment law. *Psychology, Public Policy, and Law, 3,* 499–588.

Haney, C. (1997c). Violence and the capital jury: Mechanisms of moral disengagement and the impulse to condemn to death. *Stanford Law Review, 46,* 1447–1486.

Haney, C. (1997d). *The worst of the worst: Psychological trauma and psychiatric symptoms in punitive segregation.* Unpublished manuscript, University of California, Santa Cruz.

Haney, C. (1998). *Limits to prison pain: Modern psychological theory and rational crime control policy.* Washington, DC: American Psychological Association.

Haney, C., Banks, W., & Zimbardo, P. (1973). Interpersonal dynamics in a simulated prison. *International Journal of Criminology and Penology, 1,* 69–97.

Haney, C., & Lynch, M. (1997). Regulating prisons of the future: A psychological analysis of supermax and solitary confinement. *New York Review of Law and Social Change, 23,* 101–195.

Haney, C., & Pettigrew, T. (1986). Civil rights and institutional law: The role of social psychology in judicial implementation. *Journal of Community Psychology, 14,* 267–277.

Haney, C., & Specter, D. (2001). Legal considerations in treating adult and juvenile offenders with special needs. In J. Ashford, B. Sales, & W. Reid (Eds.), *Treating adult and juvenile offenders with special needs.* Washington, DC: American Psychological Association.

Haney, C., & Zimbardo, P. (1977).The socialization into criminality: On becoming a prisoner and a guard. In J. Tapp & F. Levine (Eds.), *Law, justice, and the individual in society: Psychological and legal issues* (pp. 198–223). New York: Holt, Rinehart & Winston.

Hepburn, J. (1973). Violent behavior in interpersonal relationships. *Sociological Quarterly, 14,* 419–429.

Masten, A., & Garmezy, N. (1985). Risk, vulnerability and protective factors in developmental psychopathology. In F. Lahey & A. Kazdin (Eds.), *Advances in clinical child psychology* (pp. 1–52). New York: Plenum.

Mauer, M. (1992). Americans behind bars: A comparison of international rates of incarceration. In W. Churchill & J. J. Vander Wall (Eds.), *Cages of steel: The politics of imprisonment in the United States* (pp. 22–37). Washington, DC: Maisonneuve Press.

Mauer, M. (1995). The international use of incarceration. *Prison Journal, 75,* 113–123.

McConville, S. (1989). Prisons held captive. *Contemporary Psychology, 34,* 928–929.

McEwan, A., & Knowles, C. (1984). Delinquent personality types and the situational contexts of their crimes. *Personality & Individual Differences, 5,* 339–344.

Milgram, S. (1974). *Obedience to authority: An experimental view.* New York: Harper & Row.

Mischel, W. (1979). On the interface of cognition and personality: Beyond the person–situation debate. *American Psychologist, 34*, 740–754.

Monahan, J., & Klassen, D. (1982). Situational approaches to understanding and predicting individual violent behavior. In M. Wolfgang & G. Weiner (Eds.), *Criminal violence* (pp. 292–319). Beverly Hills, CA: Sage.

National Advisory Commission on Criminal Justice Standards and Goals. (1973). *Task force report on corrections.* Washington, DC: U.S. Government Printing Office.

Newman, G. (1988). Punishment and social practice: On Hughes's *The Fatal Shore. Law and Social Inquiry, 13*, 337–357.

Patterson, G., DeBaryshe, B., & Ramsey, E. (1989). A developmental perspective on antisocial behavior. *American Psychologist, 44*, 329–335.

Ross, L., & Nisbett, R. (1991). *The person and the situation: Perspectives of social psychology.* New York: McGraw-Hill.

Sampson, R., & Lauritsen, J. (1994). Violent victimization and offending: Individual-, situational-, and community-level risk factors. In A. Reiss, Jr. & J. Roth (Eds.), *Understanding and preventing violence: Vol. 3. Social influences* (pp. 1–114). Washington, DC: National Research Council, National Academy Press.

Toch, H. (1985). The catalytic situation in the violence equation. *Journal of Applied Social Psychology, 15*, 105–123.

Veroff, J. (1983). Contextual determinants of personality. *Personality and Social Psychology Bulletin, 9*, 331–343.

Wenk, E., & Emrich, R. (1972). Assaultive youth: An exploratory study of the assaultive experience and assaultive potential of California Youth Authority wards. *Journal of Research in Crime & Delinquency, 9*, 171–196.

Wilson v. Seiter. 501 U.S. 294 (1991).

Wright, K. (1991). The violent and victimized in the male prison. *Journal of Offender Rehabilitation, 16*, 1–25.

Zimbardo, P. (1973). On the ethics of intervention in human psychological research: With special reference to the Stanford Prison Experiment. *Cognition, 2*, 243–256.

Zimbardo, P. (1975). On transforming experimental research into advocacy for social change. In M. Deutsch & H. Hornstein (Eds.), *Applying social psychology: Implications for research, practice, and training* (pp. 33–66). Hillsdale, NJ: Erlbaum.

Zimbardo, P. G. (1977). *Shyness: What it is and what to do about it.* Reading, MA: Addison-Wesley.

Zimbardo, P. G. (1979a). The psychology of evil: On the perversion of human potential. In T. R. Sarbin (Ed.), *Challenges to the criminal justice system: The perspective of community psychology* (pp. 142–161). New York: Human Sciences Press.

Zimbardo, P. G., & Andersen, S. (1993). Understanding mind control: Exotic and mundane mental manipulations. In M. Langone (Ed.), *Recover from cults: Help for victims of psychological and spiritual abuse* (pp. 104–125). New York: Norton.

Zimbardo, P. G., Haney, C., Banks, C., & Jaffe, D. (1974). The psychology of imprisonment: Privation, power, and pathology. In Z. Rubin (Ed.), *Doing unto others: Explorations in social behavior* (pp. 61–73). Englewood Cliffs, NJ: Prentice Hall.

Zimbardo, P. G., Pilkonis, P. A., & Norwood, R. M. (1975, May). The social disease called shyness. *Psychology Today*, pp. 69–70, 72.

NO ↩

David T. Lykken

PSYCHOLOGY AND THE CRIMINAL JUSTICE SYSTEM: A Reply to Haney and Zimbardo

More than 25 years ago, Haney, Banks, and Zimbardo (1973) transformed the basement hallway of Stanford University's Psychology Department into a make-believe prison block where a group of male student volunteers posed either as inmates or as guards. Some of the "guards" behaved badly and some of the students "begged to be released from the intense pains of less than a week of merely simulated imprisonment" (Haney & Zimbardo, 1998, p. 709.) The experiment was therefore aborted after just six days and nights. Apparently many who read about the Stanford Prison Experiment (SPE), as this six day venture came to be called, agreed with the authors that it had demonstrated "the way in which social contexts can influence, alter, shape, and transform human behavior" pp. 709-10). Based on studies of this kind, some of them Gedanken experiments as in the following quotation from Mischel's influential textbook, many psychologists came to believe that social learning determines personality and that social context determines behavior.

> "Imagine the enormous differences that would be found in the personalities of twins with identical genetic endowment if they were raised apart in two different families.... Through social learning vast differences develop among people in their reactions to most stimuli they face in daily life." (Mischel, 1981, p, 311.)

It was natural, therefore, to believe that crime is largely a consequence of criminogenic contexts that could be eliminated by social engineering. It follows also that prisons, should they be necessary at all, provide an excellent opportunity for the rehabilitation of misdirected youth through the provision of healthy social learning and a more beneficent behavioral context. Haney and Zimbardo (1998) devote most of their article to a regretful discussion of the five-fold increase since the early 1970s in the proportion of Americans serving time in prison, of the change in prison policy since then from rehabilitation to mere segregation, and of what they call "the racialization of prison pain." The enormous recent increase in the rate of imprisonment of convicted

From *The General Psychologist*, vol. 35:1, Spring 2000, pp. 11–15. Copyright © 2000 by Division Services. Reprinted by permission of the Society of General Psychology, American Psychological Association, Division Services.

offenders was not in response to a corresponding increase in the proportion of citizens victimized by violent crime, at least not according to the National Crime Victimization Survey. This increase in numbers of inmates is therefore attributed to an apparently willful refusal by "correctional administrators, politicians, policymakers, and judicial decision makers" to appreciate "most of the lessons that emerged from the SPE" (p. 718). According to Haney and Zimbardo, these lessons are:

1. "SPE demonstrated the power of situations to overwhelm psychologically normal, healthy people and to elicit from them unexpectedly cruel...behavior" (p. 719).
2. "SPE also revealed how easily even a minimalized prison could become painful and powerful" (p. 719).
3. If situations matter and people can be transformed by them when they go into prisons, they matter equally, if not more, when they come out of prison" (p.720).
4. "In prison, explanations of disciplinary infractions and violence [should] focus more on the context in which they transpired and less on the prisoners who engaged in them" (p.720).
5. "Good people with good intentions are not enough to create a good prison...the SPE and the perspective it advanced also suggest that prison change will come about only when those who are outside of this powerful situation are empowered to act on it."
6. "Finally, the SPE implicitly argued for a more activist scholarship in which psychologists engage with the important social and policy questions of the day" (p. 721).

I agree with at least some of these rather vague prescriptions, although I am astonished by these authors' claim that a handbook for prison reform (indeed, a basic text in enlightened criminology) can be harvested from watching a handful of college students role-playing guards and inmates for six days in a Stanford basement. But I disagree strongly with some of the more specific claims or assumptions made by Haney and Zimbardo.

Personality Is More Important than Context

The situational model still embraced by Haney and Zimbardo is wrong. The Gedanken experiment suggested by Mischel has now been conducted by Bouchard et al. (1990) and the results were opposite to Mischel's expectation. Identical twins separated in infancy and reared apart are as similar in personality as identical twins reared together, and that is very similar indeed (Tellegen, et al., 1988). About half of the variance (more than half of the stable variance) in basic traits of temperament or personality is associated with genetic differences between people.

   Anyone familiar with the realities of prison life knows that some inmates are predictably violent and dangerous while some are predictably passive or tractable. We recently obtained scores on the Multidimensional Personality Inventory (Tellegen & Waller, 1994) from 67 inmates at Minnesota's maximum security prison, Oak Park Heights[1], men whose mean age was 32. We collected MPQs also from more than 850 male twins aged 30-33 (Lykken, 2000). The men in our inmate sample had been convicted of serious crimes, usually murder. Because the MPQ is a self-administered inventory and requires high school reading skills, a considerable proportion of the inmate population could not be sampled but there is no reason to think that the participants differed temperamentally from the non-readers.

Figure 1

Inmate Personality Profiles. **Mean MPQ profiles of inmates in a maximum security prison who scored highest or lowest on aggression. A T-score of 50 represents the mean for some 850 non-criminal males aged 30–33; a T-score of 70 is 2 standard deviations above the normal mean; etc.**

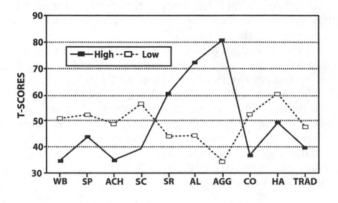

Figure 1 shows the profiles of the 22 inmates scoring highest and the 22 scoring lowest on the aggression scale of the MPQ, plotted using the data from the non-criminal male twins as norms. The most aggressive inmates are deviant also on most of the other MPQ scales; they are more than one SD below the normal mean on well being, achievement, and social closeness, the traits that comprise the Positive Emotionality super-factor of the MPQ. The aggressive inmates are more than one SD above the mean on stress reaction and on alienation which, with aggression, comprise the Negative Emotionality super-factor. And they are more than one SD below the normal mean on control (vs. impulsiveness), and on traditionalism, two of the traits that comprise the Constraint super-factor. The non-aggressive inmates, on the other hand, yield essentially normal profiles except for that low score on aggression and an elevation on harm avoidance. In spite of their confinement in the same "Painful and powerful" prison environment, these men show great variability, one from another, not only in personality but also in their tendencies to make or to stay out of trouble in that environment.

Modern Prisons Are not Places of Unremitting Pain

Because the six day SPE "had painful, even traumatic consequences for the prisoners [Stanford students pretending to be inmates] against whom it was directed" (p. 719), Haney and Zimbardo concluded that real prisons must have devastating psychological effects upon real inmates serving long sentences. Perhaps because they are situationists, rather than trait psychologists, they neglected our extraordinary human capacity to adapt to circumstances, good or bad. Suh, Diener, & Fujita (1966) have shown that both positive and negative life experiences have usually lost their effect on subjective well being after six months. A year after either winning the lottery or being permanently crippled in an accident, most people experience about the same average level of happiness that they felt before that event. In a study I did long ago in another Minnesota prison (Lykken, 1957), one inmate, the pitcher on the prison baseball team, had been paroled the previous fall. He made it back in time for the spring baseball season by the expedient of breaking the display window of a jewelry store and then leisurely collecting rings and watches until arrested on the spot. He admitted he was happier back in prison than he'd been on the outside.

Figure 2

Inmate Personality Profiles. MPQ profiles of the 22 men who scored highest on Well Being, and the 22 who scored lowest, among 67 inmates of a maximum security prison.

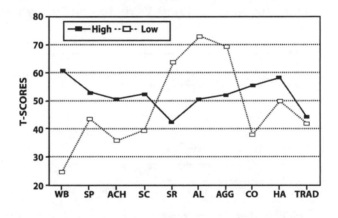

The mean expected release date for our sample of Oak Park Heights inmates is the year 2030 yet, after having been there for an average period of 37 months, many of them appear to have become well-adjusted to prison life and many are surpisingly happy. Figure 2 shows that, while the lowest-scoring third professed considerable pain and alienation, the upper-third scored higher on well being than three-fourths of our 850 noncriminal young men. Oak Park Heights is a modern prison, well run and reasonably safe because the staff, rather than the inmates, are in control. The well adjusted inmates can take classes, learn skills, find peaceful ways to pass the time. I would not wish to be incarcerated at Oak Park Heights, not even if I was made pitcher of the baseball team, but at least I could get a lot of reading done.

The Epidemic of Imprisonment Is Due to an Epidemic of Crime

The National Crime Victimization Survey, on which Haney and Zimbardo rely, has summarized annually since 1973 the reports of more than 90,000 Americans over age 12 concerning whether they have been the victims of specified crimes during the past year. These reports are from members of a stratified sample of families interviewed either in person or by telephone by (mostly female) employees of the U.S. Census Bureau. The Uniform Crime Reports, compiled by the FBI since 1929, summarize crimes actually reported to the police. As Figure 3 reveals, these two methods of measuring violent crime tell very different stories. The FBI data indicate an increase since 1973 of 54% (a peak increase of 73%) while the NCVS data indicate an actual decrease in violent crime of 15%. NCVS interviewers do not contact transients, people who are in hospital or in jail, nor do they venture into the more dangerous regions of the inner city. The NCVS tells us about middle-class crime while the UCR includes the rapid rise that ghetto crime has been displaying since the early 1960s.

Figure 3

NCVS vs UCT Data: Violent Crimes. Trends since 1973 in violent crime as revealed by the National Crime Victimization Survey versus the FBI's Uniform Crime Reports.

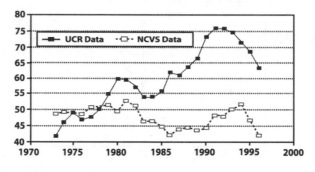

Figure 4 reveals that the increase in the rate of imprisonment actually lagged the increase in the crime rate, beginning its acceleration only about 1980. The figure also displays the much-heralded dip in violent crime that has occurred since about 1993. The most likely explanation for this modest decline is the fact that 1.3 million potential perpetrators, compared to about 200,000 in 1970, are now behind bars. Because the typical prison inmate committed some 12 serious crimes during the year prior to his last arrest (Bhunstein, Cohen, & Farrington, 1988), taking a million such men off the streets and into prison is bound to yield at least a temporary diminution in the crime rate. Haney and Zimbardo consider it "barbaric" that we have so many men in prison. While it is not a satisfactory solution to our crime problem, I believe with most Americans that sequestering violent criminals is preferable to just turning them loose.

Rehabilitation Does Not Work

If Haney and Zimbardo are correct in what they think they learned from the SPE, everyone-including prison inmates—should respond to socialized environments in a socialized manner. By creating such conditions in our prisons then, after perhaps a fairly short period of acclimation and habituation, formerly unsocialized inmates should become accustomed to behaving like law-abiding citizens and be ready for release. As Haney and Zimbardo point out, it would be necessary also to provide socialized environments for these parolees to return to, adequate jobs, housing in good neighborhoods, and the like.

Figure 4

U.S. Illegitimacy Rate. The increase since 1960 in the rates of violent crimes reported to the police and in the proportion of the U.S. male population serving terms in state or federal prisons.

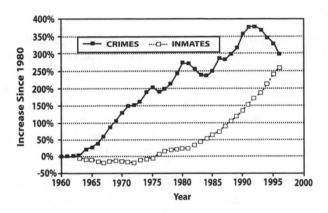

And there is no doubt that some inmates, after serving their time even in our current unenlightened prisons, manage to remain within the law (or at least unapprehended) after their release. Some inmates, after all, are reasonably normal, socialized persons who were unfortunate enough to be too strongly tempted; some, indeed, were actually innocent of the crimes for which they were convicted. Because recidivism is only frequent and not inevitable, one may be led to believe that some criminals are rehabilitated even by the present system and, therefore, that many more might similarly benefit from a more enlightened correctional system.

The fact is, however, that Haney and Zimbardo cannot point to a single convincing study indicating that prison reforms designed to augment rehabilitation have ever been successful. I am not about to claim that every reasonable method has been tried. In fact, I should be very interested to see what would happen if each new inmate were to learn that his future supervisor, teacher, and disciplinarian was to be a distant computer, "John," with whom he could communicate by means of a very sturdy keyboard and monitor inset into the wall of his cell. The computer would provide programmed learning tasks appropriate to the inmate's ability and interests. By doing what the patient but implacable computer required, the inmate could earn more palatable food, TV time, access to a telephone, and other privileges. Only after he had achieved appropriate basic educational goals, and had demonstrated his willingness to live by the computer's rules, would an inmate begin to be allowed to mix with other inmates and take further steps in demonstrating his improved level of socialization.

But I am not so naive as to claim, as Haney and Zimbardo seem to believe that, even with unlimited resources and control, I (or they) could turn Oak Park Heights into a prison with single-digit recidivism rates. A young person who has managed to reach his or her late teens almost wholly unsocialized is likely to remain a danger to society for life. Like our talent for language, our human proclivities for socialization require to be elicited, shaped, and reinforced in childhood or they may be forever lost. As Judge C.D. Gill (1994) has wisely observed, "The place to fight crime is in the cradle."...

Summary

While I agree with Haney and Zimbardo that psychologists should try to play a stronger and more constructive role in advising those responsible for social policy, I am persuaded that the vague and politically correct nostrums that they recommend cannot be helpful. We have too many men (and increasing numbers of women) in prison because we have too much crime. We have too much crime because an ever-increasing proportion of our children are reaching adolescence essentially unsocialized. Some of these youngsters can be described as psychopaths, meaning that their innate temperaments from early childhood made them very difficult to manage, too difficult for the average parent. But crime has increased far too rapidly to be attributable to dysgenic factors. Most of these troublesome youth are what I call sociopaths, meaning that their rearing environment failed to elicit, shape, and reinforce their inherent human capacity to develop an effective conscience as well as their instincts of empathy and altruism and social responsibility. All but the most difficult children become adequately socialized in the extended-family environments of traditional societies that most resemble the environment of human evolutionary adaptation in which our ancestors evolved their innate talent for social living. Such traditional societies have very little crime....

Note

I am indebted to Dr. Kenneth Carlson at Oak Park Heights Correctional Facility for collecting these data and sharing them with me.

CHALLENGE QUESTIONS

Does the Stanford Prison Experiment Help Explain the Effects of Imprisonment?

1. If you were placed in the same situation as the participants in the Stanford Prison Experiment, how do you think you would react?
2. In your opinion, why have the recommendations of Haney & Zimbardo and the lessons learned from the experiment not been heeded by policy makers?
3. Is rehabilitation of prisoners a plausible social policy, as Haney & Zimbardo believe, or are most prisoners beyond hope of reform?
4. Do you think that the Stanford Prison Experiment was ethical? Why or why not?

ISSUE 12

Is Subliminal Persuasion a Myth?

YES: Anthony R. Pratkanis, from "The Cargo-Cult Science of Subliminal Persuasion," *Skeptical Inquirer* (*16*, 1992

NO: Nicholas Epley, Kenneth Savitsky, and Robert A. Kachelski, from "What Every Skeptic Should Know about Subliminal Persuasion," *Skeptical Inquirer* (*23*, 1999)

ISSUE SUMMARY

YES: Social psychologist Anthony Pratkanis argues that research claiming to demonstrate the efficacy of subliminal persuasion is either fraudulent or flawed. Carefully controlled experiments do not demonstrate that subliminal persuasion can have any effect on behavior.

NO: Nicholas Epley, Kenneth Savitsky, and Robert Kachelski agree that much of the research examining subliminal persuasion is flawed. However, more recent research using better methodologies has demonstrated that subliminal stimuli can influence behavior.

How easily are people persuaded to change their attitudes or behavior? This is an important question in social psychology and in the business world, where companies spend billions annually on advertising in an effort to try to persuade people to buy a particular product. Social psychologists study persuasion in order to determine what kinds of persuasive appeals are most effective. As part of their study of persuasion, some social psychologists have studied the impact of subliminal messages on people's attitudes and behavior. Subliminal messages are those persuasive appeals that are not consciously perceived—we are unaware of their content. These messages differ greatly in terms of their form and content. Some subliminal messages are presented as auditory stimuli. For example, some self-help tapes may attempt to use subliminal persuasion in which a subliminal message is masked by classical music, leaving the listener unaware of the content of the message. Other subliminal messages are delivered visually, in which the presentation of the message is so brief that it cannot be consciously perceived. For example, in the 2000 presidential election, a Republican campaign commercial allegedly tried to subliminally attack Democrats by briefly flashing the word "Rats" during a campaign commercial that was critical of the Democratic Party.

Are messages like these effective? In the first selection, social psychologist Anthony Pratkanis reviews the research examining subliminal persuasion. According to Pratkanis, much of the research examining the effectiveness of subliminal persuasion is either flawed or fraudulent. When carefully conducted double-blind experiments are performed, they provide no evidence that subliminal stimuli can influence behavior. Despite the lack of convincing evidence, the general public continues to believe that companies use subliminal persuasion techniques in advertising and that these types of advertisements are effective.

Social psychologists Nicholas Epley and Kenneth Savitsky and cognitive psychologist Robert Kachelski agree that many have overstated the effectiveness of subliminal persuasion techniques. However, they argue that subliminal persuasion is real and has been demonstrated in carefully controlled experiments. Although caution is warranted because these techniques have only been reliably demonstrated in psychology experiments and not in the "real world," some forms of subliminal advertising may prove to be effective.

POINT

- Most studies that claim to demonstrate the effectiveness of subliminal persuasion are flawed.
- Well-controlled experiments demonstrate that subliminal messages do not influence behavior.
- The general public erroneously believes that subliminal advertising can be effective.

COUNTERPOINT

- More recent research has carefully tested the effectiveness of subliminal persuasion.
- Some research, also using carefully controlled experiments, demonstrates that subliminal stimuli can influence behavior.
- Some forms of subliminal advertising may actually turn out to be effective.

Anthony R. Pratkanis

 **YES**

The Cargo-Cult Science
of Subliminal Persuasion

Imagine that it is the late 1950s—a time just after the Korean War, when terms like *brainwashing* and *mind control* were on the public's mind and films like The *Manchurian Candidate* depicted the irresistible influence of hypnotic trances. You and your friend are off to see *Picnic*, one of the more popular films of the day. However, the movie theater, located in Fort Lee, New Jersey, is unlike any you have been in before. Unbeknownst to you, the projectors have been equipped with a special device capable of flashing short phrases onto the movie screen at such a rapid speed that you are unaware that any messages have been presented. During the film, you lean over to your companion and whisper, "Gee, I'd love a tub of buttered popcorn and a Coke right now." To which he replies, "You're always hungry and thirsty at movies, shhhhh." But after a few moments he says, "You know, some Coke and popcorn might not be a bad idea."

A short time later you hear that you and your friend weren't the only ones desiring popcorn and Coke at the theater that day. According to reports in newspapers and magazines, James Vicary, an advertising expert, had secretly flashed, at a third of a millisecond, the words "Eat Popcorn" and "Drink Coke" onto the movie screen. His studies, lasting six weeks, involved thousands of moviegoing subjects who received a subliminal message every five seconds during the film. Vicary claimed an increase in Coke sales of 18 percent and a rise in popcorn sales of almost 58 percent. Upon reading their newspapers, most people were outraged and frightened by a technique so devilish that it could bypass their conscious intellect and beam *subliminal* commands directly to their subconscious....

In an article titled "Smudging the Subconscious," Norman Cousins (1957) captured similar feelings as he pondered the true meaning of such a device. As he put it, "if the device is successful for putting over popcorn, why not politicians or anything else?" He wondered about the character of people who would dream up a machine to "break into the deepest and most private parts of the human mind and leave all sorts of scratchmarks." Cousins concluded that the best course of action would be "to take this invention and everything connected to it and attach it to the center of the next nuclear explosive scheduled for testing."

Cousins's warnings were taken to heart. The Federal Communications Commission immediately investigated the Vicary study and ruled that the use of subliminal messages could result in the loss of a broadcast license. The National Association of Broadcasters prohibited the use of subliminal advertising by its members. Australia and Britain banned subliminal advertising. A Nevada judge ruled that subliminal communications are not protected as free speech.

The Vicary study also left an enduring smudge on Americans' consciousness—if not their *sub*conscious. As a teacher of social psychology and a persuasion researcher, one of the questions I am most frequently asked is, "Do you know about the 'Eat Popcorn/Drink Coke' study that *they* did?" At cocktail parties, I am often pulled aside and, in hushed tones, told about the "Eat Popcorn/Drink Coke" study. Indeed, my original interest in subliminal persuasion was motivated by an attempt to know how to respond to such questions.

Three public-opinion polls indicate that the American public shares my students' fascination with subliminal influence (Haber 1959; Synodinos 1988; Zanot, Pincus, and Lamp 1983). By 1958, just nine months after the Vicary subliminal story first broke, 41 percent of survey respondents had heard of subliminal advertising. This figure climbed to 81 percent in the early 1980s, with more than 68 percent of those aware of the term believing that it was effective in selling products. Most striking, the surveys also revealed that many people learn about subliminal influence through the mass media and through courses in high school and college.

But there is a seamier side to the "Eat Popcorn/Drink Coke" study—one that is rarely brought to public attention. In a 1962 interview with *Advertising Age*, James Vicary announced that the original study was a fabrication intended to increase customers for his failing marketing business. The circumstantial evidence suggests that this time Vicary was telling the truth. Let me explain by recounting the story of the "Eat Popcorn/Drink Coke" study as best I can, based on various accounts published in academic journals and trade magazines (see Advertising Research Foundation 1958; "ARF Checks" 1958; Danzig 1962; McConnell, Cutler, and McNeil 1958; "Subliminal Ad" 1958; "Subliminal Has" 1958; Weir 1984).

Advertisers, the FCC, and research psychologists doubted Vicary's claims from the beginning and demanded proof. To meet these demands, Vicary set up demonstrations of his machine. Sometimes there were technical difficulties in getting the machine to work. When the machine did work, the audience felt little compulsion to comply with subliminal commands, prompting an FCC commissioner to state, "I refuse to get excited about it—I don't think it works" ("Subliminal Has" 1958).

In 1958, the Advertising Research Foundation pressed Vicary to release his data and a detailed description of his procedures. They argued that it had been more than a year since the results were made public and yet there had been no formal write-up of the experiment, which was necessary to evaluate the claims. To this day, there has been no primary published account of the study, and scientists interested in replicating the results must rely on accounts published in such magazines as the *Senior Scholastic* ("Invisible Advertising"

1957), which, although intended for junior-high students, presents one of the most detailed accounts of the original study.

Pressures for a replication accumulated. Henry Link, president of Psychological Corporation, challenged Vicary to a test under controlled conditions and supervised by an independent research firm. No change occurred in the purchase of either Coke or popcorn (Weir 1984). In one of the more interesting attempted replications, the Canadian Broadcast Corporation, in 1958, subliminally flashed the message "Phone Now" 352 times during a popular Sunday night television show called *Close-up* ("Phone Now" 1958). Telephone usage did not go up during that period. Nobody called the station. When asked to guess the message, viewers sent close to five hundred letters, but not one contained the correct answer. However, almost half of the respondents claimed to be hungry or thirsty during the show. Apparently, they guessed (incorrectly) that the message was aimed at getting them to eat or drink.

Finally, in 1962 James Vicary lamented that he had handled the subliminal affair poorly. As he stated, "Worse than the timing, though, was the fact that we hadn't done any research, except what was needed for filing for a patent. I had only a minor interest in the company and a small amount of data—too small to be meaningful. And what we had shouldn't have been used promotionally" (Danzig 1962). This is not exactly an affirmation of a study that supposedly ran for six weeks and involved thousands of subjects.

My point in presenting the details of the Vicary study is twofold. First, the "Eat Popcorn/Drink Coke" affair is not an isolated incident. The topic of subliminal persuasion has attracted the interest of Americans on at least four separate occasions: at the turn of the century, in the 1950s, in the 1970s, and now in the late 1980s and early 1990s. Each of these four flourishings of subliminal persuasion show a similar course of events. First, someone claims to find an effect; next, others attempt to replicate that effect and fail; the original finding is then criticized on methodological grounds; nevertheless the original claim is publicized and gains acceptance in lay audiences and the popular imagination. Today we have reached a point where one false effect from a previous era is used to validate a false claim from another. For example, I recently had the occasion to ask a manufacturer of subliminal self-help audiotapes for evidence of his claim that his tapes had therapeutic value. His reply: "You are a psychologist. Don't you know about the study they did where they flashed 'Eat Popcorn and Drink Coke' on the movie screen?"

During the past few years, I have been collecting published articles on subliminal processes—research that goes back over a hundred years (Suslowa 1863) and includes more than a hundred articles from the mass media and more than two hundred academic papers on the topic (Pratkanis and Greenwald 1988). In none of these papers is there clear evidence in support of the proposition that subliminal messages influence behavior. Many of the studies fail to find an effect, and those that do either cannot be reproduced or are fatally flawed on one or more methodological grounds, including: the failure to control for subject expectancy and experimenter bias effects, selective reporting of positive over negative findings, lack of appropriate control treatments, internally inconsistent results, unreliable dependent measures, presentation of stimuli in a manner that is not truly subliminal, and multiple experimental confounds specific to each study. As Moore 1992 points out, there is considerable evidence for subliminal perception or the detection of information outside of self-reports of awareness. However, subliminal perception should *not* be confused with subliminal persuasion or influence—motivating or changing behavior—for which there is little good evidence (see McConnell, Cutler, and McNeil 1958; Moore 1982 and 1988).

My second reason for describing the Vicary study in detail is that it seems to me that our fascination with subliminal persuasion is yet another example of what Richard Feynman (1985) called "cargo-cult science." For Feynman, a cargo-cult science is one that has all the trappings of science—the illusion of objectivity, the appearance of careful study, and the motions of an experiment—but lacks one important ingredient: skepticism, or a leaning over backward to see if one might be mistaken. The essence of science is to doubt your own interpretations and theories so that you may improve upon them. This skepticism is often missing in the interpretation of studies claiming to find subliminal influence. Our theories and wishes for what we would like to think the human mind is capable of doing interferes with our ability to see what it actually does.

The cargo-cult nature of subliminal research can be seen in some of the first studies on the topic done at the turn of the century. In 1900, Dunlap reported a subliminal Müller-Lyer illusion—a well-known illusion in which a line is made to appear shorter or longer depending on the direction of angles placed at its ends. Dunlap flashed an "imperceptible shadow" or line to subliminally create this illusion. He claimed that his subjects' judgment of length was influenced by the imperceptible shadows. However, Dunlap's results could not be immediately replicated by either Titchener and Pyle (1907) or by Manro and Washburn (1908). Nevertheless, this inconsistency of findings did not stop Hollingworth (1913) from discussing the subliminal Müller-Lyer illusion in his advertising textbook or from drawing the conclusion that subliminal influence is a powerful tool available to the advertiser.

I contend that it was no accident that subliminal influence was first investigated in America at the turn of the century. The goal of demonstrating the power of the subliminal mind became an important one for many people at that time. It was a time of great religious interest, as illustrated by academic books on the topic, religious fervor among the populace, and the further development of a uniquely American phenomenon—the spiritual self-help group. One such movement, popular in intellectual circles, was called "New Thought," which counted William James among its followers. The doctrine of New Thought stated that the mind possesses an unlimited but hidden power that could be tapped—if one knew how—to bring about a wonderful happy life and to exact physical cures. Given the rise of industrialization and the anonymity of newly formed city life, one can see how a doctrine of the hidden power of the individual in the face of realistic powerlessness would be well received in some circles.

The historian Robert Fuller (1982; 1986) traces the origins of New Thought and similar movements to early American interest in the teachings of

Franz Anton Mesmer. Fuller's point is that the powerful unconscious became a replacement for religion's "soul." Mesmer's doctrines contended that each person possessed a hidden, though strong, physical force, which he termed *animal magnetism*. This force could be controlled by the careful alignment of magnets to effect personality changes and physical cures. On one level, mesmerism can be viewed as a secularization of the metaphor of spiritual humans that underlies witchcraft. Animal magnetism replaced the soul, and good and bad magnets replaced angels and devils that could invade the body and affect their will. Mesmerism was introduced to America at the beginning of the nineteenth century and, characteristic of Yankee ingenuity, self-help movements soon sprang up with the goal of improving on Mesmer's original magnet therapy; they did so by developing the techniques of hypnotism, séances, the healing practices of Christian Science, positive thinking, and the speaking cure.

With the distance of a century, we overlook the fact that many journals of the nineteenth century were devoted to archiving the progress of mesmerism and with documenting the influence of the unconscious on the conscious. As Dunlap (1900) said in the introduction to his article on the subliminal Müller-Lyer illusion, "If such an effect is produced, then we have evidence for the belief that under certain conditions things of which we are not and can not become conscious have their immediate effects upon consciousness." In other words, we would have one of the first scientific demonstrations that the unconscious can powerfully influence the conscious. A simple step perhaps, but who knows what wonderful powers of the human mind wait to be unleashed.

As a postscript to the subliminal Müller-Lyer affair, I should point out that 30 years later Joseph Bressler—a student of Hollingworth—was able to reconcile the empirical differences between Dunlap and his opponents. Bressler (1931) found that as the subliminal angles increased in intensity—that is, as they approached the threshold of awareness—the illusion was more likely to be seen. This finding, along with many others, served as the basis for concluding that there is no absolute threshold of awareness—it can vary as a function of individual and situational factors—and led to the hypothesis that, on some trials, subjects could see enough of the stimulus to improve their guessing at what might be there. (See also Holender 1986 and Cheesman and Merikle's 1985 distinction between objective and subjective thresholds.)

Other manifestations of "subliminal-mania" illustrate additional aspects of a cargo-cult science. In the early 1970s, during the third wave of popular interest in subliminal persuasion, the best-selling author Wilson Bryan Key (1973; 1976; 1980; 1989) advanced the cargo-cult science of subliminal seduction in two ways. (See also Creed 1987.) First, Key argued that subliminal techniques were not just limited to television and movies. Cleverly hidden messages aimed at inducing sexual arousal are claimed to be embedded in the photographs of print advertisements. Key found the word *sex* printed on everything from Ritz crackers to the ice cubes in a Gilbey Gin ad. Second, Key was successful in linking the concept of subliminal persuasion to the issues of his day. The 1970s were a period of distrust by Americans of their government, businesses, and institutions. Key claimed that big advertisers and big government are in a conspiracy to control our minds using subliminal implants.

The legacy of Key's cargo-cult science is yet with us. I often ask my students at the University of California, Santa Cruz, if they have heard of the term *subliminal persuasion* and, if so, where. Almost all have heard of the term and about half report finding out about it in high school. Many received an assignment from their teachers to go to the library and look through magazine ads for subliminal implants.

These teachers miss an opportunity to teach science instead of cargo-cult science. Key (1973) reports a study where more than a thousand subjects were shown the Gilbey Gin ad that supposedly contained the word *sex* embedded in ice cubes. Sixty-two percent of the subjects reported feeling "aroused," "romantic," "sensuous." Instead of assuming that Key was right and sending students out to find subliminals, a science educator would encourage a student to ask, "But where is the control group in the Gilbey Gin ad study? Perhaps an even higher percentage would report feeling sexy if the subliminal "sex" was removed—perhaps the same, perhaps less. One just doesn't know.

Now in the late 1980s and early 1990s, we see a fourth wave of interest in subliminal influence. Entrepreneurs have created a $50-million plus industry offering subliminal self help audio- and video tapes designed to improve everything from self-esteem to memory, to employee and customer relations, to sexual responsiveness, and—perhaps most controversial—to overcoming the effects of family and sexual abuse (Natale 1988). The tapes work, according to one manufacturer, because "subliminal messages bypass the conscious mind, and imprint directly on the subconscious mind, where they create the basis for the kind of life you want." Part of the popularity of such tapes no doubt springs from the tenets of New Age. Like its predecessor New Thought, New Age also postulates a powerful hidden force in the human personality that can be controlled for the good, not by magnets, but by crystals, and can be redirected with subliminal commands.

Accusations concerning the sinister use of subliminal persuasion continue as well. In the summer of 1990, the rock band Judas Priest was placed on trial for allegedly recording, in one of their songs, the subliminal implant "Do it." This message supposedly caused the suicide deaths of Ray Belknap and James Vance.

What is the evidence that subliminal influence, despite not working in the 1900s, 1950s, and 1970s, is now effective in the 1990s? Tape company representatives are likely to provide you with a rather lengthy list of "studies" demonstrating their claims. Don't be fooled. The studies on these lists fall into two camps—those done by the tape companies and for which full write-ups are often not available, and those that have titles that sound as if they apply to subliminal influence, but really don't. For example, one company lists many subliminal perception studies to support its claims. It is a leap of faith to see how a lexical priming study provides evidence that a subliminal self-help tape will cure insomnia or help overcome the trauma of being raped. Sadly, the trick of claiming that something that has nothing to do with subliminal influence really does prove the effectiveness of subliminal influence goes back to the turn of the century. In the first footnote to their article describing a failure to replicate Dunlap's subliminal Müller-Lyer effect, Titchener and Pyle (1907) state: "Dunlap finds a parallel to his own results in the experiments of Pierce and Jastrow on small difference of sensations. There is, however, no resemblance whatever between the two investigations." In a cargo-cult science, any evidence—even irrelevant facts—is of use and considered valuable.

Recently, there have been a number of studies that directly tested the effectiveness of subliminal self-help tapes. I conducted one such study in Santa Cruz with my colleagues Jay Eskenazi and Anthony Greenwald (Pratkanis, Eskenazi, and Greenwald 1990). We used mass-marketed audiotapes with subliminal messages designed to improve either self esteem or memory abilities. Both types of tapes contained the same supraliminal content—various pieces of classical music. However, they differed in their subliminal content. According to the manufacturer, the self-esteem tapes contained subliminal messages like "I have high self-worth and high self-esteem." The memory tape contained subliminal messages like "My ability to remember and recall is increasing daily."

Using public posters and ads placed in local newspapers, we recruited volunteers who appeared most interested in the value and potential of subliminal self-help therapies (and who were probably similar to those likely to buy such tapes). On the first day of the study, we asked our volunteers to complete three different self-esteem and three different memory measures. Next they randomly received their subliminal tape, but with an interesting twist. Half of the tapes were mislabeled so that some of the subjects received a memory tape, but thought it was intended to improve self-esteem, whereas others received a self-esteem tape that had been mislabeled as memory improvement. (Of course half the subjects received correctly labeled tapes.)

The volunteers took their tapes home and listened to them every day for five weeks (the period suggested by the manufacturer for maximum effectiveness). During the listening phase, we attempted to contact each subject about once a week to encourage their daily listening. Only a handful of subjects were unable to complete the study, suggesting a high level of motivation and interest in subliminal therapy. After five weeks of daily listening, they returned to the laboratory and once again completed self-esteem and memory tests and were also asked to indicate if they believed the tapes to be effective.

The results: the subliminal tapes produced *no* effect (improvement or decrement) on either self-esteem or memory. But our volunteers did not believe this to be the case. Subjects who thought they had listened to a self-esteem tape (regardless of whether they actually did or not) were more likely to be convinced that their self-esteem had improved, and those who thought they had listened to a memory tape were more likely to believe that their memory had improved as a result of listening to the tape. We called this an illusory placebo effect—placebo, because it was based on expectations; illusory, because it wasn't real. In sum, the subliminal tapes did nothing to improve self-esteem or memory abilities but, to some of our subjects, they appeared to have an effect. As we put it in the title of our report of this study, "What you expect is what you believe, but not necessarily what you get."

Our results are not a fluke. We have since repeated our original study twice using different tapes and have yet to find an effect of subliminal messages upon behavior as claimed by the manufacturer (Greenwald, Spangenberg, Pratkanis, and Eskenazi 1991). By combining our data from all three studies, we gain the statistical power to detect quite small effects. Still, there is no evidence of a subliminal effect consistent with the manufacturers' claims.

Other researchers are also finding that subliminal self-help tapes are of no benefit to the user. In a series of three experiments, Auday, Mellett, and Williams (1991) tested the effectiveness of bogus and real subliminal tapes designed either to improve memory, reduce stress and anxiety, or increase self-confidence. The subliminal tapes proved ineffective on all three fronts. Russell, Rowe, and Smouse (1991) tested subliminal tapes designed to improve academic achievement and found the tapes improved neither grade point average nor final examination scores. Lenz (1989) had 270 Los Angeles police recruits listen for 24 weeks to music with and without subliminal implants designed to improve either knowledge of the law or marksmanship. The tapes did not improve either. In a recent test, Merikle and Skanes (1991) found that overweight subjects who listened to subliminal weight-loss tapes for five weeks showed no more weight loss than did control subjects. In sum, independent researchers have conducted 9 studies to evaluate the effectiveness of subliminal self-help tapes. All 9 studies failed to find an effect consistent with the manufacturers' claims. (See also Eich and Hyman 1991.)

It appears that, despite the claims in books and newspapers and on the backs of subliminal self help tapes, subliminal-influence tactics have not been demonstrated to be effective. Of course, as with anything scientific, it may be that someday, somehow, someone will develop a subliminal technique that may work, just as someday a chemist may find a way to transmute lead to gold. I am personally not purchasing lead futures on this hope however.

The history of the subliminal controversy teaches us much about persuasion—but not the subliminal kind. If there is so little scientific evidence of the effectiveness of subliminal influence, why then do so many Americans believe it' works? In a nutshell, I must conclude, with Feynman, that despite enjoying the fruits of science, we are not a scientific culture, but one of ill-directed faith as defined in Hebrews 11:1 (KJV): "Now faith is the substance of things hoped for, the evidence of things not seen."

We can see the workings of this faulty faith, not science, in the more than a hundred popular press articles on the topic of subliminal persuasion. Many of the articles (36 percent) deal with ethical and regulatory concerns of subliminal practices—assuming them to be effective. Only 18 percent of the articles declare flatly that subliminal influence is ineffective, with the remaining either claiming that it works or suggesting a big "maybe" to prompt readers' concern. In general, popular press articles fail to rely on scientific evidence and method to critically evaluate subliminal findings. Positive findings are emphasized and null results rarely reported. Problems with positive subliminal findings, such as lack of control groups, expectancy effects, setting subliminal thresholds, and so on, are rarely mentioned. If negative information is given, it is often presented at the end of the article, giving the reader the impression that, at best, the claims for subliminal effectiveness are somewhat controversial. Recent coverage of subliminal self-help tapes, however, have been less supportive of subliminal claims—but this may reflect more of an attack on big business than an embrace of science.

Instead of the scientific method, those accused of subliminal persuasion (mostly advertisers) are subjected to what can be termed the "witch test." During the Middle Ages, one common test of witchcraft was to tie and bind the accused and throw her into a pond. If she floats, she is a witch. If she drowns, then her innocence is affirmed. Protestations by the accused were taken as further signs of guilt.

How do we know that subliminals work and that advertisers use them? As Key notes, advertisers spend a considerable amount of money on communications that contain subliminal messages. Why would they spend such vast sums if subliminal persuasion is ineffective? The fact that these subliminal messages cannot be readily identified or seen and that the advertisers deny their use further demonstrates the craftiness of the advertiser. After all, witches are a wiley lot, carefully covering their tracks. It appears that the only way that advertisers can prove their innocence, by the logic of the witch test, is to go out of business at the bottom of the pond, thereby showing that they do not possess the arts of subliminal sorcery. In contrast, just as the motives of the Inquisition for power and fortune went unquestioned, so too the motives of the proponents of subliminal seduction, who frequently profit by the sale of more newspapers, books, or audiotapes, are rarely (or have only recently been) questioned.

The proponents of subliminal persuasion make use of our most sacred expectations, hopes, and fears. Each manifestation of interest in subliminal influence has been linked to the important philosophies and thinking of the day—New Thought in the 1900s, brainwashing in the 1950s, the corruption of big governments in the 1970s, and New Age philosophy today.

But the belief in subliminal persuasion provides much more for the individual. We live in an age of propaganda; the average American will see approximately seven million advertisements in a lifetime. We provide our citizens with very little education concerning the nature of these persuasive processes. The result is that many may feel confused and bewildered by basic social processes (see Pratkanis and Aronson 1992). The negative side of subliminal persuasion is presented as an irrational force outside the control of the message recipient. As such, it takes on a supernatural "devil made me do it" quality capable of justifying and explaining why Americans are often persuaded and can seemingly engage in irrational behavior. Why then did I buy this worthless product at such a high price? Subliminal sorcery. On the positive side, a belief in subliminal persuasion imbues the human spirit at least with the possibility of overcoming the limitations of being human and of living a mundane existence. We can be like the gods—healing ourselves, finding enjoyment in everything we do, working for the benefit of humankind by tapping our own self potentials. Perhaps our theories of what should be or what we would like to be have caused us to be a little less critical of the claims for the power of subliminal influence.

But belief in subliminal persuasion is not without its cost. Perhaps the saddest aspect of the subliminal affair is that it distracts our attention from more substantive issues. By looking for subliminal influences, we may ignore more powerful, blatant influence tactics employed by advertisers and sales agents. We may ignore other, more successful ways—such as science—for reaching our human potentials.

Consider the tragic suicide deaths of teenagers Ray Belknap and James Vance that were brought to light in the recent trial of Judas Priest. They lived troubled lives—lives of drug and alcohol abuse, run-ins with the law, learning disabilities, family violence, and chronic unemployment. What issues did the trial and the subsequent mass-media coverage emphasize? Certainly not the need for drug treatment centers; there was no evaluation of the pros and cons of America's juvenile justice system, no investigation of the schools, no inquiry into how to prevent family violence, no discussion of the effects of unemployment on a family. Instead, our attention was mesmerized by an attempt to count the number of subliminal demons that can dance on the end of a record needle.

In this trial, Judge Jerry Carr Whitehead (*Vance & Belknap v. Judas Priest & CBS Records* 1990) ruled in favor of Judas Priest, stating: "The scientific research presented does not establish that subliminal stimuli, even if perceived, may precipitate conduct of this magnitude. There exist other factors which explain the conduct of the deceased independent of the subliminal stimuli." Perhaps now is the time to lay the myth of subliminal sorcery to rest and direct our attention to other, more scientifically documented ways of understanding the causes of human behavior and improving our condition.

References

Advertising Research Foundation. 1958. *The Application of Subliminal Perception in Advertising.* New York, N.Y.

ARF checks data on subliminal ads; verdict: "Insufficient." 1958. *Advertising Age,* September 15.

Auday, B. C., J. L. Mellett, and P. M. Williams. 1991. Self-improvement Using Subliminal Self-help Audiotapes: Consumer Benefit or Consumer Fraud?" Paper presented at the meeting of the Western Psychological Association, San Francisco, Calif., April.

Bressler, J. 1931. Illusion in the case of subliminal visual stimulation. *Journal of General Psychology,* 5:244–251.

Cheesman, J., and P. M. Merikle. 1985. Word recognition and consciousness. In *Reading Research Advances in Theory and Practice,* vol. 5, ed. by D. Besner, T. G. Waller, and G. E. MacKinnon, 311–352. New York: Academic Press.

Cousins, N. 1957. Smudging the subconscious. *Saturday Review,* October 5, p.20.

Creed, T. T. 1987. Subliminal deception: Pseudoscience on the college lecture circuit. *SKEPTICAL INQUIRER,* 11:358–366.

Danzig, F. 1962. Subliminal advertising—Today it's just historic flashback for researcher Vicary. *Advertising Age,* September 17.

Dunlap, K. 1900. The effect of imperceptible shadows on the judgment of distance. *Psychological Review*, 7:435–453.

Eich, E., and R. Hyman. 1991. "Subliminal Self-help." In *In the Mind's Eye: Enhancing Human Performance*, ed. by D. Druckman and R. A. Bjork, 107–119. Washington, D.C.: National Academy Press.

Feynman, R. P. 1985. *Surely You're Joking, Mr. Feynman!* New York: Bantam Books.

Fuller, R. C. 1982. *Mesmerism and the American Cure of Souls*. Philadelphia: University of Pennsylvania Press.

———.1986. *Americans and the Unconscious*. New York: Oxford Press.

Greenwald, A. G., E. R. Spangenberg, A. R. Pratkanis, and J. Eskenazi. 1991. Double-blind tests of subliminal self-help audiotapes. *Psychological Science*, 2:119–122.

Haber, R. N. 1959. Public attitudes regarding subliminal advertising. *Public Opinion Quarterly*, 23:291–293.

Holender, D. 1986. Semantic activation without conscious identification in dichotic listening, parafoveal vision, and visual masking: A survey and appraisal. *Behavior and Brain Sciences*, 9:1–66.

Hollingworth, H. L. 1913. *Advertising and Selling*. New York: D. Appleton.

Invisible Advertising. 1957. *Senior Scholastic*, October 4.

Key, W. B. 1973. *Subliminal Seduction*. Englewood Cliffs, N.J.: Signet.

———. 1976. *Media Sexploitation*. Englewood Cliffs, N.J.: Signet.

———. 1980. *The Clam-plate Orgy*. Englewood Cliffs, N.J.: Signet.

———. 1989. *The Age of Manipulation*. New York: Holt.

Lenz, S. 1989. "The Effect of Subliminal Auditory Stimuli on Academic Learning and Motor Skills Performance Among Police Recruits." Unpublished doctoral dissertation, California School of Professional Psychology, Los Angeles, Calif.

Manro, H. M., and M. F. Washburn. 1908. The effect of imperceptible line on the judgment of distance. *American Journal of Psychology*, 19:242.

McConnell, J. V., R. I. Cutler, and E. B. McNeil. 1958. Subliminal stimulation: An overview. *American Psychologist*, 13:229–242.

Merikle, P., and H. E. Skanes. 1991. "Subliminal Self-help Audiotapes: A Search for Placebo Effects." Unpublished manuscript, University of Waterloo, London, Ontario.

Moore. T. E. 1982. Subliminal advertising: What you see is what you get. *Journal of Marketing*, 46:38–47.

———. 1988. The case against subliminal manipulation. *Psychology & Marketing*, 5:297–316.

———.1992. Subliminal perception: Facts and fallacies. *Skeptical Inquirer*, 16:273–281.

Natale, J. A. 1988. Are you open to suggestion? *Psychology Today*, September, pp. 28–30.

"Phone now," said CBC subliminally—but nobody did. 1958. *Advertising Age*, February 10, p. 8.

Pratkanis, A. R., and E. Aronson. 1992. *Age of Propaganda: The Everyday Use and Abuse of Persuasion*. New York: W. H. Freeman.

Pratkanis, A. R., and A. G. Greenwald. 1988. Recent perspectives on unconscious processing: Still no marketing applications. *Psychology & Marketing*, 5:339–355.

Pratkanis. A. R., J. Eskenazi, and A. G. Greenwald. 1990. "What You Expect Is What You Believe (But Not Necessarily What You Get): On the Effectiveness of Subliminal Self-help Audiotapes." Paper presented at the meeting of the Western Psychological Association, Los Angeles, Calif., April.

Russell, T. G., W. Rowe, and A. D. Smouse. 1991. Subliminal self-help tapes and academic achievement: An evaluation. *Journal of Counseling & Development*, 69:359–362.

Subliminal ad is transmitted in test but scores no popcorn sales. 1958. *Advertising Age*, January 20.

Subliminal has a test, can't see if it works. 1958. *Printer's Ink*, January 17.

Suslowa, M. 1863. Veranderungen der hautgefule unter dem einflusse electrischer reizung. *Zeitschrift fur Rationelle Medicin*, 18:155–160.

Synodinos, N. E. 1988. Subliminal stimulation: What does the public think about it? *Current Issues & Research in Advertising*, 11:157–187.

Titchener, E. B., and W. H. Pyle. 1907. The effect of imperceptible shadows on the judgment of distance. *Proceedings of the American Philosophical Society*, 46:94–109.

Vance and Belknap v. Judas Priest and CBS Records. 86-5844/86-3939. Second District Court of Nevada. August 24,1990.

Weir, W. 1984. Another look at subliminal "facts." *Advertising Age*, October 15, p. 46.

Zanot, E. J., J. D. Pincus, and E. J. Lamp. 1983. Public perceptions of subliminal advertising. *Journal of Advertising*, 12:37–45.

NO    **Nicholas Epley, Kenneth Savitsky,
and Robert A. Kachelski**

What Every Skeptic Should Know
About Subliminal Persuasion

The report of my death was an exaggeration.

— Mark Twain, in a note to the *New York Journal*, June 1, 1897

Readers of the Skeptical Inquirer are well acquainted with instances of mismatch between popular belief and scientific evidence. Despite an utter lack of scientific support, for example, many individuals place a great deal of belief in such topics as astrology (Carlson 1985; Dean 1987), facilitated communication (Dillon 1993; Mulick, Jacobson, and Kobe 1993), homeopathy (Barrett 1987), alien abductions (Carlsburg 1995; Randles 1993; Turner 1994) and even Elvis sightings (Moody 1987). Issues such as these are "slam dunks" for skeptics: There can be little reconciling such beliefs with evidence that simply does not exist.

In other cases, though, where there is *some* scientific support on which to pin one's belief, there may still be more belief than is warranted. Graphologists, for example, who use samples of individuals' handwriting to determine enduring aspects of their personalities, consistently claim greater predictive validity than can be supported empirically (Nevo 1986; Scanlon and Mauro 1992). Some might argue the same for ESP, for which some evidence might actually exist (Bern and Honorton 1994; but see Hyman 1994). It is in domains such as these that the skeptic's role is more subtle, but just as important. One key aspect of this role is to determine what the available scientific evidence does and does not support. With this in mind, our purpose here is to explore the psychological research on subliminal persuasion, an area in which popular belief may again outstrip available evidence.

Subliminal persuasion refers to the use of subliminally presented stimuli, or messages presented to individuals beneath their level of conscious awareness, that are intended to influence their attitudes, choices, or actions. Not surprisingly, reports that unscrupulous marketers were using this technique to influence consumer behavior have historically prompted alarm (Cousins 1957; Key 1980). Yet, as many writers have suggested, such panic is probably unwarranted: There is simply no good evidence to support the conclusion that subliminal messages implanted in advertisements can exert an influence over whether one drinks Coke or Pepsi, endorses a particular view-point, or votes for candidate X over candidate Y (Moore 1988; Pratkanis and Greenwald 1988; Trappey 1996; Vokey and Read 1985).

Or is there? We will explore why the notion of subliminal persuasion might not be as far-fetched as some have supposed. Our point of departure, in particular, is an article appearing in the Skeptical Inquirer in 1992 by Anthony Pratkanis (see also Moore 1992). In his article, Pratkanis traced the historical roots of the belief in the powers of the unconscious, nicely debunked James Vicary's famous "Eat Popcorn/Drink Coke" hoax, and described the compel-ling results of some of his own research on the ineffectiveness of subliminal self-help audio tapes.

Still, for all its strengths, we believe the Pratkanis article, and others like it, may have left readers with an incomplete picture of the state of the art regarding subliminal presentation of stimuli. Accordingly, we endeavor to acquaint readers of the Skeptical Inquirer with the varied (and thriving) use of subliminally presented stimuli in cognitive and social psychological research. Specifically, we review evidence suggesting that cognition can occur without conscious awareness, and that this unconscious cognition can be affected by subliminal stimuli, thereby influencing individuals' judgments, attitudes, and even their behavior. Indeed, this recent evidence suggesting that subliminal stimuli can influence behavior gives us pause in contemplating the possible effectiveness of subliminal persuasion in advertising.

Clarifying Ambiguities

The exact meaning of "subliminal" has been a source of controversy and con-fusion for decades. A common definition, however, is that a stimulus is sub-liminal (that is, below threshold) if it cannot be verbally identified (e.g., Cheesman and Merikle 1986; Fowler 1986, Greenwald and Draine 1997). The threshold used in this definition is that of conscious awareness, sometimes called a *subjective* threshold (Cheesman and Merikle 1986). This definition, of course, allows for the possibility that an individual perceives that *some* mate-rial was presented, but requires that its exact nature be unidentifiable. Nearly all of the studies we review use this definition, while the remaining adhere to a more conservative one: that individuals be unable to report even the pres-ence of the stimulus.

Furthermore, there is a critical distinction to be made between sublimi-nal *perception* and subliminal *persuasion*. Subliminal perception refers simply to the perception of stimuli that are below the threshold of conscious aware-ness. Subliminal persuasion, on the other hand, requires that the subliminally presented stimulus have some *effect*, not simply on an individual's judgments, but on his or her attitudes or behavior. As others have noted, subliminal per-ception need not imply subliminal persuasion (e.g., Moore 1988).

In this article, we restrict our discussion of subliminally presented stimuli to only those methods that are well supported by research evidence. Thus, audio self-help tapes with subliminal suggestions to "lose weight" or "be assertive" are not considered, nor are "backmasked" messages hidden in recorded music, or instances of messages embedded within pictures (such as the word "sex" air-brushed onto ice cubes or Ritz crackers). Research has shown convincingly that none of these methods is effective (Greenwald, Spangenberg, Pratkanis, and Eskenazi 1991; Moore 1982, 1988; Pratkanis 1992; Pratkanis and Greenwald 1988; Thorne and Himelstein 1984; Vokey and Read 1985). We focus instead on sublimi-nal visual priming techniques, whereby stimuli are presented very quickly, and are typically followed immediately by a "pattern mask," such as a geometric shape or a series of random letters. This mask is intended to disrupt the individ-ual's conscious processing of the stimuli—a bit like immersing pasta in cold water to halt the cooking process.

Unconscious Processing: Out of Sight, But Not Out of Mind

Ask people to name a psychologist and there is disappointingly little variation in their answers. Virtually all of them name Sigmund Freud (with Dr. Joyce Brothers and TV'S Frasier Crane running a distant second and third). Many people might be surprised to learn, then, that contemporary psychology bears little resemblance, either in substance or in methodology, to the work of Freud (Stanovich 1992). That said, at least one idea often attributed to Freud—the unconscious—has made a comeback in contemporary cognitive and social psychology (Bornstein and Pittman 1992; Cohen and Schooler 1997; Erdelyi 1996; Greenwald 1992; Kihlstrom 1987; Uleman and Bargh 1989). Modern psy-chologists do not subscribe to all of Freud's notions regarding the uncon-scious; instead, the term refers simply to those mental processes that occur without conscious monitoring or guidance. Viewed in this way, the uncon-scious figures prominently in many contemporary psychological theories (Greenwald and Banaji 1995; Wegner 1994). For example, numerous studies have shown that some memories that cannot be recalled consciously may nev-ertheless exert influence on a variety of mental processes (Schacter 1987). Others have noted that stereotypes can be readily applied without any con-scious effort or awareness (Gilbert and Hixon 1991; Spencer, Fein, Wolfe, Fong, and Dunn 1998). Indeed, stereotypes seem to be most readily applied at those times when one's conscious capacities are the most limited (Boden-hausen 1990; Bodenhausen and Lichtenstein 1987; Macrae, Milne, and Boden-hausen 1994).

Furthermore, the causal determinants of behavior—why we do what we do—can also be unavailable to conscious awareness. People are notoriously poor at articulating the true causes of their actions and recognizing the importance of critical causal stimuli (Nisbett and Wilson 1977). In one exper-iment, participants were given a sentence-completion task containing a num-ber of words related to the elderly (e.g., *old, wise, retired*). Later, after the experiment had ostensibly ended, these individuals walked more slowly to the elevator than participants in a control group, as if they had internalized the concept of "elderly." None of them showed any recognition of their decreased walking speed or of the high frequency of words related to the elderly in the sentence-completion task (nor could the effect be attributed to other plausible alternative factors, such as depressed mood). The result, concluded the researchers, was a direct effect of unconscious processing on behavior (Bargh, Chen, and Burrows 1996).

Thus, ample evidence attests to the fact that much of what goes on in the mind is unavailable to conscious awareness. Note, however, that the "elderly words" experiment, as well as the research on stereotype activation, used stimuli that were, or could have been, consciously perceived. Since this article's primary concern is the influence of *subliminal* stimuli, we turn to whether subliminally presented stimuli can actually be perceived, while still remaining unavailable to conscious awareness.

We believe that the research literature leaves little doubt that the answer is yes. Many researchers have reported, for example, that words presented subliminally can influence subsequent judgments. Dixon (1981, see also Epley 1998a) found that participants given a subliminal prime (e.g., the word *pencil*) were faster than those who had not seen the prime to later identify a related word (e.g., *write*). Likewise, Marcel (1983) found that participants' identification of a color on a computer screen was facilitated when it was preceded subliminally by the name of the color, but was delayed when preceded by the name of a different color. Although these early studies have been criticized on methodological grounds (Holender 1986; Merikle 1982), similar effects have been found using methodologies developed to address these criticisms (Greenwald Draine, and Abrams 1996; Greenwald and Draine 1997; Merikle and Joordens 1997).

In all, dozens of studies using implicit tests of perception now attest to the fact that subliminally presented stimuli can be perceived (for reviews, see Bornstein and Pittman 1992; Greenwald 1992). But can they persuade?

Ghosts In the Machine: Subliminal Influences on Cognition

For many, the Eiffel Tower is a beloved symbol of Paris. But this was not always true. When the structure was built in 1889, it was despised by many—some Parisians even advocated its destruction (Harrison 1977). Likewise, popular reactions to new artistic movements that are now cherished, from Impressionist painting to rock and roll music, were initially negative (Sabini 1995).

How can these changes of heart be understood? One answer has been proposed by Robert Zajonc (1968), who suggests that "mere exposure" leads to liking: The more one sees something, the more one comes to like it. Thus, the more times people were exposed to the Eiffel Tower, paintings by Monet and Renoir, and the music of Elvis and the Beatles, the more positive their evaluations became.

Experiments have demonstrated that this mere exposure effect is reliable, and, furthermore, that the phenomenon does not depend on one's conscious awareness of the exposure. In one study using subliminal stimuli, for example, participants were shown several irregular polygons for one millisecond, five times each. In a subsequent phase of the study, they were given pairs of figures, one that had been flashed to them previously and one they had never seen. Participants were then asked to make two judgments: which one had they seen before, and which one did they like better. Although they were unable to determine which figure they had seen (these guesses did not depart reliably from a chance base-rate of 50 percent), participants did show an increased liking for the familiar shapes, preferring them 60 percent of the time (Kunst-Wilson and Zajonc 1980; see also Epley 1998b; Seamon, Marsh, and Brody 1984).

Other experiments have broadened the generalizability of this result. In one study, participants were subliminally exposed to a photograph of one of two males who posed as research subjects. Later, when participants engaged in a task with both confederates that involved several scripted disagreements between the two, they sided more often with the one whose picture they had previously seen, and also reported liking that individual more than his counterpart (Bornstein et al. 1987). Mere exposure evidently leads to liking, even when that exposure is beneath the level of conscious awareness.

In other research, experimenters have shown that subliminal exposure to words related to various personality traits can influence how people judge others around them. In particular, exposure to words related to hostility (Bargh and Pietromonaco 1982), kindness, and shyness (Bargh, Bond, Lombardi, and Tota 1986) have been found to produce corresponding personality judgments (i.e., rating others as hostile, kind, or shy). Other investigators have demonstrated that subliminal exposure to pleasant and unpleasant photographs can also affect how target individuals are judged (Krosnick, Betz, Jussim, and Lynn 1992).

Subliminally presented stimuli can also affect judgments about the self, a point made in one of our favorite experiments in this literature. Psychology graduate students were asked to write down three of their ideas for possible research projects. They were then either exposed to a photograph of a familiar postdoctoral student from their laboratory or of the scowling face of their faculty advisor. Unaware that they had seen anything but flashes of light, the students were then asked to rate the quality of the research ideas they had listed. As predicted, those who had been exposed to the scowling face of their advisor rated their own ideas less favorably than did those who had been exposed to the smiling postdoc (Baldwin, Carrel, and Lopez 1991).

A follow-up experiment by the same authors makes a similar point. Catholic undergraduate women rated themselves more negatively on a series of trait adjective scales (e.g., honest/dishonest, moral/immoral) after subliminal exposure to a picture of the pope, but not after exposure to the advisor photograph used in the first study. Moreover, this was true only for participants who indicated that they practiced their religion regularly (Baldwin et al. 1991). This suggests that the effect of subliminal stimuli can be quite complex, mediated here by the personal relevance of the stimuli.

In all, these studies serve to demonstrate that subliminal stimuli can influence high-level cognitive processes, including preferences for geometric shapes, liking of individuals, personality judgments, and ratings of one's self-concept. Of course, to be of any use in a consumer context, these effects must go further. In addition to altering a consumer's *attitudes*, a marketer desires to affect his or her *behavior*. (It is not enough that one likes Pepsi, one has to buy some!) And as students of social psychology know, one need not follow from the other: There is often less correspondence between individuals' attitudes and behaviors than one might expect (LaPiere 1934; Regan and Fazio 1977; Wicker 1969). Therefore, it is incumbent upon us to document instances in which subliminally presented stimuli influence individuals' behavior. Such influence has only recently been documented, and only a handful of supportive experiments exist. Nevertheless, we find these experiments interesting and compelling. A full accounting of the possibility (or impossibility) of subliminal advertising warrants their consideration.

Subliminal Influences on Behavior

Can subliminally presented stimuli influence behavior? Recent investigations suggest that the answer may be yes. For example, Neuberg (1988) has argued that subliminally presented stimuli can influence behavior indirectly, by way of activating concepts that can influence the way individuals interpret the behavior of others. These interpretations, then, can lead individuals to opt for certain behavioral responses. For example, if the concept of hostility were activated subliminally, and caused individuals to "read" hostility into the behavior of others, these individuals might then choose to adopt a hostile course of action themselves. Though such an indirect effect is a far cry from the mindlessly acquiescent behavior conjured by the words "subliminal advertising," it nonetheless would represent an instance of subliminally presented stimuli affecting behavior.

To test this hypothesis, Neuberg confronted participants with a "Prisoner's Dilemma," an exercise in which individuals must choose to either cooperate or compete with another participant (Luce and Raiffa 1957). Before choosing, participants completed questionnaires designed to assess their proclivity toward cooperation versus competition, and were exposed subliminally to either neutral words (e.g., *house, water, sound*) or competition-related words (e.g., *hostile, adversary, cutthroat*). Although the primes did not influence the behavior of those with a cooperative orientation, participants predisposed to compete did so to a greater extent when they were exposed to competitive words than when exposed to neutral words (Neuberg 1988).

More recently, Bargh and colleagues have provided even more compelling evidence that subliminal stimuli can influence behavior (Bargh et al. 1996; Bargh 1997). In contrast to Neuberg's notion of an indirect influence on behavior, Bargh suggests that subliminally presented stimuli can influence behavior *directly*—that the influence is unmediated by conscious thought and results from a direct perception-behavior link that operates not unlike a reflex. How might this hypothesis be put to the test? Previous research has established that exposing white participants to words stereotypically associated with African Americans tends to automatically activate the concept of hostility (Devine 1989). To find out if such exposure might also induce hostile behavior, Bargh and colleagues (1996) asked participants to perform a tedious task on a computer. Unbeknownst to the participants, the computer not only administered the task but also exposed them, subliminally, to photographs of either black or white faces. Then, after many trials, the computer presented them with a bogus error message— "F11 error: failure saving data"—and informed them that they would have to start the task again from the beginning.

Participants' reactions to this news were videotaped using a hidden camera and were rated by judges (who were unaware of the participants' experimental condition) to determine the amount of hostility they exhibited. Results indicated that those exposed to black faces did indeed respond in a more hostile, frustrated manner than those exposed to white faces.

In an extension of this work, Chen and Bargh (1997) exposed participants to photographs of black or white faces and asked them to play a game with another participant who had not seen any photographs. Ratings provided by the second, naive participant once again indicated greater hostility among those presented with black faces as opposed to white faces. Indeed, these naive participants responded to the original participants' hostility with hostility of their own, causing the entire interaction to be rated by outside observers as more hostile when the original participant had been exposed to black faces, as opposed to white.

Finally, direct evidence of subliminal influences on behavior is also surfacing from neuropsychologists who are taking advantage of recent advances in brain imaging. For example, after participants have learned to respond to an odd number with their right hand and an even number with their left, the subliminal presentation of a number (odd or even) produces cortical activation in the corresponding hemisphere of the brain (left or right). This activation is located in the motor cortex, the area of the brain that controls movement (Dehaene et al. 1998).

These experiments raise more questions than they answer. What exactly are the mechanisms that allow subliminally presented stimuli to influence behavior? Is the process indirect, as Neuberg (1988) argues, direct and unmediated, as Bargh and colleagues (1996) maintain, or both? In addition the magnitude and generalizability of these effects have yet to be investigated. Extraordinary claims demand extraordinary evidence, and the evidence we have reviewed in this section falls short of extraordinary. Still, the topic is intriguing, and we eagerly await the results of future investigations.

What About Subliminal Advertising?

For some, the bottom line of research on subliminal persuasion is, well, the bottom line—whether the effects of subliminal stimuli can be harnessed in a consumer setting. Although we hesitate to offer any conclusions, we note that several of the critical requirements for subliminal advertising have been met through scientific research. In particular, as we have detailed, subliminally presented stimuli can influence high-level cognitive processes, and, in some cases, can even influence behavior. Nevertheless, many remain skeptical (Moore 1982, 1988, 1992; Pratkanis 1992; Pratkanis and Greenwald 1988), and it is easy to see why. In each of the studies we reviewed, care was taken to be certain that conditions were perfect: Participants were seated at specific distances from the video or computer screen, their attention was focused in just the right direction, at just the right moment, and extraneous stimuli were kept to a minimum. Such variables are notoriously difficult to control in the real world. In addition, influence from weak, subliminal stimuli is likely to pale in comparison to the highly salient and powerful stimuli already competing for our attention (Moore 1982).

The phenomena we have reviewed may well represent the hot-house products of cleverly crafted laboratory experiments, delicate flowers that would wilt in the harsh environment of the everyday marketplace. Even if this were the case, however, we hasten to point out that it would not challenge the basic validity of the studies we discussed in this article (Mook 1983). It would, instead, merely highlight the challenge of applying insights based on laboratory experiments to consumer behavior. Moreover, despite a lack of evidence for the applicability of subliminal messages to advertising, we suggest there is not a priori reason why such applications are not possible.

In sum, we offer no conclusions regarding the plausibility or effectiveness of subliminal advertising; we only suggest that it may, in fact, be possible, and acquaint readers with the empirical research upon which we base that suggestion. To assert that it is *impossible* for subliminally presented stimuli to influence behavior—even consumer behavior—would be, not unlike the premature reports of Mark Twain's death in the *New York Journal*, an exaggeration.

References

Baldwin, M.W., S.E. Carell, and D.F. Lopez. 1991. Priming relationship schemas: My advisor and the pope are watching me from the back of my mind. *Journal of Experimental Social Psychology* 26: 435–454.

Bargh, J.A. 1997. The automaticity of everyday life: In *Advances in Social Cognition*, ed. R.S. Wyer. 10: 1–61. Mahwah, N.J.: Lawrence Erlbaum Associates, Inc.

Bargh, J.A., R.N. Bond, W.J. Lombardi, and M.E. Tota. 1986. The additive nature of chronic and temporary sources of construct accessibility. *Journal of Personality and Social Psychology* 50: 869–878.

Bargh, J.A., M. Chen, and L. Burrows. 1996. Automaticity and social behavior: Direct effects of trait construct and stereotype activation. *Journal of Personality and Social Psychology* 71: 230–244.

Bargh, J.A., and P. Pietromonaco. 1982. Automatic information processing and social perception: The influence of trait information presented outside of conscious awareness on impression formation. *Journal of Personality and Social Psychology* 43: 437–449.

Barrett, S. 1987. Homeopathy: Is it medicine? Skeptical Inquirer 12: 56–62.

Bem, D.J., and C. Honorton. 1994. Does psi exist? Replicable evidence for an anomalous process of information transfer. *Psychological Bulletin* 115: 4–18.

Bodenhausen, G.V. 1990. Stereotypes as judgmental heuristics: Evidence of circadian variations in discrimination. *Psychological Science* 1: 319–322.

Bodenhausen, G.V., and M. Lichtenstein 1987. Social stereotypes and information processing strategies: the impact of task complexity. *Journal of Personality and Social Psychology* 52: 871–880.

Bornstein, R.F. 1989. Exposure and affect: Overview and meta-analysis of research, 1968–1987. *Psychological Bulletin* 106: 265–289.

Bornstein, R.F., and P.R. D'Agostino. 1992. Stimulus recognition and the mere exposure effect. *Journal of Personality and Social Psychology* 63: 545–552.

Bornstein, R.F., and P.R. D'Agostino. 1994. The attribution and discounting of perceptual fluency: Preliminary tests of a perceptual fluency/attributional model of the mere exposure effect. *Social Cognition* 12: 103–128.

Bornstein, R.F., D.R. Leone, and D.J. Galley. 1987. The generalizability of subliminal mere exposure effects: Influence of stimuli perceived without awareness on social behavior. *Journal of Personality and Social Psychology* 53: 1070–1079.

Bornstein, R.F, and T.S. Pittman, eds. 1992. *Perception Without Awareness*. New York: The Guilford Press.

Carlsburg, K. 1995. *Beyond My Wildest Dreams: Diary of a UFO Abductee*. Santa Fe, N.M.: Bear and Company.

Carlson, S. 1985. A double-blind test of astrology. *Nature* 318: 419–425.

Cheesman, J., and P.M. Merikle. 1986. Distinguishing conscious from unconscious perceptual processes. *Canadian Journal of Psychology* 40: 343–367.

Chen, M., and J.A. Bargh. 1997. Nonconscious behavioral confirmation processes: The self-fulfilling consequences of automatic stereotype activation. *Journal of Experimental Social Psychology* 33: 541–560.

Cohen, J.D., and J.W. Schooler, eds. 1997. *Scientific Approaches to Consciousness*. Mahwah, N.J.: Erlbaum.

Cousins, N. 1957. Smudging the subconscious. October 5. *Saturday Review* p. 20.

Dehaene, S., L. Naccache, G. Le Clec'H, E. Koechlin, M. Mueller, G. Dehaene-Lambertz, P. van de Moortele, and D. LeBihan. 1998. Imaging unconscious semantic priming. *Nature* 395: 597–600.

Dean, G. 1987. Does astrology need to be true? Part 2: The answer is no. *Skeptical Inquirer* 11: 257–273.

Devine, P.G. 1989. Stereotypes and prejudice: Their automatic and controlled components. *Journal of Personality and Social Psychology* 56: 5–18.

Dillon, K.M. 1993. Facilitated communication, autism, and Ouija. *Skeptical Inquirer* 17: 281–287.

Dixon, N.F. 1981. *Preconscious Processing*. New York: Wiley.

Epley, N. 1998a. Subliminal semantic priming and facilitation effects. Unpublished manuscript.

Epley, N. 1998b. Whatever it was, I like it: Unconscious familiarity produces conscious liking. Unpublished manuscript.

Epley, N., and T. Gilovich. in press. Just going along: Nonconscious priming and conformity to social pressure. *Journal of Experimental Social Psychology*.

Erdelyi, M.H. 1996. *The Recovery of Unconscious Memories*. Chicago: The University of Chicago Press.

Fowler, C. 1986. An operational definition of conscious awareness must be responsible to subjective experience. *Behavioral and Brain Sciences* 9: 33–35.

Gilbert, D.T., and J.G. Hixon. 1991. The trouble of thinking: Activation and application of stereotypic beliefs. *Journal of Personality and Social Psychology* 60: 509–517.

Greenwald, A.G. 1992. New Look 3: Unconscious cognition reclaimed. *American Psychologist* 47: 766–779.

Greenwald, A.G., and M.R. Banaji. 1995. Implicit social cognition: Attitudes, self-esteem, and stereotypes. *Psychological Review* 102: 4–27.

Greenwald, A.G., and S.C. Draine. 1997. Do subliminal stimuli enter the mind unnoticed? Tests with a new method. In *Scientific Approaches to Consciousness*, ed. J.D. Cohen and J.W. Schooler, 83–108. Mahwah, N.J.: Erlbaum.

Greenwald, A.G., S.C. Draine, and R.L. Abrams. 1996. Three cognitive markers of unconscious semantic activation. *Science* 273: 1699–1702.

Greenwald, A.G., E.R. Spangenberg, A.R. Pratkanis, and J. Eskenazi. 1991. Double-blind tests of subliminal self-help audiotapes. *Psychological Science* 2: 119–122.

Harrison, A.A. 1977. Mere exposure. In *Advances in Experimental Social Psychology*, ed. L. Berkowitz, 10: 39–83. New York: Academic Press.

Holender, D. 1986. Semantic activation without conscious identification in dichotic listening, parafoveal vision and visual masking: A survey and appraisal. *Behavioral and Brain Sciences* 9: 1–66.

Hyman, R. 1994. Anomaly or artifact? Comments on Bem and Honorton. *Psychological Bulletin* 115: 19–24.

Key, B.W. 1980. *The Clam-plate Orgy and Other Subliminal Techniques for Manipulating Your Behavior*. Englewood Cliffs, N.J.: Prentice-Hall.

Kihlstrom, J.F. 1987. The cognitive unconscious. *Science* 237: 1445–1452.

Krosnick, J.A., A.L. Betz, L.J. Jussim, and A.R. Lynn. 1992. Subliminal conditioning of attitudes. *Personality and Social Psychology Bulletin* 18: 152–162.

Kunst-Wilson, W.R., and R.B. Zajonc. 1980. Affective discrimination of stimuli that cannot be recognized. *Science* 207: 557–558.

LaPiere, R.T. 1934. Attitudes vs. actions. *Social Forces* 13: 203–237.

Luce, R.D. and H. Raiffa. 1957. *Games and Decisions*. New York: Wiley.

Macrae, C. N., A.B. Milne, and G.V. Bodenhausen. 1994. Stereotypes as energy-saving devices: A peek inside the cognitive toolbox. *Journal of Personality and Social Psychology* 66: 37–47.

Marcel, A.J. 1983. Conscious and unconscious perception: Experiments on visual masking and word recognition. *Cognitive Psychology* 15: 197–237.

Merikle, P.M. 1982. Unconscious perception revisited. *Perception and Psychophysics* 31: 298–301.

Merikle, P.M., and S. Joordens. 1997. Measuring unconscious influences. In *Scientific Approaches to Consciousness*, ed. J.D. Cohen and J.W. Schooler, 109–123. Mahwah, N.J.: Erlbaum.

Moody, R.A., Jr. 1987. *Elvis After Life*. Atlanta: Peachtree.

Mook, D.J. 1983. In defense of external invalidity. *American Psychologist* 38: 379–387.

Moore, T.E. 1982. Subliminal advertising: What you see is what you get. *Journal of Marketing* 46: 38–47.

Moore, T.E. 1988. The case against subliminal manipulation. *Psychology and Marketing* 5: 297–316.

Moore, T.E. 1992. Subliminal perception: Facts and fallacies. *Skeptical Inquirer* 16: 273–281.

Mulick, J.A., J.W. Jacobson, and F.H. Kobe. 1993. Anguished silence and helping hands: Autism and facilitated communication. *Skeptical Inquirer* 17: 270–280.

Neuberg, S.L. 1988. Behavioral implications of information presented outside of conscious awareness: The effect of subliminal presentation of trait information on behavior in the prisoner's dilemma game. *Social Cognition* 6: 207–230.

Nisbett, R.E., and T.D. Wilson 1977. Telling more than we can know: Verbal reports on mental processes. *Psychological Review* 84: 231–259.

Nevo, B., ed. 1986. *Scientific Aspects of Graphology: A Handbook.* Springfield, Illinois: Charles C. Thomas.

Pratkanis, A.R. 1992. The cargo-cult science of subliminal persuasion. *Skeptical Inquirer* 16: 260–272.

Pratkanis, A.R., and A.G. Greenwald. 1988. Recent perspectives on unconscious processing: Still no marketing applications. *Psychology and Marketing* 5: 337–353.

Randles, J. 1993. *Alien Contacts and Abductions. The Real Story From the Other Side.* New York: Sterling Publishing.

Regan, D.T., and R. Fazio. 1977. On the consistency between attitudes and behavior. *Journal of Experimental Social Psychology* 13: 435–443.

Sabini, J. 1995. *Social Psychology*, 2nd ed. New York: Norton.

Scanlon, M., and J. Mauro. 1992. The lowdown on handwriting analysis: Is it for real? *Psychology Today* 80(6) 46–53.

Schacter, D.L. 1987. Implicit memory: History and current status. *Journal of Experimental Psychology: Learning, Memory, and Cognition* 13: 501–518.

Seamon, J.G., R.L. Marsh, and N. Brody. 1984. Critical importance of exposure duration for affective discrimination of stimuli that are not recognized. *Journal of Experimental Psychology: Learning, Memory, and Cognition* 10: 465–469.

Stanovich, K.E. 1992. *How to Think Straight About Psychology*, 3rd ed. New York: Harper Collins.

Spencer, S.J., S. Fein, C.T. Wolfe, C.T. Fong, and M.A. Dunn. 1998. Automatic activation of stereotypes: The role of self-image threat. *Personality and Social Psychology Bulletin* 24: 1139–1152.

Thorne, S.B., and P. Himelstein. 1984. The role of suggestion in the perception of satanic messages in rock-and-roll recordings. *Journal of Psychology* 116: 245–248.

Trappey, C. 1996. A meta-analysis of consumer choice and subliminal advertising. *Psychology and Marketing* 13: 517–530.

Turner, K. 1994. *Taken: Inside the Alien-Human Abduction Agenda.* Roland, Arkansas: Kelt Works.

Uleman, J.S., and J.A. Bargh, eds. 1989. *Unintended Thought.* New York: Guilford.

Vokey, J.R., and J.D. Read. 1985. Subliminal messages: Between the devil and the media. *American Psychologist* 40: 1231–1239.

Wegner, D.M. 1994. Ironic processes of mental control. *Psychological Review* 101: 34–52.

Wicker, A.W. 1969. Attitudes versus actions: The relationship of verbal and overt behavioral responses to attitude objects. *Journal of Social Issues* 25: 41–78.

Zajonc, R.B. 1968. Attitudinal effects of mere exposure. *Journal of Personality and Social Psychology Monograph* 9: 1–27.

CHALLENGE QUESTIONS

Is Subliminal Persuasion Real?

1. Is subliminal advertising ethical? Or is it unethical to try to influence consumer behavior without the knowledge of the consumer? Should the use of subliminal advertising be banned?
2. Should social psychologists study subliminal persuasion, even if it means exposing participants to subliminal stimuli without their awareness?
3. Assume for a moment that subliminal advertising is effective. Why would a company use subliminal persuasion to sell its product, rather than a more traditional advertising campaign?

ISSUE 13

Can People Really Be Brainwashed?

YES: Trudy Solomon from "Programming and Deprogramming the Moonies: Social Psychology Applied," *The Brainwashing/Deprogramming Controversy* (Edwin Mellen Press, 1983)

NO: James T. Richardson from "A Social Psychological Critique of Brainwashing Claims about Recruitment to New Religions," *The Handbook of Cults and Sects in America* (JAI Press, 1993)

ISSUE SUMMARY

YES: Psychologist Trudy Solomon argues that well-known social psychological principles may explain the process by which brainwashing can occur. Also Solomon argues that some religious movements, generally referred to as cults, use these principles to recruit new members.

NO: Sociologist James T. Richardson believes that social psychological principles do not necessarily suggest that brainwashing is commonly used in new religious movements. Instead he believes that these organizations use the same the recruitment tactics used by many organizations and therefore cannot be considered "brainwashing."

The term "brainwashing" is a recent invention. It first became widely used during the Korean War, after a substantial number of American prisoners of war collaborated with the enemy, and a handful of Americans actually renounced their U.S. citizenship and remained in China following the end of the war. What could explain their actions? According to many, brainwashing was the answer. Brainwashing is the use of coercive psychological tactics to force people to adopt new beliefs and values. The term "brainwashing" has subsequently come into common usage, and the process of brainwashing was even depicted in the widely acclaimed film *The Manchurian Candidate*. More recently, brainwashing has been invoked as an explanation for the recruitment of people into new religious movements. It is widely believed that many new religious movements, which are often referred to as "cults," use brainwashing techniques to coerce impressionable people into joining their organization.

Social psychologist Trudy Solomon argues that some of the methods used by cults to influence their members can indeed be characterized as brainwashing, although she will use the term "programming" rather than "brainwashing." By applying principles of social influence that are well-known to social psychologists, she argues that some cults use their influence to manipulate cult members. Solomon will focus on the Unification Church, whose followers are sometimes referred to as "Moonies" after the leader of the group, Reverend Sun Myung Moon. The Unification Church is often times referred to as a cult, and some critics, including former members of the church, have claimed that it uses overly aggressive tactics to recruit and retain new members. These tactics, critics argue, can be characterized as brainwashing. Solomon will take a similar position. She argues that the Unification Church uses "programming" procedures that are designed to manipulate members of the Church.

Is it fair to characterize new and unconventional religious movements as cults—a label that has a clear pejorative connotation? And does labeling a group as a cult, and referring to the recruitment of new members as "brainwashing," unfairly associate peaceful religious movements with violent incidents that have occurred in some cults in the past, such as the Jonestown massacre in which over 900 cult members were either killed or committed suicide? These are precisely the questions that James Richardson will address in the second reading. He argues that the recruitment tactics used by new religious organizations should not be characterized as brainwashing. Rather, he believes that new spiritual movements use the same tactics that nearly all organizations employ in order to recruit and retain new members. He believes that membership in a new religious movement is better characterized as an ongoing interaction between a group and its members. It is only when we find the beliefs of a particular group to be strange or frightening that we label the recruitment process as "brainwashing" and brand the group as a "cult."

POINT

- Some new religious movements employ "programming" techniques that are designed to manipulate members of the group.
- Many well-known social psychological principles can be used to explain the coercive effect of these programming techniques.
- These tactics make it more difficult for members to voluntarily leave the organization.

COUNTERPOINT

- The recruitment tactics used by new religious movements are rarely coercive.
- Social psychological principles do not necessarily indicate that new religious movements use excessively manipulative techniques.
- Membership in a new religious movement is better characterized as an ongoing interaction between the group and its members.

Trudy Solomon

➡ **YES**

Programming and Deprogramming the Moonies: Social Psychology Applied

T he rapid proliferation of new religious movements in America during the last two decades has awakened not only a host of social scientists attempting to explain the phenomenon, but also a plethora of legal scholars caught in the concomitant constitutional crisis it has spawned. For by their very existence these movements have brought into focus the meaning and application of one of our nation's most coveted guarantees, the First Amendment. Questions concerning religious freedom, freedom of speech, of association, and of travel, thought to be fundamental to the American culture have been shown to be dependent upon the values and beliefs of those who interpret them. At issue is whether young people, the most frequent adherents to these new religions, are free to participate and believe as they choose, or if opposing parents and governmental agencies will be premitted to intervene and thereby limit individual participation.

Should this kind of intervention be allowed in light of what appears to be flagrant violations of First Amendment rights? The answer, though far from simple, rests on the assumption of the opponents of these new religions that there exists an even more fundamental right than those guaranteed by the First Amendment—freedom of thought—which is allegedly taken away by these movements. It is the contention of opponents to new religions that without this most basic human right, freedom of religion, speech, association, and its ancillary liberties are rendered utterly meaningless.

In a desperate search for remedy, both sides of this controversy are embroiled in a protracted battle whose outcome will most probably be determined through the courts. The issues involved are far from black and white. It is hoped that the following discussion will shed light on methods used by these new religions to gain converts....

Social Psychology Applied

...Numerous studies have shown that a change in attitude produced by the social influence of a persuasive message is often unrelated to behavior change.... An investigation of the programming...process...could reveal evidence of this as yet elusive link. The mysterious feature of these processes is that peoples' *beliefs* can apparently be changed. Clearly coercion can affect *behavior,* but what can persuade people to radically change their beliefs?

Traditional social psychology studies which discuss attitude or behavior change reveal that, even when a link has been found it is difficult to generalize from the laboratory experiment to the field with any confidence....

In addition these experiments often have been "artificial," making it difficult to draw general conclusions for use in interpreting reactions in more "real life" situations. The types of influences exerted in a laboratory rarely approximate the existing pressures felt by prisoners undergoing thought reform in Korea, new recruits training to be "Moonies," or deeply committed Moon movement members experiencing deprogramming. Indeed, laboratory analogues have often consisted of merely a subject's hearing a report on the adjustment being made by others to the situation... Nonetheless, several theories advanced from such studies, if taken in their proper perspective, can be useful in explaining these processes.

Thus, the following discussion of applied social psychology is put forth to make the processes ot programming...understandable. The discussion will focus on the seven component techniques touched upon earlier which have been used as evidence to equate brainwashing with the methods used during the programming process (isolation, group pressures, sleep and food deprivation, repetition, reinforcement, monopolization and coercion). These seven techniques are here collapsed into three general categories: (1) isolation; (2) group pressures... and (3) coercion....

Isolation

One of the most effective ways of producing a break with a person's present identity is to isolate him from all contact with present and past environments. Through isolation, it is possible to externally impose a stripping of self akin to the "mortification process" which Goffman...states new mental patients experience upon entering an institution. It is also possible through this method to foster an in-group (present) out-group (past) animosity which helps to maintain cohesion and loyalty within the new environment.... This cohesion is further strengthened by the censorship of informational input producing a contextual vacuum within which reality rapidly becomes relativistic.

Programming
The Unification Church isolates its converts and new recruits and in so doing shields them both from their old environment and from any negative information that environment could give them about the Moon movement. Members stress that isolation is necessary to be separate from the "temptations of evil" and to increase concentration without undue interferene.... Critics of the Unification Church charge that through isolation members are being "turned against their parents" and are even taught not to visit or communicate with them since they are "agents of the devil."

It is not difficult to see how this kind of isolation could readily foster the notion that all inside the movement is good while all outside is evil. Within this system, converts quite usually experience an intensification of affective bonds to replace any familial and friendship ties lost or damaged when the decision to become a "Moonie" was made. As inside ties become stronger, outside ties usually grow weaker, furthering the insulation and isolation of the movement. This is either accomplished by choice or by the rejection of the recruit's newly found belief and "family" by those outside the movement. Interestingly, persecution of the movement from the outside has most probably made it even more cohesive and resistant than before. Thus critics may be working at cross purposes by strengthening the movement's defenses through their attacks....

However, several researchers have provided evidence for the thesis that many recruits had weak or non-existent external ties before joining the movement and that in some cases disaffection with geographically distant families, spouses, or friends was one of the original problems they were seeking to solve.... More often than not, however, an intense belief in the new produces an intolerance of deviation and a total rejection of old beliefs. Sometimes converts even change their names, ridding themselves of that symbol of their old self conception as well....

The recent proliferation of new religious groups has, not surprisingly, elicited fear and anger from some parents who cannot understand why their children affiliate with movements the parents consider alien and antithetical to their beliefs and values. It is instructive to note that parents who approve of their children's new beliefs, or at least tolerate them, do not espouse the same accusations. Thus, it was proposed by Thomas Szasz... that: "Parents want to believe in brainwashing so badly because otherwise they have to admit to themselves that the kid they devoted 15 or 20 years has rejected them and their values." Zaretsky...emphasizes that such movements do not necessarily change a pre-existing parent-child relationship but rather that "the cults often become scapegoats for the problems of both parents and their sons and daughters." Indeed, it is common knowledge among deprogrammers that in a majority of cases, deep-seated family problems which have perhaps been festering for years are uncovered during the intense drama of the deprogramming situation. It has been proposed that such problems are among the primary reasons why many of the individuals initially joined....

Group Pressures

At the core of any attitudinal behavior changes which occur during the programming...processes are group pressures or social influence techniques. Experimental research on small groups has provided an opportunity for detailed investigations into the conditions and determinants of change induced in an individual's behavior through his or her direct or indirect experience of the behavior of other people....

One of the most significant theories in this area is Festinger's theory of cognitive dissonance which...as assumes that when two or more cognitions (thoughts, perceptions, implications of behavior) are inconsistent with each other, this inconsistency creates dissonance which motivates the individual to do something which will reduce this state. Dissonance can be reduced either by changing beliefs or changing ones behavior. Since the latter is usually much more difficult to accomplish, the former is the most common response. One of the most frequent situations which creates dissonance is an individual engaging in behavior at odds with his or her beliefs. It should not be difficult to see the relevance of this theory to the two processes under the study.

An alternative interpretation of Festinger's cognitive dissonance phenomena was more recently proposed by Daryl Bem.... Self-perception theory, states that we come to know our own attitudes in much the same way that we evaluate another's beliefs, by observing our own behavior. Thus, Bem...suggested that self-descriptive attitude statements can be based on the individual's observation of his or her own overt behavior and the external stimulus conditions under which that behavior occurs.

Evidence has been gathered by a number of researchers to confirm that behavioral commitment and active participation are key devices in producing attitude change. For example, role-playing or forced public compliance have been shown to be useful in changing attitudes previously contrary to one's beliefs.... Subjects came to believe what they had said more than what they had heard or read. Lieberman...found that workers promoted to foreman would change their attitudes in the direction of prevailing foreman attitudes within a matter of months, and, if demoted, would readopt the prevailing attitudes of the worker group. In related research, inducing subjects to comply with a small behavioral request has been shown to increase their tendency to comply with a bigger, more discrepant request—the "foot-in-the door technique.... All of these studies lend strong support to the conception that active participation and behavioral commitment are key devices for producing attitude change.

The famous studies of group pressure conducted by Asch...although they explain only modifications in a single perceptual response rather than an integrated series of beliefs or attitudes, did nonetheless show how individual judgments can yield to group pressure even when that majority opinion is obviously wrong. Asch's findings have obvious relevance to several aspects of the programming and deprogramming processes, especially that of documenting the tremendous influencing potential of an unanimous majority. Thus, theoretical interpretations seem to indicate that both perception and behavior can be made to conform to group definitions when the other members of the group define the situation consistently.

From the earliest days of psychology, a great deal of research has been done on the effects of repetition on persuasion, in part because of its relevance to the popular topics of learning.... Researchers have found that a certain amount of repetition facilitates attitude change...and that in conformity situations, the impact increases as the size of the unanimous majority grows from one to four persons....

Programming

Group pressure is an integral part of the entire indoctrination process and is an effective method in the long-term maintenance of beliefs within the Unification Church. If after the initial contact with a Unification Church member an individual accepts the subsequent invitation to a dinner or lecture, that person will seldom if ever be outside a group situation from that point forward while a member. The new recruit's contact person is far more than merely his or her "spiritual parent," but rather the contact becomes an appendage of sorts, following each bodily movement, anticipating questions, and taking care of the recruit's material and social needs. This kind of intense contact creates an affective bond quite rapidly, a process greatly facilitated by the fact that new recruits are usually brought into the movement by a Unification Church member of the opposite sex. Thus, new recruits are made a part of the "Family" and made to feel loved and needed. The member's sincerity and concern give the newcomer a sense of belonging, perhaps for the first time. Acceptance in a new group also helps to restore one's level of self esteem. New recruits become convinced that if other people care about them then they are surely worthy of care.... Thus, the development or presence of some positive, interpersonal response seems necessary to bridge the gap between exposure and conversion. As Balance Theory...would predict, affective bonding also furthers the acceptance by the new recruit of the ideology and beliefs embodied in the *Divine Principle*.

All activities, including eating, fund-raising, lectures, and games within the Moon movement take place in groups, many of which are sex-segregated. without time for private reflection new recruits and more advanced members have little time to dwell on doubts or to think about social and material characteristics of the outside world. This technique, then, is useful in breaking up past memories and external ties as well as keeping the information input to members sufficiently convoluted to avoid contact with the environment outside the Unification Church.

At weekend workshops, usually the first major step in new recruit training, group pressures become even more pronounced. Small groups are formed upon arrival at the retreat. These groups consist of a majority of committed unification Church members and a sprinkling of recruits in each. Thus, recruits are always surrounded by a larger proportion, of members more advanced in their training. During the exhausting weekend schedule these groups do everything together and become a crucial component in the training process.

One of the most effective methods used by the Moonies to gain conformity and compliance within these groups is a technique known as "sharing." Through this method group members are counseled to open up their hearts and share their experiences and thoughts with the group. Cohesion in the groups is greatly emphasized. Focal topics for this technique include discussions of lecture concepts, personal backgrounds, reactions to the weekend's experiences, and anything else a group leader decides is relevant to the growth of the group and its members. These "sharings" usually begin with testimonials of more advanced members and are followed by the recruits. Regardless of the topic, Unification Church members tend to be somewhat uniform in content and surely set the tone for the group. As in the test situation designed by Aseh, if a person hears five people say X, chances are that person will also speak to X rather than Y, even if X is not something in which he or she truly believes. As one visitor to a weekend workshop put it...:

> For two days I was swooshed and swished around in a maelstrom of conflicting messages and emotional appeals. I was told I was free to say what I liked and also strongly pressured not to rock the boat. I was assured I was experiencing the "unconditional love" of the-whole "family" and yet not permitted to engage in casual conversation with anyone. I heard "creativity" touted and saw only conformity.

It would almost seem that the Moon movement has learned one of the most basic rules of social psychology and applied it to nearly every form of human interaction, namely: social and especially positive social reinforcement is far more effective in shaping human behavior then are material or negative reinforcements. With love as a reward and its withdrawal as a punishment, behavior and beliefs can be molded and influenced. Movement members, therefore, engage in a great deal of touching, smiling, direct eye contact and emotional espousals of fellowship and love, all of which are allegedly withdrawn if "deviant" behavior is exhibited. Some comments from recent recruits are instructive:

> I realized I had to believe like them to get their love. That conditional love made me very uncomfortable.

> How can you expect me to make a decision when you are controlling all the social reinforcements?

> When you have no time to reflect, to think your own thoughts, to talk with people with whom you have something in common, you have to survive somehow. The easiest way to do that, I found, is to please.

The message is clear: conformity is praised and deviation from the group is unacceptable. To those for whom the Moon movement is particularly attractive, conformity to the norm becomes that much more important as a step toward acceptance.

Repetitive singing and chanting are also a regular part of the "Moonie" regime. Although critics suggest that such repetition produces a kind of "mind-numbing" through a variant on Pavlovian conditioning, this has not as yet been proven. More realistically, this kind of repetition in songs and chants creates an artificial feeling of togetherness while the repetition of lecture concepts serves to reinforce key ideas (e.g., Satan, evil, negativity) and desensitizes recruits to potentially mind boggling restructurings of biblical and historical facts. It should be clear that even though at this stage recruits may not believe the words they utter or accept their behavior as parts of their own repertoire, the groundwork has been laid for future acceptance. Whether one adheres to Festinger's notion of cognitive dissonance or Bern's theory of self-perception, it is not hard to see how in time and with the aid of more intensive training and contact, change on both the attitudinal and behavioral levels will be forthcoming....

Coercion

The use of sheer physical coercion, as in the extreme brainwashing situation, in an effort to change both attitudes and behavior, has been shown to produce little in the way of permanent effects. Although one can relatively easily gain temporary compliance in such a coercive environment, once people are removed from the coercive setting their attitudes and behavior will usually shift back toward their preimprisonment repertoire. Though mere behavioral compliance (a change in behavior to gain reward or avoid punishment) may be an acceptable end-product in the brainwashing situation, it is clearly not the desired result of either programming or deprogramming. For either of these processes to be effective (in the absence of an extremely totalistic environment such as a prisoner of war camp) any overt change in behavior must be accompanied by a higher order of attitudinal change. Such changes include identification, where one conforms to others to establish a satisfying relationship, or internalization, where one changes because of a recognition that the content of the new behavior is intrinsically motivating and it therefore fulfills some need....This shift from extrinsic sources to motivation to intrinsic ones is crucial in the maintenance of change over time. Once behavior or beliefs are no longer being conditioned by external motivators (i.e., compliance, reinforcement) and are instead replaced by internal or intrinsic motivators, the changes which such process produces can be quite dramatic and permanent....In addition, Zimbardo...has argued that attitudes shift into line with behavior when the individual perceives him or herself to have chosen the behavior and that attitudes fail to do so when the behavior is under the control of environmental contingencies and constraints.

Programming

Arguments over whether the Unification Church physically restrains its members or uses physical coercion to gain and maintain converts has been a central element in the brainwashing charges that have been levied against them. Leaders of the Unification Church deny the use of coercion in the conversion and maintenance of beliefs, but it is clear that the self-generated pressure members feel toward Church dictated beliefs and behavior must have derived from sources external to the individual. However, force and captivity are simply not conditions that apply to Moon's recruits. Movement members and leaders may use emotional and psychological pressure to be sure, but they do not *force* anyone to join or believe. As Rice...put it:

> While one might, question the independence of a convert's mind, no one has proven the Church holds its members against their will. It might be fairer to use the term conversion instead of brainwashing. If conversion requires the suspension of critical faculties, at least the Moonies do so willingly.

Labeling as brainwashing of any indoctrination, teaching, or philosophy that is engaged in voluntarily is surely an erroneous if not dangerous practice. This potential danger and the key issue of coercion was recently addressed by the American Civil Liberties Union (ACLU) in a statement opposing the use of temporary conservatorships, mental incompetency proceedings, or denial of government protection as a method of depriving people who have reached the age of majority of the free exercise of religion. That statement read in part:

> Modes of religious proselytizing or persuasion for a continued adherence that do not employ physical coercion or threat of same are protected by the free exercise of religion clause of the First Amendment against action of state laws or by state officials. The claim of free exercise may not be overcome by the contention that "brainwashing" or "mind control" has been used, in the absence of evidence that the above standards have been violated.

Yet critics of the Unification Church are quick to point out that the fallacy of making such analogies between the methods used by the Moon movement and those utilized by other secular and religious institutions is that people enter the latter of their own volition and therefore know the consequences of joining. These critics claim that converts to the Unification Church do not join voluntarily and furthermore that they are actually lured into conversion by deception. This accusation derives from a practice known within the Church as "heavenly deception." Members will sometimes disguise their true association or identity for proselytizing or fund-raising purposes. Its use has been widely criticized within the Bay Area by Moon himself, and it is reported to be on the wane. Further, "heavenly deception" is not employed as frequently on the East coast or in Europe as on the West coast....Although the origins of heavenly deception are not certain, leaders within the movement have ascribed it to the priority orientals have sometimes given to the accomplishment of duty rather than to the means of its fulfillment.... Critics of the practice of heavenly deception see it this way (Day of Affirmation and Protest Hearings, 18 February 1976):

> In the Unification cult, two wrongs make a right. Because in the Garden of Eden, Satan deceived God's children, now God's children—that is, the Unification Church members—are justified to deceive Satan, that is the Satan-controlled world.

Further evidence that attests to the lack of physical coercion and the charge of involuntary detainment of recruits and converts can be found in statistical data collected on the Unification Church. It has been shown that the movement has a 55 percent turnover rate in recruits during their first year. This means that over half of the new recruits will not even fulfill one year of their commitment to the movement....

Yet simply because physical coercion may not be a part of the Moonie regime does not exempt them from claims of psychological or mental coercion, which though far more subtle, might in some cases be more salient. The kind of mental coercion that can be readily studied stems from the *Divine Principle* itself which states that everyone outside the Unification Church is influenced by Satan. Implicit in this ideology is the notion that if a convert leaves the fold he or she will also "be of Satan." Deprogrammed Moonies have asserted that leaders use this threat often by teaching that if a member leaves the Unification Church they automatically damn not only themselves but also their ancestors and descendents to eternal hell. Leaders also are alleged to counsel that "Satan works through your loved ones to get you away," as well as its corollary, "Anyone who tries to get you to leave the movement is Satanic." It is easy to see how these could be potentially horrifying instruments of fear, guilt, and superstition which some would argue constitute a form of mental coercion....

Conclusion

By utilizing this applied social psychology perspective to explain program-ming...these processes become far less sensational and more comprehensible to researchers and laypeople alike. Additionally, each component of these two processes can be explored using a variety of social science techniques includ-ing, participant observation, survey research methodology, interviews, and or quasi-experimental design. In this way, programming...need no longer be viewed within the inapplicable and untestable perspective of brainwashing, but rather as phenomena amenable to research and study.

NO

James T. Richardson

A Social Psychological Critique of "Brainwashing" Claims about Recruitment to New Religions

Large numbers of young people have been involved with new religious groups—sometimes pejoratively called "cults"—over the past two or three decades in American society and other Western countries. These young people have often been from dominant class groups, and among the most affluent and better educated of all youth in their societies. Huge controversies have erupted about the meaning of this participation, as parents, friends, and political and opinion leaders have attempted to understand why this "collective desertion" by many of its youth has occurred and as methods are sought to control such involvement.

Joining the groups, some of which appear culturally strange in their beliefs and organizational patterns, has seemed to many to be an act of ultimate rejection of American or even Western culture. The act of participating in new religions has appeared to be an overt rejection of American and Western values and institutions—including religious, economic, and familial. This "culture-rejecting" explanation has been difficult for many to accept, prompting a search for alternative explanations for involvement.

One of the most appealing alternatives has been so-called "brainwashing," "mind control," or "thought reform" theories (Bromley and Richardson 1983). According to those espousing these ideas, youth have not joined the new religions volitionally, but have instead been manipulated or forced into participating by leaders and members of groups using powerful psychotechnology practiced first by communist, anti-Western societies. This psychotechnology allegedly traps or encapsulates young people in the new religions, allowing subsequent control of their behavior by leaders of the groups (see, for example, Shapiro 1977; Delgado 1977; Singer 1979). It was originally developed, according to these claims, in Russian purge trials of the 1930s, and later refined by the Chinese communists after their assumption of power in China in 1949. The techniques also were used against POWs during the Korean War of the 1950s. Now these techniques are allegedly being used by foreign-based

From HANDBOOK OF CULTS AND SECTS IN AMERCIA, vol. 3, 1993, Part B, pp. 75–97. Copyright © 1993 by Elsevier Science, Ltd. Reprinted with permission.

and inspired religious leaders against young people in Western countries, who are supposedly virtually helpless before such sophisticated methods.

When questioned about the obvious logical problem of applying these theories to situations without physical coercion, proponents have ready, if problematic, answers. They claim that physical coercion has been replaced by "psychological coercion," which is actually more effective than simple physical coercion (Singer 1979). These ideas are referred to as "second generation" brainwashing theories, which take into account new insights about manipulation of individuals. It is not necessary to coerce recruits physically if they can be manipulated by affection, guilt, or other psychological influences. Simple group pressures and emotion-laden tactics are revealed as more effective than those used by officials in physically coercive Russian, Chinese, and Korean POW situations.

These theories might be thought of as quaint ideas developed for functional reasons by those who have an interest in their being accepted. They plainly are a special type of "account" which "explains" why people join the groups and why they stay in them for a time (see Beckford 1978; Bromley and Shupe 1979 on conversion accounts; Richardson, Balch, and Melton, this volume, for problems with such accounts). Whatever the origin, and no matter that the veracity of such accounts is questionable, these ideas have become commonly accepted among the general public. For instance, DeWitt (1991) reports that 78 percent of a randomly drawn sample of 383 individuals from an urban county in Nevada said they believed in brainwashing, and 30 percent agreed that "brainwashing is required to make someone join a religious cult." A similar question asked of a random sample of 1,000 residents in New York prior to the tax evasion trial of Reverend Moon (Richardson 1992) revealed that 43 percent agreed "brainwashing is required to make someone change from organized religion to a cult." Latkin (1986) reported on results from a random sample of Oregon residents who were asked about the controversial Rajneesh group centered in Eastern Oregon. Sixty-nine percent of respondents agreed that members of the group were brainwashed. Bromley and Breschel (1992) report that 73 percent of 1,700 randomly drawn respondents in a national survey support legislation prohibiting conversion of teenagers by religious cults. This strong finding may derive from concern about perceived brainwashing-based recruitment techniques allegedly used by new religions.

These notions about brainwashing and mind control have pervaded institutional structures in our society as well. Such views have influenced actions by governmental entities and the media (van Driel and Richardson 1988; Richardson, Kilbourne, and van Driel 1989; Bromley 1984). The legal system has seen a number of efforts to promote brainwashing theories as explanations of why people might participate in new religions (Richardson 1991a; Post 1988; Anthony 1990; Anthony and Robbins 1992). A number of these initiatives have resulted in multimillion dollar judgments against religious groups allegedly using brainwashing techniques on recruits (Bromley 1988).

Thus it appears that ideas about brainwashing of recruits to new religions have developed momentum of their own in our society and other Western countries (Bromley and Shupe 1994; Beckford 1985; Barker 1984). These notions are impacting society in many ways, including as contributors to a possible severe limitation on religious freedom in American society (Post 1988; Richardson 1991a). Thus, we need to examine the brainwashing thesis more closely, in order to see if it might be a proper explanation of what takes place when people join and participate in a new religion. This paper begins with a critique of brainwashing theories from a social science perspective, followed by an attempt to explain the recruitment process from another point of view—generic social psychological theories developed to explain changes in behavior and attitudes. The paper closes with an application of a more activist perspective of the process of recruitment and participation, building on some creative work by Moreland and Levine (1985) and Levine and Russo (1988)....

Social Psychology of the Recruitment Process

...The following section presents some rather straightforward applications of theories and research from social psychology to aid in understanding recruitment and participation, relying in major part on a few explicit efforts to apply social psychology to new religions. Following that discussion, the area of "minority influence" from social psychological studies of nonconformity will be reviewed. This latter effort relies on creative work based on an assumption of a more independent and active individual functioning within the group context and influencing group culture through a process of negotiation with the group and its leaders. Such theorizing and research belies many of the claims made by so-called brainwashing theorists.

Coverage of New Religions in Text Books

Two well-known text books in social psychology, in an apparent effort to be current, discuss participation in new religions. Zimbardo, Ebbesen, and Maslach (1977) open their text with discussion of two situations bound to attract readers' attention. They describe in detail the circumstances of the kidnapping of Patty Hearst, and make the point that simplistic claims about "brainwashing" cannot be used to explain her odd behavior. The authors point out that efforts were made to present a brainwashing defense in the Hearst trial (also see Fort 1983), but they did not succeed. Their brief discussion of the classical theorists discussed above is sound.

However, the authors then discuss the Unification Church (sometimes referred to in the text using the negative descriptor, "Moonies"), under the subtitle, "A (Reverend) Moon for the Misbegotten." The authors' description of the Unification Church follows many of the stereotypes about this group, and their treatment suggests that something as sinister as the kidnapping of Patty Hearst occurs in this group. They also include a copy of a very derogatory editorial cartoon about the Unification Church that appeared in a recent *APA Monitor*. The text indicates that a student of theirs who visited a Unification Church training camp came away "shaken...by the brief, two day experience" (Zimbardo et at. 1977, p. 19).

Later in the text Zimbardo et at. (1977, pp. 182–189) offer more detail about the experiences of this student who feigned an interest in the Unification Church. They are making a similar point to the overall thrust of this section— that the influence techniques are actually quite mundane and ordinary. However, the reader cannot help but deduce that Zimbardo and company do not care for the Unification Church or the content of the influence processes being used. Several social psychological concepts are mentioned as being apropos, including deindividuation, social reinforcement, informational control, "foot in the door" techniques, dissonance, personal attraction, and semantic distortion. The following quote about the recruitment process shows the approach being taken in this text (Zimbardo et at. 1977, p. 185):

> (T)here are informational inputs to be listened to uncritically. An "open mind" means a nonevaluative vulnerable mind set of acceptance. A child-like atmosphere filled with simple demands that are easy to satisfy recreates the passivity, dependence, and obedience of childhood (and evokes our elementary school conditioning). Minimal obedience is all that is required at first. Dissonance follows once the foot is in the door, and then attitudes fall into line to justify compliant actions.

Thus Zimbardo et at. have built an excellent and socially acceptable "straw man" to show how useful and powerful social psychological techniques are for changing people.

Another prominent social psychology text that includes discussion of participation in new religions is Cialdini's (1985) widely cited and very readable *Influence: Science and Practice*. Cialdini discusses the Peoples Temple tragedy, using concepts such as social isolation and pluralistic ignorance to explain the 900 plus suicides and murders that occurred in the South American jungle. He refutes the idea that personal attributes of Jim Jones led directly to the tragedy, but gives Jones credit for knowing how to manipulate the situation so that his wishes would be followed.

This text contains as well a fairly lengthy treatment of the famous "new religion" examined by Festinger et al. (1956). The infiltration of this small group by Festinger's colleagues yielded some fascinating detail about how a group prophesying the end of the world can overcome the obstacle of a failed prophecy. Cialdini posits "social proof" as the mechanism of explanation about what happened with this group which managed to talk itself into an acceptable interpretation of why the end did not come. There was no physical proof of the events they have predicted, but an acceptable social account was developed which most members were able to adopt and even propagate rather forcefully to those who wanted to know why the end had not occurred. Cialdini ignores (as do Festinger et al. 1956) the significant impact of the infiltration and subsequent actions of the covert researchers (see Richardson 1991b). However, his discussion is relatively objective and informative, even if it overlooks the importance of the researcher intervention.

Cialdini also uses the Hare Krishna as an excellent example of the power of reciprocity in social affairs. He notes that the Krishna, a stigmatized group, were able to raise large amounts of money from strangers who did not care for them or want to talk with them, simply by offering them a token (usually a flower or book) in exchange for a donation. This example relates to participation and thus is germane to an examination of brainwashing theories explaining such activities.

Other Applications of Social Psychology to New Religions

Solomon (1983) has done the most thorough job of analyzing recruitment to new religions from a social psychological perspective. Her analysis begins by offering a provocative comparison of Russian and Chinese brainwashing techniques, which she claims differ in important ways. Her analysis reveals that the Chinese approach allegedly is more similar to the practices of new religions in the United States. Unlike the earlier Russian model, the objective of the Chinese approach was a person who was usable after the process. Chinese methods thus seek "conversion," which implies a change of attitude, instead of just compliance, and uses persuasion instead of physical coercion as a major tool. The approach is "evangelistic" instead of "scientific" in orientation, uses a social group as the change agent instead of an individual interrogator, and practices "overstimulation" as contrasted to the "understimulation" (through isolation) of the Russian model. With its emphasis on group processes and on making the convert a functioning member of the group through focused interaction, the Chinese model is obviously social psychological in orientation.

Solomon (1983, p. 169) then launches into a discussion two major issues in social psychology:

> (1) how and under what circumstances can social influence processes impact upon individual participants, and (2) what is the nature of the relationship and direction of causality between attitudinal and behavioral changes.

These issues demonstrate the problematic nature of simplistic views of social influence. Individual behavior can be modified through group pressure, as the classic studies of Asch (1960) and Sherif (1936) demonstrated long ago. However, it is not clear why this occurs or what conditions cause some people to appear to conform to group pressures while others do not. The relationship of attitudes and behavior also remains unspecified. Were peoples' minds actually changed in the classic experiments on social influence, or were those who gave incorrect answers simply conforming to avoid conflict or to get along with their fellow subjects? If their minds were changed, did this occur before or after the incorrect behavioral response? These questions are, of course, important to understanding what happens when an individual is in a recruitment situation with a new religious group.

Solomon focuses her analysis of the process of recruitment on three general factors: (1) isolation from contact with other environments; (2) group pressures that seem to influence attitudinal and behavioral changes; and (3) coercion of a physical nature, including food and sleep deprivation. Her discussion gives extended treatment to some topics covered briefly in the two texts just mentioned, and thus her delineation will be used to offer detail needed to flesh out our assertion that social influence processes in new religions are easily understood.

Isolation

Isolation of recruits can be found in a number of new religions, as efforts are made to reduce potential recruits' ties with family and friends, and "encapsulate" them in the new milieu (Greil and Rudy 1984). In some groups, such as the Unification Church, this effort is often quite systematic, whereas in others, particularly noncommunal groups, facilities do not exist for much isolation from normal life. Whatever efforts the groups make are often complemented by actions and predispositions of the recruits. Considerable research has shown that many potential recruits already had weak ties with their family and former friends. Indeed, many were "on the road," looking for alternative lifestyles and belief structures (Straus 1976, 1979; Lofland and Skonovd 1981; Long and Hadden 1983; Richardson 1985). The combination of group efforts at isolation and individual willingness to become isolated sometimes has produced a situation in which few or weak ties remain to anyone outside the recruiting group. Such a circumstance allows a greater impact from various group pressures which might develop within the group.

New religions are not the only groups seeking to influence behavior which have encouraged isolation and the weakening of ties with former friends and with family. Parental restriction of dating partners or otherwise monitoring contact with other youth exemplify the technique of isolation. College sororities and fraternities which discourage contact with home or with certain groups of students on campus are also implementing isolation techniques. Marine boot camp or juvenile detention halls are less benign examples of organizations which isolate "recruits" to improve chances of modifying behavior and belief.

Group Pressures

Group pressures can take many forms, including repetition, monopolization of time, and positive reinforcement of desired behaviors and beliefs (Solomon 1983, p. 170). The combination of such techniques can influence behavior and perhaps beliefs. The classic experiments of Asch clearly show that a significant minority of people will, under certain conditions, change their behavioral response to one which is obviously incorrect but nonetheless conforming. It is not clear, however, whether attitudes and beliefs were actually impacted in these experiments. Social psychology assumes that beliefs and attitudes can be modified through group processes, but there are competing theories to explain this phenomenon.

Treatments such as Solomon, Zimbardo et al., and Cialdini generally assume a cognitive perspective with the person actively seeking an understanding of what they encounter. Solomon discusses cognitive theories that have been developed to explain attitude changes in individuals, including Festinger's (1957) dissonance theory and Bem's (1972) self-perception theory. Both theories place emphasis on the primacy of behavior. Festinger suggests that when cognitions and behavior differ, there is a tendency to alleviate the dissonance that occurs (the actual occurrence of dissonance is a key but untestable assumption of dissonance theory). It is usually easier to modify beliefs than behaviors, or, more accurately, to align beliefs with the behaviors in which a person has engaged.

In contrast to Festinger's ideas, Bem argues that a person's self-perception develops from observing his or her own behavior, which is the same way that individuals make sense of other peoples' behaviors. Individuals attribute beliefs and attitudes to others by observing them, and Ben claims they do the same with themselves.

Both these theories assume that getting a person to act can lead to changes of belief. Thus, the theories suggest that getting potential recruits to participate in the round of group activities is the best way to begin the process of changing their belief structures to ones more closely aligned with those of the group. A number of new religions and some traditional ones as well seem to understand this concept at least intuitively, and seek to involve the potential recruit in many activities from fund raising to proselytizing. The groups welcome the recruit, and reinforce behaviors fitting the group lifestyle and values.

One example of such actions would be Mormon Church encouragement of participation by young people in the two-year volunteer mission program of the church. Whether this and similar practices are cynical manipulation or the actions of a group concerned about demonstrating a caring atmosphere to recruits and others depends in significant measure on the intentionality of the actors. In the case of highly controversial groups, manipulation may be "in the eye of the beholder," and nowhere else.

One criticism that can be made about the phenomenon group pressure and about the classic experiments which undergird this approach is that the experiment occurs in an artificial and relatively nonsalient situation in which subjects are usually only passive recipients of actions by a majority. In Asch's classic experiment the subjects were not allowed to interact with the confederate majority, to question them, or seek information about why they were giving incorrect responses. In a situation with a task of low saliency to most individuals, many who responded with incorrect answers probably just conformed to avoid conflict. In later refinements of this and similar experiments, when even one confederate was instructed to give a correct response, the conforming responses of the subjects plummeted from over 30 percent to around five percent (van Avermaet 1988).

The recruitment situation for most new religions more closely resembles a situation in which interaction is possible between recruits and between recruits and recruiters, with questions being raised by recruits. Recruitment is often an active interaction situation, with the possibility of dissenters from group views being present. Social support would typically be available from other potential recruits who are present. Most importantly, potential recruits were usually present because they chose to be there, and they could leave if they desired.

This is not to say that every recruitment situation allows maximum conditions for dissent. Indeed, new religious groups and other types of recruiting organizations are usually attempting to discourage contacts with dissenters and to "make the sale" without being impeded by other influences. Few used car salespersons deliberately introduce a client to someone who just refused to buy a car from them. Instead, for obvious reasons, they want to have the client interact with other satisfied customers. The salesperson wants to monopolize the time of the client and to have them hear positive repetitions about the value of the car they are considering. And positive behaviors, such as wanting to take a test drive, are reinforced. A less mundane example might be actions taken by members of a convent when interacting with potential recruits. Interactions with defectors would usually be kept to a minimum, while repetitions of positive experiences would be demonstrated, and actions which signaled interest in becoming a nun would be reinforced by the group of already committed nuns and their leaders.

Coercion

This concept has already been discussed in the context of examining assumptions about how brainwashing occurs in new religions. There is little evidence that actual physical coercion occurs in recruitment situations, although there have been a limited number of reports of food and sleep deprivation in a few groups. Food deprivation may be a function of limited group resources, however, and sleep deprivation may be the result of a very full round of group activities designed to accomplish group tasks rather than to tire potential recruits deliberately (see, e.g., Richardson, Stewart, and Simmonds 1979).

It should be noted, however, that if physical coercion did occur, social psychological research would predict that it would not have long-term effects on attitudes and beliefs. Indeed, forced behavioral change may lead to a backlash against the beliefs of those forcing the behavior. As dissonance theory suggests, only when behaviors are freely chosen will they lead to a commensurate change in attitudes about the object of the behavior. Only when the person chooses to behave in a certain fashion will there be an aligning of cognitions with behaviors, according to this line of thought. Cialdini (1985, pp. 60–63) makes a similar point in his examination of the ways in which Chinese captors manipulated the behavior of Korean POWs. He focuses on a kind of "foot in the door" approach, coupled with subsequent labelling of the prisoner as a collaborator to explain behavior changes which occurred.

It bears repetition that most scholars dealing with recruitment into new religions or other groups would not agree that psychological coercion can be equated with physical coercion in terms of impact on recruits (see Anthony 1990). Psychological coercion of various types is simply a fact of life with which contemporary people have to deal. Most handle psychological coercion by ignoring it and going about their business. Only a rare and unique set of circumstances would call for serious concern about the impact of psychological coercion in our society. Solomon includes physical coercion in her analysis because she is also analyzing the social psychology of "deprogramming," and those situations often do involve direct physical coercion (Solomon 1983, pp. 181–182).

Recruitment as an Interaction/Negotiation Situation

As indicated above in the discussion of group pressure phenomena, there are some difficulties with the paradigm adopted in most majority influence research, starting with the classical studies of Sherif and of Asch. A key meta-theoretical assumption of most such work is that the subject is relatively passive in the face of majority pressures, with the majority acting upon the individual subject with relative impunity. Such a perspective cannot be sustained in the face of considerable evidence that people in real recruitment situations not involving physical coercion are quite active, seeking out opportunities to engage in personal change (Straus 1976, 1979; Richardson 1985a).

In order to understand this different, more activist perspective, one must recast the recruitment situation. Instead of conceiving of a group or organization acting upon an individual who is relatively helpless in the face of unwelcome group pressures, the situation should be thought of as one in which recruits are seeking alternatives, find one in which they are tentatively interested, and then engage in open interaction with the group to "feel them out." If the results of the initial contact are positive for the recruits and the group as well, then negotiations are opened to determine what the recruits *as well as the group* must do in order for a longer-term relationship to be agreed upon.

Such a perspective implies relative autonomy on the part of individual potential recruits, and it assumes that the group is not all-powerful. The individual can decide to withdraw from the interaction situation, and the group must allow this autonomous act, unless force is used. In short, the relative power of the group and the recruit(s) is not as highly asymmetrical as assumed by proponents of brainwashing theories. There is rough symmetry, simply because the individual recruits can withdraw. In fact, either side in the negotiations can withdraw. The group can decide that the potential member is not worth the effort of recruitment, and individual recruits may decide that the group is simply too strange or too demanding to be worth the effort to meet entrance requirements; see Galanter (1980) for examples of the Unification Church deciding that some potential recruits were not acceptable, and Richardson et al. (1986) for a general discussion of "expulsion" by new religions....

Conclusions

This analysis of the brainwashing metaphor has demonstrated its ideological foundation, as well as its lack of scientific support. The simplistic perspective inherent in the brainwashing metaphor appeals to those attempting to locate an effective social weapon (Robbins, Anthony, and McCarthy 1983) to use against disfavored groups. The fact that such efforts at social control have been relatively successful should not detract from the lack of scientific basis for such opinions.

A much more fruitful way to view recruitment processes into new religions is to treat them as small groups making use of well-known social psychological techniques to gain recruits. The classical studies of Sherif and Asch give some hints about how this view might be developed, and the work of several social psychologists, particularly Solomon (1983), offers systematic application of the classical tradition of social influence research to new religions' recruitment practices.

The classical work on conformity, however, suffers from metatheoretical assumptions which may mislead scholars somewhat. The traditional paradigm in social influence assumes a relatively passive subject and seems quite anti-interactionist. The work of Moreland and Levine (1985) attempted to develop a more interactionist general theory of socialization into small groups which seems quite valuable when applied to recruitment into new religions. Their perspective emphasizes the reciprocal influences of the group and individual recruit have on one another, as well as assuming that the relationship between the individual recruit and the group is constantly changing.

The follow-up research done by Moreland and Levine (1985) and Levine and Russo (1988) on minority influence over majorities within a small group setting adds another element to the understanding of what happens when recruits participate in new religions. Recruits can and do influence the group, sometimes in dramatic ways. Such situations of minority "conversion" of the majority offer evidence that the process of recruitment into religious groups should not be characterized as situations of majoritarian influence in which the majority always wins totally and dominates all recruits. Such a view misleads, and it detracts from fruitful lines of research which might be pursued by more knowledgeable researchers willing to admit that recruits can and do seek participation, and that they can also influence the groups which they join.

References

Anthony, D. 1990. "Religious Movements and Brainwashing litigation: Evaluating Key Testimony." Pp. 295–344 in *In Gods We Trust*, edited by T. Robbins and D. Anthony. New Brunswick: NJ: Transaction Books.

Anthony, D., and T. Robbins. 1992. "Law, Social Science and the 'Brainwashing' Exception in the First Amendment." *Behavioral Sciences and the Law* 10: 5–30.

Asch, S. 1960. "Effects of Group Pressure Upon the Modification and Distortion of Judgments." Pp. 189–200 in *Group Dynamics*, edited by D. Carlwright and A. Zander. New York: Harper and Row.

Barker, E. 1984. *The Making of a Moonie: Choice or Brainwashing?* Oxford: Blackwell.

Beckford, J. 1978. "Accounting for Conversion." *British Journal of Sociology* 29: 249–262.

——1985. *Cult Controversies: The Societal Response to the New Religious Movements*. London: Tavistock.

Bem, D. 1972. "Self-Perception Theory." Pp. 2–62 in *Advances in Experimental Social Psychology*, edited by L. Berkowitz. Vol. 6. New York: Academic Press.

Bromley, D. 1984. "Conservatorships and Deprogramming: Legal and Political Prospects." Pp. 267–294 in *The Brainwashing/Deprogramming Controversy: Sociological, Psychological, Legal and Historical Perspectives*, edited by D.G. Bromley and J.T. Richardson. Lewiston, NY: Edwin Mellen Press.

Bromley. D., and E. Breschel. 1992. "General Population and Institutional Elite Support for Social Control of New Religious Movements: Evidence from National Survey Data." *Behavioral Sciences and the Law* 10: 39–52.

Bromley, D.G., and J. Richardson, eds. 1983. *The Brainwashing/Deprogramming Controversy: Sociological, Psychology, Legal, and Historical Perspectives*. Lewiston, NY: Edwin Mellen Press.

Bromley, D., and A. Shupe. 1979. "Atrocity Tales, the Unification Church, and the Social Construction of Evil." *Journal of Communication* 29: 42–53.

———. 1994. *Strange Gods and Cult Scares*. Boston: Beacon Press.

Cialdini, R. 1985. *Influence: Science and Practice*. Glenview, IL: Scott, Foresman.

Delgado R. 1977. "Religious Totalism: Gentle and Ungentle Persuasion Under the First Amendment." *Southern California Law Review* 51: 1–99.

———.1982. "Cults and Conversion: The Case for Informed Consent." *Georgia Law Review* 16: 533–574.

DeWitt, J. 1991. "Novel Scientific Evidence and the Juror: A Social Psychological Approach to the *Frye*/Relevancy Controversy." Ph.D. dissertation in Social Psychology, University of Nevada, Reno.

Festinger, L. 1957. *A Theory of Cognitive Dissonance*. Evanston, IL: Row, Peterson.

Festinger, L., H. Riecken, and S. Schachter. 1956. *When Prophecy Fails*. New York: Harper.

Fort, J. 1985. "What is Brainwashing and Who Says So?" Pp. 57–63 in *Scientific Research and New Religions: Divergent Perspectives*, edited by B. Kilbourne. San Francisco: American Association for the Advancement of Science, Pacific Division.

Galanter, M. 1980. "Psychological Induction in the Large-Group: Findings from a Modern Religious Sect." *American Journal of Psychiatry* 137: 1574–1579.

Greil, A., and D. Rudy. 1984. "What Have We Learned About Process Models of Conversion? An Examination of Ten Studies." *Sociological Analysis* 54: 115–125.

Latkin, C. 1986. "Rajneeshpuram, Oregon—An Exploration of Gender and Work Roles, Self-Concept, and Psychological Well-Being in an Experimental Community." Ph.D. dissertation in Psychology, University of Oregon, Eugene.

Levine, J., and E. Russo. 1988. "Majority and Minority Influence." Pp. 13–54 in *Group Processes*. edited by C. Hendrick. Newbury Park, CA: Sage.

Lofland, J., and N. Skonovd. 1981. "Conversion Motifs." *Journal for the Scientific Study of Religion* 20: 375–385.

Long, T., and J. Hadden. 1983. "Religious Conversion and Socialization." *Journal for the Scientific Study of Religion* 24: 1–14.

Moreland, R., and J. Levine. 1985. "Socialization in Small Groups: Temporal Changes in Individual-Group Relations." Pp. 143–169 in *Advances in Experimental Social Psychology*, edited by L. Berkowitz. New York: Academic Press.

Post, S. 1988. The *Molko* Case: Will Freedom Prevail?" *Journal of Church and State* 31: 451–464.

Richardson, J. T. 1985. "Active versus Passive Converts: Paradigm Conflict in Conversion/Recruitment Research" *Journal for the Scientific Study of Religion* 24: 163–179.

———. 1991a. "Cult/Brainwashing Cases and Freedom of Religion." *Journal of Church and State* 33: 55–74.

———. 1991b. "Reflexivity and Objectivity in Research on Controversial New Religions." *Religion* 21: 305–318.

———. 1992. "Public Opinion and the Tax Evasion Trial of Reverend Moon." *Behavioral Sciences and the Law* 10: 53–64.

Richardson, J.T., B. Kilbourne, and B. van Driel. 1989. "Alternative Religions and Economic Individualism." Pp. 33–56 in *Research in the Social Scientific Study of Religion*, edited by M. Lynn and D. Moberg. Vol. I. Greenwich, CT: JAI Press.

Richardson, J.T., M. Stewart and R. Simmonds. 1979. *Organized Miracles: A Study of the Contemporary Youth, Communal, Fundamentalist Organization*. New Brunswick, NJ: Transaction.

Richardson, J. J. van der Lans, and F. Derks. 1986. "Leaving and Labeling: Voluntary and Coerced Disaffiliation from Religious Social Movements." pp. 99–126 in *Research in Social Movements, Conflict and Change*, edited by M. Lang and G. Lang. Vol. 9. Greenwich, CT: JAI Press.

Robbins, T., and D. Anthony. 1982. "Deprogramming, Brainwashing, and the Medicalization of Deviant Religious Groups." *Social Problems* 29: 283–297.

Robbins, T., D. Anthony, and J. McCarthy. 1983. "Legitimating Repression." Pp. 319–328 in *The Brainwashing Deprogramming Controversy*, edited by D. Bromley and J. Richardson. Lewiston, NY: Edwin Mellen Press.

Shapiro, E. 1977. "Destructive Cultism." *American Family Foundation* 15: 80–87.

Sherif, M. 1936. *The Psychology of Social Norms*. New York: Harper and Row.

Singer, M. 1979. "Coming Out of the Cults." *Psychology Today* 12: 72–82.

Soloman, T. 1983. "Programming and Deprogramming the 'Moonies': Social Psychology Applied." Pp. 163–181 in *The Brainwashing/Deprogramming Controversy*, edited by D. Bromley and J. Richardson. Lewiston, NY: Edwin Mellen Press.

Straus, R. 1976. "Changing Oneself: Seekers and the Creative Transformation of Life Experience." Pp. 252–272 in *Doing Social life*, edited by J. Lofland. New York: Wiley.

———. 1979. "Religious Conversion as a Personal and Collective Accomplishment." *Sociological Analysis* 40: 158–165.

van Avermaet, E. 1988. "Social Influence in Small Groups." Pp. 350–380 in *Introduction to Social Psychology*, edited by M. Hewstone, W. Stroebe, J. Codol, and G. Stephenson. New York: Basil Blackwell.

van Driel, B., and J. Richardson. 1988. "Print Media Coverage of New Religious Movements: A Longitudinal Study." *Journal of Communication* 36: 37–61.

Zimbardo, P., E. Ebbesen, and C. Maslach. 1977. *Influencing Attitudes and Influencing Behavior*. Reading, MA: Addison-Wesley.

CHALLENGE QUESTIONS

Can People Really Be Brainwashed?

1. What words come to mind when you hear the words "brainwashing" or "cult"? Should unconventional spiritual organizations, such as the Unification Church, be called "new religious movements" instead of cults? Or is that terminology simply political correctness, as come cult critics claim?
2. Is it always unfair for an organization - any organization - to use psychologically manipulative techniques in order to influence people? Or are some mild forms of psychological coercion acceptable?
3. Occasionally some members of new religious movements have been forcibly removed from the organizations by family members in order to "deprogram" them and reunite them swith their family. Is kidnapping people, and removing them from the group without their consent, an acceptable practice?

Understanding Prejudice

Social psychologist Scott Plous hosts this excellent Web site that contains many resources that are useful for people who are interested in the psychology of prejudice, including interactive demonstrations and slide shows.

http://www.understandingprejudice.org/

Reducing Prejudice

Social psychologist Elliot Aronson and his colleagues have developed an intervention called the Jigsaw Classroom that is designed to reduce prejudice in schools. This Web site explains how to implement this technique in any classroom.

http://www.jigsaw.org/

International Association for Relationship Research

This is a Web site for a group of social scientists who study relationships. It contains information on prominent scholars in the field and additional sources of information about relationship research

http://www.iarr.org/

Online Relationship Research

This site contains several online relationships studies that are being conducted by social psychologist Joshua Foster. At this site, you can either participate in an ongoing study or examine the results of previous research.

http://www.psycdawgs.com/

Helping Behavior

This site compiles anecdotal stories of heroic behavior.

http://www.heroicstories.com

International Society for Research on Aggression

A number of social scientists specialize in the study of aggression and aggressive behavior. This is the Web site for the professional organization to which many aggression researchers belong.

http://www.israsociety.com/

PART 4

Social Relations

*S*ocial *psychologists who study social relations examine how differ-ent people and different groups of people get along with one another. Why are we attracted to some people but not others? What are the ori-gins of prejudicial attitudes and beliefs? Under what circumstances are we likely to offer assistance to those in need? These are just a few of the questions that social psychologists seek to answer.*

- Is Stereotyping Inevitable?
- Can Stereotypes Lead to Accurate Perceptions of Others?
- Does True Altruism Exist?
- Does Media Violence Cause Aggression?
- Does Evaluation Help Explain Gender Differences in Jealousy?

ISSUE 14

Is Stereotyping Inevitable?

YES: Patricia G. Devine from "Stereotypes and Prejudice: Their Automatic and Controlled Components," *Journal of Personality and Social Psychology* (56, 1989)

NO: Lorella Lepore and Rupert Brown from "Category and Stereotype Activation: Is Prejudice Inevitable?" *Journal of Personality and Social Psychology* (72, 1997)

ISSUE SUMMARY

YES: Social psychologist Patricia G. Devine argues that some forms of stereotyping may be automatic and therefore inevitable. In order to prevent these automatic stereotypes from being biased, whites must make a conscious effort to avoid responding in a prejudicial manner.

NO: Social psychologists Lorella Lepore and Rupert Brown believe that automatic stereotyping may not be so universal and automatic as Patricia Devine believes. Some whites may be more likely to engage in automatic stereotyping than others, and as a result stereotyping is not necessarily inevitable among all whites.

Stereotyping, prejudice, and discrimination have long been among the most frequently studied topics in social psychology. Consistent with most social psychologists' desire to address serious social problems (see Issue 2), research aimed at understanding and ultimately reducing prejudice has been underway since at least the 1930s (LaPiere, 1934). Certainly the most influential figure in the study of prejudice is Gordon Allport, whose groundbreaking book, *The Nature of Prejudice*, would foretell the course of research in the field for 50 years. In his book, Allport convincingly argued that prejudice is a natural by-product of the human tendency to categorize objects in our environment. For example, automatically categorize a chair as such in order to quickly recognize and react to it. Similarly, individuals may automatically categorize people on the basis of the groups to which they belong, in order to quickly recognize and react to them. This process has subsequently become known as *social categorization*. Once we have categorized others as being similar to ourselves ("us") or different from ourselves ("them"), prejudice and discrimination will quickly follow.

In Patricia Devine's influential article, she introduces a model of prejudice, comprised of separate and distinguishable psychological processes, which may be responsible for the prejudice of white Americans directed against African-Americans. She proposes that since all white Americans have been exposed to a racist culture, which favors white over black, most whites have been automatically conditioned to have negative views of African-Americans. According to this view, the "gut" reaction of whites to blacks is largely negative. Only a deliberate effort to override this initial negative reaction will result in unprejudiced perceptions and behavior. Thus whites must intentionally try to break the habit of prejudice in order to avoid discriminating against black Americans. (Note that this idea runs contrary to the idea the unprejudiced behavior will result if we simply ignore race.) In a subsequent and important piece, Lepore and Brown argue that the gut reaction of whites toward blacks may not be so uniformly bleak. They present data that suggest that different stereotypes come to mind for people who differ in their level of prejudice; some whites may have more favorable automatic thoughts and reactions towards blacks than others.

POINT

- White Americans, who live in a culture that favors whites over blacks, hold negative stereotypes of blacks that are automatically activated.
- If these stereotypes go unchecked, most whites will have biased perceptions of black Americans.
- The only way whites can avoid being biased against blacks is to make a deliberate attempt to inhibit the effects of these negative stereotypes.

COUNTERPOINT

- Not all whites possess automatic negative stereotypes of blacks to the same extent. Some whites may associate negative characteristics with blacks to a lesser degree than others
- For those whites who are low in prejudice, these stereotypes are less likely to lead to biased perceptions of blacks.
- Some whites who are low in prejudice may not necessarily hold automatic negative stereotypes of blacks.

Patricia G. Devine   ➡ YES

Stereotypes and Prejudice: Their Automatic and Controlled Components

Social psychologists have long been interested in stereotypes and prejudice, concepts that are typically viewed as being very much interrelated. For example, those who subscribe to the tripartite model of attitudes hold that a stereotype is the cognitive component of prejudiced attitudes (Harding, Proshansky, Kutner, & Chein, 1969; Secord & Backman, 1974). Other theorists suggest that stereotypes are functional for the individual, allowing rationalization of his or her prejudice against a group (Allport, 1954; LaViolette & Silvert, 1951; Saenger; 1953; Simpson & Yinger; 1965).

In fact, many classic and contemporary theorists have suggested that prejudice is an inevitable consequence of ordinary categorization (stereotyping) processes (Allport, 1954; Billig, 1985; Ehrlich, 1973; Hamilton, 1981; Tajfel, 1981). The basic argument of the *inevitability of prejudice* perspective is that as long as stereotypes exist, prejudice will follow. This approach suggests that stereotypes are automatically (or heuristically) applied to members of the stereotyped group. In essence, knowledge of a stereotype is equated with prejudice toward the group. This perspective has serious implications because, as Ehrlich (1973) argued, ethnic attitudes and stereotypes are part of the social heritage of a society and no one can escape learning the prevailing attitudes and stereotypes assigned to the major ethnic groups.

The inevitability of prejudice approach, however, overlooks an important distinction between knowledge of a cultural stereotype and acceptance or endorsement of the stereotype (Ashmore & Del Boca, 1981; Billig, 1985). That is, although one may have *knowledge of a stereotype*, his or her *personal beliefs* may or may not be congruent with the stereotype. Moreover, there is no good evidence that knowledge of a stereotype of a group implies prejudice toward that group. For example, in an in-depth interview study of prejudice in war veterans, Bettleheim and Janowitz (1964) found no significant relation between stereotypes reported about Blacks and Jews and the degree of prejudice the veterans displayed toward these groups (see also Brigham, 1972; Devine, 1988; Karlins, Coffman, & Walters, 1969).

Although they may have some overlapping features, it is argued that stereotypes and personal beliefs are conceptually distinct cognitive structures.

From *Journal of Personality and Social Psychology*, vol. 56, no. 1, 1989, pp. 5–18. Copyright © 1989 by American Psychological Association. Reprinted with permission.

Each structure represents part of one's entire knowledge base of a particular group (see Pratkanis, 1989, for a supporting argument in the attitude domain). Beliefs are propositions that are endorsed and accepted as being true. Beliefs can differ from one's knowledge about an object or group or one's affective reaction toward the object or group (Pratkanis, 1989). To the extent that stereotypes and beliefs represent different and only potentially overlapping subsets of information about ethnic or racial groups, they may have different implications for evaluation of and behavior toward members of the ethnic and racial groups. Previous theorists have not adequately captured this distinction and explored its implications for its implications for responding to stereotyped group members. The primary goal of the three studies reported here was to examine how stereotypes and personal beliefs are involved in responses toward stereotyped groups.

This work challenges the inevitability of prejudice framework and offers a model of responses to members of stereotyped groups that is derived largely from work in information processing that distinguishes between automatic (mostly involuntary) and controlled (mostly voluntary) processes (e.g., Posner & Snyder, 1975; Schneider & Shiffrin, 1977; Shiffrin & Schneider, 1977). Automatic processes involve the unintentional or spontaneous activation of some well-learned set of associations or responses that have been developed through repeated activation in memory. They do not require conscious effort and appear to be initiated by the presence of stimulus cues in the environment (Shiffrin & Dumais, 1981). A crucial component of automatic processes is their inescapability; they occur despite deliberate attempts to bypass or ignore them (Neely, 1977; Shiffrin & Dumais, 1981). In contrast, controlled processes are intentional and require the active attention of the individual. Controlled processes, although limited by capacity, are more flexible than automatic processes. Their intentionality and flexibility makes them particularly useful for decision making, problem solving, and the initiation of new behaviors.

Previous theoretical and empirical work on automatic and controlled processes suggests that they can operate independently of each other (Logan, 1980; Logan & Cowan, 1984; Neely, 1977; Posner & Snyder, 1975). For example, by using a semantic priming task, Neely demonstrated that when automatic processing would produce a response that conflicted with conscious expectancies (induced through experimenter instructions), subjects inhibited the automatic response and intentionally replaced it with one consistent with their conscious expectancy.

For example, Neely (1977) examined the influence of a single-word prime on the processing of a single-word target in a lexical decision task (i.e., whether the target was a word). The prime was either semantically related to the target (e.g., *body*-arm) or related to the target through experimenter instructions (e.g., subjects were told that *body* would be followed by a bird name such as sparrow). In this latter condition, subjects had a conscious expectancy for a bird name when they saw the *body* prime, but *body* should also have automatically primed its semantic category of body parts.

Neely (1977) found that with brief intervals between the prime and target (i.e., 250 ms), the prime facilitated decisions for semantically related targets regardless of experimenter instructions. Neely argued that this facilitation was a function of automatic processes. At longer delays (i.e., 2,000 ms), however, experimenter-induced expectancies produced both facilitation for expected targets and inhibition for unexpected targets regardless of their semantic relation to the prime. Before such inhibition of automatically activated responses can occur, there has to be enough *time* and *cognitive capacity* available for the conscious expectancy to develop and inhibit the automatic processes.

Automatic and Controlled Processes: Implications for Activation of Stereotypes and Personal Beliefs

The dissociation of automatic and controlled processes may provide some theoretical leverage for understanding the role of stereotypes and personal beliefs in responses to members of racial or ethnic groups. In the model proposed, interest centers on the conditions under which stereotypes and personal beliefs are activated and the likelihood that personal beliefs overlap with the cultural stereotype. There is strong evidence that stereotypes are well established in children's memories before children develop the cognitive ability and flexibility to question or critically evaluate the stereotype's validity or acceptability (Allport, 1954; P. Katz, 1976; Porter, 1971; Proshansky, 1966). As a result, personal beliefs (i.e., decisions about the appropriateness of stereotypic ascriptions) are necessarily newer cognitive structures (Higgins & King, 1981). An additional consequence of this developmental sequence is that stereotypes have a longer history of activation and are therefore likely to be more accessible than are personal beliefs. To the extent that an individual rejects the stereotype, he or she experiences a fundamental conflict between the already established stereotype and the more recently established personal beliefs.

The present model assumes that primarily because of common socialization experiences (Brigham, 1972; Ehrlich, 1973; P. Katz, 1976; Proshansky, 1966), high- and low-prejudice persons are equally knowledgeable of the cultural stereotype of Blacks. In addition, because the stereotype has been frequently activated in the past, it is a well-learned set of associations (Dovidio, Evans, & Tyler, 1986) that is *automatically* activated in the presence of a member (or symbolic equivalent) of the target group (Smith & Branscombe, 1985). The model holds that this unintentional activation of the stereotype is equally strong and equally inescapable for high- and low-prejudice persons.

A major assumption of the model is that high- and low-prejudice persons differ with respect to their personal beliefs about Blacks (Greeley & Sheatsley, 1971; Taylor, Sheatsley, & Greeley, 1978). Whereas high-prejudice persons are likely to have personal beliefs that overlap substantially with the cultural stereotype, low-prejudice persons have *decided* that the stereotype is an inappropriate basis for behavior or evaluation and experience a conflict between the automatically activated stereotype and their personal beliefs. The stereotype conflicts with their nonprejudiced, egalitarian values. The model assumes that the low-prejudice person must create a cognitive structure that represents his or her newer beliefs (e.g., belief in equality between the races, rejection of the stereotype, etc.). Because the stereotype has a longer history of activation (and thus greater frequency of activation) than the newly acquired personal beliefs, overt nonprejudiced responses require intentional inhibition of the automatically activated stereotype and activation of the newer personal belief structure. Such inhibition and initiation of new responses involves controlled processes.

This analysis suggests that whereas stereotypes are automatically activated, activation of personal beliefs require conscious attention. In addition, nonprejudiced responses require both the inhibition of the automatically activated stereotype and the intentional activation of nonprejudiced beliefs (see also Higgins & King, 1981). This should not be surprising because an individual must overcome a lifetime of socialization experiences. The present model, which suggests that automatic and controlled processes involved in stereotypes and prejudice can be dissociated, posits that the inevitability of prejudice arguments follow from tasks that are likely to engage automatic processes on which those high and low in prejudice are presumed not to differ (i.e., activation of a negative stereotype in the absence of controlled stereotype-inhibiting processes). Interestingly, the model implies that if a stereotype is automatically activated in the presence of a member of the target group and those who reject the cultural stereotype do not (or perhaps cannot) monitor consciously this activation, information activated in the stereotype could influence subsequent information processing. A particular strength of the model, then, is that it suggests how knowledge of a stereotype can influence responses even for those who do not endorse the stereotype or have changed their beliefs about the stereotyped group....

Several studies have demonstrated that increasing the temporary accessibility of trait categories available in memory influences subsequent evaluations of a target person who performs ambiguous trait-relevant behaviors. These findings have been produced with conscious processing of the primes (Carver, Ganellin, Froming, & Chambers, 1983; Srull & Wyer, 1979, 1980) and with priming that is reported to be nonconscious (Bargh, Bond, Lombardi, & Tota, 1986; Bargh & Pietromonaco, 1982). That is, Bargh and Pietromonaco (1982) demonstrated that even when subjects were unaware of the content of the primes, priming increased the likelihood that the primed category was used to interpret subsequently presented ambiguous category related information.

Nonconscious priming was of particular interest in this research because it is this type of processing that would allow the clearest dissociation of automatic and controlled processes involved in responses to members of a stereotyped group. Thus, the priming technique developed by Bargh and Pietromonaco (1982) was used in this study to automatically or passively prime the racial stereotype. Because the priming task activates the stereotype without conscious identification of the primes, the effects of stereotype activation can be studied independently of controlled stereotype-related processes. Specifically, interest

centered on the effect of automatic racial stereotype activation on the interpretation of ambiguous stereotype-related behaviors performed by a race-unspecified
target person.

In this study, evaluation of ambiguously hostile behaviors was examined
because the assumption that Blacks are hostile is part of the racial stereotype
(Brigham, 1971; Study 1) and because it has guided research in intergroup perception (Duncan, 1976; Sager & Schofield, 1980; Stephan, 1985). Because interest centered on the effects of activation of the stereotype on the ratings of a
target person's hostility, no words directly related to hostility were used in the
priming task. This study explicitly examined Duncan's (1976) hypothesis that
the activation of the racial stereotype, which presumably activates a link
between Blacks and hostility, explains why ambiguously aggressive behaviors
were judged as being more aggressive when performed by a Black than a
White actor.

According to the assumptions of the present model, priming will automatically activate the cultural stereotype for both those high and low in prejudice. Because hostility is part of the racial stereotype, increased priming
should lead to more extreme ratings on the hostility-related scales for both
high- and low-prejudice subjects.

Thus, following Bargh and Pietromonaco (1982), during an initial perceptual vigilance task, subjects were asked to identify the location of stimuli,
which were actually words, presented rapidly in subjects' parafoveal visual
field. These strategies were used to prevent subjects from consciously identifying the content of the primes. During the vigilance task either 20% or 80% of
the words presented were related to the racial stereotype. Then, during an
ostensibly unrelated impression-formation task, subjects read a paragraph
describing a race-unspecified target person's ambiguously hostile behaviors
and rated the target person on several trait scales. Half of the trait scales were
related to hostility and thus allowed a test of the effect of stereotype activation on ratings of the target person's hostility. The remaining trait scales were
not related to hostility and provided the opportunity to examine the possibility that stereotype activation led to a global negative evaluation that generalized beyond hostility ratings.

The data from this study could have important theoretical implications
regarding the role of controlled processes and automatic processes involved in
prejudice. However, the criteria required to establish automatic activation
have been debated (see Holender, 1986, and Marcel, 1983b, for reviews).
Greenwald, Klinger, and Liu (1989) recently suggested that automatic activation can be achieved through either *detectionless processing* or *attentionless processing*, both of which have been shown to produce reliable priming effects.
Detectionless processing involves presenting stimuli below subjects' threshold level for reliable detection (Bolota, 1983; Fowler, Wolford, Slade, & Tassinary, 1981; Greenwald et al.,1989; Marcel, 1983a). Attentionless processing
involves processing stimuli that, although detectable, cannot be recalled or
recognized (Klatzky, 1984).

In this study attentionless processing was accomplished by presenting
the primes parafoveally (Bargh & Pietromonaco, 1982) followed immediately

with a pattern mask. With phenomenal awareness of the semantic content of the primes as the criterion for conscious processing (Marcel, 1983a, 1983b), any effects of priming in this study without immediate conscious identification of the primes or recognition for them will be taken as evidence of attentionless automatic processing effects.

Method

Subjects and selection criteria.   Data were collected over two academic quarters. Introductory psychology students were pretested on the seven-item Modern Racism Scale embedded in a number of political, gender, and racial items. This was done to minimize the likelihood that subjects would identify the scale as a measure of prejudice. The experimenter told subjects that completion of the questionnaire was voluntary and that responses would be kept confidential. Subjects were also provided with a form concerning participation in subsequent experiments and provided their names and phone numbers if they were willing to be contacted for a second study for which they could earn extra credit.

Over the two quarters a total of 483 students filled out the Modern Racism Scale. Participants from the upper and lower third of the distribution of scores were identified as potential subjects.... High-prejudice subjects' scores on the Modern Racism Scale fell within the upper third of scores (between +2 and +14), and low-prejudice subjects scores fell within the lower third of scores (between –9 and –14)....

The experimenter remained blind to subjects' prejudice level, priming condition, and stimulus replication condition. Subjects were telephoned by one experimenter, who prepared the materials (with no treatment information) for the second experimenter, who conducted the experiment.

The method and procedure for this study were modeled after Bargh and Pietromonaco (1982). The only difference between their procedure and the one in this study was that in this study, stimuli were presented tachistoscopically rather than on a computer monitor. The experimental room contained a Scientific Prototype two-channel tachistoscope connected to an experimenter-controlled panel for presenting stimuli. Subjects placed their heads against the eyepiece such that the distance from subjects' eyes to the central fixation point was constant. The presentation of a stimulus activated a Hunter Model 120 Klockounter on which the interval between stimulus onset and the response was recorded to the nearest millisecond. Subjects indicated their responses by pushing one of two buttons (labeled *left* or *right*) on a response box. The experimenter recorded each response and its latency.

The stimuli were black and presented on a white background. Each stimulus was presented for 80 ms and was immediately followed by a mask (a jumbled series of letters). In addition, following Bargh and Pietromonaco (1982), the interstimulus interval was 2–7 s. The stimuli (words) were centered in each quadrant, with the center of each word being approximately 2.3 in. (0.06 m) from the central fixation point. The eye-to-dot distance was 31 in. (0.79 m) for the Scientific Prototype tachistoscope. As a result, to keep the stimulus within the parafoveal visual field (from 2° to 6° of visual angle), words could not be presented closer than 1.08 in. (0.03 m) or farther than 3.25 in. (0.08 m) from the fixation point. Twenty-five of the 100 trials within each replication were randomly assigned to each quadrant.

Stimulus materials.   Words that are labels for the social category *Blacks* (e.g., Blacks, Negroes, niggers) or are stereotypic associates (e.g., poor, lazy, athletic) were the priming stimuli. Twenty-four primes were used to generate two stimulus replications. Efforts were made to produce roughly equivalent content in the two replications. Replication 1 primes included the following: nigger, poor, afro, jazz, slavery, musical, Harlem, busing, minority, oppressed, athletic, and prejudice. Replication 2 primes included the following: Negroes, lazy, Blacks, blues, rhythm, Africa, stereotype, ghetto, welfare, basketball, unemployed, and plantation. Twelve neutral words (unrelated to the stereotype) were included in each replication. All neutral words were high-frequency words (Carrol, Davies, & Richman, 1971) and were matched in length to the stereotype-related words. Neutral words for Replication 1 included the following: number, considered, what, that, however, remember, example, called, said, animal, sentences, and important. Replication 2 neutral words included the following: water, then, would, about, things, completely, people, difference, television, experience, something, and thought. Ten additional neutral words were selected and used during practice trials.

Within each stimulus replication, the stereotype-related and neutral words were used to generate two separate 100-word lists. One list contained 80 stereotype-related words (the rest were neutral words) and the other contained 20 stereotype-related words (the rest were neutral words). The lists were organized into blocks of 20 words. In the 80% stereotype-priming condition, each block contained 16 stereotype-related words and 4 neutral words. Within each block, to make 16 stereotype-related words, 4 of the 12 stereotype-related words were randomly selected and presented twice.

For both stimulus replications, the words within each block were randomly ordered with the restriction that the first stereotype-related word was a label for the group (e.g., Negro or nigger). The positions of the minority items (stereotype-related words in the 20% priming list and neutral words in the 80% priming list) were the same for the 20% and 80% priming lists. Each of the 12 stereotype-related and the 12 control words appeared approximately the same number of times as the other stereotype-related and neutral words, respectively.

Judgment condition.   The experimenter told subjects that they would participate in two separate tasks. First, they were seated at the tachistoscope and then provided with a description of the vigilance task. The experimenter told subjects that the vigilance task involved identifying the location of stimuli presented for brief intervals. Subjects also learned that stimuli could appear in one of the four quadrants around the dot in the center of the screen. They were to identify as quickly and as accurately as possible whether the stimulus was presented to the left or the right of the central dot. Subjects indicated their responses by pressing the button labeled *left* or *right* on the response panel. The experimenter informed subjects that the timing and the location of the stimuli were unpredictable. Because both speed and accuracy were emphasized, subjects were encouraged to concentrate on the dot, as this strategy would facilitate detection performance. All subjects first completed 10 practice trials and then 100 experimental trials. Overall, the vigilance task took 11–13 min to complete.

Following the vigilance task, the second task was introduced. Subjects were told that the experimenter was interested in how people form impressions of others. They were asked to read a paragraph describing the events in the day of the person about whom they were to form an impression. This paragraph is the now familiar "Donald" paragraph developed by Srull and Wyer (1979, 1980; see also Bargh & Pietromonaco, 1982, and Carver et al., 1983). This 12-sentence paragraph portrays Donald engaging in a series of empirically established ambiguously hostile behaviors. For example, Donald demands his money back from a store clerk immediately after a purchase and refuses to pay his rent until his apartment is repainted.

After reading the paragraph, subjects were asked to make a series of evaluative judgments about Donald. Subjects rated Donald on each of 12 randomly ordered trait scales that ranged from 0 (*not at all*) to 10 (*extremely*). Six of the scales were descriptively related to hostility; 3 of these scales were evaluatively negative (hostile, dislikeable, and unfriendly) and 3 were evaluatively positive (thoughtful, kind, and considerate). The remaining 6 scales were not related to hostility; 3 of these scales were evaluatively negative (boring, narrow-minded, and conceited) and 3 were evaluatively positive (intelligent, dependable, and interesting).

After completing the rating scales, the experimenter questioned subjects about whether they believed that the vigilance task and the impression-formation task were related. No subject reported thinking the tasks were related or indicated any knowledge of why the vigilance task would have affected impression ratings. The experimenter then explained the nature of priming effects to the subjects. During this debriefing, however, the fact that subjects had been selected for participation on the basis of their Modem Racism Scale scores was not revealed. Subjects were thanked for their participation....

Guess condition.   The experimenter told subjects in this condition that the words would be presented quickly in one of four locations around the central fixation point. Their task was to guess each word immediately following its presentation. The experimenter instructed subjects to maintain their gaze on the fixation point, as this was the best strategy for guessing words given their unpredictable location and timing. Subjects saw either the 80% list of Replication 1 or the 80% list of Replication 2. Subjects were to make a guess for each word presented, even making blind guesses if necessary, and were prompted to guess if they failed to do so spontaneously. This requirement was introduced to lower subjects guessing criterion so as to provide a fair test of their immediate awareness of the stimuli (Bargh & Pietromonaco, 1982).

Results

Guess condition: A check on immediate awareness.   Six high- and 6 low-prejudice subjects were run in this condition. Half of each group were presented
with the 80% list of Replication 1 and half with the 80% list of Replication 2.
If word content were truly not available to consciousness under the viewing
conditions of this study, then subjects should not have been able to guess the
content of the stereotype-related or neutral words. Subjects reported that this
was a difficult task and that they had no idea of the content of the stimuli.
Overall, they made few accurate guesses.

Of the 1,200 guesses, subjects guessed 20 words accurately, a hit rate of
1.67%. Overall, subjects guessed 1.4% of the stereotype-related words and
3.33% of the neutral words. Replicating Bargh and Pietromonaco (1982), the
neutral word hit rate was appreciably higher than that for stereotype-related
words. The neutral words were high-frequency words and thus would presumably be more easily detectable under the viewing condition in this study.

Incorrect guesses were examined for their relatedness to the racial stereotype. Only three of the incorrect guesses could be interpreted as being
related to the stereotype. Twice *Black* appeared as a guess, once from a high-
prejudice subject and once from a low-prejudice subject. These data suggest
that neither high- nor low-prejudice subjects were able to identify the content
of the priming words at the point of encoding, thus satisfying one criterion
for attentionless processing....

Automatic stereotype activation and hostility ratings.   The   major   issue
concerned the effect of automatic stereotype activation on the interpretation
of ambiguous stereotype-congruent (i.e., hostile behaviors performed by a
race-unspecified target person.... Two subscores were computed for each subject. A hostility-related subscore was computed by taking the mean of the six
traits denotatively related to hostility (hostile, dislikeable, unfriendly, kind,
thoughtful, and considerate). The positively valenced scales (thoughtful, considerate, and kind) were reverse scored so that higher mean ratings indicated
higher levels of hostility. Similarly, an overall hostility-unrelated subscore was
computed by taking the mean of the six hostility-unrelated scales. Again, the
positive scales were reverse scored.

The mean ratings were submitted to a mixed-model ANOVA, with prejudice
level (high vs. low), priming (20% vs. 80%), and replication (1 vs. 2) as between-
subjects variables and scale (hostility related vs. hostility unrelated) as a within-subjects variable. The analysis revealed that the Priming × Scale interaction was significant, $F(1, 70) = 5.04$, $p < .03$. Ratings on the hostility-related scales were more
extreme in the 80% ($M = 7.52$) than in the 20% ($M = 6.87$) priming condition. The
hostility-unrelated scales, however, were unaffected by priming ($Ms = 5.89$ and 6.00
for the 20% and 80% priming conditions, respectively). Moreover, the three-way
Prejudice Level × Priming × Scale interaction was not significant, $F(1, 70) = 1.19$, $p = .27$. These results were consistent with the present model and suggest that the
effects of automatic stereotype priming were equally strong for high- and low-prej-
udice subjects....

These analyses suggest that the automatic activation of the racial stereotype affects the encoding and interpretation of ambiguously hostile behaviors for both high- and low-prejudice subjects....

Discussion

[This study] examined the effects of prejudice and automatic stereotype priming on subjects' evaluations of ambiguous stereotype-related behaviors performed by a race-unspecified target person under conditions that precluded the possibility that controlled processes could explain the priming effect. The judgment data of this study suggest that when subjects' ability to consciously monitor stereotype activation is precluded, both high- and low-prejudice subjects produce stereotype-congruent or prejudice-like responses (i.e., stereotype-congruent evaluations of ambiguous behaviors).

These findings extend those of Srull and Wyer (1979, 1980), Bargh and Pietromonaco (1982), Bargh et al. (1986), and Carver et al. (1983) in demonstrating that in addition to trait categories, stereotypes can be primed and can affect the interpretation of subsequently encoded social information. Moreover, it appears that stereotypes can be primed automatically by using procedures that produce attentionless processing of primes (Bargh & Pietromonaco, 1982). The effects of stereotype priming on subjects' evaluation of the target person's hostility are especially interesting because no hostility-related traits were used as primes. The data are consistent with Duncan's (1976) hypothesis that priming the racial stereotype activates a link between Blacks and hostility. Unlike Duncan's research, however, stereotype activation was achieved through attentionless priming with stereotype-related words and not by the race of the target person....

In summary, the data from [this study] suggest that both those high and low in prejudice have cognitive structures (i.e., stereotypes) that can support prejudiced responses. These data, however, should not be interpreted as suggesting that all people are prejudiced.... [The current study] suggested that when the racial category is activated and subject ability to consciously monitor this activation is bypassed, their responses reflect the activation of cognitive structures with a longer history (i.e., greater frequency) of activation. As previously indicated, it appears that these structures are the culturally defined stereotypes (Higgins & King, 1981), which are part of people's social heritage, rather than necessarily part of subjects' personal beliefs.

This analysis suggests that the effect of automatic stereotype activation may be an inappropriate criterion for prejudice because to use it as such equates knowledge of a stereotype with prejudice. People have knowledge of a lot of information they may not endorse. Feminists, for example, may be knowledgeable of the stereotype of women. Blacks and Jews may have knowledge of the Black or Jewish stereotype. In none of these cases does knowledge of the stereotype imply acceptance of it (see also Bettleheim & Janowitz, 1964). In fact, members of these groups are likely to be motivated to reject the stereotype corresponding to their own group. In each of these cases, however, the stereotypes can likely be intentionally or automatically accessed from memory.

The present data suggest that when automatically accessed the stereotype may have effects that are inaccessible to the subject (Nisbett & Wilson, 1977). Thus, "even for subjects who honestly report having no negative prejudices against Blacks, activation of stereotypes can have automatic effects that if not consciously monitored produce effects that resemble prejudiced responses....

General Discussion

The model examined in these studies makes a clear distinction between knowledge of the racial stereotype,... and [the current study] suggested that automatic stereotype activation is equally strong and equally inescapable for high- and low-prejudice subjects. In the absence of controlled stereotype-related processes, automatic stereotype activation leads to stereotype-congruent or prejudice-like responses for both those high and low in prejudice....

The present model suggests that a change in one's beliefs or attitude toward a stereotyped group may or may not be reflected in a change in the corresponding evaluations of or behaviors toward members of that group. Consider the following quote by Pettigrew (1987):

> Many southerners have confesseci to me, for instance, that even though in their minds they no longer feel prejudice toward blacks, they still feel squeamish when they shake hands with a black. These feelings are left over from what they learned in their families as children. (p. 20)

It would appear that the automatically activated stereotype congruent or prejudice-like responses have become independent of one's current attitudes or beliefs. Crosby, Bromley, and Saxe (1980) argued that the inconsistency sometimes observed between expressed attitudes and behaviors that are less consciously mediated is evidence that (all) White Americans are prejudiced against Blacks and that nonprejudiced responses are attempts at impression management (i.e., efforts to cover up truly believed but socially undesirable attitudes). (See also Baxter, 1973; Gaertner, 1976; Gaertner & Dovidio, 1977; Linn, 1965; Weitz, 1972.) Crosby et al. argued that nonconsciously monitored responses are more trustworthy than are consciously mediated responses....

...[In] contrast to the pessimistic analysis by Crosby et al. (1980), the present framework suggests that rather than all people being prejudiced, all are victims of being limited capacity processors. Perceivers cannot attend to all aspects of a situation or their behavior. In situations in which controlled processes are precluded or interfered with, automatic processing effects may exert the greatest influence on responses. In the context of racial stereotypes and attitudes, automatic processing effects appear to have negative implications.

Inhibiting stereotype-congruent or prejudice-like responses and intentionally replacing them with nonprejudiced responses can be likened to the breaking of a bad habit. That is, automatic stereotype activation functions in much the same way as a bad habit. Its consequences are spontaneous and undesirable, at least for the low-prejudice person. For those who have integrated egalitarian ideals into their value system, a conflict would exist between these ideals and expressions of racial prejudice. The conflict experienced is likely to be involved in the initiation of controlled stereotype-inhibiting processes that are required to eliminate the habitual response (activation). Ronis, Yates, and Kirscht (1989) argued that elimination of a bad habit requires essentially the same steps as the formation of a habit. The individual must (a) initially decide to stop the old behavior, (b) remember the resolution, and (c) try repeatedly and decide repeatedly to eliminate the habit before the habit can be eliminated. In addition, the individual must develop a new cognitive (attitudinal and belief) structure that is consistent with the newly determined pattern of responses....

In conclusion, it is argued that prejudice need not be the consequence of ordinary thought processes. Although stereotypes still exist and can influence the responses of both high- and low-prejudice subjects, particularly when those responses are not subject to close conscious scrutiny, there are individuals who actively reject the negative stereotype and make efforts to respond in nonprejudiced ways. At least in situations involving consciously controlled stereotype-related processes, those who score low in prejudice on an attitude scale are attempting to inhibit stereotypic responses (e.g., Study 3; Greeley & Sheatsley, 1971; Taylor et al., 1978; see also Higgins & King, 1981). The present framework, because of its emphasis on the possible dissociation of automatic and controlled processes, *allows for the possibility* that those who report being nonprejudiced are in reality low in prejudice....

References

Allport, G. W. (1954). *The nature of prejudice.* Reading, MA: Addison-Wesley.

Ashmore, R. D., & Del Boca, F. K. (1981). Conceptual approaches to stereotypes and stereotyping. In D. L. Hamilton (Ed.), *Cognitive processes in stereotyping and intergroup behavior* (pp. 1–35). Hillsdale, NJ: Erlbaum.

Bargh, J. A., Bond, R. N., Lombardi, W. J., & Tota, M. E. (1986). The additive nature of chronic and temporary sources of construct accessibility. *Journal of Personality and Social Psychology, 50,* 869–878.

Bargh, J. A., & Pietromonaco, P. (1982). Automatic information processing and social perception: The influence of trait information presented outside of conscious awareness on impression formation. *Journal of Personality and Social Psychology, 43,* 437–449.

Baxter; G. W. (1973). Prejudiced liberals? Race and information effects in a two person game. *Journal of Conflict Resolution, 17,* 131–161.

Bettleheim, B., & Janowitz, M. (1964). Social change and prejudice. New York: Free Press of Glencoe.

Bolota, D. A. (1983). Automatic semantic activation and episodic memory encoding. *Journal of Verbal Learning and Verbal Behavior, 22,* 88–104.

Billig, M. (1985). Prejudice, categorization, and particularization: From a perceptual to a rhetorical approach. *European Journal of Social Psychology, 15,* 79–103.

Brigham, J. C. (1971). Ethnic stereotypes. *Psychological Bulletin, 76,* 15–33.

Brigham, J. C. (1972). Racial stereotypes: Measurement variables and the stereo-type-attitude relationship. *Journal of Applied Social Psychology, 2,* 63–76.

Carrol, J. B., Davies, P., & Richman, B. (1971). *The American Heritage word frequency book.* New York: Houghton Mifllin.

Carver, C. S., Ganellin, R. J., Froming, W. J., & Chambers, W. (1983). Modeling: An analysis in terms of category accessibility. *Journal of Experimental Social Psychology, 19,* 403–421.

Crosby, F., Bromley, S., & Saxe, L. (1980). Recent unobtrusive studies of black and white discrimination and prejudice: A literature review. *Psychological Bulletin, 87,* 546–563.

Devine, P. G. (1988). *Stereotype assessment: Theoretical and methodological issues.* Unpublished manuscript, University of Wisconsin—Madison.

Dovidio, J.F. Evans, N.E., & Tyler, R.B. (1986). Racial stereotypes: The contents of their cognitive representations. *Journal of Experimental Social Psychology, 22,* 22-37.

Duncan, B.L. (1976). Differential social perception and attribution of intergroup violence: Testing the lower limits of stereotyping of blacks. *Journal of Personality and Social Psychology, 34,* 590–598.

Ehrlich, H. J. (1973). *The social psychology of prejudice.* New York: Wiley.

Fowler, C. A., Wolford, G., Slade, R., & Tassinary, L. (1981). Lexical access with and without awareness. *Journal of Experimental Psychology: General, 110,* 341–362.

Gaertner, S. L. (1976). Nonreactive measures in racial attitude research: A focus on "liberals." In P. A. Katz (Ed.), *Towards the eliminalion of racism* (pp. 183–211). New York: Pergamon Press.

Gaertner, S. L., & Dovidio; J. F. (1977). The subtlety of white racism, arousal, and helping. *Journal of Personality and Social Psychology, 35,* 691–707.

Greeley, A., & Sheatsley, P. (1971). Attitudes toward racial integration. *Scientific American, 222,*13–19.

Greenwald, A. G., Klinger, M., & Liu, T. J. (1989). Unconscious processing of word meaning. *Memory & Cognition.*

Hamilton, D. L. (1981). Stereotyping and intergroup behavior: Some thoughts on the cognitive approach. In D. L. Hamilton (Ed.), *Cognitive processes in stereotyping and intergroup behavior* (pp. 333–353). Hillsdale, NJ: Erlbaum.

Harding, J., Proshansky, H., Kutner, B., & Chein, I. (1969). Prejudice and ethnic relations. In G. Lindzey (Ed.), *Handbook of social psychology* (Vol. 5). Reading, MA: Addison-Wesley.

Higgins, E. T., & King, G. (1981). Accessibility of social constructs: Information-processing consequences of individual and contextual variability. In N. Cantor & J. F. Kihlstrom (Eds.), *Personality and social interaction* (pp. 69–121). Hillsdale, NJ: Erlbaum.

Holender, D. (1986). Semantic activation without conscious identification in dichotic listening, parafoveal vision, and visual masking: A survey and appraisal. *Behavioral and Brain Sciences, 9,* 1-66.

Karlins, M., Coffman, T. L., & Walters, G. (1969). On the fading of social stereo-types: Studies in three generations of college students. *Journal of Personality and Social Psychology, 13,* 1–16.

Katz, P. A. (1976). The acquisition of racial attitudes in children. In P. A. Katz (Ed.), *Towards the elimination of racism* (pp. 125–154). New York: Pergamon Press.

Klatzky, R. L. (1984). *Memory and awareness.* San Francisco: Freeman.

LaViolette, F., & Silvert, K. H. (1951). A theory of stereotypes. *Social Forces, 29,* 237–257.

YES / Patricia G. Devine   307

Linn, L. S. (1965). Verbal attitudes and overt behavior: A study of racial discrimination. *Social Forces, 43*, 353–364.

Logan, G. D. (1980). Attention and automaticity in Stroop and priming tasks: Theory and data. *Cognitive Psychology, 12*, 523–553.

Logan, G. D., & Cowan, W. G. (1984). On the ability to inhibit thought and action: A theory of act control. *Psychological Review, 91*, 295–327.

Marcel, A. J. (1983a). Conscious and unconscious perception: Experiments on visual masking and word recognition. *Cognitive Psychology, 15*, 197–237.

Marcel, A. J. (1983b). Conscious and unconscious perception: An approach to the relations between phenomenal experience and perceptual processes. *Cognitive Psychology, 15*, 238–300.

Neely, J. H. (1977). Semantic priming and retrieval from lexical memory: Roles of inhibitionless spreading activation and limited-capacity attention. *Journal of Experimental Psychology, 106*, 226–254.

Nisbett, R. E., & Wilson, T. D. (1977). Telling more than we can know: Verbal reports on mental processes. *Psychological Review, 84*, 231–259.

Pettigrew, T. (1987, May 12): "Useful" modes of thought contribute to prejudice. *New York Times*, pp. 17,20.

Porter, J. D. R. (1971). *Black child, white child: The development of racial attitudes.* Cambridge, MA: Harvard University Press.

Posner, M. I., & Snyder, C. R. R. (1975). Attention and cognitive control. In R. L. Solso (Ed.), *Information processing and cognition: The Loyola Symposium.* Hillsdale, NJ: Erlbaum.

Pratkanis, A. R. (1989). The cognitive representation of attitudes. In A. R. Pratkanis, S. J. Breckler, & A. G. Greenwald (Eds.), *Attitude structure and function.* Hillsdale, NJ: Erlbaum.

Proshansky, H. M. (1966). The development of intergroup attitudes. In L. W. Hoffman & M. L. Hoffman (Eds.), *Review of child development research* (Vol. 2, pp. 311–371). New York: Russell Sage Foundation.

Ronis, D. L., Yates, J. F., & Kirscht, J. P. (1989). Attitudes, decisions, and habits as determinants of repeated behavior. In A. R. Pratkanis, S. J. Breckler, & A. G. Greenwald (Eds.), *Attitude structure and function.* Hillsdale, NJ: Erlbaum.

Saenger, G. (1953). *The social psychology of prejudice.* New York: Harper.

Sager, H. A., & Schofield, J. W. (1980). Racial and behavioral cues in black and white children's perceptions of ambiguously aggressive acts. *Journal of Personality and Social Psychology, 39*, 590–598.

Schneider, W., & Shiffrin, R. M. (1977). Controlled and automatic human information processing: I. Detection, search, and attention. *Psychological Review, 84*, 1–66.

Shiffrin, R. M., & Dumais, S. T. (1981). The development of automatism. In J. R. Anderson (Ed.), *Cognitive skills and their acquisition* (pp. 111–140). Hillsdale, NJ: Erlbaum.

Shiffrin, R. M., & Schneider, W. (1977). Controlled and automatic human information processing: II. Perceptual learning, automatic attending, and a general theory. *Psychological Review, 84*, 127–190.

Simpson, G. E., & Yinger, J. M. (1965). *Racial and cultural minorities* (rev. ed.) New York: Harper & Row.

Smith, E. R. (1984). Model of social inference processes. *Psychological Review, 91*, 392–413. Smith, E. R., & Branscombe, N. R. (1985). *Stereotype traits can be processed automatically.* Unpublished manuscript, Purdue University, West Lafayette, IN.

Srull, T. K., & Wyer, R. S., Jr. (1979). The role of category accessibility in the interpretation of information about persons: Some determinants and implications. *Journal of Personality and Social Psychology, 37,* 1660–1672.

Srull, T. K., & Wyer, R. S., Jr. (1980). Category accessibility and social perception: Some implications for the study of person memory and interpersonal judgments. *Journal of Personality and Social Psychology, 38,* 841–856.

Tajfel, H. (1981). *Human groups and social categories: Studies in social psychology.* Cambridge, England: Cambridge University Press.

Taylor, D. G., Sheatsley, P. B., & Greeley, A. M. (1978). Attitudes toward racial integration. *Scientific American, 238,* 42–49.

Weitz, S. (1972). Attitude, voice, and behavior: A repressed affect model of interracial interaction. *Journal of Personality and Social Psychology, 24,* 14–21.

NO ⤸

Lorella Lepore and
Rupert Brown

Category and Stereotype Activation: Is Prejudice Inevitable?

> A man and a woman, both obviously Italian to judge from their looks and language, are engaged in an apparently confidential conversation that culminates with the man passing the woman an envelope.

Is it romantic love or a mafia-related exchange? Both interpretations are stereo typic and two hypothetical observers would probably *know* both aspects of the stereotype. However, would both stereotypic interpretations immediately spring to mind once the category *Italian* is activated? It seems unlikely. Rather, an observer with mainly positive beliefs about Italian people would readily think of a romantic gesture, such as a love letter, and one with mainly negative views would just as easily infer an illicit transaction. That is, different aspects of the stereotype would be activated in the two observers.

The present research was concerned with the relation between categobz.ation and stereotyping. In particular, it investigated the automaticity of stereotype activation upon categorization and the role played by people's prejudice level in the occurrence and pattern of such activation.

The Inevitability of Prejudice Argument

A long tradition has conceived of stereotyping and prejudice as an automatic and inevitable consequence of categorization (Allport, 1954; Hamilton, 1981; Tajfel, 1969), which, in turn, has been regarded as an adaptive and functional process (Brewer, 1988; Bruner, 1957; Fiske & Neuberg, 1990; Rosch, 1978). Specifically, people's memberships in fundamental categories such as age, gender, and race seem to be attended to automatically (e.g., Brewer, 1988; Bruner, 1957; Fiske & Neuberg, 1990). The associated stereotypes become activated upon perception of the category and influence judgments and behaviors (Hamilton & Sherman, 1994; Hamilton, Sherman, & Ruvolo, 1990; Stangor & Ford, 1992; Stangor & Lange, 1994). Negative group stereotypes can be thought of as the cognitive component of prejudice (Brown, 1995) . Thus, prejudice springs from normal cognitive processes and seems to be inevitable. As Billig (1985) summarized this view, "people will be prejudiced so as long as they continue to think" (p. 81).

From *Journal of Personality and Social Psychology*, vol. 72, no. 2, 1997, pp. 275–287. Copyright © 1997 by American Psychological Association. Reprinted with permission.

Automatic Stereotype Activation

It is generally assumed that stereotypes are automatically activated upon perception of a category member (e.g., Allport, 1954; Deaux & Lewis, 1984; Fiske & Neuberg, 1990; also see Hilton & von Hippel, 1996; Stangor & Lange, 1994). Often stereotypes are seen as networks of linked attributes variously conceptualized. The representation of the social group results from the associative links between discrete nodes (e.g., Carlston, 1992; Fiske, 1982; Stephan & Stephan, 1993). The traits become associated with the group node (category) through frequency and consistency of activation (e.g., Fazio, Sanbonmatsu, Powell, & Kardes, 1986; Higgins & King, 1981; Stephan & Stephan, 1993). When encountering a category member the group node is activated, and the excitation spreads from it to other connected nodes, the stereotypic characteristics. Are all characteristics known to be stereotypic automatically activated? Probably not, since within the representation some links may be stronger than others (Anderson, 1983; Collins & Loftus, 1975; Rumelhart, Hinton, & McClelland, 1986) if they are activated more often. The attributes corresponding to these links are the ones that will be activated automatically (e.g., Bargh, 1984; Posner & Snyder, 1975; Shiffrin & Schneider, 1977; Smith & Lerner, 1986; also see Stangor & Lange, 1994, for a discussion of the sources of associative strength). What links become stronger might vary systematically with a person variable such as prejudice level, as argued later.

The expression *automatic stereotype activation* has been applied to both the direct priming of stereotypic characteristics and the stereotypic responses resulting from priming the category (see Bargh, 1994; Greenwald & Banaji, 1995; von Hippel, Sekaquaptewa, & Vargas, 1995). To specify how stereotypes are elicited upon perception of a category member (or some other cue symbolic of the category), category and stereotype priming should be distinguished. The two modes of stereotype activation can also affect judgments differently. For example, Pratto and Bargh (1991) found that category and stereotype priming had distinct effects on impression formation. This is consistent with their model, in which categories are represented at a level distinct from the concrete attributes associated with them (Andersen & Klatzky, 1987). Neely (1977) and Fazio et al. (1986) proposed similar models in other domains. Ford, Stangor, and Duan (1994) also reported different effects for category and stereotype priming in impression formation, thus the distinction between them.

Stereotype Priming

Automatic stereotype activation is not a consequence of categorization when stereotypic characteristics—with or without category labels—are primed directly. Rather, it is a cause of stereotypic judgments. For example, Banaji, Hardin, and Rothman (1993) found that the applicability (Higgins, 1996) of the primed stereotypic concept to the associated gender category increased ratings of the male targets as aggressive and female targets as dependent.

In a highly influential study, Devine (1989, Experiment 2) primed sub-consciously both the category *Blacks* and the stereotype content. High- and low-prejudice people did not differ in their subsequent impression of a target person. This was rated more extremely on the hostility- (and stereotype-) related scales than on the hostility-unrelated scales. Although this study has been quoted widely as demonstrating that high- and low-prejudice people automatically activate the stereotype in the same negative way, it does not actually do so. In fact, both category labels and stereotypic attributes were present in the prime. Thus, whether the strength of association between the category and the traits varies with prejudice level remains an unanswered question. Devine's results sometimes have been explained as being attribut-able to semantic priming. Many primes had clear negative connotations (e.g., "lazy," "nigger," "welfare," "busing," "ghetto") that could have directly cued hostility (see Greenwald & Banaji, 1995; Hamilton & Sherman, 1994). The absence of differences between high- and low-prejudice people can have another explanation. As with all knowledge, stereotypes are *available* in mem-ory and can be primed, thus becoming accessible *temporarily* (Bargh, 1994; Higgins, 1989). The recent activation of available knowledge results in the well-documented assimilation effects on applicable constructs (e.g., Bargh & Pietromonaco, 1982; Erdley & D'Agostino, 1988; Higgins, Bargh, & Lombardi, 1985; Srull & Wyer, 1979, 1980). In Devine's (1989) study, the primed stereo-type was applicable only to the hostility- (and stereotype-) related scales. Thus, the hostility ratings increased as an assimilation-type effect, which is likely to occur for all participants. It therefore cannot be inferred that high- and low-prejudice people would *spontaneously* activate the cultural stereo-type in this way as an automatic response to a group member (or a symbolic equivalent.

Category Priming

Automatic stereotype activation is an effect of categorization when only the category is primed. Other research that has examined differences between high- and low-prejudice people in automatic processing typically has used category priming. This research makes the implicit assumption that the traits are differentially associated with the category in high- and low-prejudice peo-ple, but it presents an ambiguous picture as to how stereotype activation occurs. Gaertner and McGlaughlin (1983) found no differences in the attribu-tion of positive and negative traits to the category *Blacks*. The same stereotype activation was present for both high- and low-prejudice people. Locke, MacLeod, and Walker (1994) used a Stroop-like paradigm to activate the cate-gory *Aborigines*. Only high-prejudice people demonstrated greater interference in naming the stereotype-related words (compared with the unrelated words). Low-prejudice respondents were unaffected by word stereotypicality, suggest-ing less responsiveness to category activation. No effect attributable to valence of the words was found. Since our own work was conducted, Wittenbrink, Judd, and Park (1997) reported two lexical decision studies in which ethnic category primes presented subliminally facilitated responses to "Black" negative and "White" positive stereotypic words. This effect was correlated with prejudice level. Thus, people higher in prejudice showed greater activation of positive in-group and negative out-group stereotypes. Fazio, Jackson, Dunton, and Williams (1995) observed that the automatic evaluation of the category Blades varied from negative to positive, although not reliably with prejudice level.

Studies that have not involved prejudice level do not all show automatic stereotype activation upon categorization. Perdue and Gurtman (1990) and Perdue, Dovidio, Gurtman, and Tyler (1990) found that subliminal in-group primes facilitated responses on positive target words and out-group primes on negative words. However, *semantic* stereotype activation was not demonstrated directly in these studies because the target words were not stereotypical of the categories primed. Gilbert and Hixon (1991) showed that category activation may not result in stereotype activation. Participants under cognitive overload did not increase the number of stereotypic completions on a word fragment task when the assistant presenting the stimuli was Asian. However, they still categorized her correctly.

In summary, a model of automatic stereotype activation is still incomplete (see Bargh, 1994; Stangor & Lange, 1994). Stereotype activation resulting from categorization and its qualification by prejudice level need further investigation. The present studies sought to disentangle the effects of direct stereotype activation and category activation on an impression formation task. This is particularly important because Devine's (1989) study is the only one involving prejudice level directly related to person perception. Different patterns of stereotype activation may be possible for high- and low-prejudice people if category and stereotype priming are separated.

Social Group Representations

To challenge the view of prejudice as inevitable, Devine (1989) distinguished between stereotype knowledge and endorsement (Ashmore & Del Boca, 1981). In her model, differential stereotype endorsement affects only controlled (Neely, 1977; Posner & Snyder, 1975) processes. High- and low-prejudice respondents listed different thoughts about Black people (Devine, 1989). In contrast, common stereotype knowledge should determine an absence of difference between high- and low-prejudice people in automatic responses. As discussed, Devine (1989) did not really prove this point because both category and stereotypic content were present in the prime. However, the conceptual argument is considered here. Even though low-prejudice people do not endorse the stereotype, stereotype knowledge is thought to be activated automatically because of its longer history of activation than personal beliefs (Higgins & King, 1981). Thus, low-prejudice people's response to a stimulus evocative of a stereotyped group is nonprejudiced only if the automatic prejudiced reaction can be inhibited. This conclusion still implies that prejudice is inevitable, at least at an automatic level.

In Devine's (1989) model, the divergent stereotypic associations described in our opening vignette are impossible. Smith (1989) noted that

Devine's (1989) theory of the automatic activation. of stereotype knowledge presents a conceptual problem. In associational models of stereotypes, the links between the group node and associated characteristics usually represent tbe perceiver's beliefs that the group possesses those attributes (also see Hilton & von Hippel, 1996; Stangor & Lange, 1994). If low- and high-prejudice people's automatic responses are the same, the links (i.e., the beliefs and hence their representations) do not differ. Thus, it is not clear how low-prejudice people's rejection of the negative stereotype is represented cognitively in such a model.

Research has shown that high- and low-prejudice people have *available* to them the full range of stereo typic attributes culturally associated with a given out-group but *endorse* different beliefs about it (Augoustinos, Innes, & Ahrens, 1994; Devine, 1989; Devine & Elliot, 1995). In particular, high-prejudice people endorse more the negative and low-prejudice people the positive stereotypic features (Augoustinos et al., 1994, Experiment 2; Devine & Elliot, 1995). Thus, their evaluations of the group differ, possibly strengthening the links with negative traits for high-prejudice people and positive traits for the low-prejudice within the network (see the model by Stephan & Stephan, 1993). Augoustinos et al. (1994, Experiment 2) provided some evidence that stronger associative links may correspond to such different beliefs within the representation. Low-prejudice people were not only more likely to endorse the positive descriptions of Aborigines, but also faster than high-prejudice individuals in doing so. High-prejudice participants endorsed the negative descriptions more and faster than low-prejudice respondents.

Thus, high- and low-prejudice people's representations of the social group may not necessarily differ in terms of *content* (at least for stereotype knowledge) but because stronger *links* may have developed for different characteristics. Some of the research reviewed earlier hints at differences in high- and low-prejudice people's representations of a social group due to associative strength (Locke et al., 1994; Wittenbrink et al., 1997).

As part of knowledge accepted as true (Devine, 1989), beliefs should be activated frequently to process incoming information. The stronger endorsed connections between the group and the frequently activated characteristics should be the ones activated automatically (Bargh, 1984; Higgins & King, 1981; Posner & Snyder, 1975; Stangor & Lange, 1994; Stephan & Stephan, 1993).

If low-prejudice people reject the negative stereotype and high-prejudice people endorse it, the category-negative attribute linkages should be stronger for high-prejudice people. Thus, only high-prejudice people should show automatic activation of the negative stereotypic components. Because low-prejudice people endorse the positive stereotypic features (Augoustinos et al., 1994; Devine & Elliot, 1995), they could traverse their category-positive attributes linkages more frequently, resulting in activation of the positive stereotypic components. This does not exclude another possibility. Because stereotypes of the outgroup are mainly negative (e.g., Dovidio, Evans & Tyler, 1986), low-prejudice people's rejection of the stereotype could mean that all their category-trait pathways are weaker. This would result in less stereotype activation altogether, as some empirical data suggest (Locke et al., 1994)....

Differences in Automatic Responses to Category Activation

If knowledge of the cultural stereotype of Black people is available to the same extent for high- and low-prejudice people, how easily is that knowledge, or part of it, activated? As discussed earlier, endorsement could lead to differential strength of association between stereotypic characteristics and group node in high- and low-prejudice people through frequency of activation. Thus, different stereotypic traits should be automatically activated in these two groups upon perception of a category member (or its symbolic equivalent), resulting in divergent stereotypic judgments.

If it can be shown that high- and low-prejudice people differ in their automatic responses to category activation, this would suggest that they hold different representations because of their beliefs and despite their common stereotype knowledge.

A parafoveal subliminal priming procedure similar to that used by Bargh and Pietromonaco (1982) and Devine (1989) was employed to reveal the effects of preconscious automaticity, a kind that requires only a triggering stimulus (Bargh, 1989). In this case, the triggering stimuli were category labels and some category-evocative words, but not valenced stereotypic content. The use of such primes should prevent any effect due to purely semantic priming or recent priming of the cultural stereotype (e.g., Higgins et al., 1985). The subsequent judgments should reflect only a preconscious automatic operation (Bargh, 1994). Unlike most priming studies, in which the construct or concept is primed and then measured (but see Bargh, Raymond, Pryor, & Strack, 1995), here the category was primed and the differential activation of the associated stereotype assessed in the subsequent impression-formation task. With such a procedure, any effects are due to spreading activation. Thus, the differential strength of association between the category and traits in high- and low-prejudice people can be revealed in the form of divergent stereotypic judgments.

Other researchers have used a brief ambiguous paragraph for the impression formation task (Srull & Wyer, 1979). However, here the target person was described by behavioral sentences (Hamilton & Gifford, 1976) containing four stereotypic dimensions (two positive and two negative). Thus, the stimulus ambiguity was achieved with a "mixed" description (see Higgins, 1996) comprising evaluatively opposite constructs (Smith, 1989). This kind of description was designed to enable participants to use positive or negative stereotypic constructs differentially in their judgment as divergent automatic associations were predicted. Note that although the specific behaviors were clearly interpretable (each was carefully chosen to be representative of part of the stereotype), the combination of positive and negative dimensions rendered the overall description of the target person more genuinely ambiguous than proved possible with Srull and Wyer's (1979) type of task. Thus, it should be more sensitive to differential stereotype activation.

Because stronger links are more strongly activated and influence judgments (see Stangor & Lange, 1994), high-prejudice participants in the prime condition should rate the target person more extremely on the negative stereotypic dimensions and less so on the positive dimensions. Low-prejudice people may tend to do the opposite.

Method

Participants.   Fifty-one unversity students took part in the study. They were White British nationals who had agreed to participate when approached by the experimenter on campus. They were paid £2.

Design.   The design was a 2 (high vs. low prejudice) × 2 (prime vs. no-prime condition) between subjects. Participants were randomly assigned to the prime or the no-prime condition.

Materials and procedure.   The experiment was conducted using a Macintosh Quadra 650 computer. The height of the computer was adjusted so that the center of the screen was at eye level. The eye-to-screen distance was maintained at 70–80 cm. Participants were tested individually.

Priming task.   The priming phase, described as "Experiment 1," was composed of 100 trials grouped in four blocks. Participants had to respond to a series of scrambled letters, appearing at random locations and intervals on the screen, by pressing a key to indicate if the stimulus was at the left or right of the central fixation dot that preceded it. They were instructed not to lean forward, to look at the center of the screen to facilitate stimulus detection, and to be fast and accurate.

Within each block of trials, the stimulus was presented an equal number of times in four parafoveal positions (2–6° of the visual field). No word began farther away than 6.5 cm from the center of the screen or ended closer than 3.5 cm. In the prime condition, 13 words evocative of the category *Black people* were used. They were category labels themselves and neutral associates of the category, based on free responses in pretesting. The words used were as follows: Blacks, AfroCaribbean, West Indians, colored, afro, dreadlocks, Rastafarian, reggae, ethnic, Brixton, Notting Hill,[2] rap, and culture. Each word appeared on the screen for 100 ms and was then masked by a 14-letter string (xqfbzrpmqwhgbx) that stayed on the screen for 100 ms. The intertrial interval varied from 2 to 6.5 s. The first trial of each new block had an intertrial interval of 7.5 s.

Similar parameters have been used repeatedly to ensure the subliminality of such parafoveal priming, confirmed by the results of the recognition and guess conditions (Bargh, Bond, Lombardi, & Tota, 1986; Bargh & Pietromonaco, 1982; Devine, 1989). In the current experiment, the central dot appeared on the screen for 1 s immediately before each presentation, whereas in previous studies the fixation point was visible on the screen at all times. By cuing participants attention to the center of the screen right before the stimulus came up, it was less likely for the eye to wander around the screen and hence occasionally catch a glimpse of a particular word.

The procedure was the same in the no-prime condition, except that no real words were used as primes. Instead, the mask flashed up on the screen twice, creating the same subjective experience as in the prime condition (a double flashing, according to participants' reports in both conditions).

Neutral words unrelated to the category *Blacks* were used for the 10 practice trials. These were accommodation, methodology, fireplace, notebook, apple, success, orange, tree, stairs, and danger.

Impression formation task and dependent measures. Immediately after the priming task, the instructions on screen stated that we also were interested in the way people form impressions of others and introduced "Experiment 2." Eight behavioral sentences described a person whose ethnicity was not specified. The participants then rated this target person on a number of trait scales (randomly ordered for each participant). Of the eight sentences, two were descriptive of the construct *athletic* (e.g., "He plays football regularly"), two of the construct *fun loving* (e.g., "He goes to parties most weekends"), two of the construct *aggressive* (e.g., "He can easily get angry at people who disagree with him"), and two of the construct *unreliable* (e.g., "He cannot be bothered to be on time for meetings and appointments"). These four constructs had been generated spontaneously in pretesting to describe Black people[3].... The selected sentences were chosen from a bigger pool of pretested sentences; they were descriptive of their respective contructs, but not too extremely, The final sentences were pretested further for the impression they conveyed when presented together to ensure that the balance among the four constructs was maintained. This meant that the overall image of the target person was ambiguous yet also contained different stereotypic features that might be accessed more or less easily by high- and low-prejudice participants.

Twenty-one rating scales followed the behavioral sentences. Four traits were descriptive of the dimension *athletic* (i.e., athletic, fit, sporty, and active), six represented the dimension *fun-loving* (i.e., outgoing, fun loving, flamboyant, lively, easy going, and relaxed), five were related to the dimension *unreliable* (i.e., unreliable, irresponsible, careless, disorganized, and lazy), and six were descriptive of the dimension *aggressive* (i.e., aggressive, hostile, dislikable, quarrelsome, quick tempered, and touchy). To demonstrate these constructs' internal coherence, an independent sample ($N = 15$) of respondents was provided with the defining attribute of the construct (e.g., athletic) and asked to rate how much a person who had that attribute also possessed each of the other associated attributes (e.g., fit, sporty, and active) using scales ranging from 1 (*not at all*) to 7 (*extremely*). All individual traits were rated above 4.0 (the scale midpoint), and the composite ratings for each of the four constructs all were significantly greater than 4.0 ($p <$ .001 in each case), In the event, we elected to simplify the analysis by combining the four dimensions into two, one positive one negative. All scales ranged from *not at all* (1) to *extremely* (9). Participants therefore had a choice of two positive and two negative stereo typic dimensions on which to judge the target person.

The prejudice scale was presented as an "opinion survey," the last task in the study.[4] Anonymity of the answers and complete freedom to agree or disagree with each item were emphasized.

An extensive individual debriefing then took place. Any observations were recorded, particularly whether participants perceived any connection between the tasks (none did). Finally, the experimenter thanked, paid, and dismissed the respondent.

Recognition condition. Twelve additional participants were run in a recognition condition to check on the awareness of the content of the primes. After the priming task, the experimenter explained that words had been flashed on the screen and that in the next part of the experiment the participant should select one of three words after each trial. The experimenter reminded the participant to look at the center of the screen and not to lean forward; the computer was then made to proceed. A computer-based administration of the prejudice scale followed the 33 recognition trials.

To ensure maximum sensitivity, the recognition test was designed as in Bargh and Pietromonaco (1982, Experiment 2): Instead of choosing the words at the end of the experiment, when the immediate awareness of some words could have worn off, participants had to indicate their choice after each trial when the word had just been presented. More powerfully still, the test was not administered after the impression formation task (see Bargh et al., 1986; Bargh & Pietromonaco, 1982, Experiment 1) but after the priming phase. Each priming word appeared three times in the 39 trials of the recognition test This gave participants another opportunity to detect the target words because they were presented more than once. After each trial, the target word came up on the screen together with two other words. The distractors were matched in length as much as possible to the target words and were similar to these either in meaning or phonetically. Across the three repetitions, the relative positions of the words was varied. Following each choice, the computer proceeded with the next trial, which was presented after a random interval (2–6.5 s)

Results

Recognition test and self-reports. The presentation of the primes appears to have been subliminal, as intended. Participants in, the recognition condition did not score better than chance. The mean proportion correct was .35, which did not differ significantly from the chance value of .33, $t(11) = 0.66$, *ns*. In addition, only 1 participant in the prime condition reported being aware of (one or two) words. This individual was excluded from all subsequent analyses. Given that in total some 2,800 presentations were made, this is a low percentage indeed and indicates that cuing attention to the center of the screen immediately before each trial successfully prevented awareness of the primes.

Prime and no-prime conditions. Participants were divided at the median into high- ($n = 25$) and low-prejudice ($n = 25$) groups on the basis of their score on the prejudice scale (Mdn = 71.5; Ms and SDs for the high- and low-prejudice groups were 59.10 and 9.85 and 80.28 and 7.29, respectively; α = .84).

To simplify the analysis, the 10 scales making up the two positive constructs were combined into a single positive index with good internal reliability (α = .76). Similarly, the 11 scales tapping the negative constructs were combined into a single negative index, also with high reliability (α = .82). These two indexes were incorporated into the design as a within-subjects variable: 2 (high and low prejudice) × 2 (prime and no-prime condition) × 2 (positive and negative valence). Our hypothesis specified that high-prejudice people would form a more negative and less positive impression and that low-prejudice people would do the reverse in response to the prime. Therefore, the predicted effect of interest was a three-way interaction.

An ANOVA revealed several significant effects: a main effect for valence, $F(1, 46)$ = 11.40, p < .002, showing that the positive scales had higher ratings than the negative scales (Ms = 6.70 and 5.99, respectively) and a Prejudice × Valence interaction, $F(1, 46)$ = 4.01, p < .051. All of these effects were qualified by the expected three-way interaction, Condition × Prejudice × Valence, $F(1, 46)$ = 6.06, p < .02 (see Figure 1).

Figure 1

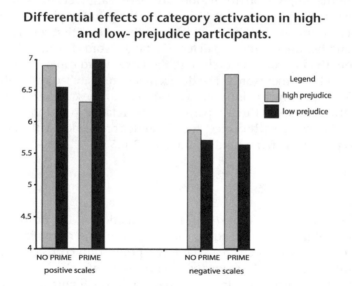

Differential effects of category activation in high- and low- prejudice participants.

Analysis of the simple effects of priming revealed that the Condition × Valence interaction was significant only for high-prejudice participants, $F(1,47)$ = 6.07, p < .02. High-prejudice participants in the prime condition rated the target person more extremely on the negative construct (Ms = 6.76 vs. 5.88), $t(46)$ = 3.43, p < .005 and less extremely on the positive construct (Ms = 6.31 vs. 6.88), $t(46)$ = 2.22, p < .025. Low-prejudice participants increased their ratings on the positive scales (Ms = 6.98 vs. 6.54), $t(46)$ = 1.69, p < .05, but showed no difference on the negative ones (Ms = 5.65 vs. 5.73). Simple effects analysis also revealed that the Prejudice × Valence interaction was significant in the prime condition, $F(1, 47)$ = 10.26, $p < .002$, but not in the no-prime condition, $F(1, 47)$ = 0.18, ns. High- and low-prejudice participants did not differ in the absence of prime. When primed, however, high-prejudice participants rated the target person more negatively than did the low-prejudice (Ms = 6.76 vs. 5.65), $t(46)$ = 4.48, $p < .0005$, and less positively than did low-prejudice participants (Ms = 6.31 vs. 6.98), $t(46)$ = 2.70, $p < .005$. Note that the direction of the effect of the prime on the positive and negative stereotypic construct was exactly the opposite for high- and low-prejudice.

Discussion

As predicted high- and low-prejudice people differed from each other in response to a subliminally presented prime. In particular, high-prejudice participants increased their ratings of the target person on the negative stereotypic dimensions and decreased them on the positive constructs. Low-prejudice participants appeared to be less affected by category activation altogether; although they tended in the opposite direction, showing activation of the positive stereotypic components. Thus, upon category activation the unintentional activation of the stereotype did not occur in an all-or-none fashion (Fiske & Dyer, 1985; Hayes-Roth, 1977) but selectively. One finding deserves some comment. High-prejudice participants' ratings on the positive scales were lower in the prime than in the no-prime condition. This finding, although not predicted, can be explained by considering that most associative models allow for the operation of both excitatory and inhibitory processes (e.g., Carlston, 1992; Stephan & Stephan, 1993). The excitation of the negative stereotypic dimensions might have inhibited the positive ones in these respondents.

By restricting the prime to category labels and neutral associates, semantic priming effects or recency effects were eliminated as explanations of the findings. The preconscious automatic activation of the stereotype proved different for high- and low- prejudice participants. Despite common stereotype knowledge, differential endorsement can make certain stetotypic features more accessible than others. This implies that the strength of association between positive or negative stereotypic traits and category varies in high- and low-prejudice people and therefore so does the resulting mental representation of the group. This pattern of results is completely consistent with the model outlined earlier. As predicted, there seem to be individual differences in the strength of association between the category and various characteristics, resulting, we speculate, from different histories of endorsement of prejudiced (and nonprejudiced) stereotypic beliefs....

Notes

1. Pretesting showed that Srull and Wyer's (1979) "Donald" paragraph graph was perceived by our participants in unambiguously negative terms, thus obscuring differences between the prime and no-prime conditions and also not permitting an impression of the person in positive or negative ways.

2. Briston and Notting Hill are two well-known areas of London with high concentrations of Afro-Caribbean people.
3. Our choice of constructs perhaps deserves some comment. We chose *athletic* and *fun loving* as the two positive constructs because pretesting had indicated that these were both unambiguously positive and could also be captured in behavioral sentences. *Musical and colorful*...were less convenient in these respects. Similar considerations applied to *unreliable*.... *Aggressive* was chosen rather than *criminal* to provide some comparability with previous work (e.g., Devine, 1989).
4. For practical reasons, it was not possible to pretest participants in their level of prejudice. However, given that responses to prejudice measures like this presumably are rather stable, it seems unlikely that any of the preceding procedures could have affected the participants' prejudice scores. Moreover, such posttest measurements of prejudice level has been used successfully in several other comparable studies (e.g., Augoustinos et al., 1994; Devine & Elliot, 1995; Locke, MacLeod, & Walker, 1994; Wittenbrink et al., 1997).

References

Allport, G. W. (1954). *The nature of prejudice*. Reading, MA. Addison-Wesley.

Andersen, S. M., & Klatzky, R. (1987). Traits and social stereotypes: Levels of categorization in person perception. *Journal of Personality and Social Psychology, 53*, 235–246.

Anderson, J. R. (1983). *The architecture of cognition*. Cambridge, MA: Harvard University Press.

Bargh, J. A. (1989). Conditional automaticity: Varieties of automatic influence in social perception and cognition. In J. S. Uleman & J. A. Bargh (Eds.), *Unintended thought* (pp. 3–51). New York: Guilford Press.

Bargh, J. A. (1994). The four horsemen of automaticity: Awareness, intention. efficiency, and control in social cognition. In R. S. Wyer, Jr., & T. K. Srull (Eds.), *Handbook of social cognition* (Vol. 1, 2nd ed., pp. 1–40). Hillsdale, NJ: Erlbaum.

Bargh, J. A., Raymond, P., Pryor, J. B., & Strack, F. (1995). Attractiveness of the underling: An automatic power–sex association and its consequences for sexual harassment and aggression. *Journal of Personality and Social Psychology, 68*, 768–781.

Billig, M. (1985). Prejudice, categorization and particularization: From a perceptual to a rhetorical approach. *European Journal of Social Psychology, 15*, 79–103.

Brewer, M. B. (1988). A dual process model of impression formation. In T. K. Srull & R. S. Wyer. Jr. (Eds.), *Advances in social cognition* (Vol. 1. pp. 1–36). Hillsdale, NJ: ErJbaum.

Brown, R. (1995). *Prejudice: Its social psychology*. Oxford, England: Blackwell.

Bruner, J. S. (1957). On perceptual readiness. *Psychological Review, 64*, 123–152.

Carlston, D. E. (1992). Impression formation and the modular mind: The associated systems theory. In L. L. Martin & A. Tesser (Eds.), *The construction of social judgments* (pp. 301–341). Hillsdale, NJ: Erlbaum.

Collins, A. M., & Loftus. E. F. (1975). A spreading-activation theory of semantic processing. Psychological Review, 82, 407–428.

Deaux, K., & Lewis, L. L. (1984). Structure of gender stereotypes: Interrelations among components and gender label. *Journal of Personality and Social Psychology, 46*, 991–1004.

Devine, P. G. (1989). Stereotypes and prejudice: Their automatic and controlled components. *Journal of Personality and Social Psychology, 56*, 5–18.

Erdley, C. A., & D'Agostino, P. R. (1988). Cognitive and affective components of automatic priming effects. *Journal of Personality and Social Psychology, 54*, 741–747.

Fazio, R. H., Jackson, J. R., Dunton, B. C., & Williams, C. J. (1995). Variability in automatic activation as an unobtrusive measure of racial attitudes: A bona fide pipeline? *Journal of Personality and Social Psychology, 69*, 1013–1027.

Fazio, R. H., Sanbonmatsu, D. M., Powell, M. C., & Kardes, F. R. (1986). On the automatic activation of attitudes. *Journal of Personality and Social Psychology, 50*, 229–238.

Fiske, S. T., (1982). Schema-triggered affect: Applications to social perception. In M. S. Clark & S. T. Fiske (Eds.), *Affect and cognition* (pp. 55–78). Hillsdale, NJ: Erlbaum.

Ford, T. E., Stangor, C., & Duan, C. (1994). Influence of social category accessibility and category-associated trait accessibility on judgments of individuals. *Social Cognition, 12*, 149–168.

Gaertner, S. L., & McLaughlin, J. P. (1983). Racial stereotypes: Associations and ascriptions of positive and negative characteristics. *Social Psychology Quarterly, 46*, 23–30.

Gilbert, D. L., & Hixon, J. G. (1991). The trouble of thinking: Activation and application of stereotypic beliefs. *Journal of Personality and Social Psychology, 60*, 509–517.

Greenwald, A. G., & Banaji, M. R. (1995). Implicit social cognition: Attitudes, self-esteem, and stereotypes. *Psychological Review, 102*, 4–27.

Hamilton, D. L., (Ed.). (1981). *Cognitive processes in stereotyping and intergroup behavior*. Hillsdale, NJ: Erlbaum.

Hamilton, D. L., & Gifford, R. K. (1976). Illusory correlation in interpersonal perception: A cognitive basis of stereotypic judgment. *Journal of Personality and Social Psychology, 12*, 392–407.

Hayes-Roth, B. (1977). Evolution of cognitive structure and processes. *Psychological Review, 84*, 260–278.

Higgins, E. T. (1989). Knowledge accessibility and activation: Subjectivity and suffering from unconscious sources. In J. S. Uleman & J. A. Bargh (Eds.), *Unintended thought* (pp. 75–123). New York: Guilford Press.

Higgins, E. T. (1996). Knowledge activation: Accessibility, applicability, and salience. In E. T. Higgins & A. W. Kruglanski (Eds.), *Social psychology: Handbook of basic principles* (pp. 133–168). New York: Guilford Press.

Locke, V., MacLeod, C., & Walker, I. (1994). Automatic and controlled activation of stereotypes: Individual differences associated with prejudice. *British Journal of Social Psychology, 33*, 29–46.

Neely, J. H. (1977). Semantic priming and retrieval from lexical memory. Roles of inhibitionless spreading activation and limited-capacity attention. *Journal of Experimental Psychology: General, 106*, 226–254.

Perdue, C. W., Dovidio, J. F., Gurtman, M. B., & Tyler, R. B. (1990). Us and them: Social categorization and the process of intergroup bias. *Journal of Personality and Social Psychology, 59*, 475–486.

Posner, M. I., & Snyder, C. R. R. (1975). Attention and cognitive control. In R. L. Solso (Ed.), *Information processing and cognition: The Loyola Symposium* (pp. 55–85). Hillsdale, NJ: Erlbaum.

Pratto, F., & Bargh, J. A. (1991). Stereotyping based on apparently individuating information: Trait and global components of sex stereotypes under attention overload. *Journal of Experimental Social Psychology, 27*, 26–47.

Rosch, E. (1978). Principles of categorization. In E. Rosch & B. B. Lloyd (Eds.), *Cognition and categorization* (pp. 27–48). Hillsdale, NJ: Erlbaum.

Rumelhart, D. E., Hinton, G. E., & McClelland, J. L. (1986). A general framework for parallel distributed processing. In D. E. Rumelhart, J. L. McClelland, & the PDP Research Group (Eds.), *Parallel distributed processing* (pp. 45–76). Cambridge, MA: MIT Press.

Shiffrin, R. M., & Schneider. W. (1977). Controlled and automatic human information processing: Perceptual learning. automatic attending, and a general theory. *Psychological Review, 84*, 127–190.

Smith, E. R. (1989). Procedural efficiency: General and specific components and effects on social judgment. *Journal of Experimental Social Psychology, 25*, 500–523.

Srull, T. K., & Wyer, R. S., Jr. (1980). Category accessibility and social perception. Some implications for the study of person memory and interpersonal judgments. *Journal of Personality and Social Psychology, 38*, 841–856.

Stangor, C., & Ford, T. E. (1992). Accuracy and expectancy-confirming orientations and the development of stereotypes and prejudice. *European Review of Social Psychology, 3*, 57–89. New York: Wiley.

Stephan, W. G., & Stephan, C. W. (1993). Cognition and affect in stereotyping: Parallel interactive networks. In D. M. Mackie & D. L. Hamilton (Eds.), *Affect, cognition, and stereotyping: Interactive processes in group perception* (pp. 111–136). San Diego, CA: Academic Press.

Tajfel, H. (1969). Cognitive aspects of prejudice. *Journal of Social Issues, 23*, 79–97.

von Hippel, W., Sekaquaptewa, D., & Vargas, P. (1995). On the role of encoding processes in stereotype maintenance. *Advances in Experimental Social Psychology, 27*, 177–254.

Wittenbrink, B., Judd, C. M., & Park, B. (1997). Evidence for racial prejudice at the implicit level and its relationship with questionnaire measures. *Journal of Personality and Social Psychology, 72*, 262–274.

CHALLENGE QUESTIONS

Is Stereotyping Inevitable?

1. Can you think of any real-world contexts in which automatic stereotypes might have a detrimental effect on how whites treat blacks?
2. If automatic stereotyping is real, what are the implications of this psychological process for social policies that deal with race, such as affirmative action?
3. If stereotyping is at least partially an automatic response, as both readings suggest, how can prejudice be reduced? What interventions can be designed to reduce prejudice and discrimination?

ISSUE 15

Can Stereotypes Lead to Accurate Perceptions of Others?

YES: Lee J. Jussim, Clark R. McCauley, and Yueh-Ting Lee, from "Why Study Stereotype Accuracy and Inaccuracy?" *Stereotype Accuracy: Toward Appreciating Group Differences* (APA, 1995)

NO: Charles Stangor, from "Content and Application Inaccuracy in Social Stereotyping," *Stereotype Accuracy: Toward Appreciating Group Differences* (APA, 1995)

ISSUE SUMMARY

YES: Lee Jussim, Clark McCauley, and Yueh-Ting Lee believe that stereotypes have been stereotyped. Stereotypes are not always inaccurate and do not invariably lead to biased judgments of others, as most social psychologists seem to believe.

NO: Charles Stangor draws a distinction between the *content* accuracy and *application* accuracy in the use of stereotypes. According to Stangor, even if the content of a stereotype is accurate, using the stereotype to judge others will still likely yield inaccurate perceptions.

Before the word *stereotype* took on its current meaning, it was originally used to refer to metal printing plates that are used to make identical copies of newspapers and books (J. M. Jones, *Prejudice and Racism*, 2nd edition, McGraw-Hill, 1997). Author Walter Lippman (*Public Opinion*, Harcourt, Brace and World, 1922) used the word "stereotype" to describe the beliefs that people hold about members of various social groups. His choice of words was deliberate—stereotypes make members of a group appear to be identical to one another, just like identical copies of a book. So from the beginning, stereotypes have been regarded in a negative light as inaccurate and undesirable beliefs. In fact, some definitions of *stereotype* explicitly describe them as inherently inaccurate beliefs about social groups. Gordon Allport (*The Nature of Prejudice*, Addison Wesley, 1954), one of the first social psychologists to write extensively on the topic of stereotypes, defined a stereotype as "an exaggerated belief." But are stereotypes always exaggerated as Allport believed?

Some social psychologists have begun to challenge this traditional conception of stereotypes. According to Lee Jussim, Clark McCauley, and Yueh-Ting Lee, stereotypes have been stereotyped. Many social psychologists unfairly characterize all stereotypes as irrational and dysfunctional instruments of prejudice that inevitably lead to biased judgments of others. Contrary to this widely shared view, Jussim, McCauley, and Lee argue that stereotypes are not universally inaccurate, or even generally mistaken. As a result, they call on social psychologists to devote more effort to studying stereotype accuracy so that social psychologists can examine the stereotypes that are likely to have a negative impact and distinguish them from the innocuous stereotypes that do not have negative consequences and may actually enhance the accuracy of social beliefs. Having a better understanding of the differences between groups that are real and those that are imagined will lead us to appreciate differences between groups, rather than dismiss them.

Social psychologist Charles Stangor believes that the study of stereotype accuracy is misguided and is not likely to yield new and important insights. He also rejects the notion that stereotypes may often lead to accurate perceptions of others. In making this argument, Strangor draws a distinction between the *content* of stereotypes and the *application* of stereotypes. While it is possible for the content of a stereotype to be accurate, according to Stangor the stereotype may still lead to biased, inaccurate judgments when the stereotype is applied to a particular individual. Thus even accurate stereotypes lead to inaccurate judgments of others and all forms of stereotyping should be discouraged.

POINT

- Stereotypes have been stereotyped.
- Since stereotypes are not always inaccurate, they do not necessarily lead to inaccurate judgments of others.
- It is important to study the accuracy of stereotypes.

COUNTERPOINT

- It is appropriate to view stereotypes in negative light.
- Even if the content of a particular stereotype may be accurate, it may still result in inaccurate perceptions of others.
- The study of stereotype accuracy is misguided.

Lee J. Jussim, Clark R. McCauley,
and Yueh-Ting Lee

 **YES**

Why Study Stereotype Accuracy
and Inaccuracy?

Are Stereotypes Necessarily Inaccurate?

The answer to this question depends on whether one defines stereotypes as inaccurate beliefs about groups (see, e.g., Brigham, 1971; Mackie, 1973). If so, then, by definition, they must be inaccurate. However, defining stereotypes in this way creates serious conceptual problems. This definition would seem to require that researchers interested in stereotypes study only beliefs about groups for which invalidity has been clearly documented. For example, one could study the belief that the Jews run the banks or the belief that most African American people are on welfare. Both beliefs are demonstrably false (e.g., Marger, 1991).

Defining stereotypes as inaccurate would also appear to preclude the study of the belief that American Jews are wealthier than are most other ethnic groups or that the majority of people on welfare are minorities. Both beliefs are true (DeParle, 1994; Marger, 1991) and, therefore, would not qualify as stereotypes. This definition would also seem to preclude study of stereotypes that Germans are efficient, gay men are effeminate, or librarians are introverted. There is no evidence documenting the invalidity of these beliefs.

In fact, most reviews of stereotyping conclude that there is very little evidence regarding the validity of beliefs about groups (e.g., Brigham, 1971; Judd & Park, 1993; Jussim, 1990; McCauley, Stitt, & Segal, 1980; Ottati & Lee, chapter 2, this volume). Furthermore, it may be very difficult to obtain objective information about many attributes (such as efficiency, effeminacy, or laziness). To take seriously a definition of stereotypes as inaccurate beliefs would lead to a drastic reduction in empirical research on stereotypes. Few beliefs about groups have been empirically demonstrated to be false; therefore, few beliefs about groups would qualify as stereotypes.

Conceptually, it seems more parsimonious to leave *inaccurate* out of any definition of stereotypes (see also Ashmore & Dell Boca, 1981). If someone believes that Jews are wealthier than other groups, is this not a stereotype (even if it is true)? Scientifically, is there any advantage to saying that the belief that Jews run the banks is a stereotype, but that the belief that Jews are

From STEROTYPE ACCURACY: TOWARD APPRECIATING GROUP DIFFERENCES, pp. 275–293.
Copyright © 1995 by American Psychological Association. Reprinted with permission.

wealthier than are other groups is not? We see no reason to assume that accurate beliefs about groups function differently than inaccurate beliefs. By definition, when people hold a belief, they think that belief is true.

We do not define stereotypes in this chapter, that task is left to the authors of the chapters that constitute this volume (see also Ashmore, Del Boca, 1981, for a review). Regardless of differences in definition, however, all authors in this book agree that stereotypes constitute people's beliefs about groups—beliefs that may be positive or negative, accurate or inaccurate. Nonetheless, many laypeople and social scientists still seem to assume that stereotypes are inaccurate, rigid, and pernicious. In the next sections, therefore, we identify the typical accusations leveled against stereotypes and evaluate their scientific status. Are stereotypes factually incorrect? Are they rigid? Are they illogical? Do they lead people to exaggerate differences among groups?

What Is Wrong with Stereotypes?

The Classic Charges

From Katz and Braly (1933) to the present, stereotypes have been condemned as factually incorrect, illogical in origin, and irrationally resistant to new information about the stereotyped group. Each of these charges is well-founded if a stereotype is understood as an exceptionless generalization about the target group (e.g., "All Asians are smart"). However, each is baseless if a stereotype is understood as a probabilistic prediction about how the target group differs from others (McCauley et al., 1980). Below we show how few, if any; of the classic charges against stereotypes would apply to a belief that Asians are likely to do better academically than individuals from most other groups. This distinction between all-or-none beliefs and probabilistic beliefs is crucial for evaluating the validity of some of the most common charges against stereotypes.

Stereotypes are factually incorrect.   This must be true if a stereotype is an all-or-none generalization about members of the stereotyped group. It cannot be the case that every German is efficient. If there is even one inefficient German, the stereotype is incorrect. Allport (1954) took this approach in distinguishing stereotypes from valid beliefs about group characteristics. For Allport, "all lawyers are crooked" is a stereotype; "lawyers are more crooked than most people" is not (p. 192).

Do people hold such all-or-none stereotypes? The research evidence on this question is clear: Although people often perceive differences among groups, we are not aware of a single study identifying a single person who believed that all members of a social group had a particular stereotype attribute (see reviews by Brigham, 1971; Judd & Park, 1993; Jussim, 1990; McCauley et al., 1980).

But if stereotypes are not 100% generalizations, then it is no longer clear that they are factually incorrect. Rather, it is clear that we are in no position to evaluate the accuracy of many everyday stereotypes. Where are the data that could tell us, for instance, the percentage of Germans who are efficient or whether Germans are probabilistically more efficient than other groups?

Stereotypes are illogical in origin.   It is often suggested that stereotypes are based on illogical or irrational foundations because they do not arise from personal experience. That stereotypes can be hearsay was already evident when Katz and Braly's (1933) Princeton students reported strong agreement that Turks were cruel and treacherous—even though these students also reported never having met a Turk. To accept such a pernicious group generalization on the basis of hearsay would appear to be dubious indeed.

But was it really that dubious? One must remember that in the early part of this century, Turks massacred millions of Armenians. Is it so unreasonable that college students strongly agreed about the cruelty of Turks? Would it have been unreasonable in 1950 for college students to agree on the aggressiveness of the Germans? Would it be unreasonable today for college students to agree on the cruelty of the Serbs?

But the "hearsay" charge suffers an even more serious problem: the assumption that learning about groups from other people is necessarily illogical and incorrect. We cannot help but wonder, How can any teacher suggest that only personal experience is valid learning? Must we go to the moon to learn about it? Must we go to Guatemala to learn about the rain forest? Must we go to Indonesia to learn about Indonesians?

Stereotypes are based in prejudice.   This is actually a variant of the "illogical in origin" charge, and it reflects an assumption underlying much of the first 30 years of research in stereotypes (e.g., Adorno, Frenkel-Brunswick, Levinson, & Sanford, 1950; Katz & Braly, 1933; LaPiere, 1936). Especially if prejudice is considered an affective predisposition to a group (an attitude of liking or disliking a social group), there is considerable historical evidence suggesting that stereotypes may sometimes serve to justify prejudice. National stereotypes, in particular, can change quickly with changing international attitudes and alliances (e.g., Americans had negative views of Germans and positive views of Russians during World War II, but positive views of Germans and negative views of Russians after World War II; see Oakes, Haslam, & Turner, 1994, for a review).

Interestingly, however, there has been little empirical study of the relation between strength or accuracy of stereotyping and attitude toward the stereotyped group. One example of this kind of inquiry is a study by Eagly and Mladinic (1989), which found that strength of gender stereotyping correlated only about .2 to .3 with attitudes toward men and women (although the study found considerably higher correlations between stereotypes of and attitudes toward Democrats and Republicans). Similarly, McCauley and Thangavelu (1991) found that strength of gender stereotyping of occupations was unrelated to attitude toward women in nontraditional occupations, although stereotype strength was positively correlated with accuracy.

On conceptual grounds, there are many stereotypes that are unlikely to be based in affect or prejudice. For example, it is hard to imagine much of a role for prejudice in the beliefs that men are taller than women, that professional basketball players are tall and athletic, or that art majors tend to be creative. Thus, the role of affect and attitude in creating stereotypes would seem to be an interesting empirical question rather than a defining component of stereotypes.

Stereotypes are irrationally resistant to new information.   People   rarely change their beliefs about groups when confronted with a single individual who does not fit their stereotype. Does this represent irrational resistance to new information? The answer to this is yes under only one condition: when the stereotype is an all-or-none generalization. If one meets a German who is all thumbs, never has a plan, and takes forever to accomplish anything, and still maintains a stereotype of all Germans as efficient, then one is dearly being irrational.

As noted earlier, however, we know of no research documenting the existence of people who believe all members of any stereotyped group have any particular attribute. In casual conversation, when people say things like "New Yorkers are loud and aggressive," we doubt that they mean all New Yorkers. Instead, they most likely mean that in general, or on average, New Yorkers are louder and more aggressive than most other people. Are these people being irrational if they do not change their belief when confronted with a calm, passive New Yorker? We do not think so. Should you change your belief that Alaska is colder than New York, even if we can show you evidence that one day last month, it was warmer in Alaska? Again, we do not think so. In fact, it would be irrational in a statistical sense if you did change your belief on such minimal evidence (see Tversky & Kahneman, 1971, on the "law of small numbers"). Similarly, if 12 million people live in the New York area, and if "New Yorkers are loud and aggressive," means something like "three fourths of all New Yorkers are loud and aggressive; then there are still 3 million New Yorkers who are not loud and aggressive. It would be irrational to change a belief about millions of New Yorkers on the basis of a few disconfirming individuals.

Some More Sophisticated Charges

Beginning with Campbell (1967) and LeVine and Campbell (1972), there has been a more sophisticated critique of stereotypes that goes beyond the metaphor of stereotypes as all-or-none pictures of the stereotyped group (see also Brown, 1965). LeVine and Campbell see stereotypes as probabilistic predictions that are not known to be wrong. They argued that what is wrong with stereotypes is that they are likely to be exaggerations of real group differences, that they are ethnocentric, and that they imply genetic rather than environmental causes of group differences. Again we consider these charges briefly.

Stereotypes are exaggerations of real group differences.   LeVine and Campbell (1972) cite the substantial literature on contrast effects in human perception to suggest that contrast effects in perception of group differences are essentially unavoidable. As dark grey looks darker and light grey looks lighter across a contour line, so Germans should look more efficient and Italians less efficient across a group boundary. In general, if there is a real difference between two groups, the perception of that difference—the stereotype—should be incorrect at least to the extent of exaggerating the real difference.

This exaggeration hypothesis comes with impeccable credentials from sensation–perception psychology, but there is little evidence for it (Martin, 1987)—at least not when the criterion of group difference is some kind of objective measure (McCauley & Stitt, 1978; McCauley & Thangavelu, 1991; McCauley, Thangavelu, & Rozin, 1988; Swim, 1994). McCauley examines relevant research in this volume (chapter 9); here, we note only that the exaggeration hypothesis is so far only a hypothesis.

Stereotypes are ethnocentric.   Brown (1965) has been perhaps the most explicit in suggesting that stereotypes are wrong because they include evaluating outgroup characteristics by ingroup standards. Certainly it is true that there is evaluation as well as description in the trait words with which stereotypes have been assessed since Katz and Braly (1933). *Efficient* is not just a summary of a behavior pattern, not just a comparison with others on a dimension of individual difference, but a positive evaluation of the upper percentiles of this dimension. Similar descriptive content, but a very different evaluation, is conveyed by traits such as *aggressive* and *assertive*. Brown objects to smuggling in an evaluative component of the stereotype as if it were as objective as the description.

Perhaps the easiest way to put the ethnocentrism charge in perspective is to recognize that personality-trait words are only one of many kinds of characteristics on which groups can be seen to differ. Perceptions of group differences may include physical appearance, behaviors, occupations, preferences, and values. At most, the charge of ethnocentrism is an argument against personality-trait stereotypes. The ethnocentrism charge has little relevance for more objective attributes. The stereotype of African Americans as having a higher percentage of female-headed families, the stereotype of women as having lower math Scholastic Achievement Test (SAT) scores, and the stereotype of business school students as less interested in taking a poetry course—these are not stereotypes that are wrong because they smuggle in an evaluation by local standards.

In addition, although stereotypes regarding personality attributes may be more subject to ethnocentrism than are more objective characteristics, there is no evidence suggesting that even stereotypes about personality attributes are *always* influenced by ethnocentrism. Like the exaggeration hypothesis, the ethnocentrism hypothesis is an interesting one. Although ethnocentrism undoubtedly *sometimes* influences evaluations (e.g., Campbell, 1967), it is premature to conclude that even stereotypes about personality *necessarily* reflect ethnocentrism.

Stereotypes imply genetic origins of group differences. This   charge   implies that we already know that many or most group differences do not have substantial genetic foundations. The truth is, of course, that we do not know any such thing. Indeed, many have been surprised by recent evidence suggesting that even political and religious views may be more similar in separated monozygotic twins than in separated dizygotic twins (Bouchard, Lykken, McGue, Segal, et al., 1990). Although many psychologists may prefer environmental explanations to biological ones, most researchers also agree that it is exceedingly difficult to distinguish biological and environmental contributions to group differences (e.g., Gould, 1981; Mackenzie, 1984).

If we do not know the extent to which genetics causes differences among groups, we are in no position to declare that people who believe in genetic differences are inaccurate. Their beliefs may not be supported by scientific evidence, but this is because the evidence is sparse or its interpretation unclear, not because the evidence disproves genetic sources of group differences.

Even more important, this charge suffers a fundamentally flawed assumption—that people actually assume a genetic basis for group differences. We are aware of only one recent study that examined the degree to which nonpsychologists attribute group differences to biological as opposed to environmental causes (Martin & Parker, 1995; cf. Buchanan & Cantril, 1953). This study showed that a sample of undergraduate students believed that differences in socialization and opportunities were a stronger basis for gender and race differences than were differences in biology. Whether people other than undergraduates hold similar beliefs is currently an open question.

"They all look alike to me" (outgroup homogeneity).   Another more sophisticated accusation against stereotypes is that they lead people to assume that members of outgroups are more similar to one another than they really are (the outgroup is seen as more homogeneous than it really is). This is one of the few accusations against stereotypes that have received some empirical attention. Although there may be some tendency for people to see outgroups as less diverse than they really are (see Judd & Park, 1993, for a review), outgroup homogeneity is far from universal (see, e.g., Linville, Fischer, & Salovey, 1989; Simon & Pettigrew, 1990). In fact, outgroup and minority group members often see themselves as more homogeneous than they see ingroup or majority group members (Brewer, 1993; Lee, 1993; Simon & Brown, 1987). Americans and Chinese perceivers both judge Americans to be more diverse than are the Chinese—which, on many dimensions, they really are (Lee & Ottati, 1993). Like many of the other charges, outgroup homogeneity seems to be a hypothesis worth pursuing rather than an established fact.

Stereotypes' Role in Person Perception

Thus far, the charges we have reviewed all focus on stereotypes as perceptions of groups. A second set of charges focuses on the errors and biases produced by stereotypes when people interact with, perceive, or evaluate individuals from the stereotyped group. We briefly review these charges.

Stereotypes lead people to ignore individual differences.   This is a variant on the "rigidity" claim: Not only is it difficult to change people's perceptions of groups, but people supposedly automatically assume that each member of a group fits the group stereotype, no matter how different any particular member may be. Before obtaining individuating information about a particular target person, perceivers often do *expect* that person to fit a stereotype of their group, but this is completely appropriate. In the absence of any other information, most people would probably expect any given day in Alaska to be colder than that day in New York, and they would expect a professional basketball player to be taller than most other people. However, we doubt that there are many perceivers who would still judge that particular day as colder in Alaska than in New York if they were also told that it was sunny, mild, and 55°F in Anchorage and cloudy, windy, and 40°F in New York. Similarly, we doubt that many people would consider Mugsy Bogues very tall if they met him; he is a professional basketball player and is listed at about 5 ft, 4 in. tall.

But do stereotypes function this way? Yes. When individuating information is ambiguous or difficult to detect (e.g., Darley & Gross, 1983; Nelson, Biernat, & Manis, 1990), people often rely on their stereotypes rather than individuating information. However, of all the studies that have manipulated both group information (e.g., ethnicity, gender, social class, and profession) and the personal characteristics of targets (e.g., job competence and academic success), we are not aware of a single one that has shown that people *ignore* individual differences (see Funder, chapter 6, this volume). Perceivers base their judgments far more on the personal characteristics of targets than on targets' gender or membership in ethnic groups (e.g., Jackson, Sullivan, & Hodge, 1993; Jussim, Coleman, & Lerch, 1987; Krueger & Rothbart, 1988; Linville & Jones, 1980; Locksley, Borgida, Brekke, & Hepburn, 1980; Rokeach & Mezei, 1966; see Jussim, 1990, for a review). Although someday some researcher may identify a condition under which stereotypes really do lead people to ignore individual differences, this hypothesis has so far only been falsified: It has been repeatedly tested, but never confirmed.

Stereotypes lead to biased perceptions of individuals.   This is a weaker counterpart to the "ignore individual differences" charge. That is, although people may not *ignore* individual differences, stereotypes may still influence or bias judgments. For example, teachers may evaluate students who perform above the mean on a math test more favorably than students who score below the mean; but regardless of where students score, teachers may evaluate most boys more favorably than they deserve, and they may evaluate most girls less favorably than they deserve (see Jussim & Fleming, 1996, for a detailed presentation of this argument). Undoubtedly, stereotypes do sometimes lead to these types of biases (see Jussim, 1990, 1991, for reviews). Interestingly, however, stereotypes sometimes lead to counterstereotypic judgments of individuals. Girls have been viewed as more aggressive than boys (Condry & Ross, 1985), and African American job applicants and law school candidates have been evaluated more favorably than equally qualified Whites (e.g., Jussim et al., 1987; Linville & Jones, 1980). Other studies show no evidence of stereotypes biasing judgments of individuals (e.g., Krueger & Rothbart, 1988, Study 2; Locksley et al., 1980). In general, it seems that the more information people have about individual targets, the less they rely on their social stereotypes in arriving at judgments about those individuals (Eagly, Ashmore, Makhijani, & Longo, 1991; Jussim, 1990). Although stereotypes *sometimes* lead to biased perceptions of individuals, it is a misrepresentation of the research evidence to claim or imply that stereotypes *generally* lead to biased perceptions.

Stereotypes create self-fulfilling prophecies.   A self-fulfilling prophecy occurs when "an originally false definition of a situation becomes true" (Merton, 1948). For example, in the early part of this century, most unions barred African American workers from membership. Union members often claimed that African Americans were strikebreakers and could not be trusted. This severely limited African Americans' job opportunities. When faced with a strike, companies often offered jobs to all takers, and African Americans often jumped at the chance for work. Thus, the union's beliefs about African Americans were confirmed.

Undoubtedly, stereotypes are sometimes self-fulfilling (see Jussim & Fleming, 1996, for a review). Often, however, the effects of expectations are small or nonexistent (see Chapman & McCauley, 1993, for a natural experiment testing the power of the expectations associated with the title, National Science Foundation graduate fellow). Furthermore, stereotypes are not necessarily inaccurate (as documented throughout this volume), and in the absence of an inaccurate expectation, a self-fulfilling prophecy cannot occur. Even inaccurate expectations do not necessarily produce self-fulfilling prophecies (Jussim, 1986, 1991).

It is worth noting that the claim that stereotypes are inaccurate contradicts the claim that stereotypes create self- fulfilling prophecies. If stereotypes create a self-fulfilling prophecy, then the stereotyped belief *becomes* true (even if it was false to begin with). For example, we know that at least part of the physical attractiveness stereotype is not self-fulfilling. That is, people believe attractive individuals are smarter than less attractive individuals, which is false (see meta-analyses by Eagly et al., 1991; Feingold, 1992). But if it is false, we know that this stereotyped belief cannot possibly be self-fulfilling. Although understanding when and how stereotypes may be self-fulfilling is an important and interesting question, it is also a misrepresentation of the research evidence to claim or imply that stereotypes *generally* lead to self-fulfilling prophecies.

Why Study Stereotype Accuracy (and Inaccuracy)?

Stereotypes Have Been Stereotyped!

We have just argued that the typical charges against stereotypes are inaccurate, unjustified, exaggerated, and not based on empirical evidence. Sound familiar? However, the frequency with which these charges are repeated in the scientific literature (often without reference to empirical studies)—combined with sociopolitical factors (a desire by many social scientists to help and defend oppressed groups and to remedy injustice; a fear of being labeled *racist* or *sexist*)—has led social scientists to premature conclusions regarding stereotype accuracy and inaccuracy. If we all "know" that stereotypes are inaccurate, rigid, and ethnocentric, and that only racists and sexists say otherwise, then clearly there is no need for empirical research.

However, the current state of our scientific knowledge cannot support broad, sweeping statements about stereotypes' inaccuracy, rigidity, or irrationality. This is not because the typical charges against stereotypes are unequivocally or always false. Rather, broad generalizations are inappropriate because there is little evidence regarding many of the claims, and because when there is considerable evidence, it presents a decidedly mixed picture.

References

Adorno, T., Frenkel-Brunswick, E., Levinson, D., & Sanford, R. N. (1950). *The authoritarian personality*. New York: Harper.

Allport, G. (1954). *The nature of prejudice*. Cambridge, MA: Addison-Wesley.

Ashmore, R. D., & Del Boca, F. K. (1981). Conceptual approaches to stereotypes and stereotyping. In D. L. Hamilton (Ed.), *Cognitive processes in stereotyping and intergroup behavior* (pp. 1–35). Hillsdale, NJ: Erlbaum.

Bouchard, T. J., Lykken, D. T., McGue, M., Segal, N. L., et al. (1990). Sources of human psychological differences: The Minnesota study of twins reared apart. *Science, 250,* 223–228.

Brewer, M. (1993). Social identity, distinctiveness, and ingroup homogeneity. *Social Cognition, 11,* 150–164.

Brigham, J. C. (1971). Ethnic stereotypes. *Psychological Bulletin, 76,* 15–38. Brown, R. (1965). *Social psychology*. New York: Free Press.

Buchanan, W., & Cantril, H. (1953). *How nations see each other*. Urbana: University of Illinois Press.

Campbell, D. T. (1967). Stereotypes and the perception of group differences. *American Psychologist, 22,* 817–829.

Chapman, G., & McCauley, C. (1993). Early career achievements of National Science Foundation (NSF) graduate applicants: Looking for Pygmalion and Galatea effects on NSF winners. *Journal of Applied Psychology, 78,* 815–820.

Condry, J. C, & Ross, D. F. (1985). Sex and aggression: The influence of gender label on the perception of aggression in children. *Child Development, 56,* 225–233.

Darley, J. M., & Gross, P. H. (1983). A hypothesis-confirming bias in labeling effects. *Journal of Personality and Social Psychology, 44,* 20–33.

DeParle, J. (1994, June 19). Welfare as we've known it. *The New York Times* ("The Week in Review"), p. 4.

Eagly, A. H., Ashmore, R. D., Makhijani, M. G., & Longo, L. (1991). What is beautiful is good, but...: A meta-analytic review of research on the physical attractiveness stereotype. *Psychological Bulletin, 110,* 109–128.

Eagly, A. H., & Mladinic, A. (1989). Gender stereotypes and attitudes toward men and women. *Personality and Social Psychology Bulletin, 15,* 543–558.

Feingold, A. (1992). Good-looking people are not what we think. *Psychological Bulletin, 111,* 304–341.

Gould, S. J. (1981). *The mismeasure of man.* New York: Norton.

Jackson, L. A., Sullivan, L. A., & Hodge, C N. (1993). Stereotype effects on attributions, predictions, and evaluations: No two social judgments are quite alike. *Journal of Personality and Social Psychology, 65,* 69–84.

Judd, C. M., & Park, B. (1993). Definition and assessment of accuracy in social stereotypes. *Psychological Review, 100,* 109–128.

Jussim, L. (1986). Self-fulfilling prophecies: A theoretical and integrative review. *Psychological Review, 93,* 429–445.

Jussim, L. (1990). Social reality and social problems: The role of expectancies. *Journal of Social Issues, 46,* 9–34.

Jussim, L. (1991). Social perception and social reality: A reflection–construction model. *Psychological Review, 98,* 54–73.

Jussim, L., Coleman, L., & Lerch, L. (1987). The nature of stereotypes: A comparison and integration of three theories. *Journal of Personality and Social Psychology, 52,* 536–546.

Jussim, L., & Fleming, C. (1996). Self-fulfilling prophecies and the maintenance of social stereotypes. In N. Macrae, M. Hewstone, & C. Stangor (Eds.), *The foundations of stereotypes and stereotyping.* New York: Guilford Press.

Katz, D., & Braly, K. (1933). Racial stereotypes of one hundred college students. *Journal of Abnormal and Social Psychology, 28,* 280–290.

Krueger, J., & Rothbart, M. (1988). Use of categorical and individuating information in making inferences about personality. *Journal of Personality and Social Psychology, 55,* 187–195.

LaPiere, R. T. (1936). Type-rationalizations of group antipathy. *Social Forces, 15,* 232–237.

Lee, Y. (1993). Ingroup preference and homogeneity among African American and Chinese American students. *Journal of Social Psychology, 133,* 225–235.

Lee, Y., & Ottati, V. (1993). Determinants of in-group and out-group perceptions of heterogeneity: An investigation of Sino-American stereotypes. *Journal of Cross-Cultural Psychology, 24,* 298–318.

LeVine, R. A., & Campbell, D. T. (1972). *Ethnocentrism: Theories of conflict, ethnic attitudes, and group behavior.* New York: Wiley.

Linville, P. W., Fischer, G. W., & Salovey, P. (1989). Perceived distributions of the characteristics of in-group and out-group members: Empirical evidence and a computer simulation. *Journal of Personality and Social Psychology, 57,* 165–188.

Linville, P. W., & Jones, E. E. (1980). Polarized appraisal of out-group members. *Journal of Personality and Social Psychology, 38,* 689–703.

Locksley, A., Borgida, E., Brekke, N., & Hepburn, C. (1980). Sex stereotypes and social judgment. *Journal of Personality and Social Psychology, 39,* 821–831.

Mackenzie, B. (1984). Explaining race differences in IQ: The logic, the methodology, and the evidence. *American Psychologist, 39,* 1214–1233.

Mackie, M. (1973). Arriving at "truth" by definition: The case of stereotype inaccuracy. *Social Problems, 20,* 431–447.

Marger, M. N. (1991). *Race and ethnic relations.* Belmont, CA: Wadsworth.

Martin, C. (1987). A ratio measure of sex stereotyping. *Journal of Personality and Social Psychology, 52,* 489–499.

Martin, C. L., & Parker, S. (1995). Folk theories about sex and race differences. *Personality and Social Psychology Bulletin, 21,* 45–57.

McCauley, C., & Stitt, C. L. (1978). An individual and quantitative measure of stereotypes. *Journal of Personality and Social Psychology, 36*, 929–940.

McCauley, C., Stitt, C. L., & Segal, M. (1980). Stereotyping: From prejudice to prediction. *Psychological Bulletin, 87*, 195–208.

McCauley, C. R., & Thangavelu, K. (1991). Individual differences in sex stereotyping
of occupations and personality traits. *Social Psychology Quarterly, 54*, 267–279.

McCauley, C., Thangavelu, K., & Rozin, P. (1988). Sex stereotyping of occupations
in relation to television representations and census facts. *Basic and Applied Social
Psychology, 9*, 197–212.

Merton, R. K. (1948). The self-fulfilling prophecy. *Antioch Review, 8*, 193–210.

Nelson, T. E., Biernat, M. R., & Manis, M. (1990). Everyday base rates (sex stereotypes):
Potent and resilient. *Journal of Personality and Social Psychology, 59*, 664–675.

Oakes, P. J., Haslam, S. A., & Turner, J. C. (1994). *Stereotyping and social reality.*
Cambridge, MA: Basil Blackwell.

Rokeach, M., & Mezei, L. (1966). Race and shared belief as factors in social choice.
Science, 151, 167–172.

Simon, B., & Brown, R. J. (1987). Perceived intragroup homogeneity in minority-
majority contexts. *Journal of Personality and Social Psychology, 53*, 703–711.

Simon, B., & Pettigrew, T. F. (1990). Social identity and perceived group homogeneity: Evidence for the ingroup homogeneity effect. *European Journal of Social
Psychology, 20*, 269–286.

Swim, J. K. (1994). Perceived versus meta-analytic effect sizes: An assessment of the
accuracy of gender stereotypes. *Journal of Personality and Social Psychology, 66*,
21–36.

Tversky, A., & Kahneman, D. (1971). Belief in the law of small numbers. *Psychological Bulletin, 2*, 105–110.

NO ↵

Charles Stangor

Content and Application Inaccuracy in Social Stereotyping

Athough we are currently enjoying a "second coming" of accuracy research within the span of only several decades in social psychology as a whole, such rapid change has decidedly not been true of work within the area of social stereotyping. By any account, the focus of stereotyping researchers has been consistent and steady, involving a persistent concern with the potential inaccuracy of stereotypes and the negative outcomes of stereotyping on the victims of the stereotyping process. The themes of inaccuracy and injustice have been part and parcel of the writings of all influential scholars in the field, beginning with Lippman (1922), Katz and Braly (1933), and Allport (1954), and continuing with the work of Tajfel (1981) and the contemporary theorists (Brewer, 1988; Fiske & Neuberg, 1990; Hamilton, 1981).

Despite this historical focus on error, inaccuracy, and unfairness, the notion that stereotypes are, at least in part, accurate is now being taken seriously for the first time within social psychology. This shift was apparent not only in the meeting of the present congress on stereotype accuracy, but also in the publication of an important book from a highly influential group of stereotype researchers (Oakes, Haslam, & Turner, 1994). The prevailing theme of both conference and book is that stereotypes are, at least in part, accurate and constitute the "social reality" of the individual. Of course, such statements are not entirely novel, for they have existed for many years in the form of the kernel-of-truth hypothesis (Brigham, 1971; Eagly & Steffen, 1984; Vinacke, 1957), which states that most stereotypes are, at least in part, accurate. And although this basic truth has frequently been lost in the focus on error, most contemporary work on stereotyping is entirely based on the assumption that there are real group differences that are perceived in everyday life and then exaggerated and distorted through cognitive and motivational biases (cf. Stangor & Lange, 1994).

Changes in the approach to a field of inquiry, such as a switch from a focus on inaccuracy to a focus on accuracy, are usually either the outcome of a decline in the utility of the current scientific paradigm or are the result of changes in the political and social climate surrounding the researchers. Although it is possible that a waning utility of the "bias" approach to social

From STEROTYPE ACCURACY: TOWARD APPRECIATING GROUP DIFFERENCES, pp. 4–27. Copyright © 1995 by American Psychological Association. Reprinted with permission.

knowledge has prompted the recent turn of events in studying stereotypes, it is also possible that the social context is, at least in part, the determining cause. Political events in the sixties brought social psychology, along with the United States as a whole, into an era of concern with political correctness. During this time, we became sensitive (and perhaps overly so) to the use of stereotypes in everyday life. Today, the social context has radically changed. "Backlash" politics has brought with it an open discussion of the realities of intergroup differences, the explicit inequality of affirmative action programs, and a concern with the impact of true cultural differences on the future of our society. Even if not a contributing causal factor, the contemporary social context certainly provides an appropriate climate for the renewed study of stereotype accuracy.

The historical tradition of social stereotyping research within social psychology is also a contributing factor to the possibility of a focus on stereotype accuracy. Stereotype research has operated in a sort of social vacuum, in which only certain types of questions have been addressed. Most important, we have proceeded as if studying stereotyping meant that we study the stereotyper. Our literature is filled with articles documenting the development, maintenance, use, and potential change of stereotypes within the stereotyper; yet, we have virtually ignored the question of how those who are the targets of stereotyping respond to being stereotyped or to the implications of stereotyping on their social lives (for some few exceptions, see recent work by Crocker & Major, 1989; Frable, Blackstone, & Scherbaum, 1990; Lord & Saenz, 1985). This focus on the stereotyper, rather than the stereotyped, has determined how the accuracy question is itself framed. Our traditions lead us to be more likely to ask whether it is accurate for a stereotyper to use his or her stereotypes than to ask whether the outcomes of stereotype use are accurate for, or fair to, the targets of stereotyping.

Although from an empirical and scientific point of view, there is much to be learned by reconsidering issues of stereotype accuracy, in doing so we must continually remember that this research is located in a social and political context. It is my hope not only that the current focus on stereotype accuracy will be beneficial in a scientific sense in terms of advancing our theorizing about stereotypes and stereotyping, but also that this work will lead to a more explicit consideration of the impact of stereotypes on the targets stereotyping, a concern that has long been neglected within the field.

Content and Application Inaccuracy in Stereotyping

In this chapter, I draw a distinction between *content inaccuracy and application inaccuracy* in the area of social stereotyping. This distinction reflects the relationship between stereotypes (as cognitive representations of social groups and their members) and stereotyping (the use of this knowledge as a basis of responding to others; cf. Brewer, 1996). I consider both factors that are likely to produce either accurate or inaccurate social stereotypes (content effects), as well as factors that may lead to inappropriate, unfair, or inaccurate use of such stereotypes in the judgments of others (application effects).

In the course of this review, I come to the conclusion that measuring the content accuracy (or inaccuracy) of social stereotypes is a venture that is premature, that will at best produce relatively limited payoffs, and that at worst may result in our unintentionally communicating to the society at large that stereotypes are by and large accurate and, thus, generally appropriate to use as a basis for judging others. Fundamentally, I believe that a focus on the content accuracy of stereotypes is premature because we do not yet have a well-established method for documenting those group differences themselves. I believe that cataloging the nature of group differences is an important first step in producing an adequate remedy for negative intergroup behavior. We need to know both how big existing group differences are and how to communicate the extent of those differences to people. And we need to develop appropriate methodologies for assessing those differences. Yet I also believe that the likelihood that we will be able to draw broad conclusions about the general or even the specific accuracy of the *perceptions* of those differences (social stereotypes) is small. And even if ultimately successful, cataloging the accuracy of those stereotypes is a project that will have little importance for the study of intergroup relations more broadly.

Although I am not sanguine about the goal of assessing the content accuracy of stereotypes, I believe that studying accuracy in their application (the process of stereotyping others) represents a very important line of inquiry and one that should be a prime focus of those interested in the stereotyping process. Of course, such an interest is not a new one. Indeed, the major part of stereotyping research over the past two decades has been focused on the question of when and how stereotypes are used as a basis of judgment (Brewer, 1996, Fiske & Neuberg, 1990; Locksley, Borgida, Brekke, & Hepburn, 1980). I believe that a focus on application rather than content has been due partly to the perception that application inaccuracy is an extremely important question with direct social relevance.

My conclusion that application accuracy is more important than content accuracy is based on my belief that stereotypes, as one type of social belief, are inherently neutral entities. Stereotypes, even when objectively inaccurate or overly negative, are neither "good" nor "bad." A person who holds the belief that most Jews are stingy may be factually incorrect and may be deceiving him- or herself, but holding this belief does not in itself represent a grave danger to Jews or to the society at large. On the other hand, the inappropriate use of stereotypic beliefs as a basis of responding to others, *even if those beliefs are entirely accurate*, is potentially damaging to the stereotyped individuals.

The distinction between content and application inaccuracy leads to the potential question of whether application effects should be considered as accuracy or whether stereotype accuracy refers only to the issue of content. Yet, I see no reason to consider one question more relevant to the accuracy issue than the other. Content accuracy and application accuracy represent two different issues, each of which can be studied in terms of accuracy or inaccuracy.

Factors Likely to Produce Accurate or Inaccurate Stereotypes

Although I do not believe that studying the content accuracy of social stereotypes is a particularly fruitful endeavor, an analysis of the processes underlying stereotype development more generally may be useful for those interested in understanding when and why stereotypes are likely to be accurate or inaccurate. Stereotypes are frequently conceptualized as "tools" (Gilbert & Hixon, 1991; Macrae, Milne, & Bodenhausen, 1994) that individuals create to help them solve a variety of everyday social needs. If this utilitarian conceptualization of stereotypes has validity, then we may well expect that stereotypes that develop to fulfill different functions will have differential content accuracy. Although my analysis of the content accuracy issue is based on this assumption, I actually know of no research that has directly tested these predictions.

Some social stereotypes develop because they serve for the stereotyper the function of providing diagnostic information about social groups. In this case, stereotypes allow the individual to understand, predict, control, and "master" their social worlds. It is useful to know that lawyers are likely to be rich and nurses poor when one is choosing a marriage partner or even a date for the evening. This goal of creating social reality and "enriching" social perception forms the theme of Oakes et al.'s analysis of stereotypes (Oakes et al., 1994). There is existing evidence to support the idea that some stereotypes develop due to their diagnostic functions. For instance, Ford and Stangor (1992) found that traits that most highly distinguished among social groups became more stereotypic (in the sense of becoming strongly connected with the group representation in memory) in comparison with traits that were less differentiating. In this sense, more diagnostic information became stereotypic.

The finding that some stereotypes develop on the basis of their informational value does not, however, mean that all or even most stereotypes are accurate. For one, accuracy *motives* do not necessarily lead to accurate *beliefs* (cf. Kruglanski, 1989). Just as opponent processes in visual and auditory perception, which have developed because they serve the basic function of providing useful information about the environment, provide useful information by routinely exaggerating perceptual differences, adopting a goal of accurate group perceptions may result in exaggerations of perceived between-groups differences and minimizations of perceived within-group variability (Tajfel, 1970; Tajfel & Wilkes, 1963). Indeed, the basic process of cognitively representing groups (the mapping of a categorical dimension onto a continuous one) is well known to result in such perceptual biases (Eiser & Stroebe, 1972).

Furthermore, the goal of accurately summarizing the characteristics of social groups and differentiating among them is only one of the many motivations that stereotypes serve. An additional function is to simplify a complex social environment (Macrae, Milne, & Bodenhausen, 1994; Stangor & Ford, 1992). Stereotypes develop more strongly under cognitively demanding conditions, such as when the number of groups that individuals have to learn about increases or when individuals are distracted by a secondary task

NO / Charles Stangor

(Stangor & Duan, 1991). Parallel results have been found in the area of individual differences. Individuals with high "need for structure" (Neuberg & Newsom, 1993; Schaller, Boyd, Yohannes, & O'Brien, 1995) develop stronger stereotypes. It would be expected that stereotypes that develop to fulfill the function of cognitive parsimony would be particularly likely to be less variable and more extreme than their objective basis, for it is exactly such "simplified" beliefs that are most functional in simplifying the social world.

Perhaps the most basic function of stereotypes is that they provide positive feedback about the self and the ingroup. Stereotypes help create both individual and social self-esteem. Stereotypes that are developed to fulfill such needs will likely be not only distorted, but systematically biased in the sense that the perceived content of stereotypes about the ingroup will be more positive than the content of stereotypes ascribed to outgroups. Again, such biases have been well documented in the literature (cf. Brewer, 1979; Diehl, 1990; Howard & Rothbart, 1980) and develop even in "minimal" situations, where there is little need for self-enhancement.

Finally, stereotypes may function to justify existing attitudes or social situations (cf. Jost & Banaji, 1994). At the collective level, groups of individuals may develop collective beliefs that serve to justify or support the superiority of their own group over other groups (Stangor & Schaller, 1996). As with self-enhancement motives, such justification functions lead individuals to focus on dimensions that favorably differentiate them from others.

In addition to potential inaccuracy that may result from the motivational functions of stereotypes reviewed above, there is also a host of cognitive mechanisms that may produce inaccurate group beliefs. The wellknown *illusory correlation phenomenon* suggests that people are likely to develop overly negative beliefs about minority groups. And once such negative stereotypes begin to develop, they may be maintained through selffulfilling prophecies, biased social memory (Fyock & Stangor, 1994), confirming information search, and biased exposure to members of the groups (cf. Hamilton, 1981; Macrae, Stangor, & Hewstone, 1996....)

On the Limitations of Studying Content Inaccuracy

Even if I thought it were desirable or important to catalog the accuracy of social stereotypes, I would be pessimistic about our ability to make definitive statements in this regard. This is because I believe the prognosis for developing unambiguous criteria on which to make such statements is small. The problem is that stereotypes often represent beliefs about the trait characteristics of a social group rather than beliefs about more objective criteria, such as group attitudes or behaviors. And the criteria for assessing the accuracy of trait beliefs are simply not clear. Consider two individuals who are in perfect agreement regarding behaviors that are evidenced by a group (i.e., "not holding a job" and "not spending much money"), and consider also the possibility that these beliefs are objectively accurate, as indexed by current unemployment rates or percentage of yearly income that is saved versus spent. And yet these two individuals may still differ dramatically in how they interpret these behaviors and, thus, differ substantially in the stereotypes they form about the group. One individual may interpret high rates of savings as "thrifty," whereas another may interpret the same behavior as "stingy" (see Maass & Arcuri, 1996, Peabody, 1968): Indeed, it is expected that the same behavior will be differentially interpreted by different perceivers because these beliefs are inherently bound up in the host of motivational and social functions that stereotypes serve. Because an aggressive behavior does not necessarily denote an aggressive personality, a person who makes that inference is no more "right" or "wrong" no more "accurate" or "inaccurate," than a person who does not. Both people have perceived reality correctly and yet have developed very different interpretations of it (cf. Oakes et al., 1994, chapter 8).

Conclusion

My review of the current state of empirical and theoretical approaches to the issue of stereotype accuracy has led me to question the utility of an approach that is based primarily on assessing the content accuracy of social stereotypes...I do not believe that this approach will be highly productive in terms of producing a better understanding of the causes or consequences of stereotyping. And I believe this study could also have negative social consequences if readers of our research interpret our conclusions to indicate that stereotypes are by and large accurate and, thus, generally appropriate to use. Furthermore, I believe that a focus on content may distract us from other, more important, questions regarding issues of stereotypes and stereotyping.

A focus on the application of stereotypes makes it clear to me that the issue of content of the stereotype itself is entirely irrelevant to an understanding of the stereotyping process. This is because stereotypes are never true of every group member. Thus, using a stereotype, regardless of its accuracy, is potentially inaccurate and unfair. When a man denies an opportunity for employment to a woman because he believes that "women are not assertive without attempting to assess whether the individual candidate in question is or is not assertive, it is entirely irrelevant (and especially so from the point of view of the applicant) whether 24% or 94% of women actually are assertive! *All* that matters is the assertiveness of the candidate herself.

One could consider the problem a different way by imagining a simple thought experiment: What would be learned by categorizing all beliefs about all social groups as either accurate or inaccurate? Would this knowledge inform us that it is appropriate to use one set of stereotypes, but not another? Or would it provide a convenient rationalization for the use of stereotypes in all situations? The implications of conceptualizing stereotype accuracy go far beyond that of scientific investigation, and we must consider these ramifications carefully. Imagine a legal case in which an employer denied employment to a qualified woman on the basis of his belief that women are too emotional to hold a management position. Yet, what would be different about this situation if it had previously been, determined, on the basis of careful scientific study, that women are indeed more emotional, on average, than men and that this employer's beliefs about those differences are entirely accurate? This information is irrelevant to the judgment of this particular woman. Yet, it is not difficult to imagine that it would be used to justify the type of decision that the employer made.

Of course, one could argue that *all* information can potentially be misused and, thus, question why my concen is with the misuse of stereotypes rather than the misuse of other potentially inaccurate information. Social psychologists have historically been concerned about the use of stereotypes when these beliefs are based on *ascribed* rather than *achieved* characteristics. Ascribed characteristics are those that are attained by birth or by accident and that are out of the control of the individual. Achieved characteristics are those that are freely chosen by the individual. I would be less concerned when an employer assumes a conservative outlook for a person who identifies herself or himself as a Republican or assumes an evil personality for an individual who is an acknowledged member of the Ku Klux Klan. When an individual freely chooses a category membership, he or she is well aware of the potential stereotypes that may follow this decision. Yet, stereotyping on the basis of ascribed social group membership, such as race, sex, age, religion, and body type, has the potential for more serious outcomes on the targets of these judgments, because these categories are not actively chosen by the individual and, thus, the potential negative stereotyping is out of the person's own control.

Although the practice of using beliefs about social groups to judge others can be harmful when the stereotypes are individual beliefs, the negative outcomes of stereotyping are dramatically increased when many people within a society share these beliefs (Stangor & Schaller, 1996). It matters less if one employer believes that Blacks are not fit for managerial positions. It matters much more when that belief is shared by many different employers. Thus, although both individual and collective stereotypes can be harmful, the latter are more serious. And the implications of collective group beliefs on individuals have not heretofore been adequately studied within social psychology.

As scientists concerned with improving the social condition, we must be wary of arguments that can be used to justify the use of stereotypes. While it may be tempting to argue that a person's beliefs that most Blacks are stupid, lazy, and aggressive represents a "social reality" and, thus, that these beliefs enrich, inform, and enhance his or her social perception, we cannot allow a bigot to continue to use his or her stereotypes, even if those beliefs seem to them to be accurate. Allowing this would be to ignore the potential damage that can result when stereotypes are misapplied. This argument is not the same as saying that it is only other people's beliefs that are incorrect (see Oakes, Haslam, & Turner, 1996,p. 206). All stereotypes, if inappropriately applied, are unfair to the targets of judgment.

There are certainly social, political, and economic causes of group inequalities that do not involve stereotyping. And it is possible that we have overestimated the role of stereotypes as determinants of inequities in our society. Certainly, not all people who hold stereotypes practice discrimination, nor is all discrimination the result of stereotypes. Yet the role of individual and collective perceptions, such as social stereotypes, as determinants of group relationships has been well documented in the social psychological literature, and research has clearly shown that stereotypes have powerful, and frequently unintended, influence on social behavior (Macrae et al.,1996).

Arguments that stereotypes are by and large accurate are premature. It is tempting, from a purely scientific point of view, to argue that stereotypes are just other pieces of social information that should be used to the extent that they provide diagnostic information about a target. Yet the cost of misusing these beliefs is potentially high, and most important, these costs are not equally distributed between the perceiver and the receiver of the judgment. It is relatively easy for individuals with power and status to convince themselves that their social beliefs are accurate and that their use is appropriate. But it is the stigmatized and the powerless for whom the inappropriate use of stereotypes really matters. The misuse of stereotypes can have grave consequences for the victims of stereotyping; thus, it behooves everyone of us to think twice or even three times before using category memberships as a basis of thinking about others.

References

Allport, G. W. (1954). *The nature of prejudice.* Reading, MA: Addison-Wesley.

Brewer, M. B. (1979). In-group bias in the minimal intergroup situation: A cognitive-motivational analysis. *Psychological Bulletin, 86,* 307–324.

Brewer, M. B. (1988). A dual process model of impression formation. In T. K. Srull & R. S. Wyer (Eds.), *Advances in social cognition* (Vol. 1, pp. 177–183). Hillsdale, NJ: Erlbaum.

Brewer, M. B. (1996). When stereotypes lead to stereotyping: The use of stereotypes in person perception. In C. N. Macrae, C. Stangor, & M. Hewstone (Eds.), *Foundations of stereotypes and stereotyping.* New York: Guilford Press.

Brigham, J. C. (1971). Ethnic stereotypes. *Psychological Bulletin, 76,* 15–38.

Crocker, J., & Major, B. (1989). Social stigma and self-esteem: The self-protective properties of stigma. *Psychological Review, 96,* 608–630.

Diehl, M. (1990). The minimal group paradigm: Theoretical explanations and empirical findings. In M. Hewstone & W. Stroebe (Eds.), *European review of social psychology* (Vol. 1, pp. 263–292). Chichester, England: Wiley.

Eagly, A. H., & Steffen, V. J. (1984). Gender stereotypes stem from the distribution of women and men into social roles. *Journal of Personality and Social Psychology, 46,* 735–754.

Eiser, R. J., & Stroebe, W. (1972). *Categorization and social judgment.* New York: Academic Press.

Fiske, S. T., & Neuberg, S. L. (1990). A continuum of impression formation, from category based to individuating processes: Influences of information and motivation on attention and interpretation. *Advances in Experimental Social Pychology, 23,* 1–74.

Ford, T. E., & Stangor, C. (1992). The role of diagnosticity in stereotype formation: Perceiving group means and variances. *Journal of Personality and Social Psychology, 63,* 356–367.

Frable, D. E. S., Blackstone, T., & Scherbaum, C. (1990). Marginal and mindful: Deviants in social interaction. *Journal of Personality and Social Psychology, 59,* 140–149.

Fyock, J., & Stangor, C. (1994). The role of memory biases in stereotype maintenance. *British Journal of Social Psychology, 33,* 331–344.

Gilbert, D. T., & Hixon, J. G. (1991). The trouble of thinking: Activation and application of stereotypic beliefs. *Journal of Personality and Social Psychology, 60,* 509–517.

Hamilton, D. L. (Ed.). (1981). *Cognitive processes in stereotyping and intergroup behavior.* Hillsdale, NJ: Erlbaum.

Howard, J. W., & Rothbart, M. (1980). Social categorization and memory for ingroup and out-group behavior. *Journal of Personality and Social Psychology, 38,* 301–310.

Jost, J. T., & Banaji, M. R. (1994). The role of stereotyping in system-justification and the production of false consciousness. *British Journal of Social Psychology, 33,* 1–27.

Katz, D., & Braly, K. W. (1933). Racial stereotypes of one hundred college students. *Journal of Abnormal and Social Psychology, 28,* 280–290.

Kruglanski, A. W. (1989). The psychology of being "right": On the problem of accuracy in social perception and cognition. *Psychological Bulletin, 106,* 395–409.

Lippmann, W. (1922). Public opinion. New York: Harcourt & Brace.

Locksley, A., Borgida, E., Brekke, N., & Hepburn, C. (1980). Sex stereotypes and judgments of individuals. *Journal of Personality and Social Psychology, 39,* 821–831.

Lord, C., & Saenz, D. (1985). Memory deficits and memory surfeits: Differential cognitive consequences of tokenism for tokens and observers. *Journal of Personality and Social Psychology, 49,* 918–926.

Maass, A., & Arcuri, L. (1996). Language and stereotyping. In C. N. Macrae, C. Stangor, & M. Hewstone (Eds.), *Foundations of stereotypes and stereotyping.* A New York: Guilford Press.

Macrae, C. N., Milne, A. B., & Bodenhausen, G. V. (1994). Stereotypes as energy saving devices: A peek inside the cognitive toolbox. *Journal of Personality and Social Psychology, 66,* 37–47.

Macrae, C. N., Stangor, C., & Hewstone, M. (Eds.). (1996). *Foundations of stereotypes and stereotyping.* New York: Guilford Press.

Neuberg, S. L., & Newsom, J. T. (1993). Personal need for structure: Individual differences in the desire for simple structure. *Journal of Personality and Social Psychology, 65,* 113–131.

Oakes, P. J., Haslam, S. A., & Turner, J. C. (1994). *Stereotyping and social reality.* Oxford, England: Basil Blackwell.

Peabody, D. (1968). Group judgments in the Philippines: Evaluative and descriptive aspects. *Journal of Personality and Social Psychology, 10,* 290–300.

Schaller, M., Boyd, C., Yohannes, J., & O'Brien, M. (1995). The prejudiced personality revisited: Personal need for structure and the formation of erroneous group stereotypes. *Journal of Personality and Social Psychology, 68,* 544–555.

Stangor, C., & Duan, C. (1991). Effects of multiple task demands upon memory for information about social groups. *Journal of Experimental Social Psychology, 27,* 357–378.

Stangor, C., & Ford, T. E. (1992). Accuracy and expectancy-confirming processing orientations and the development of stereotypes and prejudice. *European Review of Social Psychology, 3,* 57–89.

Stangor, C., & Lange, J. (1994). Cognitive representations of social groups: Advances in conceptualizating stereotypes and stereotyping. *Advances in Experimental Social Psychology, 26,* 357–416.

Stangor, C., & Schaller, M. (1996). Stereotypes as individual and collective representations. In C. N. Macrae, C. Stangor, & M. Hewstone (Eds.), *Foundations of stereotypes and stereotyping*. New York: Guilford Press.

Tajfel, H. (1970). Experiments in intergroup discrimination. *Scientific American, 223,* 96–102.

Tajfel, H. (1981). Social stereotypes and social groups. In J. C. Turner & H. Giles (Eds.), *Intergroup behavior* (pp. 144–167). Chicago: University of Chicago Press.

Tajfel, H., & Wilkes, A. L. (1963). Classification and quantitative judgment. *British Journal of Psychology, 54,* 101–114.

Vinacke, W. E. (1957). Stereotypes as social concepts. *Journal of Social Psychology, 46,* 229–243.

CHALLENGE QUESTIONS

Can Stereotypes Lead to Accurate Perceptions of Others?

1. Do you think it is possible to determine whether a stereotype is accurate? How would you go about measuring the accuracy of a stereotype?
2. Is it ever acceptable to use stereotypes? Or is using a stereotype to judge a person always immoral, regardless of whether it leads to accurate perceptions?
3. Does appreciating differences between groups necessarily lead to stereotyping? In other words, how does one learn to honor the cultures and traditions of various social groups without stereotyping members of that group?

ISSUE 16

Does True Altruism Exist?

YES: C. Daniel Batson, Bruce D. Duncan, Paula Ackerman, Terese Buckley, and Kimberly Birch, from "Is Empathic Emotion a Source of Altruistic Motivation?" *Journal of Personality and Social Psychology* (40, 1981)

NO: Robert B. Cialdini, Mark Schaller, Donald Houlihan, Kevin Arps, Jim Fultz, and Arthur L. Beaman, from "Empathy-Based Helping: Is It Selflessly or Selfishly Motivated?" *Journal of Personality and Social Psychology* (52, 1987)

ISSUE SUMMARY

YES: Social psychologist C. Daniel Batson and his colleagues believe that people sometimes help for purely altruistic reasons. He proposes that empathy is the key factor responsible for altruism and describes the results of an experiment that supports his position.

NO: Social psychologist Robert Cialdini and his colleagues are not convinced that empathy alone can motivate helping. He proposes an alternative explanation, called the Negative State Relief Model, which proposes that people help others in order to make themselves feel better.

Do people ever behave selflessly? Is it possible that we help simply out of genuine concern for another person's welfare and nothing else? These are fundamental questions for social psychologists who study altruism. Altruism can be defined as an unselfish interest in helping others. At first glance, it may seem as if altruistic behavior is commonplace—philanthropists donate to charities, public safety workers risk their lives on a daily basis, and everyday people often lend a helping hand to others for no apparent ulterior motive. However, if we look more closely at helping, it becomes evident that there may be other factors, besides a concern for the welfare of others, that may motivate helping. For example, philanthropists who donate money to a charity are likely to feel good about themselves after making their donation. If these positive feelings were the primary factor that motivated the donation—

the person donated the money to feel good—then this act of charity could not be considered truly altruistic. It would be considered an *egoistic* act because it was ultimately aimed at improving the welfare of the person giving the help rather than the person receiving help, even if the donation had positive consequences for others. But how can we tell if it is altruism or more self-centered motives that are responsible for helping? When helping occurs in the real world, it can be difficult to ascertain the true motivation of those who provide help. A social psychology laboratory is likely to be a more promising place to determine whether true altruism exists; in the laboratory the causes of helping behavior can be isolated and systematically studied.

In the first selection, Daniel Batson and his colleagues propose that empathy plays a key role in altruistic behavior. Empathy is the ability to experience someone else's feelings by imagining what it would feel like to be in the same situation as another person. According to Batson, when we feel empathy for another person we become genuinely concerned for their well-being and are more likely to help for altruistic reasons. Batson will describe a laboratory experiment designed to test this hypothesis.

Robert Cialdini and his colleagues propose a different model to explain helping behavior, which they call the Negative State Relief Model. According to this model, people help others in order to avoid the negative feelings that they might experience if they did not help. Imagine that you are witnessing someone suffering. How would it make you feel to watch them suffer? It would probably bother you and make you feel personally distressed. According to Cialdini, you would be likely to take action to reduce this person's suffering in order to reduce the distress that *you* were currently experiencing. If this were your motivation for helping then it would not be altruism, because the ultimate goal of your behavior would be to increase your own welfare. So according to this perspective, we often help in order to avoid negative consequences for ourselves—such as feelings of sadness, anxiety, or guilt that would result if we did not help.

It should be noted that the two selections you will read were only the initial exchange in a series of articles that have debated the existence of altruism. In response to Cialdini's Negative State Relief Model, Batson has produced additional research that he believes demonstrates the existence of true altruism. Despite Batson's efforts, the debate over altruism continues to this day.

POINT

- We sometimes help others for altruistic reasons
- Altruistic helping is a result of empathic feelings for others.
- Experimental evidence supports the importance of empathy in generating altruistic helping behavior.

COUNTERPOINT

- Other motivations besides altruism can explain helping behavior.
- We may help others to reduce our own distress rather than to reduce the distress of others.
- Experimental evidence has not conclusively demonstrated that people have purely altruistic reasons.

C. Daniel Batson, Bruce D. Duncan,
Paula Ackerman, Terese Buckley,
and Kimberly Birch

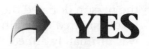 **YES**

Is Empathic Emotion a Source of Altruistic Motivation?

Evidence indicates that feeling empathy for the person in need is an important motivator of helping (cf. Aderman & Berkowitz, 1970; Aronfreed & Paskal, cited in Aronfreed, 1970; Coke, Batson, & McDavis, 1978; Harris & Huang, 1973; Krebs, 1975; Mehrabian & Epstein, 1972). In the past few years, a number of researchers (Aronfreed, 1970; Batson, Darley, & Coke, 1978; Hoffman, 1975; Krebs, 1975) have hypothesized that this motivation might be truly altruistic, that is, directed toward the end-state goal of reducing the other's distress. If the empathy-altruism hypothesis is correct, it would have broad theoretical implications, for few if any major theories of motivation allow for the possibility of truly altruistic motivation (cf. Bolles, 1975, for a review). Current theories tend to be egoistic; they are built on the assumption that everything we do is ultimately directed toward the end-state goal of benefiting ourselves.

The egoistic orientation of modern psychology should not be dismissed lightly; it has prevailed for decades, and it can easily account for what might appear to be altruistic motivation arising from empathic emotion. To illustrate: You may answer the question of why you helped someone in other-directed, altruistic terms—you felt sorry for that person and wished to reduce his or her distress. But this apparently altruistic concern to reduce another's distress may not have been the end-state goal of your action but rather an intermediate means to the ultimate end of reducing *your own* distress. Your own distress could have arisen not only from the unpleasant emotions you experienced as a result of knowing that the other person was suffering (shock, disgust, fear, or grief) but from the increase in unpleasant emotion you anticipated if you did not help (guilt or shame). Interpreted in this way, your helping was not altruistic. It was an instrumental egoistic response. You acted to reduce the other person's distress because that reduced your own distress.

If we allow that apparently altruistic helping may be no more than an instrumental egoistic response, and we believe that we must, then there is no clear empirical evidence that empathic emotion leads to altruistic motivation to help. The difficulty in providing evidence is, of course, that egoism and altruism are motivational concepts, and we cannot directly observe motiva-

From *Journal of Personality and Social Psychology*, vol. 40, no. 2, 1981, pp. 290–302. Copyright ©
1981 by American Psychological Association. Reprinted with permission.

350

tion, only behavior. If we are to provide empirical evidence that empathic emotion leads to altruistic motivation, we need to identify some point at which the egoistic and altruistic interpretations differ at a behavioral level. If no such point can be found, then we must conclude that the claim that empathy evokes altruistic motivation is of no real theoretical significance.

Conceptual Distinction between Egoism and Altruism

In an attempt to find a point of behavioral difference, it is important, first, to be clear about the points of conceptual difference. Therefore, let us be explicit about what we mean by egoistic and altruistic motivation for helping. As we shall use the terms, a person's helping is egoistic to the degree that he or she helps from a desire for personal gain (e.g., material rewards, praise, or self-esteem) or a desire to avoid personal pain (e.g., punishment, social castigation, private guilt, or shame). That is, *egoistically motivated helping is directed toward the end-state goal of increasing the helper's own welfare.* In contrast, a person's helping is altruistic to the degree that he or she helps from a desire to reduce the distress or increase the benefit of the person in need. That is, *altruistically motivated helping is directed toward the end-state goal of increasing the other's welfare.*

This conceptual distinction between egoism and altruism leads to three observations: (a) Helping, as a behavior, can be either egoistically or altruistically motivated; it is the end-state goal, not the behavior, that distinguishes an act as altruistic. (b) Motivation for helping may be a mixture of altruism and egoism; it need not be solely or even primarily altruistic to have an altruistic component. (c) Increasing the other's welfare is both necessary and sufficient to attain an altruistic end-state goal. To the degree that helping is altruistically rather than egoistically motivated, increasing the other's welfare is not an intermediate, instrumental response directed toward increasing one's own welfare; it is an end in itself. Although one's own welfare may be increased by altruistically motivated helping (for example, it may produce feelings of personal satisfaction or relief), personal gain must be an unintended by-product and not the goal of the behavior. This conception of altruism and of the distinction between it and egoism seem quite consistent not only with Auguste Comte's (1875) initial use of the term but also with modern dictionary definitions, for example, "unselfish concern for the welfare of others."

Empirical Distinction between Egoism and Altruism

Equipped with this conceptual distinction, we may turn to the problem of making an empirical distinction between egoistic and altruistic motivation for helping. As we have said, all we can directly observe is the behavior, helping. The challenge is somehow to use the behavior as a basis for inferring whether the motivation underlying it is egoistic or altruistic.

Batson and Coke (1981) have recently proposed a technique for doing this. Building on the work of Piliavin and Piliavin (1973), they point out that the effect on helping of a cost variable—the cost of escaping from the need situation without helping—should be different, depending on whether the bystander's motivation is egoistic or altruistic. If the bystander's motivation is egoistic, his or her goal is to reduce personal distress caused by seeing the other suffer. This goal can be reached either by helping, and so removing the cause of one's distress, or by escaping (physically or psychologically) and so removing contact with the cause; either behavior can lead to the desired goal. The likelihood that the egoistically motivated bystander will choose to help should, therefore, be a direct function of the costs associated with choosing to escape. These costs include the physical effort involved in escaping from the need situation (often minimal) and, more importantly, the feelings of distress, guilt, and shame anticipated as a result of knowing that the person in need is continuing to suffer. Thus, if the bystander were egoistically motivated and all other variables were held constant, increasing the cost of escaping by, for example, preventing the bystander from leaving the scene of the accident and so making it hard to avoid thinking about the continuing distress of the unhelped victim should increase the rate of helping. Conversely, reducing the costs of escaping by, for example, making it easy for the bystander to leave the scene of the accident and thus avoid thinking about the victim's continuing distress should decrease the rate of helping.

If the bystander's motivation is altruistic, his or her goal is to reduce the other's distress. This goal can be reached by helping, but not by escaping. Therefore, the likelihood that the altruistically motivated bystander will help should be independent of the cost of escaping because escaping is a goal-irrelevant behavior. Increasing or decreasing the cost of escaping should have no effect on the rate of helping; the rate should remain as high when escape is easy as when it is difficult.

These predictions suggest a way of determining whether the motivation for helping is egoistic or altruistic. The motivation cannot be inferred from any single behavioral response, but it can be inferred from the *pattern* of helping responses presented in Table 1. To the extent that the motivation for helping is egoistic, the helping rate should be affected by the difficulty of escaping. The easier it is to escape continued exposure to the need situation, the lower the cost of escaping and the less chance of a bystander's helping. But to the extent that the motivation for helping is altruistic, the helping rate should be unaffected by the difficulty of escaping; helping should be just as high when escape is easy as when it is difficult.[1]

Table 1
Rate of Helping When Difficulty of Escape Is Varied and Motivation Is Egoistic or Altruistic

Difficulty of escape	Type of motivation (level of empathic emotion)	
	Egoistic (low empathy)	Altruistic (high empathy)
Easy	Low	High
Difficult	High	High

Application to the Problem of the Motivation Resulting From Empathic Emotion

Now let us apply this general technique for discriminating between egoistic and altruistic motivation to the specific question of whether empathic emotion leads to altruistic motivation to help. If the motivation associated with feeling empathy for the person in need is altruistic (the empathy–altruism hypothesis), individuals induced to feel a high degree of empathy should help regardless of whether escape is easy or difficult (column 2 of Table 1); individuals feeling little empathy should help only when escape is difficult (column 1). Thus, if empathy leads to altruistic motivation to help, one can relabel the columns in Table 1, as has been done in parentheses. If, however, the motivation to help resulting from empathic emotion is egoistic, as seems to be implied by those who speak of "empathic pain," helping in the high-empathy condition should be affected by the ease of escape. Then we would expect to observe two main effects: As in previous research, high empathy should lead to more helping than low empathy, presumably as a result of an increase in feelings of personal distress or in anticipated guilt or shame. And in each empathy condition difficult escape should lead to more helping than easy escape.

Note that the entire one-versus-three interaction pattern depicted in Table 1 is important if one is to provide evidence for the empathy–altruism hypothesis. If, for example, one were to compare the easy and difficult escape cells only in the column marked altruistic motivation (high empathy), the altruistic prediction is for no difference in the rate of helping. Such a result could easily occur simply because the escape manipulation was too weak or the behavioral measure was insensitive. If, however, an escape manipulation has a significant effect on helping when a bystander feels little empathy but does not when a bystander feels much empathy, the evidence that empathic emotion evokes altruistic motivation is much stronger. Then the evidence cannot be dismissed as being the result of a weak escape manipulation or an insensitive measure.

It is also clear that one must be on guard for a possible ceiling effect. A ceiling effect in the high-empathy column could obscure the two-main-effect pattern that would be expected if the motivation were egoistic, making it look like the one-versus-three interaction that would be expected if the motivation were altruistic.

Present Research

We conducted two experiments to test the hypothesis that empathic emotion leads to altruistic motivation to help. As suggested by the preceding analysis, a 2×2 design was used in each. Subjects observed a young woman named Elaine receiving electric shocks; they were given an unanticipated chance to help her by volunteering to take the remaining shocks in her stead. Cost of escaping without helping was manipulated by making escape either easy or difficult. Subjects believed that if they did not take Elaine's place, either they would continue to observe her take the shocks (difficult escape condition) or they would not (easy escape condition). Level of empathic emotion (low versus high) was manipulated differently in the two experiments. Following the classic studies of Stotland (1969) and Krebs (1975), in Experiment 1 we used similarity information to manipulate empathy. In Experiment 2 we sought to manipulate empathy more directly through the use of an a emotion-specific misattribution to a placebo. In both experiments, the empathy–altruism hypothesis predicted that helping responses would conform to the one-versus-three pattern depicted in Table 1.

Experiment 1

There is evidence (e.g., Hornstein, 1976; Krebs, 1975; Stotland, 1969) that people are more likely to identify with a person they perceive to be similar to themselves and, as a result, to feel more empathy for a similar than for a dissimilar other. In the clearest demonstration of this relationship, Krebs (1975) manipulated male subjects' perceptions of their similarity to a young man (an experimental confederate) prior to having them watch him perform in a roulette game in which he received money if the ball landed on an even number and an electric shock if the ball landed on an odd number. Similarity was manipulated by telling subjects that their responses to a personality test completed several days earlier indicated that they and the performer were either similar or different. In addition, subjects received information suggesting that the performer's values and interests were either similar or different from their own. Compared with subjects in the dissimilar condition, subjects who perceived themselves to be similar to the performer showed greater physiological arousal in response to his pleasure and pain, reported identifying with him to a greater degree, and reported feeling worse while waiting for him to receive shock. These subjects also subsequently helped him more. But it was not clear whether the motivation to help was egoistic or altruistic. To clarify this issue, we used a procedure similar to Krebs's but varied perceived similarity and difficulty of escape in a 2 × 2 factorial design.

Method

Subjects

Subjects were 44 female introductory psychology students at the University of Kansas participating in partial fulfillment of a course requirement. They were randomly selected from those who had completed a personal value and interest questionnaire, which formed the basis for the similarity manipulation, at a screening session held a few weeks earlier. Subjects were assigned to the four conditions of the 2 (easy versus difficult escape) × 2 (similar versus dissimilar victim) design through the use of a randomized block procedure, 11 subjects to each cell. Four additional participants, one from each cell, were excluded from the design because they suspected Elaine was not actually receiving shocks.

Procedure

...On arrival, subjects were told that they would have to wait a few minutes for the arrival of a second subject, Elaine (actually a confederate). They were given an introduction to read while waiting:

> In this experiment we are studying task performance and impression projection under stressful conditions. We are investigating, as well, whether any inefficiency that might result from working under aversive conditions increases proportionately with the amount of time spent working under such conditions.
>
> Since this study requires the assistance of two participants, there will be a drawing to determine which role will be yours. One participant will perform a task (consisting of up to, but not more than, ten trials) under aversive conditions; the aversive conditions will be created by the presentation of electric shock at random intervals during the work period. The other participant will observe the individual working under aversive conditions, This role involves the formation and report of general attitudes towards the "worker" so that we may better assess what effect, if any, working under aversive conditions has upon how that individual is perceived.

After reading the introduction and signing a consent form, subjects drew lots for their role. The drawing was rigged so that they always drew the observer role.

Subjects were then escorted to the observation room and given more detailed instructions. They learned that they would not actually meet the worker but would instead observe her over closed-circuit television as she performed up to 10 2-min, digit-recall trials. At random intervals during each trial, the worker would receive moderately uncomfortable electric shocks. The instructions went on to explain that equipment limitations made it impossible to capture visually all of the worker's reactions and that this was a problem, since prior research suggested that nonverbal cues were important in assessing another person's emotional state. To compensate for this lost information, the worker would be connected to a galvanic skin response (GSR) monitor, which would be visible in the lower right-hand corner of the television screen. The level of arousal indicated on the monitor would enable the subjects to assess more accurately the worker's emotional response, and help them form an impression.

Difficulty of escape manipulation.   To manipulate difficulty of escape without helping, the last line of the detailed instructions varied the number of trials that subjects expected to observe. In the easy-escape condition, subjects read: "Although the worker will be completing between two and ten trials, it will be necessary for you to observe only the first two." In the difficult escape condition they read: "The worker will be completing between two and ten trials, all of which you will observe." All subjects were later to learn that Elaine agreed to complete all 10 trials, and they were given the chance to help her by trading places after the second trial. Therefore, in the easy-escape condition, subjects who did not help would not have to watch Elaine take any more shocks; in the difficult-escape condition they would.

Similarity manipulation.   After the subject finished reading the detailed instructions, the experimenter handed her a copy of the personal values and interest questionnaire administered at the screening session, explaining that this copy had been filled out by Elaine and would provide information about her that might be of help in forming an impression. Elaine's questionnaire was prepared in advance so that it reflected values and interests that were either very similar or very dissimilar to those the subject had expressed on her questionnaire. In the similar-victim condition, Elaine's responses to six items that had only two possible answers (e.g., "If you had a choice, would you prefer living in a rural or an urban setting?") were identical to those the subject had given; her responses to the other eight items were similar but not identical (e.g., "What is your favorite magazine?" Answers: *Cosmopolitan* for the subject, *Seventeen* for Elaine; *Time* for the subject, *Newsweek* for Elaine). In the dissimilar-victim condition, Elaine's responses to the six two-answer items were the opposite of those the subject had given, and her responses to the other eight were clearly different (e.g., *Cosmopolitan* for the subject, *Newsweek* for Elaine)....

While the subject looked over Elaine's questionnaire, the experimenter left to see if Elaine had arrived. She returned to say that she had and that the subject could now begin observing her over the closed-circuit television. So saying, the experimenter turned on a video monitor, allowing the subject to see Elaine. Unknown to the subject, what she saw was actually a videotape.

Need situation.   On the videotape, subjects first saw Elaine, a moderately attractive young woman, tell the research assistant (female) that she would complete all 10 of the digit-recall trials. As the assistant was going over the procedure, Elaine interrupted to ask about the nature of the electric shocks that were to be used. The assistant answered that the shocks would be of constant intensity and, although uncomfortable, would cause "no permanent damage." "You know if you scuff your feet walking across a carpet and touch something metal? Well, they'll be about two to three times more uncomfortable than that."

After GSR electrodes were attached to the first and third fingers on Elaine's nondominant hand and a shock electrode was attached to her other arm, the digit-recall trials began. The experimenter left subjects alone at this point. As the first trial progressed, Elaine's facial expressions, body movement, and the GSR monitor all indicated that she was finding the shocks extremely unpleasant. By midway through the second trial, her reactions were so strong that the assistant interrupted the procedure to ask if Elaine were all right. Elaine answered that she was but would appreciate having a glass of water. The assistant readily agreed to this request and went to get the water....

Returning with the glass of water, the assistant asked Elaine if she had ever had trouble with shocks before. Elaine confessed that she had—as a child she had been thrown from a horse onto an electric fence. The doctor had said at the time that she suffered a bad trauma and in the future might react strongly to even mild shocks. (This information was provided to ensure that subjects would view Elaine's extreme reaction to the shocks as atypical and would not expect to find the shocks as unpleasant if they chose to take her place.) Hearing this, the assistant said that she did not think Elaine should continue with the trials. Elaine replied that even though she found the shocks very unpleasant, she wanted to go on: "I started; I want to finish. I'll go on ... I know your experiment is important, and I want to do it." At this point, the assistant hit upon an idea: Since the observer was also an introductory psychology student, maybe she would be willing to help Elaine out by trading places. Elaine readily consented to the assistant checking about this possibility. The assistant said that she would shut off the equipment and go talk with the experimenter about it. Shortly thereafter, the video screen went blank.

Dependent measure: Helping Elaine.   About 30 sec later, the experimenter entered the observation room and said:

> First of all, let me say that you're under no obligation to trade places. I mean, if you would like to continue in your role as observer that's fine; you did happen to draw the observer role. If you decide to continue as the observer, ([easy-escape condition] you've finished observing the two trials, so all you need to do is answer a few questions about your impression of Elaine and you'll be free to go) ([difficult-escape condition] I need you to observe Elaine's remaining trials. After you've done that and answered a few questions about your impression of Elaine, you'll be free to go). If you decide to change places with Elaine, what will happen is that she'll come in here and observe you, and you'll do the aversive conditioning trials with the shocks. And then you'll be free to go.
>   What would you like to do? [Experimenter gets response from subject.] OK, that's fine. [If subject says she wants to trade places with Elaine, the experimenter continues.] How many trials would you like to do? Elaine will go ahead and do any of the eight remaining trials that you don't want to do. [Experimenter gets response.] Fine.

The experimenter then left, ostensibly to go tell the assistant what had been decided. In fact, she recorded whether the subject wanted to trade places and, if so, how many of the eight remaining trials she would do. This information provided the dependent measure of helping. Then the experimenter made herself aware of the subject's similarity condition.

Debriefing.   The experimenter returned promptly and fully debriefed the subject. Subjects seemed readily to understand the necessity for the deception involved in the experiment, and none seemed upset by it. After debriefing, subjects were thanked for their participation and excused.

Results and Discussion
Relieving Elaine's Distress by Helping
The proportion of subjects in each experimental condition who offered to help Elaine by trading places is presented in Table 2.... The 2 × 2 analysis revealed a highly significant main effect for similarity, $\chi^2(1) = 11.69$, $p < .001$ qualified by a significant Escape × Similarity interaction, $\chi^2(1) = 4.19$, $p < .04$. The main effect for difficulty of escape did not approach significance, $\chi^2(1) = 1.34$, $p < .20$.

Table 2

Proportion of Subjects Agreeing to Trade Places with Elaine in Each Condition of Experiment 1

| | Similarity condition | | | |
| | Dissimilar victim | | Similar victim | |
Difficulty of escape condition	Proportion	M no.[a]	Proportion	M no.[a]
Easy	.18	1.09	.91	7.09
Difficult	.64	4.00	.82	5.00

Note. $n = 11$ in each condition.
[a] Mean number of shock trials (from 0 to 8) that subjects agreed to take for Elaine ($MS_e. = 9.70$, $df = 40$).

Inspection of the proportion of helping each condition revealed that the interaction, was of the form predicted by the empathy–altruism hypothesis; the proportion in the easy-escape–dissimilar–victim condition was much lower than in the other three conditions. To test the statistical significance of this predicted one-versus-three pattern, the rate of helping in this condition was contrasted with the rate in the other three conditions. This planned comparison revealed a highly significant difference, $\chi^2(1) = 14.62$, $p < .001$.... Individual cell comparisons revealed that, as predicted, the proportion of helping in the easy-escape–dissimilar-victim condition was significantly lower than the proportion in each of the other three conditions (zs ranging from 2.27 to 3.87, all $ps < .015$, one-tailed). Comparisons among the other three conditions revealed no reliable differences (all $zs < 1.60$).

With one exception, an identical pattern of significant effects emerged from analysis of variance and planned comparisons one the number of shock trials subjects in each condition volunteered to take for Elaine. The one exception was that the number of trials was significantly lower in the two difficult-escape conditions (pooled) than in the easy-escape–similar-victim condition, $t(40) = 2.25$, $p < .03$, two-tailed.

These results were quite consistent with the empathy–altruism hypothesis; they were not consistent with the view that empathy simply increases egoistic motivation to help. In the dissimilar-victim condition, where empathic emotional response to Elaine's distress was expected to be relatively low and according to the empathy–altruism hypothesis, the motivation to help was expected to be primarily egoistic, the difficulty of escape manipulation had a dramatic effect on helping. When escape was easy, subjects were not likely to help, presumably because a less costly way to reduce any personal distress caused by watching Elaine receive shock was to answer the experimenter's final questions and leave. When escape was difficult, subjects were likely to help, presumably because taking the remaining shocks themselves was less costly than sitting and watching Elaine take more.

In the similar-victim conditions, however, where empathic emotional response to Elaine's distress was expected to be relatively high and, according to the empathy–altruism hypothesis, the motivation to help should be at least in part altruistic, difficulty of escape had no effect on subjects' readiness to help. Presumably, because their concern was to reduce Elaine's distress and not just their own, they were very likely to help, even when escape was easy....

Overall, the results of Experiment 1 seemed to conform closely to the one-versus-three pattern that, according to Table 1, would be expected if increased empathic emotion led to altruistic motivation; they did not conform to the two-main-effect pattern that would be expected if increased empathy led to egoistic motivation. Still, although Stotland (1969) and Krebs (1975) had provided rather strong evidence that a similarity manipulation like the one used in Experiment 1 manipulated empathic emotion, the manipulation was indirect. Therefore, a second experiment was conducted in which we sought to test the empathy-altruism hypothesis by manipulating empathic emotion more directly....

General Discussion

As we noted at the outset, the hypothesis that empathic emotion produces truly altruistic motivation contradicts the egoistic assumption of most, if not all, current theories of motivation. Because egoism is a widely held and basic assumption, it is only prudent to require that the evidence supporting altruism be strong before this hypothesis is accepted.

To the degree that the conceptual analysis and resulting predictions presented in Table 1 provide an adequate framework for an empirical test of truly altruistic motivation, the two experiments reported here seem to make an initial step toward providing such evidence....

It may be, then, too early to conclude that empathic emotion can lead to altruistic motivation. But if future research produces the same pattern of results found in the experiments reported here, this conclusion, with all its theoretical and practical implications, would seem not only possible but necessary. For now, the research to date convinces us of the legitimacy of *suggesting* that empathic motivation for helping may be truly altruistic. In doing so, we are left far less confident than we were of reinterpretations of apparently altruistically motivated helping in terms of instrumental egoism.

Note

1. It is worth noting that another cost variable, the cost of helping, is frequently thought to be the key to altruism. If helping occurs when the cost of helping is high (at the extreme, when the helper's life is in danger), this is thought to be evidence of altruistic motivation. A little reflection shows that such an inference is unfounded, for even highly costly helping could easily be an instrumental egoistic response, motivated by a desire to avoid guilt or to attain praise and honor either in this life or an anticipated life to come.

References

Aderman, D., & Berkowitz, L. Observational set, empathy, and helping. *Journal of Personality and Social Psychology*, 1970, *14*, 141–148.

Aronfreed, J. M. The socialization of altruistic and sympathetic behavior: Some theoretical and experimental analyses. In J. Macaulay & L. Berkowitz (Eds.), *Altruism and helping behavior*. New York: Academic Press, 1970.

Batson, C. D., & Coke, J. S. Empathy: A source of altruistic motivation for helping. In J. P. Rushton & R. M. Sorrentino (Eds.), *Altruism and helping behavior*. Hillsdale, N.J.: Erlbaum, 1981.

Batson, C. D., Darley, J. M., & Coke, J. S. Altruism and human kindness: Internal and external determinants of helping behavior. In L. Pervin & M. Lewis (Eds.), *Perspectives in interactional psychology*. New York: Plenum Press, 1978.

Bolles, R. D. *Theory of motivation* (2nd ed.). New York: Harper & Row,1975.

Coke, J. S., Batson, C. D., & McDavis, K. Empathic mediation of helping: A two-stage model. *Journal of Personality and Social Psychology*, 1978, *36*, 752–766.

Comte, I. A. *System of positive polity* (Vol. 1). London: Longmans, Green, 1875.

Harris, M. B., & Huang, L. C. Helping and the attribution process. *Journal of Social Psychology*, 1973, *90*, 291–297.

Hoffman, M. L. Developmental synthesis of affect and cognition and its implications for altruistic motivation. *Developmental Psychology*, 1975, *11*, 607–622.

Hornstein, H. A. *Cruelty and kindness: A new look at aggression and altruism*. Englewood Cliffs, N.J.: Prentice-Hall, 1976.

Krebs, D. L. Empathy and altruism. *Journal of Personality and Social Psychology*, 1975, *32*, 1134–1146.

Mehrabian, A., & Epstein, N. A measure of emotional empathy. *Journal of Personality*, 1972, *40*, 525–543.

Piliavin, J. A., & Piliavin, L. M. *The Good Samaritan: Why does he help?* Unpublished manuscript, University of Wisconsin, 1973.

Stotland, E. Exploratory investigations of empathy. In L. Berkowitz (Ed.), *Advances in experimental social psychology* (Vol. 3). New York: Academic Press, 1969.

NO ↵

**Robert B. Cialdini, Mark Schaller,
Donald Houlihan, Kevin Arps,
Jim Fultz, and Arthur L. Beaman**

Empathy-Based Helping:
Is It Selflessly or Selfishly Motivated?

The existence of pure altruism among humans has been a topic of long-standing debate in both philosophical and general psychological circles (see, e.g., Bentham, 1789/1879; Campbell, 1975; Comte, 1851/1875; Hoffman, 1981; Hume, 1740/1896; McDougall, 1908). Recent attention to this issue within social psychology has been stimulated by the contributions of Batson and his associates (Batson, 1984; Batson & Coke, 1981; Batson, Duncan, Ackerman, Buckley, & Birch, 1981; Batson, O'Quin, Fultz, Vanderplas, & Isen, 1983; Coke, Batson, & McDavis, 1978; Toi & Batson, 1982). The significance of the work of these last authors lies in their presentation of an experimental method for assessing the possibility of selflessly motivated aid and in their presentation of systematic empirical support for the existence of such aid among empathically oriented subjects. If research continues to verify their data and conceptual analysis, they will have provided the first persuasive argument that we are capable of truly selfless action. The implications for fundamental characterizations of human nature are considerable.

In constructing their experimental method, Batson and his colleagues proposed that an observer of a suffering other is likely to react in one of two primary ways to the victim's plight: by reducing the other's need through helping or by escaping the situation. The egoistically motivated observer would be expected to choose the option entailing the smallest personal cost (Piliavin, Dovidio, Gaertner, & Clark, 1981). An altruistically motivated observer, however, should be principally concerned with reducing the other's suffering. Although the operations have changed from study to study, the basic paradigm of these researchers is as follows: Subjects are exposed to the plight of a suffering victim under conditions of high or low empathy for the victim. The subjects are next given the opportunity to aid the victim under conditions that allow them easy or difficult escape from the helping situation. The consequence is a factorial design crossing two levels of the empathy factor (high vs. low) with two levels of the escape factor (easy vs. difficult).

On the basis of the hypothesis that selflessly motivated helping occurs under conditions of high empathic concern for a victim, Batson and his colleagues predicted a three-versus-one pattern of helping within the design.

From *Journal of Personality and Social Psychology*, vol. 52, no. 4, 1987, pp. 749–758. Copyright © 1987 by American Psychological Association. Reprinted with permission.

That is, they suggested that the factor of ease of escape from the helping situation should play a role in a subject's helping decision only when the subject's behavior is motivated by egoistic concerns. Thus, when subjects are not oriented toward others (low empathy), they should help less when escape from helping is easy than when it is difficult. However, when empathy is high, egoistic concerns such as ease of escape are dwarfed by the subject's primarily altruistic motive to relieve the victim's suffering; highly empathic subjects, then, should help at elevated levels whether escape from the helping situation is easy or difficult. This predicted pattern—that subjects in the low-empathy, easy-escape condition will help less than subjects in the other three cell of the design—has been borne out repeatedly in the previously cited studies (e.g., Batson et al., 1981; Batson et al., 1983; Toi & Batson, 1982).

A critical piece of support for the selfless altruism explanation of this data pattern has come from the elevated helping scores of subjects in the high-empathy, easy-escape condition of the design. According to the selfless altruism interpretation, the heightened benevolence of these subjects occurs because their empathic state motivates them to help the victim with little regard for egoistic considerations (such as the ease of escape) that would otherwise reduce aid. Yet, there is at least one alternative interpretation that could explain this finding in egoistic terms. That is, it may be that an empathic orientation causes individuals viewing a suffering victim to feel enhanced sadness. A substantial body of research exists to indicate that temporary states of sadness or sorrow reliably increase helping in adults (for reviews see Cialdini, Kenrick, & Baumann, 1982, and Rosenhan, Karylowski, Salovey, & Hargis, 1981), especially when the sadness is caused by another's plight (Thompson, Cowan, & Rosenhan, 1980). Moreover, the research of Cialdini and his associates has suggested that these saddened subjects help for egoistic reasons: to relieve the sadness in themselves rather than to relieve the victim's suffering (Baumann, Cialdini, & Kenrick, 1981; Cialdini, Darby, & Vincent, 1973; Cialdini & Kenrick, 1976; Kenrick, Baumann, & Cialdini, 1979; Manucia, Baumann, & Cialdini, 1984). Because helping contains a rewarding component for most normally socialized adults (Baumann et al., 1981; Harris, 1977; Weiss, Buchanan, Alstatt, & Lombardo, 1971), it can be used instrumentally to restore mood.

Thus, it may be that in the typical experiment of Batson and his associates the high-empathy procedures increased helping not for selfless reasons, but for an entirely egoistic reason: personal mood management. It is important to recognize that the mood at issue is rather specific to the temporary state of sadness or sorrow. Cialdini and his coworkers have argued (see Cialdini, Baumann, & Kenrick, 1981) that their data on negative mood effects implicate only temporary sadness in the enhancement of helping, and they have repeatedly asserted that other negative moods that are normally not reduced through benevolence (e.g., anger, frustration, agitation, anxiety) consequently would not be expected to increase helping. This distinction among negative moods may help explain why, in the research of Batson and associates, an index of personal distress has not been systematically related to helping among high-empathy subjects. The adjectives making up this index (e.g., *alarmed, disturbed, upset, worried*) are agitation or anxiety based rather than sadness based. Because empathic concern, sadness, and distress all involve negative feelings, we would expect them to be strongly intercorrelated. At the same time, however, we see them as functionally distinct in their relation to helping.

A major implication of our analysis, then, is that empathy-induced helping in the Batson et al. design is mediated by the increased sadness of high-empathy subjects witnessing a suffering other and that the help is an egoistic response designed to dispel the temporary depression. This interpretation is crucially different from that of Batson and his colleagues, in which empathy is said to stimulate helping through a selfless concern for the welfare of others. To test these alternative explanations against one another, it would be necessary to separate subjects' feelings of sadness from the empathic orientation that is said to bring about that sadness. Our first experiment sought to provide such a test by (a) replicating the basic Batson et al. empathy procedures for all subjects; (b) presenting some subjects with a gratifying event (money or praise) designed to relieve any sadness that an empathic orientation may have produced, without simultaneously interfering with that empathic orientation; (c) allowing subjects the opportunity to help a victim or escape the situation; and (d) assessing whether subjects' helping tendencies are related primarily to Batson's measures of empathic concern or to traditional measures of sadness.

The experimental design, then, included a replication of the standard four cells of the paradigm of Batson and his associates (two levels of empathy orientation and two levels of ease of escape). We also included additional high-empathy orientation cells in which subjects received a gratifying event (either money or praise) between the empathy manipulation and the chance to help. From our egoistic, sadness-based interpretation of helping in the Batson et al. paradigm, we made the following predictions. First, subjects in the high-empathy conditions of the Batson et al. design would show (Prediction 1a) greater empathic concern and (Prediction 1b) greater sadness than would those in the low-empathy conditions of that design. This pair of predictions, if confirmed, would establish the possibility that the helping pattern of previous Batson et al. studies was not caused by the action of empathic concern but by the action of sadness. Second, high-empathy subjects who received a gratifying intervention would have their (Prediction 2a) greater sadness but (Prediction 2b) not their greater empathic concern canceled by the gratifying events. This pair of predictions, if confirmed, would provide the basis for a test of whether empathic concern or sadness was functionally related to helping in this design. Third, high-empathy subjects who did not receive a sadness canceling intervention (i.e., those subjects expected to show the greatest sadness) would show greater helping than all other subjects (i.e., those subjects in whom enhanced sadness was canceled or in whom enhanced sadness had not been experimentally induced). If confirmed, this prediction (Prediction 3) would support the idea that empathically oriented subjects in this study and in the general Batson et al. paradigm help for a primarily egoistic reason (i.e., personal mood management) rather than a primarily selfless reason (i.e., concern for the other's welfare).

Experiment 1

Method

Subjects   Eighty-seven introductory psychology students at Arizona State University participated in the study as partial fulfillment of a course requirement. Six subjects were dropped from the analyses because they expressed suspicion about the legitimacy of the need situation. These subjects were distributed approximately evenly across experimental conditions.

Procedure.   With the exception of a different empathy manipulation and several changes necessary for the inclusion of the rewards manipulation, the procedures of the study followed those of Batson et al. (1981, Experiment 1) and Batson et al. (1983, Experiment 1). Only the manipulations and important changes are described in detail here.

All subjects were randomly assigned to conditions and run individually by either a male or a female experimenter. On arrival, subjects read a short introduction while waiting for the other subject, "Elaine," to appear. They read that one subject—the worker—would be performing a series of learning trials while receiving mild electric shocks, and the other—the observer—would watch her and form impressions. The instructions went on to say that because the study involved personal perceptions of others, it would be necessary to have subjects take a short personality test as well. The subject then drew lots to determine whether she would be the worker or the observer. The drawing was rigged so the subject always drew the role of the observer. The experimenter then ushered the subject into an experimental room where she was told she would be watching the worker over closed-circuit television.

At this point, the subject was given the "Remington–Hughe Scale of Social Abilities." The experimenter stated that this was a previously validated instrument that was shown to measure social abilities very reliably. The test was actually the Marlowe-Crowne Social Desirability Scale (Crowne & Marlowe, 1964). The experimenter left, announcing that she or he would check to see if the other subject had arrived yet.

Ease-of-escape manipulation.   When subjects finished the scale, the experimenter returned and began telling them what they would be watching over the closed-circuit television. At this time, the experimenter introduced the escape manipulation. Subjects in the easy-escape condition were told, "Although the worker will be completing between two and ten trials, it will be necessary for you to observe only the first two." Subjects in the difficult-escape condition were told, "The worker will be completing between two and ten trials, all of which you will observe."

Empathy-set manipulation.   Just before turning on the television monitor, the experimenter presented subjects with written instructions on the perspective they should adopt while observing Elaine. These instructions were adapted from those used in research by Batson and his colleagues (Fultz, Batson, Fortenbach, McCarthy, & Varney, 1986; Toi & Batson, 1982). The experimenter was blind to the empathy-set manipulation. Subjects in the low-empathy-set condition read the following:

> While you are observing the trials, try to pay careful attention to the information presented. Try to be as objective as possible, carefully attending to all the information about the situation and about the person performing the trials. Try not to concern yourself with how the person performing the trials feels about what is happening. Just concentrate on trying to watch and listen objectively to the information presented.

Subjects in the high-empathy-set condition read the following:

> While you are observing the trials, try to imagine how the person performing them feels. Try to take the perspective of the person performing the trials, imagining how she feels and how it is affecting her. Try not to concern yourself with all of the information presented. Just try to imagine how the person performing the trials is feeling.

The videotape showed Elaine reacting more and more strongly to the shocks presented to her during the learning trials. Toward the end of the second trial, the assistant stopped the procedure and asked Elaine if she was all right. Elaine responded that she was, but would like a glass of water. The assistant agreed and left. During this break, the experimenter returned to the experimental room, turned off the television monitor and announced that as long as there was this break, they could do some things they would have to do anyway during the experiment.

Reward manipulation   To subjects in the high-empathy/money condition the experimenter said, "First of all, we were awarded some additional funding for this experiment to pay subjects, so everyone who participates gets one dollar." The experimenter gave the subject a $1 bill and then presented two short questionnaires to till out: a mood questionnaire and an emotional-reactions questionnaire. To subjects in the high-empathy/praise condition, the experimenter said that he or she had just scored the subject's responses on the Remington-Hughe scale and noted that the subject had scored a 26, indicating a high level of social ability. The subject was shown a brief explanation of her score:

> People scoring in this category have fine social abilities. They are normally liked by their peers, who enjoy spending time with them. This is so partially because people scoring in this category tend to be interesting and versatile conversationalists who can contribute intelligently on a fairly wide range of topics. They also bring a creative flare to the social situations they find enjoyable. Finally, they are known for their capacity for recognizing which of their friends and acquaintances will get along together.

After reading this false feedback, subjects were given the two questionnaires to fill out. In the high-empathy/no-rewards condition and the low-empathy condition, the experimenter simply presented subjects with the two questionnaires.

Mood and emotional-reactions questionnaires.   The order of the two questionnaires was counterbalanced across subjects. The mood questionnaire consisted of nine 7-point bipolar scales. On the first of these scales subjects were asked to rate how much happier or sadder they were relative to how they felt before the experimental session. On the other eight scales subjects were asked to rate how they presently felt. The poles of these eight scales were *depressed– elated, happy–sad, hopeful–hopeless, active–passive, good–bad, exhilarated– dejected, useless–useful,* and *satisfied–dissatisfied.* The emotional-reactions questionnaire was an abridged form of the list of 28 adjectives used in previous research (Batson et al, 1981, Experiment 2; Batson et al., 1983) and consisted of the 20 adjectives Batson and Coke (1981) found to load highly on either an empathic-concern factor (e.g., moved, compassionate, sympathetic) or a personal distress factor (e.g., *alarmed, upset, worried*). Subjects were asked to rate on 7-point scales the extent to which they were presently experiencing each of the emotions.

When the subject had finished filling out the questionnaires, the experimenter returned, announced that Elaine was about ready to start again, turned on the monitor, and left. Subjects saw the assistant ask Elaine about her strong reaction to the shocks and Elaine hesitantly reply that she had previously experienced problems with electric shock. The assistant suggested she not continue. Elaine resisted until the assistant suggested that perhaps the other subject—the observer—might be willing to help her out by trading places. Elaine acquiesced, the assistant left, and the screen went blank.

Dependent measure: Helping Elaine.   After about half a minute, the experimenter returned to the experimental room and began explaining to the subject what her options were, following verbatim the script used by Batson et al. (1981; 1983, Experiment 1). During this discourse, the experimenter reiterated the subject's escape condition: In the easy-escape condition, subjects were reminded that if they chose not to trade places they would be free to go; in the difficult-escape condition subjects were reminded that if they chose not to trade places they would have to remain and continue to watch Elaine perform the trials. Subjects were asked what they would like to do. If they volunteered to take Elaine's place, they were asked how many of the remaining trials they would like to do, as Elaine had agreed to do any of the remaining eight that the subject did not. The dependent measure was the number of trials subjects chose to do.

Debriefing.   The experimenter left briefly to note the subject's helping response and then returned and presented the subject with a brief questionnaire to assess subjects' suspicions about the procedures. This questionnaire asked subjects to describe what they thought the hypothesis of the experiment was and to note if they had entertained any doubts about any aspects of the procedures. After responding to these questions, subjects were verbally probed for suspicion and then fully debriefed.

Results

Reported empathic concern and distress.   To measure empathic concern, three adjectives from the emotional-response questionnaire were averaged to comprise an empathy index: *compassionate, moved,* and *sympathetic* (Cronbach's alpha = .60). These adjectives were selected to be consistent with those currently refined for use by Batson and his colleagues (e.g., Batson et al., 1983). To measure personal distress, five other adjectives from the same questionnaire were similarly selected: *alarmed, worried, upset, disturbed,* and *grieved* (Cronbach's alpha = .89). Two subjects were dropped from the analyses on reported empathy, and three were dropped from the analyses on reported distress because they did not respond to all the items on the appropriate index.

Two of the predictions of this experiment involved subjects' reported empathy scores. The first (la) stated that in the four replication cells of the Batson et al. paradigm, high-empathy-set subjects would report more empathic concern than would low-empathy-set subjects, replicating the prior Batson et al. results. This was the case, as the two high-empathy-set/no-reward cells (M = 5.40) showed greater empathic concern than did the two low-empathy-set/no-reward cells (M = 4.63), $F(1, 71)$ = 4.10, $p < .05$. The second empathy-related prediction (2b) suggested that the reward interventions of the current design would not interfere with the heightened empathic concern produced in the high-empathy-set conditions. Therefore, it was expected that the empathy index scores in the four high-empathy-set cells with a reward intervention (M = 5.10) would not differ from the two such cells without a reward intervention (M = 5.40) This prediction was also supported, $F(1, 71) < 1$....

Reported sadness.   It was suggested that an empathic orientation toward a suffering other may depress one's mood, leading to a state of temporary sadness or sorrow. Three of the 7-point scales on the mood questionnaire were relevant to this type of affect. On the first, subjects rated how much happier or sadder they felt relative to their mood before the experiment. On the other two, subjects rated their present mood on bipolar scales of *elated–depressed* and *happy–sad*. Responses on these three scales were averaged for each subject to form an overall index of mood (lower numbers indicating sadder mood). Not surprisingly, this resulting mood index was correlated with both the empathy index (r = −.44) and the distress index (r = −.49). The relation to empathy is clearly predicted by the Negative State Relief model; the relation to distress is not formally a part of the model but is to be expected, as both measure a negative emotion and both are related to empathy. Apparently because of a confusing placement in the mood questionnaire, 12 subjects failed to respond to the scale assessing relative change in mood, and these subjects were therefore dropped from the mood analyses.

A pair of experimental hypotheses directly involved the mood measure. The first (1b) predicted that within the four replication conditions (i.e., the no-reward cells of the present design), high-empathy-set subjects would show greater sadness than would low-empathy-set subjects. This prediction was confirmed, $F(1, 61) = 5.73$, $p < .02$ (Ms = 2.63 and 3.47, respectively). This outcome supports the contention that empathically oriented subjects experience a saddened mood when observing a suffering other. The second mood-related experimental prediction (2a) stated that the greater sadness of high-empathy set subjects would be canceled through the presentation of an unexpected reward such as money or praise. This prediction was tested by a set of contrasts showing that the high-empathy-set subjects who received a reward (M = 3.25) were equivalent in mood to the low-empathy-set subjects (M = 3.47), $F(1, 61) < 1$, and were less sad than the high-empathy-set subjects who had not received a reward (M = 2.63), $F(1, 61) = 3.81$, $p < .06$. Combined with the outcomes of the earlier analyses, these results support the argument that rewards such as those of this study will cancel the saddened mood but not the empathic orientation of subjects empathizing with a suffering other.

Helping.   The nature of the dependent variable allows for two, different helping measures: a continuous measure based on the number of learning trials for which subjects volunteered in taking Elaine's place, and a dichotomous measure based on the proportion of subjects in each condition who chose to help Elaine. Table 1 presents results on both measures. The analyses reported here are on the continuous measure. Parallel analyses were performed on the dichotomous measure, which yielded results consistent with those reported but short of conventional levels of significance.

Table 1

Experiment 1: Mean Scores on Empathic Concern, Mood, and Helping Measures

	High-empathy set			Low-empathy set
Ease of escape	Money	Praise	No reward	No reward
Easy				
Empathic concern	4.29	5.23	4.90	4.84
Mood	3.61	3.10	2.50	3.42
Helping	1.71 (29)	2.27 (45)	3.60 (50)	1.75 (33)
n	7	11	10	12
Difficult				
Empathic concern	5.24	5.41	5.85	4.40
Mood	3.40	2.92	2.73	3.52
Helping	1.82 (36)	4.00 (56)	4.73 (73)	2.60 (40)
n	11	9	11	10

Note. For the mood measure, lower scores represent more depressed mood; for the other measures, high scores indicate more of the quality. For the helping measure, proportions of helpers are presented in parentheses.

In keeping with our predictions, a pair of planned contrasts was performed. First, the helping scores of the high-empathy set subjects who did not receive a reward intervention ($M = 4.19$) were contrasted with the helping scores of the subjects in the other cells of the design (i.e., those subjects in whom enhanced sadness had been canceled or had not been experimentally induced; $M = 2.34$). This contrast proved significant, $F(1, 73) = 4.09$, $p < .05$. Second, the helping scores of the high-empathy-set subjects who received a reward intervention ($M = 2.45$) were tested against those of the low-empathy-set subjects ($M = 2.14$) and, as predicted, were found to be no different, $F(1, 73) < 1$. An additional contrast, somewhat redundant with the two reported above, showed that the difference in helping between high-empathy-set/reward and high-empathy-set/no-reward subjects was marginally significant, $F(1, 73) = 3.19$, $p < .08$.

Besides the tests of the experimental prediction regarding the helping measure, an additional analysis was conducted to determine whether the basic one-versus-three pattern of the Batson et al. paradigm showed the form of the traditional pattern, in that the easy-escape/low-empathy-set subjects helped the least ($M = 1.75$) compared with subjects in the other three no-reward conditions (combined $M = 3.68$), $F(1, 73) = 2.53$, $p < .12$. Although this difference is not conventionally significant, it would appear to be sufficient for the purpose of replication. The failure of this analysis to reach conventional significance is in large part a function of the unexpectedly low level of helping in the low-empathy-set/difficult-escape cell. Fortunately, helping scores in that particular cell hold relatively minor theoretical weight in our argument....

Discussion

In this study we sought to provide data to help to explain the frequently demonstrated tendency for empathically oriented individuals to be more helpful toward a needy other (Eisenberg & Miller, 1987). The Empathy–Altruism model of Batson and associates, which views empathically concerned individuals as primarily selfless in their approach to helping, was examined relative to the Negative State Relief model of Cialdini and associates, which posits the egoistic desire to manage personal sadness as a primary cause of helping in such individuals. To pose a proper test of these conceptually opposed models of helping, we considered it necessary to demonstrate several effects within the Batson et al. empathy–altruism paradigm: first, that empathic orientation toward a sufferer not only increased a person's empathic concern but also that person's sadness and, second, that the receipt of a gratifying event (money or praise) would serve to reduce the increased sadness but not the increased empathic concern. The results of the study supported both of these sets of conditions. Relevant high-empathy-set subjects reported greater empathic concern and sadness than did low-empathy-set subjects; furthermore, the receipt of a rewarding event by high-empathy-set subjects relieved their sadness but not their empathic concern. With these two sets of conditions in place, it was then possible to examine whether helping was related to manipulated levels of sadness or empathic concern. It was found that high-empathy-set subjects did show elevated helping scores, except when they had received a sadness-canceling reward, whereupon they were no more helpful than low-empathy-set subjects. Therefore, it appeared to be personal sadness rather than empathic concern that accounted for the increased helping motivation of our empathically oriented subjects....

Conclusion

The nature of benevolent motivation has been a long-standing issue of philosophical and psychological inquiry. Recently, psychologists have examined the role of empathy in the generation of and explanation of such motivation (see Eisenberg & Miller, 1987, and Hoffman, 1981, for reviews). An impressive and important body of research by Batson and his associates has repeatedly provided evidence for the selfless mediation of helping under conditions of heightened empathy for a needy other. The two studies reported here offer a reinterpretation of that evidence by associating increased personal sadness with such empathy and by supporting the egoistic motive of sadness reduction as the mediator of this form of helping. We recognize fully that no mere pair of experiments is capable of resolving so fundamental a question as the motivational nature of benevolence; accordingly, we do not see our studies in such light. Instead, we view them as providing a plausible egoistic explanation for the first powerful experimental evidence for pure altruism.

References

Batson, C. D., & Coke, J. S. (1981). Empathy: A source of altruistic motivation for helping? In J. P. Rushton & R. M. Sorrentino (Eds.), *Altruism and helping behavior: Social, personality, and developmental perspectives* (pp. 167–187). Hillsdale, NJ: Erlbaum.

Baumann, D. J., Cialdini, R. B., & Kenrick, D. T. (1981). Altruism as hedonism: Helping and self-gratification as equivalent responses. *Journal of Personality and Social Psychology, 40,* 1039–1046.

Bentham, J. (1879). *An introduction to the principles of morals and legislation.* Oxford, England: Clarendon Press. (Original work published 1789)

Cialdini, R. B., Darby, B. L., & Vincent, J. E. (1973). Transgression and altruism: A case for hedonism. *Journal of Experimental Social Psychology, 9,* 502–516.

Coke, J. S., Batson, C. D., & McDavis, K. (1978). Empathic mediation of helping: A two-stage model. *Journal of Personality and Social Psychology, 36,* 752–766.

Comte, L. A. (1875). *System of positive polity* (Vol. 1). London: Longmans, Green. (Original work published 1851)

Kenrick, D. T., Baumann, D. J., & Cialdini, R. B. (1979). A step in the socialization of altruism as hedonism: Effects of negative mood on children's generosity under public and private conditions. *Journal of Personality and Social Psychology, 37,* 747–755.

Manucia, G. K., Baumann, D. J., & Cialdini, R. B. (1984). Mood influences on helping: Direct effects or side effects? *Journal of Personality and Social Psychology, 46,* 357–364.

CHALLENGE QUESTIONS

Does True Altruism Exist?

1. Do you think it is possible for research to distinguish between selfish motivations for helping and truly altruistic motivations?
2. Try to think of a time when you gave assistance to someone in need. Do you think that your behavior was altruistic, or can you think of egoistic reasons why you may have helped? Explain.
3. Can you think of any practical applications for the research examining helping behavior? How might the results of this research be used to promote helping behavior in the real world?

ISSUE 17

Does Media Violence Cause Aggression?

YES: Brad Bushman and Craig A. Anderson from "Media Violence and the American Public: Scientific Facts Versus Media Misinformation," *American Psychologist* (56, June/July 2001)

NO: Jonathan L. Freedman from *Media Violence and Aggression* (University of Toronto Press, 2002)

ISSUE SUMMARY

YES: Brad Bushman and Craig Anderson contend that an overwhelming amount of research indicates that media violence is a significant cause of violent and aggressive behavior. Despite this overwhelming evidence, media corporations irresponsibly downplay the impact that media violence may have.

NO: Jonathon Freedman argues that the evidence linking aggression to media violence is not as strong as is it believed to be. Psychologists who contend that such a link has been proven are misunderstanding or misrepresenting what the data actually indicates.

A twelve-year-old boy kills his friend after imitating a professional wrestler whom he saw on television. A teenager commits suicide after listening to heavy metal music. In tragedies like these, the media is sometimes cited as an important and dangerous influence that promotes violent behavior among young people. But does media violence actually cause aggressive and violent behavior? Or is the media just a convenient scapegoat? The incident that sparked some of the most heated debate about this issue was the Colombine Massacre in which one teacher and twelve students were killed by students Dylan Klebold and Eric Harris. Klebold and Harris were avid fans of violent computer games called "first person shooters" in which the player of the game gains points for shooting and killing other characters in the game. Did playing these games encourage Klebold and Harris to act out their violent impulses? Evidently the families of the victims believed the games had a significant impact; they filed a $5 *billion* lawsuit in which they alleged that the manufacturers of video games should have known that playing these games could result in tragic consequences. Is such a lawsuit frivolous, or is there some truth to these arguments?

Brad Bushman and Craig Anderson contend that there is an overwhelming amount of evidence from psychological research indicating that media violence can promote aggressive and violent behavior. Not only does the media have an impact on aggression, but the magnitude of this effect is substantial. According to Bushman and Anderson, the link between media violence and aggression is similar in magnitude to the link between cigarette smoking and lung cancer. Despite the evidence that clearly indicates the serious nature of the problem, media corporations continue to irresponsibly ignore the problem and dismiss the evidence that comes from social psychological research.

Jonathan Freedman believes that the results of social psychological research are not nearly as convincing as Bushman and Anderson claim. He argues that social scientists, including many prominent psychologists, frequently misinterpret the evidence that presumably documents the negative impact of media violence. When the evidence is interpreted properly, it does not indicate that the link between media violence and aggressive behavior has been proven. Nonetheless, scientific organizations continue to irresponsibly contend that the link has been definitively established without properly reviewing the research.

POINT

- An overwhelming amount of evidence suggests that exposure to media violence can lead to aggressive behavior.
- Not only does the media have an impact on aggression, but the magnitude of this effect is substantial.
- Media companies irresponsibly downplay the impact of the media on aggression and violence.

COUNTERPOINT

- The evidence presumably demonstrating the harmful effect of media violence is not very strong.
- Even if we could trust the evidence that supposedly demonstrates the effect of media violence on aggressive behavior, the magnitude of this effect would still be small.
- Psychologists irresponsibly inflate the degree to which the media may influence violence and aggression without properly reviewing the evidence.

Brad J. Bushman and
Craig A. Anderson

 **YES**

Media Violence and the American Public: Scientific Facts Versus Media Misinformation

The Mass Media Explosion

A mass media explosion occurred in the 20th century. Inventions such as the television set, the digital computer, and the videocassette player forever changed the way people gain information about the world, including information about how violent the world is. Television was introduced to the United States at the 1939 World's Fair in New York. Two years later, on July 1, 1941, the Federal Communications Commission licensed and approved the first commercially available television stations. Because of World War II, however, full-scale television broadcasting was suspended until 1946. In 1950, about 9% of American homes had TV sets. It didn't take long for television ownership in the United States to increase. By 1955, it was up to about 65%, and by 1965, it reached about 93%. Since 1985, television ownership has been about 98% (Nielsen Media Research, 1998). More recent types of electronic media have also become ubiquitous implements in modern society. About 97% of homes with children have a VCR, 90% have a CD player, and 89% have either a personal computer or other video-game-capable equipment (Federal Trade Commission, 2000).

The American public has consumed media as if they were ambrosia. A recent national study reported that consuming media is a full-time job for the average American child, who spends about 40 hours per week doing it (Kaiser Family Foundation, 1999). More than half of this time is spent watching television programs, movies, or videos. One telling statistic is that at 10 a.m. on any Saturday morning, more than 60% of all children in America are watching TV (Comstock & Scharrer, 1999).

Violence in the Reel World

Violence in drama is as old as drama itself—from ancient Greek drama, through the Elizabethan theater, to modern electronic dramas. In William Shakespeare's play *Macbeth*, for example, Macbeth's head is brought on stage

From *American Psychologist*, June/July 2001, pp. 477–489. © 2001 by The American Psychological Association. Reprinted by permission.

at the close of the play. In 1903, Edwin S. Porter directed a film called *The Great Train Robbery* (Edison & Porter, 1903). This 11-minute film is usually considered the first film ever made to tell an organized story (Turan, 1972). In one scene, there is a large close-up of a cowboy firing his pistol directly at the camera. The first audiences who saw the film reacted by running out of the theater screaming.

Americans get a heavy dose of media violence. A recent content analysis of more than 8,000 hours of programming on cable and broadcast television in the United States found that about 60% of TV programs contained violence (*National Television Violence Study*, 1996, 1997, 1998). By the time the average American child graduates from elementary school, he or she will have seen more than 8,000 murders and more than 100,000 other assorted acts of violence (e.g., assaults, rapes) on network television (Huston et al., 1992). The numbers are higher if the child has access to cable television or a videocassette player, as most do. Violence dominates the big screen as well as the small screen. The percentage of PG films produced has steadily dropped over the years (Auletta, 1993). Even G-rated films contain more violence now than they ever have before (Yokota & Thompson, 2000). Violence is also frequently found in video games. For example, Provenzo (1991) found that 85% of the most popular video games were violent. Even young children are exposed to many violent video games. Buchman and Funk (1996) found that fourth-grade girls and boys reported that the majority of their favorite games were violent ones (59% for girls, 73% for boys).

One plausible explanation for the media emphasis on violent materials is that violent media are easy to export to foreign markets, perhaps because they lose less in translation than do other types of media. Comedies, for example, often require some knowledge of the popular culture. In time, violent media might become America's most exportable commodity (Hamilton, 1998).

The Explosion of Violence in the Real World

Violence is as American as cherry pie.

—H. Rap Brown

Among industrialized countries, the United States is one of the most violent (Zimring & Hawkins, 1997). Scholars have been investigating media violence as a potential contributor to societal violence in the United States since the early 1960s. One possible reason for the early interest in a link between media violence and societal violence is that violence in the United States began to increase fairly dramatically in 1965, exactly when the first generation of children raised on TV began to reach the prime ages for committing violent crimes (see Figure 1). Indeed, studies of violent crime rates before and after the introduction of television have shown similar effects in several countries (e.g., Centerwall, 1989, 1992).

Figure 1

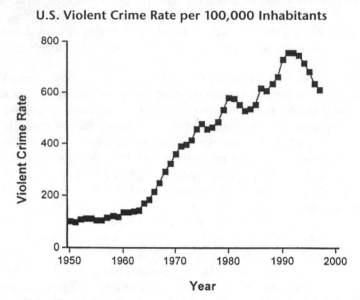

U.S. Violent Crime Rate per 100,000 Inhabitants

Note. Data were obtained from *Uniform Crime Reports* (U.S. Federal Bureau of Investigation, 1951–1999)

Of course, such comparisons of demographic trends are not proof of any causal relationship between violent media and violent crime. Numerous factors influence violent crime rates, including simple demographic trends (e.g., changes in age distribution) in the population. Thus, large numbers of empirical studies of media violence have ben conducted over the past 40 years using more traditional psychological research methods. Before examining the outcomes of those studies, we first consider the claim that media violence mirrors what is happening in contemporary society.

Does the Level of Violence in the Reel World Mirror the Level of Violence in the Real World?

The entertainment industry often claims that violent media simply reflect the violence that already exists in society. Consider the following statements from representatives of the three major television networks. According to Leonard Goldenson of ABC, "We are presently reaping the harvest of having laid it on the line at a time when many Americans are reluctant to accept the images reflected by the mirror we have held up to our society" ("Fighting Violence," 1968, p. 59). Julian Goodman of NBC agreed. "The medium is being blamed for the message" ("Fighting Violence," 1968, p. 59). Howard Stringer of CBS claimed that the TV industry is "merely holding a mirror to American society" (West, 1993). Zev Braun, also of CBS, said, "We live in a violent society. Art imitates the modes of life, not the other way around. It would be better for

Congress to clean that society than to clean up the reflection of that society" ("Violence Bill Debated in Washington," 1990).

However, even in reality-based TV programs, violence is grossly overemphasized. For example, one study compared the frequency of crimes occurring in the real world with the frequency of crimes occurring in the following reality-based police TV programs: *America's Most Wanted, Cops, Top Cops, FBI, The Untold Story,* and *American Detective* (Oliver, 1994). The real-world crime rates were obtained from the U.S. Federal Bureau of Investigation (FBI: 1951–1999) *Uniform Crime Reports,* which divide seven major types of crimes into two categories, violent and nonviolent. About 87% of the crimes occurring in the real world are nonviolent crimes, whereas only 13% of crimes occurring in reality-based TV programs are nonviolent crimes. The largest discrepancy between the real world and the world depicted on television is for murder, the most violent crime of all. Only 0.2% of the crimes reported by the FBI are murders, whereas about 50% of the crimes shown in reality-based TV programs are murders (Oliver, 1994).

According to film critic Michael Medved (1995), the claim that the entertainment industry merely reflects the level of violence in society is a lie.

> If this were true, then why do so few people witness murders in real life but everybody sees them on TV and in the movies? The most violent ghetto isn't in South Central L.A. or Southeast Washington D. C.; it's on television. About 350 characters appear each night on prime-time TV, but studies show an average of seven of these people are murdered every night. If this rate applied in reality, then in just 50 days everyone in the United States would be killed and the last left could turn off the TV. (pp. 156–157)

In summary, there is far more violence in the reel world than in the real world.

Is There Strong Evidence Linking Exposure to Media Violence with Increased Aggression?

The "Logical" Debate

The television and motion picture industries often claim that violent media have no influence on aggressive behavior. For example, Jack Valenti, president of the Motion Picture Association of America, said, "If you cut the wires of all TV sets today, there would still be no less violence on the street in two years" (Moore, 1993, p. 3007). However, this same industry makes all of its money from commercials, charging hundreds of thousands of dollars for a few minutes of commercial airtime. As former Federal Communications Commission Chairman Reed Hundt said, "If a sitcom can sell soap, salsa and cereal, then who could argue that TV violence cannot affect to some degree some viewers, particularly impressionable children?" (Eggerton, 1994, p. 10).

Sometimes, the entertainment industry goes one step further and claims that violent media influence behavior in a beneficial way. For example, TV scriptwriter Grace Johnson said that violent TV shows "often serve as a release valve for aggressive impulses which would otherwise be bottled up, only to explode later" ("See No Evil?", 1954, p. 8). Similarly, film director Alfred Hitchcock said, "One of television's greatest contributions is that it brought murder back into the home where it belongs. Seeing a murder on television can be good therapy. It can help work off one's antagonism" (Myers, 1999, p. 412).

The first recorded description of this "catharsis hypothesis" occurred more than one thousand years ago, in Aristotle's (trans. 1970) *Poetics*. He taught that viewing tragic plays gave people emotional release (*katharsis*) from negative feelings such as pity and fear. The tragic hero in a Greek drama did not just grow old and retire—he often suffered a violent demise. By watching the characters in the play experience tragic events, the viewer's own negative feelings were presumably purged and cleansed. This emotional cleaning was believed to benefit both the individual and society.

The ancient notion of catharsis was revived by Sigmund Freud and his associates. For example, A. A. Brill, the psychiatrist who introduced Freud's psychoanalytic techniques to the United States, prescribed that his patients watch a prizefight once a month to purge their angry, aggressive feelings into harmless channels (Feshbach & Price, 1984). While serving as chairman of the National Board of Review of Motion Pictures, Brill said,

> You remember that the Greeks spoke of the play as effecting a "catharsis" of the emotions. The movies serve this purpose. So do hockey and football games. People get rid of pent-up aggression when they go to a prizefight, and society approves of this release. Children, too, have plenty of bottled up protest against life's little tyrannies—keeping clean, learning lessons, behaving themselves—and the screen is the great medium for giving the child an outlet for this revolt. (Mackenzie, 1940, p. 9)

The Scientific Evidence

Psychologists have studied the effect of violent media on aggression for several decades. Hundreds of studies have been conducted on this topic. Scientific evidence from a collection of studies, such as those on media-related aggression, can be integrated and summarized in a narrative (qualitative) review or in a meta-analytic (quantitative) review. Both types of reviews have been conducted on the research literature about media violence and aggression, and all have come to the same conclusion: that viewing violence increases aggression (e.g., Hearold, 1986; Hogben, 1998; Huston et al., 1992; National Institute of Mental Health, 1982; Paik & Comstock, 1994; Surgeon General's Scientific Advisory Committee on Television and Social Behavior, 1972; Wood, Wong, & Chachere, 1991). On the basis of such findings, in July 2000, six major professional societies—the American Psychological Association (APA), the American Academy of Pediatrics, the American Academy of Child and Adolescent Psychiatry, the

American Medical Association, the American Academy of Family Physicians, and the American Psychiatric Association—signed a joint statement on the hazards of exposing children to media violence, noting that "at this time, well over 1,000 studies...point overwhelmingly to a causal connection between media violence and aggressive behavior in some children "(*Joint Statement*, 2000, p. 1).

One common industry response to the conclusions of such literature reviews is to deny the findings. For example, Jim Burke of Rysher Entertainment said, "I don't think there is any correlation between violence on TV and violence in society" (Stern, 1995, p. 28). Another is to claim that the effects of media violence on aggression are so small or that they affect so few people that the risks to society are negligible and can and should be ignored. For example, a *Time* magazine writer concluded, "While the bulk of published research has indeed found some correlation between watching fictitious violence and behaving aggressively, the correlation is statistically quite modest" (K. Anderson, 1993, p. 66).

But is the effect so small? How is one to judge? This type of question begs for a quantitative answer, and meta-analysis techniques have been developed to help address such questions. In the remainder of this article, we use the correlation coefficient, denoted by r, as the quantitative measure of the effect of one variable (e.g., exposure to media violence) on another variable (e.g., aggression).[1]

Earlier meta-analytic reviews of studies of media violence on aggression have reported average effect sizes ranging from $r+ =.11$ (Hogben, 1998) to $r+ =.31$ (Paik & Comstock, 1994). In all cases, the reviews found a significant positive relation. That is, greater exposure to media violence is strongly linked to increases in aggression.

Just how small are these estimates of the media violence effect? Figure 2 presents the results of the largest published meta-analysis on violent-media-related aggression (Paik & Comstock, 1994, included 217 studies in their meta-analysis), along with the results from a number of meta-analyses done in other (primarily medical) domains. All of the correlations in Figure 2 are significantly different from zero. Note, however, that the second largest correlation is for violent media and aggression. Most people would agree that the other correlations displayed in Figure 2 are so strong that they are obvious. For example, most people would not question the assertion that taking calcium increases bone mass or that wearing a condom decreases the risk of contracting HIV, the virus that causes AIDS.

Why, then, do some individuals question the assertion that viewing violence increases aggression? One possible reason is that people do not understand psychological processes as well as they understand physiological processes. Another possibility is that people might (mistakenly) believe that the media violence data are merely correlational. A third possibility that we examine in more detail later in this article is that news media reports of media violence research might not be accurately presenting the state of scientific knowledge, much like news media reports on the relationship between cigarette smoking and lung cancer in the 1950s, 1960s, and 1970s seemed to inaccurately portray that research as being weaker than medical scientists knew it to be.

Figure 2

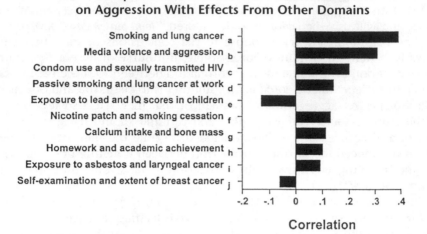

**Comparison of the Effect of Violent Media
on Aggression With Effects From Other Domains**

Note. All correlations are significantly different from zero. a = the effect of smoking tobacco on lung cancer, as estimated by pooling the data from Figures 1 and 3 in Wynder and Graham's (1950) classic article. The remaining effects were estimated from meta-analyses: b = Paik and Comstock (1994); c = Weller (1993); d = Wells (1998); e = Needleman and Gatsonis (1990); f = Fiore, Smith, Jorenby, and Baker (1994); g = Welten, Kemper, Post, and van Staveren (1995); h = Cooper (1989); i = Smith, Handley, and Wood (1990); j = Hill, White, Jolley, and Mapperson (1998).

More Logical Analyses

The Smoking and Media Violence Analogy

There are at least six instructive parallels between the smoking and lung cancer relationship and the media violence and aggression relationship. First, not everyone who smokes gets lung cancer, and not everyone who gets lung cancer is a smoker. Similarly, not everyone who watches violent media becomes aggressive, and not everyone who is aggressive watches violent media.

Second, smoking is not the only factor that causes lung cancer, but it is an important factor. Similarly, watching violent media is not the only factor that causes aggression, but it is an important factor.

Third, the first cigarette can nauseate a person. Repeated exposure reduces these sickening effects, and the person begins to crave more cigarettes. Similarly, the first exposure to violent media can make a person (especially children) anxious and fearful (Cantor, 2000). Repeated exposure reduces these effects and leaves the viewer wanting stronger doses of violence.

Fourth, the short-term effects of smoking are relatively innocuous in most cases and dissipate fairly rapidly. Smoking one cigarette has numerous physiological effects that are rarely serious and that dissipate within an hour or so. Similarly, watching one violent TV program on film increases aggressive thoughts, feelings, and behaviors, but these effects usually dissipate within an hour or so (Bushman & Huesmann, 2001).

Fifth, the long-term cumulative effects of smoking are relatively severe. One cigarette has little impact on lung cancer. However, repeated exposure to tobacco smoke, for example, smoking one pack of cigarettes a day for 15 years, seriously increases the likelihood of a person contracting lung cancer (and other diseases). Similarly, watching one violent TV show has little impact on the likelihood of a child becoming a habitual violent offender, but the empirical evidence now clearly shows that repeated exposure to violent media, for example, a couple of hours a day for 15 years, causes a serious increase in the likelihood of a person becoming a habitually aggressive person and occasionally a violent offender (Huesmann, Moise, Podolski, & Eron, 2000).

One final parallel also deserves consideration. In the long fight of medical science against the tobacco industry, the big money interests of the tobacco industry apparently led them to deny publicly that there was any scientific evidence supporting the claim that tobacco products caused lung cancer. Many of the same arguments used in this war of deception have been and continue to be made by the entertainment industry regarding reports that exposure to violent media causes aggression. In both cases, the industry claims that there is no good evidence have persisted long after the scientific data clearly indicated there could be no reasonable doubt about the seriousness of the causal impact. That point in the history of scientific developments in the smoking case was reached quite some time ago: In 1964, the U.S. Surgeon General concluded that the evidence on the harmful effects of tobacco smoke was overwhelming enough to warn the American public about it (U.S. Department of Health, Education, and Welfare, 1974). In the next section of this article, we show that the no-reasonable-doubt point in the data on media violence effects was also reached some time ago: The U. S. Surgeon General issued such a statement in 1972 (Surgeon General's Scientific Advisory Committee on Television and Social Behavior, 1972).

When Small Is Big

Obviously, exposure to media violence does not produce violent criminals out of all viewers, just as cigarette smoking does not produce lung cancer victims out of all smokers. This lack of perfect correspondence between heavy media violence exposure and violent behavior simply means that media violence exposure is not a necessary and sufficient cause of violence. When an ad is shown on TV, no one expects that it will sell the product to everybody. If the ad influences only 1% of viewers, it is considered to be a great success (Medved, 1995). Suppose violent media make only 1% of the population more aggressive. Should society be concerned about a percentage so small? The answer is a resounding "Yes!" Suppose 10 million people watch a violent TV program. If only 1% of the viewers will become more aggressive afterward, then the violent TV program will make 100,000 people more aggressive! Because so many people are exposed to violent media, the effect on society can be immense even if only a small percentage of viewers are affected by them. It takes only one or two affected students to wreak murderous havoc in a school, as demonstrated in recent years in Jonesboro,

Arkansas; West Paducah, Kentucky; Pearl, Mississippi; Stamps, Arkansas; Springfield, Oregon; Littleton, Colorado; and Santee and Elcajon, California. (See Abelson, 1985, and Rosenthal, 1990, for example of how small effect sizes can yield large effects.)...

General Discussion

In 1995, *Newsweek* magazine published an article that claimed there was no solid evidence that exposure to media violence increases aggression (Leland, 1995). We wrote a letter to the editor in an attempt to correct this factually incorrect statement. The reply said that they were not interested in publishing our letter. More recently, *The New York Times* published an op-ed article (Rhodes, 2000) that similarly attacked extant media violence research in general and specifically targeted the pioneering and ongoing research of Rowell Huesmann and Leonard Eron (e.g., Huesmann et al., 2000). Despite protests from a variety of sources, including a very thoughtful reply by Huesmann and Eron, no rebuttal, retraction, or reply was ever published (International Society for Research on Aggression, 2001). In an age of multinational, multimedia mega-corporations, perhaps it should not be surprising that truth in journalism has been forced to the back of the bus, as if it is not as important or valuable as profits or a good story. Nonetheless, the *Newsweek* incident was a shock to us, one that instigated the present research. *The New York Times* incident confirms the generality of this problem, as does Figure 3.

Figure 3

Effect of Media Violence on Aggression: News Reports Versus Scientific Studies

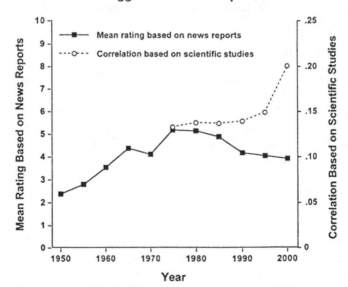

Note. Ratings based on news reports are positive if the article said that exposure to media violence is positively related to aggression. Correlations based on scientific studies are positive if media violence was postively related to aggression.

Figure 3 reveals a major problem in the public reporting of social science information. Mass media magazines and newspapers have consistently failed to capture the changes in the scientific state of knowledge as research evidence supporting the causal link between exposure to media violence and aggression has accumulated. By 1975, the effect was clear, yet major news sources continue today to suggest to the U.S. public that there is relatively little reason to be concerned about media violence. Indeed, since the mid-1980s, the average news story has actually softened a bit on the media violence problem, even though the cumulative evidence is now more overwhelming in showing that short- and long-term exposure to media violence causes significant increases in aggression.

There are several plausible explanations for this apparently irresponsible reporting pattern. The simplest, perhaps, is that the print news media industry has a vested interest in denying a strong link between exposure to media violence and aggression. There are at least three ways in which such a denial might serve the profits of the news media companies. First, many print news media companies are part of larger conglomerates that directly profit from the sale of violent media such as television and movies. Second, many print news media get a lot of their advertising revenue from companies that produce and sell violent media. For example, almost all newspapers advertise movies. Third, the print news media may fear they will offend their readers by printing stories with which their readers might disagree. Given the large number of people who consume violent media and who allow their children to do likewise, such fears might be legitimate, even though the biased reporting of scientific "fact" is not.

A second plausible explanation for the apparent misreporting of the state of media violence evidence concerns a misapplied fairness doctrine. There may be a sort of journalistic "fairness" heuristic guiding the reporting of scientific findings that systematically leads to an overemphasis on minority views. Specifically, an attempt to get both sides of the story may itself lead to a final story that puts too little emphasis on the findings and opinions of leading researchers and puts too much emphasis on the few dissidents who can be found on almost any scientific issue. Indeed, a reading of even a small sample of the print media reports on media violence reveals that this fairness doctrine extends even to the public opinions of people who clearly have a monetary interest in befuddling the general public. Of course, the mass media industry has the money and the expertise to hire top guns to create such obfuscations and to deliver them in a convincing fashion, much as the tobacco industry successfully did for several decades.

A third plausible explanation involves the failure of the research community to effectively argue its case. There are at least four contributing factors involved. First, research scientists typically do not see themselves as public policy advocates. It is not normally considered a part of their jobs to take on the task of educating the general public. Second, the scientist role itself includes a very conservative norm against publicly making the kinds of claims that scientists privately believe to be true, especially concerning the generalizability of their results and the ability to draw causal inferences from their studies. It is deemed more proper to discuss limitations of a particular study, especially if it is a scientist's own study. Third, research scientists do not have the time needed to educate reporters or to respond to the hired guns whose only job is to attack the research base of the undesired findings. Fourth, attempting to educate the general public is very costly in many ways, not just in the amount of time required. For instance, hate mail is one additional cost that must be borne by anyone who appears in mass media sources with an opinion on a controversial issue. The Internet has made such hate mail easier to send and seemingly more prevalent. Also, there are security risks associated with becoming a more public figure. A more mundane yet real cost involves expenses accrued in presenting scientific information to appropriate sources. For instance, as one of us—Craig A. Anderson—recently discovered, the U.S. Senate does not pay travel expenses associated with testifying for one of their myriad committees. In addition, public debates about media violence effects make it more difficult to continue to conduct research on media-related aggression, because the participant pool becomes less naive and more suspicious of the research.

It is likely that all three of the explanations—the vested interests of the news media industry, a misapplied fairness doctrine, and communication failures—are operative, in both the specific case of research on media violence and aggression and more generally. The research community can do relatively little about the first two. However, we believe that the research community can more effectively present the research findings.

One major step would be to realize that the conservative scientist role and the public educator role are two very different roles with different norms. When the U.S. Senate, CNN, *The New York Times,* or the *London Daily Observer* asks researchers whether they believe that exposure to violent media causes an increase in aggression, they are not asking for the overly conservative, self-defensive kind of answer that is appropriate when discussing their latest research projects at an APA convention. They are asking for their opinions, based on their knowledge of the research literature and their general knowledge of their scientific fields. For instance, in recent testimony before the U.S. Senate Committee on Commerce, Science, and Transportation, Craig A. Anderson testified that there is now a sufficient empirical database to state that exposure to violent video games can cause increases in aggression (C.A. Anderson, 2000). This assessment was based on a thorough review of the video game literature, our own recent research on this topic (C.A. Anderson & Bushman, 2001), knowledge of the vast TV and movie violence literature, and knowledge about the key psychological processes at work in the media violence phenomenon. This is not to say that scientists should abandon all caution and deliver outlandish, quotable statements. For instance, we also testified that although there are good reasons to expect that the negative effects of exposure to violent video games will be larger than the comparable TV violence effects, there currently was not sufficient research evidence to claim this effect had been demonstrated as a fact. (Of course, many newspaper and Web-based accounts misreported what was actually said.)

One way to decide the proper response for the public education role might be for scientists to ask themselves what sort of actions they are taking in their personal lives relevant to the issue being considered. For instance, in deciding whether to state that they believe that playing violent video games can cause increases in aggression, scientists might ask whether they allow (or would allow) their children to play such violent games. If their answer is "no," and if that answer is based on their knowledge of the research literature, then the proper answer to the question, "Can playing violent video games cause increases in aggression?" would be some version of "Yes, on the basis of the research in the TV literature as well as the video game literature, I believe that exposure to violent video games can cause increases in aggression and that this effect is serious enough to lead me to prevent my own children from playing such games." Admittedly, this is not a great sound bite, but it is appropriate. Additional caveats may be appropriate, of course, but in our view, it would not be appropriate to hide behind the conservative scientist role and deny a belief in the causal role of media violence.

Another major step that researchers can take is to realize that the role of disseminating insights gained from their research *is* a part of their job, along with restructuring evaluation systems so that they explicitly include a public education component. For the typical faculty member at a research university, this suggests that departments need to add a public-education-efforts dimension to the annual performance evaluations (it could be part of the research service or teaching components).

A third step—public education efforts by relevant professional associations—is already being taken to some extent. Both APA and the American Psychological Society have made such efforts. For example, APA's Science Advocacy Training Workshops bring in a group of researchers who are experts on a particular topic, create a forum in which to discuss some of the issues involving the future of research on this topic, and arrange meetings with appropriate congressional staff. A recent report revealed that one such workshop group succeeded in getting language incorporated into a house committee report accompanying the Veterans Administration–Department of Housing and Urban Development bill "urging the NSF (National Science Foundation) to increase efforts to fund research on the impact of emerging media on children's cognitive, social and emotional development" (Kobar, 2000, p. 6).

We believe that more efforts along this line can be made. For instance, when a major news source such as *Newsweek* magazine misrepresents the current state of psychological science knowledge, one or more of the relevant professional associations could take an active role in countering that misrepresentation, perhaps by issuing a press release.

Finally, scientists must be willing to pay some of the unavoidable costs, both monetary and personal, associated with educating the public. Some of the monetary costs can be defrayed by relevant organizations: For example, APA generously picked up some of the travel costs for some of the participants in the Senate hearings mentioned earlier. However, other costs, such as time or having to deal with hate mail, are costs that individual researchers may simply have to pay on their own. We believe that the benefit to society of more effectively communicating to a broad general audience the knowledge gained from psychological research is worth the cost. We also hope that the research presented in this article helps to correct the continuing public misrepresentation of what is known about the effects of exposure to media violence on aggressive behavior.

Note

1. The correlation coefficient measures the magnitude of (linear) relation between two variables. The value of a correlation coefficient can range from –1 (a perfect negative correlation) to +1 (a perfect positive correlation), with 0 indicating no correlation between the two variables. In research, however, virtually no correlations are perfect. According to Cohen (1988), a *small* correlation is ± .1, a *medium* correlation is ± .3, and a *large* correlation is ± .5, respectively. According to Cohen, most of the correlations in the social sciences are small-to-medium in size. The correlation coefficient can be calculated between two continuous measures, such as number of hours of violent TV watched per week and teacher ratings of aggressiveness, as well as between one dichotomous and one continuous measure, such as in experiments wherein children are randomly assigned to watch either a violent or a nonviolent TV show (dichotomous variable) followed by a free-play period in which the number of times the child hits another child is recorded (continuous variable). If the correlation is between two continuous variables, it is called the Pearson product-moment correlation coefficient; if it is between a continuous and dichotomous variable, it is called a pointbiserial correlation.

References

Abelson, R. P. (1985). A variance explanation paradox: When a little is a lot. *Psychological Bulletin, 97,* 129–133.

Anderson, C. A. (2000). *Violent video games increase aggression and violence.* [Testimony at the U. S. Senate Committee on Commerce, Science, and Transportation hearing on "The Impact of Interactive Violence on Children"]. Retrieved April 9, 2001, from the World Wide Web: http://www.senate.gov/~brownback/00032land.pdf

Anderson, C. A., & Bushman, B. J. (2001). Effects of violent video games on aggressive behavior, aggressive cognition, aggressive affect, physiological arousal, and prosocial behavior: A meta-analytic review of the scientific literature. *Psychological Science.*

Anderson, K. (1993, July 12). The great TV violence hype. *Time, 142*(2), 66–67.

Aristotle. (1970). *Poetics* (G. F. Else, Trans.). Ann Arbor: University of Michigan Press.

Auletta, K. (1993, May 17). What won't they do? Hollywood decision-makers discuss the social impact of the big screen and the small screen—and where the entertainment industry's responsibilities end. *New Yorker, 69,* 45–53.

Buchman, D. D., & Funk, J. B. (1996). Video and computer games in the '90s: Children's time commitment and game preference. *Children Today, 24,* 12–16.

Bushman, B. J., & Huesmann, L. R. (2001). Effects of televised violence on aggression. In D. Singer & J. Singer (Eds.), *Handbook of children and the media* (pp. 223–254). Thousand Oaks, CA: Sage.

Cantor, J. (2000, August). *Media violence and children's emotions: Beyond the "smoking gun."* Paper presented at the annual convention of the American Psychological Association, Washington, DC. Retrieved November 3, 2000, from the World Wide Web: http://www.joannecantor.com/EMOTIONS2_sgl.htm

Centerwall, B. S. (1989). Exposure to television as a risk factor for violence. *American Journal of Epidemiology, 129,* 643–652.

Centerwall, B. S. (1992). Television and violence: The scale of the problem and where to go from here. *Journal of the American Medical Association, 267,* 3059–3063.

Comstock, G. A., & Scharrer, E. (1999). *Television: What's on, who's watching, and what it means.* San Diego, CA: Academic Press.

Edison, T. A. (Producer), & Porter, E. S. (Writer/Director). (1903). *The great train robbery* [Motion picture]. United States: Edison Manufacturing.

Eggerton, J. (1994, January 31). Hundt hits television violence. *Broadcasting and Cable, 124*(5), 10–12.

Federal Trade Commission. (2000). *Marketing violent entertainment to children: A review of self-regulations and industry practices in the motion picture, music recording, & electronic game industries—Appendix B.* Washington DC: Author.

Feshbach, S., & Price, J. (1984). Cognitive competencies and aggressive behavior: A developmental study. *Aggressive Behavior, 10,* 185–200.

Fighting violence. (1968, December 27). *Time, 92,* 58–59.

Hamilton, J. T. (1998). *Channeling violence: The economic market for violent television programming.* Princeton, NJ: Princeton University Press.

Hearold, S. (1986). A synthesis of 1043 effects of television on social behavior. In G. Comstock (Ed.), *Public communication and behavior* (Vol 1., pp. 65–133). New York: Academic Press.

Hogben, M. (1998). Factors moderating the effect of television aggression on viewer behavior. *Communication Research, 25,* 220–247.

Huesmann, L. R., Moise, J., Podolski, C. P., & Eron, L. D. (2000). *Longitudinal relations between childhood exposure to media violence and adult aggression and violence: 1977–1992.* Manuscript submitted for publication.

Huston, A. C., Donnerstein, E., Fairchild, H., Feshbach, N. D., Katz, P. A., Murray, J. P., Rubinstein, E. A., Wilcox, B. L., & Zuckerman, E. (1992). *Big world, small screen: The role of television in American Society.* Lincoln: University of Nebraska Press.

International Society for Research on Aggression. (2001). Editor's note. *Bulletin of the International Society for Research on Aggression, 23,* 5–6.

Joint statement on the impact of entertainment violence on children: Congressional Public Health Summit. (2000, July 26). Retrieved December 4, 2000. from the World Wide Web: http://www.senate. gov/brownback/violence1.pdf

Kaiser Family Foundation. (1999, November). *Kids and media at the new millennium.* Menlo Park, CA: Author.

Kobar, P. C. (2000). Policy news you can use: A federal funding update for NSF and NIH. *Psychological Science Agenda, 13*(4), 6.

Leland, J. (1995, December 11). Violence, reel to real. *Newsweek,* 46–48.

ISSUE 17 / Does Media Violence Cause Aggression?

Mackenzie, C. (1940, June 23). Movies and the child: The debate rages on. *New York Times Magazine,* 9–10.

Meved, M. (1995, October). Hollywood's 3 big lies. *Reader's Digest, 147*(882), 155–159.

Moore, J. W. (1993, December 18). Lights! Camera! It's gun control time. *National Journal,* 3007.

Myers, D. G. (1999). *Social psychology* (6th ed.). Boston: McGraw-Hill.

National Institute of Mental Health. (1982). *Television and behavior: Ten years of scientific progress and implications for the eighties (Vol. I): Summary report.* Washington, DC: U.S. Government Printing Office.

National television violence study (Vol. 1). (1996). Thousand Oaks, CA: Sage

National television violence study (Vol. 2). (1997). Studio City, CA: Mediascope.

National television violence study (Vol. 3). (1998). Santa Barbara: Center for Communication and Social Policy, University of California.

Nielsen Media Research. (1998). *Galaxy explorer.* New York: Author.

Oliver, M. B. (1994). Portrayals of crime, race, and aggression in "reality-based" police shows: A content analysis. *Journal of Broadcasting and Electronic Media, 38,* 179–192.

Paik, H., & Comstock, G. (1994). The effects of television violence on antisocial behavior: A meta-analysis. *Communication Research, 21,* 516–546.

Provenzo, E. F. (1991). *Video kids: Making sense of Nintendo.* Cambridge, MA: Harvard University Press.

Rhodes, R. (2000, September 17). Hollow claims about fantasy violence. *The New York Times,* Sect. 4. p. 19.

Rosenthal, R. (1990). How are we doing in soft psychology? *American Psychologist, 43,* 775–777.

See no evil? (1954, November 10). *Scholastic,* 7–8.

Stern, C. (1995, January 30). Syndicators say Clinton off base on violence. *Broadcasting and Cable, 125*(5), 28–30.

Surgeon General's Scientific Advisory Committee on Television and Social Behavior. (1972). *Television and growing up: The impact of televised violence.* Washington, DC: U. S. Government Printing Office.

Turan, K. (1972, June). The new violence in films. *Progressive, 36,* 40–44.

U.S. Department of Health, Education, and Welfare. (1974). *The health consequences of smoking.* Washington, DC: U. S. Government Printing Office.

U.S. Federal Bureau of Investigation. (1951–1999). *Uniform crime reports.* Washington, DC: U. S. Government Printing Office.

Violence bill debated in Washington: Most panelists argued against legislation. (1990, February 5). *Broadcasting, 118*(6), 77–79.

West, W. (1993, July 5). TV's bigwigs are a smash at the Capitol Hill comedy club. *Insight on the News, 9*(27), 40–41.

Wood, W., Wong, F. Y., & Chachere, J. G. (1991). Effects of media violence on viewers' aggression in unconstrained social interaction. *Psychological Bulletin, 109,* 371–383.

Yokota, F., & Thompson, K. M. (2000, May 24/31). Violence in G-rated animated films. *Journal of the American Medical Association, 283,* 2716–2720.

Zimring, F. E., & Hawkins, G. (1997). *Crime is not the problem: Lethal violence in America.* New York: Oxford University Press.

NO ↵

Jonathan L. Freedman

Villain or Scapegoat?
Media Violence and Aggression

On 20 April 1999, at around 11:20 a.m. local time, two students wearing black trenchcoats walked into Columbine High School in Littleton, Colorado. Eric Harris, eighteen, and Dylan Klebold, seventeen, were armed with semiautomatic handguns, shotguns and explosives. They killed twelve students, one teacher, and then themselves.

On 1 December 1997, Michael Carneal killed three students at Heath High School in West Paducah, Kentucky.

On 30 April 1999, a fourteen-year-old Canadian boy walked into the W.R. Myers High School in Taber, a quiet farming community of 7,200 people two hours southeast of Calgary, Alberta. He shot and killed one seventeen-year-old student and seriously injured another eleventh-grade student.

It is difficult to imagine events more terrible than our young people deliberately killing each other. These horrifying incidents have caused almost everyone to wonder what has gone wrong with North American society. How can it be that in quiet, affluent communities in two of the richest countries on earth, children are taking guns to school and killing their classmates?

Many answers have been suggested. It was the parents' fault; it was Satanism and witchcraft; it was lack of religion in the schools and at home; it was moral breakdown; it was the availability of guns; it was the culture.

One answer proposed whenever events like this occur is that they are a result of exposure to media violence. Children who watch television and go to the movies see thousands of murders and countless other acts of violence. They see fistfights, martial arts battles, knifings, shootings, exploding cars, and bombs. These acts of violence are committed by heroes and villains, by good guys and bad guys. They are committed by live actors and animated figures; they appear in the best movies and TV programs as well as in the worst. It is almost impossible for children to avoid witnessing these violent acts time and time again. All of this has caused many people to ask whether watching violent television programs and movies causes people, especially children, to be more aggressive and to commit crimes.

Another reason some people worry about the effects of media violence is that television became available in the United States and Canada in the 1950s and violent crime increased dramatically in both countries between 1960 and 1990. Many people see a connection. They think that watching violence on television makes children more aggressive and causes them to grow into adults who are more likely to commit violent crimes. Brandon Centerwall, a psychiatrist and epidemiologist, has even suggested that the increase in violent crime during this period was due entirely to television. As he put it, 'if, hypothetically, television technology had never been developed, there would today be 10,000 fewer homicides each year in the United States, 70,000 fewer rapes, and 700,000 fewer injurious assaults.'

The belief that media violence is harmful is widespread. In a recent poll in the United States, 10 percent of people said that TV violence is the major cause of the increase in crime. This tendency to blame media violence has been fostered by some social scientists and whipped up by politicians and lobby groups. It has led politicians to propose bills restricting access to violent movies, banning violent television programs during certain hours, forcing television companies to rate every single program in terms of violence, and requiring that all television sets be fitted with V-chips to enable parents to block out programs they find offensive. We are told that all of this will reduce crime and make children better behaved, and that if we do not deal with media violence our society will continue to experience increased violence and crime....

Although it may seem as if youth violence is increasing, it is actually declining. In 1999 the rate of murder by white youths in California was at a record low, 65 percent less than in 1970, and the rates for Black, Latino, and Asian youths were also low. According to FBI records, elementary-school students are much less likely to murder today than they were in the 1960s and 1970s. And, both Black and white children feel less menaced now by violence in their schools than twenty-five years ago. True, over the past seven years there has been an increase in incidents in schools in which more than one person was killed. However, the number of children killed in schools in the United States and Canada has dropped during the same period, from a high of fifty-five in the 1992–93 school year to sixteen in 1998–99. This last year included one killing in Canada, which shocked a country not used to this kind of violence in its schools, but it is the only case of its kind in this decade.

Moreover, the rates for all violent crimes have been dropping steadily and dramatically since the early 1990s. The number of homicides in the big American cities has plunged to levels not seen since the early 70s, and the numbers for other violent crimes have been falling as well. This, at a time when movies and television shows are as violent as ever. Add to this the rising popularity of rap music, with its violent language and themes; and of video games, which are just as violent and just as popular. If violence in the media causes aggression, how can real-life violence and crime be dropping?

None of this proves that television violence plays no role in aggression and violence. The point is that stories about its effects are often false and that obvious effects may be explainable in other ways. People's intuitions and observations are sometimes wrong, and may be this time. That is why we have to rely on scientific research to answer the question whether exposure to media violence really makes children more aggressive; and that is why I have conducted the extensive review of the research that is presented in this book.

What about Pronouncements by Scientific Organizations?

The public has been told by panel after panel, organization after organization, that media violence causes aggression. A long list of prestigious scientific and medical organizations have said that the evidence is in and the question has been settled. The American Psychiatric Association and the Canadian Psychological Association have all weighed in on this matter. Recently, under some prodding by a congressional committee, the American Medical Association, the American Academy of Pediatrics, the American Psychological Association, and the American Academy of Child and Adolescent Psychiatry issued a joint statement. According to these groups, it is now proven that media violence causes aggression and probably causes crime. The pediatric group went so far as to urge that children under two should watch no television because it interferes with their normal development. The National Institute of Mental Health has published an extensive report on television in which it concludes that media violence causes aggression.

If all these respectable scientific organizations agree that media violence is harmful, surely it must be. Well, it isn't. Although they have all made unequivocal statements about the effects of media violence, it is almost certain that not one of these organizations conducted a thorough review of the research. They have surely not published or made available any such review. If they made these pronouncements without a scientific review, they are guilty of the worst kind of irresponsible behaviour. If they were in court as expert witnesses, they could be convicted of perjury. It is incredible that these organizations, which purport to be scientific, should act in this manner. Yet that seems to be the case.

Consider the policy statement from the American Academy of Pediatricians published in August 1999. It states: 'More than 1000 scientific studies and reviews conclude that significant exposure to media violence increases the risk of aggressive behavior in certain children and adolescents, desensitizes them to violence, and makes them believe that the world is a "meaner and scarier" place than it is.' Apparently not satisfied, in its November 2001 Policy Statement on Media Violence the AAP stated: 'More than 3500 research studies have examined the association between media violence and violent behavior [and] all but 18 have shown a positive relationship.' That sounds pretty impressive. After all, if over 3500 scientific studies reached this conclusion, who could doubt it? The only problem is that this is not true. There have not been over 3500 or even 1000 scientific studies on this topic. This vastly exaggerates the amount of work that has been done. That the pediatricians give such an inflated figure is only one indication that they do not know the research. Imagine the response if an organization of economists asserted that there were serious economic problems in over 150 American states. No one would bother asking for their statistics, since if they were so sloppy as to think there were that many states, who could possibly trust the rest of their statement? In the same way, since the pediatricians say that they are basing their statement on over 3500 scientific studies, it must be clear that they have not read the research because there are not anywhere near that many studies.

To make matters worse, the studies that do exist do not all reach the conclusion that media violence has any of the effects listed by the AAP. Indeed, ... most of the studies show no ill effects of exposure to media violence. And there is virtually no research showing that media violence desensitizes people to violence. Why do these presumably well-meaning pediatricians make these unsupported and inaccurate statements? Who knows.

To cap it off, the policy goes on to 'urge parents to avoid television viewing for children under the age of 2 years.' It supports this extreme recommendation by saying that 'research on early brain development shows that babies and toddlers have a critical need for direct interactions with parents ... for healthy brain growth and the development of appropriate social, emotional and cognitive skills.' I am not a neuroscientist and I have not reviewed the relevant research. However, an article in the *New York Times* quotes neuroscientists at Rockefeller University, the University of Minnesota, and the Washington University Medical School, as saying that there is no evidence to support the pediatricians' advice. 'There is no data like that at all,' according to Charles Nelson. The author of the *Times* article goes on to say that the person who wrote the pediatric academy's report agreed that there was no evidence but that they had 'extrapolated' from other data.

This is incredible. This organization is giving advice to medical doctors who deal directly with millions of American parents and children. And it is telling these doctors to urge their patients (i.e., the parents of their patients) to keep children under two away from television—not just limit their exposure but to keep them away from television entirely. Given the role that television plays in the lives of most families, following this advice would be a major undertaking. In the first place, it would be very difficult for the parents to manage it. Television keeps children occupied, stimulates them, entertains them, and educates them. Even if it did none of these things, imagine how difficult it would be for parents who like to watch television themselves or have older children who like to watch. Would they have to turn off the television whenever the under-two children are in the room? Or are they supposed to keep the young children out of the room with the television? Be serious.

Yet the pediatricians are supposed to tell parents that watching television will harm their children by preventing them from developing normally. This is quite a threat. Many parents will presumably take it to heart, worry about doing damage to their children, and try to follow the advice. This is not a matter of reducing fat intake a little or giving them enough milk—this is telling them to alter the social environment in their home, supposedly on the basis of hard, scary, scientific facts. Do *this* or your child will not grow up normally.

But there is no scientific evidence that television harms children under two—nothing at all to support this recommendation. It is junk science; pop psychology of the worst sort based on nothing but some vague extrapolations from research that is not cited and may not exist. This is truly irresponsible. Fortunately, I think we can trust most pediatricians to ignore this nonsensical policy and not give the advice; and if they do give it, we can probably trust most sensible parents to ignore it....

Then there is the group that represents my field—the American Psychological Association. Psychologists are trained to do and interpret research; the whole focus of their graduate education is research; they are required to do a research thesis. Most of the relevant research was done by psychologists and published in psychology journals. Surely APA can be trusted.

Think again. The APA is probably the worst offender in this whole story, not because its statements are any worse than the others, but because it should know better. The APA has taken the lead in the battle against media violence. It has issued many press statements and policy positions and has testified often in front of the U.S. Congress. Lest I be accused of being unfair to American psychologists, let me add that the Canadian Psychological Association has been just as bad, though less active. If the psychologists had taken careful, principled positions thoroughly supported by systematic research, this would be cause for applause. As it happens, this is a sad chapter in the organization's history, since it is probably the case that most of the other organizations have based their stands on what the psychologists have had to say.

The APA published a report called *Violence and Youth* that deals with the effects of media violence. It states in no uncertain terms that viewing media violence has all sorts of negative effects. Consider this extract, published in bold type in the report: 'There is absolutely no doubt that higher levels of viewing violence on television are correlated with increased acceptance of aggressive attitudes and increased aggressive behavior.' And this one: 'In addition, prolonged viewing of media violence can lead to emotional desensitization toward violence.' In support of these definitive statements, the report refers to three major national studies: the Surgeon General's Commission report of 1972, the National Institute of Mental Health ten-year follow-up of 1982 (which I'll discuss in detail below), and its own Committee on Media in Society of 1992. The APA says that these groups 'reviewed hundreds of studies to arrive at the irrefutable conclusion that viewing violence increases violence.'

There are many inaccuracies and misstatements in these few statements. First, none of these reviews looked at 'hundreds' of studies, because there are not that many studies now, and there certainly were not that many when these reviews were done. This is mere puffing to inflate the numbers to make the reviews sound more impressive. The psychologists do not claim 'over 1000,' like the pediatricians do, but they are still inflating (unless, I suppose, what they mean is 'two hundreds,' since that is about the right number). Second, the first two reviews were done by other groups, and presumably the psychologists should only make a pronouncement if they have looked at the research themselves. Third, although there is pious talk of a thorough review by the APA committee, this committee did not conduct the kind of open hearings that might have allowed people with divergent views to appear. In any case, this committee released a statement, but never released an actual review. In sum, the APA's bold report is not based on an independent review of the research, or if they did conduct such a review they have never released it for public consumption, comment, and—God forbid—criticism.

In addition, the APA makes serious factual errors. Let me put aside for now the question whether the research shows that media violence has an effect on violence—that, after all, is what this book is about. The APA says that viewing violence is associated with increased acceptance of aggressive attitudes. Now that's a new one. Not even the other organizations mentioned that, and it appears more or less out of the blue. Yes, it has been the subject of speculation, but there has been almost no research on changes in attitudes due to viewing violence. It may be true, but surely the APA does not know it is true—so why do they say there is 'no doubt' about it?

Then the report mentions emotional desensitization toward violence. Again, there has been speculation about this, and a few relevant studies have been done. But there is no reason for the APA to believe that this effect of media violence has been demonstrated definitively. As we shall see, my review shows that it is probably not true. For now the important point is that so little research has been done that no serious scientist could have faith in the existence or non-existence of the effect. So why does the APA mention it?

This lack of concern with actual research was evident again in testimony given for the APA to the U.S. Senate Subcommittee on Juvenile Justice. John Murray, speaking for the APA, was slightly more careful than the APA report. In answer to his own question 'Does televised violence produce aggressive behavior?' he said that 'the answer seems to be yes.' Not 'yes'; not 'proven beyond a doubt'; but 'seems to be yes,' Good for him. Unfortunately, the rest of his testimony had the effect of changing the 'seems' into 'does.'

Perhaps the most interesting part of his testimony—and, incidentally, of the report issued by the APA committee described earlier—was the research he mentioned. Both Murray and the report offered very few references to studies. Yet both referred to a study in which preschool children were shown various types of programs. Indeed, this study by Friedrich and Stein (1973) is often cited as showing the harmful effects of violent television. Now remember, of all of the studies that could have been cited, this is one of the very few that the APA chose to mention in its report and in its presentation to Congress. Presumably it was chosen because it produced such clear, unambiguous, and powerful results.

Here is the way Murray described it to the Senate committee: 'They found that the youngsters who watched the Batman and Superman cartoons were more likely to hit their playmates, start arguments, disobey the teacher and be more impatient.' This description is similar to the one in the report of the committee on violence.

Yet it is just plain wrong. That is not what the study found. The study used four basic measures of aggression and one additional, computed measure that combined two of the others. It found no difference between children who watched the aggressive cartoons and those who watched *Mister Rogers* (the prosocial program) on any of these measures. That is, just to make this perfectly clear, there was no difference on physical aggression, verbal aggression, object aggression, fantasy aggression, or interpersonal aggression (which combined physical and verbal). Those who watched the cartoons were *not* more likely to hit their playmates or start arguments. (They were also *not* more likely to disobey or be impatient, but this review is not about those effects so I will not focus on them.) There was a complex, marginally significant relationship between initial levels of aggression and type of film, but even this did not show any increase in aggression due to the 'violent' cartoons. In other words, Murray was wrong and the APA committee was wrong to cite this study as showing an increase in physical aggression due to watching Batman and Superman cartoons. There was no such effect.

Several years ago I debated this issue at a conference at the Hoffstra Law School. Murray was also there. In arguing that media violence is harmful, he cited this same study. When it was my turn to talk, I happened to have figures that proved he was wrong—the study did not show what he said it showed. His response to this was that you could always poke holes in any particular study. This surely is a classic instance of *chutzpah*. As I said to him, 'You picked the study, I didn't pick it. You chose it to make your point and you were wrong.'

Think about it. In testimony to Congress and in its report, the APA claimed that the scientific research definitively shows that exposure to media violence causes aggression, and it cited a study to support this assertion. *And that study is wrong—it does not show what the APA said it shows.* It could have chosen any study it wanted to mention; it could have picked one that *did* show an effect, because there are some. But no, it picked one that did not show an effect of media violence. I hope this makes people doubt the APA's assertion, since if it was wrong on this, why think it is correct in its more sweeping statements? That the APA selected this study shows just how sloppy that group is, and how little concerned with ensuring it has the science right. Embarrassing!

Thus the APA—the organization that represents many psychologists in the United States and around the world—pronounced that media violence causes aggression without doing a thorough review of the literature, without consulting those who disagree with this conclusion, without any hearings, and apparently with little concern for scientific accuracy. Perhaps the APA was worried about its public image. It knew that the public was concerned about media violence. Maybe the APA worried that if it took a more moderate stand or did not take a stand, the public would be upset. A more likely explanation is that the APA was worried about the reaction in Congress. The APA knew that many members of Congress were blaming television violence for the increase in crime rates. It also knew that psychologists depended on Congress for funding and for all sorts of other issues. Maybe its strong stand against media violence was to appease Congress. Or maybe it was simply that some psychologists believe in the causal effect and convinced the rest to go with them. Whatever the reason, the APA failed to be scientific....

It is a sad state of affairs when one cannot trust scientific and professional bodies to review the research carefully before making public pronouncements. It is likely that the APA and the rest have been influenced by public concerns and political considerations, and also presumably by the self-interest of those who have based their careers on demonstrating the harmful effects of media violence. Many of these people—perhaps most of them—are entirely sincere and mean well. They are worried about aggression and crime; they believe that media violence causes both; this makes sense to them. And they then make the dangerous leap from intuition to truth. They conclude that because they care and because it makes sense, it must be true. But this is not science, and it should not be passed off as science.

The real problem is that they are presenting views as scientific and proven when they are neither. Yet those views may have a direct effect on the public. People are extremely concerned about the effects of media violence. They base their concerns in part on their own intuitions, but also in large part on what they are told are the findings of scientific research. Because their intuitions are supported (or so they think) by hard science, they have no doubt that media violence is dangerous. This has led many people in the United States to believe that media violence is the major cause of violent crime in our society. With a few exceptions, even those scientists who are the most fervent believers in the causal hypothesis would not go this far. Rather, the conventional wisdom among these scientists is that media violence may account for about 10 percent of aggression and crime. This is still a lot, but it is far from the major cause of crime. However, this view is rarely heard or publicized, perhaps because it is not exciting. So people are told that media violence causes aggression and crime, and that scientific research proves this, and they come to believe that reducing media violence will greatly reduce aggression and crime.

Given the public pronouncements from professional organizations and the strong recommendations to avoid exposure to media violence, people naturally worry about their children being exposed to it, and even more about other people's children being exposed to it. Some people are so upset about this that they devote their lives to trying to reduce media violence. Indeed, I heard one such person accuse a mother of child abuse because she let her children watch the 'Mighty Morphin Power Rangers'. This is admittedly an extreme view, but why shouldn't she think that? If she had accused the mother of child abuse for smoking in the room of her infant son, many might agree with her. Well, I have heard a social scientist tell a large audience that the effect of media violence on aggression is as strong as the effect of smoking on lung cancer. This is, of course, total nonsense, but that is what the public is hearing from the experts. Is it any wonder that people are concerned?

The public is also affected indirectly through the actions of the U.S. Congress. Many members of Congress strongly favor reducing media violence. They support their position by citing the scientific evidence. Presumably they have not read the research themselves, and we would not expect them to have the time or expertise to do so. Instead they rely on the APA, ... and other scientific and quasi-scientific bodies to evaluate the evidence for them. When the APA ... and all the other organizations state unequivocally that media violence causes all sorts of harm, it would be irresponsible for Congress not to do something about it.

The difficulty is that these organizations have not reviewed the research either. Everyone is trusting everyone else to do it for them. The public and Congress have not done it and probably are not equipped to do it; the psychiatrists and pediatricians also have not done it and also are probably ill-equipped to do it. Fine. These groups can and should rely on the experts. And the experts are the psychologists. They are trained to review scientific research of this kind.... But they also have not done it....

In short, every organization has avoided the job of reviewing the research in detail. If they had acknowledged this, it would not be so bad. The real difficulty is that they have acted as if they *had* reviewed it. They have made definitive, powerful statements about the findings of the scientific research when they had no solid, independent basis for making them. Instead, presumably they have relied on what other people said and on their own intuitions. Sad!

CHALLENGE QUESTIONS

Does Media Violence
Cause Aggression?

1. Do you think that your behavior has ever been influenced by what you have seen on television or in other forms of mass media?
2. Considering that some psychological research does suggest a link between media violence and aggressive behavior, should media corporations ever be held legally or financially responsible when it appears that exposure to a violent media message may have been a factor in the crime?
3. If Bushman and Anderson are correct and media violence is an important cause of aggression, should action be taken in order to reduce the exposure of young people to its harmful effects? If so, why kind of action may be necessary?

Does Evolution Help Explain Gender Differences in Jealousy?

YES: David M. Buss, Randy J. Larsen, Drew Westen, and Jennifer Semmelroth, from "Sex Differences in Jealousy: Evolution, Physiology, and Psychology," *Psychological Science* (3, 1992)

NO: Christine R. Harris and Nicholas Christenfeld, from "Gender, Jealousy, and Reason," *Psychological Science* (7, 1996)

ISSUE SUMMARY

YES: According to David Buss and his colleagues, men and women have evolved different emotional reactions to the infidelity of their partners in response to different reproductive challenges. Men are likely to be particularly bothered by their partner's sexual infidelity while women are likely to be particularly bothered by emotional infidelity.

NO: Christine Harris and Nicholas Christenfeld argue that there is a serious methodological problem in the study described by David Buss and his colleagues. They are skeptic of the evolutionary interpretation.

How do women and men feel about relationship infidelity? Of course when one partner cheats on another, the reaction is invariably a negative one. But do both genders react with the same amount of scorn? And do different kinds of infidelity, whether emotional or sexual, evoke different amounts of anger and jealousy? These questions have important theoretical significance because they provide an opportunity to test the relevance of evolutionary principles to the study of emotion; addressing this question allows social psychologists to determine whether evolution has played an important role in determining how people experience emotion.

Evolutionary psychologist David Buss believes that men are likely to be particularly bothered by their partner's sexual infidelity, while women are likely to be particularly bothered by emotional infidelity. This prediction is based on two assumptions, both of which are derived from evolutionary principles. Buss argues that men are more likely to be bothered by sexual infidelity because men face concerns over paternity uncertainty. Paternity uncertainly is the degree to which a father is unsure that a child he is raising is actually his offspring. Buss reasons that fear over paternity uncertainty leads men to experience intense feelings of jealousy in response to the possibility of a partner's sexual infidelity.

Buss also argues that women are more likely to be bothered by emotional infidelity. According to evolutionary principles, women seek out partners who are willing to invest resources in their offspring. Emotional infidelity—when a partner falls in love with another person—should be particularly distressing to women because it signals that the partner will invest resources in a different partner. As a result, women have evolved to be sensitive to emotional infidelity and should be more likely to experience jealousy in response to the emotional indiscretions of their partner.

In the first selection, Buss and his colleagues present the results of a study in which they asked participants to imagine acts of sexual and emotional infidelity, and examined whether women and men experience different levels of jealously in response. However, Christine Harris and Nicholas Christenfeld believe that there is a serious flaw in the methods used by Buss and his colleagues. According to Harris and Christenfeld, an act of infidelity performed by a man usually has different implications than an act of infidelity performed by a woman. When one imagines an act of male sexual infidelity, one might imagine that the act of infidelity may not have also involved emotional infidelity. It could be sex without love. However, when one imagines an act of female sexual infidelity, one is likely to imagine that the act also involved emotional infidelity as well. Sex without love is less likely for women. The different scenarios that we might imagine for acts of infidelity among women and men make the results of Buss' study difficult to interpret. Harris and Christenfeld conclude that the results of Buss' study do not support the notion that there are gender differences in sexual and emotional jealousy.

POINT

- In the course of human evolution, women and men have faced different concerns over the rearing of offspring.
- Gender differences in sexual and emotional jealousy provide support for the evolutionary perspective.

COUNTERPOINT

- Evolutionary principles are not necessary to explain gender differences in jealousy.
- The evidence suggesting that women and men differ in their reaction to infidelity is flawed.
- Gender differences in jealousy may occur because a women's act of sexual infidelity has different implications than a man's act of sexual infidelity.

David M. Buss, Randy J. Larsen,
Drew Westen, and Jennifer Semmelroth ➡ **YES**

Sex Differences in Jealousy:
Evolution, Physiology, and Psychology

In species with internal female fertilization and gestation, features of reproductive biology characteristic of all 4,000 species of mammals, including
humans, males face an adaptive problem not confronted by females—uncertainty
in their paternity of offspring. Maternity probability in mammals rarely or never
deviates from 100%. Compromises in paternity probability come at substantial
reproductive cost to the male—the loss of mating effort expended, including time,
energy, risk, nuptial gifts, and mating opportunity costs. A cuckolded male also
loses the female's parental effort, which becomes channeled to a competitor's
gametes. The adaptive problem of paternity uncertainty is exacerbated in species
in which males engage in some postzygotic parental investment (Trivers, 1972).
Males risk investing resources in putative offspring that are genetically unrelated.

These multiple and severe reproductive costs should have imposed
strong selection pressure on males to defend against cuckoldry. Indeed, the literature is replete with examples of evolved anticuckoldry mechanisms in lions
(Bertram, 1975), bluebirds (Power, 1975), doves (Erickson & Zenone, 1976),
numerous insect species Thornhill & Alcock, 1983), and nonhuman primates
(Hrdy, 1979). Since humans arguably show more paternal investment than any
other of the 200 species of primates (Alexander & Noonan, 1979), this selection pressure should have operated especially intensely on human males.
Symons (1979), Daly, Wilson, and Weghorst (1982), and Wilson and Daly
(1992) have hypothesized that male sexual jealousy evolved as a solution to
this adaptive problem (but see Hupka, 1991, for an alternative view). Men who
were indifferent to sexual contact between their mates and other men presumably experienced lower paternity certainty, greater investment in competitors'
gametes, and lower reproductive success than did men who were motivated to
attend to cues of infidelity and to act on those cues to increase paternity probability.

Although females do not risk maternity uncertainty, in species with
biparental care they do risk the potential loss of time, resources, and commitment from a male if he deserts or channels investment to alternative mates
(Buss, 1988, Thornhill & Alcock, 1983, Trivers, 1972). The redirection of a
mate's investment to another female and her offspring is reproductively costly

From *Psychological Science*, vol. 3, no. 4, July 1992, pp. 251–255. Copyright © 1992 by Blackwell
Publishers, Ltd. Reprinted by permission.

for a female, especially in environments where offspring suffer in survival and reproductive currencies without investment from both parents.

In human evolutionary history, there were likely to have been at least two situations in which a woman risked losing a man's investment. First, in a monogamous marriage, a women risked having her mate invest in an alternative woman with whom he was having an affair (partial loss of investment) or risked his departure for an alternative woman (large or total loss of investment). Second, in polygynous marriages, a woman was at risk of having her mate invest to a larger degree in other wives and their offspring at the expense of his investment in her and her offspring. Following Buss (1988) and Mellon (1981), we hypothesize that cues to the development of a deep emotional attachment have been reliable leading indicators to women of potential reduction or loss of their mate's investment.

Jealousy is defined as an emotional "state that is aroused by a perceived threat to a valued relationship or position and motivates behavior aimed at countering the threat. Jealousy is 'sexual' if the valued relationship is sexual" (Daly et. al. 1982, p. 11, see also Salovey, 1991, White & Mullen, 1989). It is reasonable to hypothesize that jealousy involves physiological reactions (autonomic arousal) to perceived threat and motivated action to reduce the threat, although this hypothesis has not been examined. Following Symons (1979) and Daly et. al. (1982), our central hypothesis is that the events that activate jealousy physiologically and psychologically differ for men and women because of the different adaptive problems they have faced over human evolutionary history in mating contexts. Both sexes are hypothesized to be distressed over both sexual and emotional infidelity, and previous findings bear this out (Buss, 1989). However, these two kinds of infidelity should be weighted differently by men and women. Despite the importance of these hypothesized sex differences, no systematic scientific work has been directed toward verifying or falsifying their existence (but for suggestive data, see Francis, 1977, Teismann & Mosher, 1978, White & Mullen, 1989).

Study 1 Subjective Distress over a Partner's External Involvement

This study was designed to test the hypothesis that men and women differ in which form of infidelity—sexual versus emotional—triggers more upset and subjective distress, following the adaptive logic just described.

Method

After reporting age and sex, subjects ($N = 202$ undergraduate students) were presented with the following dilemma.

> Please think of a serious committed romantic relationship that you have had in the past, that you currently have, or that you would like to have. Imagine that you discover that the person with whom you've been seriously

involved became interested in someone else. What would distress or upset you more (*please circle only one*).

A. Imagining your partner forming a deep emotional attachment to that person
B. Imagining your partner enjoying passionate sexual intercourse with that other person

Subjects completed additional questions, and then encountered the next dilemma, with the same instructional set, but followed by a different, but parallel, choice.

A. Imagining your partner trying different sexual positions with the other person
B. Imagining your partner falling in love with that other person

Results

Shown in Figure 1 (upper panel) are the percentages of men and women reporting more distress in response to sexual infidelity than emotional infidelity. The first empirical probe, contrasting distress over a partner's sexual involvement with distress over a partner's deep emotional attachment, yielded a large and highly significant sexual difference ($\chi^2 = 47.56$, $df = 3$, $p < .001$). Fully 60% of the male sample reported greater distress over their partner's potential sexual infidelity, in contrast, only 17% of the female sample chose that option, with 83% reporting that they would experience greater distress over a partner's emotional attachment to a rival.

This pattern was replicated with the contrast between sex and love. The magnitude of the sex difference was large, with 32% more men than women reporting greater distress over a partner's sexual involvement with someone else, and the majority of women reporting greater distress over a partner's falling in love with a rival ($\chi^2 = 59.20$, $df = 3$, $p < .001$).

Study 2 Physiological Responses to a Partner's External Involvement

Given the strong confirmation of jealousy sex linkage from Study 1, we sought next to test the hypotheses using physiological measures. Our central measures of autonomic arousal were electrodermal activity (EDA), assessed via skin conductance, and pulse rate (PR). Electrodermal activity and pulse rate are indicators of autonomic nervous system activation (Levenson, 1988). Because distress is an unpleasant subjective state, we also included a measure of muscle activity in the brow region of the face—electromyographic (EMG) activity of the *corrugator supercilu* muscle. This muscle is responsible for the furrowing of the brow often seen in facial displays of unpleasant emotion or affect (Fridlund, Ekman, & Oster, 1987). Subjects were asked to image two scenarios in which a partner became involved with someone else—one sexual intercourse scenario and one emotional attachment scenario. Physiological responses were recorded during the imagery trials.

Figure 1

Reported comparison of distress in response to imagining a partner's sexual or emotional infidelity. The upper panel shows results of Study 1—the percentage of subjects reporting more distress to the sexual infidelity scenario than to the emotional infidelity (left) and the love infidelity (right) scenarios. The lower panel shows the results of Study 3—the percentage of subjects reporting more distress to the sexual infidelity scenario than to the emotional infidelity scenario, presented separately for those who have experienced a committed sexual relationship (left) and those who have not experienced a committed sexual relationship (right).

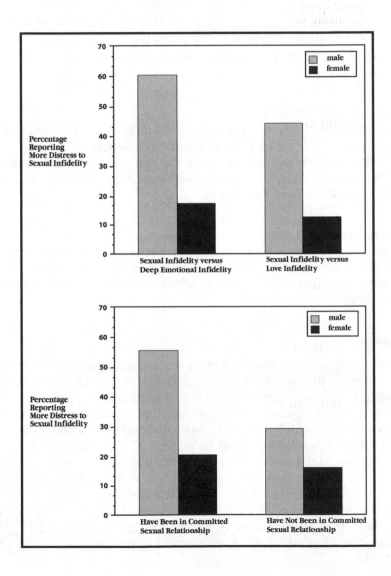

Subjects

Subjects were 55 undergraduate students, 32 males and 23 females, each completing a 2-hr laboratory session.

Physiological Measures

Physiological activity was monitored on the running strip chart of a Grass Model 7D polygraph and digitized on a laboratory computer at a 10-Hz rate, following principles recommended in Cacioppo and Tassinary (1990).

Electrodermal Activity
Standard Beckman Ag/AgCl surface electrodes, filled with a 05 molar NaCl solution in a Unibase paste, were placed over the middle segments of the first and third fingers of the right hand. A Wheatstone bridge applied a 0 5-V voltage to one electrode.

Pulse Rate
A photoplethysmograph was attached to the subject's right thumb to monitor the pulse wave. The signal from this pulse transducer was fed into a Grass Model 7P4 cardiotachometer to detect the rising slope of each pulse wave, with the internal circuitry of the Schmitt trigger individually adjusted for each subject to put PR in beats per minute.

Electromyographic Activity
Bipolar EMG recordings were obtained over the *corrugator supercilu* muscle. The EMG signal was relayed to a wide-band AC-preamplifier (Grass Model 7P3), where it was band-pass filtered, full-wave rectified, and integrated with a time constant of 0 2 s.

Procedure

After electrode attachment, the subject was made comfortable in a reclining chair and asked to relax. After a 5-min waiting period, the experiment began. The subject was alone in the room during the imagery session, with an intercom on for verbal communication. The instructions for the imagery task were written on a form which the subject was requested to read and follow.

Each subject was instructed to engage in three separate images. The first image was designed to be emotionally neutral. "Imagine a time when you were walking to class, feeling neither good nor bad, just neutral." The subject was instructed to press a button when he or she had the image clearly in mind, and to sustain the image until the experimenter said to stop. The button triggered the computer to begin collecting physiological data for 20 s, after which the experimenter instructed the subject to "stop and relax."

The next two images were infidelity images, one sexual and one emotional. The order of presentation of these two images was counterbalanced. The instructions for sexual jealousy imagery were as follows. "Please think of a serious romantic relationship that you have had in the past, that you currently have, or that you would like to have. Now imagine that the person with whom you're seriously involved becomes interested in someone else. *Imagine you find out that your partner is having sexual intercourse with this other person.* Try to feel the feelings you would have if this happened to you."

The instructions for emotional infidelity imagery were identical to the above, except the italicized sentence was replaced with *"Imagine that your partner is falling in love and forming an emotional attachment to that person."* Physiological data were collected for 20 s following the subject's button press indicating that he or she had achieved the image. Subjects were told to "stop and relax" for 30 s between imagery trials.

Results

Physiological Scores

The following scores were obtained: (a) the amplitude of the largest EDA response occurring during each 20-s trial, (b) PR in beats per minute averaged over each 20-s trial, and (c) amplitude of EMG activity over the *corrugator superculi* averaged over each 20-s trials. Difference scores were computed between the neutral imagery trial and the jealousy induction trials. Within-sex t tests revealed no effects for order of presentation of the sexual jealousy image, so data were collapsed over this factor.

Jealousy Induction Effects

Table 1 shows the mean scores for the physiological measures for men and women in each of the two imagery conditions. Differences in physiological responses to the two jealousy images were examined using paired-comparison t tests for each sex separately for EDA, PR, and EMG. The men showed significant increases in EDA during the sexual imagery compared with the emotional imagery ($t = 2.00$, $df = 29$, $p < .05$. Women showed significantly greater EDA to the emotional infidelity image than to the sexual infidelity image ($t = 2.42$, $df = 19$, $p < .05$. A similar pattern was observed with PR. Men showed a substantial increase in PR to both images, but significantly more so in response to the sexual infidelity image ($t = 2.29$, $df = 31$, $p < .05$. Women showed elevated PR to both images, but not differentially so. The results of the *corrugator* EMG were similar, although less strong. Men showed greater brow contraction to the sexual infidelity image, and women showed the opposite pattern, although results with this nonautonomic measure did not reach significance ($t = 1.12$, $df = 30$, $p < .14$, for males. $t = -1.24$, $df = 22$, $p < .12$, for females). The elevated EMG contractions for both jealousy induction trials in both sexes support the hypothesis that the affect experienced is negative.

Table 1

Means and Standard Deviations on Physiological Measures during Two Imagery Conditions

Measure	Imagery type	Mean	SD
	Males		
EDA	Sexual	1.30	3.64
	Emotional	–0.11	0.76
Pulse rate	Sexual	4.76	7.80
	Emotional	3.00	5.24
Brow EMG	Sexual	6.75	32.96
	Emotional	1.16	6.60
	Females		
EDA	Sexual	–0.07	0.49
	Emotional	0.21	0.78
Pulse rate	Sexual	2.25	4.68
	Emotional	2.57	4.37
Brow EMG	Sexual	3.03	8.38
	Emotional	8.12	25.60

Note: Measures are expressed as changes from the neutral image condition. EDA is in microsiemen units, pulse rate is in beats per minute, and EMG is in microvolt units

Study 3 Contexts that Activate the Jealousy Mechanism

The goal of Study 3 was to replicate and extend the results of Studies 1 and 2 using a larger sample. Specifically, we sought to examine the effects of having been in a committed sexual relationship versus not having been in such a relationship on the activation of jealousy. We hypothesized that men who had actually experienced a committed sexual relationship would report greater subjective distress in response to the sexual infidelity imagery than would men who had not experienced a high-investing sexual relationship, and that women who had experienced a committed sexual relationship would report greater distress to the emotional infidelity image than women who had not been in a committed sexual relationship. The rationale was that direct experience of the relevant context during development may be necessary for the activation of the sex-linked weighting of jealousy activation.

Subjects

Subjects for Study 3 were 309 undergraduate students, 133 men and 176 women.

Procedure

Subjects read the following instructions.

> Please think of a serious or committed romantic relationship that you have had in the past that you currently have, or that you would like to have. Imagine that you discover that the person with whom you've been

seriously involved became interested in someone else. What would distress or upset you more (*please circle only one*).

A. Imagining your partner falling in love and forming a deep emotional attachment to that person
B. Imagining your partner having sexual intercourse with that other person

Alternatives were presented in standard forced-choice format, with the order counterbalanced across subjects. Following their responses, subjects were asked "Have you ever been in a serious or committed romantic relationship? (yes or no)" and "If yes, was this a sexual relationship? (yes or no)."

Results

The results for the total sample replicate closely the results of Study 1. A much larger proportion of men (49%) than women (19%) reported that they would be more distressed by their partner's sexual involvement with someone else than by their partner's emotional attachment to, or love for, someone else (χ^2 = 38.48, df = 3, p < .001).

The two pairs of columns In the bottom panel of Figure 1 show the results separately for those subjects who had experienced a committed sexual relationship in the past and those who had not. For women, the difference is small and not significant. Women reported that they would experience more distress about a partner's emotional infidelity than a partner's sexual infidelity, regardless of whether or not they had experienced a committed sexual relationship (χ^2 = 0.80, df = 1, ns).

For men, the difference between those who had been in a sexual relationship and those who had not is large and highly significant. Whereas 55% of the men who had experienced committed sexual relationships reported that they would be more distressed by a partner's sexual than emotional infidelity, this figure drops to 29% for men who had never experienced a committed sexual relationship χ^2 = 12.29, df = 1, p < .001). Sexual jealousy in men apparently becomes increasingly activated upon experience of the relevant relationship.

Discussion

The results of the three empirical studies support the hypothesized sex linkages in the activators of jealous. Study 1 found large sex differences in reports of the subjective distress individuals would experience upon exposure to a partner's sexual infidelity versus emotional infidelity. Study 2 found a sex linkage in autonomic arousal to imagined sexual infidelity versus emotional infidelity, the results were particularly strong for the EDA and PR. Study 3 replicated the large sex differences in reported distress to sexual versus emotional infidelity, and found a strong effect for men of actually having experienced a committed sexual relationship.

These studies are limited in ways that call for additional research. First, they pertain to a single age group and culture. Future studies could explore the degree to which these sex differences transcend different cultures and age groups. Two clear evolutionary psychological predictions are (a) that male sexual jealousy and female commitment jealousy will be greater in cultures where males invest heavily in children, and (b) that male sexual jealousy will diminish as the age of the male's mate increases because her reproductive value decreases. Second, future studies could test the alternative hypotheses that the current findings reflect (a) domain-specific psychological adaptations to cuckoldry versus potential investment loss or (b) a more domain-general mechanism such that any thoughts of sex are more interesting, arousing, and perhaps disturbing to men whereas any thoughts of love are more interesting, arousing, and perhaps disturbing to women, and hence that such responses are not specific to jealousy or infidelity. Third, emotional and sexual infidelity are clearly correlated, albeit imperfectly, and a sizable percentage of men in Studies 1 and 3 reported greater distress to a partner's emotional infidelity. Emotional infidelity may signal sexual infidelity and vice versa, and hence both sexes should become distressed at both forms (see Buss, 1989). Future research could profitably explore in greater detail the correlation of these forms of infidelity as well as the sources of within-sex variation. Finally, the intriguing finding that men who have experienced a committed sexual relationship differ dramatically from those who have not, whereas for women such experiences appear to be irrelevant to their selection of emotional infidelity as the more distressing event, should be examined. Why do such ontogenetic experiences matter for men, and why do they appear to be irrelevant for women?

Within the constraints of the current studies, we can conclude that the sex differences found here generalize across both psychological and physiological methods—demonstrating an empirical robustness in the observed effect. The degree to which these sex-linked elicitors correspond to the hypothesized sex-linked adaptive problems lends support to the evolutionary psychological framework from which they are derived. Alternative theoretical frameworks, including those that invoke culture, social construction, deconstruction, arbitrary parental socialization, and structural powerlessness, undoubtedly could be molded post hoc to fit the findings—something perhaps true of any set of findings. None but the Symons (1979) and Daly et. al. (1982) evolutionary psychological frameworks, however, generated the sex-differentiated predictions in advance and on the basis of sound evolutionary reasoning. The recent finding that male sexual jealousy is the leading cause of spouse battering and homicide across cultures worldwide (Daly & Wilson, 1988a, 1988b) offers suggestive evidence that these sex differences have large social import and may be species-wide.

References

Alexander, R.D., & Noonan, K.M. (1979). Concealment of ovulation parental care, and human social evolution. In N Chagnon & W Irons (Eds) *Evolutionary biology and human social behavior* (pp 436–453), North Scituate, MA: Duxbury.

Bertram, B.C.R. (1975). Social factors influencing reproduction in wild lions, *Journal of Zoology, 177*, 463–482.

Buss, D.M. (1988). From vigilance to violence: Tactics of mate retention, *Ethology and Sociobiology, 9*, 291–317.

Buss, D.M. (1989). Conflict between the sexes: Strategic interference and the evocation of anger and upset, *Journal of Personality and Social Psychology, 56*, 735–747.

Cacioppo, J.T., & Tassinary, L.G. (Eds.). (1990). *Principles of psychophysiology: Physical social and inferential elements*, Cambridge, England: Cambridge University Press.

Daly, M., & Wilson, M. (1988a). Evolutionary social psychology and family violence, *Science, 242*, 519–524.

Daly, M., Wilson, M., & Weghorst, S.J. (1982). Male Sexual jealousy, *Ethology and Sociobiology, 3*, 11–27.

Erickson, C.J., & Zenone, P.G. (1976). Courtship differences in males ring doves: Avoidance of cuckoldry? *Science, 192*, 1353–1354.

Francis, J.L. (1977). Toward the management of heterosexual jealousy, *Journal of Marriage and Family Counseling, 10*, 61–69.

Fridlund, A., Ekman, P., & Oster, J. (1987). Facial expressions of emotion. In A Siegman & S Feldstein (Eds), *Nonverbal behavior and communication* (pp 143–224), Hillsdale, NJ: Erlbaum.

Hrdy, S.B.G. (1979). Infanticide among animals: A review classification, and examination of the implications for the reproductive strategies of females, *Ethology and Sociobiology, 1*, 14–40.

Hupka, R.B. (1991). The motive for the arousal of romantic jealousy: Its cultural origin. In P Salovey (Ed), *The psychology of jealousy and envy* (pp 252–270), New York: Guilford Press.

Levenson, R.W. (1988). Emotion and the autonomic nervous system: A prospectus for research on autonomic specificity. In H Wagner (Ed), *Social psychophysiology: Theory and clinical applications* (pp 17–42), London: Wiley.

Mellon, L.W. (1981). *The evolution of love*, San Francisco: W H Freeman.

Power, H. W. (1975), Mountain bluebirds: Experimental evidence against altruism, *Science, 189*, 142–143.

Salovey, P. (Ed.) (1991). *The psychology of jealousy and envy*, New York: Guilford Press.

Symons, D. (1979). *The evolution of human sexuality*, New York: Oxford University Press.

Teismann, M.W., & Mosher, D.L. (1978). Jealous conflict in dating couples, *Psychological Reports, 42*, 1211–1216.

Thornhill, R., & Alcock, J. (1983). *The evolution of insect mating systems*, Cambridge, MA: Harvard University Press.

Trivers, R. (1972). Parental investment and sexual selection. In B Campbell (Eds), *Sexual selection and the descent of man, 1871–1971* (pp 136–179), Chicago: Aldine.

White, G.L., & Mullen, P.E. (1989). *Jealousy: Theory research and clinical strategies*, New York: Guilford Press.

Wilson, M., & Daly, M. (1992). The man who mistook his wife for a chattel. In J Barkow, L Cosmides, & J Tooby (Eds), *The adapted mind: Evolutionary psychology and the generation of culture*, New York: Oxford University Press.

NO ↩   Christine R. Harris and
Nicholas Christenfeld

Gender, Jealousy, and Reason

Buss, Larsen, Westen, and Semmelroth (1992) have suggested that men and women are intrinsically different in the magnitude of their responses to sexual and emotional infidelity, as a result of differing reproductive costs over human evolutionary history. Women, seeking to ensure males' long-term involvement, have evolved to care about their mates falling in love with others and not to be so concerned about their mates having sex with others. Men, keen not to expend resources on other men's children, should be concerned about their women having sex with others, and not care so much about their falling in love with others. Buss et. al. supported their argument with data indicating that when asked to choose whether sexual or emotional infidelity would be more bothersome, more women than men selected emotional infidelity, and more men than women selected sexual infidelity. We argue here that these results can be explained without suggesting that men and women are innately different in how much they are disturbed by emotional and sexual infidelity.

Although Buss et. al. and other investigators before them (Daly & Wilson, 1983, Symons, 1979) proposed an evolutionary account for men caring about sexual infidelity and women about emotional infidelity, Buss et. al. argued that "emotional infidelity may signal sexual infidelity and vice versa, and hence both sexes should become distressed at both forms" (p. 255). We suggest instead that men and women may be equally upset by each type of infidelity and that the crucial difference may lie in how much they think that each form of infidelity signals the other.

Imagine a man returning from work one day to discover incontrovertible proof of his wife's sexual infidelity. He might well think that because women have sex only when in love, it is quite certain that she has fallen in love with this other man as well. A woman, however, finding the same evidence about her husband, might think that because men often have sex without being in love, there is no reason to assume he is in love with the other woman. The man, then, is upset by what he takes to be sexual and emotional infidelity, whereas the woman is concerned only about sexual infidelity. The man will be more bothered by the sexual infidelity than is the woman because he draws a more troubling conclusion from that evidence. The man should have a stronger response to sexual infidelity even if the man and woman care equally about their spouses' actual sexual exploits.

From *Psychological Science,* vol. 7, no. 6, November 1996, pp. 364–366. Copyright © 1996 by Blackwell Publishers, Ltd. Reprinted with permission.

The situation should be reversed with evidence of emotional infidelity. The man, on coming across evidence of this sort, should reason that women can be in love without having sex, and so he need not assume that there is sexual infidelity as well. The woman, however, thinking that men in love are certainly having sex, will assume that both sorts of treachery have occurred, and be doubly bothered.

Thus, emotional infidelity should especially trouble women, and sexual infidelity should especially trouble men. This prediction follows not from any postulated innate difference in responses to the specific infidelities, but rationally from the hypothesis that men think women have sex only when in love and women think men have sex without love. We tested this hypothesis in a survey, and also sought to replicate the original finding of Buss et. al.

Method

Subjects were 137 undergraduate students (55 males and 82 females) who individually and anonymously completed a survey of attitudes about relationships as part of a requirement for experimental participation. Among other questions about sexuality and dating were three questions about sexual and emotional infidelity. The first was taken from Buss et. al. and was included to replicate their finding, the other two were designed to measure how much men and women think each form of infidelity implies the other.

1. Please think of a serious romantic relationship you have had in the past, currently have, or would like to have. Imagine that you discover that your romantic partner has become interested in someone else. What would upset you more?
   a. Imagining your partner trying different sexual positions with that other person.
   b. Imagining your partner falling in love with that other person.
2. Please think of a serious romantic relationship you have had in the past, currently have, or would like to have. Imagine that you discover that your mate is engaging in sexual intercourse with someone else. How likely do you think it is that your mate is in love with this person?
3. Please think of a serious romantic relationship you have had in the past, currently have, or would like to have. Imagine that you discover that your mate is in love with someone else. How likely do you think it is that your mate is also engaging in sex with this other person?

The latter two questions were answered on 5-point Likert scales ranging from "not at all likely" to "very likely."

Results

Results for the first question replicated the results of Buss et. al. In choosing between the two forms of infidelity, more males than females selected sexual infidelity as more upsetting, whereas more women than men selected emotional infidelity, $\chi^2(1, N = 136) = 9.39, p < .005$. (One female failed to answer this question.) The data are shown in Table 1. Overall, subjects were bothered

Table 1

Comparison of Men's and Women's Distress in Response to Imaging Emotional and Sexual Infidelity in a Partner (in Percentages)

Gender	More bothered by	
	Sex	Love
Females (n = 81)	12	88
Males (n = 55)	47	53

more by emotional than sexual infidelity, a bias that Buss et. al. found also. In fact, in both our data and those reported by Buss et. al., the men were close to equally split about which would bother them more, and it is the women's strong aversion to emotional infidelity that produced the effect.

To analyze whether the sexes differ in the extent to which they think one form of infidelity implies the other, we subjected the second and third questions to a mixed factorial analysis of variance, with gender as the between-subjects factor and the two questions as the within-subjects factor. There was no main effect of gender, $F(1, 132) = 1.03$, n.s., and overall subjects thought that emotional infidelity implies sexual infidelity more than sexual infidelity implies emotional infidelity, $F(1, 132) = 12.17$, $p < .001$. (One female and 2 males failed to answer one of these questions.) The specific prediction, that men think that sex implies love for their partners more than do women, whereas women think that love implies sex more than do men, was tested with the interaction, which was significant, $F(1, 132) = 11.32$, $p < .001$. An inspection of the means, which are presented in Table 2, indicates that the dominant effect was that women think men can have sex without being in love.

Discussion

The findings provide strong support for the predicted interaction in the extent to which men and women think each form of infidelity implies the other. The pattern suggests that it is reasonable for men to be more concerned than women by evidence of a partner's sexual infidelity and for women to be especially concerned by evidence of a partner's emotional infidelity. Women may report less concern over scenarios of sexual infidelity because they believe that their partners have sex without being in love, men care more about sexual infidelity because they think it is unlikely to occur without emotional infidelity as well. It need not be the case that men care more about the sex, but may just be that sexual infidelity accompanied by emotional infidelity is worse than sexual infidelity alone.

Both the approach taken by Buss et. al. and our own interpretation can explain why women are more bothered by emotional than sexual infidelity. Buss et. al. suggested that this is an innate response based on women's desire that their offspring have involved fathers. We suggest it may be due to women's belief that men may have sex without being in love, but are less likely to be in love without having sex. Emotional infidelity is thus logically a more troubling indicator. The account offered by Buss et. al. however, has dif-

Table 2

Subjects' Rating of How Much Sexual Infidelity Implies Emotional Infidelity and How Much Emotional Infidelity Implies Sexual infidelity

Gender	Sex implies love	Love implies sex
Females (n = 81)	2.70	3.75
Males (n = 53)	3.43	3.32

Note: Cells indicate means on a 5-point Likert scale, from 1 (*not at all*) to 5 (*very*).

ficulty explaining men's indifference between sexual and emotional infidelity, a pattern that Buss et. al. found in their survey (even after discarding men who have never had a committed sexual relationship), and one replicated here. The evolutionary account predicts that men, not wanting their partners bearing others' children, but not caring so much about their partners loving others, should care far more about sexual than emotional infidelity. Our account, that men care about both kinds of infidelity, and our finding that they think the two signal each other about equally, is perfectly compatible with men reporting they would be equally concerned to discover evidence of either type of infidelity.

The different inferences about the relationship of love and sex that are documented here could well reflect actual differences in the behavior of men and women in the world. That is, our subjects may be correct in suspecting that women tend to have sex only when in love, and this tendency may reflect an innate dispositional difference (Symons, 1979). However, even if it does, our account would not require one to postulate an innate gender difference in the intensity with which men and women experience sexual or romantic jealousy. Whether or not the difference in sexual behavior is real, and whether or not it is based in innate biological differences, does not matter. As long as women think that men have sex without love but not love without sex, it is rational for them to be bothered more by reports of emotional infidelity than by reports of sexual infidelity.

Ultimately, all differences between men and women have a genetic origin, because the difference between man and woman is one of genes, however, the path from genes to attitudes and behavior may be circuitous and based on reasoning (Harris & Pashler, 1995). It is not, for example, an innate preference that causes men to micturate standing and women sitting, but a reasonable response to an innate difference. Gender differences in affective responses to jealousy also need not be innate.

One can think of many examples of gender differences in emotions that are based on reasoned interpretations of evidence. Men and women will have very different emotional reactions to lipstick stains on a partner's collar—not because of a difference in their innate responses to lipstick, but rather as a result of their rationally interpreting the evidence differently. What suggests an affair to one sex implies mere sloppiness to the other. Responses to infidelity may likewise not be innate reactions, but instead a result of differences in the way the evidence is interpreted. Men and women need not differ in how much they care about each sort of infidelity, but only in what they think each implies.

References

Buss, D. M., Larsen, R. J., Westen, D., & Semmelroth, J. (1992). Sex differences in jealousy: Evolution physiology, and psychology, *Psychological Science, 3,* 251–255.

Daly, M., & Wilson, M. (1983) *Sex evolution and behavior* (2nd ed.), Belmont, CA: Wadsworth.

Harris, C. R., & Pashler, H. E. (1995). Evolution and human emotions, *Psychological Inquiry, 6,* 44–46.

Symons, D. (1979). *The evolution of human sexuality,* New York: Oxford University Press.

CHALLENGE QUESTIONS

Does Evolution Help Explain Gender Differences in Jealousy?

1. Do you think that there are any ethical concerns raised by these studies? Is imagining a partner committing an act of sexual and emotional infidelity likely to induce excessively severe emotional distress?
2. Do you agree that the evolutionary principles cited by Buss do, in fact, predict that there should be gender differences in jealousy? Or do you disagree with the reasoning that Buss and his colleagues use to derive their hypotheses?
3. What other studies could be conducted that would perhaps be a better test of the hypotheses proposed by Buss and his colleagues?

Contributors to This Volume

EDITOR

Jason A. Nier is an Assistant Professor of Psychology at Connecticut College in New London, CT. He received his undergraduate degree from The Pennsylvania State University and his masters and doctorate in psychology from the University of Delaware. Dr. Nier is a social psychologist who specializes in the study of intergroup relations. Within the field of intergroup relations, his research has focused primarily on the measurement of intergroup attitudes and the development of interventions that reduce bias and conflict between groups. He has authored or co-authored numerous articles and book chapters, which have appeared in journals such as the *Journal of Personality and Social Psychology, Personality and Social Psychology Bulletin,* and *Group Processes and Intergroup Relations.* Nier also co-authored a book chapter that won the 1998 Gordon Allport Intergroup Relations Prize, awarded annually to the best paper in the field of intergroup relations.

STAFF

Larry Loeppke   Managing Editor
Jill Peter   Senior Developmental Editor
Nichole Altman   Developmental Editor
Lori Church   Permissions Coordinator
Beth Kundert   Production Manager
Jane Mohr   Project Manager
Kari Voss   Lead Typesetter
Craig Purcell   eContent Coordinator
Maggie Lytle   Cover Designer

AUTHORS

PAULA ACKERMAN is a former student at the University of Kansas.

CRAIG A. ANDERSON is professor of psychology and chair of the psychology department at Iowa State University. Dr. Anderson is the author of numerous journal articles and book chapters. Much of his research examines the psychology of aggressive behavior, including the impact of the media on aggression.

ARTHUR ARON is professor of psychology at the State University of New York, Stony Brook. His research examines the cognitive overlap between self and others, and how this may relate to many social psychological phenomena, including romantic relationships, friendships, and prejudice.

ELAINE N. ARON is a clinical psychologist and psychotherapist who is the author of numerous books in the field of psychology, including *The Highly Sensitive Person*.

KEVIN ARPS teaches psychology at Paradise Valley Community College.

DANIEL C. BATSON received his Ph.D. in psychology from Princeton University in 1972 and is now professor of psychology at the University of Kansas. He has conducted a number of experiments on various forms of prosocial motivation, is the author of *The Altruism Question: Toward a Social-Psychological Answer*, and the chapter in *The Handbook of Social Psychology* titled "Altruism and Prosocial Behavior."

ROY F. BAUMEISTER is professor of psychology and the Francis Eppes Eminent Scholar at Florida State University. He is the author of sixteen books and dozens of journal articles and books. His current research interests include the psychology of self-control, self-destructive behavior, and the need to belong.

DIANA BAUMRIND is a research psychologist at the Institute for Human Development located at the University of California, Berkeley. She is the author of over 50 journal articles and book chapters.

ARTHUR L. BEAMAN received his doctoral degree from the University of Washington. He has taught at the University of Montana.

DARYL J. BEM is professor of psychology at Cornell University. Bem began his academic career as a graduate student in the Physics Department at MIT, but eventually enrolled in the social psychology doctoral at the University of Michigan, where he received his Ph.D. in 1964. Dr. Bem is the author of several books and has published research on a variety of different topics including self-perception, group decision making, sexual orientation, and extrasensory perception.

KIMBERLY BIRCH is a former student at the University of Kansas.

JACK BLOCK is Emeritus professor of psychology at the University of California, Berkeley. Dr. Block received his Ph.D. in clinical psychology from Stanford University in 1950. A member of faculty at UC–Berkeley since

1957, Dr. Block has written extensively in many different areas of psychology including social, personality, and developmental psychology.

JONATHON D. BROWN is professor of psychology at the University of Washington. His research examines the nature, origins, and consequences of self-esteem. He is the author of dozens of journal articles and book chapters.

RUPERT J. BROWN is professor of psychology at Sussex University (UK). His research examines the social psychology of prejudice. His numerous publications include the books *Prejudice: Its Social Psychology* and *Group Processes: Dynamics within and between Groups*.

TERESE BUCKLEY is a former student at the University of Kansas.

BRAD J. BUSHMAN is professor of psychology at the Institute for Social Research at the University of Michigan. He has written extensively on the topic of aggression, with an emphasis on the impact of the media on aggressive behavior. He has also served as associate editor of *Personality and Social Psychology Bulletin*.

DAVID M. BUSS has taught at Harvard University, University of Michigan, and currently holds a professorship at the University of Texas at Austin; he is author or more than 180 scientific publications, and has authored six books, including *The Evolution of Desire: Strategies of Human Mating*, and *Evolutionary Psychology: The New Science of the Mind*.

JAMES M. CARLSMITH received his Ph.D. from Harvard University in 1963. He was professor of psychology at Stanford University. He was the author of numerous journal articles and books including textbooks in social psychology and research methods.

NICHOLAS CHRISTENFELD is professor of psychology at the University of California, San Diego. His research examines a wide variety of topics including procrastination, memories for emotions, and stress.

ROBERT B. CIALDINI received his doctoral degree from the University of North Carolina, Chapel Hill. He is currently Regents' professor of psychology at Arizona State University. He is author of the widely read book *Influence*.

C. RANDALL COLVIN is associate professor of psychology at Northeastern University. Dr. Colvin's research examines the accuracy of personality judgments and the implications of these judgments for psychological adjustment. He is the author of numerous journal articles and has also served as associate editor for the *Journal of Research in Personality*.

BELLA M. DEPAULO received her Ph.D. from Harvard University in 1979, and she is currently a visiting professor of psychology at the University of California, Santa Barbara. Dr. DePaulo has numerous publications in her areas of interest including the psychology of deception, non-verbal communication and self-presentation.

PATRICIA DEVINE is professor of psychology at University of Wisconsin–Madison. Her research interests focus primarily on prejudice in contemporary society, including the distinction between implicit and explicit forms of prejudice and the use of stereotypes. She is currently serving as editor of the *Journal of Personality and Social Psychology*.

DAVID DUBOIS is associate professor of psychology at the University of Missouri–Columbia. Dr. Dubois' research examines child and adolescent developmental psychopathology, with a particular emphasis on the role of self-esteem. Dr. Dubois received his Ph.D. from the University of Illinois, Urbana–Champaign.

BRUCE D. DUNCAN is a former graduate student in the department of psychology at the University of Kansas.

ALICE EAGLY is professor of psychology and Faculty Fellow at the Institute for Policy Research at Northwestern University. Dr. Eagly has two primary research interests—the psychology of attitudes and the psychology of gender. She has written extensively on these topics, including two books and many journal articles and book chapters. She has also served as president of the Midwestern Psychological Association and the Society for Personality and Social Psychology.

ALAN C. ELMS is Emeritus professor of psychology at the University of California, Davis. Dr. Elms' work examines psychobiography as a research methodology in personality psychology. As a former research assistant in Stanley Milgram's Obedience Experiments, he has also written about his first-hand experience with Milgram's research.

NICHOLAS EPLEY is assistant professor of psychology at Harvard University. Dr. Epley received his Ph.D. from Cornell University prior to becoming a member of the faculty at Harvard in 2001. He has won numerous honors and awards for his scholarly work and is author of over a dozen journal articles and book chapters.

LEON FESTINGER was professor of psychology at the University of Minnesota, Stanford University, and the New School for Social Research, as well as former director of Research Center for Group Dynamics at the University of Michigan. Festinger, who was a former student of Kurt Lewin, was one of the most influential social psychologists of his generation who is best known for his theory of cognitive dissonance.

JONATHAN L. FREEDMAN is professor of psychology at the University of Toronto. Dr. Freedman is best known for his work that critically examines the impact of the media on aggressive behavior.

JIM FULTZ received his doctoral degree from the University of Kansas. He has taught at Northern Illinois University.

DAVID C. FUNDER is professor of psychology at University of California, Riverside. His research examines the circumstances under which social judgments are likely to be accurate. His most recent research focuses on the Realistic Accuracy Model, which proposes that accurate judgments of personality are a result of a four-stage psychological process.

JAMES GEARY is a journalist and editor for *Time* magazine.

CRAIG HANEY is professor of psychology at the University of California, Santa Cruz. His research examines the application of social psychology to various legal and civil rights issues.

CHRISTINE R. HARRIS is assistant professor of psychology at the University of California, San Diego, where she received her Ph.D. in 1998. Her research examines the function of various emotions including jealousy, embarrassment, and shame.

DONALD HOULIHAN is a former student at Arizona State University.

LEE JUSSIM received his Ph.D. from the University of Michigan in 1987 and is currently professor of psychology at Rutgers University. His research examines a variety of topics including social perception, political correctness, and stereotyping. Dr. Jussim is the author of over 50 journal articles and book chapters. He is also Director of the Social Psychology Graduate Program at Rutgers University.

DAVID KIPNIS was professor of psychology at Temple University. Dr. Kipnis was a social and industrial-organizational psychologist who was best known for his work examining the influence of power and technology on society. He was author of three books and numerous articles.

RICHARD P. KLUFT is clinical professor of psychiatry, Temple University School of Medicine. Dr. Kluft has written extensively on the topic of dissociative identity disorder. He has edited two books on the topic including *Childhood Antecedents of Mutliple Personality Disorder* and *Clinical Perspectives on Multiple Personality Disorder*, which he co-edited with Catherine Fine.

RANDY J. LARSEN is Stuckenberg Professor of Human Values and Moral Development at Washington University in St. Louis. Dr. Larsen is a personality psychologist who is interested primarily in mood regulation. He has published extensively on a variety of topics relating to his research interests and has served as associate editor for the *Journal of Personality and Social Psychology*.

YUEH-TING LEE received his Ph.D. in social psychology from the State University of New York at Stony Brook and completed his postdoctoral work at the University of Pennsylvania. He is currently chairperson and professor of ethnic studies at Minnesota State University, Mankato. Dr. Lee's research examines stereotyping, social identity, and intergroup conflict from cross-cultural and experimental perspectives.

LORELLA LEPORE is Lecturer in Psychology at the University of Reading (UK). Dr. Lepore received her Ph.D. in psychology from the University of Kent. She won the Dissertation Award from the Society of Experimental Social Psychology for her doctoral work, which examined the automatic stereotype activation and prejudice.

ELIZABETH LOFTUS is Distinguished professor of psychology and Social Behavior at the University of California, Irvine. She has also taught at the University of Washington, Harvard University, New School University,

Georgetown Law School, and the University of Nevada. Dr. Loftus is an expert on memory and is best known for her research examining the formation of false memories. She has also served as president of the American Psychological Society.

DAVID T. LYKKEN is Emeritus professor of psychology at the University of Minnesota. He has published numerous articles on a diverse array of topics including behavior genetics, psychophysiology, statistics, psychopathology, and the psychology of criminal behavior.

CLARK R. MCCAULEY received his Ph.D. in social psychology from the University of Pennsylvania in 1970. Dr. McCauley is currently professor of psychology at Bryn Mawr College. He also co-directs the Solomon Asch Center for Study of Ethnopolitical Conflict along with his colleague Paul Rozin.

FLORENCE R. MIALE is a former psychiatrist and member of the United Nations Commission on German National Character. She has been a visiting professor at several universities and hospitals.

RICHARD NISBETT is Theodore M. Newcomb Distinguished University professor of psychology at the University of Michigan. His research examines how people reason and draw conclusions about the world around them. He has written extensively on this topic, and has authored or co-authored ten books in addition to a variety of journal articles and book chapters.

ANTHONY R. PRATKANIS is professor of psychology at University of California, Santa Cruz. His research examines how the social environment influences our attitudes, beliefs, and behavior. He is co-author of a book entitled *The Age of Propaganda: The Everyday Use and Abuse of Persuasion* which he wrote with his colleague Elliot Aronson.

JAMES T. RICHARDSON is professor of sociology and judicial studies at the University of Nevada, Reno. Dr. Richardson has published six books and over 150 articles and book chapters. He is an internationally known expert in the area of minority religious movements.

LEE ROSS is Stanford Federal Credit Union professor of psychology at Stanford University. His research examines attributional biases and shortcomings in lay judgments. He has published dozens of journal articles and book chapters.

JOHN P. SABINI is professor of psychology at the University of Pennsylvania. His research focuses primarily on the study of emotions such as jealousy, embarrassment, and shame. Dr. Sabini is also the Director of Graduate Studies.

MARK SCHALLER is professor of psychology at the University of British Columbia. His research interests include stereotypes and prejudice, culture, and evolutionary psychology. He has published numerous book chapters, journal articles, and two books. His research has been supported by institutions such as the Social Sciences and Humanities Research Council and the National Institute of Health.

MICHAEL SELZER is a former Professor of Political Science at Brooklyn College and is the author of several books.

JENNIFER SEMMELROTH is a former graduate student in the department of psychology at the University of Michigan.

MAURY SILVER currently teaches psychology at Yeshiva University. He is author of a number of publications, including *The Individual in a Social World*, which he co-edited along with his colleagues Stanley Milgram and John Sabini.

TRUDY SOLOMON is a former graduate student at the University of California, Berkeley.

CHARLES STANGOR is professor of psychology at the University of Maryland. Dr. Stangor has received research grants from the National Institute of Mental Health and from the National Science Foundation. The author of 7 books and over 50 journal articles, Dr. Stangor has written extensively on the development of stereotypes, prejudice, and the impact of discrimination on its victims.

SHELLEY E. TAYLOR is professor of psychology at the University of California, Los Angeles. Dr. Taylor's primary research interests focus on the manner in which beliefs may affect the course of physical illnesses. Dr. Taylor is internationally known as one of the pioneers in the field of health psychology, an interdisciplinary area of research that lies at the intersection of psychology and medicine.

HEATHER D. TEVENDALE received her Ph.D. in clinical psychology from the University of Missouri–Columbia.

DREW WESTEN received his Ph.D. in clinical psychology from the University of Michigan. Before moving to Emory University where he is currently professor of psychology, he held positions at the Harvard Medical School and Boston University. Dr. Westen has a variety of research interests including personality disorders, emotion regulation, and adolescent psychopathology.

WENDY WOOD received her Ph.D. in social psychology from the University of Massachusetts. She is currently professor of psychology at Duke University. Dr. Wood's research focuses on sex differences in attitudes and behavior.

PHILIP ZIMBARDO is professor of psychology at Stanford University. Dr. Zimbardo is probably best known for serving as host of the popular *Discovering Psychology* educational films. Dr. Zimbardo is also former president of the American Psychological Association and an internationally recognized scholar who has over 300 publications to his credit.

Index